Reinventing Film Studies

Reinventing Film Studies

Edited by

Christine Gledhill

Professor of Cinema Studies, Staffordshire University,
Stoke on Trent, UK

and

Linda Williams

Director of Film Studies, University of California,
Berkeley, California, USA

A member of the Hodder Headline group
LONDON
Co-published in the United States of America by
Oxford University Press Inc., New York

First published in Great Britain in 2000 by
Arnold, a member of the Hodder Headline Group,
338 Euston Road, London NW1 3BH

http://www.arnoldpublishers.com

Co-published in the United States of America by
Oxford University Press Inc.,
198 Madison Avenue, New York, NY10016

Thanks are due to Oxford University Press and Christopher Williams for permission to reproduce
'After the classic, the classical and ideology: the differences of realism' *Screen* **35**(3), 275–93, 1994

British Library Cataloguing in Publication Data
A catalogue record for this book is available from the British Library

Library of Congress Cataloging-in-Publication Data
A catalog record for this book is available from the Library of Congress

ISBN 0 340 67722 8 (hb)
ISBN 0 340 67723 6 (pb)

2 3 4 5 6 7 8 9 10

Production Editor: Rada Radojicic
Production Controller: Iain McWilliams
Cover Design: Terry Griffiths

Typeset in 11 on 13 Minion by Phoenix Photosetting, Chatham, Kent
Printed in Great Britain by Redwood Books Ltd

What do you think about this book? Or any other Arnold title?
Please send your comments to feedback.arnold@hodder.co.uk

For Miriam

Contents

Figures

Contributors

Gill Branston teaches and researches in Film and TV Studies in the School of Journalism, Media and Cultural Studies, Cardiff University, Wales. She is co-author of *The media student's book* with Roy Stafford and is currently completing a book on the relationship between cinema and cultural modernity.

Noël Carroll is the Hilldale Professor as well as the Monroe C. Beardsley Professor in the Philosophy of Art at the University of Wisconsin–Madison. He is the President of the American Society for Aesthetics. His most recent books are *Philosophy of mass art* and *Philosophy of art: a critical introduction*.

Rey Chow is Andrew W. Mellon Professor of the Humanities at Brown University. She is the author of several books, the most recent of which is *Ethics after idealism: theory–culture–ethnicity–reading*. Her latest essays on literature, film, and cultural politics can be found in the journals *boundary 2, Postcolonial Studies, Communal/Plural, Camera Obscura*, and *differences*, among others.

Carol J. Clover is Class of 1936 Professor of Rhetoric (Film) and Scandinavian (Medieval Languages and Literatures). She is the author of *Men, women and chain saws: gender and the modern horror film* and is at work on *Trials, lies and movies*.

Steven Cohan is Professor of English at Syracuse University. He is co-author of *Telling stories* (1988), co-editor of *Screening the male* (1993) and *The road movie book* (1997), and author of *Masked men: masculinity and the movies in the fifties* (1997).

James Donald is Professor of Media at Curtin University of Technology, Perth, Western Australia. He was the editor of the journal *Screen Education*, 1978–80, and founding editor of the journal *New Formations*. He is the author of *Sentimental education: schooling, popular culture and the regulation of liberty* and *Imagining the modern city*.

Stephanie Hemelryk Donald is Senior Lecturer in Media Studies at Murdoch University. She is the author of *Public secrets, public spaces; Cinema and civility in China*, and *The state of China atlas* (with Robert Benewick) and is co-editor of *Picturing power in the People's Republic of China: posters of the Cultural Revolution* (with Harriet Evans); *Belief in China: art and politics, deities and mortality* (with Robert Benewick) and a special issue of the journal *New Formations*, 'Culture/China'.

Anne Friedberg is Associate Professor of Film Studies at UC Irvine. Author of *Window shopping: cinema and the postmodern* and co-editor with James Donald and

Laura Marcus of *Close up 1927–1933: cinema and modernism*. She is currently working on a book which offers a cultural history of windows and screens entitled, *The virtual window: the architecture of spectatorship*.

Jane M. Gaines is Associate Professor of Literature and English and Director of the Program in Film and Video at Duke University, Durham, NC. She recently co-edited *Collecting visible evidence* and completed *Fire and desire: mixed blood relations in early cinema*.

Christine Geraghty is Senior Lecturer in Media and Communications at Goldsmiths' College, University of London. She is author of *Women and soap opera*, co-editor of *The television studies book*, and has written extensively on issues of representation and women in film. She is currently working on a study of British cinema in the 1950s.

Christine Gledhill is Professor of Cinema Studies at Staffordshire University. She has written widely on feminist film criticism and melodrama and is currently working on a study of British cinema in the 1920s.

Tom Gunning is a Professor in the Art Department and the Cinema and Media Committee at the University of Chicago. Author of *D. W. Griffith and the origins of American narrative film* and *The films of Fritz Lang: allegories of modernity and vision*, he has written numerous essays on early silent cinema, and on the development of later American cinema, in terms of Hollywood genres and directors as well as the avant garde film. He has lectured around the world and his works have been published in a dozen different languages.

Miriam Bratu Hansen is Ferdinand Schevill Distinguished Service Professor in the Humanities at the University of Chicago, where she also teaches in the Department of English and the Committee on Cinema and Media Studies. She is a co-editor of *New German Critique*. Her most recent book is *Babel and Babylon: spectatorship in American silent film*. She is currently completing a study on the Frankfurt School's debates on cinema, mass culture, and modernity.

Henry Jenkins is the Director of the Comparative Media Studies Program at the Massachusetts Institute of Technology. He is the author/co-author of seven books on various aspects of popular culture, including *Textual poachers: television fans and participatory culture*, *The children's culture reader*, and *Hop on pop: the politics and pleasure of popular culture*.

Ana M. López teaches Film and Cultural Studies at Tulane University and has published widely on Latin American and Latino film, television, and video. Her *Third and imperfect: the new Latin American cinema* is forthcoming from the University of Minnesota Press.

Bill Nichols is Director of the Graduate Program in Film Studies at San Francisco State University. He has recently edited *Maya Deren: radical transformations* for the University of California Press. His previous books include *Blurred boundaries: questions of meaning in contemporary culture*.

Geoffrey Nowell-Smith is Professor of Cinema Cultures at the University of Luton and Director of the Joint European Filmography. He is the editor of *The Oxford history of world cinema* and author of a British Film Institute Film Classic on Michelangelo Antonioni's *L'avventura*.

Tessa Perkins is Principal Lecturer in, and Subject Leader of, Media Studies at Sheffield Hallam University and Treasurer of MECCSA (the Media, Communications and Cultural Studies Association). She has published on stereotypes and representations of women, including 'Rethinking stereotypes', 'The politics of Jane Fonda' and 'Two weddings and two funerals', and a book on women's part-time employment, *A matter of hours*. She is currently working on a book on stereotypes and the politics of representation.

Ella Habiba Shohat is Professor of Cultural Studies and Women's Studies at the City University of New York. A writer, curator, and activist, she is the author of *Israeli cinema: East/West and the politics of representation* and the co-author (with Robert Stam) of the award-winning *Unthinking Eurocentrism: multiculturalism and the media*. She has co-edited *Dangerous liaisons: gender, nation and postcolonial reflections* and is the editor of *Talking visions: multicultural feminism in a transnational age*.

Vivian Sobchack is an Associate Dean and Professor of Film and Television Studies at the UCLA School of Theater, Film and Television. Her books include *Screening space: the American science fiction film* and *The address of the eye: a phenomenology of film experience*; two edited anthologies, *The persistence of history: cinema, television and the modern event* and *Meta-morphing: visual transformation and the culture of quick change*; and a forthcoming collection of her own essays, *Carnal thoughts: bodies, texts, scenes and screens*.

Robert Stam is Professor of Film Studies at New York University. He is the author of 10 books on cinema and cultural studies, including *Brazilian cinema* (with Randal Johnson); *Reflexivity in film and literature, Subversive pleasures, Unthinking Eurocentrism* (with Ella Shohat), and *Film theory: an introduction*. He is also the recipient of Fulbright, Rockefeller, and Guggenheim Fellowships.

Ravi S. Vasudevan is with the Centre for the Study of Developing Societies, Delhi, and on the editorial advisory board of *Screen*. He has taught courses on Indian cinema in India and the USA, and has edited *Making meaning in Indian cinema* (Delhi: Oxford University Press, forthcoming).

Christopher Williams is Reader in Film and Television and Chair of the Criticism and Creativity Research Group at the University of Westminster. He is editor of the anthologies, *Realism and the cinema* and *Cinema: the beginnings and the future*.

Linda Williams is Professor of Film Studies and Rhetoric, and director of the Program in Film at the University of California, Berkeley. She is an editor at *Film Quarterly*. Her books include *Hard core: power, pleasure and the 'frenzy of the visible'* and the edited volume *Viewing positions: ways of seeing film*. She is completing a book, *The race card:*

American melodramas of black and white from Uncle Tom to O.J. Simpson for Princeton University Press.

Sharon Willis is Associate Professor of French and Visual and Cultural Studies and Director of the Film Studies Program at the University of Rochester. A co-editor of *Camera obscura: feminism, culture, media studies,* she is the author of *Marguerite Duras: writing on the body* and *High contrast: race and gender in contemporary Hollywood film,* and co-editor of *Male trouble.*

Introduction

There is no shortage of anthologies introducing key theories and figures in the field of film studies. This anthology does not aim to join them. Less dutifully, our aim is not to pay homage to the past but instead to distil key issues and problems of the contemporary field that are, as the British Workers' Education Association once demanded of the knowledge it sought, 'really useful' for the future. In this, the second century of moving images, new questions, and new knowledge, animate the field. The essays collected here, many of them published for the first time, offer not grids to be applied, but tools of investigation through which to open up and explore the questions that confront us at the start of the new century. They begin by asking of the specific areas with which they are concerned: What do we need to know now? What theories, concepts, and methodologies will help us to know? From this starting point they move on either to reframe or to depart from the concerns of the 1970s when film first became an academic subject of study. The first aim of this collection is thus to explore the field in the light of these reorientations. In the process we are not so much discarding the old questions and knowledge, but rethinking, refiguring, and restructuring what is most useful from this past. It is in the spirit of postmodernist self-fashioning of new identities out of old that we call this book *Reinventing film studies*.

This reinvention centres around five key issues: the interdisciplinary location of film studies as a means of engaging with the 'massness' of cinema; film understood as a sensory as well as meaning-producing medium; the conception of cinema as constituting an 'alternative public sphere'; history and the postmodern; and, finally, the impending dissolution of cinema within globalised multimedia and of Western film studies in their transnational theorisation.

First, then, film studies can no longer afford to ignore its interdisciplinary location. For some writers in this volume film studies reinvents itself by intersecting with neighbouring disciplines – media studies, cultural studies, visual culture – in an engagement with film as popular and mass culture. This theoretical move relocates the 'massness' of the media at the heart of our theories of mass culture. It aims, as Jane Gaines argues in her return to Ernst Bloch, to produce a theory *for* the mass rather than *about* them. Previous efforts to establish film studies as a distinct field elaborated aesthetic, psychic, and ideological structures which separated film from the mess of movie-making and movie-going, providing disciplinary distance and professional justification, while depending on the silent presence of the mass, interpellated as film theory's intellectual 'other'. For its part, media studies focused on issues of mass communications, political economy, public policy, and media imperialism, and detached itself from the 'soft' issues of aesthetics, fantasy, and the body. Paradoxically, the politically despairing perception of postmodernity as the saturation of the public sphere by the mass-produced image has driven many critics back to the Frankfurt School. This encounter permits new readings of its work which allows us to face up to, rather than reject out of hand, the massness of modernity and to include the analyst as situated within, rather than outside, the mass (Chapters 6, 7, 9, and 18).

This retrieval of the massness of modernity paves the way to a second key issue of reinvention: attention to the sensory experience of the cinematic mass medium. Where earlier film studies had tended either to ignore or condemn the apparently mindless, sensual, and affective pleasures of film viewing, many of the essays in this collection confront the need to take account of movie-going as a concrete, physical experience with distinctive, and historically changing, sensory appeal. Without shirking the 'mass-produced' nature of the cinematic 'production of the senses', several authors locate this physical–sensual appeal as the very hallmark of modernism now reconceived under the influence of postmodernism (Chapters 3, 17, 18, and 19).

Film studies' suspicion of the massness of cinema rested to a large degree on the perception of dominance – by ideology, by complicit formal structures, by an underlying psychic substructure to which all difference would be reduced. Dominance locked film studies into an unproductive binarism of progressive versus reactionary text. The political point of film analysis was to separate the progressive from the ideologically contaminated or the retrogressively nostalgic. Now the reinsertion of the body and the affective into film reconceives the social, cultural, and aesthetic as equally significant but distinct factors, mutually determining but not reducible to one another. This suggests for some that ideology as formerly conceived is no longer useful as the basis of a totalising theory of film (Chapters 6 and 11), while others argue that a way of reconceptualising the relation of films and the political is urgently needed (Chapters 3, 5, and 20).

Understanding 'our mass-mediated culture' as the only terrain on which we have to work has thus gradually led to a third major reinvention: the displacement of binarism by a dialogical conception of the media as constituting arenas of exchange and negotiation, in what is now conceived as an 'alternative public sphere' (Chapters 7 and 18). This shift has enabled many of these essays to reinfuse aesthetic concepts such as realism, melodrama, genre, and fantasy with analytical purchase on the cinema's location within mass culture and on the way it works as public sphere. Thus aesthetic concepts that had until recently been caught up either in a deliberately self-distancing formalism or trapped in an ideological binarism have again become useful. Many of these essays wrest the concept of an 'imaginary' from its narrowly psychoanalytic definition to define the space where reality is discursively shaped and a resulting 'social imaginary' becomes materially and aesthetically concrete. A key perception emerging from these essays is the significance of the 'image' and 'imaginary' as sites of cultural construction (Chapter 15) and contest (Chapter 12). In particular, the rethinking and use of genre in many of these essays (Chapters 12, 13, 15, and 18) suggest its renewed value for exploring the location of cinema at the heart of a social imaginary. So where genres, modes, and cultural formations were once viewed as in the service of an overarching dominant narrative, we can now relocate them in a more complex matrix of cultural forms, practices, and effects that do not necessarily add up to 'master narratives' (Chapter 3) but which have political purchase.

The present challenge of postmodernity – even if one does not accept the radical rupture of the modern by the postmodern and of old technologies by new – has, if nothing else, compelled a new urgency in the understanding of film history. As Tom Gunning demonstrates in his essay on cinema's forgotten future (Chapter 17), 'written after 100 years of films', history is never fully about then and always about now. A fourth reinvention thus occurs as the pressure of the notion of the postmodern has created a new perception of the massness of the public sphere and opened up the possibility of a new kind of history – a history for the present. The essays included in Part 4, on the 'Return to History' (Chapters 16–19), along with several others (Chapters 7, 20, and 23), share a sense of fluid identities and total mediation of all aspects of life that necessitates a reinvention of the very concept of cinema.

The massness and global reach of film raise for some of these essays the issue of different national conditions of modernisation. These include the ambivalent formation of the popular in the encounter between indigenous cultural traditions, Western media imperialism, national politics, and the appropriateness of the theories and protocols of Western film studies. For Rey Chow, writing about Chinese cinema (Chapter 21), a key question is how a 'third world' cinema manufactures an alterity that it gives back to the 'first world' but also what alterity it sees in its own reflection. For Ravi Vasudevan, writing about Bombay cinema (Chapter 8), a key question is how the spectator of a transitional/national cinema is addressed, while Ana López, writing about Latin American cinemas (Chapter 22), examines the various ways they have 'faced up' to Hollywood. For all of these writers the film medium constitutes a vital political issue. As mass media break down national barriers and national attempts to reinvent discrete cultural identities, the reviewing of film studies from positions outside the West forces the field to a fifth arena of reinvention – remaking itself as a site of international exchange (Chapters 6, 8, and 20–22).

Predominantly, however, this volume – with its British and US co-editors – represents a self-reflexive venture on the part of a specifically located Anglo-American film studies. In asking 'Where is film studies now?' many of these essays localise the grand theories that once guided the establishment of the discipline in the 1970s while at the same time seeking more global understanding. The essays written on either side of the Atlantic suggest the impact of their different historical, cultural, and political locations on the development of the discipline and the uses of theory for each. The inception of film studies in Britain outside the academy, and its continuing political struggles for existence within it, account for a stronger sense of frustration in some of the British essays with both the political stagnation of a 'grand theory' based on ideological and subjective interpellation and postmodernism's apparent loss of grip on cultural politics. In contrast, the blockage perceived in some of the American essays lies in a textual totality which, distilled from the neo-Marxist and structuralist theoretical ferment of the 1970s, emphasises a universal poetics and cognitive effectivity of a narrative form remote from the mess of daily cultural practice and political demands.

Reinventing film studies has five sections of four to five chapters each. The first two or three essays of each section open up key problems, issues, and debates, exploring the consequences of particular theoretical approaches. A case study in each section offers a concrete example of what these approaches can deliver in relation to a particular work or genre. Part 1, 'Really useful theory', begins with questions about film meaning and film theory, asking why we need film theory and what are the 'really useful' theories today. Part 2, 'Film as mass culture', poses the relation of film studies to mass culture, refiguring the nature of the Hollywood dream factory in relation to hopeful wish-fulfilment, reception research, stardom, and the public sphere. Its case study looks at Bombay cinema, one of the most popular cinemas in the world. Part 3, 'Questions of aesthetics', tackles the formal and fantasmatic dimensions of cinema, rethinking such key topics as the 'classical' text, ideology, genre, and aesthetics. Its case study is of a genre that has heretofore gone unrecognised in film studies: the ubiquitous and essential trial movie. Part 4, 'The return to history', then takes up the many new ways historians have engaged in theoretically informed historiography, asking first what film history is, then engaging in historical research on the mass audience's sensory involvement in the medium. Part 5, 'Cinema in the age of global multimedia', concludes with essays investigating local and global identities in a postmodern, international context which includes unequal exchanges of media products and theories, a case study on the labour of social fantasy in Chinese cinema, and new directions for technologies of multimedia.

Acknowledgements: Special thanks go to Lesley Riddle for patience and enthusiasm, to Paul Fitzgerald, Matthew Collins, and Luke Collins for friendly sustenance, and to all our friends and colleagues whose work and support have contributed to this book.

PART 1

Really useful theory

Editors' introduction

Most of the contributors to this section on theory agree that whatever film
theory is today it can no longer be the kind of overarching, 'grand' theory that
flourished in the 1970s. These theories tended towards totalising philosophical
or scientific quests for big truths, whether truths of history and revolution (Marx,
Althusser), self and identity (Freud, Lacan), or language (Saussure, semiotics).
Each writer may define the nature, the pitfalls, and the ultimate value of 'grand'
theory differently, but all agree that the kind of theorising about cinema that
needs to be done today must be more concretely located and, as Bill Nichols
puts it in Chapter 3, historicised. Theory must now be seen as having
debatable historical legacies rather than philosophical essences. Once placed
within these debatable contexts, Nichols argues, theories can become 'really
useful' conceptual frames within which historically situated generalisations can
address significance and value. Theory, like cinema itself, thus comes to be
seen as a socially constructed, historical category, serving socially significant
and historical and therefore politicised ends.

Geoffrey Nowell-Smith, in the opening essay, 'How films mean, or, from
aesthetics to semiotics and half-way back again', reviews the current state of
film theory by asking how the emphasis on film meaning came about and
whether it can be sustained in the relative absence of the grand theories that
once animated the field. Arguing that the grand theories of history, linguistics,
and psychoanalysis had displaced an earlier concern with aesthetics, Nowell-
Smith illustrates the various ways in which aesthetic questions, albeit in a
different form, are back on the agenda. Yet if Nowell-Smith, along with other
contributors to this part of the book, is critical of overarching grand theories,
he does not will the end of theory or even the end of the (now more limited and
situated) political goals and foundational concerns of many of those earlier
'grand' theories.

In similar vein, in Chapter 2, Gill Branston dissects some of the blockages of grand theory for those who have most practical need of it – teachers and their students seeking to understand the work of media in the world in which we find ourselves. Nevertheless she endorses the value of theory (and curiosity) as '"life skills" for the twenty-first century' (page 31). Arguing for both the 'ordinary' nature of theory as well as its necessarily distanced and reflexive specialisation, Branston answers the question, 'Why theory?' with an account of some of the more modest yet irrefutable theoretical achievements that have absolutely changed the way we think and argue about films: the recognition of the ways realism is coded, the recognition of genres that depict repetition *and* difference, and the recognition of stars as constructed.

In endorsing the kind of 'middle range theorising that moves easily from bodies of evidence to more general arguments and implications' (page 29) favoured by Bordwell and Carroll in their, perhaps inaptly, named book *Post-theory*, Branston stresses their political value. This call to political situatedness is pursued by Bill Nichols in Chapter 3. He vigorously argues the value for film theory of three key concepts – visual culture, representation, and rhetoric – that retain a foundation in grand theory but provide a more culturally and multiculturally sensitive perspective. While not specific to film theory, but rather inhabiting a cultural studies framework, these concepts, unlike the cognitive psychology of Bordwell, enable us to think about film in relation to the social, political, and identificatory concerns that motivated grand theory but in more historically and locally specific ways. These concepts are broad and fluid enough to situate film studies within larger interdisciplinary frameworks within which it can carry on conversations that will continue to vitalise its work.

Nichols interestingly situates film studies, along with other new disciplines such as women's studies and gay and lesbian studies, within a problematic of cultural visibility that encompasses both cultural difference and the appeal to the senses as a crucial, but often unacknowledged, form of knowledge production. Thus visual culture, a field of study and a conceptual frame that extends well beyond the specific medium of film, allows film studies to take up issues such as the appeal of cinema to the senses (addressed in Part 4 in the chapters by Hansen and Williams (Chapters 18 and 19)) that have been dismissed in earlier theory.

Steven Cohan, in a case study on *Singin' in the Rain*, demonstrates the usefulness of theory in generating film interpretation (Chapter 4). Interpreting an enduringly popular, now canonical, musical of the 1950s from a number of different, theoretically informed, perspectives, Cohan elegantly illustrates how meaning changes according to the theoretical framework applied. By demonstrating how films exist as textual objects of inquiry that lend themselves to theoretically informed interpretation Cohan reasserts the value of textual reading even as he shows how various it can be. These different perspectives do not rigorously duplicate the march from totalising 'grand theory' to the more situated cultural studies theories described by some of the other authors in this section. However, the initial structuralist analysis of the film's narrative opposition does follow a rough development from structuralism through cultural studies and queer theory. Structural opposition gives way to a 'post-structuralist' Derridian deconstruction which gives way to a psychoanalytic and feminist interpretation of sexual difference to a cultural studies interpretation of Gene Kelly's star status to a queering of this image. As Cohan shows, each of these theoretical interpretations also yields an analytical method and a politics that determines what we see and why it matters.

In asking the question, 'Who (and what) is it for?', Tessa Perkins explores the relationship between the academy, theory, film-making, and politics (Chapter 5). Like Bill Nichols she revisits the 'grand theories' of the 1960s and 1970s and the various 'turns' taken by film studies since in an attempt to dissolve the problems they posed and to accommodate the changing contexts of both political and academic scenes. In so doing Perkins outlines a somewhat different, British, theoretical history from that described by Nichols. For British film studies, 'empiricism' rather than 'formalism' has been the main problem, with 'politics', arising outside higher education, forcing theory – especially the 'continental', neo-Marxist and psychoanalytic kind – on to the reluctant agendas of a number of academic disciplines. In the heady decades of the 1960s and 1970s, film theory was developed in the pages of *Screen*, in British Film Institute Summer Schools, and among the widening circles of teachers, cultural activists, and film-makers in order to promote a larger 'film culture' as part of an interventionist cultural politics. Tessa Perkins offers an acute analysis of the political, theoretical, and cultural reasons for the dispersal of this energy, while reminding us not only of its achievements but also of the paramount importance, exemplified in the needs of marginalised, oppressed, and unrepresented groups, of developing holistic theoretical frameworks capable of grasping the shifting relations of capitalism, the media, audiences, and the workings of cultural power.

1 How films mean, or, from aesthetics to semiotics and half-way back again

Geoffrey Nowell-Smith

The revolution which took place in film studies in the 1970s was, to use the jargon of the time, highly overdetermined. It had a significant political dimension, spun off from the radicalism of 1968. Philosophically it vaunted its materialism, in opposition to idealisms of every kind. Thirdly (this list is not intended to be exhaustive), it was aligned with the grand structuralist project to understand human culture as a whole in terms of patterns of meaning.

In a sense this revolution has done its work too well. It has successfully shifted the focus of film study. Theory has come first and foremost to concern itself with meaning, often with the aim of bringing to the surface those aspects of meaning which can be characterised as ideological. Meanwhile, the impulse behind the shift in focus has been lost or mislaid, leaving unexplained the reasons why it was thought to be necessary and what it was that the revolution set out to overthrow. Changes in intellectual fashion – structuralism has been 'post'-ed and Marxism overhastily consigned to the capacious dustbin of history – have left much of film theory high and dry, no longer supported by the more general theories on which it used to rely.

In reviewing the current state of film theory it is therefore worth focusing on two questions in particular: first, how did the current focus on meaning come about; and, second, can it be sustained in the absence of the impulses that gave it force at the beginning?

In the definition given to it by the magazine *Screen* in the mid-1970s, film theory was seen as addressing three distinct but overlapping problems: the relation of the film to the world it represents; the internal organisation of filmic discourses; and the reception of the film by the spectator. The methodologies for investigating these problems were derived, respectively, from historical materialism, semiotics, and psychoanalysis. Subsequent developments have seen historical materialism sidelined, psychoanalysis contested, and semiotics, at a scientific level, more or less abandoned. But the problem of representation, and with it the problem of meaning, has remained central to all forms of modern film theory, including those which claim to have broken definitively with the *Screen* problematic. Indeed, without a theory of representation there can hardly be said to be a theory of film at all.

Strictly speaking, the problems of representation and of meaning are not the same. The problem of representation is an extremely broad one. It covers both the formation of mental events and their relation to outside stimuli and the more narrowly artistic question of how representation is produced within the work of art itself. The sort of representations films produce and the extent to which their nature can be derived from the underlying photographic character of the film image have been central concerns of film theory since the 1920s. But these problems were on the whole seen as problems of aesthetics – of artistic expressivity and of the spectator's emotional response – rather than as semiotic concerns. The idea that, interlaced with the problem of representation, there was also an apparently simpler one of what films meant and how they did so did not occur to early theorists as a problem.

The problem of meaning in films is, in fact, one of those problems which is only a problem when you come to think about it. Films are, for the most part, pretty easy to understand – if only because in the great majority of cases they have been designed to be instantly accessible to audiences with no special esoteric competence. It is only a minority of films which see themselves as repositories of hidden meanings accessible only to the enlightened. The problem therefore, as Christian Metz put it, is not how films are to be understood but how come they are understood, what the process is by which we make sense of what we see on the screen. This is not on the whole a problem that audiences are much concerned with. Nor on the whole are film-makers, except on the rare occasions when they want to try something unusual and wonder whether they can get away with it. But for theory it is the kind of problem which, once raised, does not want to go away.

Negatively, one might say the problem of meaning in the cinema is a bit like the problem faced by the centipede who had no problem with walking until asked how she did it, whereupon she became paralysed by the thought of which leg she put in front of which in order to create locomotion, More positively, it can be seen as opening up the Pandora's box of what the cinema is and what it does for us, its spectators.

The problem of meaning

The problem of meaning in the cinema takes on a different aspect according to whether it is seen as in the first instance a philosophical, linguistic-semiotic, or psychological (psychoanalytic or cognitive) problem, and yet further complications are revealed depending on the school of philosophy, linguistics-semiotics, or psychology one first turns to for help. The tendency in film studies in the 1970s was to draw on linguistics and psychoanalysis – more specifically on semiotic extensions of Saussurean tradition of structural linguistics, on the one hand, and on the psychoanalysis of Jacques Lacan, on the other. In the 1980s, however, another school emerged, initially from a similar base as far as linguistic theory was concerned (the Russian-born linguist and poeticist Roman Jakobson was for a long time a common reference point), but increasingly psychological theories were drawn from the emergent field of so-called cognitive science. Relations between the cognitivist and the semiotic (or post-semiotic) schools are occasionally acrimonious and it is not my purpose here to add to the acrimony. While reasons have to be found to explain the divergences, I propose to concentrate as much as possible on what might be held as common ground.

Why films mean

It is easier to say why films mean than how. Films mean because people want them to mean. Meaning is not something inert, a passive attribute of books, films, computer programs, or other objects. Rather it is the result of a process whereby people 'make sense' of something with which they are confronted. This making sense goes on in the presence of real-life situations as well as artefacts. If I find myself face-to-face with a scene in which there is a car smashed up against a lamp post, a body on the ground being given resuscitation, and a policewoman directing traffic, my response will be composed in more or less equal measure of emotional shock and an intellectual (or intellectualising) desire to reconstruct what has happened. Is the body that of a pedestrian? Did the car perhaps swerve to avoid him, strike him a glancing blow, and then end up crosswise against the lamp post? Nobody compels me to perform this sense-making activity but nevertheless I do it. Furthermore, the sense I make takes the form of a narrative. Even though nothing is happening, I turn the scene into a story, reformulating the spatial layout into a possible sequence of events.

A similar process of making sense goes on in the presence of a film – with the difference that the meanings on offer have been channelled in a particular direction as a result of actions undertaken by the film-makers. The film's makers – plural rather than singular, everyone from scriptwriter to editor passing through art director, costume designer, even hairdresser – have devised a spectacle whose elements are meaningful. Before the star even opens her mouth the spectator can tell from some indicator (maybe it is the lighting, maybe the make-up) what sort of character she is likely to be playing. Prompts to understand the scene in particular ways abound. These prompts can be seen as, on the one hand, creating meaning and, on the other hand, as limiting it. No longer do I make up my own story to account for what I see. The story is now being told to me and even its ambiguities are likely to be strictly circumscribed.

The reason for putting things this way is that the role of the spectator is often misunderstood. The often-asked question 'Is the spectator active or passive?' is a stupid one. Of course the spectator is active. He or she is motor active to a slight extent, eyes scanning the screen, body sometimes shifting or squirming in the seat. But intellectually and emotionally active he or she has to be. Questions that might arise concern the extent of this activity 'Is it greater in the presence of certain films than others?' – or its nature – 'Exactly *how* is the spectator active and at what level?' But of the fact of activity there can be no doubt, because there is no possibility of the film meaning anything without the creative intervention of the spectator in determining what to pay attention to and what sense to give it.

Cinema and language

Thus far common sense. It is only common sense to suppose that the brain is constantly engaged in processing information that comes to it in the form of external stimuli. It is also only common sense to suppose the meaning-making process emerges, in the case of artefacts such as films, from a desire to communicate. But common sense may need to be supplemented. A problem arises, for example, as soon as one asks how the communication takes place. Is it really the case that situations are so transparent that a film-maker only requires to present one in order to be understood? Since this is patently not the case, the question must then be asked, 'What fills the channel through which the communication must pass in order for a meaning to take shape?' The answer to this question has generally been that in some sense – precise or imprecise, literal or metaphorical – cinema is a language. This idea originated in the silent period, when the cinema made very little use of words. Descriptively it could be observed of silent cinema that it produced meaning in a fairly systematic way without much recourse to verbal language to back it up. More contentiously it could be – and occasionally was – argued that its essence was to do precisely that and that the consummation of cinema was to do without words entirely. But even while arguing for the cinema as *photogénie* (Louis Delluc) or for the image as the antithesis of 'the word' (Béla Balázs), the theorists of silent cinema accepted the notion that the communication effected by the cinema was the product of a systematic ordering of its material. For Balázs, cinema rejects the word (and thereby gives access to a level of feeling often denied within Western culture) but this makes it an alternative system to a linguistic one, rather than not a system at all. By contrast, Eisenstein was quite explicit in ascribing to cinema linguistic capacity.

The idea of cinema as a language or maybe anti-language fell out of favour with the coming of sound. Since the cinema now used language – verbal language, that is – as part of its communicative armoury, it was hard to argue that cinema *per se* either provided an autonomous alternative to language or that it was a language in itself. (This did not stop writers such as Raymond Spottiswoode, writing in the early sound period, from expounding theories of cinema as possessed of a 'grammar'.) Instead, verbal communication came more and more to be seen as the heart of a film , with montage and *mise en scène* as mere effect. When a sense of the wholeness of a film's construction returned to film criticism, as most notably with André Bazin and *Cahiers du cinéma* in the 1950s, it was under the auspices of a very different aesthetic. Cinema as language became a distant memory.

Even Bazin, however, recognised that the systematic communicative power of the cinema had to be accounted for somehow other than just by the properties of the photographic image as a simulacrum of reality. '*D'autre part*', he wrote in 'Ontologie de l'image photographique' (1945),[1] '*le cinéma est un langage*'. This can be translated as 'meanwhile, cinema is also a language'. In French and other romance languages, however, a distinction is made between language in the generic sense (as in 'musical language' or 'the language of bees'), for which the word is *langage*, and language in the more specific sense of a natural language (such as French or English) and the system subtending it; the word here is *langue*. In recognising that cinema was *langage*, therefore, Bazin was making a merely precautionary and not particularly contentious statement.

But even as Bazin's writings were becoming more widely known through publication in book form (the first volume of *Qu'est-ce que le cinéma?* appeared in 1958), film theory was in for a series of seismic shocks. The first of these was administered by the publication in 1957 of the essay 'Myth today' in Roland Barthes's *Mythologies*. This essay set out a model, derived from the Swiss linguist Ferdinand de Saussure, for charting the relationships between different forms of signifying procedure, pictorial or linguistic. Within a few years Barthes followed this up with his *Eléments de sémiologie* (1964) and, in France at least, a revolution was underway.

In retrospect it is clear that the influence of Saussure on theories of what subsequently came to be called semiotics was not an unalloyed blessing. Although credited as the founder of semiotics, Saussure never did more than prospect its possible existence as a science which would bear the same relation to sign systems in general as linguistics does to language. Saussurean linguistics was a powerful intellectual construction, though not particularly useful for solving the problems practical linguists were interested in. The same was to prove the case with the application of his linguistic theories to cinema. The intellectual leap taken by Saussure in comparison with previous linguistics was to understand language as a system – '*un système où tout se tient*' – where everything holds together, in his own words. Famously Saussure also declared that '*dans la langue il n'y a que des différences*': 'in language there are only differences'. Both these remarks were to prove intellectually fertile in various fields, but dangerously distracting when applied to cinema. If cinema were a system, it could be argued that its components could be analysed in terms of the differences they bear to each other in the way that linguists can analyse the system of, say, consonants in terms of voiced as opposed to unvoiced (*b* versus *p*) or labial as opposed to dental (*b* versus *d*). But cinema is a not a system of this type. If it is to be regarded as a system, then it is what the Soviet[2] semiotician Yuri Lotman calls a secondary modelling system – that is, an artistic language which draws on communicative resources from different registers.

The first person systematically to apply Saussurean linguistics to cinema was Christian Metz. Metz was a rigorous thinker with a rationalistic cast of mind. When faced with a theoretical problem he always looked for an elegant solution at a high level of abstraction. If a simple and elegant solution was not possible (and in the nature of the beast it often was not), he would adjust his model to take account of difficulties so tiresomely thrown up by the real situation. He started out in 1964 by trying to discover if it could be proved that cinema either was or was not a language (*langue*) in the sense that Saussure and his followers gave to the term. Having proved that it was not, he turned his mind to lesser problems one by one: did cinema nevertheless have a syntax; did it work by denotation or connotation or a mixture? In his book *Langage et cinéma*, published in 1971, he set out reconstruct in the most systematic way possible what he took to be the remaining languages of cinema. Recognising that in default of a unitary language (*langue*) cinema had to be seen as a composite artistic language, he recomposed the world of the fiction film as an elaborate web of filmic and cinematic codes and subcodes, systems and subsystems. The guiding assumption behind this, of Saussurean inspiration, was that languages, of whatever sort, exist as networks deployed as it were horizontally, so that concrete instances of meaning need to be analysed by means of a vertical probe through the various levels in play at any given time. As Metz himself seems to have recognised, the kind of analysis promoted by this assumption is going to be of a very refined type and remote from ordinary experience. This is not to say that it is wrong; merely that the problems it can solve are in many cases going to be of interest only to specialists.

Where the Saussurean notion of language as a system of differences proved to have an unexpected payoff was when it came to applying psychoanalysis to cinema. Saussurean linguistics deals with signification – the process whereby signifiers relate to their signifieds. It does not deal with questions of how individual human subjects construct meaning for themselves. In itself it is neutral in respect of psychology. But a theory of language which can be interpreted (rightly or wrongly) as privileging the signifier could also be used to support a revision of psychoanalysis such as that being carried out in France by Jacques Lacan. The availability of a Saussurean semiotics for this purpose was quickly seized on by film theorists on the lookout for ways of completing the jigsaw society–ideology–individual. In the event, this was to prove a contentious move.

Signification and information

Rebellion against the Metzian approach to signification and its extension in the direction of psychoanalysis was not slow to develop. There was always dissent but it took a little time for this dissent to articulate itself around an alternative theory. Such a theory was to emerge in the early 1980s with the publication of David Bordwell's *Narration in the fiction film* (1985). Compared with the intricacies of *Langage et cinéma*, the model proposed by Bordwell has an almost Copernican simplicity. Bordwell sweeps away Metz's semiotic apparatus (apart from a shared dependence on Roman Jakobson) and proposes instead that a theory of the workings of cinema – or at any rate of the fiction film – can be based on a single active principle, which he calls the narration. Bordwell's model sees the film as producing not so much signification as information. This information is contained in the dialogue and in the various movements of the picture – shots from changing angles, reframings, etc. The relevant parts of this information are delivered by the film-maker and picked up by the spectator in the form of cues, and inferences are then made by the spectator as to how the information can be pieced together to form a coherent narrative. In this scheme, the narration (the form of which can vary from film to film) is the sequential ordering given by the film-maker to the supply of information. In many films the narration is extremely straightforward, but it can be complex (as in Hitchcock) or it can be inflected by a set of quasi-arbitrary parameters applied to it by an artist of a distinctive stamp (as with Ozu). Whatever the variants, however, the basic principle is the same: film is organised as a diegesis (literally, a leading through), and what does the leading is the narration.

This theory, as well as being elegant, is also plausible. But I do not think it is adequate for more than a very basic purpose, the reason for this being the impoverished and hypothetical nature of the underlying theory of cognition. What makes the theory plausible is that, as already mentioned, the majority of films, particularly Hollywood films, are in fact put together with an emphasis on comprehension. The film's makers work together to ensure that the plot line can be followed, and at this level their thought processes prefigure those that the audience is supposed to follow on watching the film. But the idea that we understand by forming inferences is itself an inference, and a suspect one. The cognitivist model with which Bordwell works imagines the mind as an inferring machine. It asks the question, 'How could a mind get from point A (the film begins and the audience does not yet know what is going to happen) to point B (the film ends, the characters have had their say and gone through their moves in front of the camera, and the audience is clear about the outcome)?' It also says, 'A well-ordered thinking machine could be designed which made a set of inferences and as a result was clear about the outcome: therefore this is how spectators do it.' That is, it infers from the possibility of an inferential reading of the film that inferential readings are what spectators produce in reality. This is itself, however, no more than a possibility, and assumes that our minds work when watching a film rather as they do when doing a crossword puzzle or as policemen's minds do in detective stories. Indeed, the theory is at its most plausible when applied to the watching of detective films, in which the role of inference (on the part of the hero and following him on the part of the audience) is paramount. But as a general model for aesthetic perception it is deficient. The more a film resembles a crossword puzzle, the better the model works. The less a film is anchored to a principle of narrativity, and the more it is polysemic, or assimilable to other artistic forms, the less applicable it turns out to be. I would not deny that inference plays a role in aesthetic appreciation, in understanding a Bach partita or a Jimi Hendrix guitar solo, or piecing together the elements of an allegorical painting, or making sense of the hero's behaviour in *Hamlet*, or anticipating the rhyme in a sonnet or song. But there is more to it than that. There is more to films than is allowed for in the theory of narration, and more to the mind than is allowed for in even the most sophisticated cognitivist model. The theory is open-ended enough to allow for the fact that narration is not everything and that there are pleasures to a film which can even derive from the fact that narrativity is suspended. But it is hamstrung by its intellectualisation of the activity of spectating.

This intellectualisation can appear in two guises. On the one hand there is the construction of the spectator preferred by Bordwell as, in the jargon, a 'rational agent'. The sort of reason being appealed to is that of the ideal consumer in economics who optimises his or her choices in the marketplace, and by analogy the rational spectator is one who comes up with optimal readings of films on the basis of the available evidence. Hypothesising this sort of rationality is a useful (if ideologically motivated) simplification when practised by economics trying to account for the workings of a system. It is somewhat less useful in trying to understand how flesh and blood humans come to terms with the experience offered to them by the viewing of a film. On the other hand the spectator is also viewed by some writers as a computational device, which implies a slightly different conceptualisation of viewing activity. The 'rational agent', although deeply implausible as an entity, is a human subject of a type familiar from traditional philosophy and assumed capable of constructing meaning. The spectator of the hardline cognitivist stamp is not lacking in computational powers, but it is uncertain whether these powers extend to the construction of meaning, since it has yet to be shown how 'computational devices' can make the step that human and other higher animals undoubtedly make from syntax to true semantic understanding.

The question that therefore has to be asked is how dependent are theories of film on corresponding theories of psychology. I suggested above that semiotics can be used with or without a psychoanalytic theory of the subject, though there are valuable gains to be made from putting the two together. But can the historical poetics favoured by David Bordwell survive without rational agents and other pieces of armature borrowed from cognitive science? The answer is a qualified yes. At the level where one is talking about criteria of understanding, a film-maker can be imagined as proposing a certain style to an audience confident in the knowledge that the aesthetic procedures in play will meet with acceptance and it does not matter in the slightest whether either film-maker or audience is posited as rational agent or computational device or any other kind of creature.[3] But there does remain a gap to be filled between this level of understanding and the level properly speaking of meaning. Meaning comes into being only with the person who experiences it. The American philosopher Charles Sanders Peirce defined the sign as 'something which stands to somebody for something in some respect or capacity' (1931: 135; quoted in Silverman, 1983: 14) and the status of that somebody is an essential component of any theory of meaning in cinema or anywhere else. Of themselves neither signification nor information guarantees meaning. In the case of information, it only means something if someone interprets it. In the case of signification, the fact that a certain signifier relates to a certain signified is a purely formal matter until and unless the signified comes to rest somewhere.[4] At this level the issue is between theories of meaning which assume a conscious subject to whom things mean something and those which allow for a subject both conscious and unconscious, as in psychoanalysis. This issue is unlikely to be resolved in a hurry.

Semiotics and aesthetics

How much does all this matter? Concern with questions of meaning arose because it seemed important to be able to establish unequivocally that certain combinations of sign had certain effects and that particular signs stood in for more general statements. Theories of meaning were used as supports for a politics of representation. Struggles over meaning in this sense – the meaning of stereotypes, for example – have rather lost their urgency. Much of what theorists in the 1970s sought to give theoretical grounding to is now part of common culture. If today's spectators watch a film in which there is one black character and five who are white they know without having to be told that meaning of a certain type is being created. They do not need to be given the vocabulary of pertinence and synecdoche to realise that the black character bears a massive weight of collective representation on his or her shoulders. Departments of film studies can supply the analytic tools, but the political lesson has been learned. The problem is now a different one. Finding meaning has become an academic exercise, in both good and bad senses of the phrase. It is useful work to set students to carry out but it is in danger of being routinised. Films mean. But they do not just mean. Because they can be described with the aid of language we can be led to think that description can substitute for the film. This is the perennial temptation of what I have called the linguistic analogy. But films also work in less describable ways. They work as painting or music do, partly through meaning but partly in other ways; partly in ways that have linguistic equivalents and partly in ways that do not. The move in the direction of semiotics in the 1970s was, at least in part, a reaction against the kind of aesthetics that dealt in concepts that were 'indeterminate' and could not be brought within a rational schema. But the need for such a rational schema has become questionable. Too many of the things that films do evade attempts to subsume them under the heading of meaning. This is not to say there is no place for historical poetics or for the semiotics of culture in film study. Clearly, there is. But it is also time to consider a return to theories of the aesthetic so thoughtlessly cast aside a quarter of a century ago.

Endnotes

1   Reprinted in Bazin (1958).
2   Lotman's career was based in the now independent Estonia but his writings are in Russian.
3   In his book *Engaging characters* (1995), Murray Smith criticises the semiotic-psychoanalytic approach to character prevalent in film studies from a standpoint which has a lot in common with the cognitivist approach. It is not necessary to swallow the implausibilities of the cognitivist full Monty in order to recognise the validity of Smith's critique.
4   This is better expressed in the terminology proposed by Louis Hjelmslev, according to whom signification is a relation (r) between an Expression (E) and a Content (C). The formula ErC applies in a variety of contexts – to the relation between dot–dot–dot dash–dash–dash dot–dot–dot and S–O–S, for example, or that between S–O–S ('Save our souls') and the notion of a distress signal for sailors. As those examples show, the mere presence of that relation is not enough to create meaning. On the other hand, the fact that signs can circulate without coming to rest in the form of meanings recognised as such by the individual to whom the sign 'means something' is noteworthy in its own right.

References

Barthes, R. 1964: *Eléments de sémiologie*. Paris: Editions de Seuil; English translation, *Elements of semiology*. London: Cape, 1967.
Bazin, A. 1958: *Qu'est-ce que le cinéma?* Vol. 1. Paris: Cerf; English translation, *What is cinema?* Berkeley, CA: University of California Press, 1971.
Bordwell, D. 1985: *Narration in the fiction film*. London: Methuen.
Metz, C. 1964: Le cinéma: langue ou langage? Originally in *Communications* **4**; reprinted in *Essais sur la signification au cinéma*. Paris: Klincksieck, 1968.

Metz, C. 1971: *Langage et cinéma*. Paris: Larousse; English translation, *Language and cinema*. The Hague: Mouton, 1974.

Peirce, C.S. 1931: *The collected papers of Charles Sanders Peirce*, Vol. II. Cambridge, MA: Harvard University Press.

Silverman, K. 1983: *The subject of semiotics*. New York: Oxford University Press.

Smith, M. 1995: *Engaging characters*. Oxford: Oxford University Press.

2   Why theory?

Gill Branston

'Film studies' is in a state of reconfiguration as the boundaries of what we call 'film' shift from celluloid, cameras and photochemistry into video, television, digital and computer technologies and screens. All this before we even begin to consider changes to those other 'objects of study': audiences, industries and identities, and the ways that movies, key contemporary entertainments of the visible, impact on notions of the 'public'. New kinds, hierarchies and guarantees of knowledge and analytical skills, claiming to be the core of teaching and researching about 'media', emerge, converge and disappear. Such changes necessarily affect the study of cinema, and its academic location, which is often now within cultural and media studies.

The question, then, is not only 'Why theory?' but also 'Which theories, when, where?' That apparent block, 'Theory', needs breaking up and historicising. It need not always and only mean the 'grand' theories of the 1960s and 1970s, nor is it ever a non-purposeful, coolly distanced entity. I want also to ask: 'Who is asking "Why theory?"' Film studies often celebrates popular cultures which themselves imply that 'intellectualising' is unnecessary, or that 'theories' simply serve a callow kind of 'political correctness' – even while quantities of style journalism, cultural comment and public relations proliferate in precisely those areas broached by the questions posed in theories. So the apparently simple question 'Why theory?' touches on cultural nerves and interest groups. It also asks 'Theory' once more to describe and justify its existence.

Histories, locations

'Academic theory' has had a bad press, especially in Britain. It is regularly placed in opposition to such blockbuster terms as 'practice', 'experience', 'common sense', 'the real'. Other sets of association invoke highly classed and gendered distinctions: theory in 'popular' discourses is often called 'airy-fairy', 'high', 'highbrow', 'grand', 'abstract' – along with even more insulting (if sometimes justified) suggestions that theory disdains the ordinary. It is also acquiring the patina prevalent in many US discourses, where 'theory' sometimes stands as a kind of shorthand for that type of cultural politics which used to be called progressive but which is now dismissed, not by argument, but by the talismanic phrase 'political correctness'.[1]

Perhaps equally damaging in an era of (relatively) massified higher and further education[2] is the opposition 'theory/information', or 'theory/know-how'. Film studies is now part of systems of mass education asked, not for the first time, to present their credentials for the creation of 'skills, and no longer ideals . . . [in which] the transmission of knowledge is no longer designed to train an elite capable of guiding the nation' (Lyotard, 1984: 48). Why teach or learn theory within education systems expected to fit students for the world of post-Fordist work, for employers who value 'intellectual capital' only insofar as it will create (corporate) wealth or smooth the way of 'impression management'? Surely all you need is information, to be easily found on the Internet or in pop-up videos, which is then combined with the New-Age-speak of contemporary management theory? Even more cynical is Lyotard's perception that, while some will continue, in elite institutions, to be educated for 'guiding the nation', many more are effectively being trained as a 'lumpen intelligentsia' (see McGuigan, 1999), without sufficient jobs or pay in the career openings of their disciplines. Such accounts are often made to fuel concern about 'theory' (rather than about the fate of massified higher education within deeply unequal social orders), attacked as a cheap and intellectually worthless alternative to practical media work in film courses. How does 'theory' have relevance alongside 'opinion', 'know-how' and other kinds of quiz knowledge, let alone next to 'practice'? Is it the same as being 'smart', that current term of highest praise, whether for modes of thought, drugs, bombs or credit cards: making quick connections, being efficient and, in the end, user-friendly and obedient within larger structures?

Academic work has usually been concerned with making links and testing out general propositions, sometimes very speculative ones, in order to produce conceptual maps of the fields it is interested in. These, like any other maps, are necessarily at some distance from the particular, in order to carve a path through their study (see Geraghty, 1998; Gray, 1997).[3] Of course, this attempted distance can easily come to seem a privileged divide from commonly held sense, so readily presented as 'theory-free' or as somehow escaping discursivity. If academic theorising were more open about its own histories, locations and ways of operating, then its connection to other, very ordinary, skills might be better appreciated and worked for.

Theories take the form of sets of productive generalisations which result from defining a problem or a striking characteristic of a given field and then trying to solve or explain it via key concepts. Theories contribute to the systematic organisation of ways of thinking an area and have been defined as existing in between a law ('a theory which is open to no objection from practice') and a speculation ('an idea that feels no need to prove its relation to practice') (Williams, 1983: 316–18). If a theory is put to research use, it furthermore produces a methodology, a way of working which seeks to be coherently related to certain theoretical premises and to systematically linked concepts and propositions (see Andermahr et al., 1997: 223–4).

Academic theories have usually been productive in two broad fields of knowledge, each with different histories and locations, and often with a disciplinary interest in accentuating those differences. In the (traditionally male-dominated) physical sciences, theories have usually related to events made to happen in controlled conditions, and are seen, often rightly, as being verifiable by results, by the real, the empirical and even as being available for codification into laws. In the human and social sciences (traditionally more 'woman-friendly', which is not the same as 'woman-dominated'), where film studies have been located, the same rules of proof and the stance of objectivity are not usually expected. There has often been more reliance placed on metaphor and certain kinds of rhetoric; and more recently an emphasis on the extent to which scientific theory is also rhetorical, narrativised, constructed. Moreover, some writers suggest that impulses from very different directions have worked to produce a disproportionate ambivalence towards empirical evidence or experiential accounts (for a useful discussion of the concept of 'experience', see Gray, 1997; for stimulating discussions of the 'proof' offered by textual and other approaches, see Barker and Brooks, 1998). These different impulses range from totalising post-structuralist and postmodern scepticisms, which emphasise the impossibility of evidence or proof for *any* position whilst nevertheless going along with fairly speculative positions themselves, to the very different political challenge of feminist or black cultural emphases, 'from below', emphasising for very different ends the impossibility of godlike theoretical objectivity. Experience and the empirical in such a climate can easily be constructed as the 'Other' of theory, as simple raw data, along with a rhetorical implication that theories need not consider the test and difficulties of proof.

Oddly, such very contemporary emphases meld with the histories of Western academic theorising. Like much scholarship, theory in European universities originated in religious practices, with their own purposes: the secluded scholar's role of making evident the word of God as revealed in 'His' creations by the work of exegesis or textual explanation. Even in the early nineteenth century in Britain a university education meant a course of Greek and Latin (in that order of importance) at Oxford or Cambridge, usually leading to holy orders and often a college living – for white, upper-class males, of course (see Stray, 1998). This is echoed in the gendered and classed language with which 'theory' is often justified: said to possess 'rigour', 'proper distance/objectivity' as opposed to the 'emotion' and 'instinct' of raw encounters with the object of study. A further rhetorical legacy is that of scholarly deference in the drive to name and pay homage to key experts and terms within the field as a way of accrediting and displaying status and expertise.

By the early twentieth century, however, 'the material bases for intellectual life (replacing politics and the church) were education and the press' (Frith and Savage, 1993: 110) with a resulting hostility between academics and journalists which was encouraged to blossom during the Thatcher and Reagan years, following the systematic reduction of the status of teachers, teaching and intellectuality. Cultural debate in the UK is still often characterised as belonging to 'the chattering classes', with its implication of purposeless idleness – a peculiarly revealing way of describing an intelligentsia.

But in many ways challenges to the religious, gender and class sanctions of 'cloistered' (that is, Oxbridge-referenced) 'higher' education have been tonic. Academics had rarely been understood as operating within particular institutional and historical contexts which in fact strongly formed the kinds of theories and publications they produced: there have always been purposes and bodies of ambition for that apparently disembodied, non-purposeful, abstract activity, theory. Geographical–historical–

institutional and even governmental contexts have always shaped theorising, depending on whether it was being pursued, to take a French example, in an elite Ecole, training state functionaries, or in a university – but then, Catholic or Calvinist? In Germany, writers of the 1930s such as those of the Frankfurt School were concerned to theorise the impact and possible results of the propaganda campaigns of German Fascism, which in turn shaped later theories of the 'public sphere', largely ignored until recently for film study (though see Donald and Donald, Chapter 7, and the recent work of Hansen referenced therein; see also Hansen, Chapter 18). In the USA (to which several of the Frankfurt School eventually fled) there was a different kind of preoccupation with 'public' opinion and with an aggressive new advertising industry, which, as part of its market researches, deployed an instrumental, socially uncritical version of cognitive psychology. These early contexts, for film studies, have meant an often tense relationship, both for and against 'Continental' theory, sometimes defined in terms of that 'other' 'psychology': Freudian–Lacanian psychoanalysis.[4]

In the British version of these 1930s' 'founding moments', long-standing literary–intellectual concerns with declining cultural values associated with the name of F.R. Leavis ironically set the agenda for pioneering work, initially around film and advertising but eventually also television. This was premised on the ambition to 'inoculate' students against powerful media forms through the acquisition of critical reading skills, based on literary theories of creative response and often resulting in a high profile for debates on the nature of 'quality' film and television. Powerful stereotypes emerged of different ways of theorising: English and US distrust of (yet fascination with) 'Continental' high theory often produced the figures of a plodding, oversystematic, rationalist German theory and of French high-flying, boulevardier thought (the 'fancy French theory' of the Thatcherite view). In return, from home and foreign commentators, came images of a kind of drizzling British empiricism, often confused with a simple 'fact' collecting, and for many years seen as the enemy of theory rather than itself constituted in its own theoretical forms. Such histories of the founding moments of film theory in different national contexts continue to shape the tenor and expectations of theorists who inhabit them, and the 'home'-based debates they have to engage in.

Theorising has also been institutionally situated in such processes as the histories of journals (see Willemen and Pines, 1998: 1–11), of the proliferation of academic and textbook publishing houses and, recently, of journals, related, like so much else in the field of British higher education in the last 10 years, to the mechanisms of research funding.[5] Theory is also shaped by the career stages of academics, involved in the display of expertise and claimed innovation on which, in part, depend employment, publication, security and promotion within 'the academy'. Different institutional motivations might include working with theories in a well-established subject area such as English in the 1930s, or in an area, such as film studies in the 1950s–1970s, eager to gain accreditation and legitimacy via the incorporation of difficult, higher status 'scientific' theories.[6] These different communities of practice produce theories within highly directive processes and locations such as the 20-minute conference paper, the 5000 to 10 000 word article, the 100 000 word book or dissertation (all with a very specified role for footnotes and other unofficial spaces as the locus of tentative thought and talk). The lecture form or performance itself has been argued to be the direct descendant of the mediaeval sermon (and as such its authority is eroded by the acceleration of resource-based learning). These structures, then, shape theorising very differently for undergraduate students, learning to deploy their knowledge of theory to get grades; for newly qualified, untenured staff, perhaps anxious to assert their difference, at least in this area, from the students they teach; and, finally, for securely tenured, perhaps even celebrity, academics, moving easily between the worlds of journalism, celebrity soundbite and the academy, worlds previously so separate.

The academic theoretical style broadly shared across such histories is a tool of thought with advantages and drawbacks. Academic writing usually makes more effort than most journalism to be scrupulous in, for example, referencing clearly, trying to avoid plagiarism, trying to make explicit its own conceptual basis, guaranteeing anonymity for research interviewees, etc. But it is also driven in other, more politically situated, directions: to underplay the politics of different higher educational contexts in what constitutes its research priorities (the British five-yearly Research Assessment Exercise (RAE) and its impact on different institutions is a crucial determinant here); to make large claims from small samples (see Gray, 1997); to exaggerate 'breaks' and 'crises' in the subject area in order to justify the production of new theories and paradigms, often, oddly, combining deference to established authorities with this need to proclaim innovation (see Bordwell, 1989). The declaration and inflation of the term 'post-modernism' are a key example here (see Hayward and Kerr, 1987; Morley, 1996; McGuigan, 1999). Like news, theory cannot simply keep reporting equilibrium in a particular area; it is the sexy 'new' story or hypothesis that will get the ratings. And within the soundbite dynamics of an intensely written, even literary, research practice which relies on key quotes, the resonance (at worst, simple punning) of certain terms and phrases across several fields of knowledge production is sometimes overvalued as a way to make broad, interdisciplinary affiliations and connections. A contemporary example might be the word 'performance', which is 'sexy' because of the way it resonates with the skills consciousness (via 'performance outcomes and indicators') of much contemporary educational and business assessment, and with broad cultural interest in the 'performativity' of identities, as well as with the more familiar sense from theatre which it has always had for film study. Yet in seeming to mean so much, there is a real danger such terms get spread very thin, and come to mean very little.

Why theory?

What, then, given all these qualifications, is the value of this highly structured activity 'theory'? How can it be justified in an era when, despite the massification of higher education, there is evidence that fewer students expect or even want to continue in academic work, often assumed to be the only place where theory has any currency? How does it relate to areas of 'practice' which are themselves deeply destabilised by new technologies and the 'downscaling' of employment prospects and which may in any case need quite different approaches for the sustaining of creativity? In Britain the question is sometimes dramatised as: 'Why film theory? Does a car mechanic need the history of the internal combustion engine to fix a car?' which in fact sets up a very odd comparison between a car and a movie, of which more later. Alternatively, in echoes of some contemporary management and business theory, it is conflated with the 'intellectual capital' of firms and corporations, which is said to be produced when 'human resources' work with information technology to produce wealth through innovative ideas. Teaching about theory might be justified, within this highly instrumental scheme, as building up the brain as muscle, or as megacomputer, choosing your (weighty) thought training from the local college's software packages. But the 'smartness' of all this is usually premised on a kind of obedience (ultimately to existing structures of profitability). The more political–cultural kinds of film studies theorising might rather risk this, given the broader, egalitarian ambitions which have largely formed it and which, it seems, will not go away despite the implication in some contemporary 'postmodern' writing that we all just 'shut up and (theory) shop'.

There are other problems to confront in justifying the place of theory. Pat Holland (1997) has suggested that media practice makes hard demands on skills not tested by theory: manual dexterity, speed of response, the 'brute facts' of production. She suggest that, contrary to such theories as those sustaining 1970s' 'countercinema', there may be some truth in the claim that the reflective effort of critical thinking may 'hold up' production and even be inimical to creativity. Certainly, theories of movies could well involve more awareness and even celebration of the creative processes of production. But even for film courses involving only production, it is hard to imagine what a 'purely vocational' course (that is, one stripped of this thing 'theory') would look like. Is it possible to teach editing without in some way relating it to the changing histories of editing practices and how those are imbricated with such questions as the various 'looks' of cinema/camera, the imperatives of narrative construction in entertainment cinema, changing gender relations and how audience theory studies these? Can theorising be separated from empirical work, as though it were possible to utilise or even collect 'information' outside conceptual frameworks or as though theorising simply reproduced itself, without reference to any 'outside'? Even a simple history of technologies needs to be theoretically alert to the words and phrases that signal uncritical 'evolutionary' or 'technologicial determinist' assumptions and to the various strengths and weaknesses of such models. There is evidence within the industry[7] of mounting concern at the effects of cost cutting in the training sectors of the British cinema and television industries, for example, which suggests that 'learning on the job' or reliance on homilies extolling the 'marvellous creativity' of the Hollywood studio system will not sustain the next generation of producers.

Theory as ordinary and special

I want to suggest two main arguments 'for theory':

- theory is an ordinary, inescapable and alluring activity which deserves full recognition inside as well as outside universities and college courses;

- theory is a rather special part of a spectrum of activities within film studies.

Theory's generalising and critical methods necessarily involve quite marked kinds of distance, of generalisation and deliberation ('the ivory tower' for which it is attacked) but this distance cannot be absolute, guaranteed or unreflexive and is best thought of as a kind of to-ing and fro-ing engagement or mapping.

Theory is ordinary

It may seem odd to begin defending a specialised activity such as theory by arguing that it is partly ordinary: it tries to shape an approach to certain kinds of problems or questions about an area you are interested in and which may be quite everyday, involving how you are treated on the street, or at work, or, at a more immediate level, why you so enjoyed, or perhaps were unable to enjoy, or even get to see a particular film. This connection to the ordinary, and, incidentally, to a politics in which there is still 'something at stake' (Hall, 1992: 285–94) in cultural–theoretical work, is worth emphasising. The divide of 'theory' and 'practice' has often been a sharp one, with theory, in the most distasteful extremes, the haughty downlooker on practice, history, the everyday, secure in its self-proclaimed possession of totalising accounts – for example, of the ideological 'suturing' processes of editing or the 'closure' of narratives. Without such objective knowledge, it was implied, practice was benighted and ignorant – though it was not always apparent what practice could do to escape such large control mechanisms, or how difference and indeed change occurred. The breakdown of such forms of generalisation, which seemed to speak from a godlike nowhere, about everything (though usually in the accents of the white, male, West and often from purely film-textual evidence), can only be welcome. They are now more likely to be tested by uncertainties, by different, often more 'ordinary', voices often on the Internet.[8] For ironically it was often the case that the radical, even revolutionary/guerrilla language of much *Screen* theory ('regimes' of truth; 'economies' and 'interrogations' or 'subversions' of texts, films, concepts, etc; 'hostile terrain', etc.) was actually part of a 'rabid textuality' (McArthur, 1997) relatively uninterested in audiences.

   Yet the move into more relaxed and pluralistic alignments (such as the engagement with postfeminism charted by Brunsdon, 1997) can be hard to distinguish from the relativist, resolutely apolitical 'turn' of much postmodern theory let alone the caution often engendered in some writers by anxieties about employment prospects. It raises the problem of how to argue for 'cultural political' theoretical positions, many of which connect to older, more essentialist politics in film studies and to the dissatisfactions as well as the much vaunted pleasures of audiences. How, for example, do our offerings improve upon the best cultural journalism? Just about everything (even, as Frith and Savage (1993) point out, something as extraordinary as Madonna, or Michael Jackson) seems available for fluent theorisation, especially within the huge, cruelly tenure-driven US cultural studies 'academic market'. Even when the rhetoric is still of power, inequality, difference, politics, within such easy-seeming textualisation of everything, it becomes difficult to see exactly where are the connections to the ordinary (now usually called 'vulgar', 'crude') processes of economics, of everyday unequal access to style and cyber objects of desire. In order for the 'ordinary' of our students' experience of cinema to enter our thinking, and such discussions, we need to argue the necessary distance between their 'ordinary' viewing pleasures and dissatisfactions and the special space of theories.

Theory is specialised

Paradoxically our students, as audiences, fans, are sometimes the object of studies which celebrate their powers to remake and resist almost any media resource, in other words those films previously (or elsewhere) so securely and separately interpreted as 'the text' by the specialist theorist. In such a context, we need metaphors of far less distanced theorising than is often given in the seminar request that newcomers 'pretend to be a visitor from Mars and look at it this way'. But we still need to equip students with some sense of what is specific and special to the activity of theorising.

Emphasis on the 'ordinary viewer' within formal film theorising has been a crucial move away from the arrogance of political textualism. But theory defines and requires a rather different and special space than 'ordinary viewing'. In many cases this is what students have indeed chosen in opting for formal study of film, hoping to engage in a more energetic study of one of the most powerful modern cultural forms than can be offered by even the best journalism or ain't it coolnews.com, let alone the marketing discourses of the film conglomerates. They are usually quite well aware that such study offers the possibility of making explicit, exploring and changing their own assumptions which media imagery has helped to form.

But in suggesting that 'special' degrees of engagement with theory are rewarding, we need to take seriously the strengths of the 'ordinary' of students' interest in film and cultural debate, which is often formed by engagement with cultural journalism. Theories, even the newest and wildest, are the bread and butter of such journalism, rendering the boundaries between the academy and this journalistic 'outside' far from watertight. For example in contemporary British journalism and television film criticism such columnists are (or have been) usually ex-students and often ex-academics or part-time academics: Mark Kermode, Ros Coward, Simon Frith, Linda Grant, Lisa Jardine, Suzanne Moore, Judith Williamson. Globally indeed the commanding 'star' heights of this journalistic intellectual economy are often occupied by celebrity academics (Camille Paglia comes to mind) participating as regularly in television discussions and print journalism as in their (highly paid) academic careers (for further discussion of the academic star system, see Moran, 1998).

The downside of these permeable boundaries between everyday 'style' journalism and the academy can mean that students may feel that they have 'been there, done that' when asked to make a study of film theories. Paradoxically, though, this sense of having already vaguely tasted its theories goes along with one of the commonest objections, in the early stages of film study: 'Studying on this course means I can't just enjoy movies any more, I'm always at a kind of distance'. Urging 'step back a moment' still feels particularly tricky as applied to movies, whose very name suggests the ways they seek to move us, to have us leaning forward in our seats, holding on to the roller-coaster, or being magically entranced by a moment. Even so, the simplest after-movie comment ('that was a great performance') can still be prised open to raise huge questions: What counts as 'performance'? How does casting relate to it? What is the possibility of non-performance being understood as acting (for example the debates over the 'Kuleshov effect' in early Soviet cinema, where an actor's blank look was itself said to have signified as performance through editing)?

And there exist theoretical 'breaks' or achievements which absolutely change the way you can think and argue about an area, though not forever, and not in any guaranteed way. These 'breaks' often link to the inherited political ambitions of the subject area, as well as to equally valid desires to explore the very textures of cinema: performance, colour, voices, costume. For example, you cannot now discuss realism and cinema with any sophistication and ignore a valuable tool such as the idea of cultural verisimilitude. This replaces a simple sense that films relate to 'the real' with demands that attention be paid to the ways in which 'the real' itself is coded and appealed to in movies (Neale, 1990). A term such as 'signification', which implies codes being put into play rather than a truth being shown, valuably replaces earlier art discourses shaping film study ('search for the truth which is revealed in this great work of art'), or even in some kinds of content analysis which shaped earlier cultural–political approaches ('How many successful career women are allowed happy personal lives in studio Hollywood films? How does this relate statistically to the real world?'). Other theoretical achievements include: the understanding that film genres work with both repetition and difference which replaces antipopular discourses of banal sameness and repetition as being inevitable in genre products; the move away from talking only about the 'magic' and 'charisma' of star presence to thinking about the constructedness of stars even in their physical presence; the prising open of a distinction between historical 'audiences' and textual 'spectators' so that the 'effects' of movies can no longer be read, complacently, by the film critic sitting in front of the Steenbeck (for a clear account of such changes, see Gripsrud, 1998). Of course they will in turn be rendered irrelevant by new social movements, discourses and technologies which will put new pressures on theories. But for the foreseeable future they render obsolete previous ways of theorising, and are part of what many students are hoping to encounter in 'brained-up' film study.

Theories now

There are, however, a number of blocks to a student developing the confidence to handle such a body of theory. Like some of the films we use, certain theories, as embodied in now-standard textbooks, and even quotes within them, have acquired the status of the blockbuster/canonical. Theories such as Bordwell, Staiger, and Thompson's (1985) formulation of the 'classical Hollywood narrative' or Burch's (1969) 'institutional mode of representation' (IMR), however carefully argued and voluminously illustrated, make it difficult, in their chosen scale, for difference to breathe.

Any theory, of course, in order to be productive, needs to carve out its own approach or model of its object/subject, ignoring huge areas that it cannot or does not want or need to incorporate or see as relevant. And for teaching purposes a canonical theory or film has the advantage of having accrued a lot of easily available published debate and discussion. Conversely, though, it may seem to have precisely the character of a sacred relic, to be brought out, in selected phrases, at exam time. Tracing the genealogy of older theories can easily seem to be on the syllabus for its own sake, especially where these are often difficult, partly inherited from earlier intellectual accreditation of the subject area. While lecturers are loath to abandon them, since they were learnt with great travail, many students, not surprisingly, may feel they are 'old hat' precisely because of their status. They may wonder, for example, why so much time is spent in some film classes on the classic Mulvey 'male gaze' position (1989a; first written in 1973), especially when so much of its psychoanalytic underpinnings seem no longer key, when Mulvey herself refined and critiqued it only a few years later (Mulvey, 1989b) and when others have taken the critique even further (see Gamman and Marshment, 1988; Gledhill, 1995; Linda Williams, Chapter 19 in this volume). Ironically, the commitment to developing and therefore openly self-critiquing positions (as in the long-term work of theorists such as Mulvey), so central to debate-centred theorising, can seem like simple indecision to such students, timetabled for an hour, probably in a mass lecture, for each particular weighty dilemma of Western thought. They may then understandably learn how to ventriloquise those theoretical soundbites which have the most prestige – which can also, of course, partly because of the overlap between journalism and theory, function as contemporary style accessory ('I love it when you talk post-structuralist').

Also daunting to newcomers to theory can be its intensely deliberative, *written* mode, as they come to realise that its debates are often registered in small nuances of phrasing. The imagery of film theory is still often saturated with radical political rhetoric and with the sediments of a Marxist language of the materiality of labour (involving lamps, scalpels, tools, maps, engineering, geological shifts). For the actual persistence of a particular theoretical model is revealed 'only' in words. Theory being usually a written discourse (unfortunately even when it is spoken as a conference paper) it is necessarily denser than speech, a contrast which students can find slowing and irritating: 'Why can't s/he just put it simply?' It takes a time for the apprentice theorist to realise that a single word or naming ('postmodernism', 'thick accounts') can imply allegiance to whole continents of emphasis; that outdated models can be returned to, unwittingly, via 'slips of the tongue' ('the *spectator* [not *audience member*] is *forced* [not *invited*] into the position of . . .', 'though *merely a routine* western . . .') and that these habits take time to work through and to change. And student time now is subject to very urgent, competing claims.

The social theory and activism which underpinned 1970s' *Screen* theory – that it might help change the world politically in huge ways – has been highly complicated by subsequent history, even as a globally triumphant contemporary capitalism falters so alarmingly. Oddly enough there are similarities as well as differences between the 'moment' of 'Grand Film Theory', promising power to its apprentices, and our pluralised present. Those ambitious theories of semiotics, Marxism, structuralism and feminism broke onto the world of film study, along with the formation of the British

New Left and cultural studies, at a moment, in the 1960s, which, like the present, experienced the disintegration of a kind of state socialist Marxism, and the entry into higher education of numbers of students whose families had never seen anyone go to university before.[9] Both also share a major reconfiguration of the culturally popular and elite under the impact of new technologies, conditions of profitability and forms of ownership. But whereas in the 1960s this produced, for the emerging field of cultural studies, a tense political engagement with Marxism, feminism and culture, it is harder to say how the current upheavals and relativist emphases in the field will shape the cultural politics of cinema studies.

There is now a long-standing crisis in that totalising and essentialising rhetoric which has always been necessary to still-powerful forms of political action and decision-making. Even as political parties seek product differentiation for themselves rather than total-identity rhetorics, it is still true that in many areas of political action you still have to vote either/or; politics involves decisions, and therefore temporary closures. But with the power of totalising rhetoric has also gone the guarantee of the value of that effort which theory makes to 'stand back' in order to map the outlines essential to such political argument and action. There is a growing sense not only of the value of non-political theories of cinema (see Bordwell and Carroll, 1996) but that theories are needed which are not:

> the will to truth ... but ... a set of contested, localised, conjunctural knowledges, which have to be debated in a dialogical way ... a practice which always thinks about its intervention in a world in which it would make some difference, in which it would have some effect.
>
> (Hall, 1992: 286)

Alluring challenges exist here, not least in the relationship between films and the attempts at a politics of representation which they often provoke in their audiences. It is now harder to settle for 'misrepresentation' or 'stereotyping' alone as fully satisfying theories of how a film 'works' politically: somehow politics and textuality need to be held in a kind of tension rather than theory promising access to a body of guaranteed politically effective knowledge, to be applied to movies. We need to engage with questions of aesthetics, or, for example, with the various ways of looking in cinema (for women-looking-at-men, as well as for men-looking-at-women, men-at-men, women-at-women) or with the powerfully inherited modes of melodrama which continue to shape contemporary cinema (for a striking exploration of these strands, see Gledhill, 1995).

Yet despite the importance of such historical–constructivist rethinking, it is still the case that for women, and for other groups with a material stake in shifting the conditions of representation, and thus of employment, and of 'the personal', the risk of essentialism is one worth taking, that is, the risk of speaking as I have just done as though there were unified groups which, for the purposes of political change, can be called 'women' or even where the word 'we' can be used. The problems with this attempt to continue the political projects of film studies now are partly the changed conditions of politics in general, and, specifically, a cynical knowingness which when it hears the words 'cultural politics' is likely to reach for the words 'political correctness'.

The current rise of 'queer theory' illustrates some of the excitement, and the persistence and problems, of attempted cultural–political connections now. As Jackie Stacey writes, queer theory is 'in some ways taken as the guarantor of a sustained political edge to cinema studies; it both celebrates the diversity of visual cultures in the 1990s and explores the intersections of marginal positionalities' (Stacey, 1996: 389). With its emphasis (close to a canon) on certain writers and themes such as 'the body', drag, parody, style, pleasure, multiple and shifting identities, performance, it is attractive to students, and as 'theory' runs well with certain kinds of fine art practice courses, and, indeed, with some of the skills needed for future employment in the media industries, especially advertising and public relations. But its high-style way of working by pun, metaphor and symbolisation, rather than evidence, criteria, histories, means that some valuable theoretical approaches to the social, historical and economic are lost – and then are difficult for the apprentice theorist to grasp. Huge problems of methodology are raised by the question of what is to count as a 'queer' (*authentically* queer'?) text or reading, within an emphasis on the rhetorical/inauthentic nature of *all* identities (see McArthur, 1997: 82).

As Stuart Hall has suggested we do not know what it is like to conduct a politics without a guarantee (1996) and theorising, too, often seems nostalgic for cultural–political guarantees even though 'film theory' often now takes the form of a fluid emphasis on 'middle range theorising which moves easily from bodies of evidence to more general arguments and implications' (Bordwell and Carroll, 1996: xiii). The language is less frequently that of height, depth, distance, rigour but more often process of – 'theorising' (fluid, provisional) or 'thickness' (a contrast to the 'height' of God's-position theory) implying a situatedness, an awareness that other paradigms than your chosen one impinge on your topic.

Theory is becoming understood as itself partly rhetorical, as not conforming to fantasies of utterly objective thought. The relatively new sense of give and take, to and fro, even of a proper scale for the importance of theorising compared with other activities, is a welcome change from an emphasis on a too narrow range of theories and on too little engagement with other, related fields of study and even of life outside the lecture hall. Any theory which is not simply playing out the more grandiose fantasies of control of its operator is now much more likely to be aware of the challenges which the empirical, or the political, or the aesthetic might pose to its arguments. It is now much better understood that the history of theory in film and cultural studies is partly one of social movements (such as those raising questions of class, race, gender, or of the protest movement against the Vietnam War in the 1960s) or even technologies (sound, colour, widescreen and now digitalisation). These have provoked theoretical breaks and new paradigms, often without the theory acknowledging that the 'break', the 'surprise' from experience, has come from 'outside' itself. This is also true of the earliest 'classic' (that is, 'pre-semiotic', from the 1910s to the 1930s) theorists of cinema, often ignored now in favour of a rattling yarn of serial monogamy, film theorists besotted by one Big Theory after another, then settling for scattered affairs or theory shopping. Yet the 'classic' theorists were engaging with these new technologies in the full blast of modernity and in some cases, such as Eisenstein or Bazin, more or less directly with film's relationship to the representation of huge political upheavals and movements such as the Russian Revolution or the post-(First World) war settlements in Europe. Their responses were to debate on cinema as an art form: questions of how it is aligned with other arts/technologies; cinema as a popular form, as an economic practice, as, like photography, 'too' closely linked to the real for its images to be accredited as art. These in many ways resemble those currently shaping the multimedia ecology of cinema, trying to locate its specificity within all its combinations with digital, electronic, globalised, conglomerate media, its survival in forms where the existence of the projector and even of a camera have been questioned. Early theoretical debates on the relationship between the real, realism and film (for which André Bazin is a key figure) likewise anticipate anxieties around the capacity of digitalisation to destabilise the reliability of the evidence apparently offered by photographic and filmic images. And as more historical work is done on early theorists, the surprisingly modern tenor of work such as Emilie Altenloh's 1914 empirical study of audiences becomes available for study (see Gripsrud, 1998: 207).

Conclusions

Theory, always historically positioned, is inescapable in any considered practice. Our hypothetical car mechanic may find her work intolerable, and indeed replaceable, if it consists entirely of behaving like a competent machine. She will be using some sense of the whole engine to fix bolts successfully; she has to operate creatively with something close to theories – those buried traces of theories which we call assumptions or even, if more elaborated, definitions – of energy, combustion. Should she ever want to drive the car she will need maps. Maybe here we should halt this parallel, for cars and movies are such different kinds of product. Films, as cultural industries, sell precisely on a blend of repetition and difference, on magical-seeming moments: of a face in motion, or a burst of screen energy which cannot be exactly predicted in advance yet on which 'standards' and sales depend. Car engines, whatever their differences, need a sameness or machine-tooled standardisation which only the thinnest and most hostile accounts could attribute to cinema.

Theorising has to be a part of any serious study of cinema, a set of sophisticated and engaged activities, necessarily working alongside others, in the case of an entity as complex as cinema; attempting what should be the goal of any 'postmodern' education (if postmodernism allowed us to talk of goals): a fully interdisciplinary approach to the range of cultural–political and aesthetic processes that make up 'cinema'. It will always have to operate with tensions, such as its necessary distance from 'common sense' or 'lived experience', even as it tries to get close to those. Or it will be pulled by the attractions of relativist approaches, but with awareness that the 'absolute relativism' of post-structuralism or postmodernism is not only itself a totalising position but, more importantly, one which can sustain no social theory of truth, so important for feminist, black cultural and other democratising impulses within film studies. It will need to register the urgencies of practical/creative media-making and of production histories of films which will always impinge on analysis. These to-and-fro processes of curiosity and theorising, applied to a never-still, and hugely significant, object of study sound to me like the best kind of 'life skills' for the twenty-first century, and still a central method for mapping the terrain of cinema.

Endnotes

1   See Noël Carroll's essay 'Prospects for film theory' (1996) which lists 'political correctness' as the third of his major 'impediments to film theory'. His account gave this British reader a sense of how powerfully that term has become established in the USA to stand in for political dogmatism.

2   British further education (post-16 years old but not to degree level) and higher education (post-18 years old, usually to degree level) are strikingly distinguished by their adjectives of direction and height.

3   It is worth noting that though contemplative distance is still a key part of the imagery of theorising, the word's origins, in 'theoria', are shared with the Greek word for 'gods' and for the 'theatre' interested in influencing them, suggesting a more rhetorical origin for 'theory' than is present in the pure 'distance' model. See also Barker and Brooks (1998) for a striking re-thinking of the supposed virtues of 'distance' and involvement in relation to specialism, in audience responses to *Judge Dredd* texts.

4   Bordwell and Carroll's (1996) recent collection against 'theory', though wonderfully acerbic (like Bordwell, 1989) on many of the absurdities and lack of evidence of what passed for 'high theory', still hugely privileges psychoanalysis as theory itself. This is then set up against cognitivism, which surely raises equally profound problems in its application to film.

5   For example, consider the five-yearly Research Assessment Exercise in British universities, or the 'free-market' rhetoric and differently driven 'star system' of much US higher education.

6   See the ways in which Althusserian Marxism or Lacanian psychoanalysis deployed the notion of science. The basis of the apparent scientificness of the Lacanian and other post-structuralist models has been attacked (and given spectacular amounts of journalistic coverage) by Sokal and Bricmont (1999). Conversely, Norris (1995) provides a valuable corrective to absolute relativism.

7   See the current London School of Economics project, *Study of Industrial Modes of Production of Television Drama* (SIMPTD), funded by the Economic and Social Research Council (ESRC).

8   See for example the work of Jackie Stacey (1993) or the ongoing work by Annette Kuhn for the Economic and Social Research Council (ESRC) 'Cinema Culture in 1930s Britain' project based at Glasgow University, for work connecting academic scholarship and theory to 'ordinary' viewers' memories of 1930s–1950s' cinema.

9   For the 1960s this was dramatised by Soviet tanks rolling into Hungary and Czechoslovakia, prompting rethinking of Soviet state socialism. For the 1990s the collapse of that Eastern bloc state socialism was symbolised by the demise of the Berlin Wall in 1989. Later crises, such as the collapse of the Eastern and Russian stock markets in 1998, may augur deeper change in what can still most adequately be described as global capitalism.

References

Andermahr, S., Lovell, T. and Wolkowitz, C. 1997: *A concise glossary of feminist theory*. London and New York: Arnold.

Barker, M. and Brooks, K. 1998: *Knowing audiences: Judge Dredd, its friends, fans and foes.* Luton: University of Luton Press.

Bordwell, D. 1989: *Making meaning: inference and rhetoric in the interpretation of cinema.* Cambridge, MA: Harvard University Press.

Bordwell, D. and Carroll, N. (eds) 1996: *Post-theory: reconstructing film studies* (especially Bordwell's chapter, 'Contemporary film studies and the vicissitudes of grand theory'). Madison, WI: University of Wisconsin Press.

Bordwell, D., Staiger, J. and Thompson, K. 1985: *The classical Hollywood cinema – film style and mode of production to 1960.* New York: Columbia University Press.

Bordwell, D. and Thompson, K. 1979; 1985; 1990; 1993; 1997: *Film art: an introduction.* New York: Alfred A. Knopf; Reading, MA: Addison-Wesley; New York: McGraw-Hill.

Brunsdon, C. 1997: Post-feminism and shopping films. In Brunsdon, C. *Screen tastes: soap opera to satellite dishes.* London and New York: Routledge.

Burch, N. 1969: *Theory of film practice.* Princeton, NJ: Princeton University Press.

Carroll, N. 1996: Prospects for film theory. In Bordwell, D. and Carroll, N. (eds), *Post-theory reconstructing film studies.* Madison, WI: University of Wisconsin Press.

Frith, S. and Savage, J. 1993: Pearls and swine: the intellectuals and the mass media. *New Left Review* number 198: 107–16.

Gamman, L.and Marshment, M. (eds) 1988: *The female gaze: women as viewers of popular culture.* London: the Women's Press.

Geraghty, C. 1998: Audience and 'ethnography': questions of practice. In Geraghty, C. and Lusted, D. (eds), *The television studies book.* London and New York: Arnold.

Gledhill, C. 1995: Women reading men. In Kirkham, P. and Thumim, J. (eds), *Me Jane: masculinity, movies and women.* London: Lawrence and Wishart.

Gray, A. 1997: Learning from experience: cultural studies and feminism. In McGuigan, J. (ed.), *Cultural methodologies.* London: Sage.

Gripsrud, J. 1998: Film audiences. In Hill, J. and Church Gibson, P. (eds), *The Oxford guide to film studies.* Oxford and New York: Oxford University Press.

Hall, S. 1992: Cultural studies and its theoretical legacies. In Grossberg, L., Nelson, C. and Treichler, P. (eds), *Cultural studies.* New York and London: Routledge.

Hall, S. 1996: The problem of ideology: Marxism without guarantees. In Morley, D. and Kuan-Hsing, C. (eds), *Stuart Hall: critical dialogues in cultural studies.* London and New York: Routledge, 25–46.

Hall, S. 1997: *Race: the floating signifier.* VHS tape, The Media Education Foundation.

Hayward, P. and Kerr, P. 1987: Introduction. *Screen* **28**(2).

Holland, P. 1997: Thinking the impractical: doing the unthinkable – the uneasy meeting of theory and practice. Paper delivered to the Association for Media Cultural and Communication Studies Conference, Sheffield, December 1997.

Lyotard, J.-F. 1984: *The postmodern condition: a report into the condition of knowledge.* Manchester: Manchester University Press: 48.

McArthur, C. 1997: Report on Screen Studies Conference. *Screen* **38**(1).

McGuigan, J. 1999: *Modernity and postmodern culture.* London: Open University Press.

Moran, J. 1998: Cultural studies and academic stardom. *International Journal of Cultural Studies* **1**(1).

Morley, D. 1996: Postmodernism: the rough guide. In Curran, J., Morley, D. and Walkerdine, V. (eds), *Cultural studies and communications.* London and New York: Arnold.

Mulvey, L. 1989a: Visual pleasure and narrative cinema. In Mulvey, L., *Visual and other pleasures.* London: Macmillan, 14–26.

Mulvey, L. 1989b: Afterthoughts on 'Visual pleasure and narrative cinema' inspired by King Vidor's *Duel in th sun* (1946). In Mulvey, L., *Visual and other pleasures*. London: Macmillan, 29–38.

Neale, S. 1990: Questions of genre. *Screen* **31**(1).

Norris, C. 1995: Culture, criticism and communal values: on the ethics of enquiry. In Adam, B. and Allan, S. (eds), *Theorizing culture*. London: UCL Press.

Sokal, A. and Bricmont, J. 1999: *Fashionable nonsense: postmodern intellectuals' abuse of science*. New York: Picador.

Stacey, J. 1993: *Stargazing: Hollywood cinema and female spectatorship*. London and New York: Routledge.

Stacey, J. 1996: Report of The Society for Cinema Studies Conference, 1996. *Screen* **37**(4).

Stray, C. 1998: *Classics transformed: schools, universities and society in England, 1830–1960*. Oxford: Clarendon Press.

Willemen, P. and Pines, J. (eds) 1998: *The essential framework: classic film and TV essays*. London: Epigraph Publications.

Williams, R. 1983: *Keywords*. London: Collins.

3　Film theory and the revolt against master narratives

Bill Nichols

The accumulation of a wide variety of theories and methods over the past 80-odd years represents a dynamic, critical engagement with cinema. It also signals a clear obligation to locate historically theories that now sediment into what can be recounted as the story of film theory past. Such activity fits squarely with the onus of academic scholarship to preserve and use the past. But to the extent that the preservation of things past becomes an end in itself, 'it's history', in the vernacular sense of over and done with. Clearly, past theory is far too vital and formative of present effort to deserve such a fate. Within this nexus of previous thought and debate we locate ourselves and orientate our own work toward a future in part determined by the nature and quality of our engagement with the past.

A temptation exists to reify film theory into blanket assumptions and essentialized categories such as Bordwell's glib 'SLAB theory' catch-all for work based on 'Saussurean semiotics, Lacanian psychoanalysis, Althusserian Marxism and Barthesian textual theory' (1989: 385). Rather than treat film theory as congealed dogma, we can regard it as a historically situated process of conceptualization and generalization. The object of this process is to ask of film, its related media (television, video, digital images), and its various forms (classic fiction, art cinema, third and fourth world cinema, non-fiction or documentary, and experimental or avant-garde film) how they work and why they matter, both here and now and there and then. To theorize is to step back, to assemble categories and concepts that will allow us to formulate ideas about film that have greater extension than a single instance. These ideas now have, as do the films and movements, genres and periods examined, a history. We, through our engagement with this history, make it part of our contemporary participation in its extension forward.

The process of stepping back from particular films to ask questions about what films generally say and do, what they have in common in structure or use, encourages a philosophic pose. From this position, those preexisting theories or prevailing methods with sufficient explanatory power to account for most of cinema – narrative film most centrally – have obvious appeal. Numerous candidates have gained nomination and each has generated valuable results. These include:

- a Marxist concept of culture as a realm of symbolic production linked to a society's economic mode of production and the perpetuation of its existing, hierarchical relations (James and Berg, 1996; Jameson, 1992; Shohat and Stam, 1994);
- a semiotic theory of sign systems that can grasp the organizational subtleties of film form (Metz, 1974a, b; Nichols, 1976; Silverman, 1983);
- formalist and neoformalist notions of film structure as a semi-autonomous domain with an internal history of development and a self-contained system of signification (Burch, 1973; Thompson, 1981);
- a psychoanalytic theory of the subject whose use of sign systems is always tied to issues of gender, desire and the unconscious (Doane, 1987; Heath, 1981; Kaplan, 1990; Silverman, 1983; Studlar, 1988);
- a post-structural theory of narrative as a process of lending meaning to the historical world by investing the historical world with those meanings narrative form provides (Mitchell, 1981; Polan, 1990; White, 1987); and
- a phenomenology of film experience as a visceral, existential mode of encounter irreducible to concepts and categories (Andrew, 1978; Sobchack, 1992).

At their best, these theories have not engendered 'master narratives' for film so much as *conceptual frames* within which historically situated processes of generalization address significance and value in variable ways. Continual transformations occur in relation to time and place. The cumulative result traces out a pattern that is neither linear nor predictable. It is a pattern of socially and historically conscious engagement that remains at odds with a more classically philosophic or detached pose. It is in relation to this pattern that the theorist must locate himself or herself if history, politics and ethics are to serve as an articulated basis for theory itself.

Theorization about film shares a common pattern, divisible into three moments, with modern literary and cultural study (Patterson, 1995). In very simplified form, the profile of previous theorization looks like a series of possible answers to some deceptively simple questions: What is cinema? How does it work? Why does it affect us? The first moment of film theorizing shared classic historicist assumptions with literary and art historical scholarship. The external, historical world provided the yardstick by which to measure all attempts at representation. This world was made available through factual sources – artifacts and documents – that would, once carefully assembled and examined, provide entry into the spirit, or Zeitgeist, of the times. This Zeitgeist, in turn, informed or colored all cultural production. Such a procedure gave theory a social bent and works like Siegfried Kracauer's *From Caligari to Hitler* (1947) their political potency. The subjective work of art corresponded to the objective, historical world in ways that the attentive and diligent scholar could specify. Not only Kracauer but Rotha and Griffith (1950), Leyda (1960), Bazin (1967; 1971) and other early critics and theorists adopted this point of view.

The social, sometimes Marxist, strain to early film theory subsided in the 1960s and 1970s. In this second moment, pronouncedly formal methods gained prominence. For example, semiotics was an attempt to elucidate a structural coherence to cinema; auteur theory was a vehicle by which to identify authorship in elements of style and structure, and a revival of Russian formalism and Brechtian reflexivity was a way to elaborate the techniques governing narrative construction. Later, psychoanalysis became a way to account for transcendental, ideological 'effects' of the cinematic apparatus as a whole, including its representation of women as scopophilic objects of desire, to-be-looked-at and either revered or punished.

All these methods provided a clearly formalist turn to film study and coincided, not accidently, with the rise of film studies as an academic discipline. Metz's *Film language* (1974b) and *The imaginary signifier* (1982), Mulvey's 'Visual pleasure and narrative cinema' (1975), Wollen's *Signs and meaning in the cinema* (1969) and Wood's *Howard Hawks* (1968) exemplify these tendencies as does the more recent *New vocabularies in film semiotics* (Stam *et al.*, 1992). Principles of cinematic structure, effects of the apparatus, qualities of formal organization and aspects of directorial artistry provide necessary mediations for social and political effects. A rhetoric of political regard often persists but fails to generate concepts as powerful as those of semiotics, auteurism or formalism, except for a strongly feminist current within psychoanalytic theory. Film studies' gain in disciplinary status by these approaches is also its loss in social consequence and historical significance outside the frame of a self-contained, disciplinary development.

These methods also did for cinema what both romantic and formalist methods such as new criticism had done for literature: they redeemed cinema from the material and historical determinants of the marketplace. They legitimated its study as a liberal art or humanities, rather than as a social science, discipline. These methods displaced film theory from the level of movies and their consequences to that of cinema and its qualities. They granted to cinema the (classic) status of art as a disinterested, non-practical form of engagement first formulated by Kant (1851) and perpetuated by formalist theories ever since.

Ironically, however, this redeeming gesture only sanctioned yet another form of commodity fetishism now tied to the non-practical or aesthetic: objects of artistic merit regain in economic exchange value what they forfeit in use value when they become the esteemed work of named artists with distinctive styles (Bourdieu, 1984; Kavolis, 1979).

Like formal literary theory and criticism, these approaches gave substantive weight to claims for a distinctive status to cinema as an object of academic study. Cinema became an art *form* whose distinct, formal properties nominated it for academic consideration alongside the other liberal arts: 'the seventh art'. In Roman Jakobson's influential terms, literature and, by extension, art cinema, stressed the poetic function of communication in contrast to phatic, referential or imperative functions, among others (1960). In Jacques Lacan's equally influential formulations cinema became a perfect medium to explore the relationships between images, identity and desire, especially in relation to gender but not necessarily history (1977). Film might serve social or political ends but these ends provided less specificity and less promise of guaranteeing institutional (academic) security than the formal and artistic properties of the medium itself. Questions related to the place of *film in history* yielded to questions of the *history of film*.

The third, contemporary, moment of cultural study acknowledges the importance of its two predecessors but inflects the sediments of these earlier moments in new ways. This, like the first moment, is a more social and historical method of inquiry. What has changed from the first moment is that the formal marks of distinction accorded film, or literature, are no longer taken as subjective interpretations of a preexistent, objective reality. Film form is now seen as part and parcel of a larger, social process of constructing concepts and categories that are always relative to alternative constructs and always subject to historical transformation. Rather than a reality/representation, content/form, denotation/connotation, or norm/deviance model that accepts one set of terms and conditions as a given by which to measure others, this third, post-structural, moment acknowledges realities and norms but treats them as social constructions like any others. The subordination of systems of representation, form, connotation and deviance to a factual base of reality, content, denotation and norms comes to be seen as the social mechanism by which a classically historicist view of the world gains dominance.

In this third moment, the positivist dimension of historicism falls by the wayside: no longer does the lived world offer up indisputable artifacts and documents that attest to the historical truth against which all representations can be measured. Artifacts and documents are themselves seen as representations. These representations allow for the formulation of statements that acquire the patina of truth not because they are facts and nothing but facts but because they conform to the protocols governing what counts as truth within a given institutional, discursive or representational frame (Foucault, 1972, 1979, 1980; Lyotard, 1984; Nichols, 1981; Plantinga, 1997; Rosenstone, 1995; Sobchack, 1996). The social location of the theorist once again becomes integral to the work of conceptualization. My own location in this post-structural moment and my own commitment to a historically situated, politically or ethically informed theory belong to this moment and the institutional frame it has generated. Cinema becomes less a semi-autonomous series of formal patterns and shifts that stress the poetic aspect of communication in ways that defamiliarize previous or common usage than another representational system that constructs the sense of reality it simultaneously claims to represent (Jameson, 1988).

Cinema now comes to be regarded as a socially constructed category serving socially significant ends. Like theory itself, cinema has less a privileged ontological status than a variable historical purpose. This allows for considerable exploration of its similarities and differences with other media and art forms since its 'essential nature' is no longer jeopardized by such syncretism and its social function is, in fact, further elucidated. Cinema no longer eludes the marketplace but retains, often in dialectical or conflictual fashion, its status as a material commodity and an idealized, even utopian, representation of socially repressed possibility.

The historicist assumptions of earlier theorizing that proposed virtually causal links between Zeitgeist and cultural objects, between the dominant ideology and the most prevalent art, also collapse in this third moment of film theory. Idealist categories of holistic world-views, unitary Zeitgeists, and clear-cut periodizations fracture into more localized and materially based concepts such as gender, ethnicity and class. Each concept entails multiple viewpoints, contending perspectives and conflictual relations of hierarchy, power and hegemony.

In the case of psychoanalysis this collapse has been, until recently, partial. A certain causal linkage persists between cinema and gender, particularly in arguments that male desire controls the camera's gaze at the expense of women, a category that remains undifferentiated as to class, nationality or ethnicity. As in the transformations of Sartre's existential philosophy at the hands of Frantz Fanon (1964; 1967) to address the specificities of the colonial situation, some psychoanalytic theory has begun to rethink questions of desire and the cinema in terms of categories other than that of women as an overarching generality (Butler, 1993; Mulvey, 1996; Silverman, 1992). Claims that cinema itself yielded universal 'ideological effects' (Baudry, 1970), a position more characteristic of the first phase of cultural study, no longer seems convincing from the multiple points of view of women of color, gays and lesbians, African-Americans or Asian-Americans, Pakistani-British or Caribbean-British working-class or subaltern subjects. Cinema's consequences return to the fore as they regain historical nuance and social specificity (Bobo, 1995; Friedman, 1991; Gabriel, 1982; James and Berg, 1996).

In this third moment, the preexisting and overarching theories mentioned earlier (Marxism, psychoanalysis, formalism, etc.) retain their usefulness but their disposition toward a teleology of revolution, cure or formal self-renewal comes to be seen as a debatable, historical legacy rather than as the essentialist core of the theory. The goal of providing explanations for cultural forms and social practices loses its appeal in favor of an emphasis on the (preferably thick) interpretation of specific forms, practices and effects (Bobo, 1995; Clover, 1992; Gaines, 1991; Nichols, 1994; Russo, 1981; Williams, 1989). It is in particulars rather than abstractions that larger generalities take on forms that have emotional impact, social effect and ideological import. Contemporary film theory, like the cultural anthropology proposed by Geertz (1973) and the new historicism of Greenblatt (1980), works out from the specific or particular to tell stories, offer interpretations, make arguments and propose conceptual frames that do not aspire to the status of 'master narratives' but strive to demonstrate their usefulness in specific situations and for specific ends.

The telescoped review of film theory provided here not only reveals how the general pattern of its history parallels that of literary and cultural study generally, it also lends added prominence to what seems closest to us: the present moment. In accord with this emphasis the final main section of this chapter sets out to explore some of the pressure points within contemporary theory. In this section I will be discussing three concepts of signal importance: visual culture, representation and rhetoric. These concepts are not issues internal to a specific form of theorizing nor are they specific to film theory alone. They are, instead, concepts nominated for consideration because of their striking and, ideally, foundational centrality to theorizing about film in materialist, situated ways still capable of confronting the work of desire and the unconscious, conflict and class struggle, value and symbolic exchange in both theory and practice.

The concept of visual culture signals the importance of both culture and the visual to contemporary theory. The importance of *visual* culture corresponds to the importance of *multi*culturalism, or identity politics, where the struggle to bring diverse, potentially incompatible, identities into being entails an effort to give visual representation to what had been previously homogenized, displaced or repressed. Like ideology, culture has acquired a weighty accretion of meanings and uses (Williams, 1976). Contemporary concepts of culture depart from previous ones that defined culture as a discrete domain of artistic production or an observable repertoire of ritualized social practices common to a people or nation. Culture now stands for something closer to a symbolic economy. Culture represents the aggregation of all those embodied forms of social practice that stand over against us yet also require our participation for their perpetuation and transformation (Berger and Luckmann, 1966). As an economy, culture involves the management of desire and the law, subjectivity and the social order, meaning and form. As such it is open-ended but not teleological; it changes but neither predictably nor necessarily for the better.

Modern cultural study spans multiple media and diverse, interrelated cultures. Multiculturalism disputes the idea that American, Western or European culture can serve as the civilizing 'glue' to bind citizens into one nation and one people. Historically, culture pegged the exchange rate of its symbolic capital to the value of its high cultural products, those more elite forms of culture that affirmed national identity and social status among the dominant classes, partly by providing a common set of – idealized and sometimes unattainable – reference points for all citizens. Multiculturalism regards such a culture as one defined and maintained (managed as an economy) by a distinct and dominant stratum of society for the purpose of building national consensus (Bishop, 1989; Chow, 1993; Ferguson *et al.*, 1990; Gilroy, 1987; Jameson, 1992; Said, 1978; Williams and Christian, 1994; Wilson and Dissanayake, 1996). Visual culture provides one key domain in which questions of identity and difference, self and other, representation and self-representation actively contend.

The modern university and its academic disciplines are one specific site where different conceptions of culture come to be institutionalized. The twentieth-century university initially granted disciplinary status to the study of national culture – in terms of indigenous art and literature – not only because they could be seen to possess the formal integrity of disciplines but also because they served the purpose of 'general education' for a predominantly technocratic society. Art and literature offered idealized and visible reference points to complement the all too invisible hand of the marketplace. If industrial and post-industrial society characteristically atomizes and commodifies social relationships, culture promises to do what the market could not: put the organic sense of lived community back together again. Culture is an aesthetic means to a political end. It need not produce avid nationalists but it should generate a common ground of universalized subjectivity for all citizens. From this ground particularized technocratic, managerial and professional knowledge takes root and diverges. Through culture, and certainly the *visual* culture of movies, television, fashion, architecture and landscape, citizens come to see the national forest from the individual trees.

By contrast, multiculturalism emphasizes diversity and difference within a nation rather than commonality.[1] The earlier emphasis on art, form and the poetic dimension to texts as the core of a great (national or European) tradition conflicts dramatically with the priorities of groups and collectivities who see in cinema, as in visual culture more broadly, an arena of political contestation. Formalist concepts and aesthetic categories become incorporated within interpretations aimed at bringing diverse identities and distinct cultural formations into a condition of visibility: 'Visibilities are preeminently social and the bringing into the condition of visibility is always apolitical or a political act' (Soussloff, 1997: 78). This shift relocates history from its position as the 'background' for a formal system to the position of *the ground* for all systems of communication and exchange that themselves constitute the very terrain we take as preexistent and external to formal structure.

The gaps that culture promised to anneal earlier in this century – most notably of socio-economic class with its burden of undue privilege and unequal opportunity – have cracked open along a number of fault lines from gender orientation to ethnic and racial identity. Alternative group identities have gained a visible sense of common purpose in relation to a diversity of races, ethnicities, gender orientations and creeds rather than a diversity of internally homogenous nation-states.

In contrast to assimilationist politics, identity politics asks whether different forms of collectivity are, in fact, incommensurate rather than ultimately in accord with one another. Such a politics opposes the pluralism of an earlier, more officially optimistic, period (1940s–1950s). The rise of distinct cultures to a condition of visibility accompanies a radical shift away from democratic ideals of universalism (equality under the law for all regardless of gender, color, sexual orientation and so on) toward a particularism that insists on equality precisely in relation to differences of gender, color, sexual orientation and the like (Zizek, 1992; 1994).

The newer academic disciplines that arose in the second half of the twentieth century, from film studies, women studies and ethnic studies to gay and lesbian studies and cultural studies, accompany this reconception of diversity. No longer are class and the uneven distribution of wealth the great divide; group identities and the hierarchical imposition of stigma (visible signs of subordinate status) become of central importance. Stereotyping, discrimination, bias and harassment by others contribute to the manifestation of a contestatory affirmation of group identity. Inequities of wealth and class difference, however, often remain an internal tension within each group's identity.

In the academy, these new disciplines often play a role in a new 'general education' initiative that seeks less to build national consensus than to promote diverse interpretations of a once common culture and to grant recognition to new social constituencies whose interests these new academic disciplines serve. Rather than a binding glue, culture becomes a contested arena, with administrative forms of multiculturalism stressing 'respect' and 'tolerance' for a diversity of viewpoints. If, however, different cultures and perspectives are incommensurate, tolerance, a disposition primarily available to those who already possess the power to abuse it, no longer suffices. Tolerance must yield to a more thoroughgoing consideration of the ethics and politics of representation and visual culture (Druckery, 1996; Gross *et al.*, 1988; Heidegger, 1977; Soussloff, 1997; Virilio, 1988).

Much of the important theorizing in cinema in the past 10 years addresses those forms of independent, documentary, third and fourth cinemas that have contributed significantly to making these new forms of diversity and identity visible. In what ways are modes of self-representation among minority populations or within other cultures commensurate with the documentary and ethnographic film tradition in the West? How does a gay or lesbian symbolic economy intersect with the cinematic mechanisms of the gaze and desire? What role does narrative play in telling the stories of repressed histories and in constructing a consciousness of future alternatives? Film study seems centrally implicated in questions of what forms of cultural affiliation can be constructed, what identities can be assumed or understood, what degrees of commensurateness can be forged and what levels of incommensurateness can be recognized among the diverse cultures that constitute our postmodern condition.

In this context, film theory has undertaken a radical revision of previous positions both to bring to light what was evident on the surface all along – stereotyping, bigotry, bias – and to reveal what was not – alternative subjectivities and orientations. Incommensurate differences may persist, masked but not vanquished by an ideology of tolerance. Lesbian desire may mark out a terrain and a trajectory at odds with male quest narratives; ethnic identity may only sustain its vitality when assimilation becomes an acute form of the paradox of identity on the other's terms and ethnographic forms of realism may serve more as a point of departure than as a universal model. In pursuing such issues the study of visual culture serves less as a universalizing glue than as a particularizing tool, cracking open myths of commonality based on abstract principles of equality to examine the specific operations whereby subcultural identities and subjectivities take shape around the concrete principles of racially, socio-economically and gender-specific forms of social relationship. What we might call, in parallel with historical consciousness, cultural consciousness becomes an issue of negotiation, performativity and representation rather than one of essentialized origins. Such consciousness is less instilled or affirmed than produced.

The emphasis on *visual* culture also compels us to rethink some central tenets of cultural theory. Ever since Plato, visual forms of representation have earned many epithets but seldom have these included knowledge. Knowledge, and especially, truth, remain reserved as the province of language (arbitrary sign-systems whose units bear no necessary relation to their referents). It then fell to that distinctive discursive formation known as philosophy to lay down the rules of reason, or logic, to which all claimants to more specialized knowledge would be bound. Culture, then, might in some views be tolerated as a symbolic economy of pleasure (Aristotle, Kant) and, in others, not tolerated at all (Plato, Descartes).

Recognition of visual culture as a field of study acknowledges appeals to the senses as a form of knowledge production. This form of knowledge production is distinct from appeals to the intellect or cognitive faculty. For the intellect, logic prevails over affect; for the senses the converse holds, bringing with it a distinct form of knowledge. The intellect, according to classic distinctions, devoted itself to processing the signifieds of linguistic systems that had been stripped of the sensuous, material, form of their signifiers. This is what philosophy has always done, segregating itself from rhetoric by this very means. Rhetoric and affect, though, are fundamental to visual culture and the knowledge of self, other, history and culture it affords.

In this regard, the most regressive current in contemporary film study is the nomination of analytic philosophy and cognitive psychology as global theoretical frameworks rather than occasionally useful adjuncts (Bordwell and Carroll, 1996; Carroll, 1996). These approaches uphold the rule of reason and a philosophic tradition that can only accommodate affect, emotion, subjectivity, desire, the unconscious or the historical, material, body within bounds that deny them foundational status or systematic integrity. Analytic philosophy and cognitive psychology cling to the same assumptions of abstract rationality and democratic equality that led to a politics of consensus (based on a denial of bodily, material difference) and the repression of a politics of identity. Most commensurate with social science forms of game theory, logic-based problem-solving and theories of cognitive processing that can be replicated by computer software, these approaches offer considerable challenge to the intellect but appreciably less reward to cultural studies. They dissociate the theorist from any sense of historical situatedness and allow theory to stand with its feet firmly planted in the air. Cognitive psychology and analytic philosophy, in fact, themselves exemplify a conceptual framework radically incommensurate with a politics of multiculturalism and social representation.[2]

The study of visual culture as a sensuous, affective domain capable of producing distinct forms of knowledge and consequences outside a classic subjective/objective dichotomy follows from reconceptualizations of ideology and language (Belsey, 1980; Bennett, 1979; Coward and Ellis, 1977; Hebdige, 1979; Taussig, 1993). The figurative aspects of language, rather than being consigned to the arid taxonomy of a denatured rhetoric, become crucial: metaphor and the other rhetorical tropes become not the enemies of logic but the allies of knowledge and power. It is figuration, the ability to make visible what had lain dormant, present but unseen, that governs the seventeenth-century idea of wit and modern ideas of insight and interpretation. Figuration *makes* visible, it restores insight. It generates an embodied form of knowledge in rhetoric, in historiography, in interpretative writing and expressive practice. Figuration is crucial to the formalist concept of defamiliarization as well as to Althusser's (1971) concept of ideology as an imaginary relation to our actual situation and Foucault's notion of modern disciplinary regimes that bring knowledge into a condition of visibility, be it through discourse or images (Foucault, 1972). For these reasons, visual culture becomes a vital arena in the contemporary symbolic economy of law and desire (Apter and Pietz, 1993; Berger, 1972; Gonzalez-Crussi, 1995; Jenks, 1995; Nichols, 1981; Wollen, 1993; Wollen and Cooke, 1995).

Characterizations of modernity as the society of the spectacle is one consequence of placing figuration centrally. A turn toward visual culture collectively, from film, video and digital graphics to art, performance pieces and virtual realities as symbolic economies of knowledge production pertinent to the identities of diverse groups and social formations is another. The visual is no longer a means of verifying the certainty of facts pertaining to an objective, external world and truths about this world conveyed linguistically. The visual now constitutes the terrain of subjective experience as the locus of knowledge, and power.

Jonathan Crary (1990) argues that this radical shift in the role of vision and visibility occurs as early as 1810, symbolically marked by Goethe's use of the camera obscura not to obtain an accurate picture of an external reality as others did with this same technology but to explore the subjective images, and after-images, that no longer correspond to mimetic principles of representation. The 'objective description of an external referent became the precise examination of subjective experience' (Soussloff, 1997: 80), a formulation applicable not only to Goethe but also to the third moment of cultural study. Bruno (1993) pursues such a notion fruitfully as she resituates the work of Elvira Notari in a methodologically complex web of political, historical and feminist reflections. The ontological basis for objectivity in a world to which linguistic systems ideally correspond yields to a symbolic field of subjectivity in a world constituted and disciplined, conjured and controlled, by techniques of visibility.

The study of visual culture invites a reconfiguration of disciplinary boundaries, dissolving some, constructing others, and encourages a reordering of prevalent hierarchical relations among disciplines (philosophy over literature, history over anthropology, cultural anthropology over visual anthropology, economics over art or film). Ethnographic film, for example, potentially gives embodied, representational expression to what it means to live among others that complicates many of the protocols of written ethnography. These protocols erect a barrier between the experience of 'fieldwork' and the practice of writing ('experiencing' abroad, writing 'at home'). Like some reflexive and most performative documentary film-making, ethnographic film in its more experimental approaches to enunciative certainty, linear narrative causality and spatio-temporal continuity can function as a model of how to address the challenge of interpersonal encounter, intersubjective experience and cross-cultural representation where knowledge, power, affect and pleasure are constantly at issue (Devereaux and Hillman, 1995; Nichols, 1991; 1994).

Visual culture also invites a more rigorous conceptualization of ideology and ethics as these terms intersect with power, discipline, pleasure, fetishism, symbolic exchange, historical consciousness, representation and identity, among others. Film study has the potential to play a tutelary role in proposing the ways and means for exploring the techniques of the visible in both theory and practice. As a recently constituted discipline it bears within its history fewer of the traces of previous methods and more of the vitality of contemporary methods. As a study of poetic, expressive and affective forms, be they narrative or non-narrative, fiction or non-fiction, film study offers viable models for cultural studies, visual anthropology, new historicism and art history in their own distinct efforts to address the contemporary 'turn to the visual'.

Representation is a term that bears much of the burden of mediating the relationship between symbolic forms of communication and the social or historical context in which they occur and to which they refer. Representation always involves an externalization of inner experience or thought. What was once interior takes form in something exterior. This exteriority is material (marks on paper, images on film, activated pixels on a screen), sensuous (it moves and pleases) and symbolic (representations stand for something else: 'cat' stands for this particular species of creature in English; 'love' stands for an emotional state quite different from a mere word (Mitchell, 1995)).

The fact that representations 'stand alone', existing in a world of objects alongside the rest of the stuff that surrounds us, gives them an apparent certainty and solidity, but the fact that they 'stand for' something else confers on them an elusive quality. They are not 'just stuff'. We may not know what it is that a representation, a symbolic sign system or utterance, a film or painting, stands for if we do not share the cultural context from which it stems. And even if we do understand a message, we may still discover that any representation can appear to be one thing only to turn out to be another.

Representation makes possible fetishism, as we invest in the representation what we would have invested in that for which it stands, and misrepresentation, as the recourse to signs allows deceptions and confusions to occur. Both misrepresentation and misunderstanding inevitably arise when what a representation stands for is itself a social construct, open to permutation. Signifiers, the material signs we attend to, do not invariably correspond either to fixed signifieds, the meanings we associate with them, or to precise referents, the things they refer to outside their own code or language. The emphasis on one possible signified may be at the expense of other, suppressed, signifieds. The linkage of 'America' to 'freedom' and 'equality', for example, may occlude reference to 'poverty' and 'discrimination'. The linkage of white characters in films with universal themes such as ambition or betrayal may suppress the ethnic distinctiveness of white, middle-class, Anglo-American cultural norms for success or failure while also intensifying the ethnic 'burden of representation' placed on non-white characters; such characters are then expected to provide the situated inflections of cultural difference erased for representations of whiteness (Dyer, 1997).

The world that a camera records is often called the pro-filmic; it may correspond to everyday social reality or a specially designed stage set. In either case, the pro-filmic is already heavily coded with meanings and laden with representations (Stam *et al.*, 1992: 112). The likelihood that the referent itself belongs to another signifying system also raises the question whether any referent exists outside the (endless) chains of discourse that constitute a culture. This, however, is not merely a formal problem but a political one as well. The 'remains' of the referent, no matter how tattered or mediated, function to affirm distinctive qualities to the historical world, to anchor signification to beliefs and to orientate subjectivity toward possible action. A multiplicity of referential 'remains' are quite commensurate with different, multicultural ways of seeing: theorizing how such frameworks correspond with one another and with what degree of compatibility, though, calls for a stress on comparative methods that have been slow to arise in relation to an identity politics that emphasizes the autonomy and often insularity of one group from another.

The possibility of fetishism hinges on representations becoming invested with value in excess of their material worth. Like commodities, representations are the product of labor that distinguishes them from other material things. Labor imbues them with both use and exchange values that may far exceed the cost of the raw materials from which they are fashioned. As a fetish object, the specific, even unique, qualities of an object present a mystery: from such mystery is born what Marx called the 'primitive religion of sensuous desire' which is, in turn, the basis for commodity fetishism as a symptomatic expression of the symbolic economy of capital. We overinvest in the material form of things that embody an excess and disguise a lack – the excess of our own (alienated) labor, the lack of what we fear we have lost.

Such fetishism bears close proximity to a romantic aesthetic in which creative works present a mystery. This mystery we label creativity or genius and then find it embodied in but not reducible to the specific, material form of the work. The sensuous desire, or love, for things aesthetic becomes a symptomatic expression of the symbolic economy of culture. The ultimate commodity fetish is then one that frees the object of its commodity status entirely as 'pure' art or beauty. A law of inverse value pertains: the more a thing is valued as art, the less it is acknowledged as a commodity; the more we value a film aesthetically, the less we want to treat it as an industrial product like any other. The more we invest ourselves in a movie's representations, the less we concern ourselves with its commodity status or ideological operations. A fetishistic relation prevails akin to the 'suspension of disbelief' invited by realist fiction or the classic posture of the fetishist who can say in all honesty, 'I know very well, but all the same'. Addressing this dynamic of desire and denial, awareness and forgetting gives representation an acute complexity lacking from approaches restricted to formal, text-centered interpretations.

A representation may stand for and, in some sense, be a compelling manifestation of that which has not yet received tangible representation, that which has not yet been brought into a condition of visibility, even though socially present. Gay and lesbian subjectivities that have been historically enacted but not symbolically represented would be a case in point (Holmlund and Fuchs, 1997). The relations between cinematic representation and actual social practices, between films and contending ideologies, between images and their referents or the impulse that produced them is terrain still rich with challenge. Who gets to represent what to whom and why; what image, icon or person shall stand for what to whom are questions in a form that allows issues of visibility and cinematic representation to tie into issues of social and political consequence.

Rhetoric has been most influential as a concept in relation to the study of documentary film but it need not be so limited. I take rhetoric to be far more than a bag of elocutionary techniques or propagandistic protocols. In its most root sense (as the arts of oratory and persuasion) rhetoric addresses the symbolic economy of corporeal expression. It always engages the body and voice, gesture and sight in the service of representation. (When Marcel Mauss wrote a monograph entitled 'Les Techniques du corps' he was proposing a rhetoric of anthropological investigation (1979).)

Rhetoric is embodied, impassioned, situated and purposeful. Logic no longer stands as an end in itself; it becomes placed in the service of speaking well and moving others. In this sense, rhetoric cannot misrepresent: symbolic action, effect, 'seduction' and pleasure are its stated goals. The effects of rhetoric are effects corporeally experienced in fact. Though produced or constructed, such effects are truly felt. The sign of rhetorical eloquence is tangible: it moves us. The sign of philosophic truth is uncertain: it can be simulated. Where rhetoric and philosophy potentially join is in the realm of erotics and desire: even for Plato knowledge 'follows the model of an erotic encounter' (Lichtenstein, 1993: 85).

Rhetoric refers not to abstract universals but to existential situations, although its effect can be far-reaching indeed. In the classic, and finally, unproductive hierarchy dictated by a disembodied philosophy, logic is rational, abstract, universal and detached (or non-purposeful). *Logos*, the word, bears a truth transcendent to the materiality of its signifiers and what they refer to. *Imago*, the image, deceives when its signifiers appear to take the place of the material reality they can only refer to. This mimetic bond fools the senses, befuddles logic and disqualifies the image from the realm of reason. Before Marx, Freud and the phenomenon of the commodity fetish, religion challenged philosophy to the ground of truth. The paradox of the trinity is a spiritualized way of representing the idea of the Word made flesh that began, in the West, with Greek oratory and the rhetoric of embodied thought and that painting, sculpture, poetry and music carried forward. It continues with cinema and visual culture.

This materialist, sensuous idea of bodily speech as a form of knowledge, more specifically that form of knowledge we might call wisdom, displaces a fetishism of signs, commodities and representations to yield an erotics of knowledge and a politics of representation. This approach to representation ties in with the inventive, even transgressive, adaptations of form in performative documentary, third cinema and experimental narrative – initiatives themselves closely allied to bringing the symbolic economies of diverse social groupings into a condition of visibility (Haraway, 1991; Leong, 1991; Mercer, 1994; Nichols, 1994; Rony, 1996).

Rhetoric, as the art of persuasion, aims to move (*movere*) us bodily, existentially, in our way of seeing and being in the world, not simply to convince only our mind of a truth. What we tend to consider in narrative forms as style would be to a rhetorician one (central) aspect of this purpose as would plot (under the traditional term of arrangement). The story told, in genres of fiction or non-fiction, exists as a formal entity in vital connection with its social ground, as something that stands for something to others in ways that affect and move them. Such concerns often register as 'excess' to structural and even post-structural theories of narrative, cognition and reception, but, from the point of view of rhetorical engagement where the criterion of effect is paramount, their role is central.

Rhetoric, as a principle rather than technique, reverses philosophic priorities. It places reason in the service of effect. Rhetoric abandons the universal (disembodied) subject of philosophy, the universal 'man' of democratic idealism, in favor of particular subjects, specific cultures, situated issues.

Rhetoric swings us in the direction of particularity. It invites inductive theorization that begins with immediate experience before it moves to abstract generalization. Rhetoric returns us to the body – the entangled bodies of texts and viewers. The emphasis of rhetoric is on materiality not ideality. Debates about color versus drawing in art history, about ornamental versus 'plain' style in rhetoric, about expressivity versus objectivity in cinema revolve around a dissociation between mind and body, reason and emotion, science and art that then proposes conditions of possibility (determined by mind, reason and science) that render the recognition of alternative conditions impossible. The dichotomy persists hierarchically, in terms defined by the dominant pole of what is in fact a continuous spectrum.

Classic philosophy bequeathed us a false dichotomy between reason and experience, thought and affect:

On the one hand is a discourse of truth whose strictly demonstrative arguments address an abstract audience's universal reason; on the other is an effective discourse that seeks to gain the support of particular listeners by acting on their belief .... According to Cicero, this opposition between truth and effectiveness is deadly not only for rhetoric, which it deprives of any relation to knowledge, but also for philosophy, which it condemns to an impotence that has afflicted many philosophers.

(Lichtenstein, 1993: 78)

Rhetoric here shares a common project with a materialist, multicultural project of representation and self-representation. Rhetoric enjoins the theorist to speak from the heart, to construct a conceptual frame that embodies purpose and to situate generalizations in the historical moment from which they arise and to which they return.

Performative speech acts ('I pronounce you man and wife', for example), like rhetoric, or cinematic expressivity generally, embody an effect where saying and doing are one. The misrepresentational possibility of referential communication (where we use signs that stand for something else) subsides beneath the actual effect of speech that is its own referent and yet is vividly distinct from a recursive reflexivity: rhetorical and performative speech have real consequences.

Catherine MacKinnon grasps much of this point in her attacks on heterosexual pornography as acts of discrimination against women but fails to understand that these acts, as speech, remain *representations* and hence belong to the symbolic economy of culture rather than the brute reality of physical forces (1993). MacKinnon returns us to the days of Louis Lumière's *Arrivée d'un train* (1895) where audiences reputedly mistook the image of an onrushing train for an actual train. Similarly, MacKinnon responds to representations of explicit heterosexual sex, and especially explicit, heterosexual, *violent* sex (pornography) as if it were always and actually violent sex (rape).

Considered as action rather than speech, the production of explicit sexual representations that require actual sexual conduct by performers would clearly fall under the jurisdiction of labor law and workplace safety regulations. Though crucial for sex workers, the extension of principles constraining production to principles constraining reception totally fails to understand speech, representation, visual culture and rhetoric as distinct forms of communication and exchange that engage fantasy and desire as fully as reality and reason and that invoke fetishism and misrepresentation more readily than logic or truth. Pornography, like rhetoric, strives for effect. To philosophy this disqualifies it as non-reason. To moralists this disqualifies it as prurient. To the rhetorician and materialist film scholar it only demands that we examine and assess these effects in all their ramifications rather than assume a repugnance identical to what, for some, the actions these representations *stand for* might typically induce (Williams, 1989).

Visual culture, representation and rhetoric themselves stand for a larger array of terms with which we could continue to explore contemporary directions in film theory. What they are meant to represent most of all, in the foreshortened, exaggerated perspective adopted here, is the urgency of this question: How may we conceptualize the work of film within the domain of visual culture in ways that matter to our individual and collective well-being? This is somewhat less of a 'theoretical' (abstract) question than a 'rhetorical' (real, imperative) one. To call it a 'rhetorical' question only underscores the ways in which both traditional and some post-structural theory have continued to denigrate the rhetorical, and for reasons similar to those suggested by Martin Jay (1993) for the denigration of vision in a world where the power to make visible is very great power indeed. Like that peculiar corporate name for a toy store, Toys 'Я' Us, where toys are clearly another dimension of our symbolic, cultural economy, we might say that Theories 'R' Us. Our theorizing stands as a representation of how we wish to engage with the world; of how we wish to bring its relations of power and pleasure, structure and meaning into a condition of visibility, and of how we wish to engage our wisdom and deploy our power in the service of 'really useful' knowledge. To do or expect any less than this is to settle for rhetorical representations of theory that will, in a regrettably derogatory sense, be 'only academic'.

Endnotes

1   Multiculturalism accompanies significant change in the composition of the modern university. The US university is no longer the institution it was in 1960. Then, 94 per cent of all students were white, and over two-thirds of these students male. By contrast, in 1993 20 per cent of all students were non-white (with some state colleges and universities showing whites as the largest minority group on campus) and a full 55 per cent of college students were women (Menand, 1995: 344.)

2   The limitations of cognitive psychology have been most conspicuous where its totalizing claims have been most persistent, in the social sciences. In calling for an *interpretative* science of cultural anthropology some 25 years ago, Clifford Geertz clearly recognized the inadequacy of all reductions of culture to schema, protocols, structures and algorithms. To follow such rules would presumably allow an outsider (or a sophisticated computer program) to 'pass' for a native (or simulate a native's behavior). This leads to an eager search for the most accurate taxonomies, tables and formulae to simulate what others say and do. As Geertz then notes,

> [I]f we take, say, a Beethoven quartet as an, admittedly rather special but, for these purposes, nicely illustrative, sample of culture, no one would, I think, identify it with its core, with the skills and knowledge needed to play it, with the understanding of it possessed by its performers or auditors nor, to take care, *en passant*, of the reductionists and reifiers, with a particular performance of it or with some mysterious entity transcending material existence. The 'no one' is perhaps too strong here, for there are always incorrigibles. But that a Beethoven quartet is a temporally developed tonal structure, a coherent sequence of modeled sound – in a word, music – and not anybody's knowledge of or belief about anything, including how to play it, is a proposition to which most people are, upon reflection, likely to assent ... . The cognitivist fallacy – that culture consists (to quote another spokesman for the movement, Stephen Tyler) of 'mental phenomena which can [he means 'should'] be analyzed by formal methods similar to those of mathematics

and logic' – is as destructive of an effective use of the concept as are the behaviorist and idealist fallacies to which it is a misdrawn correction.

(1973: 11–12)

Acknowledgements: This chapter has benefitted immeasurably from conversation with and comments from Catherine Soussloff. Catherine also read an earlier draft of the chapter and offered extremely beneficial observations, often seeing what I had intended to write through the camouflage of what I actually wrote. Linda Williams also made numerous suggestions on earlier versions of the chapter, from which I profited greatly. Her encouragement and advice have helped this become a better essay than I could have otherwise hoped to produce.

References

Althusser, Louis, 1971: *Lenin and philosophy and other essays*. London and New York: Monthly Review Press.

Andrew, Dudley, 1978: The neglected tradition of phenomenology in film theory. In Bill Nichols (ed.), 1985: *Movies and methods*. Berkeley, CA: University of California Press, 625–32.

Apter, Emily and Pietz, William, (eds), 1993: *Fetishism as cultural discourse*. Ithaca, NY, and London: Cornell University Press.

Baudry, Jean-Louis, 1970: Ideological effects of the cinematographic apparatus. In Bill Nichols (ed.), 1985: *Movies and methods*. Berkeley, CA: University of California Press, vol. 2, 531–42.

Bazin, André, 1967: *What is cinema?* Berkeley, CA, and London: University of California Press.

Bazin, André, 1971: *What is cinema?* vol. 2. Berkeley, CA, and London: University of California Press.

Belsey, Catherine, 1980: *Critical practice*. London and New York: Methuen.

Bennett, Tony, 1979: *Formalism and Marxism*. London and New York: Routledge.

Berger, John, 1972: *Ways of seeing*. London: BBC and Penguin Books.

Berger, Peter L. and Luckmann, Thomas, 1966: *The social construction of reality*. New York: Doubleday.

Bishop, Peter, 1989: *The myth of shangri-la: Tibet, travel writing and the western creation of sacred landscape*. Berkeley, CA: University of California Press.

Bobo, Jacquelyne, 1995: *Black women as cultural readers*. New York: Columbia University Press.

Bordwell, David, 1989: Historical poetics of cinema. In R. Barton Palmer (ed.), *The cinematic text: methods and approaches*. New York: AMS Press, 369–98.

Bordwell, David and Carroll, Noël, (eds), 1996: *Post-theory: restructuring film studies*. Madison, WI: University of Wisconsin Press.

Bourdieu, Pierre, 1984: *Distinction: a social critique of the judgment of taste*. Cambridge, MA: Harvard University Press.

Bruno, Giuliana, 1993: *Streetwalking on a ruined map: cultural theory and the city films of Elvira Notari*. Princeton, NJ: Princeton University Press.

Burch, Noël, 1973: *Theory of film practice*. New York: Praeger.

Butler, Judith, 1993: *Bodies that matter*. New York and London: Routledge.

Carroll, Noël, 1996: *Theorizing the moving image*. Cambridge: Cambridge University Press.

Chow, Rey, 1993: *Writing diaspora: tactics of intervention in contemporary cultural studies*. Bloomington, IN: Indiana University Press.

Clover, Carol, 1992: *Men, women, and chain saws: gender in the modern horror film*. Princeton, NJ: Princeton University Press.

Coward, Rosalind and Ellis, John, 1977: *Language and materialism: developments in semiology and the theory of the subject*. London: Routledge and Kegan Paul.

Crary, Jonathan, 1990: *Techniques of the observer: on vision and modernity in the nineteenth century.* Cambridge, MA, and London: MIT Press.

Devereaux, Leslie and Hillman, Roger, (eds), 1995: *Fields of vision: essays in film studies, visual anthropology and photography.* Berkeley, CA, and London: University of California Press.

Doane, Mary Ann, 1987: *The desire to desire: the woman's film of the 1940s.* Bloomington, IN: Indiana University Press.

Druckery, Timothy (ed.), 1996: *Electronic culture: technology and visual representation.* New York: Aperture.

Dyer, Richard, 1997: *White.* London and New York: Routledge.

Fanon, Frantz, 1964: *The wretched of the earth.* New York: Grove Press.

Fanon, Frantz, 1967: *A dying colonialism.* New York: Grove Press.

Ferguson, Russell, Martha Gever, Trinh T. Minh-ha and Cornel West (eds), 1990: *Out there: marginalization and contemporary cultures.* Cambridge, MA, and London: MIT Press.

Foucault, Michel, 1972: *The archaeology of language.* London: Tavistock Publications.

Foucault, Michel, 1979: *Discipline and punish: the birth of the prison.* New York: Vintage Books.

Foucault, Michel, 1980: *The history of sexuality,* vol. 1. New York: Vintage Books.

Friedman, Lester D. (ed.), 1991: *Unspeakable images: ethnicity and the American cinema.* Chicago, IL: University of Illinois Press.

Gabriel, Teshome H., 1982: *Third cinema in the third world: the aesthetics of liberation.* Ann Arbor, MI: UMI Research Press.

Gaines, Jane, 1991: *Contested culture: the image, the voice, and the law.* Chapel Hill, NC, and London: University of North Carolina Press.

Geertz, Clifford, 1973: *The interpretation of cultures.* New York: Basic Books.

Gilroy, Paul, 1987: *'There ain't no black in the union jack'.* Chicago, IL: University of Chicago Press.

Gonzalez-Crussi, Frank, 1995: *Suspended animation: six essays on the preservation of bodily parts.* New York and London: Harcourt Brace.

Greenblatt, Stephen, 1980: *Renaissance self-fashioning: from More to Shakespeare.* Chicago, IL: University of Chicago Press.

Gross, Larry, Katz, John Stuart and Ruby, Jay (eds), 1988: *Image ethics: the moral rights of subjects in photographs, film and television.* New York, Oxford: Oxford University Press.

Haraway, Donna J., 1991: *Simians, cyborgs and women: the reinvention of nature.* New York and London: Routledge.

Heath, Stephen, 1981: *Questions of cinema.* Bloomington, IN: Indiana University Press.

Hebdige, Dick, 1979: *Subculture: the meaning of style.* London and New York: Routledge.

Heidegger, Martin, 1977: *Martin Heidegger: basic writings.* New York: Harper and Row.

Holmlund, Chris and Fuchs, Cynthia (eds), 1997: *Between the sheets, in the streets: queer, lesbian, gay documentary.* Minneapolis, MN, and London: University of Minnesota Press.

Jakobson, Roman, 1960: Linguistics and poetics. In Thomas A. Seboek (ed.), *Style in linguistics.* Cambridge, MA: MIT Press, 296–322.

James, David E. and Berg, Rick, (eds), 1996: *The hidden foundation: cinema and the question of class.* Minneapolis, MN, and London: University of Minnesota Press.

Jameson, Fredric, 1988: Symbolic inference: or, Kenneth Burke and ideological analysis. In Fredric Jameson, *The ideology of theory.* Minneapolis, MN: University of Minnesota Press, vol. 1, 137–52.

Jameson, Fredric, 1992: *The geopolitical aesthetic: cinema and space in the world system.* Bloomington, IN: Indiana University Press/London: British Film Institute.

Jay, Martin, 1993: *Downcast eyes: the denigration of vision in twentieth-century French thought.* Berkeley, CA, and London: University of California Press.

Jenks, Chris (ed.), 1995: *Visual culture.* London and New York: Routledge.

Kant, Immanuel, 1851: *The critique of judgement*. New York: Macmillan.

Kaplan, E. Ann (ed.), 1990: *Psychoanalysis and cinema*. New York: Routledge.

Kavolis, Vytautas, 1979: Arts, social and economic aspects of the arts. In *Encyclopedia Britannica, Macropedia* **1**: 100–5.

Kracauer, Siegfried, 1947: *From Caligari to Hitler: a psychological history of the German film*. Princeton, NJ: Princeton University Press.

Lacan, Jacques, 1977: The mirror-stage as formative of the function of the I. In Jacques Lacan, *Ecrits: a selection*. New York: Norton, 1–7.

Leong, Russell (ed.), 1991: *Moving the image: independent Asian Pacific American media arts*. Los Angeles, CA: UCLA Asian American Studies Center.

Leyda, Jay, 1960: *Kino: the history of the Russian and Soviet cinema*. London: George Allen and Unwin.

Lichtenstein, Jacqueline, 1993: *The eloquence of color: rhetoric and painting in the French classical age*. Berkeley, CA: University of California Press.

Lyotard, François, 1984: *The postmodern condition: a report on knowledge*. Manchester: Manchester University Press.

MacKinnon, Catherine, 1993: *Only words*. Cambridge, MA: Harvard University Press.

Mauss, Marcel, 1979: Les techniques du corps (Body techniques). In Ben Brewster (ed.), *Sociology and psychology*. London: Routledge, 95–123.

Menand, Louis, 1995: Diversity. In Frank Lentricchia and Thomas McLaughlin (eds), *Critical terms for literary study*. London and Chicago, IL: University of Chicago Press, 336–53.

Mercer, Kobena, 1994: *Welcome to the jungle: new positions in black cultural studies*. London and New York: Routledge.

Metz, Christian, 1974a: *Language and cinema*. The Hague and Paris: Mouton.

Metz, Christian, 1974b: *Film language: a semiotics of cinema*. New York: Oxford University Press.

Metz, Christian, 1982: *The imaginary signifier: psychoanalysis and the cinema*. Bloomington, IN: Indiana University Press.

Mitchell, W.J.T. (ed.), 1981: *On narrative*. Chicago, IL: University of Chicago Press.

Mitchell, W.J.T., 1995: Representation. In Frank Lentricchia and Thomas McLaughlin (eds), *Critical terms for literary study*. London and Chicago, IL: University of Chicago Press, 11–22.

Mulvey, Laura, 1975: Visual pleasure and narrative cinema. *Screen* **16**(3). In Bill Nichols (ed.), 1985: *Movies and methods*, vol. 2, 303–15.

Mulvey, Laura, 1996: *Fetishism and curiosity*. London: British Film Institute/Bloomington, IN: Indiana University Press.

Nichols, Bill (ed.), 1976: Section on 'Structuralism–semiology'. In *Movies and methods*. Berkeley, CA: University of California Press, 461–628.

Nichols, Bill, 1981: *Ideology and the image*. Bloomington, IN: Indiana University Press.

Nichols, Bill (ed.), 1985: *Movies and methods*, vol. 2. Berkeley, CA: University of California Press.

Nichols, Bill, 1991: *Representing reality: issues and concepts in documentary*. Bloomington, IN: Indiana University Press.

Nichols, Bill, 1994: *Blurred boundaries: questions of meaning in contemporary culture*. Bloomington, IN: Indiana University Press.

Patterson, Lee, 1995: Literary history. In Frank Lentricchia and Thomas McLaughlin (eds), *Critical terms for literary study*. London and Chicago, IL: University of Chicago Press, 250–62.

Plantinga, Carl, 1997: *Rhetoric and representation in nonfiction film*. Cambridge and New York: Cambridge University Press.

Polan, Dana, 1990: *Power and paranoia: history, narrative and American cinema, 1940–1950*. New York: Columbia University Press.

Rony, Fatimah Tobing, 1996: *The third eye: race, cinema and the ethnographic spectacle*. Durham, NC: Duke University Press.

Rosenstone, Robert A., 1995: *Visions of the past*. London and Cambridge, MA: Harvard University Press.

Rotha, Paul and Griffith, Richard, 1950: *The film till now* and *the film since then*. New York: Funk and Wagnals.

Russo, Vito, 1981: *The celluloid closet: homosexuality in the movies*. New York and London: Harper and Row.

Said, Edward W., 1978: *Orientalism*. New York: Pantheon Books.

Shohat, Ella and Stam, Robert, 1994: *Unthinking Eurocentrism: multiculturalism and the media*. London and New York: Routledge.

Silverman, Kaja, 1983: *The subject of semiotics*. New York: Oxford University Press.

Silverman, Kaja, 1992: *Male subjectivity of the margins*. New York: Routledge.

Sobchack, Vivian, 1992: *The address of the eye: a phenomenology of film experience*. Princeton, NJ: Princeton University Press.

Sobchack, Vivian, 1996: *The persistence of history: cinema, television and the modern event*. London and New York: Routledge.

Soussloff, Catherine, 1997: The turn to visual culture: on *Visual culture* and *Techniques of the observer*. *Visual Anthropology Review* **12**(1): 77–83.

Stam, Robert, Burgoyne, Robert and Flitterman-Lewis, Sandy, (eds), 1992: *New vocabularies in film semiotics: structuralism, post-structuralism and beyond*. London and New York: Routledge.

Studlar, Gaylyn, 1988: *In the realm of pleasure: von Sternberg, Dietrich and the masochistic aesthetic*. Chicago, IL: University of Illinois Press.

Taussig, Michael, 1993: *Mimesis and alterity: a particular history of the senses*. London and New York: Routledge.

Thompson, Kristen, 1981: *Eisenstein's* Ivan the Terrible*: a neoformalist analysis*. Princeton, NJ: Princeton University Press.

Virilio, Paul, 1988: *War and cinema: the logics of perception*. New York and London: Verso.

White, Hayden, 1987: *The content of the form: narrative discourse and historical representation*. Baltimore, MD: The Johns Hopkins University Press.

Williams, Linda, 1989: *Hard core: power, pleasure and the 'frenzy of the visible'*. Berkeley, CA: University of California Press.

Williams, Patrick and Christian, Laura, (eds), 1994: *Colonial discourse and post-colonial theory*. New York: Columbia University Press.

Williams, Raymond, 1976: *Keywords*. London: Collins.

Wilson, Rob and Dissanayake, Wimal, (eds), 1996: *Global/local: cultural production and the transnational imaginary*. Durham, NC: Duke University Press.

Wollen, Peter, 1969: *Signs and meaning in the cinema*. Bloomington, IN: Indiana University Press [also published 1972].

Wollen, Peter, 1993: *Raiding the icebox: reflections on twentieth-century culture*. Bloomington, IN: Indiana University Press.

Wollen, Peter and Cooke, Lynn, (eds), 1995: *Visual display: culture beyond appearances*. Seattle, WA: Bay Press.

Wood, Robin, 1968: *Howard Hawks*. London: Secker and Warburg/New York: Doubleday.

Zizek, Slavoj, 1992: *Looking awry: an introduction to Jacques Lacan through popular culture*. Cambridge, MA and London: MIT Press.

Zizek, Slavoj, 1994: How did Marx invent the symptom? In Slavoj Zizek (ed.), *Mapping ideology*. London and New York: Verso, 296–331.

4 Case study: interpreting *Singin' in the Rain*

Steven Cohan

From its original release in 1952, when it was overshadowed by the greater success and prestige of *An American in Paris* released the year before, to its ranking as fourth three decades later in *Sight & Sound*'s listing of the 10 best films ever made (Wollen, 1992: 9), to its commodification as the signature film of MGM's Golden Era in a series of anthologies produced by that studio's various corporate successors, *Singin' in the Rain* has steadily grown in popular and critical appeal. It is still exhibited in an assortment of venues, not only old downtown movie palaces and revival houses, but also museums, home video, cable television, college classrooms, even the Hollywood Bowl in 1990 – all places its creators never anticipated. The film's meanings have undergone considerable revision since it was first made, too. Star and co-director, Gene Kelly, noted in the 1970s, 'A lot of people have called it the first camp picture', and he immediately added his reservation, 'I don't know' (BBC, 1974).

This case study on *Singin' in the Rain* demonstrates how a popular film, which has endured in value over the years to achieve canonical status as a classic, changes in its meaning, depending on the theoretical methodology applied. Each interpretive framework discussed here brings a different critical strategy to bear upon the film, causing its significance to shift. This is not to suggest that a film can mean just about anything, but that its meanings are determined through interaction with a critical theory. Interpreting therefore amounts to much more than deriving a film's theme; interpretation makes the film an object of inquiry in its own right, a text. Furthermore, as interpreters of a film, we need to recognize that a text has its own specificity but also a porous historical materiality, with regard to its fields of reference when first produced and as it continues to be viewed. A film consequently exists in history as a cultural object as well as a work of art, and this is why *Singin' in the Rain* can be appreciated today as a classic, as camp, as a commodification of popular entertainment, *and* as a case study of interpretation.

The narrative of *Singin' in the Rain*

Since the most common way audiences make sense of a commercial film is through its narrative, let us begin there. Set in Hollywood during the film industry's transition from silent films to talkies in 1927, *Singin' in the Rain* opens with the gala premiere of *The Royal Rascal*. This swashbuckler romance features the two biggest stars working for Monumental Pictures, Don Lockwood (Gene Kelly) and Lina Lamont (Jean Hagen). Before the famous couple can start their next feature, a similar costumer entitled *The Duelling Cavalier*, the success of *The Jazz Singer* forces the studio to shut down while it converts to sound. Don Lockwood's voice fits comfortably with the new technology, but Lina Lamont's voice – shrill, high, and nasal – does not. The sneak preview of their all-talking *The Duelling Cavalier* is thus a disaster from start to finish. To save the film, the studio takes advantage of Don's vaudeville background, converting the historical costume drama into an extended dream sequence set in a backstage musical. To get around the problem of Lina's inadequate voice, a talented contract player, Kathy Selden (Debbie Reynolds), dubs her songs and dialogue. Discovering that someone else's voice is being used in place of hers, Lina instigates an overnight publicity campaign promoting her own singing and dancing talents, foiling the studio's intention of acknowledging Kathy's contribution. Retitled *The Dancing Cavalier*, the musical version is an unqualified success, and at its premiere, Lina's forged performance is exposed in order to give credit to her voice double, who becomes Don's new partner, on screen and off.

As a means of opening up the narrative of *Singin' in the Rain* for interpretation, it is useful to follow the formalist distinction between 'story' and 'plot'. These are not synonymous terms. 'Story' refers to the implied chronological sequencing of events, from which one further infers the logic of cause and effect, temporality, and space governing the 'diegesis' (that is, the spectator's deduction of a film's fictive world inhabited by the characters and appearing fully coherent on its own terms). A story is easily synopsized, reducible to a summary of what happens. 'Plot', on the other hand, refers to the form through which a film narrative actually orders (or even reorders) its story in the process of recounting it. Classical Hollywood cinema of the studio era makes character the prime causal agent unifying a story, and it constructs a linear plot to reiterate this emphasis. A linear plot identifies what amounts to a syntax for the story, organizing it in sequence around four nodal points – 'an undisturbed stage, the disturbance, the struggle, and the elimination of the disturbance' (Bordwell, 1985: 157) – to keep directing attention toward closure as the key to unlocking the story's meaning.

In *Singin' in the Rain*, the showing of a Lockwood–Lamont movie at several points in the story marks out the plot's linear development. The opening establishes an undisturbed stage with the premiere of *The Royal Rascal* celebrating the reigning star couple of the silent screen (Figure 4.1). The disastrous preview of *The Duelling Cavalier* disturbs that stasis by threatening their great popularity, and the dubbing of *The Dancing Cavalier* crystalizes how that disturbance amounts to a struggle between the two screen stars over their careers. The audience's unqualified enthusiasm for *The Dancing Cavalier* at its premiere proves that the technology enabling Lina's musical performance can go

Figure 4.1 Lockwood and Lamont (Gene Kelly and Jean Hagen) arrive at the premiere of *The Royal Rascal*. Reproduced courtesy of Jerry Ohlinger, *Singin' in the Rain,* © 1951 Turner Entertainment Company.

undetected, but when the counterfeit is revealed immediately afterward, the plot achieves resolution simply by causing her elimination. The closure restores the undisturbed stage of the opening but with a significant difference, since a new star couple replaces the original one.

David Bordwell points out that a classical Hollywood narrative further complicates its linear development by arranging two plotlines. One revolves around 'heterosexual romance (boy/girl, husband/wife)', while the other one arises from action occurring in the public sphere, be it 'work, war, a mission or quest' (1985: 157). *Singin' in the Rain* conforms to this convention, too, with a romance plot involving Don and Kathy and a professional plot concerned with his career. The doubling amplifies how *Singin' in the Rain* represents the industry's conversion to sound technology. The professional plot recounts the historical transformation of the movies from a medium of popular entertainment that divorces image from sound, as epitomized by the disparity between Lina's attractive body and abrasive voice, to one that integrates them, as evident in Don's conversion to musical pictures as well as his change of partners. But the disturbance Lina poses when she will not remain mute, while motivated by the professional plot, obstructs the romance, since she functions as the primary obstacle to Don's relationship with Kathy.

Don's first encounter with Kathy encapsulates the disturbance that the double plot contains through Lina's character. Unimpressed when she learns his identity, Kathy mocks Don's profession. 'The personalities on the screen just don't impress me', she declares. 'I mean, they don't talk, they don't act, they just make a lot of dumb show. . . . You're nothing but a shadow on film'.[1] Kathy's description of silent film as 'a lot of dumb show' refers to the pantomime style distinctive of that era's acting; more subtly, it rhymes with Lina's first lines of dialogue just minutes before Don meets his future co-star. *Singin' in the Rain* pointedly delays letting us hear Lina's voice until after the premiere when, backstage, she complains about not being allowed to say anything to her admiring pubic, adding, 'What do you think I am? Dumb or something?' As used by the double plot, Lina's figure equates one meaning of 'dumb' ('muteness') with another ('stupidity') to underscore the aptness of Kathy's criticism, indicating how and why Lina's bad acting, and not the studio's own ineptitude in handling the new technology, obstructs the professional plot. *Singin' in the Rain* knots its double plot around Lina so that the closure makes it seem as if whatever complications arising from the film industry's tumultuous conversion to talkies have been satisfactorily resolved once Don finds a more authentic partner in Kathy. The final shot shows this couple admiring a billboard advertising their new musical, also entitled *Singin' in the Rain*. Because the film and its diegesis mesh so perfectly at this end point, any future disturbance seems unthinkable.

We can understand why *Singin' in the Rain* invests so much ameliorating value in the formation of this new couple by using the insights of structuralism to look beyond the plot's linearity. In a study of the Oedipus myth, anthropologist Claude Lévi-Strauss showed how it manages contradictory cultural beliefs about the origins of humankind by building its plot around two incompatible pairs of binary oppositions that appear comparable as antitheses. According to Lévi-Strauss, a myth's narrative reconciles cultural contradiction structurally, not logically, because its underlying structure demonstrates that 'contradictory relationships are identical inasmuch as they are both self-contradictory in a similar way' (1963: 216). His analysis has been productively extended to other types of narrative, and two points about the resulting method are worth emphasizing. First, a structuralist analysis takes a lateral perspective upon a plot's linearity in order to examine the binary oppositions arising at every point. Second, in identifying an underlying oppositional structure, this analysis does not dwell on the psychological conflicts between characters but instead seeks to illuminate the conceptual antitheses that the plot enacts.

Singin' in the Rain illustrates the usefulness of the structuralist paradigm. Once we notice how the professional plot pits Don against Lina to initiate the disturbance, certain binarized terms immediately emerge to dominate the entire narrative: body/voice, image/sound, naturalness/engineering, innovation/obsolescence. The film's opposi-tional structure stands out even more clearly if we recall the many musical numbers performed by stars Gene Kelly, Debbie Reynolds, and Donald O'Connor (as Don's best friend, Cosmo Brown). The numbers supplement but do not advance the plot very much, but they locate the fusion of body and voice, of sound and image, in the characters' joyous act of singing *and* dancing, and they equate musical performance with innovation and naturalness, juxtaposing these values to the plot's main source of disturbance: obsolescence and engineering.

Genre plays a significant role in highlighting this oppositional structure. According to Rick Altman, who builds upon the tenets of structuralism in his taxonomy of the Hollywood musical, the genre operates from a dual focus that, in concentrating on the couple, obeys a principle of lateral parallelism, not linear sequencing. In a musical, he comments, 'the couple is the plot' (1989: 35), and the genre works in a non-linear fashion to match the male and female leads as a potential couple through paired segments: parallel numbers, scenes, shots, dialogue, settings, and so on. Fundamental to this dual focus is a sexual opposition that associates the male with one cluster of values and the female with another. The couple's eventual union implies reconciliation of various secondary oppositions, intially 'perceived as mutually exclusive', so the couple has the important function of 'reducing an unsatisfactory paradox to a more workable configuration, a concordance of opposites' (1989: 27).

Singin' in the Rain structures its narrative according to this generic principle. Don's maturity is contrasted with Kathy's youthfulness, his stardom with her fandom, his hammy acting with her criticism, his dancing with her singing, his athletic body with her pure voice. Viewed through this dual focus, Kathy represents the innovation, spontaneity, and artlessness that Don professionally lacks at the start of the film, while the parallelism of their many differences links them as a couple. As a consequence, the opposition structuring the romance plot (masculinity versus femininity) compares with the opposition structuring the professional plot (innovation versus obsolescence), and this dual focus then reconciles the more central opposition motivating the entire narrative: the disjunction of image and sound inherent in the technology of cinema and crucial to the film's historical setting in the industry's conversion to talkies. As Peter Wollen observes, *Singin' in the Rain* closes its narrative by valuing 'the married couple' and 'the married print' (the industry's term for the joining together of image and soundtrack in the finished product) as metaphors of each other (1992: 55, 57). In their eventual teaming on screen as a couple, Don and Kathy embody the perfect synchrony of body and voice, dancing and singing, which marks the achievement of the talkie, just as the talkie's technological matching of sound and image mirrors the couple's off-screen harmonious blending of masculinity and femininity.

Dubbing, dancing, and deconstruction

The dual focus of *Singin' in the Rain* highlights another opposition underlying the binary pairings of masculine/feminine and innovation/obsolescence as they accrue around the disjunction of sound and image – that of authenticity versus artifice. This latter opposition is crucial to the film's celebration of the musical genre's authenticity as a representational art. However, since a musical's authenticity depends upon effacing the very technological artifice that makes it possible, the binary pairing of authenticity/artifice also summarizes the textual problematic, inescapable because of the film medium, that permeates *Singin' in the Rain* and cannot be worked out solely at the level of narrative structure.

A structure implies stability and containment, but 'the concept of *structure*', Jacques Derrida comments, is 'ambiguous' because 'it can simultaneously confirm and shake' (1981: 214). Deconstruction, which has become synonymous with Derrida's name, is a theory of reading a work for its textuality, its destabilizing play of differences, which critiques the logic of structuralism. A deconstructionist analysis traces the textual path through which a binary opposition, in arranging differential terms as a positive and negative relation, inevitably refers to a third term that functions to authenticate the polarity. The third term appears to stand outside the binary pair but is indispensable to its formation, revealing how 'each allegedly "simple term" is marked by the trace of another term' (Derrida, 1981: 221). In *Singin' in the Rain* dubbing has such an effect of destabilizing the binary logic by which, through the trope of dance, the film hierarchically arranges its oppositions in terms of authenticity or artifice as its primary means of mythifying the musical genre.

To be sure, with its Hollywood setting, witty script, and songs recycled from earlier films, *Singin' in the Rain* might seem too ironically aware of its place in the history of the musical to be doing anything other than demystifying the genre. But while musical entertainment is demystified by the self-reflexive narrative, which becomes increasingly preoccupied with the technology of cinema, it is remystified by the numbers, which efface technology, promoting 'the mode of expression of the musical itself as spontaneous and natural rather than calculated and technological' (Feuer, 1981: 165). Musicals value the spontaneity of singing and dancing over the careful engineering required to perfect a number for filming, giving rise to a number of familiar conventions, well explained by Jane Feuer in her book, *The Hollywood musical* (1993). These all highlight the effortlessness of performing while underscoring it *as* performance: the unrehearsed public appearance (as in Kathy's rendition of 'Singin' in the Rain' or her closing duet with Don, 'You Are My Lucky Star'); the effacement of choreography to make dancing seem as natural as walking (as in Don's 'Singin' in the Rain') and to disguise the obvious labor involved in perfecting it (as in the eruption of raucous tap-dancing in his and Cosmo's 'Moses Supposes'); the prop dance (as in Cosmo's 'Make 'Em Laugh' or the trio's 'Good Mornin''); and a direct address that surpasses diegetic spectatorship (as when the camerawork in 'Make 'Em Laugh' forgets that Cosmo is ostensibly performing for Don's benefit and ceases to follow the latter's spatial perspective).

Most of the numbers in *Singin' in the Rain* are not diegetically motivated as part of a show but meant to seem spontaneous expressions of joyful emotion and native talent, without overt reference to the technology that exposes the possible fraudulence of movie stardom in the narrative. The numbers establish an implicit comparison with the contrivance of physical action in Don's silent films on the one hand and to the insincerity of his speech when not acting on the other. The one time a number does call explicit attention to the technology of film – when Don sings 'You were meant for me' to Kathy on a studio soundstage – it initially highlights cinematic artifice only so that his lyric declaration of love can then disavow it entirely. Don begins the number by using technology (colored lights, a wind machine, and so on) to simulate a suitable romantic atmosphere copied from the movies he stars in with Lina. Once he begins to dance with Kathy, the technology fades from view. Performed on the bare soundstage, their dance confirms their mutual sexual attraction; just as importantly, it supplies the first occasion for making the musical talent each previously displayed apart in a show number seem spontaneous, thereby associating their harmony as a couple with artless musical performance.

In their synchronization of voice and body, the numbers offer a view of performing that, unlike Lina's, succeeds in integrating sound and image, so it follows, as Gerald Mast puts it, that 'the controlling myth of *Singin' in the Rain* is performance itself' (1987: 265). To support this myth, *Singin' in the Rain* has to circumvent the film medium's own representation of spontaneity through technology. The production of a musical relied upon the splitting of sound and image while simultaneously engineering the illusion of their unity: the songs and orchestra were prerecorded, often edited from numerous takes, and played back on the set during shooting; dances were usually rehearsed whole but shot in segments, as determined by the various camera set-ups planned for the number's editing; and the sound effects, including the tapping, were postrecorded, sometimes not by the dancers themselves. Thus, while carrying the force of fusing sound and image in a film's exhibition as a completed print, numbers technically depended upon their separation into multiple audio tracks and numerous cinematographic takes during their production.

Singin' in the Rain acknowledges the basis of performance in technology with an in joke that audiences frequently miss. At the point when Kathy dubs Lina's singing and speaking, Debbie Reynolds's voice is itself dubbed by others, Betty Noyes for the song and, even more self-reflectively, Jean Hagen – who plays Lina – for the dialogue. According to co-director Stanley Donen, Reynolds was dubbed in these scenes because of her regional accent, since the voice looped over Lina's 'was supposed to be cultured speech' (Fordin, 1975: 358). If that is the case, why was Reynolds not dubbed as well when Kathy has to sing for Lina 'live'? Presumably because that moment has to appear as the unmasking of Lina's counterfeiting of musical stardom and the simultaneous revelation of Kathy's – and Reynolds's – greater authenticity.

The layers of dubbing involved in the manufacturing of Lina's voice for talkies has fascinated commentators on *Singin' in the Rain* (Figure 4.2). Wollen points out, 'dubbing, here, represents the cinematic form of writing, through which sound is separated from its origin and becomes a potentially free-floating, and thus radically unreliable, semantic element' (1992: 56). By paradoxically marking the disjunction of sound and image in their technological conjunction, dubbing deconstructs the oppositional logic supporting the myth of performance through the comparable value of the married couple and the married print. Dance, by comparison, supplies *Singin' in the Rain* with a trope that, by harmonizing voice and body, re-centers the myth.

The big production number in *Singin' in the Rain*, 'The Broadway Ballet', interrupts the linear trajectory of the plot, stopping it cold for 14 minutes, but the number reinforces the significance of dance as an alternative third term reunifying sound and image. Don explains to studio head R.F. Simpson that there is one number left to shoot

Figure 4.2 Lina discovers that Kathy is dubbing her voice.
Reproduced courtesy of Cinema Collectors, *Singin' in the Rain*, © 1951 Turner Entertainment Company.

for *The Dancing Cavalier*. As Don begins to describe it, the film immediately cuts to the number itself. Interestingly, the published screenplay adds: 'This is a big production number shown as it will appear in *The Dancing Cavalier*' (Comden and Green, 1972: 63). However, while set in the 1920s, the number we see takes full advantage of 1950s' technology so it in no way duplicates what it would have looked like in 1927. After its conclusion, Simpson remarks, 'I can't quite visualize it. I'll have to see it on film first.' While that line gets the big laugh, Cosmo's retort is more telling: 'On film, it'll be better yet.' As the framing dialogue indicates, 'The Broadway Ballet' is another underlined moment of self-reflexivity in *Singin' in the Rain*, and the gap between what we actually see on the screen and what Don supposedly narrates to Simpson in the diegesis forces us to reconsider what dance means for the film.

Because of the way it is set up by Don's brief introduction, the ballet rhymes with his voiceover montage about his career at the start of the film, when gossip columnist Dora Bailey asks him to tell his life story to the crowd of fans outside Grauman's Chinese Theater. Summarized by Don's pretentious motto – 'Dignity, always dignity' – his spoken account represents an elitist class background with his formal training in dance, music, and theater leading to a career in motion pictures playing 'sophisticated' and 'suave' leading men. What we see, though, differs considerably from what he describes.

A young Don and his pal Cosmo dance for pennies in a poolroom and sneak into a nickelodeon to see a movie serial; as adults, the two friends entertain in a tavern, do a comic act on amateur night, and perform 'Fit as a Fiddle' in a third-rate vaudeville hall, until they find themselves in Hollywood, where Don accidentally gets a job as a stuntman. The voiceover montage establishes image as truth, demystifying sound as a manufactured representation. However, since *Singin' in the Rain* recounts the industry's transition to talkies, the film must eventually recuperate sound. The ballet contrasts with the montage because it offers dance as the ultimate wedding of sound and image, enacting what the couple metaphorically represents. This number's own 'star-is-born' narrative parallels the story Don tells at the premiere of *The Royal Rascal* – he plays a hoofer who rises from burlesque, to vaudeville, to the Ziegfeld Follies – but incorporates sound so that singing and music motivate physical movement in the image as dancing (Altman, 1989: 229), and the dancer himself, combining movement with music and not relying on words (Cuomo, 1996: 43), then embodies the image's unity with sound as grace, coordination, and rhythm.

Value is thus restored to sound once it is firmly subordinated to the image through dance. But dubbing deconstructs the authenticity of dance, too. After all, how can anyone tap-dance in the rain, as Gene Kelly does in this film's famous title number, unless the taps are post-recorded and then added to the image as supplementary sound? That number took a day and a half to shoot but months to find the right sounding taps to use for the dubbing (AMCN, 1994). Far from being a genuine alternative to dubbing, dancing in a musical was produced through the same technology and toward the same end: manufacturing a performance. Consequently, the more *Singin' in the Rain* self-reflexively highlights the instability that dubbing exemplifies, the more readily it exposes the profound rift between sound and image, deconstructing the text's efforts to 'wed' them, technically and metaphorically, in the married print and the married couple. Dance may therefore work as a third term to stabilize *Singin' in the Rain*'s sound/image dichotomy, but it is subject to the text's deconstructive energies too.

Spectatorship and sexual difference

We can understand what else the rhyming of the ballet with the voiceover montage puts at issue by turning to psychoanalytic film theory. When hearing 'The Broadway Ballet' described, Simpson cannot visualize it in his mind, in contrast to the way we as spectators have seen it, and he will not be able to do so until it is filmed. For as Cosmo says, it looks better filmed. In stressing that the ballet is, as far as concerns the diegesis, an *imaginary* representation right after we have been allowed to see it for ourselves, the exchange between Simpson and Cosmo condenses in a joke what psychoanalytic film theory explains is the source of pleasure in cinematic spectatorship: unconscious identification with the camera through the imagery projected on-screen.

According to Christian Metz, in identifying with the act of looking that characterizes both spectatorship and camerawork, 'the spectator can do no other than identify with the camera, too' (1977: 47). But since the camera is not present during a film's exhibition, the spectator must accept a substitute or stand-in, in Metz's term, an 'imaginary signifier': the cinematic image. It is 'imaginary' in the sense of being visual *and* fantasmatic (nothing but 'shadow on film', as Kathy says). Furthermore, the image repeatedly comes between the spectator's look and the camera's, so the viewing situation encourages while continually rending their alignment through the course of a film's unfolding. Mirroring the way that film itself is an edited or 'sutured' series of shots or 'cuts', spectatorship produces a comparably sutured viewer. With each new shot, editing ruptures and re-secures identification with the image; and since *how* a film addresses a spectator continually interacts with *what* it shows on-screen, this 'suturing' operation has profound implications. As Kaja Silverman points out, 'the entire system of suture is inconceivable apart from sexual difference' (1983: 221).

In explanation, Silverman puts Metz's theorization of spectatorial identification together with Laura Mulvey's critique of commercial narrative cinema for its perpetuation of an asymmetrical gender dualism. Whereas Hollywood films typically associate masculinity with seeing, in command of an active, voyeuristic look, they just as typically represent femininity as lacking and passive, put on exhibition and looked at. The female figure is either made an enigma to be investigated, redeemed, or punished, or she is visually fragmented in a fetishized spectacle – for example, in close-ups that direct attention to glamorized parts of her body. Either representation of femininity makes it 'reassuring rather than dangerous' (Mulvey, 1975: 21), disavowing male lack by encouraging voyeuristic identification with the camera's look at the eroticized female body and by reiterating that identification through the male character's gaze in the diegesis.

As amplified by feminism, psychoanalytic film theory reveals additional meanings for the sound/image dualism of *Singin' in the Rain*. It explains why the film goes to such lengths to discount, in both its narrative and its numbers, that the male is the initial means of rending sound from image, and why this rupture must then be outwardly attributed to the female. *Singin' in the Rain* operates upon a viewer by jeopardizing the imaginary unity of sound and image necessary for suture, disrupting the symbolic status of the female as the signifier of male authenticity, but only to restore that function in its closure. Don's voiceover montage detaches his look from the image and dramatizes his masculinity as a state of self-division. After all, in his own biography, he is himself an 'imaginary signifier', a stand-in for a stand-in; he began his career in the movies by replacing a stuntman in silent film. In order to recuperate what it initially reveals is a division in male subjectivity, *Singin' in the Rain* displaces male lack onto the female so that *she* gets blamed for the breakdown of sound and image, while *he* repairs it, restoring the voice to its proper body. As a result of this gendering of the sound/image dualism, Silverman points out about *Singin' in the Rain*, the male assumes control of the apparatus, defining the female as its object, confining her to representation, and reinvesting a transcendent authority in his voice, aligning it to his look (1988: 47, 57). When Don, Cosmo, and Simpson raise the curtain to let the audience see what it hears – Kathy, the 'real' voice behind Lina's singing performance – hearing becomes dependent upon seeing and sound is married to the image, all controlled by the male look and, once Don orders the audience to stop Kathy from running away, matched to his voice.

Lina's lack of wholeness, because her voice does not match her body, motivates her replacement by Kathy, as we have already learned by analyzing the plot. But now we can draw a further conclusion: this closure takes place only after subjecting the female to a series of substitutions that, far from restoring voice to image, subsumes her disturbing impact. Women are disruptive in *Singin' in the Rain* because they speak. 'Well, of course we *talk*', Lina declares after the studio decides to convert *The Duelling Cavalier* into a talkie. And when they talk, watch out! Kathy's outspoken criticism jeopardizes Don's masculinity by calling attention to its imaginary status as 'nothing but a shadow on film'. Dubbing regulates Kathy's insubordinate voice – diegetically when she ghosts for Lina and extradiegetically in the dubbing of Reynolds – by displacing it from her body. Even more significant, Kathy is replaced as Don's partner in 'The Broadway Ballet' by a distinctly mute dancer playing the heartless vamp, Cyd Charisse. From the first shot introducing her by way of her long legs, the choreography and camerawork fetishize Charisse's body. The female figure is thus punished (Lina) and redeemed (Kathy) in the narrative and then, in the ballet, silenced completely in order to be eroticized as pure spectacle (Charisse) (Figure 4.3). Reversing the lack depicted in the opening voiceover montage, the ballet disavows anxiety about male subjectivity, rendering the female as pure spectacle so that the male appears whole, his body and voice reunified by the repeated song lyric that drives the number, 'Gotta Dance!'.

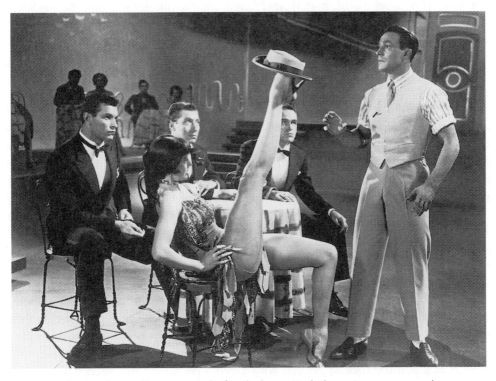

Figure 4.3 'The Broadway Ballet' eroticizes the female dancer (Cyd Charisse) as pure spectacle.
Reproduced courtesy of Cinema Collectors, *Singin' in the Rain*, © 1951 Turner Entertainment Company.

Psychoanalytic film theory has been extremely important for film studies in explaining how the cinematic apparatus embeds spectatorial pleasure in the sexual politics of representation. But for all its emphasis on the unconscious mechanism of spectatorial identification, as Judith Mayne comments, 'What has been surprisingly absent from much psychoanalytic film theory is an investigation of the ways in which the unconscious refuses the stability of any categorization' (1993: 97–98). Mayne proposes that we instead conceive of 'the cinema as a form of fantasy wherein the boundaries of biological sex or cultural gender, as well as sexual preference, are not fixed' (1993: 88). She places emphasis on the psychoanalytic theorization of fantasy not as make-believe, but as a scenario of desire offering variable positions of identification: with the subject of fantasized desire, or with its object, or with its setting in the desire itself, regardless of who is acting on it or receiving it. Fantasy allows for the possibility of shifting between those positions, even when they are gendered and fixed as male or female within the scenario. And, to link Mayne's point back to Mulvey's and Silverman's arguments, if film can be said to draw a viewer into the ideological field of sexual representation as fantasy, then it cannot guarantee for certain the identificatory positions to which viewers will suture.

Mayne defines fantasy 'as the *staging* of desire . . . a form of mise-en-scène' (1993: 88), and this description applies especially well to the musical numbers of *Singin' in the Rain* – indeed, to its self-reflexivity in general – calling for reassessment of its apparent fixing of male and female identities through the voice/image dualism. For all its disavowal of male lack, the ballet is, ultimately, premised on the hoofer's failure to sustain a heterosexual relation with the vamp; both times they meet in this number, after they dance up a storm, she leaves him for her gangster lover. In fact, only one of the numbers in *Singin' in the Rain* ('You Were Meant for Me') directly celebrates the heterosexual couple, and even this one begins with Don setting the stage – with his enacting heterosexual desire as a fantasy scenario for a spectator.

The other numbers engage even more fluid possibilities of identifying with bodies in motion and, correspondingly, with dance as a state of mobile desire not tied to the gender and sexual norms legitimated by the active-male/passive-female binary. Don watches Kathy dance with a voyeur's eye in 'All I Do is Dream of You' but he takes even more pleasure in dancing by himself in the title number, giving his joy an autoerotic dimension. Similarly, when Cosmo dances to cheer up Don in 'Make 'Em Laugh', he turns himself into a spectacle of energetic, even maniacal, movement that, not coded as feminine, problematizes Don's male perspective, leading Alex Doty to comment about the difficulty of responding to this number 'as anything but a case of overwrought, displaced gay desire' (1993: 11). The intimation that dance can stage homoerotic desire resurfaces when the two men synchronize their movement as a challenge dance in 'Moses Supposes'. Dance also takes on bisexual implications in 'Good Mornin'' when Don and Cosmo perform with Kathy, positioned between them in the dancing every step of the way except in the middle of the number. At that point, each dancer grabs someone else's raincoat, using it as a costume prop for a solo dance that is specifically inflected as a performance of gender: with Kathy's coat, Cosmo dances a Charleston; with Don's, Kathy dances a hula; with Cosmo's, Don dances a Spanish flamenco. These solos disrupt the presumed correspondence between gender and dancing as enactments of a fixed sexuality, and they point to 'the interchangeability of Kathy and Cosmo' elsewhere in *Singin' in the Rain* (Mellencamp, 1991: 6). After this number Cosmo stands in front of Kathy to show Don how her voice can be mimed, and, much later, when her dubbing of Lina is publicly revealed, Cosmo precipitates Kathy's flight from the stage by pushing her aside to sing for Lina himself.

The variable positions of sexual identification offered by the numbers extend to the entire film and may even determine, in subverting, the plot's investment in the romantic couple. Cosmo's ambiguous status as an odd man out whenever in the presence of the two lovers provides an identificatory position that, in triangulating the pairing of Don and Kathy, calls into question the plot's automatic privileging of heterosexual desire. The romantic couple in *Singin' in the Rain* is not achieved by a process of addition but by one of subtraction, exclusion of the extra male who is interchangeable with the female. The improper coupling of Don and Lina has the same resonance, since she treats Cosmo as if he were her rival, and vice versa. At the start of the film, in short, Don is *already* coupled – with Cosmo. Why Cosmo has to be marginalized in the narrative, but not the numbers, does not become clear until we see that he poses an obstacle to the heterosexual masculinity Don represents in his relationship with Kathy, which reiterates the orthodox male/female binary and its erotic premise. Because *Singin' in the Rain* forms this couple only by replacing a partner of one gender (male) with that of the other (female), Don is not fixed to that position to begin with, and neither is a spectator (Figure 4.4).

In drawing this conclusion, I do not mean to say that the film characterizes Don as homosexual or bisexual, for that is surely not the case. Rather, I have wanted to call attention to certain queer tensions regarding gender and sexuality that underlie *Singin' in the Rain* and help to determine both its representational content and the pleasures spectators may find in the film. These tensions, moreover, are not confined to the film alone but arise from its connections, as a product of the Hollywood studio system, to cultural history. We can begin to account for these tensions by examining Gene Kelly's extratextual importance for the film as both its author and its star.

Gene Kelly's authorship

It may be tempting to get around what the film's self-reflexivity exposes as the inherent instability of cinematic representation, and to evade the claims of psychoanalytic theory regarding its sexual politics and the possibility of fluid positions of identification, by reading *Singin' in the Rain* solely through the fact of Gene Kelly's authorship. The theory of auteurism interprets a film through its director as 'the expression of his individual personality', demonstrating 'that this personality can be traced in a thematic and/or stylistic consistency over all (or almost all) the director's films' (Caughie 1981: 9). Wollen's insightful monograph on *Singin' in the Rain* follows this line of thinking to legitimate Kelly, who co-directed the film with Stanley Donen, as its primary auteur. Wollen illustrates his viewpoint with a careful analysis of the title number, interpreting it as 'a summation of Gene Kelly's own work up to that point, echoing and developing numbers he had done in earlier films' (1992: 29).

Figure 4.4 The trio of Kathy (Debbie Reynolds), Don (Gene Kelly), and Cosmo (Donald O'Connor). Reproduced courtesy of Cinema Collectors, *Singin' in the Rain*, © 1951 Turner Entertainment Company.

There is a certain justice in appreciating *Singin' in the Rain* as a statement of Kelly's convictions about the musical genre and dance. His efforts to make dance cinematic as opposed to photographed theater resulted in an innovative, influential style that reflected his aesthetic views on choreography. Filmed dance, Kelly maintained, has to be conceived of solely in terms of the camera, which sees differently than the human eye watching a live stage show (Hirschhorn, 1974: 98–99). He consequently staged dances so that performers move into or away from the camera, and used editing to enhance the choreographed movement, all to compensate for 'the two-dimensional limitations imposed by film' (Delameter, 1981: 140).

It is therefore consistent with Kelly's ambitions as a director that technical as well as choreographic innovation receives so much emphasis in *Singin' in the Rain*, and that the film uses dance to ameliorate its sound/image dichotomy. 'The Broadway Ballet', even more so than the film's other dance numbers, combines tap, jazz, and ballet styles in accord with Kelly's aesthetics and formal training. The fluidity of this choreographic style metaphorically raises 'the larger issue of generic flexibility' (Cuomo, 1996: 40), and it further reflects ways in which Kelly's innovations as a director correspond to his character's career within the narrative. Dance, in Cuomo's view, exemplifies how Kelly historically reinvigorated the musical genre, so *Singin' in the Rain* can be read as a 1950s' musical responsive to post-war changes in the industry that were threatening the genre's future and the studios producing them. Dance, the sign of the body's agility at every point in the film, likewise mirrors the generic flexibility of star Don Lockwood as he turns from swashbucklers to musicals. Whereas his athleticism is initially a sign of his inauthenticity, with the change in genres, the same physical movement is set to music and becomes visible proof to the contrary.

Singin' in the Rain bears Kelly's authorial signature insofar as it became his signature film, so much so that on the night he died, for its obituary notice *ABC News* in the United States reportedly closed its broadcast by playing the title number without any spoken commentary. However, *Singin' in the Rain* actually makes it difficult to assign authorial intention to a single pair of hands (or feet!). Kelly himself spoke out against auteurism at his 1985 AFI tribute: 'There are no auteurs in musical movies. The name of the game is collaboration.' While true of all studio-produced films, this was especially the case with *Singin' in the Rain*. It was produced by the Arthur Freed unit at MGM, a team of craftspeople working together under the guidance of Freed and his assistant, Roger Edens. Freed initiated the project because he wanted to produce a film organized around songs he had co-written with Nacio Herb Brown for MGM musicals of the 1920s. The film's script was written by Betty Comden and Adolph Green, Broadway artists under contract to MGM. They wrote the screenplay independently of Kelly – in fact, they recall that it was not originally planned with the star in mind (1972: 4–8), a point that Donen disputes (Harvey, 1973: 5). Most important, because most unusual in Hollywood at that time, *Singin' in the Rain* was co-directed as well as co-choreographed by Kelly and Donen, a former dancer himself. They often split directing chores when filming *Singin' in the Rain*, shooting on different soundstages. This is not to suggest that Kelly directed the numbers and Donen the non-musical portions, because their collaboration was interactive at every point. 'Even through rehearsing the numbers, when everything would really get complicated I would be with him,' Donen said of his work with Kelly. 'So it really was a collaboration' (Harvey, 1973: 5).

In its diegesis, *Singin' in the Rain* also views film-making as a collaboration, one manufacturing an industrial product. The director of the Lockwood–Lamont series is no auteur but a studio employee who keeps referring to R.F. Simpson as 'boss', and who allows Don Lockwood great latitude in writing lines and blocking movement. The director is not present when Simpson listens to a description of 'The Broadway Ballet', so Don seems to be responsible for planning and executing the number. But his best friend Cosmo is also a strong if uncredited influence on *The Dancing Cavalier*. Cosmo devises the scheme to dub Lina with Kathy's voice, invents the plot for the musicalized *The Duelling Cavalier*, and comes up with its new title. Indeed, the Don–Cosmo relation bears a striking resemblance to the Kelly–Donen collaboration, not just in their working relationship but in the auteurist hierarchy that kept the idea man in the shadow of the dancer. Randall Duell, one of the art directors on *Singin' in the Rain*, describes the partnership in terms that evoke Don and Cosmo's in the film: 'Gene ran the show. Stan had some good ideas and worked with Gene, but he was still the "office boy" to Gene, in a sense, though Gene had great respect for him' (Delameter, 1981: 247).

In various television interviews, Kelly spoke of his collaborator as his apprentice, assistant, or protégé. Yet Donen was no 'office boy'. Throughout their collaboration, Kelly staged dance for the camera; he choreographed it in cinematic terms. Donen, far from running the camera in Kelly's place while the latter performed, planned out the dance's relation to the camera; he photographed and edited it in cinematic terms, making full use of his own technical expertise (Charness, 1977: 7, 65). The authorship of *Singin' in the Rain* is thus a complex matter that perhaps cannot be definitively settled. Kelly's signature nevertheless helps to explain why the film can be taken as his personal statement about cinematic dance, but that is also because he was equally important to the film's production and reception as its star, and his star image adds additional layers of cultural significance to *Singin' in the Rain* that further contribute to its meaning.

Stardom and culture

'A star image,' Richard Dyer writes, 'consists both of what we normally refer to as his or her "image", made up of screen roles and obviously stage-managed appearances, and also of images of the manufacturing of that "image" and of the real person who is the site or occasion of it' (1986: 7–8). Analyzing a star's image does not examine the 'real person' beneath the persona, in the way that auteurism seeks evidence of an authorial identity as the origin of a film, but reads it as a cultural text in its own right. Using the methodology of cultural studies, star studies concentrate on the discourses surrounding performers and their films, identifying the connections to beliefs and practices that embed cinema in social history.

The obituaries on Kelly after his death in 1996 summarize his popular star image as established in the 1940s and 1950s. They emphasize, to sample just some of the headlines, that he was the 'he-man dancer [who] perfected the filmusical [*sic*]' (Howard, 1996: 30); that he 'imbued dance with blue collar style' (Wolk, 1996: 2); and that he was 'the athlete who danced our dreams' (Matthews, 1996: 5). Such descriptions illustrate the widespread perception of Kelly's star image as it brought together gender and class to represent male sexuality in a way that, while appearing to give a coherent meaning to his dancing as an expression of virility, produced what Dyer calls a 'clash of codes' (1979: 38).

Richard Griffith's comments in a program for the Museum of Modern Art's tribute to Kelly in the 1960s exemplify, but without acknowledging, the contradictory views of masculinity held together by his star image throughout his career: 'Gene, a superb specimen of manly beauty, doomed, you'd say, to matinee idolatry, has neatly escaped from the trap of dancing and miming in such a way that you would never mistake him for anybody but an ordinary Joe' (1962: 3). On the one hand, Griffith admits that Kelly's 'dancing and miming' turn him into an erotic spectacle, placing his 'manly beauty' on display to be appreciated as 'a superb specimen'. On the other hand, Griffith insists that Kelly avoids that 'trap' because his films cast him as an 'ordinary Joe' to emphasize how the dancer is just another guy, thereby minimizing his spectacular screen value as a male sex object (Figure 4.5).

Like the obituary notices, Griffith's remarks indicate that Kelly was considered to be the most virile of Hollywood's musical stars, with his manliness characterized through associations with the working class as connoted by macho posturing in place of specific social detail. 'What I wanted to do,' Kelly remembered, 'was dance . . . for the common man. The way a truckdriver would dance when he would dance, or a bricklayer, or a clerk, or a postman' (AMCN, 1994). When discussing his screen roles, commentators emphasize the same characteristics: egoism and cockiness, athleticism and physicality, immaturity and ordinariness. Taken together, these attributes formed his screen persona as 'a breezy, brash, unashamedly American urban hero' (Babington and Evans, 1985: 166). But as Jerome Delameter also observes, 'The Kelly character is often a city

Figure 4.5 The spectacle of Gene Kelly: matinee idol *and* 'ordinary Joe' (publicity photograph c. 1950).

character, though one with a small town soul ... [which reveals] that there is a more personal and friendly nature hiding behind the outward appearance of the city' (1981: 147). The disclosure that a decent, smalltown 'ordinary Joe' lurks inside the pompous, hustling, urban wiseguy occurs in almost every one of Kelly's films, *Singin' in the Rain* included, and it substitutes an innate moral (and 'American') character for class as the factor delineating his character's social identity.

In trying to reconcile what had become incompatible in the post-war national consciousness, namely, the rural and urban settings of US culture, Kelly's star image further reflects tensions resulting from class difference as it intersected with conflicted beliefs about gender and sexuality. Briefly, the automatic equation of gender (identity) and sexuality (desire) in forming a person's heterosexual or homosexual preference is, as historian George Chauncey documents, a recent invention of US culture, one occurring with the middle class securing its hegemony after World War 2. Before then, the cultural category of 'gender' in working-class ideology did not necessarily correspond to or determine sexual practices, as it had begun to do for the middle class. A 'sissy' was defined by his outward behavior, not by his having male sexual partners, just as a 'manly' man could have sex with men as well as with women without impugning perceptions of his virility (Chauncey, 1994: 13, 100).

As Kelly's 'ordinary Joe' persona tries to homogenize working-class identity with middle-class sexual values, his star image brings into contention what at the time were still distinct class ideologies that differed in their presumptions of the correspondence between gender and sexuality. His gendered affiliation with the working class explains why a male sidekick such as Donald O'Connor figures as importantly as a female co-star in the casting of Kelly's films. As well as incorporating the male bonding experiences of World War 2 into his characterizations, the buddy relation provides Kelly with a male partner whose masculinity is played for laughs, building up a viewer's identification with the star's dancing as a representation of virility akin to a truckdriver's. According to Clive Hirschhorn, Kelly's biographer:

> Instead of alienating his male audiences, which he feared he might do, he made them identify with him and won them over by the virility of his dancing. There was nothing sissy or effeminate about him, and they relaxed completely in his presence. Gene was 'safe'. 'Like a guy in their bowling team – only classier', as Bob Fosse put it. Women found his smile and the cockiness of his personality most attractive and responded to his sex appeal.
>
> (1974: 157)

As Hirschhorn's carefully worded appreciation reveals, the erotic dimension of Kelly's dancing is the uneasy meaning that his star image, drawing on cultural assumptions about gender, sexuality, and class that historically converged in the 1940s and 1950s, seeks to manage. His star image projects ambivalence about dance's relation to his screen masculinity, evident in his interviews, which stress that 'dancing is a man's game' (the title of his 1958 TV special), in order to disavow the effeminacy connoted by a male dancer's spectacularity for its corresponding intimations of homoeroticism. "'Any man", he maintained, "who looks sissy while dancing is just a lousy dancer"'

(Hirschhorn, 1974: 225). The paradoxical basis of Kelly's star image, then, is that while he expresses his virility *through* a dance, he also worries about losing it *in* the dance. His typical pairing alongside a more effeminate co-star such as O'Connor gives Kelly's masculinity its social inflection of gender – the working-class man, psychologized by his dependence on post-adolescent male friendships – while allowing for the erotic spectacle of his dancing. However, at the same time that the athleticism of his dancing, like the aggression in his screen persona, tries to compensate for the eroticization of his body, his dance numbers stage a bisexual address to the film audience, because 'the virility of his dancing', as Hirschhorn terms it, is directed at men and women. Kelly's dancing consequently provides his star image with a provocative sexual context that is not as 'safe' as Hirschhorn supposes.

Whereas Kelly's MGM films generally promoted his 'reputation as the Douglas Fairbanks of dance' (Harris, 1996: A-1), when *Singin' in the Rain* uses actual footage of Kelly's 1948 non-musical version of *The Three Musketeers* (originally made by Fairbanks in 1921) as an inexpensive way to include film supposedly starring Don Lockwood, it does so to distance Kelly's star image from those erotic implications. The inserted scene of Kelly's D'Artagnan now represents Lockwood's hammy acting in *The Royal Rascal*, the trap of being a 'matinee idol' that, a decade later, Richard Griffith said Kelly could have fallen into if he were not at heart an 'ordinary Joe'. Don's behavior at *The Royal Rascal* premiere satirizes the character's star image for its pretentious, flamboyant style, and the voiceover montage exposes a working-class origin as the truth concealed by that false persona. As *Singin' in the Rain* then proceeds to demystify Don, it remystifies Kelly. In effect, the film incorporates Kelly's own screen past and attributes it to Lockwood in order to revise – through the fictive character's transformation from silent-film swashbuckler to sound-era song-and-dance man, and, correspondingly, from glamour to ordinariness – the star's erotic image. Comparison with the MGM films that, by sexualizing his athletic body through the kind of swashbuckling associated with Lockwood, established his reputation – *Du Barry Was a Lady* (1943), *Anchors Aweigh* (1945), and *The Pirate* (1948) – makes *Singin' in the Rain*'s recuperation of Kelly's star image even more pronounced.

Singin' in the Rain's revisionist incorporation of Kelly's star image figures into its mythification of Hollywood; at the same time, the film's continual attention to the production of movies keeps reminding us that the star system cannot be easily separated from its industrial setting. 'It's damn hard work to make a musical', Kelly recalled on television almost two decades after leaving MGM. 'It's hard work, it's as tough as digging a ditch.' Yet moments later he also commented: 'If the audience is aware that you're working hard, then you're not dancing well' (BBC, 1974). While meant to describe the perfectionism a finished number had to display, the comment also applies to the institution of stardom, which disguises the position of performers such as Kelly as industrial employees, commodifying their labor as stardom while effacing the work force that supports it. The title number of *Singin' in the Rain*, designed to feature Kelly's tap-dancing, relied on numerous artists who remained invisible as laborors: craftspeople and technicians, such as the musical arranger, cameraman, soundman, set designer, costumer, not to mention the anonymous crew who lit the set, installed rain pipes throughout the street, and even dug ditches, the holes in the ground for puddles that had to match Kelly's steps exactly. The number, furthermore, was shot during the day, with a black tarpaulin covering the backlot set, because the studio wanted to avoid paying the crew double time (Hirschhorn, 1974: 186).

Singin' in the Rain shows enough of the invisible work force necessary for star-driven films such as musicals to suggest that, no less than Kelly's, Don Lockwood's star value stands atop a hierarchy of laborers. Don has a freedom to control his work that Lina, Kathy, Cosmo, and all the artists and crews laboring under him lack, since they are expected to follow directions as obedient personnel. Their labor consequently has a different value for the studio; it is more easily commodified and effaced as serious work. Thus Kathy easily succeeds Lina as Don's co-star and Cosmo as easily disappears from view when his labor is no longer required. Yet as a star Don is himself a commodity; his value for the studio is as threatened by the failure of *The Duelling Cavalier* as is Lina's.

Putting cultural studies in conjunction with Marxism to analyze the labor of stars, Danae Clark points out that, economically, they 'are actors caught between the forces of production and consumption, between bodily labor and commodified image. A gap exists between an actor's use value (labor) and exchange value (image)' (1995: 21). This gap is essential to the musical genre's myth of performance, in fact, to stardom in general as a cultural phenomenon. Remembering the production date of *Singin' in the Rain*, we can perhaps see why, historically, the movies' institutionalization of stardom was under particular stress at the time, making that gap between the use value of actors' labor and its exchange value as stardom more evident than usual. By 1952, MGM had replaced studio head Louis B. Mayer with Dore Schary and had begun to drop its big stars as their contracts expired; the House Un-American Activities Committee (HUAC) was investigating the left-wing politics of Hollywood actors such as Gene Kelly (Wollen, 1992: 47–51); the film audience had diminished in size and the studio system was breaking down economically as a result of the Paramount consent decree legally requiring the film companies sell off their theater chains, their main source of profit; and the movies had to compete with a new technology and new type of stardom in television.

Using Kelly's star image to cover over the rift between labor and image, which the female characters expose, *Singin' in the Rain* plays out these industrial concerns about stardom by projecting them onto fandom. Fandom commodifies stars as images through their consumption, and it is shown to be dangerous in *Singin' in the Rain* because, in their idolizing of stars, fans collect together as a crowd to form mass culture. Anonymous fans cheer the stars as they enter Grauman's Chinese Theater, but they are safely contained. Later that evening, though, they mob Don and endanger his life. Fans disturb the institution of stardom by forcing recognition of the difference between star labor and its exchange value. One bad movie, and a fan can decide, 'I never want to see that Lockwood and Lamont again', threatening to end the stars' careers and causing the studio to face the prospect of financial ruin.

Of course, this account oversimplifies the degree to which the studio system controlled star labor and profited from actors and fans alike. As Kelly recalled about the contract system, 'we were all indentured servants – you can call us slaves if you want – like ball players before free agency. We had seven-year contracts but every six months the studio could decide to fire you if your picture wasn't a hit' (de Vries, 1994: 3). Shifting the source of power from the studio to the fans, *Singin' in the Rain* would nevertheless have us believe that the preview audience's mockery of his acting is what finally convinces Don to accept Kathy's view that he is nothing but a shadow, just an image: 'Something happened to me tonight . . . everything you said about me is true, Kathy. I'm no actor. Just a lot of dumb show. I know that now.' Enthusiastically taking to the proposal that he rethink his career and make a musical, Don confirms the value of Gene Kelly's star image for *Singin' in the Rain*. However, even at this crucial moment that meaning does not stay perfectly fixed. At the prospect of Don's returning to his vaudeville roots to sing and dance, Cosmo jests, 'The new Don Lockwood. He yodels. He jumps about to music.' Cosmo's remark implies that the new star persona for Don, like Kelly's, is as much of an erotic spectacle and industrial commodity, and no less of an effacement of the actor's labor, as the old one. And someone else still has to play the music.

Conclusions

Any closure invariably carries with it an expectation of resolution, but I have intentionally resisted synthesizing *Singin' in the Rain* to offer a totalizing meaning that accounts for each possibility of interpretation raised by this case study. We may gather that, thematically speaking, each theoretical perspective explains how *Singin' in the Rain* is about Hollywood, but that does not go very far in engaging with the specificity of the film, nor can it reconcile what are competing interpretations of the same textual elements, such as the couple, the sound/image dualism, the value of dance, the ballet, the voiceover montage, and so forth. Rather than reaching a definitive statement about this film's meaning, it will be more useful to reach some tentative conclusions about the process of interpretation that this case study has illustrated.

Each theoretical perspective yields an analytical methodology, placing *Singin' in the Rain* in a different interpretive framework, catching different emphases, and finding different value for the film. We should not rush to conclude, however, that some methods of interpreting are more objective (or 'trustworthy') because they find meanings inherent in the film, while others are more biased (or 'suspect') because they project meanings onto it, since any interpretation has to bring a set of theorized assumptions about the act of interpreting itself to a film in order to make sense of it. Without that informing ground, the film would lack meaning; all we could do is summarize it.

Even more importantly, because each theoretical method illuminates the film in different ways, the one we choose to follow is crucial not only in terms of explaining how a film means, but in determining what it means to us as critical readers. Interpreting a film delineates what significance can and cannot be attributed to it. So whether we confine our attention solely to textual detail, as in the first half of this case study, or move from there to everwidening cultural and historical contexts, as in the second, the meanings produced have great consequence. There is a politic to any interpretation, however implicit its theoretical reasoning and whatever its analytical method, because how we read film clarifies what we see there and tells us why it matters.

Endnote

1   All quotations from *Singin' in the Rain* (1952; MGM; dir. Gene Kelly and Stanley Donen) are my own transcriptions from the MGM–UA videodisc.

References

AFI, 1985: AFI life achievement awards,1985: Gene Kelly. Worldvision Home Video, 1991.

Altman, R. 1989: *The American film musical*. Bloomington, IN: Indiana University Press.

AMCN, 1994: Reflections on the silver screen with professor Richard Brown: Gene Kelly. American Movie Classics Network, 2 February.

Babington, W. and Evans, P.W.1985: *Blue skies and silver linings: aspects of the Hollywood musical*. Manchester: Manchester University Press.

BBC, 1974: *An evening with Gene Kelly*. Rebroadcast on Turner Classic Movies Network, 23 July 1995.

Bordwell, D. 1985: *Narration in the fiction film*. Madison, WI: University of Wisconsin Press.

Caughie, J. (ed.), 1981: *Theories of authorship: a reader*. London: Routledge, reprinted 1988.

Charness, C. 1977: Hollywood cine-dance: a description of the interrelationship of camerawork and choreography in films by Stanley Donen and Gene Kelly. Dissertation, New York University.

Chauncey, G. 1994: *Gay New York: gender, urban culture, and the making of the gay male world 1890–1940*. New York: Basic Books.

Clark, D. 1995: *Negotiating Hollywood: the cultural politics of actors' labor*. Minneapolis, MN: University of Minnesota Press.

Comden, B. and Green, A. 1972: *Singin' in the Rain*. New York: Viking.

Cuomo II, P. 1996: Dance, flexibility, and the renewal of genre in *Singin' in the Rain*. *Cinema Journal* **36**(1), 39–54.

Delameter, J. 1981: *Dance in the Hollywood musical*. Ann Arbor, MI: UMI Research Press.

Derrida, J. 1981: Semiology and grammatology: interview with Julia Kristeva. In Cobley, P. (ed.), *The communication theory reader*. London: Routledge, reprinted 1996, 209–24.

de Vries, H. 1994: It's been so entertaining: these days, when there are more MGM stars in heaven than on earth, there is still Gene Kelly, who is quite happy to debunk some of the myths of the studio's golden age, much as 'That's Entertainment! III' does. *Los Angeles Times* 1 May, Home Edition: Calendar 3+. *Los Angeles Times* archives, online 9 August 1996.

Doty, A. 1993: *Making things perfectly queer: interpreting mass culture*. Minneapolis, MN: University of Minnesota Press.

Dyer, R. 1979: *Stars*. London: British Film Institute.

Dyer, R. 1986: *Heavenly bodies*. New York: St. Martin's Press.

Feuer, J. 1981: The self-reflective musical and the myth of entertainment. In Altman, R. (ed.), *Genre: a reader*. London: Routledge, 159–74.

Feuer, J. 1993: *The Hollywood musical*, 2nd edn. Bloomington, IN: Indiana University Press.

Fordin, H. 1975: *The movies' greatest musicals: produced in Hollywood USA by the Freed unit*. New York: Ungar, reprinted 1984.

Griffith, R. 1962: *The cinema of Gene Kelly*. New York: Museum of Modern Art.

Harris, S. 1996: Gene Kelly dies: legendary dancer was 83. *Los Angeles Times*, 1 May, Home Edition: A-1. *Los Angeles Times* archives, online 4 August 1996.

Harvey, S. 1973: Stanley Donen. *Film Comment* **9**(4): 4–9.

Hirschhorn, C. 1974: *Gene Kelly*. New York: St. Martin's Press, reprinted 1984.

Howard, E. 1996: Gene Kelly: he-man dancer perfected the filmusical. *Memphis Business Journal* 19 February, 30; Electric Library, online 10 August 1996.

Lévi-Strauss, C. 1963: The structural study of myth. In *Structural anthropology*, trans. Claire Jacobson and Brooke Grundgest Schoepf. New York: Basic Books, 206–31.

Mast, G. 1987: *Can't help singin': the American musical on stage and screen.* Woostock, NY: Overlook Press.

Matthews, J. 1996: The athlete who danced our dreams. *Newsweek* 11 February, 5; Electric Library, online 10 August 1996.

Mayne, J. 1993: *Cinema and spectatorship.* London: Routledge.

Mellencamp, P. 1991: Spectacle and spectator: looking through the American musical comedy. In Burnett, R. (ed.), *Explorations in film theory.* Bloomington, IN: Indiana University Press, 3–14.

Metz, C. 1977: *The imaginary signifier: psychoanalysis and the cinema*, trans. Celia Britton, Annwyl Williams, Ben Brewster, and Alfred Guzzetti. Bloomington, IN: Indiana University Press, 1982.

Mulvey, L. 1975: Visual pleasure and narrative cinema. *Visual and other pleasures.* Bloomington, IN: Indiana University Press, reprint 1989, 14–26.

Silverman, K. 1983: *The subject of semiotics.* New York: Oxford University Press.

Silverman, K. 1988. *The acoustic mirror: the female voice in psychoanalysis and cinema.* Bloomington, IN; Indiana University Press.

Wolk, M. 1996: Gene Kelly dies; imbued dance with blue collar style. Reuters newservice, 2 February. Electric Library online, 10 August 1996.

Wollen, P. 1992: *Singin' in the Rain.* London: British Film Institute.

5   Who (and what) is it for?

Tessa Perkins

The question of the relationship between the academy, politics, theory and film-making practices is particularly relevant in two ways: first, because of the current educational, technological and economic changes; second, because of an apparent identity crisis within film theory specifically and cultural studies more generally. This is not unrelated to the broader social changes noted above but it has its own set of determinations as well arising from the history of the relationships between film theory, politics and film-making practices, particularly since the 1970s. In this crisis both the contribution of theory and the place (or not) of politics have played a significant role – to the extent that some wish, to all intents and purposes, to abandon both and others are determined that the former should cleanse itself of all contamination by the latter, fantasizing, perhaps, that a pseudo-scientific objectivity will emerge from the funeral pyre. There is a sense of ennui about the issue, laced through maybe with guilt. My concern in this chapter is to encourage discussion about, and reflection on, these issues rather than sweeping them under the carpet.

In recent years it has become difficult to pursue critical paths which engage students about the political work of media representations or to discuss how criticism and research may, if only by circuitous routes, influence representational practices. This implies that films, *along with other forms of representation*, play an important role in forming ideas about, and attitudes to, the world, in setting agendas, in enabling (or not) other ways of envisaging the world, in alleviating anxiety and even in defusing conflict – in short that they do do political work. This is not to argue that films have the same 'effects' on everyone, as I discuss later, or that individual films have immediate or identifiable effects *à la* hypodermic syringe model, or that all (mainstream) films do the same political work or that films have a privileged role. It is, however, to claim that films contribute to the circulation of meaning within the public sphere and thus the continued importance of a critical textual analysis. Such analysis needs to incorporate both the theoretical achievements of the past 20 years and a new commitment to locating film within a broader theoretical framework. The almost total annihilation of a socially situated 'ideological' critique from contemporary academic discourse is counterproductive. I start by addressing the question 'Who (and what) is theory for?' by means of a personal account.

Who (and what) is it for?

My own engagement with film theory has been as an 'outsider'. I am neither a 'film theorist' nor a 'film-maker' but rather someone whose political (and on occasions economic) interests led them through various forms of political activity and, within the academy, different disciplinary perspectives – sociology, women's studies, cultural studies, communication studies, film and media studies. This 'journey' was stimulated by an interest in ideology. 'To study ideology,' argues Thompson, 'is to study the ways in which meaning sustains relations of domination' (Thompson, 1984: 141). The frequency with which, whether as an 'academic' sociologist or as a 'political activist' involved in local politics and the women's movement, I came across 'explanations' of inequality, discrimination or prejudice as resulting from 'attitudes', 'values' and 'negative stereotypes' led me, like so many of my generation, to question why such 'attitudes', 'values' and 'stereotypes' existed and persisted and how they could be changed. An encounter with Richard Dyer who was already working on stereotyping in films raised a question about sociological literature on stereotyping. I realised that stereotyping was rarely referred to in sociological theory; it seemed mainly a psychological concept. And so I found myself attempting to develop a more sociologically informed approach to stereotypes, as ideological concepts. But then I experienced the difficulties of mentally crossing disciplinary boundaries. At the end of the article I wrote in 1978 about stereotypes (Perkins, 1979) I admitted I had made 'very few ... references to how stereotypes function aesthetically' despite having claimed at the beginning (*pace* Dyer, 1977) that it was politically important to understand this if we were to change them. The problem was that sociologists and film theorists typically conceptualised films very differently and I knew just enough about film and media theory to recognise this but could move no further.

I am often reminded of such problems by students' dissertations on film and media texts – especially dissertations about fictional representations of gender or race. Students fall back onto a reflection/accuracy model of the text, the 'common-sense' model assumed in much public debate about film, which severely restricts the accounts they can give. In my own engagement with film theory I recall certain ideas which shifted *how* I could think about films: Richard Dyer's 'Entertainment and utopia' (1992a) suggested films could be located within particular socio-historical contexts without depending on literalist or reflectionist models; it emphasised the affective and imaginative dimensions of audience involvement in films suggesting how qualities such as 'energy' and 'abundance' were realised filmically. Then I became involved in a debate about whether the moment of narrative closure (of *Calamity Jane* (1953)) was more significant than the 80-odd minutes of Calamity's rebellion prior to her marriage, and the pleasure that gave female audiences – a debate which opened up for me the question of 'what texts mean' and indicated that texts need to be conceptualised as fluid, as sites of negotiation which can offer 'subversive' pleasures and even allow for resistance. This debate occurred in a programme made for an Open University Women's Studies course which was stimulated by a season of Doris Day films at London's National Film Theatre in 1980 (Clarke and Simmonds, 1980; Perkins, 1981). The season (*Move Over Misconceptions*) itself exemplified a successful attempt by feminists both to intervene in film exhibition practices and to subject the conventional description of Day as the stereotyped girl-next-door to critical re-evaluation. In stark contrast was Laura Mulvey's 'Visual pleasure and narrative cinema' (1989). Although I was largely unsympathetic to her Lacanian framework, her account of the way in which the pleasures of classic Hollywood movies were organised around the control of women showed how patriarchal ideology was reproduced, forcing me to address the interplay of narrative and visual discourses. That Mulvey's article drives towards a conclusion about changing the form of mainstream narratives and finding new forms of pleasure is often forgotten. None of these different, but not totally incompatible, theoretical positions have proved total dead ends as I realised recently when reading *Framed*, an anthology about media representations of disability and the employment of people with disabilities in media industries, which recalls how much representations do still matter and how much film theory contributed to expanding our understanding of representation (Pointon and Davies, 1997).

The point of this personal account is threefold. First, I wish to show that film theory is not just for film theorists; perhaps 1970s' film theory became too focused on the specificity of film and tended to grant film a uniquely privileged place in representational practices. While film theory's strengths derived from that obsession, it was ultimately untenable. Second, I wish to emphasise that theory is a practice which develops not only in the pursuit of 'pure knowledge' (or, more cynically, academic ambition) but also in the process of trying to understand, and sometimes to change, phenomena. The point is also to demystify both theory and academics by indicating gaps in theoretical development and academics' knowledge. Last, I wish to establish that while the academy may be the primary site in which theoretical work takes place, it is by no means the only one.

Like many others at the time, both Richard Dyer and I were attempting to cross disciplinary boundaries and explicitly defined our theoretical interest in stereotypes in terms of politics. This was not unproblematic for an academic at the time. Indeed, the academic conference at which we gave a paper on stereotypes unusually received coverage in *The Sunday Times* which was scandalised by the conference's 'political' tenor. Dyer's work still demonstrates the political commitment which characterised film and cultural theory 20 years ago (for example, see his recent publication *White*, 1997) and a cursory glance at current film periodicals demonstrates that there is still considerable interest in this area. But the place of such work in the academy is being challenged both by calls to separate politics from theory and by other changes.

The academy

This term refers, in abstract, to a social institution, implying a body of knowledge and expertise, a set of professional practices and a site of scholarship and learning. Like all abstract terms, it conceals complexity and mess. Not all 'academics' in a particular field have its defining body of knowledge. A body of knowledge and expertise is, like a language system, only held collectively and not by any individual. It is easy also to slip into thinking of the academy as coterminous with higher education, which is, of course, not the case. In fact a notable change in the past 30 years for film and media studies has been their institutionalisation within higher education. A key factor in the formation of film studies, and film theory, lies, in Britain at least, in its origins outside the university sector – in art colleges, secondary schools and adult education – although many involved in the 'production' of film theory in the 1960s and 1970s also struggled to get film recognised as a 'legitimate' area of study within higher education. In the 1960s and 1970s the British Film Institute played a key role in the circulation and orchestration of debates in British film theory and, at times, the attempt to realise theories in practice. By the 1990s film studies had come in from the margins (though not all the way in) and now constitutes one of the most popular 'humanities' degrees. While no doubt the institutionalisation of film studies (along with media and cultural studies) accounts in part for the diminution of its political agenda, other factors have also been involved.

The academy, and more specifically higher education, is, like Janus, two-faced. Its goals are non-political – 'Universities provide a protected space for free inquiry and expression' (Saunders, 1999) – and its professional creed of 'academic freedom' is resolutely, if not always effectively, defended. But it is also a player in the political field. In today's political context higher education is increasingly expected to answer to 'stakeholders' – students, now conceived of as 'customers' (or, more recently, 'partners'), employers, taxpayers – and even if 'academic freedom' has never been as great as our professional creed suggests, this is a marked change. Higher education is both an instrument of control, an ideological state apparatus (ISA) in Althusser's terms, and an instrument of subversion. The frequency with which political rebellion, across the world, starts in universities or involves students (and lecturers) is testament to its intrinsic subversive potential. It is an important source of 'experts' who play a crucial role in setting agendas and in gatekeeping. It is a key player in defining fields of knowledge, in defending tradition and in 'creating' new fields of knowledge, giving (or denying them) legitimacy. Struggles to legitimate new fields of knowledge such as film and media studies as areas for 'academic' study exist both within the academy and between the academy and the outside world. The introduction of new 'disciplines' challenges existing canons and points to weaknesses and prejudices in related disciplines. The development of women's studies, ethnic studies and gay studies all exemplify this, representing the point at which theory, politics and the academy intersect (see below).

The role of the academy, and of academics and students, is changing. The expansion of student numbers has been accompanied by increased demands (not merely from employers) to 'train' students for 'employment', and many academics believe this threatens the value they have traditionally placed on developing students' capacity for analytical thought and critical reflection. There is, in Britain at least, a definite increase in governmental intervention – to oversee, through '*standard*isation' of both curriculum and research, what is delivered, how it is delivered and what counts as knowledge.

As relatively new disciplines, and in a climate of seemingly endless expansion of the media, film and media studies have been particularly pressurised to provide 'practical' rather than 'theoretical' education and undoubtedly the emphasis of teaching has changed. Students are now far more likely to be involved in making film and media texts as part of their studies and this is frequently where they devote most energy. Some 20 or 30 years ago 'production' was the preserve of one or two specialist schools or of art colleges. The increased pressure on us now explicitly to prepare students for employment comes from students as much as from elsewhere. The expansion of higher education and the contraction, and increased casualisation, of employment (not just in the film and media industries) mean that a degree is no longer the guarantee of entry into middle-class occupations it once was (for men at least). And because it is no longer a guarantee, one of the ways in which academics themselves are now assessed is in terms of graduate employment figures. In this context it is easy to see how critical theory – whether the political economy or the textual variety – could get pushed out of degrees in favour of more pragmatic 'training' needs, especially given the virulence of the media's attacks on media studies, attacks which show no sign of abating. However, the expansion of higher education also means a far larger proportion of the younger generation going to university and thus academics in universities have greater opportunity than ever before to influence both those who will work in the film and media industries and a significant proportion of the population as a whole.

This is not the place to explore the whys and wherefores, the pros and cons, of these changes but it is significant that they follow the massification of higher education which was something many on the left welcomed in the perhaps naive belief that such an expansion would lead to a more egalitarian society. Many years ago Basil Bernstein argued that different ideas about knowledge were inscribed in educational curricula at different stages of education.[1] Only at the level of higher education, the education of the elite, was 'knowledge' presented as an active and ongoing process in which undergraduates were encouraged to participate. That was the 'secret' (and privilege) of higher education to which the vast majority of the population were denied access because it was held to be inappropriate for the mass of the labour force in a capitalist society. Bernstein's arguments about the ways in which school education dulls critical faculties, about the relationship between power and knowledge and the structure of the labour force belong to that leftist critique of education which characterised the 1960s and 1970s. Currently, when all critiques of capitalism seem to have disappeared from the public domain, such a critical perspective is difficult to reintroduce (see Branston, Chapter 2). However, the spirit of Bernstein's arguments is pertinent in the current context where pressures to prepare students for employment conflict at times with the desire to develop their analytical and critical faculties and encourage them not merely to participate in the production of knowledge but even to believe that, if they want to, they can change things.

The academy is frequently described as an ivory tower, implying a separation between the university and the 'real' world. While there is some validity in this description, it is also deceptive insofar as it underplays and conceals its role in the political process. As a primary site for the production and circulation of knowledge the academy plays a key role in the formation of social and political discourses. In a recent critique of cultural studies Todd Gitlin commented: 'if we wish to do politics let us organise groups, coalitions, demonstrations, lobbies whatever; let us do politics. Let us not think that our academic work is already that' (1997: 37). It would be easy to sympathise with this comment, after a sustained, slick if sometimes pertinent, attack on 'The anti-political populism of cultural studies', but I think it is misleading because it underestimates the ways in which academic work is political. This is clearly so in curriculum changes such as the introduction of women's studies and in the way issues raised by feminism have affected so many disciplines. Furthermore, these changes gave opportunities to groups of students previously excluded from higher education, and anyone teaching on such courses knows the impact they have on students. It would be wrong to argue that the women (blacks and gays) who fought to get women's (black and gay) studies into the curricula of countless universities were not 'doing politics'. And what is one to say of those who attempted to resist these changes or who simply ignored them? Were they not also 'doing politics'? Of course they were.

Politics

Gitlin's comment, like many similar discussions, raises the confusing question of what we mean by politics. 'Politics' tends to be used to describe a mode of activity whose aims are to effect a change in the social order and the distribution of power and resources within that order. But 'politics' also describes a mode of activity, or inactivity, which aims to *maintain* an established order. The association of the word 'political' generally with those of left-wing 'progressive' persuasion, sometimes with those of right-wing, 'reactionary' persuasion encourages us to ignore the politics of the centre, of stability and maintaining things as they are, the politics which are, after all, the most successful. This point – that all positions are political – was, of course, a key theme of 1960s' radical politics and if it was on occasions overstated, it nonetheless remains important in the current climate to insist that the politics of the 'centre' are as political as any other and must be rendered visible. The concerted attack on 'political correctness' has mainly denied its own political position but been largely successful in silencing the debates which lay behind the much maligned PC (politically correct) lobby.

The term 'politics' became itself the site of political contestation and theoretical debate from the mid-1960s in a struggle to extend the term. This was fuelled partly by Marxist politics and the increasingly central role of ideology in 1960s' Marxist analysis and partly by the 'new social movements'. It took place most obviously in the women's movement where the phrase 'the personal is political' served both as a slogan around which various strands of feminism could unite and a theme around which key political and theoretical concerns could be articulated. But although most strongly associated with feminism this conceptual shift became a central feature of all the new social movements and was associated with the strategy of consciousness-raising. This is frequently discussed as if it were solely an exercise in white, middle-class feminist navel-gazing, an indulgence, but it was more complex and widespread than that and had both a personal and a public dimension concerned with raising one's own consciousness of oppression and public consciousness. Consciousness-raising drew on the Marxist distinction between a class-in-itself (an objective, descriptive category) and a class-for-itself which could act politically on its own behalf only when it recognised its shared situation and interests. At a personal level, consciousness-raising encouraged the sharing of the experience of oppression and consequent development of an identity from which oppression could be resisted and political activity take place.

Expanding the term 'political' has consequences for the cultural sphere. The political relevance of films is not restricted to films with explicit political intentions or content such as *Malcolm X* (1992), *JFK* (1991) or *Land and Freedom* (1995). The politics of such films deserve consideration in their own right but any film can be looked at in terms of its political significance, and the relationship between films and politics is neither singular nor stable. Those involved in making films may deny any political *intention*, insist that they were just telling 'a good story', just trying to entertain,[2] but lack of a conscious (or acknowledged) political intent by its makers does not make a film unpolitical. Such explanations reveal how particular 'common-sense' accounts of the world are recruited and defended in the name of entertainment or commercial viability. For example, interviewed about the representation of disability, David Puttnam responded to a question about the commercial viability of such films as follows:

> I think it's *inevitable* that the main storyline of any film regarding disability would have to allow the audience an opportunity to understand the nature of disability, and *inevitably* the able-bodied audience would regard the fact itself as something of a *tragedy*.
>
> As to *pathos*, I think that's *just* a dramatic facet of the story you decide to tell, but what is certain is that the issue of disability clearly evokes *sympathy* and it would seem to me to be a wasted opportunity not to *optimise* the emotions of the audience in watching someone *overcome* any form of severe disability.
>
> (Pointon and Davies, 1997: 53–4 [emphasis added])

This 'sympathetic' view of disability is constructed as common sense even though it is the inability to move beyond such 'tragic' and 'brave' representations that disability politics has been challenging for years and which most contributors to *Framed* argue reproduce unacceptably oppressive attitudes to disability. Embedded in Puttnam's answer are assumptions about the 'pleasure' available to 'normal' audiences in this genre and 'appropriate' narrative strategies which guide his film-making practice.[3] The similarities between this explanation and numerous justifications of class, race, gender and sexuality representations are also notable. Here perhaps the more general relevance of Mulvey's arguments about the politics of pleasure are worth remembering. As teachers (whether of theory or practice), researchers or students such justificatory accounts need analysis. One of the tools we can give our students – even if their main objective is to make commercially successful films – is the capacity for reflective thought. One way to do this is to help them consider alternative practices and different responses and to question assumptions made by media professionals about what audiences 'want' or what will be successful. Here critical textual analysis intersects with political economy and with professional training. Can film theory help us approach these issues, or should we ignore them, for fear of bringing politics into the academy or failing to equip students for employment?

Theory

My purpose now is to render the relationship between politics and theory more transparent, to situate theoretical and political changes in a broader process of socio-economic change and to explore the ways in which theories may be appropriated and become incorporated into common-sense thinking. It is hoped that by understanding these relationships better we can avoid the evils of theoryphobia, theoryworship and theorycide.

In the late 1960s and much of the 1970s 'ideology' was the concept which informed the new political and theoretical work in cultural theory (including film theory). By the early 1990s it had almost disappeared from the lexicon and was being replaced either by the Foucauldian notion of 'discourse' or by Gramscian notions of hegemony and negotiation, leading to a celebration of popular culture and resistant readers – a sort of audience anarchy. It moved from textual determinism to audience determinism. To some extent film theory's (in contrast to television theory's) 'turn to the audience' has been half-hearted, substituting another 'turn' – to history. Both turns seem to represent a desire for empirical evidence from 'outside', in which either to ground theory or to escape from it. But running alongside the rejection of 'grand theory' which these 'turns' represent, the early 1990s also saw increasing unease with what had happened to cultural studies and film theory and a call to return to a 'critical' cultural studies or to abandon it (Ferguson and Golding, 1997; Kellner, 1995; McGuigan, 1992). Recently the term 'ideology' has been spotted creeping back into the lexicon (Ferguson, 1998; Van Dijk, 1998) and renewed arguments for reintroducing political economy (Ferguson and Golding, 1997). If nothing else such diverse tendencies indicate, as does this book, that there is no theoretical perspective currently available that finds broad acceptance within the academic community of which we are part. It is hard to deny that during the Reagan and Thatcher years the critical and political edge of cultural studies, but not just cultural studies, was lost. That it was during those years that postmodernist 'theories' became dominant and identity politics were increasingly prominent is significant.

The attack on 1960s' and 1970s' theory targets what seemed to many of us an abstract theoreticism – partly because of exaggerated claims for its capacity to change things, and particularly to influence film-making practices, and partly because, disengaging from its initial concerns, it celebrated theory for its own sake. But it is important to remember where the concern with theory came from and what it contributed in its time – a time when the dominant paradigms laid claim to a value-free, politically neutral objectivity, untainted by theory or ideology – a time in which the 'end of ideology' was celebrated by Daniel Bell in a book of that name. Exposing the theoretical and ideological assumptions which underlay the so-called neutrality of the conservative position and demonstrating that different theories produced different and more adequate accounts of the world became a key weapon in the arsenal of the left. Theoretical critique and the development of alternative theoretical accounts became a political strategy.

As Gill Branston comments, 'there do . . . exist theoretical "breaks" or achievements which absolutely change the way you can think and argue about an area' (this volume, Chapter 2, page 26). The trinity of Marxism, structuralism and psychoanalysis and their awkward articulation with each other produced such a break. What they offered was a way to account for and critique the taken-for-grantedness of theoretical systems which no longer provided an adequate account of sociocultural phenomena. The impetus behind these attempts to understand how consciousness was formed was that we might change it – which is why Mulvey's article drives to the conclusion it does.

This theoretical, and accompanying empirical, work played a crucial role both in undermining a dominant paradigm and in providing new concepts and new ways of understanding the world and cultural phenomena. It proposed new forms of political activity. Sexism, racism, heterosexism, homophobia, patriarchy, orientalism, subjectivity and identity are just a few of the concepts which emerged at this time – some of them (such as sexism) were new terms,[4] some (such as patriarchy) were terms which took on a new range of meanings.

The theoretical import of such terms is that they conceptualised these 'oppressions' as being systemic rather than an effect of individual or local deviance. These were not 'empty' theoretical concepts. They produced grounds on which political action took place and around which political debates focused. Separatist politics (both black and gender) was one of the responses to this stage. They were also attempts to make sense of empirical observations. Given theory's frequently assumed disdain for empiricism, this point deserves emphasis. Much of this theoretical work either critiqued existing interpretations of empirical evidence or was based on the 'discovery' of new evidence. For feminists, blacks and gays this act of 'discovery' was explicitly political as well as theoretical. While this is obvious in a discipline such as sociology, it was equally true of film theory. Films are documents which provide empirical evidence.

New concepts such as sexism and homophobia were not just used by intellectuals in articles and books. They emerged as much from political activity 'outside' the academy as from abstract theoretical debates within it. And, of course, they have a political effectivity and become part of the political process, contributing to the formation of discourses in and around which political activity takes place – for example campaigns about domestic violence or race relations policy.

The theoretical struggles of the 1970s and early 1980s should – at the risk of oversimplifying – be placed in the context of the considerable economic, industrial and political turmoil of the time. During this period a gap opened between 'Marxism' and 'structuralism', and psychoanalysis entered the field. This gap became identified as a split between 'political economy' and 'textual analysis', which focused increasingly on subjectivity and consciousness. Early feminists' attempts to accommodate themselves within Marxism and within the British labour movement were only partly successful, and as the economic crisis developed throughout the 1970s and into the 1980s it became increasingly hard to keep women on the agenda. The collapse of Britain's industrial heartland, the enormous rise in unemployment and the increase in women's part-time employment all contributed to a crisis in gender relations and class politics. Perhaps because of the problems which were besetting the British labour movement, feminists' frustration grew as women were once again told to wait. The ways in which Marxism was 'blind' to gender, or the ways feminist research suggested that patriarchy was as significant in explaining women's oppression as capitalism, became a growing theme. A tendency to essentialist arguments which would explain patriarchy emerged and separatism, once identified as an extremist strategy, became far more acceptable. It was primarily with this strand of feminism that psychoanalysis became associated, increasingly detached from economic analysis. Within film theory the emphasis on psychoanalytic analysis becomes evident by the mid-1970s, and two articles, one by Mulvey and one by MacCabe, seemed unchallengeable touchstones, both of them notably lacking any reference to the here-and-now, to the social and cultural context. The task of grounding the analysis of film and its ideological work within the social context was lost, as McArthur's critique of MacCabe demonstrated (Mulvey, 1989; MacCabe, 1981; McArthur, 1981; Pawling and Perkins, 1992).

A key figure in the attempt to 'rethink' Marx was Louis Althusser, whose structuralist Marxism became a dominant influence on British cultural theory from the mid-1970s. While Althusser's identification of media as one of the ISAs, his attempt to 'free' ideology from a simple economic determinism, and his arguments about interpellation were interesting, his particular theorisation of the way ideology determined consciousness and its relative autonomy from the economic robbed the notion of its explanatory potential. Ideology became a static concept, especially when allied to the universalist and essentialist tendencies of psychoanalysis. It was also politically debilitating. The Althusserian variant of ideology became untenable in the face of 1970s' identity politics. It could neither explain protest nor provide an account of ideology as dynamic, changing and adaptive. Hence the turn from Althusser to Gramsci, whose conceptualisation of hegemony as never finally secure but rather subject to crises and negotiation reintroduced a dynamic concept of ideology, one which was easier to ground in specific historical conjunctures, which could account for protest and dissent – indeed presupposed it. It also provided an alternative way to understand how film contributed to the circulation of meaning. It was possible to see the ways in which films and other cultural phenomena played a role in the process of negotiation, of gaining, or even undermining, the *consent* of the population to be *led*.[5]

The turn to Gramsci represented a partial return to 'agency'. The idea that consent had to be won allowed the possibility that it could be withheld. The text was conceived as a site of struggle rather than a simple instrument of ideological imposition. Audiences could be understood as political players rather than dupes. Audiences' active participation in the production of meaning, their capacity to resist ideology and to produce alternative, possibly subversive, meanings, became a key theme.

Running alongside (or in my memory slightly behind) the turn to Gramsci was the turn to Foucault and 'discourse' which also broke with the economistic version of the Marxist notion of ideology. Sometime during the late 1970s discussions of ideology began to use the plural and theorists started talking about 'ideologies', using it increasingly to refer to any 'system of ideas' attaching to particular social groups, and this usage in turn was gradually displaced altogether by the popularisation of the Foucauldian notion of 'discourse'. While the Marxist and Gramscian notion of power was tied to the idea of a dominant (economic) class, Foucault proposed a different, if somewhat confusing, model of power. On the one hand, power was everywhere and nowhere in particular; on the other hand, Foucault stressed the important role of experts in the construction of discourses, and even though Foucault's analyses did not address the issue of the sources of power of particular groups, nonetheless the centrality of the idea of power to Foucault's model made it very attractive to a range of theorists from different disciplines and of different political persuasions. In a climate where old political alliances were breaking down, where changes in the labour process were undermining and fragmenting the class system and in which a number of 'oppressed' groups were emerging as political entities, this dispersed model of power was highly appropriate. The notions of discursive struggle and reverse discourse provided a way out of the various Marxist, structuralist and psychoanalytic strait-jackets. The turn to discourse also made it easier to trace connections between different spheres of action: to see how they might be worked out in particular ways in particular areas (for example, stereotypical representations in film genres) but nonetheless connect to discourses in other spheres (for example, legal discourse, colonial discourses). The notions of 'consciousness' and 'subjectivity' were also subsumed into the notion of discourse which emphasised the constructed nature of our experience and that we only ever know things through discourse. Finally, Foucault's work was historical – and one of the fundamental criticisms which had been made of structuralism and psychoanalysis, and indeed certain branches of radical feminism, were that they were ahistorical, universalistic and essentialist. With Foucault the analysis of historical change, of the historical contingency of power and the emergence and development of discourses was central. But lost in all this is the relationship between discourse and material conditions. It lacks reference to what is beyond discourse – to a 'real' world, to experiences with which discourses must engage.

There are, then, marked similarities between Gramsci and Foucault as well as differences. Gramsci (who of course was not writing at the same time as Foucault, but was taken up in leftist circles at more or less the same time) holds on to a notion of dominance and implicitly of ideology as in the interests of a dominant group. The critical and political thrust of Gramsci's work is absolutely clear, but this is not true of Foucault – which is perhaps why it is Foucault who eventually became the more dominant. Foucault is more compatible with pluralism and postmodernist theorists than is Gramsci.[6]

From one perspective postmodernism is a way of both theorising and managing dissent – a sort of con-dis-sensus model. So too is the emergence of the Blair or Clinton 'third way' politics. Postmodernism accounts for the breaking down of the old order with its economic certainties and related sureties about social location. Those secure identities turn out to have been an effect of discourse, which is, of course, a not unpredictable development of the social constructionist wing of identity politics and a rejection of the essentialist wing. The individual, no longer a class member, no longer a woman, is now the site of conflicting and competing discourses; the fluidity and instability of identity are celebrated. Postmodernism is not, of course, a monolithic entity but is rather the site itself of conflicting and competing discourses and identities – now social theory, now cultural description, now a sandwich. The relationship between postmodernism, economic change and identity politics is crucial and complex. In one respect the changing economic structure, and the associated decline of class politics, opened up a space for identity politics.[7]

The British film *The Full Monty* (1997) is interesting in this context, registering as it did the collapse of Sheffield's industrial base, the defeat of class politics and the consequent entry of unemployed men into the female arena of 'stripping' (albeit not exactly as things of beauty, and only comically the object of the female gaze, and not quite managing to give up the phallus but rather, in the finale, protecting it). That Sheffield was known as 'the red city of the north', during a period of municipal socialism which flowered briefly and contradictorily at a time of conservative rule but which the Thatcher government so effectively smashed, underlines the collapse of class politics. Undoubtedly a film about the relationship between economic change and identity, its quite unexpected success was interesting and explicable in terms of the way it addressed both a middle-class and a working-class audience, providing a space for working-class audiences to have class registered again briefly and to relive the bitterness of the experience of those years of industrial collapse and transformation, and for middle-class audiences to feel some sympathetic and guilty regret. The landslide victory of 'New Labour', with its 'third way', shortly after the film was released was the electoral expression of the same regret. Thinking about *The Full Monty* in this broader political and economic context I am struck by the similarities and differences between it and Ken Loach's *Days of Hope* (1975) and recall Marx's comment about history occurring first as tragedy and then as farce.

Within various identity politics the emphasis on diversity, the need to respect and recognise each other's difference and acknowledge 'our own' classism, racism, sexism, homophobia or whatever, increasingly weakened the grounds on which politics could be conducted, and this had a curiously contradictory effect whereby anti-essentialism produced new essentialisms. In recognising, for example, the difference between black and white women's experiences, that is, in recognising this diversity, something 'essential' tended to be posited about black women's experience. Respect for diversity complicated the basis on which criticism could take place. The attempt to hold on to both the commonality *and* the diversity proved harder than we anticipated and made us vulnerable.

Relativism, at one time the hallmark of liberatory discourses, became the means by which they were denied any particular space and also a means of managing conflict. 'Cultural diversity' is appropriated by and incorporated into liberal discourse and in that process wrested from the politics from which it emerged. It is used now as a means of 'acknowledging' the 'problem' (of racism, for example) and in the same breath confirming these differences as the source of the problem. In the current outrage in Britain about the Stephen Lawrence case, and the publication of a report accusing the British police of institutional racism, the Prime Minster, Tony Blair, talked about 'fighting racism': 'we must', he said, 'learn to accept cultural diversity'. This formulation suggests that racism can be reduced to a failure to accept 'cultural diversity' with its connotations of different religious beliefs, leisure pursuits, styles of behaviour and so on – all different from 'ours'. In this move 'cultural diversity' becomes 'essentialised' as a characteristic of particular groups. The groups become homogenised, and the history of oppression, which was at the root of the original insistence on 'diversity', disappears. Stephen Lawrence was not murdered because he was doing something 'culturally diverse' in Blair's diluted sense of the term – on the contrary, the evidence seems to suggest that there was little to 'mark' him off from many a conventional 'English' lad, *except* the colour of his skin. It is this *lack* of the accepted (and acceptable?) markers of cultural diversity which has made the case so shocking to liberal sensibilities – it was raw, unrepressed racism which threatened to explode the myth of liberal England.

The politics of diversity have made it hard to maintain the continued validity of arguments about connections between structures of oppression. To argue, for example, that sexism and racism serve functions for capitalism (as did early feminist and post-colonial theorists), or that the treatment of women by the Taliban is not just a case of cultural and religious diversity but a particularly extreme symptom of more widespread patriarchy, is to raise the spectre of the so-called grand theories which are no longer accepted. But we should pause a while and remember: it was only a 100 years ago that British men could imprison *their* wives if those wives tried to run away from home, however brutal their husband's behaviour; less than 50 years since the last 'marriage bar' was lifted which forced British women in certain occupations to leave *their* jobs upon marriage; less than 10 years since British men could 'rape' *their* wives because, legally, a man could not rape his wife. Whatever the differences between women, however much the category 'woman' is a discursive construction, this does not mean that there is not a commonality in our experience and history that cannot be theorised away.

How postmodernist theory entered into the public domain is important to my argument that postmodernism 'manages' dissent. It was not just an academic theory. It entered into media and political discourse as a way of describing and interpreting the world – it became part of 'common sense' in a way that Marxism never did.[8] Its liberatory potential was appropriated and the threat posed by identity politics defused

Cultural politics

I am not sure where the term 'cultural politics' originated, but it had become commonplace in academic discourse by the 1980s. 'Cultural politics', though not in itself new, described a form of politics which, from the 1960s onwards, became a marked strategy of a number of protest/liberation movements, discussed above. 'What is at stake,' wrote Dyer in a discussion of gay cultural politics in 1981, 'is who controls the definition of the category. The key significance of the gay movement is that for the first time in living memory, gay people themselves determined that they would decide the definition' (1992b: 163). Such attempts to wrest control from those who have it were common features of post-1960s' cultural politics and illustrate the emergence of 'reverse discourses', 'struggles over the sign' or 'transcoding' of which Foucault, Volosinov and Hall speak. Not just 'the personal is political' but also 'glad to be gay' and 'black is beautiful'. Of course there were many problems to be faced in 'self-definition', discovering 'our own identity', or knowing 'who we were' – to the extent that now the very question of whether there is a place from which I can speak, 'as a woman' or 'as a lesbian' has become the issue.

It was this association with 'identity politics' that gave the term 'cultural politics' its resonance and relevance. There was no single form taken by cultural politics. The strategies were many and varied, depending partly on theoretical position, partly on social or occupational location. One set of strategies belongs under the heading 'intervention into practice', subdividing into: changing forms, changing content, changing personnel, changing institutional arrangements such as funding, distribution and exhibition practices, etc. A second set was 'critical textual analysis', with a number of variants and sometimes conflicting objectives: to influence the punters and change the climate, and ultimately (by a trickle effect) the representations; to reveal the operations of ideology, the objective being partly to demonstrate that films had systematically served to reproduce oppressive images and partly to understand how it was that the oppressed groups came to collude with their oppression; to crown unsung heroes (for example, the 'discovery' of Arzner as one of the few women directors who had worked in Hollywood); to point to absences and suppressions, to the *lack* of heroes in order to show the systematic exclusion of women, blacks or homosexuals; to point to gaps and fissures and spaces for resistance.

This last is related to a third, less dominant, strategy in film culture, namely 'discovering the audience', the object of which has been primarily to rescue the audience from its theoretically passive role and to establish its potential for subversion. It is also perhaps to establish some ground from which the critic or theorist can speak as an authenticated voice. This question of the place from which the critic or theorist speaks has, as Sue Thornham (1997) demonstrates, increasingly become a problem. Does the feminist critic speak on behalf of the oppressed or as one of the oppressed, and either way can the oppressed be conceived of as 'oppressed' or as a group, as having a position from which to speak? The combination of the last two strategies (resistant readings and discovering the audience) lies behind what Clare Whatling (1997) calls a 'politics of appropriation'.

These were not simply 'film' strategies but had their parallels in other arenas. The gradual move away from strategies of intervention and of textual critique to a politics of appropriation reflects, on the one hand, the partial success of those early strategies and of identity politics, but, on the other, two theoretical shifts: first, the loss of the foundational social theories which underpinned their objectives and defined their targets, and, second, the collapse of those theories of textual analysis which were secure about what, and how, texts 'mean'.

The turn to the audience has been an important corrective both to the 'sponge' model of audiences – unproblematically and passively soaking up ideological messages from Hollywood movies – and to the view of movies as hermetically sealed, ideologically consistent texts which can have only one meaning and one effect. It turns away from the viewer as 'victim' and constructs a space for a resistant reader. Richard Dyer's chapter on the meanings of Judy Garland to gay men, and Andrea Weiss's (wonderfully titled) article on Garbo, Dietrich and Hepburn, 'A queer feeling when I look at you' (1991), were early and exciting attempts to explore this area in relation to lesbian and gay audiences. I use the word 'exciting' deliberately here, as I remember them both as 'liberating' – escaping a 'victim' mentality. Raymond Williams' discussion of 'emergent groups' – groups which are 'coming to consciousness' – provides a useful framework for cultural politics. He argues that 'to the extent that such groups are oppositional, a process of attempted incorporation ... begins', a process which 'is made much more difficult by the fact that much incorporation looks like recognition, acknowledgement, and thus a form of *acceptance*' (1977: 124).

The 'politics of appropriation' exemplifies the relationship between film theory, politics and film-making practices. It not only provides evidence of the ways in which individual members of an oppressed group strive to resist oppressive representations, but also represents a critical practice which can be shared so it becomes a collective act of resistance. It is an example of 'transcoding' in the domain of decoding rather than encoding. Describing this era Julianne Pidduck talks of the move from a 'positive images' politics of representation to one which explores the

> rhetorical possibilities of re-activating the 'place of rage' of radical politics ... . Troubling stereotypes of *femmes fatales*, lethal lesbians, enraged gay men were no longer simply ammunition 'against' us, but might be re-appropriated as a virtual arsenal to strike fear in the heart of heteropatriarchy.
>
> (1998: 3)

As a political strategy this becomes more effective as it is disseminated, and becomes a subcultural response. This is facilitated by changing media representations. 'Liberal' colonisation puts images into circulation which suggest a degree of 'acceptance'. Appropriative readings can become a collective, rather than a secret and individual, strategy, in a climate in which concessions are being made and a collective and oppositional identity is being formed.

But there are dangers to this strategy if it becomes the *only* strategy and leads to a complete abandonment of what (because of the enormous problems around the notion of 'positive' and 'negative' stereotypes) I prefer to call a 'critical politics of representation'. Here we return to the question of whether texts have 'preferred meanings' and, without going into detail, and despite the undoubted ambiguity of many contemporary films, I would argue that they do, the ambiguity itself being a meaning or explicit evasion of meaning (for example, *Basic Instinct* (1992)). Indeed the whole notion of 'resistant' readings presupposes a 'preferred reading' which is being 'resisted'. The question is whether this politics of appropriation entails abandoning other political strategies. If, as Pidduck suggests, it emerged out of a disillusionment with 'good girl' feminism and with the tedium of 'political correctness', does this mean that the objective of changing representations is abandoned? My concern is that celebrating 'killer lesbians', for example, supports precisely those images which 'sustain relations of domination' (Thompson, 1997: 141). Here we have to move beyond the lesbian and gay audience, beyond identity politics and beyond individual films to a consideration of these representations circulating within the public sphere, not as singular representations but as one of many. To quote Pidduck again,

> the 'affective force' of these representations rests not only in the instant or in the particular text, but in the continual temporal unfolding of the series – the ongoing

re-invention of the figure of the 'lethal lesbian' across mainstream, independent, and sometimes queer cinema, and her play to particular audiences in different places and times.

(1998: 1–2)

Lesbian and gay audiences are not, after all, the only audiences for these texts which are being appropriated. I think Pidduck is right in pointing to the need to 'problematise the larger political stakes of lesbian, gay, and queer representation' (1998: 7).

Before drawing the threads of my argument together, I want briefly to discuss some research I did with Jill McKenna in 1995 concerning lesbian responses to representations of lesbians in the media. The year 1995 was the year of the so-called lipstick lesbian, and the sudden emergence of lesbian characters in popular culture – most notably in the British soap operas *Brookside* and *Emmerdale Farm*, in *Heavenly Creatures* (1994) and in the KD Lang/Cindy Crawford cover of *Vanity Fair*. This certainly suggests the process of incorporation referred to by Williams. Conducting the research at this particular time highlighted this process, of which our interviewees were perfectly well aware. We discussed a whole range of film and media representations, old and new, current and 'favourite' ones, and it became clear that to characterise their reading positions as *either* 'resistant' *or* 'oppositional' *or* 'preferred' would be grossly simplistic since they adopted all these positions in articulating a perspective. Their responses to representations of lesbians in film and media texts included the following:

- They asked: What sort of representation is this and how will mainstream audiences read it? What does it mean about the way lesbians are seen? What is at stake in this representation?
- They were 'pathetically grateful' (and had at times been 'hungry') for representations which were halfway positive, partly because they didn't have them as adolescents, so they welcomed them on behalf of younger lesbians, and partly because they suggested partial acceptance by the wider community.
- They were also often anxious about the representation.

These last two points underline the *significance* of representation which becomes much more apparent if you belong to a group that is not represented or has historically been represented as a pariah group. Anxiety arises from the knowledge that as a member of such a group you are regarded as 'unrepresentable'. In order to be represented taboos must be broken, which will always lead to substantial media coverage, discussion of what you are, what you do, and perhaps more importantly, what you should be allowed to do.

- With all this, came ambivalence, criticism and cynicism, because, while welcoming 'acceptance', it was nonetheless an important part of their identity as lesbians that they 'lived on the edge', or beyond the boundary, and they resented representations that diluted or purified that – as one woman remarked, she longed to see a lesbian in dungarees. They were sick of what they called 'silk pyjama lesbians'. They also anticipated that this brief flurry of representations would be just that.

- Finally, there were the 'appropriative' readings which celebrated the killer lesbian. The discussion of *Fried Green Tomatoes* (1991) (albeit not really offering a killer lesbian) produced gales of gleeful laughter at the declared pleasure in 'cutting up your lover's husband and serving him to the cops'.

This by no means covers all the responses but illustrates two main points. First, it highlighted the multilayered responses. These do not suggest that films can mean anything. On the contrary, disagreements about what was happening, why some character did something or over the general sense of the film's position were few and far between. In this sense everyone agreed about the 'preferred meaning' of the films we discussed. It is at the level of emotional, aesthetic and political responses, judgements about the film's 'relation to the real or to the possible' and opinions about the media's role and responsibilities that both intrapersonal and interpersonal differences emerge. Second, these responses demonstrate that the media function as a site in which meanings are circulated and made available, so forming the climate in which we must live our lives. It was not that these women were avid media consumers – they weren't particularly – and in some ways they were quite distanced from media representations. But in spite of this the important role played by the media in contributing to a climate became quite apparent in discussions of what they liked and did not like, what made them angry or humiliated or irritated them. Do media representations matter? Yes, I'm afraid they do.

Conclusions

In this chapter I have been exploring the relationship between theory, politics, the academy and film-making practices from a number of points of view. Like any writer I have my own particular agenda and set of concerns which, implicitly or explicitly, I have been addressing. It is not always easy to identify the sources of these concerns precisely. You pick them up from colleagues, from articles, books and conferences, from your experience in the various academic roles you perform. It's a thoroughly messy and unscientific process and one is always anxious that one is out of step – and yet oddly one finds a considerable amount of agreement, as well, of course, as dissent. My goal has been to render the political more visible and to argue for the continued importance of a politics of representation that is more thoroughly grounded within particular sociocultural contexts. There is a tendency now to see 'cultural politics' as being coterminous with 'identity politics' and to suggest that both have had their day – now we need to get back to 'real' politics. This tends to reintroduce the split between the 'real' and the 'cultural', between 'political economy' and 'textual analysis'. To return to such a division would be to give up on the project which Nancy Fraser identified recently as 'the real task' now: 'to think integratively about the relation between cultural struggles and social and economic struggles' (Alldred, 1999: 131). That was also the project started in the 1960s and, through various theoretical and political shifts, gradually abandoned, perhaps most particularly in film theory. In losing hold of the broader ideological critique we allowed the terrain to change. Michael Rustin has argued 'the notion of capitalism as a problem in some fundamental deep structural way is being annihilated, and we're being taught to live with capitalism as part of the everyday furniture and fabric of life' (Bird and Jordan, 1999: 202–3). It will be clear from my discussion that I do not go along with the wholesale abandonment of the grand theories and believe that in order to understand our current situation we need to restore the sort of critical analytical perspective which is grounded in a social critique of which Marxism, feminism and post-colonialism are prime examples.

It is easy (and fashionable) to scorn the optimism of the 1960s because, of course, the revolution did not happen, the difference between rich and poor increased, the welfare state has more or less collapsed and 'socialism' is now a dirty word. But the changes which have occurred since then have not all been for the worse. Britain and the USA are in some ways less sexist, racist, classist, homophobic, disablest, and may be less ageist places to live. The gains are recent, insecure and inadequate, but it is important to remember these gains which were won after considerable struggle and in the face of considerable opposition. It is important not to forget the opposition, the attempts to defend or deny the various systems of oppression. The temptation to belittle the effectiveness of these social movements is dangerous and encourages us to think that political action is futile. 'It has to be said that there has been a massive effort, politically and in the media, to eradicate from popular consciousness some of our better moments' (Bird and Jordan, 1999: 211).

It is ironic that in the 1960s, hemmed in by oppressive structures, we felt able to change those structures, but in the 1990s, 'discursively' freed from such constraints, we feel powerless. What is the role of the teacher, student, critic and film-maker in all this?

Endnotes

1   Basil Bernstein was an educational theorist best known for his writing about differences between working-class and middle-class language and the ways in which the 'elaborated' code of the middle-class predisposed them to succeed in education. His work was briefly popular among radical educationalists in the 1960s but was subsequently seen as problematic by some who read him as undervaluing, and misunderstanding, the nature of working-class speech.

2   The claim that something is 'just entertainment' does not mean there is nothing else to discuss (Dyer, 1992a).

3   A typical narrative strategy is the use of an 'enlightened' (usually white, male) person (usually the hero) who makes it possible for the person with disabilities to achieve their goal, come to acceptance or whatever. Similar strategies are used in films about 'overcoming racial oppression' (*Cry Freedom* (1987)), 'sexual oppression' (*Tootsie* (1982)) and so on. The problem with the strategy is that the political struggle is diluted and incorporated.

4   The term 'sexism' illustrates this best as it came to describe what Betty Friedan, in the early 1960s, could only call 'the problem without a name' (Friedan, 1965: Chapter 1).

5   A good example of how this was taken up within British film culture, and its relationship to contemporary political debates, can be found in *National Fictions*, edited by Geoff Hurd (1984).

6   This may also explain why Foucault seems to have been taken up far more by US theorists than was Gramsci.

7   But see Doreen Massey, in Bird and Jordan (1999: 198):

> Surely it's not a question of the capital–labour settlement breaking down *and then* the other movements taking off, to fill the space as it were . . . . Feminism, sexual politics and post-colonial struggles were part of what destabilised the old, all-too-comfortable, consensus. They were part of the *cause* of the breakdown, not simply its effect.

8   See Gramsci's discussion of 'common sense': 'Every philosophical current leaves behind a sedimentation of "common sense" . . . . Common sense . . . is continually transforming itself, enriching itself with scientific ideas' (1971: 32, note 5).

Acknowledgements: Thanks are due to colleagues and students in Media, Film and Communication Studies at Sheffield Hallam University with whom, over the past 12 years, I have discussed and experienced many of the issues covered in this article. I have a long overdue debt to Victor Perkins and Richard Dyer who patiently helped me with my early attempts to grapple with what often seemed unnecessarily inaccessible film theory. And, finally, and most particularly, thanks are due to Christine Gledhill and Jill McKenna whose comments on earlier drafts were offered in a typically perceptive and supportive manner.

References

Alldred, P. 1999: Not making a virtue of a necessity: Nancy Fraser on postsocialist politics. In Jordan, T. and Lent, A. (eds), *Storming the millennium*. London: Lawrence and Wishart.

Bell, D. 1965: *The end of ideology*. New York: The Free Press.

Bird, T. and Jordan, T. 1999: Sounding out new social movements and the Left: interview with Stuart Hall, Doreen Massey and Michael Rustin. In Jordan, T. and Lent, A. (eds), *Storming the millennium*. London: Lawrence and Wishart.

Blair, T. 1999: Interview on PM, Radio 4 *News*, February 1999.

Bordwell, D. and Carroll, N. (eds) 1996: *Post-theory – reconstructing film studies*, Madison, WI: University of Wisconsin Press.

Clarke, J. and Simmonds, D. 1980: *Move over misconceptions*, dossier 4. London: British Film Institute.

Dyer, R. 1977: Stereotyping. In Dyer, R. (ed.), *Gays in film*. London: British Film Institute.

Dyer, R. 1992a: Entertainment and utopia. In Dyer, R., *Only entertainment*. London and New York: Routledge, pp. 17–34.

Dyer, R. 1992b: Identity and pleasure in gay cultural politics. In Dyer, R. *Only entertainment*. London and New York: Routledge, pp. 159–72.

Dyer, R. 1997: *White*. London and New York: Routledge.

Ferguson, M. and Golding, P. (eds) 1997: *Cultural studies in question*. London, Thousand Oaks, CA, New Delhi: Sage.

Ferguson, R. 1998: *Representing 'race': ideology, identity and the media*. London, Sydney, New York, and Auckland: Arnold.

Foucault, M. 1981: *The history of sexuality*. Vol. 1. London: Pelican, pp. 101.

Friedan, B. 1965: *The feminine mystique*. London: Penguin.

Gitlin, T. 1997: The anti-political populism of cultural studies. In Ferguson, M. and Golding, P. (eds), *Cultural studies in question*. London, Thousand Oaks, CA, New Delhi: Sage, pp. 25–38.

Gramsci, A. 1971: *Prison notebooks: selections*. London: Lawrence and Wishart.

Hall, S. 1997: The spectacle of the 'other'. In Hall, S. (ed.), *Representation: cultural representations and signifying practices*. London: Open University, pp. 223–79.

Housee, S. and Sharma, S. 1999: 'Too black too strong?': anti-racism and the making of South Asian political identities in Britain. In Jordan, T. and Lent, A. (eds), *Storming the millennium*. London: Lawrence and Wishart.

Hurd, G. (ed.) 1984: *National fictions*. London: British Film Institute.

Kellner, D. 1995: *Media culture*. London: Routledge.

MacCabe, C. 1981: Realism and the cinema: notes on some Brechtian theses. In Bennett, T., Boyd-Bownan, S., Mercer, C. and Woollacott, J. (eds), *Popular television and film*. London/Milton Keynes: British Film Institute/Open University.

McArthur, C. 1981: *Days of hope*. In Bennett, T., Boyd-Bowman, S., Mercer, C. and Woollacott, J. (eds), *Popular television and film*. London/Milton Keynes: British Film Institute/Open University, pp. 305–9.

McGuigan, J. 1992: *Cultural populism*. London and New York: Routledge.

McKenna, J. and Perkins, T. 1996: Lesbians and popular culture. Paper presented to Theory, Culture and Society conference, *Culture and identity: city, nation, world*, Berlin.

Mulvey, L. 1989: Visual pleasure and narrative cinema. In *Visual and other pleasures*. London: Macmillan.

Pawling, C. and Perkins, T. 1992: Popular TV drama and realism. In Page, A. (ed.), *Death of the playwright?* London: Macmillan.

Perkins, T.E. 1979: Rethinking stereotypes. In Barrett, M., Corrigan, P., Kuhn, A. and Wolff J. (eds), *Ideology and cultural production*. London: Croom Helm.

Perkins, T.E. 1981: Remembering Doris Day. *Screen Education* **39**.

Perryman, M. (ed.) 1994: *Altered states: postmodernism, politics, culture*. London: Lawrence and Wishart.

Pidduck, J. 1998: Framing the lethal lesbian: critical allegiances and the 'force of fantasy'. Unpublished paper delivered to Deviant Imaging conference, University of Warwick, Coventry.

Pointon, A. and Davies, C. (eds) 1997: *Framed*. London: British Film Institute.

Rodowick, D.N. 1994: *The crisis of political modernism*. 2nd edn. Berkeley, CA, Los Angeles, CA, London: University of California Press.

Saunders, J. 1999: The importance of defending academic freedom. In *The Times Higher Educational Supplement*, 12 February, p. 16.

Thompson, J.B. 1984: *Studies in the theory of ideology*. Cambridge: Polity Press.

Thornham, S. 1997: *Passionate detachments*. London, New York, Sydney, Auckland: Arnold.

Van Dijk, T.A. 1998: *Ideology*. London: Sage.

Volosinov, V.N. 1973: *Marxism and the philosophy of language*. New York: Seminar Press.

Weiss, A. 1991: A queer feeling when I look at you. In Gledhill, C. (ed.), *Stardom: industry of desire*. London and New York: Routledge, pp. 283–99.

Whatling, C. 1997: *Screen dreams*. Manchester and New York: Manchester University Press.

Williams, R. 1977: *Marxism and literature*. Oxford: Oxford University Press.

PART 2

Film as mass culture

Editors' introduction

Many of the contributors to this section argue that cinema represents the first truly mass medium, one which functions as prototype for the commodity industries and which ushers in a new kind of 'publicness'. 'Massness', 'commodification' and the 'public sphere' have traditionally been the concerns of mass communication or cultural theory, while film studies, in defining its disciplinary boundaries, largely cut film off from its industrial base and mass audience, emphasising texts and textual producers. Even in the decades of high theory, film studies' attempt to acknowledge cinema's institutional conditions drew on textually orientated concepts such as ideological interpellation and subjectivity. As a result, theoretically sophisticated critics elaborated oppositional cinematic practices and reading techniques against the grain of a shadowy mass audience as its manipulated stooge. In opposition to this view, the writers in this section all take 'our inevitably mass-mediated culture' as the starting point for film studies at the end of the twentieth century.

Several of these chapters revisit earlier responses to the emergence of mass society, especially those of the Frankfurt School. They rethink notions such as publicness, massness, utopia, fantasy, in order to conceptualise the place of cinema, audiences and analysts within rather than above and beyond the mass.

Jane Gaines opens this section by contesting the metaphor of 'bad dream factory' which imagines Hollywood as a pedlar of ideologically contaminated, consumption-orientated fantasies. Drawing on Stuart Hall's concept of the 'doubleness' of popular culture, which generates both containment and resistance, and returning to Ernst Bloch's concept of 'hope', Jane Gaines rethinks the relation of the ideological to the utopian. Whereas postmodernism may understand the utopian as regressive nostalgia, Bloch stresses the forward movement of hope. In a mass-mediated culture, consumer desire is also a gesture of hope for better things. In its embrace of both realism and spectacle,

Gaines argues that Hollywood delivers our culture's 'best hopes along with the worst tendencies' (page 108). Thus she argues that Bloch shows us how to develop theories *for* rather than *about* the audience. Gaines concludes by exhorting us to look for the dreams being generated beyond Hollywood and the West as future sources of world-transforming hope.

James Donald and Stephanie Donald address the massness of cinema through the notion of 'publicness'. They suggest how films might provide ground on which hope can operate, and, as Gaines suggests, they do indeed look beyond Hollywood to test the theory. Citing Kant on the French Revolution, they recast the aesthetics of the spectacle, condemned in film theory as commodification of the event for a voyeuristic audience. For Kant it is precisely specularity and distance that elicit the aesthetic and therefore moral judgements which found the public sphere of bourgeois democracy. Cinema, by magnifying and multiplying the spectacle, threatens this 'good public' with a 'bad mass'. Donald and Donald recast this opposition. Drawing on Miriam Hansen's conception of cinema as an alternative public sphere, they suggest that its new working-class and female audiences bring into public view a 'horizon of experience' which exists in tension with the traditional male and middle-class public sphere of the quality press and public service broadcasting. The problem for film studies is how to conceptualise the 'alternativeness' of the films themselves, a problem addressed in 1970s' film theory in terms of degrees of ideological complicity. Donald and Donald take Chinese cinema of the 1980s and 1990s, the product of a society for which the notion of the 'public' is generated not by bourgeois democracy but by the Party, as a test case for the notion of an alternative textual 'publicness'. Exchanging ideological interpellation for the concept of negotiation, they argue that in the conjuncture of history, public memory and filmic *mise en scène*, cinema as mass medium can open up moments of public space as 'cinematic symbolic space' (page 126) in which aesthetic and critical judgements may be made.

Similar questions are explored in Ravi Vasudevan's case study of Bombay cinema, which as part of the critically neglected but highly successful Indian commercial film industry worked between the 1930s and 1950s to construct a hegemonic 'nation space'. Whereas for Donald and Donald Chinese cinema's potential alternative to a totalitarian publicness arises from the historical circumstances of viewing, Vasudevan focuses on the mixed textual address developed by Bombay cinema as a means of creating a national subject for a state developing a modern democracy. The 'elaborate scenic construction' of Bombay cinema (page 151) performs a textual and cultural negotiation between iconographic, narrational and generic traditions of a pre-modern, hierarchical society and modernising Westernised narrational forms. Rather than condemning popular cinema for either clinging to pre-modern and regressive practices or celebrating them as a site of resistance to Western alienation, Ravi Vasudevan argues that traditional myths and iconographic practices provide a site of creative invention for new political conditions. Thus the relation of private and public is refigured and the individualised subject of modernity is incorporated within an imaginary form of communal subjectivity. Vasudevan concludes by examining the political resonances of these iconographic and narrative moves in the creation of national identity.

Henry Jenkins examines the different ways in which film studies has or might engage with reception theories and audience research. Warning against both the derivation of audiences from texts, and the illusion that empirical research gives direct access to the experience of viewing, Jenkins stresses that the responses which research solicits and the fan activities that provide evidence of spectating are themselves kinds of text, by which audiences respond dialogically to a 'world populated with other people's stories' (page 175). Viewers may thus 'poach' and 'rescript' film stories in ways more satisfying to their needs and fantasies. However, the conditions of fictional production and reception, the conventions of different genres, and the social protocols of interpretative communities, act as constraints on the possibilities of reading and support meaning-making as a form of social conversation or interaction. Thus Jenkins shifts the focus of audience studies from the either/or of ideological complicity or resistance to suggest how distracted audiences or reading communities may at the same time participate in the public spaces of film fictions.

This section ends with Christine Geraghty's consideration of the phenomenon most predicated on film as mass culture, the star. Stardom has traditionally been defined by its duality, premissed both on film roles and on private life, circulated through subsidiary media. Yet the separation of star image from a largely inaccessible 'real' life has favoured a textual approach to stars, their duality feeding theories of textual contradiction and resistant fan readings. However, Geraghty argues that the 'drive' to 'exploit the status of being famous across the whole range of entertainment formats' (page 188), including 'sport, television, fashion and music' (page 188) has reconfigured the conditions of stardom, both challenging cinema as the acme of stariness and confronting film actors with a range of different career routes, identified by Geraghty as celebrity, professionalism and performance. Understanding stars as products of different media career choices suggests different kinds of textual function and modes of audience engagement. While the contradictory tensions that feed resistant readings are most likely to be found in celebrity with its split between fame and personal life, professionalism, based on a 'franchise' in a specific kind of role, offers the dependable pleasure of a stable identity in which actor and image are one. Performance, on the other hand, demands aesthetic judgement on the work of acting. For the textual analyst, consideration of the institutional conditions of star production reintroduces the possibility of ideologically nuanced readings as different modes of stardom encounter each other or run on divergent tracks determined in part by gender and ethnicity. With this conclusion, Christine Geraghty returns us to the issues of textual readings and evaluation, the focus of the next section.

6 Dream/Factory

Jane M. Gaines

At the end of the twentieth century, looking all the way back to the turn of the nineteenth, it is clear that this century has been the 'Age of Commodities'. More than ever, Georg Simmel (1900) and Thorstein Veblen (1912) should be recognized as the great prophets of consumer culture, writing as they did about luxuries and money at the start of the new century. Motion picture historians and film theorists have always read Simmel and Veblen with great interest, a special interest based on the remarkable coincidence of the birth of consumer culture and the invention of motion pictures. Relative to this fortuitous moment, how often have we asked ourselves, 'Were the first theorists of mass culture thinking about motion pictures when they wrote about the visibility of consumption and the interrelatedness of the products of mass society?' This is a particularly important question to ask today, given the hypothesis of postmodernism that the representational products of consumer culture (motion pictures and television) are now indistinguishable from our lived reality. But an even more pragmatic question arises when we ask whether motion pictures are still central to theories of mass culture. And here it is that we could also begin to wonder about the history of the connection between film studies and cultural studies, the one approach that looks at the penultimate culture industry and the other that would seem to look at all of them.

I want to start by considering the way in which histories and theories of consumer culture might be seen as privileging the motion picture industry, beginning with the factory and ending with the problem of what has been understood as the 'manufacture' of dreams. Asserting what many scholars merely assume, Lary May, in his study of motion pictures and the rise of mass culture, organizes the history of popular diversion in the first decades of the century around the film industry. By 1914, he argues, motion pictures were the first genuine mass entertainment in US history (1980: xii). Not only did they become the preeminent mass amusement after they began to appeal to middle-class audiences, but, May continues, motion pictures also had something to do with a new visibility of affluence. They were, in short, 'the goose that lay [sic] the golden egg' (1980: xii). One of the sources of the 'goose that laid the golden egg' thesis is no doubt the sociology of Robert and Helen Lynd, who assign movie-going a determining function in their famous description of life in Muncie, Indiana, in the 1920s:

Week after week at the movies people in all walks of life enter, often with an intensity of emotion that is apparently one of the most potent means of reconditioning habits, into the intimacies of Fifth Avenue drawing rooms and English country houses, watching the habitual activities of a different cultural level.

(1929: 82)

More recently, Stuart and Elizabeth Ewen, carrying on where the Lynds left off, reasserted the significance of the motion picture as a cornucopia of consumer goods, even the source of important visual ideas about fashions in dress and decor. Again, as in May, the motion picture bears more responsibility than any other cultural institution: 'By 1920, the most powerful agencies of mass impression were the movies, which played a part in the rise of fashion'. As important, I would argue, is the Ewen's next point in which they see movie palaces as 'like department stores and expositions' and therefore 'grand monuments to elaborate facades' (1982: 200).

The historical similarities between the movie palace and the department store can never be stressed enough (see Friedberg, 1995; Gaines, 1989). At the turn of the century, the French *grand magasin*, the US emporium, and the motion picture palace were all designed as exquisite containers for opulence and excess – the fruits of mass production displayed in their magnitude and multiplicity (Figures 6.1 and 6.2). The multiple images on the strip have their equivalence in the rows of shelved and hanging goods, testimony to abundance, availability, and seriality or inventory. Stores and theatres alike provided spectacles of plenty in the commodity tableaux, the exemplification of dream lives as concrete and *realizable*, a concept I derive from Christine Gledhill's discussion of nineteenth-century 'realization', the transformation of the material of real life into theatrical melodrama and the terms of the stage (1992: 132). For the wares of the marketplace would always have to be transposed into the *mise en scène* of the middle-class parlor drama in such a way that narrative realism was served rather than circumvented. Exceeding the bounds of realism, however, by the 1920s, the commodity-stuffed screen was in danger of being seen by spectators as 'just advertising'. By the mid-1930s, 'product placement', the practice of planting brand name goods in the scene, had become so prevalent that audiences complained and there would be an implicit agreement among studio producers to try to keep the screen promotion-free as well as to keep hard-sell advertising off the motion picture theatre program.

Writing from the vantage of Los Angeles in the 1940s, it would seem to German émigrés Max Horkheimer and Theodor Adorno that there was nothing outside consumer culture, that there was no escape from the commodity form (although for these Frankfurt School theorists the problem was as much the waning of high culture). 'The whole world is made to pass through the filter of the culture industry', they would write (1987: 126), and again, as with Simmel and Veblen, we have to wonder whether they were thinking of the motion picture industry when they developed their influential theory of mass culture. Important would be their comparison between the factory production of automobiles and the factory production of motion pictures. Warner Brothers and Metro Goldwyn Mayer in 'The Culture Industry' essay are no different from Chrysler and General Motors:

Figure 6.1 Motion picture palace exterior, Chicago: Roosevelt Theater, *Hands Across the Table* (1935). Reproduced courtesy of The Theatrical Historical Society, Chicago.

for automobiles, there are such differences as the number of cylinders, cubic capacity, details of patented gadgets; and for films there are the number of stars, the extravagant use of technology, labor, and equipment, and the introduction of the latest psychological formulas.

(1987: 123–24)

And, finally, still holding out the hope that some aspect of existence would remain uncommodified, Adorno and Horkheimer come to the bleakest of conclusions regarding the inextricability of motion pictures and everyday existence: 'Real life is becoming indistinguishable from the movies' (1987: 126). This doomsday proclamation, coming at least 30 years before Jean Baudrillard would produce the same analysis that is now understood as basic to theories of the postmodern, clearly points the finger at the film industry. The assumption is that the film industry is more insidious than the magazine industry, the newspaper industry, the paperback book industry, the toy industry, the fashion industry, the sports industry, or the popular music industry. But where do we fit the beauty-care products, fast-food, and home-improvement industries that would today seem to be as much purveyors of culture as they are essential goods industries? Is it that motion pictures are more ubiquitous or more influential, or is it that the film industry is the prototype for all the other culture industries?

Figure 6.2 Motion picture palace interior.
Reproduced courtesy of The Theatrical Historical Society, Chicago.

Bringing us up to date, Michael Denning has argued, based on the achieved cultural saturation of these industries in the West, that this success should be understood as nothing more or less than the 'end of mass culture' as we have known it, and saturation is the swan song of mass culture because the distinction between mass, high, and working-class popular culture can no longer be made. Denning explains that whereas in the middle of the century (during the period theorized by the Frankfurt School) one could point to certain enemies of mass culture and could count on fear and hostility toward it, now there is no hold-out culture and 'All culture is mass culture under capitalism'. There is no culture other than that which is commodified, he concludes, and 'the fact is that mass culture has won; there is nothing else' (1990: 8). One wonders how contemporary film and television studies in the USA and the UK fit into this picture, and perhaps fear of television even now contributes to the engulfment of film, journalism, and radio in the category of media studies. Because this 'end of mass culture', not surprisingly, always seems to be exemplified by television, 'The great powers of broadcasting and mass spectacle(s) are second nature' (1990: 8). Once again, the film and television industry stands in for all of the culture industry, epitomizing it with a vengeance. The implications, as Denning says, are finally most significant for cultural studies, defined here by its Frankfurt School methodology as well as its object of study – the film and television industry and all the products of mass culture.

All too often we have assumed and asserted this close relationship between the film (and now television) industries and the other industries of culture. But now, at the end of the twentieth century, and certainly if 'mass culture has won', it would seem imperative that we begin to sort out this relationship. Accordingly, I would like to propose that we see the film industry as a prototype for others, as the strategically central industry, and finally as a strange and atypical industry.

Whereas the film industry was the first to institute a genuine star system, following its example others, even today the book industry, have received their inspiration if not their model from the motion picture prototype (see Geraghty, this volume, Chapter 10). Perhaps more interesting is the relationship the motion picture industry has had historically with other culture industries in an ancillary capacity. By this I mean the way the motion picture provides opportunities for advertising 'tie-ups' as well as 'product placement', as I have mentioned. Since the commodity tie-up heydays of the 1930s and into the contemporary period, the theatrical exhibition window has been seen by other producers as a publicity opportunity for their goods, as I have discussed elsewhere (Gaines, 1991: 155–64) (see also Figures 6.3 and 6.4). Consequently, new release pictures

Figure 6.3 Cosmetic tie-ups: *Lovely to Look At* (1952).
Reproduced courtesy of The Academy of Motion Picture Arts and Sciences.

Figure 6.4 Book tie-ups: *The Wizard of Oz* (1939).
Reproduced courtesy of The Academy of Motion Picture Arts and Sciences.

have been linked with automobiles, cosmetics, popular tunes, women's fashions, housewares, and, increasingly, fast-food restaurants. Beyond the easy link with candy and drink concessions in the theatre lobby and the permanent association with buttered popcorn, the popular motion picture has historically worked to magnetize other commodities. As Mary Ann Doane once remarked about the commodity tie-up, it 'disperses the fascination of the cinema onto a multiplicity of products' (1987: 25). But whereas the announcement of a new theatrical release often works to foreground the commodity status of other consumer products which are themselves 'attracted' in some (often peripheral) way to the major attraction, the commodity status of the motion picture itself remains ambiguous.

Motion pictures are strange commodities, as unlike Marx's original coal, flax, and linen as one can get, and even unlike the new atypical commodities of the twentieth century such as sex acts, sex workers, and sexual accoutrements. We often wonder, 'What exactly is the commodity involved?' Is it the film in the can, the VHS tape, or the theatrical experience for which each audience member buys a ticket? Nevertheless, with or without clear agreement as to what counts as the entertainment commodity, the film industry is often used as the example of how everything under capitalism has become commodified, and certainly this commodification of everything is exemplified in the term 'dream factory'. There is a certain ludicrous contradictoriness captured in the concept, in the idea that dreams, of all things, could be produced on the assembly line. Hortense Powdermaker used this apparent absurdity in the title to her famous anthropology of the industry in which she at one point asserts: 'Hollywood is engaged in the mass production of prefabricated daydreams' (1951: 38). But as defined by film studies, the real problem is neither that motion picture dreams are not your own nor that they have been historically produced in factory-like studios according to formulas.

The problem with the dream factory products is that the fantasies they contain are always compromised, and this question of exactly how it is that they are constrained is perhaps the most important question to have engaged film scholars since the 1970s. It is on this particular question of the degree and quality of the constraint that cultural studies has made its most important contribution to film studies. Let me state this as the question of the extent to which popular forms can be said to be 'ideological'. Since in contemporary film studies almost every analysis is now an ideological analysis it is difficult to recall the time in the mid-1970s in Britain and the USA when to perform an ideological analysis on a Hollywood film was to be in the vanguard. It was not, of course, as though this approach came discretely from the Birmingham School of Contemporary Cultural Studies and was ever formally introduced into film circles. Although one could point to the publication of the 'On Ideology' issue of *Working Papers in Cultural Studies* in 1977 as a watershed, film scholars were using the concept of ideology as well as the companion concept of hegemony well before the publication of this issue. To give only one example, in an early article in *Screen*, Terry Lovell described the methodology of cultural studies as exemplified by Barthes's *Mythologies* (1972) as an attempt to 'lay bare the ideological meaning' of the products of popular culture, even warning about the way the critique of 'bourgeois ideology' could stand in for genuine analysis (1973: 119, 121). Fortunately, the cultural studies emphasis on the *contents* of popular forms complemented well the interests of apparatus theory, the 1970s' import from France. Now the machines and the art forms they produced were as much carriers of bourgeois ideology as their more obviously ideological cultural contents.

Lovell's warning would prove to be prescient, for the 1970s and early 1980s saw many studies dedicated to demonstrating how Hollywood cinema was nothing but a purveyor of bourgeois ideology. Here, the dreams we dreamed in the dark theatre were never our own, and they turned against us even as we claimed them as deeply personal secret wishes. As Julia Lesage (1982) put it, these wishes were always 'hegemonic fantasies', dreams that, although they seemed to be ours alone, actually served our masters, whether those masters were the husbands of traditional wives or the owners of the means of production. Appropriately, Adorno and Horkheimer were rediscovered at this time and the 'bad factory' metaphor was revitalized with a new flowering of 'industry studies' within film studies.

But on the heels of the new interest in the negative pronouncements of the Frankfurt

School came the corrective to the bleak prognosis – the prognosis that the products of mass culture are hopelessly ideological. The same entertainment products that were thought to serve such reactionary ends, that produced visions of female subordination and worker capitulation, that figured the achievements of capital and the triumph of the single-minded, hard-headed individualist over the collectivity, always had within them a counter-force of some kind. Stuart Hall, in 'Notes on deconstructing "The Popular"', refers to this phenomenon as the 'double movement' of popular culture, a 'back and forth' of the text that one minute capitulates to the dreams of the dominant and the next minute resists these dreams in some way (1981: 228). If articulation of the 'ideological' has been the most important contribution cultural studies has made to film studies, the understanding of this 'double movement', the duality of mass dreams, has been the single most productive metaphor for describing how popular ideologies work in and through and on our favorite films. Even entertainment, we have come to see, can be understood dialectically, understood as organized around a productive tension that is a form of class struggle in which the forces of containment meet the forces that cannot be contained. The popular film, the dream product, is one of those places where these forces meet in fantasy form, where the highly ideological attempts to hold sway over all and where objections to its rule, tiny signs of insurrection in the text, are disguised or muffled. It should be no surprise that the experience of popular genre films for many viewers is one of doubleness – the doubleness of enjoying diversion that is so despised, or the doubleness of hating what gives so much pleasure.

This idea of the doubleness of the dream product is often formulated as the way the ideological coexists with the utopian, as in Michael Denning's overview (1990: 4). Although Stuart Hall does not elaborate the concept of utopia *per se* as much as he attends to the concept of resistance, it is generally understood that it is the utopian sensibility or strain that offsets the ideological in those popular, crowd-pleasing works that do so well at the box office. However, because the preferred theoretical term has been textual 'resistance' rather than 'utopianism', the origins of the understanding of ideology as tempered by the aspiration for something better in popular forms are in danger of being forgotten. As we know, these origins are in the famous Frankfurt School stance, the point of view on the popular that would both offer a bleak analysis and supply its theoretical antidote, an extremely influential position in the history of critical theory. Although various critics have found resistive or utopian moments in Theodore Adorno, Walter Benjamin, and, more recently, Siegfried Kracauer, the full theorization of the antidote to ideology is found in the work of one Frankfurt theorist – it is only there in Ernst Bloch's development of the concept of hope as a political vision.

Bloch packs into his concept of hope the vision of a better life and a world transformed. Not a vague feeling, 'hope' for Bloch is precise and action-orientated. Above all, it is strategic: 'Hope is thus ultimately a practical, a militant emotion, it unfurls banners' (1986: 112). Looking for the intimations of hope in mass culture, Bloch turns to those forms that are larger than life, that imagine more and reach further. Thus it is that he is be able to credit Hollywood, giving us not a bad but a *'good* dream-factory', and this in spite of all that is wrong with the motion picture industry: 'For it remains indicative that so much that is right emerges time and again in film. Amidst so much futility, so much opium, such quick turnover, so little leisure' (1986: 412). This theme of Hollywood as always delivering the best hopes along with the worst tendencies, of delivering them almost simultaneously, so that the bad dream factory never has an opportunity to work its mischief, seems also tied to the particularity of cinematic form. It is as though the characteristic realism, the notorious mimetic function (in Bloch the 'pantomimic'), could not help but deliver the aspiration along with the degradation, facing the world as it does, bringing the world to us as it finds it. In this long passage we hear an eerie summary of the cultural studies approach to film analysis, an early sketch of the paradigm that would come to organize so many discussions of Hollywood since the late 1970s, a sketch that was written by Bloch, the German émigré, while in the USA between 1938 and 1947:

> In general therefore the film, in that it is capable through photography and microphone of incorporating the whole of real experience in a stream-like mime, belongs to the most powerful mirror- and distortion- but also the concentration-images which are displayed to the wish for the fullness of life, as substitute and glossy deception, but also as information rich in imagery. Hollywood has become an incomparable falsification, whereas the realistic film in its anti-capitalist, no longer capitalist peak performances can, as critical, as stylizing film and as mirror of hope, certainly portray the mime of the days which change the world. The pantomimic aspect of the film is ultimately that of society, both in the ways in which it expresses itself and above all in the deterring or inspiring, promising contents which are set out.
>
> (1986: 408–9)

Here, then, is the statement of how classical narrative realism *can* work to pull the world-improving aspirations out of the society itself and play them back to us. And it would be that *if* there is hope in the world, *if* there is an imagining beyond things as they are, this imagining will be found in some form in the mirrorings of Hollywood realism, a realism that cannot help but bring us more at the same time that it restricts us to less.

Perhaps the best statement of how very little Hollywood actually offers, how little it *needs* to offer in order to appeal to our best sensibilities, is Fred Jameson's utilization of Bloch in his famous analysis of Steven Spielberg's *Jaws* (1975), 'Reification and utopia in mass culture'. Understood by Denning as a kind of companion essay to Stuart Hall's 'Notes on deconstructing "The Popular"' (1981), Jameson has been taken as the definitive statement of what mass culture must give us in order to lure us, or in his terms, to 'manipulate' us. Crucial here is the argument that if it did not offer us something, mass culture *would not be able* to deceive, a critical elaboration of Bloch's assertion that 'without the utopian function, class ideologies would only have managed to create transitory deception' (1986: 156). But Jameson's theorization differs from Hall's in the emphasis and proportion, what might be called the ratio, of the ideological to the utopian:

> I will now indeed argue that we cannot fully do justice to the ideological function of works like these unless we are willing to concede the presence within them of a more positive function as well: of what I will call, following the Frankfurt School, their Utopian or transcendent potential – that dimension of even the most degraded type of

mass culture which remains implicitly, and no matter how faintly, negative and critical of the social order from which, as a product and a commodity, it springs. At this point in the argument, then, the hypothesis is that the works of mass culture cannot be ideological without at one and the same time being implicitly or explicitly Utopian as well: they cannot manipulate unless they offer some genuine shred of content as a fantasy bribe to the public about to be so manipulated.

(1979: 144)

Perhaps it is the image of the 'genuine shred', the scrap, the sliver, the crumb, that is given, that makes Jameson's version of the Frankfurt School theorists come down on the side of their characteristic despair. So very little is there in the way of genuine anything, it would seem, that audiences are almost made to appear desperate and hope-deprived. The problem is put back on the audience for accepting so little. They are blamed for their own loss. And is fantasy always the inducement because, if so, this would suggest that the reality of the odd flash of political insight, the critical, and the negative, neither induces nor stirs? Bloch, it should be recalled, stakes a great deal on the appealingness of 'revolutionary interest' (1986: 95). If Jameson gives somewhat more weight to the ideological, Hall, in contrast, theorizes a swing between the two possibilities, which has the effect of making him sound less like the other Frankfurt School critics, and this is perhaps a measure of how cultural studies has reformulated the Frankfurt School. The more interesting question, one for further consideration, would be why in Jameson and Hall we have two companion essays, equally indebted to Frankfurt School theory, but whereas the latter is inside cultural studies, founding and defining it, the former is outside cultural studies, outside the tradition that continues to parallel and intersect with his work.

Film studies, however, has remained largely unaware of the great debt it owes to Ernst Bloch. With the exception of Richard Dyer's early analysis of the utopian dimension in the Hollywood musical and Carol Flynn's more recent use of Bloch to explicate the classical Hollywood score (1992), film scholars have seemed largely unaware of the applicability of his concepts of the 'hope-landscape', 'anticipatory consciousness', and the 'world-improving dream' for film theory. Bloch's specific comments on film are provocative, as well, and often call up references to classical genres, most specifically melodrama and science fiction. He refers to the 'marvels of technology' as well as to the 'wishful images' of architecture, and assigns a value to 'longing', which is always a yearning forward toward the better world that is found in the productive daydream (1986: 14, 99). It would almost seem with Ernst Bloch that yet another Frankfurt theorist were writing under the sway of cinema, here the culmination of the art forms he favors: 'The appeal of dressing-up, illuminated *display* belong here, but then the *world of fairytale*, brightened distance in *travel*, the *dance*, the dream-factory of *film*, the example of *theatre*' (1986: 13). The portrayal of the better life requires the theatricality, the ease of movement, the lighted spectacle, the spatial expanse, and the fantasy quality of motion pictures. While we might not want to argue that cinema is integrally or essentially utopian, we could argue that because of its amazing technological capabilities, capabilities that are enhancements of the magical tale, it could be said to have a *utopianizing* effect, that is, whatever subject receiving cinematic treatment can be produced as a 'wishful landscape'. The *utopianizing* effect is certainly there in the panorama, part of which involves the exploitation of scale difference and the magnification feature of cinema as seen in the extreme close-up, the minute made large as well and the large made gigantic, given wide-screen proportions and epic magnificence. Here, the exemplification of the truism that to make bigger is to make better is an easy utopian effect. The visual correlatives of the 'world-improving dream' carry the utopian sensibility in the angle of view as well as the use of scale, and just as easily in the climax of color and the virtuosity of special effects. Consider how, in addition, the classical narrative supplements the image with continuous orchestral underscoring, providing a separate system that often works at cross-purposes with the overall ideological scheme of the motion picture. If the utopian sensibility is there at all, critics seem to agree, it can be found in the melodies and rhythms of the classical score and quite possibly in certain tonalities of popular music.

The fullest implications of Bloch for film theory, however, are found in his highly original reflections on the daydream. Setting himself apart from Freud whom he associated with the backward-looking horrors of the night dream, Bloch argued that the daydream was about new possibilities, the imagination into the future of the world improved. 'There is nothing new in the Freudian unconscious,' he would write, distinguishing regression from the 'progression' of the daydream (1986: 57). 'The content of the night-dream is concealed and disguised, the content of the day-fantasy is open, fabulously inventive, anticipating, and its latency lies ahead,' explains Bloch, outlining the goals and the means of the progressive dream. For this is the drawback as well as the opportunity for any theorization informed by Bloch's early work on the utopian imagination. Bloch's theory is a theory of a purely socialist dream, not a theory of dreams or wishes in general, and, as such, although it is about the anticipation of materially better lives, it is *not* about the achievement of more in capitalist terms. Ironically, in this theory of the good dream factory, capitalism gives us glimpses of the socialism we have never known and may never know in our lifetime. Bloch's theory is a theory of the longing for change, for world-transforming revolution, and therefore it is a theory *for* the mass audience without whom the theory is incomplete.

There is at least one other point at which Bloch's notion of the dream seems to be at odds with psychoanalytic film theory, and this is in relation to the crucial question of what might be called the 'having' of the fantasy wish. In Bloch, *realization*, here, as in the actual achievement of the desired ends of the world made more perfect through socialism, would be important, even though he perhaps theorizes the anticipation at the expense of the accomplishment of the dream. But what good is a dream of socialism if it is 'only a dream'? And here is where psychoanalytic film theory diverges from Bloch's utopia, holding as it does that desire in the cinema is precisely defined by the condition of never having; the object never achieved is the object most desired. An excellent summary of the cine-psychoanalytic function of fantasy in cinema is Elizabeth Cowie's: 'Fantasy involves, is characterized by, not the achievement of desired objects, but the arranging of, a setting out of, desire; a veritable mise en scène of desire' (1997: 133). While Bloch would see the cinematic 'mise en scène of desire' as indicative of hope, the 'gathering emotion', psychoanalytic theory reads the same opulent and evocative *mise en scène* as the stage of desire, a deep wish turned in on itself (Cowie, 1997: 129). While it might seem that fantasy is a difficult approach to the question of political action, a long route as well as a long shot, psychoanalysis actually suggests a short cut, if we understand, following Cowie's discussion of Freud's theorization of fantasy as a psychic reality, that although indifferent to developments in any realm of 'the real', fantasy may still be implicated in that realm (Cowie, 1997: 129). Fantasy, it might be said, has its 'reality effect'.

So are we talking about the bad dream factory or the good dream factory? Increasingly, it has become a question of whose dreams for whom. Ernst Bloch, years before the institutionalization of the concept of hegemony, cautioned about the 'beautifying mirror' which 'often only reflects how the ruling class wishes the wishes of the weak to be', a mirror like a cinema that specializes in 'hegemonic fantasies' (Cowie, 1997: 129). So would we want to know who owns the dream factories, no longer exclusively corporate studio entities but independent production companies such as Steven Spielberg's new DreamWorks, a highly visible entity at the time of his production of *Amistad* (1998), a historical narrative featuring a slave revolt. DreamWorks, turning the concept of the culture factory to its own advantage, foregrounds the industrial and the mechanistic at the same time that it denies this aspect of the business via the associations with the thoroughly creative 'dream work', borrowed coyly from Freud. The name of Spielberg's company also contributes to an illusion of collaborative productivity, the illusion that many hands toil in the DreamWorks, that the labor is hard labor but nevertheless dream labor.

The question of whose dreams for whom is particularly relevant in relation to Spielberg who gave us boyish dreams in the Star Wars trilogy, asking all of the peoples of the world to see these dreams and to find something for themselves in them. Soon after, in his production of Alice Walker's *The Color Purple* (1985), Spielberg gave us his version of the now classic piece of African-American fiction (Walker, 1983). However, I do not want to belabor here either the question of the preoccupations of the white male auteur or the question of the portrayal of whose people in what light. More interesting and to the point here is Jackie Bobo's (1995) research on black women and their responses to Spielberg's *The Color Purple*, for Bobo's spectators reacted in ways that confirm again the doubleness of popular forms. And yet it seems improbable. How could it be that the film they found to be offensively racist was the same film that made them feel empowered? The business of the dream factory, of course, is to make the fantasy 'work' for everyone even though the fantasy may not speak to everyone.

At the end of the twentieth century there is pressure to think, to wonder, to imagine the critical future. Looking ahead it is difficult to imagine anything beyond more of the bad First World dream factory that continues to fabricate and disseminate its mixed messages, interrupted occasionally by the Third World dream that floats to the First through alternative channels. But film history leads us to skepticism about the old socialist dream. To critique the capitalist dream factory is not to ask for anything resembling Socialist Realist musicals, and not to ask for a world without the thrill of horror films or the visual feast of a big-budget blockbuster. Perhaps it is that we have learned to love our hegemonic fantasies – the more hegemonic the better – and not only to consume but also to critique because the pleasure of analysis is in finding the 'shred' of something, of anything remotely utopian, in the most crudely escapist entertainment. But maybe the challenge is not to try to imagine new forms of entertainment from the world that brought the old forms.

What would it mean to put 'hope' back into the model of analysis, back into critical theory? Since this question sounds a bit naive as phrased, let us ask if we could substitute 'hope' for 'politics', coming closer to Bloch's meaning. But how many times have Left-leaning (and even just well-meaning) critics asked for the restoration of politics in the debates over popular culture in the past several decades? That has been done. To inflect 'politics' in such a way that the transformation of the entire world is implied, would that do it? That, too, has been advocated – as revolution. But perhaps Bloch's 'world-improving dream' is not exclusively about social upheaval but about upheaval in the accompanying realm of fantasy. What if, hope beyond hope, in the next century we soon begin to see instead of First World fantasies for the Third World, Third World fantasies for the First World? Who knows what the weak wish the wishes of the rulers to be, since they have never really been asked to dream for us.

Acknowledgements: Special thanks to Christine Gledhill for her comments on this Chapter, to Susan Willis for her insights on cultural studies, and to Charlotte Herzog for the motion picture palace interior still.

References

Barthes, R. 1972: *Mythologies*. New York: Hill and Wang.

Bloch, E. 1986: *The principle of hope*. Vol. I, trans. N. Plaice, S. Plaice and P. Knight. Oxford: Basil Blackwell.

Bobo, J. 1995: *Black women as cultural readers*. New York: Columbia University Press.

Cowie, E. 1997: *Representing the woman*. Minneapolis, MN: University of Minnesota Press.

Denning, M. 1990: The end of mass culture. *International Labor and Working Class History* **37**: 4–18.

Doane, M. 1987: *The desire to desire: the woman's film of the 1940s*. Bloomington, IN: Indiana University Press.

Dyer, R. 1977: Entertainment and utopia. In Nichols, B. (ed.), *Movies and methods II*. Berkeley, CA, and Los Angeles, CA: University of California Press, pp. 2–13.

Ewen, S. and Ewen, E. 1982: *Channels of desire*. New York: McGraw-Hill.

Flynn, C. 1992: *Strains of utopia: gender, nostalgia, and Hollywood film music*. Princeton, NJ: Princeton University Press.

Friedberg, A. 1995: Cinema and the postmodern condition. In Williams, L. (ed.), *Viewing positions: ways of seeing films*. New Brunswick, NJ: Rutgers University Press.

Gaines, J. 1989: The *Queen Christina* tie-ups: convergence of show window and screen. *Quarterly Review of Film and Video* **XI**(4): 35–60.

Gaines, J. 1991: *Contested culture: the image, the voice, and the law*. Chapel Hill, NC: University of North Carolina Press.

Gledhill, C. 1992: Between melodrama and realism: Anthony Asquith's *Underground* and King Vidor's *The Crowd*. In Gaines, J. (ed.), *Classical Hollywood narrative: the paradigm wars*. Durham, NC: Duke University Press, pp. 129–67.

Hall, S. 1981: Notes on deconstructing 'The Popular'. In Samuel, R. (ed.), *People's history and socialist theory*. Boston, MA: Routledge and Kegan Paul.

Horkheimer, M. and Adorno, T. 1987: *Dialectic of enlightenment*. New York: Continuum.

Jameson, F. 1979: Reification and utopia in mass culture. *Social Text* **1**: 130–48.

Kracauer, S. 1995: *The mass ornament*. Trans. T.Y. Levin. London and Cambridge, MA: Harvard University Press.

Lesage, J. 1982: Hegemonic fantasies and *An Unmarried Woman* and *Craig's Wife*. *Film Reader* **5**: 83–94.

Lovell, T. 1973: Cultural studies. *Screen* **14**(3): 115–22.

Lynd, R.S. and Lynd, H. 1929: *Middletown: a study in contemporary American culture*. New York: Harcourt Brace and Co.

May, L. 1980: *Screening out the past: the birth of mass culture and the motion picture industry*. Chicago, IL, and London: University of Chicago Press.

Powdermaker, H. 1951: *Hollywood: the dream factory*. Boston, MA: Little, Brown.

Simmel, G. 1900: *The philosophy of money*. Reprinted in 1978. Trans. T. Bottomore and D. Frisby. Boston, MA, and London: Routledge and Kegan Paul.

Veblen, T. 1912: *The theory of the leisure class*. London: Macmillan.

Walker, A. 1983: *The color purple*. London: The Women's Press.

7   The publicness of cinema

James Donald and Stephanie Hemelryk Donald

At the heart of *The media and modernity* (1995), John B. Thompson's ambitious meditation on the social consequences of the media from the press to broadcasting, there is a curious silence. Look in the index, and you will find just two references to 'Hollywood'. Both relate solely to the development of a global media market over the past decade or two. Neither 'cinema' nor 'film' merits a mention – compared with seven entries for 'coffee houses'! Given the historical case for arguing that early cinema embodied 'the fullest expression and combination of modernity's attributes' (Charney and Schwartz, 1995: 1; also, see Friedberg, 1992; Gunning, 1986; Hansen, 1991), it seems strange to ignore film when theorising the role of communication media in the formation of modernity.

Thompson's oversight might be excused as a matter of perspective, the result of approaching modernity through grand social theory. His organising question is whether the media constitute a sphere in which effective deliberation on political and social issues takes place. Starting from there, it *is* tempting to focus on the early print media and public service broadcasting in the twentieth century. But that does not diminish what is lost as a result.

Against Thompson, we argue that cinema must be part of any account of the media and modernity, even if that means fuzzying up the neat categories of social and political theory. First, in response to Thompson's question, we show how cinema, like the press and broadcasting, makes available structures of visibility, modes of conduct, and practices of judgement, which together constitute a culture of public participation. Second, looking at the special case of China, we examine how this emphasis on the public dimension of cinema prompts new thinking about theories of spectatorship.

The backdrop to our argument, as to Thompson's, is the concept of the public sphere. Its present currency in the study of media is one symptom of a move away from, or at least a rethinking of, the ideology model of the media. To summarise with comic book starkness, that model assumed that the media are important above all because their dominant forms and practices of representation shape the way people see and experience the world, themselves, and themselves and others in the world. That, went the argument, is how the media and their products contribute to the reproduction, adaptation, or transformation of social relations of power.

In equally broadbrush terms, there have been two main objections to the ideology model. It overinflates the power of media representations and their impact on the beliefs, values, or, most decisively, actions of the people who are, for part of the time, media consumers. At the same time, it underestimates the role of media technologies, media institutions, and media discourses in shaping less the content of our thoughts than the frameworks in which those thoughts are developed.

The conception of the public sphere that has been taken up in media studies was first formulated by Jürgen Habermas in the early 1960s. It was 27 years before *Strukturwandel der Öffentlichkeit* (*The structural transformation of the public sphere*; 1962) appeared in English, in 1989 – by chance, but not without consequence, the year that the Communist regimes of East and Central Europe collapsed and the Berlin Wall was torn down. Habermas's premise was that valid knowledge can emerge only from a situation of open, free, and uninterrupted dialogue. On that basis, he attempted to show how the emergence of new institutions in early modern Europe (including the print media) contributed to the opening up of public affairs to scrutiny by citizens. This, he argued, was crucial in the transition from absolutist to liberal-democratic regimes, and established the articulation of critical public opinion through the media as a vital feature of modern democracy.

Habermas thus traces the emergence of a new political voice. This was the *public opinion* formed and articulated within the *public sphere* and given authority by its *publicness*; that is, to repeat, its openness and freedom from external constraint, whether by government, church, or economic interests. Habermas himself has freely acknowledged many of the objections to his initial formulation. The boundaries of the bourgeois public were extremely limited in both class and gender terms. It is historically wrong to suppose that there was ever a single public sphere. The bourgeois press on which he dwells was far from uncontaminated by political or economic corruption (for example, see Calhoun, 1992; Keane, 1991). Nevertheless, defenders of the concept argue that the public sphere remains useful less as an empirical description than as a yardstick by which to judge existing media systems. That is how the legal theorist Monroe E. Price sees it: as 'a technique for evaluating speech practices and media structures to measure progress towards a democratic society' (1995: 24). And certainly that is how Habermas initially used it when condemning the way the modern media developed as vehicles for the creation of a manipulated and managed *mass* opinion, not as a forum for *public* deliberation.

Monroe Price's pragmatic usage offers a clue to the interest in the public sphere among anglophone media scholars. Although derived from the Marxism of the late Frankfurt School, the concept is more in tune with our disenchanted times than the old ideology model. It is tragic rather than utopian. Recognising the fragility of human civilisation, it is sensitive to the difficulty, costs, and dangers of social change, however desirable or necessary change may be (Garnham, 1992: 375).

The emergence of mediated publics

To consider the relevance of the public sphere to cinema, it helps to go back a century before the institution came into being. As early as the 1790s, we can find a discussion of modernity in which concepts of the public and (at least by implication) the media are intertwined.[1] In his 1983 lectures on the Enlightenment, Foucault re-read Kant in order to explain the motive behind his own philosophical project in a question which Kant posed when responding to a newspaper editor's challenge, 'What is Enlightenment?' The question, paraphrased by Foucault, is this: 'What is happening today? What is happening now? And what is this "now" which we all inhabit, and which defines the moment in which I am writing?' (1986: 88). The question of what it means to live in the present imposes a new responsibility on philosophers, claims Foucault. Philosophy should provide a critical discourse on modernity.

To show this new discourse at work, Foucault turns to another text by Kant. In the second dissertation in *The contest of faculties*, Kant stages the conflict between the Faculty of Philosophy and the Faculty of Law around the question, 'Is the human race continually progressing?' Kant looks around him for a sign that this might be the case. He finds it in one of the great historical events of his time, the French Revolution. What matters is not, for him, whether the Revolution in itself was a good thing or a bad thing. Rather, the sign of progress is to be found in the feeling of *enthusiasm* provoked by the Revolution. The important thing is less the Revolution itself, than the way that people 'in states and national groups' respond to the drama of the event, the way it is perceived and judged by spectators who do not take part in it but observe it from a distance.

How is Kant's response to the French Revolution relevant to an understanding of the modern media? Note first how the historical event has been translated into a *spectacle* or *drama* through the work of representation. Note too that this is a drama represented for an *audience*, and specifically for an audience of distant spectators – Kant stresses that he is commenting from 'a country more than a hundred miles removed from the scene of the Revolution' (1991: 183). In a gesture that prefigures media critique, Kant turns away from the event and focuses his attention on its representation and its spectators.

He does so because these spectators constitute a particular type of audience: a *public*. 'We are here concerned,' he writes, 'only with the attitude of the onlookers as it reveals itself *in public* while the drama of great political changes is taking place' (1991: 182, emphasis in original). What is so important about this public? Is it that its members meet in face-to-face conversations and negotiations in coffee houses, board rooms, presbyteries, and universities? Not really; or certainly not only that. At least since Kant's time, the public has meant not so much gents in frock coats talking to each other as a public of spectators. But these spectators are neither passive nor, although distant, marginal. What, then, do they do that makes them a public? The implication is that the spectacularisation and visibility of historical–political events allow, and even demand, a new mode of political judgement. Because the Revolution is presented to this public of spectators as a dramatic spectacle, they form an opinion of it on the basis of what is primarily an *aesthetic* judgement. It is the sublimity of the Revolution that provokes their enthusiasm. This enthusiasm prompts Kant to believe that there is 'a moral disposition within the human race' which in turn provides grounds for accepting the idea of human progress.

What emerges from Kant's ruminations on the French Revolution is a new cultural–political configuration: the historical event as dramatic spectacle; an audience of distant and diffuse spectators; and an aesthetic–political mode of judgement which sustains the new force of public opinion. What is needed to make this dynamic of modernity work? The link is the medium of the press, which both represents the event and provides the forum for the articulation of public opinion.

In this context, consider Hegel's famous aphorism: 'Reading the morning paper is a kind of realistic morning prayer' (1974: 360). Hegel is not just talking about being in-the-know so that you can act the 'man of the world'. In a condensed way, he is making a far-reaching claim about the mutually constitutive relationship between government, public, and subjectivity. He makes explicit and systematic Kant's observations about the centrality of a public. It is public visibility (*Öffentlichkeit*) that gives modern constitutional government its legitimacy.[2] The public sphere is part of the network of institutionalised mediations which not only makes the exercise of legislative power possible but also, at the same time, and as part of the same process, renders the operation of power open to this legitimating deliberation – hence the mediated public discourse described by Kant, which embodies this principle of openness. The point of Hegel's quip, though, is that it is only through the *practice* of public deliberation that *Öffentlichkeit* can have any effective existence. The mutually sustaining relationship between government and public cannot be purely formal or constitutional. Because you need people to behave as members of the public, this sense of a public inscribes a particular way of life, or at least a form of conduct. What emerges, in theory at least, is that shared ethical life which Hegel saw as the ideal modern *polis*. To participate in this public ethical life, to act as a citizen and so to be a citizen, it is not enough just to vote from time to time. Nor, however, need participation take the form of the republican debate of Plato's Athens or the political activism of Rousseau's Geneva. As Kant implied, and as Hegel reaffirms, the subjective dimension of public life now consists primarily in the exercise of a specific mode of political judgement. That is how, for Hegel, the small act of reading the newspaper, if performed in the right spirit, becomes part of the *Bildung* of citizenship. It represents a minimal instance of self-formation through mediated participation in the media-constituted public sphere.

The publicness of cinema

So far, a social theorist such as John Thompson might find little reason to dissent from our story. But how does this philosophical digression make it possible to understand the public nature of quite a different medium – cinema – as it emerged a century after Kant? A Habermasian version of the story might emphasise how, certainly by the 1890s, any ideal of the media operating as a sphere of democratic deliberation on public issues had been corrupted by venality, partisanship, or the degrading logic of supply and demand. In the emerging mass market for symbolic goods, media commodities – commoditised media – not only failed to encourage the disciplines necessary for an effective reasoning public and for mediated participation in the public sphere. For Habermasian pessimists, they actually subverted them. Reading the morning paper as a spiritual exercise becomes the exception. By the end of the century, most people read the paper pragmatically (for the job advertisements, the entertainment guide, the weather forecast) or simply for amusement. The key to understanding the period at which cinema emerged is therefore not just the supposed incompatibility between the classic model of the deliberative public sphere and the mass media market. It is not a question of good public versus bad mass. The crux is that the *present* of the end of the nineteenth century – in the sense that Foucault derives from Kant – was significantly different from the *now* of a century earlier. The *mass* nature of cinema refers not only to an audience far larger and less socially discriminated than the narrowly bounded public of the earlier period. It implies a different way of living in the social and cultural space of that present: not an ethic of self-formation through public participation, but distraction, diffusion, and anonymity.

The change from forum for public participation to commodity for mass consumption is not only internal to the history of the media. It is bound up with dramatic changes in forms of perception and patterns of social interaction brought about by new methods of industrial production, the new metropolis, new techniques of government, the unprecedented speed of the railways and the automobile, and instant, long-distance communication by telegraph and telephone. In emerging human sciences such as psychology, suggests Jonathan Crary, one reaction to the undermining of stable structures of perception by this sensory speed-up was the attempt to impose a discipline of attentiveness:

> It's possible to see one crucial aspect of modernity as a continual crisis of attentiveness: a crisis in which the changing configurations of capitalism push distraction to new limits and thresholds, with unending introduction of new organisations of sensory experience, new sources of stimulation, and streams of information, and then respond with new methods of regulating but also productively harnessing perception.
>
> (1996: 275; see also Crary, 1995)

That is where cinema comes in. As Miriam Hansen elegantly demonstrates in *Babel and Babylon*, from its beginnings in the 1890s until the end of the silent era in the late 1920s, cinema both harnessed the experience of perception for profit and regulated it through the transition to the norms of spectatorship associated with the classical Hollywood style that was set in place roughly between 1907 and 1917. The shift from early cinema, observes Hansen, was characterised by 'the elaboration of a mode of narration that makes it possible to anticipate a viewer through particular textual strategies, and thus to standardize empirically diverse and to some extent unpredictable acts of reception' (1991: 16).

Kant invoked public enthusiasm for the French Revolution to show what it meant to be a member of the public in the 1790s. In a similar gesture, Hansen identifies two events that produced a different type of enthusiasm – one bordering on mass hysteria – to stand as emblems of mass publicness at the start of the twentieth century. Cinema, she argues, changed the topography of public and private domains, breaking most dramatically from earlier formations with regard to the position of women (1991: 2–3). Hansen's events are drawn not from political events of world historical importance, but from popular culture. The first is *The Corbett–Fitzsimmons Fight*, a 100-minute long 'illustration' of a heavyweight title bout which enjoyed huge popular success in the USA in 1897, especially among women. The film, suggests Hansen, redrew public–private boundaries by offering women, even if at one remove, 'the forbidden sight of male bodies in seminudity, engaged in intimate and intense physical action'. Such visceral enthusiasm is scarcely what Kant had in mind, but it was a force that lent itself to being harnessed by the emerging cinema industry. By the time of Hansen's second event, the release of *The Son of the Sheik* almost three decades later in 1926, the sadistic display of Rudolph Valentino's torso for the female consumer had become 'a calculated ingredient of star packaging': 'Valentino becomes an emblem of the simultaneous liberalization and commodification of sexuality that crucially defined the development of American consumer culture' (1991: 1, 2). Publicness, in this context, involved less participation through rational judgement and mediated deliberation than a *distance* (however absentminded or distracted) from existing social and cultural norms – an *alternative horizon of experience*, in Hansen's terms.

The gist of Hansen's revisionist history is that, even if cinema spectatorship entailed a very different public sphere from the one Hegel extrapolated from the reading of newspapers, it was just as effective in instituting a mode of self-creation through membership of a media-defined community:

> on the one hand, a specifically modern form of subjectivity, defined by particular perceptual arrangements and a seemingly fixed temporality; on the other, a collective, public form of reception shaped in the context of older traditions of performance and modes of exhibition.
>
> (1991: 3)

In its own way, cinema too provided a normative discipline for living in a mediated present.

The tension between the actual public, or publics, engendered by cinema in the early decades of the twentieth century and the normative ideal of the public sphere is not just a retrospective theoretical construction. It informed attempts to regulate cinema, of which censorship was just the most obvious, and it shaped the development of newer media. Lord Reith's BBC, for example, was set up in the early 1920s to pre-empt the emergence of a broadcasting market and to defend British national culture against its corruption by the 'American octopus' of Hollywood and Tin Pan Alley. The BBC represents a self-conscious attempt to create a new type of public sphere, or at least to recreate the simulacrum of an old one. Paradoxically, given that the new mass media were held largely responsible for the atomising, alienating nature of mass society, Reith's vision was that broadcasting should re-establish the ethos of 'the city-state of old' and so provide the integrating sinew for democracy. His strategy was to create a different type of citizen by drawing a different boundary between public and private, exploiting the technology of broadcasting to institute a public presence in the private home. His favourite image was that of Prime Minister or King speaking to citizens and their families through the radio by the domestic hearth. In the attempt to create a new sense of public participation and cultural nationhood, all the techniques of early BBC radio – the refusal of continuity, the emphasis on attentive listening, even the tone of voice – were designed to produce the listener as the well-informed, responsible citizen. It was a gesture, both forlorn and in some ways stunningly successful, to subvert the distracted publics being produced across the globe by the reach of Hollywood.

This opposition between the dangers of distraction and the ideal of self-reflexive perception and public participation structured most discussions of cinema in mass culture in the 1920s (Crary, 1996: 267). In England, it surfaced in the pages of the journal *Close Up* (see Donald *et al.*, 1998). For the most part, *Close Up* championed an avant garde film aesthetic that assumed a skilled audience. One contributor, however, the novelist Dorothy Richardson, struck a different note in her column, 'Continuous performance'. Prefiguring Hansen's argument about the public space cinema provided for understandably distracted women, she describes a visit to a picture palace in North London:

> It was a Monday and therefore a new picture. But it was also washing day, and yet the scattered audience was composed almost entirely of mothers. Their children, apart from the infants accompanying them, were at school and their husbands were at work. . . . Tired women, their faces sheened with toil, and small children, penned in the semi-darkness and foul air on a sunny afternoon. There was almost no talk. Many of the women sat alone, figures of weariness at rest. Watching these I took comfort. At last the world of entertainment had provided, for a few pence, tea thrown in, sanctuary for mothers, an escape from the everlasting qui vive into eternity on a Monday afternoon.
>
> (quoted in Donald *et al.*, 1998: 160)[3]

In contrast to Reith's vision of the public sphere penetrating the domestic hearth, Richardson recognises in the publicness of cinema an escape from the tyranny of domesticity. But as she tracked cinema's presence across London, Richardson saw how it fulfilled a variety of functions for different urban audiences. It did not just provide a haven for women in the suburbs. It offered entertainment in the West End, and acted as a 'civilising agent' in the slums. To her, cinema suggested a public, a community of spectators, being educated for modernity: Everyman, 'at home in a new world', thanks to the movies. She sees 'a vast audience born and made in the last few years, initiated, disciplined, and waiting'. 'And here we all are, as never before. What will it do with us?' (1998: 204, 174, 171).

What will cinema do with us? And so, by implication, what will modernity do with us? Richardson's question captures a defining ambivalence from the first half of the twentieth century: an anxiety about massification and standardisation, certainly, but also a desperate investment in the liberating potential of modernity. This was felt not only by intellectuals. It was also worked though by (for want of a better term) ordinary people. In an article on Weimar Germany, Miriam Hansen captures what it was about cinema that represented hope for Dorothy Richardson and danger for John Reith:

> Cinema was . . . both part and prominent symptom of the crisis as which modernity was perceived, and at the same time it evolved into a social discourse in which a wide variety of groups sought to come to terms with the traumatic impact of modernization. This reflexive dimension of cinema, its dimension of *publicness*, was recognized by intellectuals early on, whether they celebrated the cinema's emancipatory potential or, in alliance with the forces of censorship and reform, sought to contain and control it,

adapting the cinema to the standards of high culture and the restoration of the bourgeois public sphere.

(Hansen, 1995: 365–6)

For Hansen it is Siegfried Kracauer who perceived most clearly what was, at least potentially, public about popular modernity. In essays such as 'The cult of distraction' (on the picture palaces of Berlin) and 'The mass ornament' (on the Tiller Girls dance troupe) Kracauer defended forms of culture usually denounced as inauthentic. As if in response to the question, 'What is this "now" which we all inhabit?', Kracauer bluntly insists that in the Europe of the 1920s and 1930s it was a mass-mediated cultural present. If publicness was to have any critical bite, it would have to recognise the distracted aesthetic of the masses consuming mass-produced, mechanical cultural products. The old distinction between 'authentic' and 'inauthentic' no longer made sense. Kracauer, argues Hansen, 'increasingly asserted the reality and legitimacy of "*Ersatz*"' because he recognised that 'the mass media might be the only horizon in which an actual democratisation of culture was taking place' (1995: 374).

The publicness of film

That was then. Does cinema still 'offer the conditions for critical self-reflexion on a mass basis', especially if, as Miriam Hansen suggests, television now provides 'the single most expansive discursive horizon in which the effects of modernity [are] reflected, rejected or denied, transmuted or negotiated' (1995: 374)? The question recalls, for us, a debate from film theory in the 1970s, when the possibility of publicness was discussed in terms of cinema, politics, and ideology. It led to a hunt, in cinema as in other arts and media, for the Progressive Text: a Brechtian phantom that would not so much teach its audience what to think, as disturb everyday ways of seeing and understanding. It was never found, despite reported traces of 'progressiveness', sometimes in the most unlikely texts: Hollywood melodrama, the films of Douglas Sirk or Sam Fuller, wherever. The catalyst for this frantic search was the famous 'Category E' in the Althusserian taxonomy of cinema's ideological effects drawn up in the 1960s by two editors of *Cahiers du Cinema*, Jean Narboni and Jean-Louis Comolli. Their category of the 'progressive text' contained those mainstream films whose relationship to ideology was ambiguous or slyly critical.

> Looking at the framework one can see two moments in it: one holding it back within certain limits, one transgressing them. An internal criticism is taking place which cracks the films apart at the seams. If one reads the film obliquely, looking for symptoms; if one looks beyond its apparent formal coherence, one can see that it is riddled with cracks: it is splitting under an internal tension which is simply not there in an ideologically innocuous film. The ideology thus becomes subordinate to the text. It no longer has an independent existence: it is *presented* by the film.
>
> (1977: 7; see also Klinger, 1984)

The notion of *progressiveness* was always pretty fatuous. It suggested a calibration of ideological complicity, ranging from servility through subversion to militant opposition.

The progressive text was roughly at midpoint on this scale, offering a formalist get-out from the 'dominant ideology'. Alternatively, progressiveness implied a claim about the social or political consequences of a film. As John O. Thompson waspishly suggested, the measure of progressiveness would presumably then be whether people left the cinema and rushed to the barricades (1979).

Without wanting to resuscitate the salvationist connotations of progressiveness, there may be a case for linking the *style* of film spectatorship described by Narboni and Comolli to a broader, less text-obsessed notion of publicness. This suggests one (and just one) possible way of reflecting on the present, a moment of public participation made possible by the address of the film ('An internal criticism is taking place') but enacted by the spectator ('If one reads the film obliquely . . . if one looks beyond its apparent formal coherence').

This line of thought, it is true, implies not the distraction of mass cinema but a skilled and necessarily minority way of relating to film. This form of publicness is not, and never will be, the usual way in which most audiences relate to most films. However, there is a case for claiming that *under totalitarian or authoritarian political and cultural regimes*, this form of cinematic publicness continues to be significant.

We noted earlier the political context of 1989 in which the English translation of *The structural transformation of the public sphere* appeared. In the dissident movements of East and Central Europe, as well in the critiques of Western commentators, it was the lack of the institutions of 'civil society', and so the absence of a sphere for free public deliberation, that were seen as the defining flaw of the Communist regimes. Democratic parties aspired to recreate a network of autonomous associations, independent from the state, which bound citizens together in matters of common concern, and whose existence and activities would enable them not only to monitor public policy but also to influence it (Taylor, 1995: 66). In the Leninist model, the symbolic space of publicness was given a mass dimension in a sense quite different from that of either Kracauer or Habermas. Whether through the rational deliberation of a press-based public or through the more distracted spectatorship of cinema audiences, they saw publicness acting as a check on the exercise of state power. Leninist public culture was supposed to act as a relay for that power. Under the direction of a vanguard party, itself led by a core elite, press and cinema were supposed to play their part in the mass – total – mobilization of society towards the goals of revolutionary change. Although it is difficult to provide good empirical accounts of the impact of the Leninist media and their messages, one consequence seems to have been rampant self-delusion among the elite groups. (The Chinese call this 'public square consciousness' [Wang, 1996: 6].) Anecdotal evidence suggests a high degree of irony, scepticism, and cynicism amongst wider audiences.

Ideas about the public and civil society certainly had a part to play in the reorganization of East and Central European media systems in the post-1989 period. But there broadcasting and the press were more urgent issues than cinema. We therefore look at a different instance of the post-Leninist articulation of the public/mass tension: the cinema of mainland China (Berry, 1991; Chow, 1995; Clark, 1987; Lu, 1997; Yau, 1991; Zhang, X, 1997; Zhang, Y, 1996). Even without all the contextualisation this case needs and deserves, China does reveal how cinema can create a different kind of symbolic public space: an official social, national or public imaginary dedicated to 'mass' mobilisation, which nonetheless allows moments of 'public' engagement.[4]

Thinking about the public in China means working in quite a different political and social landscape from that of Western democracies, and so requires different maps. The familiar forums of civil society and public sphere, as conceived in Western political theory, simply do not exist. The Chinese Communist Party, as distinct even from state or government, monopolises many spaces or institutions in which public or civil association might be expected to appear in a Western model. It is therefore important not to fall into the 'deficit model' to which Habermasian approaches are prone. Too often, they set up 'the public sphere' as a normative criterion of judgement, and then condemn the empirical absence of that ideal. That approach to civil society can become little more than a thinly disguised and minatory search for something like the West. Of course, China is not 'like' the West, and never has been. Even today, even after Deng Xiaoping's economic reforms in the 1980s abandoned Mao's totalitarian ambitions, the Communist Party's rule remains authoritarian and at odds with international discourses of human rights. Agitating for sectional interests may now be legitimate, but it is tolerated only under the umbrella of the communist state and only so long as it ultimately fits in with the state's developmental goals (Lyman, 1996: 59).

In Communist China, the role of public culture has always been to produce revolutionary consciousness, a mass sense of belonging to a shared historical narrative. In the struggle for Liberation before 1949, the task of cinema was to mobilise a revolutionary spirit and expand it into a mass movement. After the People's Republic was created in 1949, its function became winning the loyalty of the Chinese population to the Maoist state, or at least their acquiescence.

Central to the mass mobilisation in the struggle for Liberation was the mythical status ascribed not only to Mao, but also, from the early 1940s onwards, to Yan'an, the Communist Army's headquarters during the war against the Japanese and Chiang Kaishek's Nationalist forces in previous decades. Together, the man and the place provided a rhetorical framework within which tales of individual suffering and individual redemption through absorption into the Party project were used to feed a broader narrative of universal Chinese experience. The story of how each recruit came to Yan'an would be mediated through a mythologised history of Mao's own life, told in terms of his progress across China to Yan'an. Mao was adept at recasting these individual stories as metaphorical narratives, thus (as David Apter and Tony Saich put it) recasting time from history to situation. In this bonding through storytelling, Yan'an came to represent the present of Maoism, a present containing within it both the past of oppression and a future of socialist perfection. As a utopian community, Yan'an 'was made to serve as a moral template, rather than a model, of the China yet to be born' (Apter and Saich, 1994: 114, 115; see also Donald, 1997).

Apter and Saich's notion of a 'moral template' is close to our notion of a public imaginary legislated by Maoist ideology. It refers to a regulatory principle guiding cultural production, not an achieved state of controlled public behaviour and belief. (That is how it differs from the conception of ideology to be found in Narboni and

Comolli's taxonomy.) Even during the Yan'an period there was documented – albeit purged – dissent. However carefully designed for mass mobilisation, cinema always allowed occasions for critical engagement with official imagery. Mao's vision of the future never entirely excluded public debate, either before or after the founding of the People's Republic. Chinese intellectual and political history is more subtle than that. The question is where and how debate took place. Under what conditions was it suppressed? In what circumstances did it become visible?

After 1949, all aspects of cinema were subject to the Maoist moral template. The staple fare of Hollywood reruns was gradually displaced by Soviet films, often the cult movies from the late 1940s featuring the actor Gelovani as Stalin. Film projects were subject to scrutiny and censorship before and after production, and were made in studios subsidised by a central Ministry of Film and Television. In extraordinary times the exercise of cultural power shifted to direct control by Party figures. Between 1967 and 1972, Mao's wife Jianq Qing halted production of virtually all films other than a few based on revolutionary operas.

In terms of genre and narration, the 'moral template' helps to explain the move of Chinese cinema after 1949 towards revolutionary romanticism and revolutionary realism. A comparison between pre- and post-Liberation films reveals a shift from a wistful social realism towards a starker socialist imagination. *Street Angel* (1937) and *Goddess* (1934), for example, both tell a story of women in Shanghai caught in the trap of prostitution, as a way of criticising gender relations in traditional society and the disparity between urban rich and poor. Although *The White-haired Girl* (1950) tells a similar tale of a girl raped by a rich landlord, it tells it within a post-Liberation aesthetic (Yue, 1993). Not surprisingly, given the veneration of peasants in official ideology, at least until the drive for economic efficiency under Deng Xiaoping, *The White-haired Girl* is a story about peasants, not the urban poor. And here, redemption comes not through romantic love, but through loving submission to the Party. In the final scene, the film cuts from the gaze between heroine and hero to the Liberation troops appearing over the horizon.

It is in this historical and generic context that the publicness of some films in the 1980s and 1990s can be grasped.[5] They re-deploy some strategies from revolutionary realism and romanticism, but in ways that recognise the spectatorial experience of their audience and, for the dissident or cynical among them, invite the oblique, symptomatic reading Comolli and Narboni describe.

In *The Big Parade* (1985), for example, Chen Kaige offers the very public spectacle of a national day parade in Tiananmen Square. It is a sumptuous sequence of long pans across ranks of service men and women. The film cuts to medium close-ups of drummers lifting their sticks in synchronised anticipation, trumpets set to lips, guns raised in salute. The national anthem which has been playing on the soundtrack pauses. Then in a low-angle medium close-up we see the military conductor, his eyes hidden by dark glasses, one arm raised. A moment passes in silence. The arm drops. The music plays.

Is this moment to be read solely as propaganda glorifying an enormous military machine? Or does it produce a different range of possible meanings by leaving space for the entry of the spectator into the text? The cut to the conductor takes the spectacle away from the massed bodies of the Chinese national subject 'on parade' to an image of a single man that is both sinister and enigmatic, and which evokes the presence of the Party in all manifestations of national Chineseness. That is what makes the moment at least potentially public. For the politically attuned spectator, it provokes a question. How are we to insert this man into the spectacle of a massed body of the nation when he occupies a frame which excludes the masses, and in which he faces in an opposite direction from the rest of the narrative subject?

The concept of publicness thus provides a way of framing questions about the political encoding of contemporary Chinese films. In the sequence from *The Big Parade*, narrational techniques are turned in on themselves and made visible in a way that provokes questions about contemporary Chinese politics and society. In films such as this, Chinese cinema reveals a special case of publicness in the consumption of cultural texts, even (or perhaps especially) in the absence of formal political freedoms. Authoritarianism produces audiences able to read politically in something like Narboni and Comolli's sense – obliquely, beyond apparent formal coherence. But the Chinese case reminds us that historical contingency has to be put back in alongside the textuality of film.

This means looking at the way a system of textual referentiality is organized around ironic involvement in a shared history. Films work over the past – sometimes the immediate past, as in *The Big Parade*; sometimes, as in the case of *Yellow Earth* (1984), the mythical past of the Communist Party's adolescence in Yan'an. Moments of publicness are achieved less through the story or history being told, however, than through the symbolic force of the *mise-en-scène*, often in moments (or movements) that appear to have nothing to do with either story or plot. Such moments establish the contemporaneity of the film, in the sense that their calculated frustration of generic expectations will be meaningful only to those attentive spectators who share the same imaginary, the same memories, the same terms of cultural reference.

In the films of Zhang Yimuo, this complicity of contemporaries can be glimpsed in his manipulation of luscious colours, the sensual texture of fabrics, and the sheer beauty of his female star, Gong Li. These haptic qualities are most effective when counterposed against moments of high comedy or great sexual passion. Two scenes in *Red Sorghum* (1987) come to mind. In the first, the mistress of a winery (Gong Li) lies spreadeagled in a field of sorghum waiting for sex. The camera tracks up and back until she is in an extreme high-angle shot that becomes an aerial view. In this movement, she is rendered both vulnerable and self-sufficient. Later in the film workers at the winery stand, almost naked, in front of the picture of the wine god, offering up the year's vintage for blessing. The solemnity of the moment is shattered as they break into an uproarious song about *hao jiu* (good wine). The sequence ends with the men offering a full bowl of wine to Gong Li.

Scenes such as these – especially the turning moments or reversals in them – constitute cinematic symbolic space. This space may be opened up by a break in the narrative, signalled by a subsequent release – through sex, laughter, or the excruciating poignancy of the scene in *Yellow Earth* in which the young revolutionary soldier deserts the unhappy peasant girl in order to return to Yan'an (see Donald, 1996). These disruptions allow spectators to be contemporary; that is, to engage with the present critically, through a reappraisal of the shared memories or of the 'moral template' of Maoist iconography. They are confronted with something familiar, yet disturbing: a familiar gesture or scene, but one surrounded by a questioning silence. The question is not, 'What does this mean?' but, 'What does this mean *now*?'

This, again, is Foucault's question of modernity: 'What is happening now?' A decade before the lectures on Kant and the Enlightenment, Foucault had suggested another answer in his work on film and popular memory (1989). Public memory is created to replace historical knowledge, he implied, whilst history is written in order to construct public memory. Thus a seemingly endless cycle of reproduction and reinforcement is always already in train. Foucault also observed, however, that memory works at its own pace, so that the attribution of memory to a particular set of circumstances, or singular circumstance, is difficult to maintain. There is a dynamic relationship between events, historical developments, and memory. The metamorphosis of this continuing reaction into some kind of cultural product that exemplifies public memory must be understood as merely a stage in a long, possibly unending process. If an event is categorised by its status as a mass spectacle, then a memory emerges as a product of the public imaginary. The mass becomes a public partly through the experience of producing memory for its own consumption. So Foucault ends up making a similar point to Kracauer. In the twentieth century, public space – the space of publicness – has existed in cultural products more than it has in the formal institutions of civil society. This is certainly the case in the various imaginaries, sometimes complementary and sometimes jarringly dissonant, to be found in Chinese cinema today.

Cinema as mass medium

In this chapter, we have suggested some things that media studies might learn from closer attention to cinema – which now appears historically to have been the definitively *mass* medium – and some things that film studies might learn from rethinking cinema and film spectatorship in the light of broader debates about modernity and modern publics.

The lesson of cinema for a theory of the modern media is simply this: that Hegel's disciplined and attentive reading of the newspaper is not the only way of being in public. Rational deliberation and political activity are not to be lightly dismissed, but nor should they be fetishised. Critical engagements with a public imaginary happen, however roughly and readily, in the nickelodeons of turn-of-the-century New York, on a Monday afternoon in suburban London movie houses, in Weimar picture palaces, and in the coded provocations of contemporary Chinese films. The history of publicness is also the history of distraction, of irony, of popular remembering.

Cinema thus recasts many of the assumptions about mass culture and the public sphere that are part of the conceptual legacy of the Frankfurt School. Even the notion of 'the progressive text' turns out to be closer in spirit to the cultural despair of the first generation of Frankfurt School theorists than to the scientific pretensions of Althusserianism. The guerrilla publicness proposed by Narboni and Comolli, whereby politically savvy film spectators pick up on knowing moments of critique, only really makes sense in totalitarian societies. That is pretty much how Theodor Adorno and Max Horkheimer, scarred by the experience of Nazi Germany, experienced the Hollywood-dominated mass culture of their disconcerting new home in the USA. In their chapter on 'The culture industry as mass deception', written in the 1940s, they denounced the consumer culture which Kracauer saw as an inescapable fact of modernity. Its apparent freedom 'everywhere proves to be freedom to choose what is always the same' (1979: 167). This gloomy anti-modernism was shared by Narboni and Comolli. They saw French society in the 1960s not as a flawed, imperfect, and often cynical democracy, but as repressive and incipiently totalitarian. It was only this Manichean political imagery that enabled them to present politically informed movie watching as a kind of heroism.

Even a second-generation Frankfurt intellectual such as Habermas failed, at least in his early work, to rid himself entirely of this melodramatic picture of culture and politics. That is why we reject his early treatment of publicness as a normative ideal of communication free from external constraint. We have turned to the more worldly, accommodating assessment of mass culture to be found in figures on the fringes of the Frankfurt School, such as Kracauer. If it exists anywhere, the practice of publicness involves an inventive, creative and mundane engagement with the dense symbolic *now* we inhabit. Purists may object that the ideological saturation of popular films and other media products makes them instruments of mass domination and control. But if publicness, a pragmatic critique of what is and an exploration of alternative ways of thinking and being, cannot be worked through there, then we have to say that the public sphere exists only as a non-place of deluded nostalgia.

For the study of film, we hope that our approach may contribute to an understanding of what Miriam Hansen calls the public dimension of the cinematic institution. This offers an alternative to overpoliticised, overtextualised, or overpsychologised conceptions of film. In tracing what it is that cinema has mediated, we have attempted to show that spectatorship not only invokes historically specific and technologically determinate modes of perception and interpretation, but also embodies, institutionally and textually, ways of being and acting in the symbolic space of public life.

Endnotes

1 The argument in this section is made, in similar terms, in Donald (1998).
2 *Öffentlichkeit* is often better translated as 'public-*ness*' rather than as 'the public *sphere*'.
3 Here we follow Laura Marcus's argument.
4 'Public imaginary' is based on the concept of the *social imaginary* developed by the philosopher and psychoanalyst Cornelius Castoriadis. A social imaginary is something like a grammar of social action. It makes social action possible, but at the same time it constrains it (see Curtis, 1997; for a useful discussion of Castoriadis, see Thompson, 1984).
5 Examples include *One and Eight* (Zhang Junzhao, 1983), *Yellow Earth* (Chen Kaige, 1984), *The Big Parade* (Chen Kaige, 1985), *Army Nurse* (Hu Mei, 1985), *The Black Cannon Incident* (Huang Jianxin, 1985), *Red Sorghum* (Zhang Yimu, 1987), *Ju Dou* (Zhang Yimu, 1989), *Bloody Morning* (Li Shaohong, 1990), and *Family Portrait* (Li Shaohong, 1992).

References

Adorno, Theodor and Horkheimer, Max 1979: *Dialectic of enlightenment*. London: Verso; first published 1944.

Apter, David and Saich, Tony 1994: *Revolutionary discourse in Mao's Republic*. Berkeley, CA: University of California Press.

Berry, Chris (ed.) 1991: *Perspectives on Chinese cinema*. London: British Film Institute.

Calhoun, Craig (ed.) 1992: *Habermas and the public sphere*. Cambridge, MA: MIT Press.

Charney, Leo and Schwartz, Vanessa R. (eds) 1995: *Cinema and the invention of modern life*. Berkeley, CA, Los Angeles, CA, and London: University of California Press.

Chow, Rey 1995: *Primitive passions: visuality, sexuality, ethnography and contemporary Chinese cinema*. New York: Columbia University Press.

Clark, Paul 1987: *Chinese cinema: culture and politics since 1989*. Cambridge: Cambridge University Press.

Crary, Jonathan 1995: Unbinding vision: Manet and the attentive observer. In Charney, L. and Schwartz, V.R. (eds), *Cinema and the invention of modern life*. Berkeley, CA, Los Angeles, CA, and London: University of California Press.

Crary, Jonathan 1996: Dr. Mabuse and Mr. Edison. In Ferguson, Russell (ed.), *Art and film since 1945: hall of mirrors*. Los Angeles, CA: Museum of Contemporary Art/Monacelli Press.

Curtis, David Ames (ed.) 1997: *The Castoriadis reader*. Oxford: Basil Blackwell.

Donald, James 1998: Perpetual noise: thinking about media regulation. *Continuum* 12(2): 217–32.

Donald, James, Friedberg, Anne and Marcus, Laura 1998: *Close Up, 1927–1933: cinema and modernism*. London: Cassell.

Donald, Stephanie 1996: Women reading Chinese films: between Orientalism and silence. *Screen* **36**(4): 325–46.

Donald, Stephanie 1997: Landscape and agency: *Yellow Earth* and the demon lover. *Theory, Culture and Society* **14**(1): 97–112.

Foucault, Michel 1986: Kant on Enlightenment and revolution. *Economy and Society* **15**(1): 88.

Foucault, Michel 1989: Film and popular memory. In *Foucault Live*. New York: *Semiotext(e)*; first published in *Cahiers du Cinéma*, 1974.

Friedberg, Anne 1992: *Window shopping: cinema and the postmodern*. Berkeley, CA, Los Angeles, CA, and London: University of California Press.

Garnham, Nicholas 1992: The media and the public sphere. In Calhoun, C. (ed.), *Habermas and the public sphere*. Cambridge, MA: MIT Press.

Gunning, Tom 1986: The cinema of attraction[s]. *Wide Angle*, **8**(3–4): 63–70.

Habermas, Jürgen 1962: *Strukturwandel der Öffentlichkeit*. Neuwied and Berlin: Luchterhand (2nd edn, Frankfurt: Suhrkamp, 1989).

Habermas, Jürgen 1989: *The structural transformation of the public sphere*. Cambridge, MA: MIT Press.

Hansen, Miriam 1991: *Babel and Babylon: spectatorship in American silent film*. Cambridge, MA: Harvard University Press.

Hansen, Miriam 1995: America, Paris, the Alps: Kracauer (and Benjamin) on cinema and modernity. In Charney, L. and Schwartz, V. (eds), *Cinema and the invention of modern life*. Berkeley, CA, Los Angeles, CA, and London: University of California Press.

Hegel, Georg Wilhelm Friedrich 1974: Aphorismen aus der Jenenser Zeit, No. 31. In Hoffmeister, J. (ed.), *Dokumente zu Hegels Entwicklung*. Stuttgart-Bad Cannstatt: Frommann.

Kant, Immanuel 1991: *Political writings*, 2nd edn, ed. Hans Reiss. Cambridge: Cambridge University Press.

Keane, John 1991: *The media and democracy*. Cambridge: Polity Press.

Klinger, Barbara 1984: 'Cinema/ideology/criticism' revisited: the progressive text. *Screen* **25**(1): 36–41.

Lu, Sheldon Hsiao-ping 1997: *Transnational Chinese cinemas: identity, nationhood, gender*. Honolulu, HI: University of Hawaii Press.

Lyman, H. Miller 1996: *Science and politics in post-Mao China: the politics of knowledge*. Seattle, WA, and Washington, DC: University of Washington Press.

Narboni, Jean and Comolli, Jean-Louis 1977: Cinema/ideology/criticism. In *Screen Reader 1*, London: SEFT.

Price, Monroe E. 1995: *Television, the public sphere, and national identity*. Oxford: Clarendon Press.

Taylor, Charles 1995: Invoking civil society. In Goodin, Robert E. and Pettit, Philip (eds), *Contemporary political philosophy: an anthology*, Oxford: Basil Blackwell.

Thompson, John B. 1984: *Studies in the theory of ideology*, Cambridge: Polity Press.

Thompson, John B. 1995: *The media and modernity: a social theory of the media*. Cambridge: Polity Press.

Thompson, John O. 1979: Up Aporia Creek. *Screen Education* **31**, Summer.

Wang, Jing 1996: *High culture fever: politcs, aesthetics, and ideology in Deng's China*, Berkeley, CA: University of California Press.

Yau, Esther 1991: *Yellow Earth*: Western analysis and a non-Western text. In Berry, Chris (ed.), *Perspectives on Chinese cinema*. London: British Film Institute.

Yue, Meng 1993: Female images and national myth. In Barlow, Tani (ed.), *Gender politics in modern China: writing and feminism*. Durham, NC: Duke University Press.

Zhang, Xudong 1997: *Chinese modernism in the era of reform*, Durham, NC: Duke University Press.

Zhang, Yingjin 1996: *The city in Chinese literature and film*. Stanford, CA: Stanford University Press.

8 The politics of cultural address in a 'transitional' cinema: a case study of Indian popular cinema

Ravi S. Vasudevan

Recent discussions of cinema and national identity in the 'third world' context have tended, by and large, to cluster around the concept of a 'third cinema'. Here the focus has been on recovering or reinventing local aesthetic and narrative traditions against the homogenising impulses of Hollywood in its domination over markets and normative standards. One of the hallmarks of third cinema theory has been its firmly unchauvinist approach to the 'national'. In its references to wider international aesthetic practices third cinema asserts but problematises the boundaries between nation and other. In the process, it also explores the ways in which the suppressed internal others of the nation, whether of class, sub- or counter-nationality, ethnic group, or gender, can find a voice.[1]

A substantial lacuna in this project has been any sustained understanding of the domestic commercial cinema in the 'third world'. This is important because in certain countries such as India the commercial film has, since the dawn of the 'talkies', successfully marginalised Hollywood's weight in the domestic market. This is not to claim that it has functioned within an entirely self-referential autarchy. The Indian popular cinema stylistically integrated aspects of the world 'standard', and has also been influential in certain foreign markets. But it constitutes something like a 'nation-space' against the dominant norms of Hollywood, and so ironically fulfils aspects of the role which the avant garde third cinema proclaims as its own.

Clearly, the difference in verbal, as opposed to narrative and cinematic, language cannot be the major explanation for this autonomy, for other national cinemas have succumbed to the rule of the Hollywood film. Instead, it is in the peculiarities of the Indian commercial film as an entertainment form that we may find the explanation for its ascendancy over the home market. In the Indian case the theoretical silence around the specificity of the commercial cinema is due not so much to third cinema discourse but to the discourses and institutions of art cinema in the 1950s which refused to consider seriously the commercial film as a focus of critical discussion.

Indian commercial cinema has exerted an international presence in countries of Indian immigration as in East Africa, Mauritius, the Middle East, and Southeast Asia, but also in a significant swathe of Northern Africa.[2] Here it has often been regarded by the local intelligentsia and film industry in as resentful and suspicious a way as the Hollywood cinema in Europe.[3] On the other hand, there are instances when the Bombay film's penetration of certain markets is not viewed as a threat. The popularity of the Hindi cinema in the former Soviet Union is a case in point. Such phenomena make one think of a certain arc of narrative form separate from, if overlapping at points, the larger hegemony exercised by Hollywood. From the description of the cultural 'peculiarities' of the Bombay cinema which follows, one could speculate whether its narrative form has a special resonance in 'transitional' societies. The diegetic world of this cinema is primarily governed by the logic of kinship relations, and its plot driven by family conflict. The system of dramaturgy is a melodramatic one, displaying the characteristic ensemble of manichaeism, bipolarity, the privileging of the moral over the psychological, and the deployment of coincidence in plot structures. And the relationship between narrative, performance sequence, and action spectacle is loosely structured in the fashion of a cinema of attractions.[4] In addition to these features, the system of narration incorporates Hollywood codes of continuity editing in a fitful, unsystematic fashion, relies heavily on visual forms such as the tableau and inducts cultural codes of looking of a more archaic sort.

At first glance, there would appear to be a significant echoing here of the form of early Euro-American cinema, indicating that what appeared as a fairly abbreviated moment in the history of Western cinema has defined the long-term character of this influential cinema of 'another world'. What is required here is a comparative account of narrative forms in 'transitional' societies which might set out a different story of the cinema than the dominant Euro-American one. However, to talk about transition might imply that such cinemas are destined to follow paths already set earlier. In fact, these cinemas may pose problems which will not admit of similar solutions. The problem of transition poses a cultural politics centred on the way local forms reinvent themselves to establish dialogue with and assert difference from universal models of narration and subjectivity. Recent currents in international film study have sought to recast the opposition between local and universally hegemonic norms of narration into a dialectical relationship. Here the specificity of particular cultural histories – European and American as much as 'third world' – have been constructed to understand the national and regional contexts in which the cinema was instituted,[5] how it came to assume an identity, became 'ours'.[6] At issue, then, is how traditions of identity, aesthetic form, and cultural address are deployed for a politics of creative adaptation and interrogation of social transformation in a colonial and post-colonial world. To examine this process, I will take examples primarily from the Bombay cinema, but will also refer to films from other regional film cultures in the period from the 1930s through to the first decade after Independence was won, in 1947.

In exploring these issues, I want to analyse the various types of cultural adaptation involved without losing sight of certain larger political frames. For the problem of Indian popular cinema lies not only at the interface between the local and the global in the constitution of a politics of cultural difference, but also in terms of the internal hierarchies that are involved in the constitution of a national culture. The formation of a national market is a crucial aspect of these multilayered relations of domination and subordination. Bombay became ascendant in the home market only in the 1950s. Earlier, Pune in Maharashtra and Calcutta in Bengal were important centres of film production, catering to the Marathi- and Bengali-speaking 'regional' audience as well as to the Hindi audience, the largest linguistic market in the country. Although these regional markets continued to exist, Bombay became the main focus of national film production. This ascendancy was curtailed by the emergence of important industries in Tamilnadu, Andhra Pradesh, and Kerala, producing films in Tamil, Telugu, and Malayalam. From the 1980s these centres produced as many and often more films than Bombay.[7] There has been a certain equivalence in the narrative form of these cinemas, but each region contributed its distinct features to the commercial film. In the Tamil and Telugu cases the cinema also has a strong link with the politics of regional and ethnic identity. In recent times the cinemas of the south have also made a greater effort to diversify their products than the Bombay industry.

The domestic hegemony achieved by the commercial cinema has had ambivalent implications for the social and political constitution of its spectator. All of India's cinemas were involved in constructing a certain abstraction of national identity; by national identity I mean here not only the pan-Indian one, but also regional constructions of national identity. This process of abstraction suppresses other identities, either through stereotyping or through absence. The Bombay cinema has a special position here, because it positions other national/ethnic/socio-religious identities in stereotypical ways under an overarching north Indian, majoritarian Hindu identity. The stereotypes of the 'southerner' (or 'Madrasi', a term which dismissively collapses the entire southern region), the Bengali, the Parsi, the Muslim, the Sikh, and the Christian occupy the subordinate positions in this universe. Bombay crystallised as the key centre for the production of national fictions just at the moment when the new state came into existence, so its construction of the national narrative carries a particular force.[8] In the last part of this chapter, I want to explore how such a national hegemony came to take shape in the cinema through a discussion centred on how relations between the majority Hindu population and the crucial Muslim minority have been represented in the Bombay cinema.

Indian popular cinema genres and discourses of transformation

Arguments for cultural transformation have defined Indian cinema from very early on in its history. The key theme in these discussions was the social and cultural implications of film genres. In the initial phase, Indian cinema was dominated by the mythological film, which used Hindu myths as their major resource. Very soon, other genres developed, including the social, which addressed issues of modern day life, the costume film, or the 'historical', the spectacular stunt or action-dominated film, and the devotional film, which recounted tales of popular saintly figures who criticised religious orthodoxy and hierarchy.

Our knowledge about the terms on which the industry addressed spectators through genre, and the way spectators received genres, are as yet rudimentary. Steve Hughes's work on exhibition practices in early South Indian cinema argues that Hollywood and European action serials catered to lower-class audiences.[9] And a 1950s' essay by an industry observer[10] noted that stunt, mythological, and costume films would attract a working-class audience. The film industry based this evaluation on two assumptions: first, it is believed that the plebeian spectators would delight in spectacle and emotion, uncluttered by ideas and social content. Second, publicity strategies used by the industry suggest that exhibitors believed that such audiences were susceptible to a religious and moral rhetoric. In the industry's view, therefore, the lower-class audience was motivated by visceral or motor-orientated pleasures and moral imperatives.

On the other hand, the film industry understood the devotional and social films, with their emphasis on social criticism, to be the favoured genres of the middle class. A running theme in social films was the need to maintain indigenous identities against the fascination for Western cultural behaviour. While this has become part of the armature of films devoted to contemporary society down to the present day, a substantial vein of social films was devoted to making a critique of Indian society and setting up an agenda for change. Recent discussions of Tamil film of the 1930s and 1940s argue that there were repressive and disciplinary elements to the agenda for a modern social grounding of film narratives.[11] The agenda here was for the social film to displace the mythological and the superstitious and irrational culture it founded. In the 1930s, a host of studios emerged who employed scriptwriters to develop reformist narrative, and an alliance emerged in these decades between literature and cinema, with films adapting important novels as their source material.[12]

However, by the 1950s, the industry reformulated genre and audience appeal. After the collapse of the major studios, Bombay Talkies, Prabhat, New Theatres, the new, speculative climate of the industry encouraged an eye for the quick profit and therefore the drive for a larger audience. This encouraged the induction of the sensational attractions of action, spectacle, and dance into the social film, a process explained by industry observers as a lure for the mass audience. Industry observers clearly believed the genre label to be quite superficial, and, indeed, there is something inflationary about a large number of films released in the 1950s being called 'socials'. The label of the 'social' film perhaps gave the cinematic entertainment that cobbled sensational attractions together in a slapdash way a certain legitimacy. However, arguably, the mass audiences earlier conceived of as being attracted only by sensation and themes of moral affirmation were now being solicited by an omnibus form which also included a rationalist discourse as part of its 'attractions'.[13]

We will observe a replaying of these discussions in more recent paradigms of the Indian popular cinema. One of my arguments will be that, rather than oppose different types of audience disposition on the ground of genre and subject matter, one needs to explore how forms of address may set up certain similar problems in constituting spectatorial subjectivity, whether this is played out within the domain of the mythological or the social. Especially important here is an agenda of moving beyond the deployment in Indian cinema of a rhetoric of traditional morality and identity to a focus on how cinematic address, the way spectators are positioned in terms of vision, auditory address, and narrative intelligibility, may complicate and rework the overt terms of narrative coherence.

Dominant currents in contemporary criticism

Here I want briefly to summarise some of the dominant currents in the contemporary criticism of the Indian popular cinema and the nature of its spectator. The dominant view is that of a tradition of film criticism associated with Satyajit Ray and the Calcutta Film Society in the 1950s. This school of criticism, which has proven influential in subsequent mainstream film criticism, arraigned the popular cinema for its derivativeness from American cinema, the melodramatic externality and stereotyping of its characters, and especially for its failure to focus on the psychology of human interaction. In these accounts the spectator of the popular film emerges as an immature, indeed infantile, figure, one bereft of the rationalist imperatives required for the Nehru era's project of national reconstruction.[14]

Recent analyses of the popular cinemas in the 'non-Western' world have indicated that the melodramatic mode has, with various indigenous modifications, been a characteristic form of narrative and dramaturgy in societies undergoing the transition to modernity.[15] Criticisms of this prevalent mode have taken the particular form that I have just specified, and have had both developmentalist and democratic components. The implication was that, insofar as the melodramatic mode was grounded in an anti-rationalist ethos, it would undercut the rational, critical outlook required for the development of a just, dynamic, and independent nation.[16]

This premise of modern film criticism has been taken in rather different directions. The critic Chidananda Das Gupta emerges from this earlier tradition, being one of the founder members of the Calcutta Film Society in 1948. But his book, *The Painted Face*,[17] pays greater attention to the commercial cinema than realist criticism ever has. Here his analysis develops certain insights about the narrative structure of the popular film, but it is still dogged by assumptions which spring from the earlier terms of reference. These relate to the belief that the commercial film of the early period and again after the 1950s primarily catered to a spectator who had not severed his or her ties from the countryside and so had a traditional or premodern relationship to the image, one which incapacitated him or her from distinguishing between image and reality.[18] Another of Das Gupta's theses is that the pre-rationalist spectator, *en route* from countryside to city in his mental outlook, was responsive to Bombay cinema's focus on family travails and identity, a focus which displaces attention from the larger social domain. He describes the spectator caught up in the psychic trauma brought about by threatened loss of the mother and the struggle for adult identity as adolescent and self-absorbed or 'totalist'.[19]

We have echoes here of the realist criticism of the 1950s in its reference to the spectator of the commercial film as infantile. Following on from earlier discourses underwriting the cinema as a vehicle of modernisation, he exempts the social-reform-orientated cinema of the 1930s through the 1950s from this general formulation, and underwrites its attempts to transform social perception in rationalist directions.

Such a conception of the spectator ultimately has political implications. Das Gupta sees this social and psychic configuration reflecting the gullible mentality that enabled the rise to power of the actor-politicians of the south, M.G. Ramachandran and N.T. Rama Rao.[20] The naive spectator actually believed his screen idols to be capable of the prowess they displayed on-screen. In Das Gupta's view the rational outlook required for the development of a modern nation-state is still lacking, and the popular cinema provides us with an index of the cognitive impairment of the majority of the Indian people. There is a sociological underpinning to this argument, that the middle class are bearers of a rationalist discourse and the attributes of responsible citizenship, and that the popular cinema in its earlier and later manifestations is the domain of first a premodern, and then a decultured, lumpenised mass audience.

This psychological and social characterisation of the popular spectator is pervasive, even if it is not used to the same ends as Das Gupta. The social psychologist Ashish Nandy, although working outside the realist tradition, shares some of its assumptions about the psychological address of the commercial film.[21] Nandy argues that the dominant spectator of the popular cinema holds on to a notion of traditional community quite remote from the outlook of the modern middle class; as such, this spectator is attracted to a narrative which ritually neutralises the discomfiting features of social change, those atomising modern thought-patterns and practices which have to be adopted for reasons of survival. Nandy embraces the cultural indices of a subjectivity which is not governed by the rationalist psychology and reality orientation of a contested modernity. In this sense he valorises that which Das Gupta sees as a drawback.

So a psychical and sociological matrix for understanding the address of the commercial Bombay film to its spectator, deriving in some respects from the realist criticism of the 1950s, has been extended to the more explicitly psychoanalytical interpretations of spectatorial dispositions and cognitive capacities. Ironically, these premises are shared by those critical of the commercial film and its spectator for their lack of reality orientation and by those who see popular cinema resisting modern forms of consciousness.

The most complex attempt to transcend these oppositions between tradition and modernity in thinking about Indian cinema is the recent work of Madhava Prasad. In his *Ideology of the Hindi film*[22] he argues that many of the dimensions identified as composing a non-modern outlook in Indian popular films are in fact constructed under the aegis of an ideology of modernity. For the rhetoric and narrative form of modernity has to produce a traditional 'other' in order to overcome and institute a new form of subjectivity. Prasad situates this cinematic project in terms of certain overarching political and ideological formations in post-colonial India. Foremost here is the concept of passive revolution, where a modernising state and its constituency in the bourgeoisie and bureaucracy have to adapt their transformative agenda to the realities of precapitalist power. In terms of narrative form, the political compromise at the level of the state is represented by what Prasad calls the 'feudal family romance'. This form releases a series of new drives – to individual romantic fulfilment and the formation of the couple for the nuclear family, consumerist orientations, affiliations to an impersonal state form – but ultimately subordinates them to the rule of 'traditionally regulated social relationships'. This regime of narrative coherence depicts landed gentry, urban gentlemen, representatives of social and religious orthodoxy, as ultimately capable of fulfilling or neutralising the energies unleashed by new forces. In this regard, the feudal family functions as a way both of disavowing change and, more subtly, of allowing for it without disturbing social hierarchies. This dominant narrative form exists over a long period in Prasad's rendition, running from the 1940s through to the end of the 1960s, when the ruling configuration changes and the cinematic institution is diversified under the aegis of state support and through new developments within the film industry.

The politics of Indian melodrama

Where for Das Gupta the popular form subjects the spectator to pre-modern perceptions, for Prasad the pre-modern is an ideological construction rather than a cognitive problem. The ideology of his 'feudal family romance' echoes, but is significantly distinct from, melodrama theory as it has evolved in the West.

For Peter Brooks, melodrama emerged in the nineteenth century as a form which spoke of a post-sacred universe in which the certainties of traditional meaning and hierarchical authority had been displaced.[23] The melodramatic narrative constantly makes an effort to recover this lost security, but meaning comes to be increasingly founded in the personality. Characters take on essential, psychic resonances corresponding to family identitites and work out forbidden conflicts and desires. In the process, the social dimension collapses into the familial and, indeed, the family itself becomes a microcosm of the social level.

The distinction is that the issue posed by melodrama for Prasad is not simply one of striving to recover sacred forms and traditional hierarchical meaning, but a deployment of this desire for a strategy of transformation. Here, Prasad sees the imbrication of familial and social levels as political, as a register of the way pre-capitalist enclaves function as the ideological integument under conditions of social transformation. He compares the dominant Indian narrative form of his construction to the aristocratic romances of early European stage melodrama. Implicitly, the drives to alter this form are, in turn, comparable to the more democratic social vision of later melodrama.

Prasad's identification of a hierarchical coding of address in popular narrative form leads to a suggestive thesis about the informal prohibition on the private sphere and individuated characterisation in Indian popular cinema. The argument centres on the prohibition on kissing. Whereas conventional discourses on the cinema argue that the prohibition maintains a sense of national identity against the inroads of Western cultural behaviour, Prasad places it within the coordinates of power of the dominant narrative form. He suggests that the feudal family romance seeks to contain those romantic drives that threaten traditional social authority with the spectre of secession. Here the kiss marks the incipient space of privacy and the nuclear family, understood as an infringement of the overwhelmingly public monitoring of sexuality and subjecthood under feudal scopic regimes.

Prasad argues that the pre-emption of such types of characterisation have ramifications for the forms of knowledge and modes of performance in popular cinema. Instead of a narrative form constructed around enigmas, the popular cinema is governed by forms of speech and narrative mechanisms deriving from the domain of the already-known.[24] The spectator of this cinema is then addressed through the presentation of a pre-interpreted symbolic order in contrast to the spectator of classical realist cinema who is complicit in the conversion of the raw material of re-presentation into narrative meaning.

I would like to hold onto Nandy's insight about community forms of address in complicating the terms of this very original and systematic thesis. Here one should consider Nandy's invocation of tradition, often rendered in a way that leaves the historical coordinates of how tradition is constituted unexamined, as a heuristic, an enabling function or stance with which to critique modern forms of political and cultural organisation.

In terms of narrative form, the popular imperative engages in a series of transactions, with methods and idioms marked as traditional or culturally distinctive as well as those defined as modern. Here, I would like to consider the location of the spectator's position around three issues.

- How is the ideology of the traditional constituted in cinematic narration?
- What is the function of cinematic techniques of subjectivity in the construction of narrative space?
- How does the overall attraction-based, presentational rather than re-presentational field of the popular film system address the spectator?

These questions amount to an engagement with a history of the methods of film narration, film style, as well as a history of the relationship between screen practices and audience reception.

Iconicity, frontality, and the tableau frame

The question of mode of address concerns how objects and figures are located with respect to the look of the spectator within the spatial and temporal coordinates of scenic construction. Central here is the aesthetics of frontality and iconicity noted for Indian films in certain phases and genres by Ashish Rajadhyaksha and Geeta Kapur.[25,26] The iconic mode is not used by these writers in its precise semiotic sense, to identify a relation of resemblance, but to identify a meaningful condensation of image. The term has been used to situate the articulation of the mythic within painting, theatre, and cinema, and could be conceived of as cultural work which seeks to bind a multiply layered dynamic into a unitary image. In Geeta Kapur's definition the iconic is 'an image into which symbolic meanings converge and in which moreover they achieve stasis'.[27] This concept of the iconic needs to be grounded within a conception of *mise en scène*, and it is here that the question of frontal address surfaces. At one level frontality would mean placing the camera at a 180° plane to the figures and objects constitutive of filmic space. These may display attributes of direct address, as in the look of characters into the camera, but a frontal, direct address is relayed in other ways, as in the way the knowledge of the spectator is drawn upon in constructing the scene, through the stylised performance, ritual motifs, and auditory address that arise from a host of Indian aesthetic and performance traditions.[28] This position of knowledge is not one which relays the spectator through a hermeneutic play, the enigma of what is to come, but through existing paradigms of narrative knowledge, although these may be subject to reworking. In genres such as the mythological film, the narrative process assumes audience knowledge of the narrative totality it refers to, so that a fragmentary, episodic structure can be deployed. The film song displays this function of 'frontal' address across genres, reaching over and beyond the space of the scene, locking the spectator into a direct auditory relay.

Frontal planes in cinematic composition are used to relay this work of iconic condensation and also to group characters and objects in the space of the tableau. In Peter Brooks's formulation the tableau in melodrama gives the 'spectator the opportunity to see meanings represented, emotions and moral states rendered in clear visible signs'.[29] And Barthes has noted that it is

> a pure cut-out segment with clearly defined edges, irreversible and incorruptible; everything that surrounds it is banished into nothingness, remains unnamed, while everything that it admits within its field is promoted into essence, into light, into view ... (it) is intellectual, it has something to say (something moral, social) but is also says it knows how this must be done.[30]

Barthes also argues that the tableau has a temporal dimension, what he calls the 'pregnant moment' caught between past and future.[31] In the course of this argument, I will show that the temporality of the tableau can be deployed cinematically, its shape setting the geometrical terms of the temporal construction of the scene as it extends over a series of shots. The tableau also displays interruptive, interventionist functions in the flow of scenic construction. In my argument, the function of this spatial figure is to encode a socially and communally defined address to the spectator.

The reconstruction of the icon

I will illustrate the dynamic employment of the frontal, iconic mode, and of tableau framing in a sequence from Mehboob Khan's saga of peasant life, *Mother India* (1957). This segment presents, and then upsets, a pair of relatively stable iconic instances. The mother-in-law, Sundar Chachi, is centred through a number of tableau shots taken from different angles to highlight her authority in the village just after she has staged a spectacular wedding for her son. This representation of Sundar Chachi takes place in the courtyard of her house. The other instance is of the newly wedded daughter-in-law, Radha, shown inside the house, as she massages her husband's feet. It is a classic image of the devout Hindu wife.[32]

The two instances are destabilised because of the information that the wedding has forced Sundar Chachi to mortgage the family land. The information diminishes her standing, causing her to leave the gathering and enter her house. Simultaneously, it also undermines Radha's iconic placement as submissive, devout wife. As the larger space of the scene, the actual relationship between the inside and the outside, remains unspecified, the relationship is suggested when Radha, hearing the conversation, looks up and away towards off-screen left. The likelihood of this positioning is further strengthened when Sundar Chachi enters the house, and, looking in the direction of off-screen right, confesses that she has indeed mortgaged her land. There is the use here of a Hollywood eyeline match, where the direction of looks cast is consistent with the convention that characters separated into successive shots face each other in space. The women are narrativised out of their static, iconic position through narrative processes of knowledge circulation and character movement, and by the deployment of Hollywood codes of off-screen sound and eyeline match.

The mobilisation of Radha out of one convention of iconic representation is completed when she assumes maternal functions extending beyond her family, and over the domain of village community and nation. In turn, she becomes the focal point of community norms, and her gaze acquires punitive functions in delineating the limits of permissible action. A process of the narrative dispersal of one iconic figure is thus finally brought to a close by instituting a new iconic figure to ground subjectivity. Central here is a particular reinscription in the cinema of a discourse of the image and the look in indigenous conventions.

Darsana

I refer here to *darsana*, the power exercised by the authoritative image in Hindu religious culture. In this practice, the devotee is permitted to behold the image of the deity, and is privileged and benefited by this permission, in contrast to a concept of looking that assigns power to the beholder by reducing the image to an object of the look.[33] *Darsana* has a wider purchase, being invoked in discourses of social and political authority as well. In a certain rendering of the category of *darsana* as an authoritarian form, social status derives from the degree of access which social groups and individuals have to a central icon of authority, whether of kingship, divine authority, or the extended patriarchal family and its representatives.[34] This eligibility then rests on very hierarchically coded criteria of social rank. There is a task here of identifying how the *darsanic* locates characters and is responded to by them within cinematic narration. One hypothesis would be that an authoritative figure, symbol, or space (temple, landlord's house, court of law) is mobilised to order the place of characters within a scene and over the time of the narrative. But if such a diegetic instance is located, it is not necessary that characters abide by the positions they are assigned by it, nor that filmic techniques subordinate the spectator to the sway of *darsanic* authority.

Indeed, to assume otherwise could lead to the conclusion that the cinema is merely the vehicle of an archaic way of inscribing power on the visual field. Instead of seeing the discourse of *darsana* framing cinematic narration, we need to think of *darsana* as being enframed and reconstructed by it. Here, the localised deployment of filmic techniques in the micro-narration of a scene – editing, shot-distance and angle, camera movement, lighting, sound elements – alert us to how characters and spectators are being cinematically positioned in relation to the *darsanic*. The *darsanic* is not static, and generates new sources of authority from it, and in ways not entirely comprehensible in terms of established conventions. Thus, while much of the moral authority of Radha in *Mother India* derives from the preservation of her chastity, and thereby the assertion of her devotion to her absent husband, this patriarchal rhetoric is condensed along with other features, including a solidarity with other women, and an insistence on the maintenance of community norms.

The cinematic process of iconic reconstruction may in fact deploy and subordinate modern methods of subject construction modelled on Hollywood narration. By convention, the continuity system, and especially its point-of-view editing, is associated with the drives and perception of individuated characters. However, it is quite common in popular Hindi cinema to observe the yoking of such views to the bearer of *darsanic* authority. But the emergence of such enshrining views is tied to the dynamic of reconstruction, and is mobilised to the end of a patriarchal transformation.

To suggest the transactional basis on which popular cinema inducts those methods of narration marked as modern, I will cite an example from *Devdas* (Bimal Roy, 1955), a film based on a well-known Bengali novel by Sarat Chandra Chatterjee. Devdas, the son of a powerful landed family, is prohibited from marrying the girl he desires, Parvati, because of status differences. He is a classic renouncer figure of the type favoured in Indian storytelling, a figure who is unable or refuses to conform to the demands of society, and wastes away in the contemplation of that which he could never gain. I want to refer to a scene which employs continuity conventions to the highly 'traditional' end of deifying the male as object of desire. The sequence deals with Devdas's visit to Parvati's house, and indicates a strategy of narration whereby Parvati's point of view is used to underline the desirability and the authority exercised by Devdas's image. In this sequence, Parvati returns to her house to find her grandmother and mother discussing Devdas's arrival from the city, and the fact that he has not yet called upon them (Figure 8.1). Devdas, off-screen, calls from outside the door. From this moment, Parvati's auditory and visual attention dominates the narration. Before we can see Devdas entering the house, we withdraw with Parvati to her room upstairs (Figure 8.2), and listen along with her to the conversation taking place below (Figure 8.3). Devdas announces that he will go to see Parvati himself. In anticipation of Devdas's arrival Parvati hurriedly starts lighting a *diya*, devotional lamp (Figure 8.4), and the melody of a *kirtan*, a traditional devotional song expressing Radha's longing for Krishna, is played. We hear the sound of Devdas's footfalls on the stairs, and Parvati's anxiety to light the lamp before Devdas enters her room is caught by a suspenseful intercutting between her lighting of the lamp and shots of the empty doorway (Figure 8.5). The doorframe in this sequence suggests the shrine in which the divine idol is housed. Devdas's entry is shown in a highly deifying way; first his feet are shown in the doorway, followed by a cut to the lighted lamp. Finally his face is revealed. There follows a cut to

Figure 8.1 Parvati returns to her house to find her grandmother and mother discussing Devdas's arrival from the city.
Frame still from *Devdas* (1955); reproduced courtesy of National Film Archive of India.

Figure 8.2 Parvati withdraws to her room upstairs.
Frame still from *Devdas* (1955); reproduced courtesy of National Film Archive of India.

Figure 8.3 Parvati listens to the conversation taking place below.
Frame still from *Devdas* (1955); reproduced courtesy of National Film Archive of India.

Figure 8.4 In anticipation of Devdas's arrival, Parvati lights a devotional lamp.
Frame still from *Devdas* (1955); reproduced courtesy of National Film Archive of India.

Parvati, suggesting that this is the order through which she has seen Devdas's arrival (Figure 8.6). As she looks at him, conch shells, traditional accompaniment to the act of worship, are sounded. The future husband as deity, object of the worshipful gaze, is established by the narration's deployment of Parvati's point of view. Her lighting of the devotional lamp and the extra-diegetic sound of the *kirtan* and conch shells underline the devotional nature of the woman's relationship to the male image (Figure 8.7).

Figure 8.4 *continued*

Figure 8.5 Parvati's anxiety to light the lamp before Devdas enters her room is caught by a suspenseful intercutting between her lighting of the lamp and shots of the empty doorway.

Frame still from *Devdas* (1955); reproduced courtesy of National Film Archive of India.

(a)

Figure 8.6 Devdas's entry is shown in a highly deifying way: (a) first his feet are shown in the doorway; (b) followed by a cut to the lighted lamp; (c) finally his face is revealed.

Frame still from *Devdas* (1955); reproduced courtesy of National Film Archive of India.

(b)

(c)

Figure 8.6 *continued*

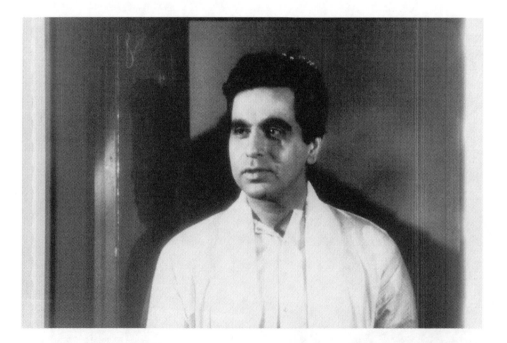

Figure 8.7 Parvati's lighting of the devotional lamp underlines the devotional nature of the woman's relationship to the male image.

Frame still from *Devdas* (1955); reproduced courtesy of National Film Archive of India.

Here we can see how the cinema reinscribes *darsana,* locating it within a new figure, that of the emergent if ultimately ineffectual patriarchal figure of Devdas, who cannot be assimilated to the reigning feudal order. And it does this in such a way as to both enable and limit the conditions of subjectivity. For, while the film mobilises point-of-view codes to represent the subjectivity of the woman, this is done in such a way as to constrain the field of her look by focusing the beloved within a discourse of divinity. This setting of certain limiting coordinates for the woman's look also significantly institutes a division between the incipient formation of a new domesticity and the wider external world: Devdas's enshrinement in the doorway converts the public space beyond the door into his domain, restricting the woman to domestic space.

Tableau, time, and subjectivity

A more complicated version of this pattern of looking is observable in Guru Dutt's *Pyaasa/Craving* (1957), a film which refers to but in many ways contraverts the narrative of *Devdas.* In the pertinent scene, the poet-hero Vijay refers to the prostitute, Gulab, as his wife in order to protect her from a policeman who is pursuing her. The prostitute is unaccustomed to such a respectful address, especially one suggestive of intimate ties to a man she loves, and is thrown into a sensual haze. Vijay ascends a stairway to the terrace of a building where he will pass the night. Gulab sees a troupe of devotional folk-singers, performing a Vaishnavite song, 'Aaj sajan mohe ang laga lo' (Take me in your arms today, O beloved) and follows Vijay up the stairs. The scene is structured by Gulab's desire for Vijay, expressed in the song, and these relations of desire are simultaneously relations of distance, as the woman follows, looks at, and almost touches the man she loves (who is entirely unaware of all this) but finally withdraws and flees as she believes herself unworthy of him.

The relation between devotional voice, devotee, and object of devotion determines the space of this scene, providing the coordinates for the extension and constraining of space. The relationship between characters is not one of the iconic frontality of traditional worship. The desired one is not framed in this way, for continuity codes dominate the scenic construction. Even in the scene I have cited from *Devdas,* continuity codes construct space and it is a shot/reverse-shot relationship which defines the ultimate moment of looking. The spectator is offered a rather complicated position. If we think of the male icon as a 'traditional' marker of authority and desire which anchors the view of the female devotee, as in *Devdas,* then the scene conforms to the logic of *darsana.*

However, within the *bhakti,* or devotional, tradition, while the female devotee's energy is channelled directly into the worship of the deity, without the mediation of the priest, the Lord still remains a remote figure. The devotional act thus becomes a somewhat excessive one, concentrating greater attention on the devotee than the devotional object,[35] and this is only underlined in the maintenance of Gulab's distance from Vijay, and his failure to see her. This rather complicated structure of spectatorship needs to be framed within the address relayed by the devotional voice. The space assigned this voice emerges from Gulab's look off-screen, but it remains autonomous, never sharing her space. The narration periodically cuts back to the singer, and cutting and camera movement closely follow the rhythms of the song. The soundtrack maintains a steady pitch to the singing, irrespective of how far the action moves away from the singer's (imaginary) space, and places it thereby at an extra-diegetic location.[36] The relatively stable articulation of these three points in the narrative construction – devotional voice, desiring woman, and her object – effects a dynamic, temporal deployment to the essentially spatial category of the tableau. The result for the spectator is neither the subordination of subjectivity to *darsanic* authority, whose circuit is left incomplete by withholding Vijay's authorizing *darsanic* look, nor the unmediated identification with the desiring woman, but a framing of these elements of scenic composition within the narrative community solicited by the *kirtan*. Here the audience is invited to participate in a culturally familiar idiom that reinvents itself by providing a supportive frame to the cultivation of new techniques for the representation of an individuated feminine subjectivity. However, the supportive frame of narrative community, while inducting a new view through the deployment of modern perceptual codes, cannot, it would seem, abjure the anchorage given by the authoritative object. In this instance, where the *darsanic* circuit is not completed, the woman ultimately lies outside the sanction provided by the man returning her look. Later, however, the *darsanic* circuit is completed, instituting a new paternalist form in the conclusion of the film. Gulab's view enshrines Vijay, as travelling point-of-view shots punctuate her running down towards the beloved as he appears at the doorway of her dwelling, and his return of her look acknowledges her eligibility to reside within the orbit of his gaze.

How the cinema deploys these discourses of visual and auditory authority, how it hierarchises them into its levels of narration, is the issue at stake: who authorises a view, locates a figure in narrative space, who speaks, who sees, who listens. Where these relations are organised to highlight the compact between the narrating instance and the spectator's attention, the place of the third look of the character is subordinated to the spectator's knowledge that it is she or he who looks and listens. As Ashish Rajadhyaksha has argued, in such instances, the concept of a third look codified by the requirements of an integral continuity narration emerges as a transaction between narrator and spectator, and does not acquire a decisive autonomy.[37] The discourse of narrative community is one such instance. But, in terms of Barthes's analysis of the tableau, narration may deploy an interventionist, intellectual rather than emotive use of this spatial figure, suggesting a distancing perspective rather than a shaping of spectatorial subjectivity into identification with characters. Thus, we may observe the emergence of a space in which the main characters are composed separately from the flow of character-grounded narrative awareness and development. The narration places us in a position superior to that of all the characters, and we are alerted to how different character attitudes are framed within normative and hierarchical social discourses. This address does not, I would argue, ask us to accept the norm, but highlights the inevitability of a social frame to meaning.

I have suggested how this works in *Andaz/Style* (Mehboob Khan, 1949).[38] However, while these community grounded and socially coded modes of direct address constitute a fundamental aspect of cinematic narration for the popular cinema, the character-driven codes of subjectivity and narration associated with Hollywood may stand quite independently of such an address, inducting another set of subjectivities or storytelling conventions into the architecture of filmic narrative. I have suggested how *Andaz* drew upon Hollywood narrative conventions in order to highlight the enigmatic dimensions of its female character's desires, and especially the conventions of hallucinations and dream to define her in terms of an ambivalent psychology and a transgressive if involuntary sexuality. Such conventions were drawn upon to be contained and disavowed. A nationalist modernising imperative had symbolically to contain those ideologically fraught aspects of modernity that derived from transformations in the social position and subjectivity of women. The result was a fascinatingly perverse and incoherent text, one whose ideological drives are complicated by the subjectivities it draws upon.[39]

I would suggest that these examples indicate that for popular Indian cinema the categories of public and private and of feudal and modern scopic regimes may not adequately comprehend the subjectivity offered the spectator, and that this would in turn have implications for the culture of citizenship. The rupturing of an integral, self-referential narrative space via direct address suggests a circuit of imaginary communication, indeed, a making of audience into imaginary community. The authorising voice of narrative community is not fixed, however. To complicate Prasad's insight, while speech may be pre-interpreted in the sense that characters do not speak in the register of everyday, naturalist conversation, but are vehicles of existing language systems, cinematic narration subjects these to a reconstitution which enables an inventive, dynamic address to contemporary issues. As I have suggested, the solicitation of the cinema audience into a familiar community of meaning via direct address may afford a certain movement, an outlining of new forms of subjectivity on the grid of the culturally recognisable. We have seen how this works in terms of a transgressive rendering of romance. An overt political address, bearing directly on questions of citizenship and state legitimacy, also emerges in new languages of direct address. The development of a new linguistic nationalist community in the direct address of the Dravida-Munnetra-Kazhagam-influenced Tamil cinema would be an obvious example.[40] In fact, Indian popular cinema has, throughout its history, deployed such modes of address to constitute imaginary political communities, around issues of social reform and nationalist mobilisation. Here, direct address may argue for change on somewhat different grounds than the protocols of narrative continuity, realism, and individual characterisation.

Community authorisation then rests alongside, and complicates, 'feudal' and 'modern' ways of organising narrative. Song sequences deployed from a host of musical traditions have often worked in this way, and, in cases such as the one I have cited from *Pyaasa*, have assumed the role of a narrational authority external to the main story. This is enacted by a source other than any of the fictional characters, and sometimes in a space separated out from theirs. In this sense the narrational song can be identified with the properties of extra-diegetic music. They both inhabit a location outside the fiction and shape a cultural space for the representation of characters. We are both inside and outside the story, tied at one moment to the seamless flow of a character-based narration from within, in the next attuned to a culturally familiar stance from without.

Not only does this narrating instance function to outline new types of subjectivity that in a sense emerge from within the community of meaning but it may also be deployed to offer a critical view on narrative development. In *Awara/Vagabond* (Raj Kapoor, 1951), the judge, Raghunath, expels his wife, Leela, on suspicion of bearing another man's child. The event is framed through a song critically invoking the mythical King Rama's expulsion of his wife Seeta, and performed by a troupe located separately from the main action. The critical stance offered by the song renders the iconic figure of the judge as an oppressive one, subjecting the *darsanic* to censure.[41]

The comic, deriving from earlier theatrical traditions of the *vidushak*, also left a mark as one of the staple figures of the commercial cinema.[42] Here the comic sometimes plays the role of a narrator external to the main narrative and is often engaged in a relationship of direct address to the audience. There is a certain didacticism involved in his functions, but this is a didacticism gone wrong, relaying authoritarian discourses voiced elsewhere through a figure entirely lacking the status and integrity carried by a *darsanic* rendering of such discourses. For example, in *Andaz*, V.H. Desai, as the charlatan and free-loading Professor Dharmadas Devdas Trivedi, or DDT (the assigning of a Brahmin name to the comic sends up the pretensions and parasitical features of upper-caste status claims), is a spokesman and even a narrative agent of what he claims to be authentic indigenous attitudes to marriage. Such attitudes are similar to those voiced by the film's patriarchal figure and his delegates, but when the comic is made their vehicle they are subjected to a lampooning idiom. In a more commonplace function, it is the very absurdity of the comic figure, quite obviously opposed to the larger-than-life attraction of the hero, which invites a less flattering point of identification for the audience, and thereby a certain narratorial distance towards the story. Further, in the very superfluousness of his functions, we could say that the comic was the spokesman within the story for a different order of storytelling, one which celebrates the disaggregative relationship to narrative and, indeed, makes coherent meaning within the world of the narrative a problematic agenda.

This would imply that, instead of only looking to the overall work of ideology that 'officially' organises the text, perhaps one should also attend to the fissiparous qualities of cinematic form to focus on the importance of non-continuity in evaluating the narrative worlds offered to the spectator. In terms of sensory experience, non-continuity would suggest a characteristic modern culture of distraction, where the spectator's world is governed by a multiplicity of focuses and not by a carefully calibrated, goal-orientated channelling of his or her investment in the narrative process. At issue here is the subjectivity arising from the development of this particular type of cinematic modernity.

The political terms of spectatorial subjectivity

The terms of cinematic narration I have sketched here are rather different from the notions of spectatorship which have emerged from that model of the successful commodity cinema, Hollywood. Historians and theoreticians of US cinema have underlined the importance of continuity editing in binding or suturing the spectator into the space of the fiction. The undercutting of direct address and the binding of the spectator into a hermetic universe on-screen heighten the individual psychic address and sideline the space of the auditorium as a social and collective viewing space. This very rich historiography and textual analysis, excellently synthesised in works by Miriam Hansen[43] and Thomas Elsaesser,[44] speaks of the fraught process through which US cinema's bourgeois address came into being. This work describes how social and ethnic peculiarities were addressed in the relation between early cinema and its viewers. The sites of filmic performance were institutions such as vaudeville, in which the one-reel and two-reel film was one in a series of 'acts' on the programme; all of these items, including films, tended to solicit audience interest by referring to the ethnic particularities of the audience. The process by which the cinema took over and came to develop its own entertainment space was a process of the formation of a national market in which the spectator had to be addressed in the broadest, non-ethnic, socially universal terms. Of course, what was actually happening was that a dominant white Anglo-Saxon norm came to be projected as universal. Along with this process there developed the guidelines for the construction of a universal spectator placed not in the auditorium but as an imaginary figure enmeshed in the very process of narration.

The mixed address of the Hindi cinema, along with the spaces which open up within the commercial film, the song and dance sequences, and comic skits, might suggest a rather different relationship of reception. Indeed, it recalls the notion of a 'cinema of attractions', a term developed by Tom Gunning to theorise the appeal of early Euro-American cinema.[45] In contrast to the Hollywood mode of continuity cinema or narrative integration, Gunning and Gaudreault argue that early cinema was exhibitionist. The character's look into the camera indicated an indifference to the realist illusion that the story tells itself. The films displayed a greater interest in relaying a series of views and sensations to their audience rather than following a linear narrative logic. These elements were to be increasingly transcended in Hollywood cinema's abstraction of the spectator as individuated consumer of its self-enclosed fictional world. In the process, the audience, earlier understood to be composed of workers and immigrants, was 'civilised' into appreciating the bourgeois virtues of a logical, cause-and-effect-driven and character-based narrative development.[46]

However, something rather more complicated is happening here. For the direct address of popular Indian cinema, while certainly inviting immersion in fragmentary ocular sensation and exhibitionist performance, does more than this by founding elaborate scenic construction. The address, whether voiced directly by characters or relayed through song, ensures a mediated relationship to processes of identification. At one level, this form of spectatorial subjectivity can deny the atomising modernity associated with the construction of individuation and a privatised sphere for the couple. The comedian, for example, often disrupts a scenic construction that verges on an intimate moment or kiss, and thereby brings the couple back within the purview of a public view, but one which entirely lacks the disciplinary drives of an authoritarian gaze. Instead, the intervention could be said to draw the couple away from a hermetic space and back into a more expansive *communitas*. However, this non-atomistic form of spectatorship may also be harnessed to cultivate an aesthetic of the private. This constitutes a narration of desire in which the relationship between zones of intimacy and socio-political arrangements need not follow a model of opposition and separation of public and private experience. As I have suggested, narrative communities, both relayed and produced afresh by the cinema, may provide sanction to privatised storytelling codes such as character point of view.

One needs to think this through in terms of the relationship between socially symbolic narrative forms and their political resonances. I would suggest that fictional processes parallel, interrogate, and question the authoritative functions communities have exercised under the colonial and post-colonial Indian states. While espousing the standard repertoire of democratic principles – civil liberties, universal suffrage – the nationalist movement also mobilised people in terms of community appeals, and this inevitably left its stamp on state and civil institutions after independence. Governments have regarded the rights of minority groups over their civil and familial laws, such as those of the Muslim community, as an area to be regarded with caution, apprehending that arguments for universal codes would take on an oppressive dimension. This has often meant the state shoring up the most retrograde patriarchal community authority in the field of women's rights to property and maintenance.[47] And the historical backwardness of ritually lower groups in the Hindu hierarchy – lower castes, and those outside the caste hierarchy – has given rise to state policies of affirmative legislation on their behalf. The assertion of the rights of such groups in government service and educational institutions has generated multicommunity strategies in larger political formations, as well as distinct political parties catering to particular swathes of the socially deprived.

While one democratic agenda urges the state to disperse such forms of community authority in favour of individual rights, others have tended to problematise the characteristic institutions of modern democracy, emphasising the unequal, assymetric terms on which modern forms of political and cultural representation have been instituted. Such theoretical work has argued that modern civil society, the domain of freely associating individuals who contract to generate institutions of representation, is not the uncomplicated vehicle of democratic politics. The individualist dispositions and educational and cultural capital associated with such representational politics is, in operative terms, the preserve of a relatively small segment of society. This argument does not so much invalidate these forms of representation, and the types of rights to freedom of expression and civil liberty which they have developed, but suggests that digits of representation of a more collective order need to be developed for strategies of social change and gender justice. The category of community has thus become central, even when contesting oppressive community practices. In this paradigm, rather than entirely vacate the discourse of community in favour of that of the individual citizen, other dissenting traditions of community need to be mobilised to develop a consensus for change.[48]

In terms of how this broader frame impinges on cultural practices, I would suggest that rather than regard the pre-modern or the traditional merely as a repressive construction engaged in by the state and ruling elites we need to see it as a source of creativity, where traditions are reinvented in accord with the dynamics of social and political transformation. In this context, I would like to draw attention to how the cinema deploys traditions such as *darsana* to enable the redefinition of collective rather than individual identity. As I have pointed out, *bhakti* constituted a form of worship which sought to circumvent the traditional mediation of the divine by the priest. As represented in saintly devotional figures of low-caste origin, the *bhakt* or devotee was dedicated to the worship of the deity through popular language rather than sacred texts monopolised by a priestly class. The establishment of direct links between worshipper and the sacred thus subverted ritual hierarchies and afforded a new sense of self. The devotional genre of the 1930s and 1940s is a case in point: critiquing brahmanical orthodoxy, films such as *Sant Tukaram* (Fatehlal and Damle, Marathi, 1937), have the reformist saint of the seventeenth century invoking the deity to provide an alternative vision of social conditions and political self-determination for the character/spectator. In a key sequence of the film, the saint, Tukaram, is involved in expounding a discourse of duty to the Maratha king Shivaji, and this extends into a more general address, as the film frames Tukaram in relation to other segments of the general public who have assembled in the shrine of Tukaram's deity, Pandurang. Tukaram's discourse of duty is designed to persuade Shivaji not to abjure his kingly role for a life of devotion, and it would appear to have conservative dimensions, fixing people to the roles they are assigned. But Tukaram's message emphasises that all will find their path to the divine, and the film then goes on to replay this message of ultimate, transcendant equality in terms of an earthly political equivalent. Shivaji's enemies, taking advantage of his absorption in the religious dialogue, descend on the shrine, and at this point Tukaram appeals to Pandurang to save his devotee. Cuts from Tukaram to Pandurang ultimately culminate in a series of phantom images of Shivaji being released from the deity and coming to repose in the assembled public; wherever the invaders look, they see Shivaji, but when they grasp the figure, he turns into a startled member of the public. This dissemination of kingship amongst the public, an image of popular sovereignty that undermines political hierarchy, is rendered through a transfer of looks: the spectator looks at the saint, who beseeches the deity, who then looks back, releasing images of the king which transform the identity of characters and spectators. In this instance the transfer is effected via a cinematic materialisation of the miraculous. But redefinitions of subjecthood through image practices are more widely observable across genres. Indeed, one may observe a plurality of cinematically constructed *darsanic* motifs within a film, setting up a conflicting political forcefield of images and image constituencies.

Nation and community

There is a suggestive containment of nationalist discourses in *Sant Tukaram*. In Hindu nationalist discourse, Shivaji is often perceived as a Hindu King whose main enemy was the Muslim Mughal rulers of India, but in this film the invader who threatens the Maratha king is not of the Mughals, but a local chieftain. Perhaps we have here an instance of how the period of the 1930s in the anti-colonial movement against British imperialism was concerned to preserve an intercommunity amity in the construction of the nation-state. That legacy was to persist, and is one of the main inheritances cultivated by the independent nation-state; but by the end of the 1930s we see the emergence of discourses about the cinema and within cinematic narratives in which a Hindu nationalist hegemony over the Muslim was being worked out.

At this time, discussions about genre surfaced as one of the key arenas in which cultural differences were conceptualised, and central here was the historical film. Historical films developed a number of subjects: the glory of ancient, pre-Islamic India (*Chandragupta*, Jayant Desai, 1945); Mughal kingship and its relation to local Hindu ruling groups, the Rajputs; (*Pukar/The Call*, Sohrab Modi, 1939; *Humayun*, Mehboob Khan, 1945); the heroism of the Maratha King Shivaji; and, after Independence, a set of films based on Indian resistance to colonial rule (*Anandmath*, Hemant Gupta, 1950; *Jhansi ki Rani/Queen of Jhansi*, Sohrab Modi, 1953). The historical genre provides an account of the relationship between foreign invaders and rulers and local Indian kings and ruling groups. These films endorsed a subtle rereading of Indian history in favour of Hindu nationalism, whereby the foreign ruler's formal authority is shown to be ultimately contingent on the real hegemonic authority that Hindu aristocrats and ruling groups exercised over indigenous society.[49]

Here we can observe a significant mobilisation and contest of *darsanic* codes. *Pukar* is organised around a series of spectacular public assemblies centred on the Mughal King Jehangir. While the camera at first places the spectator at a respectful distance and through low angles to the royal personage, subsequent scenes continuously alter these spatial relations and, in turn, the authority of the *darsanic* figure. This narrational pattern climaxes when a Rajput ally intervenes between King and diegetic audience. While the intervention is couched in the rhetoric of Rajput loyalty to the emperor, it is in effect a display of the hegemony the Rajput exercises over society, with the implicit message that Mughal rule is contingent on his power. The intervention here is also one between the Mughal king and the contemporary audience, for the order issued by the emperor to his subject is presented in an enormous frontal close-up which inducts the spectator into an overwhelming direct address. The Rajput countering of the command thus functions as a disruption of screen–audience relations. This challenge to Mughal rule and medieval Indian past is governed by an imperative of recovering Hindu pride for a present and future organisation of nationalist culture, and is defined by leadership grounded in hierarchy rather than community. For the Rajput challenge does not represent an egalitarian rendering of Indian society against Mughal absolutism, but deploys the power the upper-caste aristocrat can exercise over the lowest of this society, an untouchable washerwoman.

Pukar was understood in contemporary writing to be a film about the historical amity between Hindu and Muslim communities, and was deemed a salient corrective to the sectarian animosity that was emerging at the time. Even more explicitly orientated to the theme of intercommunity amity was the social film *Padosi/Neighbours* (V. Shantaram, Marathi, 1940), about the effects of modern technological change on relations within a village community. The film is a very moving story about how a grasping modern businessman seeks to break village opposition to his schemes of modernisation by manipulating conflict between Jiwaba and Mirza, the leaders of the village community. The estranged friends are ultimately reunited when they are martyred by the new forces, and a grieving village community builds a shrine to their memory. But here, too, suggestive hierarchies emerge in the construction of narrative. This is especially marked in the opening scene, in which a devotional hymn to the Hindu God Rama is invoked on the soundtrack and over a tableau frame of a village scene, a cottage and sacred *pipal* tree in the background. A cut in anchors the voice to the village elder, Jiwaba, who sits by the tree. As he sings, we observe his good friend and neighbour, the Muslim Mirza, arrive with his prayer mat in hand. Mirza stands at a discrete distance, waiting for Jiwaba to finish. As Patil concludes, he notices Mirza, and wryly remarks that he should have said that the time had arrived for his prayer; Mirza responds, what is the need when one gets one's requirements without asking?

The film opens on a Hindu devotional space. This is first articulated by voice, and then by a figure associated with sacred symbols who is iconised as vehicle of the discourse. Unlike the Muslim prayer which follows, this practice is defined by an enveloping auditory address from the screen, a public, communal address. Jiwaba, its expressive vehicle, is overwhelmed by the feelings it arouses in him, and wipes away a tear at its conclusion. In narrational terms, the enveloping address is of sustained duration, but its diegetic reference is to the perennial. A definite sense of time and sequence only emerges with the arrival of the Muslim, for whom a specific moment is required to conduct his prayer. The emergence of time, sequence, and narrative development is authorised by a privileged, because prior, Hindu discourse of emotive community. Jiwaba gives Mirza time, and thus is inaugurated an incipient, if never quite actualised, discourse of national origins. From the 1920s, right-wing Hindu nationalist ideologues had developed an argument that India was originally composed of Hindus, who therefore had prior rights to the country over those, especially Muslims and Christians, who arrived subsequently.[50] Central to such ideologies is a profound ahistoricism that seeks to enforce a monolithic Hindu identity across time and against the historical reality of the many, very different, traditions, conflictual and dissenting trends, and inegalitarian social hierarchies that have loosely made up a rather inchoate religious and social history. These writings have provided the foundations for a Hindu majoritarianism whose objective is to assign a subordinate status to other religious identities in the make-up of the modern Indian nation-state. Later the film implicitly invokes anxieties about Muslim dominance in the medieval period, when Mirza heads the village council that has to rule on charges levelled against Jiwaba's son. Jiwaba's feelings of ignominy and powerlessness condenses a whole, specifically modern ideology of the historical subordination of Hindus to other communities, and provides the emotional ground for drives to assert Hindu authority over the nation-state, an objective echoed in the ideological work implicit in *Pukar*.

These ideological currents are never actualised, and, as in the case of *Pukar*, are never straightforwardly expressed, but indicate that even films arguing for amity were premised on a certain privileging of modern Hindu constructions of the 'other'. These incipient hegemonic drives took an articulate form in discourses about the social film in the early 1940s. An influential film periodical, *Filmindia*, argued that the genre was the preserve of Hindu drives to reform and modernise society, and that Muslim film-makers were averse to introspection about the practices of their community, preferring to invest in genres such as the historical. In this construction, the social genre constituted modern society and reformist nationalist initiatives as Hindu, and attributed to Muslims an isolationist, conservative, and backward-looking mindset and narrative disposition. It should be underlined that this argument was a retrospective one, for the reformist films of the 1930s, while addressing change in Hindu society, never identified themselves in terms of a particular socio-religious group, and some of the issues they raised, such as the oppression of women, the contest of feudal authority, and the depiction of social inequality, could obviously have an appeal broader than the Hindu community. However, hegemonic practices tend to leave their identity unmarked in order to assume the ability to speak on behalf of society as a whole, and when the exclusionist and suborning aspects of an emerging Hindu nationalist hegemony surfaced in the 1940s, there developed a drive to pluralise unmarked categories such as the social. Thus we witness the emergence of the category of the Muslim social, films produced by Muslim-led studios which laid claim to a reform and modernisation of Muslim society. Films such as *Najma* (Mehboob Khan, 1943) and *Elaan/The Call* (Mehboob Khan, 1948) pitted liberal professionals against the effete, feudal face of Muslim society. Here the address to the particular group was not isolationist. Rather, in appealing for change in the Muslim community, they clearly staged, for a wider public, the desire of Muslims to embrace a common modern social agenda.

During the same period, we notice the emergence of a more aggressive nationalist stance, one which was to be influential in setting up certain symbolic coordinates for a Hindu hegemony. In 1937, an All India League for Censorship, a private body, was set up to lobby for stringent measures in regard to what was perceived to be an anti-Hindu dimension in the film industry.[51] It claimed that the industry was dominated by Muslims and Parsis who wanted to show the Hindus 'in a bad light'. Muslim actors and Muslim characters were used, it declared, to offer a contrast to Hindu characters portrayed as venal, effete, and oppressive. The League evidently assumed that the government of Bombay, led by the Congress Party, would be responsive to their demand that certain films be banned for their so-called anti-Hindu features. Such expectations were belied by K.M. Munshi, Home Minister in the Bombay Government, who dismissed the League as bigots. Indeed, this was how the League must have appeared at the time. But their charges do bring to light the fact that certain off-screen information, that is, the religious identity of producers, directors, and actors, was being related to the on-screen narrative, and in fact was seen to constitute a critical social and political level of the narrative.

It is against this background that we should situate the as-yet rudimentary information which suggests that in the next decade the industry itself was coming to project an address to its market which clearly apprehended and sought to circumvent Hindu alienation. Syed Hasan Manto, who had written scripts for Hindi films, recalled that he was pressurised to leave his job in the early 1940s because he was a Muslim. Indeed, Bombay Talkies, the studio Manto worked for from 1946 to 1948, came under threat from Hindu extremists who demanded that the studio's Muslim employees be sacked.[52] At a more symbolic level, a process was inaugurated by which the roles of hero and heroine, which normally remain outside the purview of stereotypes associated with other characters, had to be played by actors with Hindu names. In 1943, when Yusuf Khan was inducted as a male lead by Devika Rani at Bombay Talkies, his name was changed, as is well known, to Dilip Kumar.[53] In the actor's account, the change was quite incidental. But we have information about other Muslim actors and acresses who underwent name changes, such as Mahzabin, who became Meena Kumari,[54] and Nawab, who became Nimmi;[55] and in 1950 a struggling actor, Hamid Ali Khan, changed his name to Ajit on the advice of the director, K. Amarnath.[56] I am sure that this short-list is but the beginning of a much longer one, and an oral history might uncover nothing less than a parallel universe of concealed identities.

The transaction involved seems to have been purely symbolic. Evidence from film periodicals suggests that the true identity of such actors was mostly well known, and yet a symbolic abnegation of identity had to be undertaken if the transition to the screen was to be achieved. It was as if the screen, constituting an imaginary nation-space, required the fulfilment of certain criteria before the actor or actress could acquire a symbolic eligibility.

Following in the tracks of the Hindu communal censorship League of 1937, *Filmindia* showed that a bodily sense of communal difference had come to inflect a certain reception of film images. *Filmindia*, incensed in 1949 by the restrictions placed on Indian cinema imports by the Government of Pakistan, was delighted to see two Muslim actresses, Nimmi and Nargis, kiss the feet of Premnath and Raj Kapoor in the latter's *Barsaat*. In an ironic aside, the gossip columns of the periodical suggested that, to balance this act of submission, a Muslim director such as Kardar should now arrange to have a Hindu actress kiss Dilip Kumar's feet. Clearly, it was understood that such an inversion was not a likely scenario, and a vicarious pleasure was being taken in this symbolic triumph.[57]

How much of these off-screen discourses actually went into the structuring of on-screen narratives? It seems to me no coincidence that in the same year that *Filmindia* carried this dark communal reception of *Barsaat*, in *Andaz*, a film by a Muslim director, Mehboob, Nargis should again be seeking to touch Raj Kapoor's feet, desperate to demonstrate her virtue as a true Hindu wife, and to clear herself of charges of being involved with Dilip Kumar. The image of the star is not just reiterated in this interweaving of on-screen and off-screen narratives; there is an active working out and resolution of the transgressive features which have come to be attached to him or her. For example, speculations about Nargis's family background, and suspicions of her chastity following from her affair with Raj Kapoor, seemed repetitively to feed into and be resolved within a host of films, from *Andaz* to *Bewafa* (M.L. Anand, 1952), *Laajwanti* (Rajinder Suri, 1957), and *Mother India* (1957).[58]

The way in which this symbolic space was charted out by the Hindi commercial cinema is comparable with the way in which the white hero became the norm for North American commercial cinema, and, preeminently, his white Anglo-Saxon Protestant version. In both cases the ideological construction of this symbolic space appears to be neatly effaced, but the discourses surrounding the films clearly indicate that this was not so.

A note on recent developments

In post-Independence history there follows a complicated history, in which these coordinates of narrative form undergo important changes. To conclude this chapter I would like to isolate a broad current in these changes, centred on how discourses of state, community, and character are interwoven in new ways. Crucial here is the system of typage, that is, the employment of a recurrent, relatively fixed set of attributes to define character. I have already noted the importance of character as a vehicle of direct address, a figure who establishes a junction between screen and audience to constitute an incipient political community. The system of typage, which emerges subsequently, and especially after 1970, while carrying on some of the earlier functions of character address, introduces a new regime of representation. For in this arrangement community is not presented as something achieved in the narrative process, where events come to coalesce in a character giving voice to community. Instead, community is condensed into the iconic figure, pre-eminently into the triad of Hindu, Muslim, and Christian, whose attributes are largely fixed and unvarying. Even here there is a hierarchy, in which Hindus assume the apex position in a multicommunity image of the nation, and display the attributes of modernity: education, modern profession, nuclear domesticity. Muslims and Christians are defined as less socially dynamic, caught up, respectively, in traditional occupations and indigent behaviour. Nevertheless, romantic drives animate each group within the triad. While marriage within community remains a basic narrative rule, romantic drives are nevertheless pitted against the repressive dimensions of patriarchal community. Further, while a symbolic hierarchy is observable in films of the 1970s, assymetric hierarchies of star discourse were also deployed to pressurise narrative hierarchies. The key Bombay film star, Amitabh Bachchan, is a case in point. He could assume Muslim and Christian roles, as in *Coolie* (Manmohan Desai, 1983) and *Amar, Akbar, Anthony* (Manmohan Desai, 1977), but his commanding position in the star hierarchy put pressure on the regime of social representation which would subordinate such figures within the film. Something of a carnivalesque inversion of hierarchies then emerges; the plebian communities acquire an attractive freedom, of personality, bodily disposition, and romantic initiative, posed in marked contrast to the respectable, but also more repressed, Hindu hero of films such as *Amar, Akbar, Anthony*. It is as if the distractive, anarchic aspects normally associated with comic figures had erupted to envelop the narrative world, loosening hierarchies and coherent modes of symbolic social representation.

Such domains of possibility were significantly undermined in the climate of an aggressive Hindu nationalism in the 1990s, in which majoritarian discourses and political mobilisation relentlessly targetted the Muslim other, culminating in the destruction of a mosque at Ayodhya on 6 December 1992. Significantly, the convention of the multicommunity nation was dispersed in Bombay cinema, as the Hindu hero assumed a singular authority in expressing a social and political vision. Ironically, in the recent past it has been the re-emergence of the earlier, Hindu-led multicommunity triad which has functioned as a form of resistance to a monolithic Hindu nationalist narrative.[59]

However, narrational techniques display a certain diversification in this period. While character typage, invoking an established pattern of rhetorical discourse centred on familial duty and patriotic sentiment, remained dominant, there has also developed a modernising impulse in the deployment of point-of-view narration, naturalist acting styles, and the integration of song and dance sequences to a cause-and-effect-driven narrative economy. These new drives in the popular cinema have appropriated an earlier impulse to diversify the cinematic institution in the 1970s. At this time there emerged a distinct middle-class cinema, displacing attention from the extraordinary, large-scale figure of the star, and invoking the pleasures of the ordinary and everyday.[60]

What is remarkable is that these discourses were successfully appropriated[61] to speak of larger issues, about how citizenship and the nation-state could be consolidated against the threat of anti-nationalist forces invariably associated with the Muslim-majority nation-state of Pakistan. In a key film of the 1990s, *Roja* (Mani Ratnam, 1993, Tamil/Hindi), much of these ideological imperatives and new narrative strategies are on display, with a constant movement between character-driven narration and a condensation of the voice of (Hindu) community and nation into a character. The only signs of resistance to the dominant Hindu nationalist ideology of this film arise from its female character, who gives voice to small-scale motivations of romantic desire quite indifferent to the larger designs of patriotic duty and national interests.[62]

To point to this node of resistance is not to argue that the logic of realist characterisation will or must supplant systems of direct address in popular cinema. For the particular implication of diegetic characters and film audiences in the fictive contracts of community and nation suggest the constant need to represent imperatives larger than the individual and to stage debates about the nature of social and political subjectivity.

Endnotes

1   For a representative selection of articles, see Jim Pines and Paul Willemen (eds), *Questions of third cinema* (London: British Film Institute, 1989).

2   M.B. Billimoria, 'Foreign markets for Indian films', *Indian Talkie, 1931–56* (Bombay, Film Federation of India, 1956), pp. 53–54. A substantial deposit of Indian films distributed by Wapar France, an agency which catered to North African markets, are in the French film archives at Bois D'arcy. For the importance of Indian film imports to Indonesia and Burma, see John A. Lent, *The Asian film industry* (London, Christopher Helm, 1990), pp. 202, 223; and for patterns of Indian film exports at the end of the 1980s, see Manjumatj Pendakur, 'India', in the same book, p. 240.

3   'None of these cinemas [from Morocco to Kuwait] is doing well . . . markets are flooded with Rambos, Karate films, Hindu [*sic*] musicals and Egyptian films'. Lisbeth Malkmus, 'The "new Egyptian cinema"', *Cineaste* 16, 3 (1988), p. 30.

4   The term comes from Tom Gunning, 'The cinema of attraction: early film, its spectator and the avant-garde', *Wide Angle*, 8, (1986) 3–4. There is a more elaborate discussion of this term in relation to the Bombay cinema later in this chapter. For reflections on other 'attraction-based' cinemas, see Laleen Jayamanne, 'Sri Lankan family melodrama: a cinema of primitive attractions', *Screen*, 33, 2 (Summer 1992), pp. 145–53; and Gerard Fouquet, 'Of genres and savours in Thai film', *Cinemaya* no. 6 (1989–90), pp. 4–9.

5   For example, Ginnette Vincendeau, 'The exception and the rule', *Sight and Sound* 2, 8 (1994), which demonstrates that Renoir's *Rules of the game* (1939), invariably highlighted in the canon of world cinema by critics, should be understood within a set of local parameters of narrative form, performance tradition (boulevard plays), and cinematographic style (long takes and shooting in depth) that were shared by a number of French films of the time. Other stimulating writing on the importance of local industrial and cultural contexts includes: Ana M. López, 'Tears and desire: women and melodrama in the "old" Mexican cinema', in John King, Ana M. López and Manuel Alvarodo (eds), *Mediating two worlds: cinematic encounters in the Americas* (London, BFI publishing, 1993); Thomas Elsaesser, *A second life: German cinema's first decade* (Amsterdam, Amsterdam University Press, 1996); James Hay, *Popular film culture in fascist Italy: the passing of the rex* (Bloomington, IN, and Indianapolis, IN, Indiana University Press, 1987); see Sue Harper, *Picturing the past: the rise and fall of the British costume film* (London, British Film Institute, 1994) for an understanding of how the historical film reflected popular perceptions about British history. Susan Hayward, *French national cinema* (London, Routledge, 1994) notes the importance of systems of gesture and morphology in condensing social and political consensuses through the vehicle of the star. More generally, there is the elegant introduction on the problems and possibilities of the notion of popular cinema in Ginette Vincendeau and Richard Dyer, *Popular European cinema* (London, Routledge, 1992). Such writing is yet to evolve substantially for the 'third world cinema', as much recent writing has been centred on avant garde 'third cinema' studies.

6   This agenda would also re-set the terms of an ethnographic cultural studies seeking to recover the many ways audiences interpret texts. Distinctions have arisen between an ethnographic cultural studies for the West and that applied to the third world. Where the former is governed by democratic assumptions, and the possibilities of multiple viewpoints in the construction of texts, the latter tends to be monolithic in its characterisation of the cultural basis of interpretation. But clearly, once the West too is remade into a series of specific cultural histories, the possibility of putting the democratic and cultural together within an ethnographic approach generates a more universal agenda.

7   For the standard account, see E. Barnouw and S. Krishnaswamy, *Indian film* (London and New York, Oxford University Press, 1980); also Manjunath Pendakur, 'India', in *The Asian film industry* (London, Christopher Helm, 1990), p. 231.

8   For reflections on the subordinating implications of Bombay's national cinema, see my 'Dislocations: the cinematic imagining of a new society in 1950s India', *Oxford Literary Review* 16 (1994).

9   Steve Hughes, 'The pre-Phalke era in south Indian cinema', *South Indian Studies*, no. 2. (1996).

10 All references are to 'The Hindi film', *Indian Talkie*, p. 81.

11 Tamil film studies workshop, Madras Institute of Development Studies, Chennai, 1997.

12 Moinak Biswas, 'Literature and cinema in Bengal, 1930s–1950s', paper presented at the seminar 'Reading Indian cinema', Department of Film Studies, Jadavpur University, 1998.

13 The reasons for the restructuring of the 'social' film are complex. Artists associated with the Indian People's Theatre Association (IPTA), which had ties with the Communist Party of India, had started working in the film industry from the 1940s. Amongst these were the actor Balraj Sahni, the director Bimal Roy, and the scriptwriter K.A. Abbas, who was involved in *Awara/The Vagabond* (Raj Kapoor, 1951), a film representative of the new drive to combine a social reform perspective with ornate spectacle. However, the years after independence

were characterised by a broader ideological investment in discourses of social justice associated with the image of the new state and the personality of its first prime minister, Jawaharlal Nehru.

14 For an exploration of this influential critical tradition, see my 'Shifting codes, dissolving identities: the Hindi social film of the 1950s as popular culture', *Journal of Art and Ideas*, nos 23–4 (January 1993), pp. 51–85; reprinted in *Third Text*, 34.

15 See the collection of essays in Wimal Dissanayake (ed.), *Melodrama and Asian cinema* (Cambridge, Cambridge University Press, 1993).

16 For example, Mitsushiro Yoshimoto's account of the post-war domestic criticism of Japanese cinema, 'Melodrama, post-modernism and Japanese cinema' in Wimal Dissanayahe (ed.), *Melodrama and Asian cinema* (Cambridge, Cambridge University Press, 1993) pp. 101–26, especially pp. 110–11.

17 Chidananda Das Gupta, *The painted face* (New Delhi, Roli Books, 1991).

18 Chidananda Das Gupta, 'Seeing is believing', in *The painted face* (New Delhi, Roli Books, 1991), pp. 35–44.

19 Chidananda Das Gupta, 'City and village' and 'The oedipal hero', in *The painted face* (New Delhi, Roli Books, 1991), pp. 45–58 and 70–106, respectively.

20 Chidananda Das Gupta, 'The painted face of Indian politics', in *The painted face* (New Delhi, Roli Books, 1991), pp. 199–247.

21 All references are to Ashish Nandy, 'An intelligent critic's guide to the Indian cinema', *Deep Focus* 1, (December 1987), pp. 68–72, (June 1988), pp. 53–60; and (November 1988), pp. 58–61.

22 Madhava Prasad, *Ideology of the Hindi film: a historical construction* (Delhi, Oxford University Press, 1998).

23 Peter Brooks, *The melodramatic imagination: Balzac, Henry James, melodrama and the mode of excess*, reprint (New York, Columbia University Press, 1985); first published in 1976.

24 This part of the argument has been anticipated by several writers. See Ashis Nandy, 'The Hindi film: ideology and first principles', *India International Centre Quarterly*, 8 (1981), pp. 89–96; Rosie Thomas, 'Indian cinema: pleasures and popularity', *Screen*, 26, 3–4 (1985); and Ravi Vasudevan, 'The melodramatic mode and the commercial Hindi cinema', *Screen*, 30, 3 (1989), pp. 29–50.

25 Ashish Rajadhyaksha, 'The Phalke era: conflict of traditional form and modern technology', *Journal of Art and Ideas*, 14–15 (1987), pp. 47–78; reprinted in T. Niranjana, P. Sudhir and V. Dhareshwar (eds), *Interrogating modernity: culture and colonialism in India* (Calcutta, Seagull, 1993), pp. 47–82.

26 Geeta Kapur, 'Mythic material in Indian cinema', *Journal of Arts and Ideas*, 14–15 (1987), reprinted as 'Revelation and doubt: *Sant Tukaram* and *Devi*', in T. Niranjana, P. Sudhir and V. Dhareshwar (eds), *Interrogating modernity: culture and colonialism in India* (Calcutta, Seagull, 1993), pp. 19–46.

27 Geeta Kapur, 'Revelation and doubt, in T. Niranjana, P. Sudhir and V. Dhareshwar (eds), *Interrogating modernity* (Calcutta, Seagull, 1993), p. 23.

28 Kapur defines the formal category of frontality as arising from 'the word, the image, the design, the performative act . . . . This means, for example, flat, diagrammatic and simply contoured figures (as in Kalighat *pat* painting). It means a figure-ground design, with notational perspective (as in the Nathdwara pictures, and the photographs which they often utilise). It means, in dramatic terms, the repetition of motifs within ritual "play", as in the *lila*; it means a space deliberately evacuated to foreground actor-image performance, as in the *tamasha*.

Frontality is also established in an adaptation of traditional acting conventions to the proscenium stage, as when stylised audience address is mounted on an elaborate *mise en scène*, as in Parsi theatre.' In Kapur, 'Revelation and doubt', in T. Niranjana, P. Sudhir and V. Dhareshwar (eds), *Interrogating modernity* (Calcutta, Seagull, 1993), p. 20.

29   Peter Brooks, *The melodramatic imagination* (New York, Columbia University Press, 1985) p. 62.

30   Roland Barthes, 'Diderot, Brecht, Eisenstein', in *Image, music, text*, selected and translated by Stephen Heath (London, Collins, 1982), p. 70.

31   Roland Barthes, 'Diderot, Brecht, Eisenstein', in *Image, music, text* (London, Collins, 1982), p. 70.

32   Reference may be made here to a panel from the eighteenth-century Hindu text analysed by I. Julia Leslie in *The perfect wife: the orthodox Hindu woman according to the Stridharmapaddhati of Tryambakayajvan* (Delhi, Oxford University Press, 1989).

33   For *darsana*, see Lawrence A. Babb, 'Glancing: visual interaction in Hinduism', *Journal of Anthropological Research*, 37, 4 (1981), pp. 387–401; Diana Eck, *Seeing the divine image in India* (Chambersburg, PA, Anima Books, 1981).

34   Madhava Prasad uses the concept in this fashion, to outline the way narrative relations are organised in the 'feudal family romance'. Prasad, *Ideology of the Hindi film* (Delhi, Oxford University Press, 1998), chapter 3.

35   Kumkum Sangari has noted the following effects of the female devotional voice:

> The orthodox triadic relation between wife, husband and god is broken. The wife no longer gets her salvation through her 'godlike' husband ... *Bhakti* offers direct salvation. The intermediary position now belongs not to the human husband or the Brahmin priest but to the female devotional voice. This voice, obsessed with the relationships between men and women, continues to negotiate the triadic relationship – it simultaneously transgresses and reformulates patriarchal ideologies.

In 'Mirabai and the spiritual economy of Bhakti', Nehru Memorial Museum and Library, New Delhi, Occasional Papers on History and Society, Second Series, no. 28, pp. 59–60.

36   I owe this observation to Jim Cook.

37   Ashish Rajadhyaksha, 'Who's looking? Viewership and democracy in Indian cinema', in Ravi S. Vasudevan (ed.), *Making meaning in Indian cinema* (Delhi, Oxford University Press, forthcoming).

38   Ravi S. Vasudevan, 'Shifting codes, dissolving identities: the Hindi social film of the 1950s as popular culture', *Journal of Art and Ideas*, nos 23–4 (January 1993), pp. 51–85; reprinted in *Third Text*, 34.

39   Ravi S. Vasudevan, '"You cannot live in society – and ignore it": nationhood and female modernity in *Andaz* (Mehboob Khan, 1949)', in Patricia Uberoi (ed.), *Sexuality, social reform and the state* (New Delhi, Sage, 1996), pp. 83–108.

40   See Karthigesu Sivathamby, *The Tamil film as a medium of political communication* (Madras, New Century Book House, 1981); and S. Theodor Baskaran, *The eye of the serpent* (Chennai, East–West Books, 1997).

41   For a more detailed account, see my 'Sexuality and the film apparatus: continuity, non-continuity and discontinuity in Bombay cinema' in Mary E. John and Janaki Nair (eds), *A question of silence: the sexual economies of modern India* (Delhi, Kali for Women, 1998), pp. 192–215.

42 For an account of narrators and comics in traditional and folk theatrical form, see M.L. Varadpande, *Traditions of Indian theatre* (New Delhi, Abhinav Publications, 1978), pp. 84–5.

43 Miriam Hansen, *Babel and Babylon: spectatorship in American silent cinema* (Cambridge, MA, Harvard University Press, 1991).

44 Thomas Elsaesser, *Early cinema: space–frame–narrative* (London, British Film Institute, 1990).

45 Tom Gunning, 'The cinema of attraction', *Wide Angle*, 8, 3–4 (1986).

46 Miriam Hansen, *Babel and Babylon* (Cambridge, MA: Harvard University Press, 1991), chapters 1 and 2.

47 For an outline of the complexity of these issues, see Nivedita Menon, 'State/ gender/community: citizenship in contemporary India', *Economic and Political Weekly*, 31 January 1998, PE3–PE10. For a historical account showing that the boundaries of state law and personal law were not immutable, see Archana Parashar, *Women and family law reform in India* (New Delhi, Sage, 1993). For the mixture of codes in colonial criminal law, see Radhika Singha, *A despotism of law: crime and justice in early colonial India* (Delhi, Oxford University Press, 1998).

48 Sudipta Kaviraj, 'Democracy and development in India' in Amiya Bagchi (ed.) *Democracy and development* (London, St Martin's Press, 1995), and 'Dilemmas of democratic development in India', in Adrian Leftwich (ed.), *Democracy and development: theory and practice* (Oxford, Polity Press, 1996); Partha Chatterjee, *The nation and its fragments: colonial and post-colonial histories* (Delhi, Oxford University Press, 1994); 'Beyond the nation? Or within?', *Economic and Political Weekly* Delhi, 4–11 January 1997, 30–34, and 'Community in the East', *Economic and Political Weekly*, 7 February 1998, pp. 277–82; Veena Das, 'Communities as political actors: the question of cultural rights', in Veena Das, *Critical events* (Delhi, Oxford University Press, 1996).

49 The following discussion in text is a summary of a larger work in progress.

50 For an analysis of these aspects of Hindu nationalist ideology, see Tapan Basu, Pradip Dutta, Sumit Sarkar and Tanika Sarkar, *Khaki shorts and saffron flags: a critique of the Hindu Right* (Delhi, Orient Longman, 1993).

51 All references are taken from Bombay, Home Department, Political file no. 313/1940, Maharashtra State Archives.

52 See the introduction to Saadat Hasan Manto, *Kingdom's end and other stories*, translated from the Urdu by Khalid Hasan (London, Verso Books, 1987).

53 *Filmfare*, 26 April 1957, p. 77.

54 *Filmfare*, 17 October 1952, p. 19.

55 *Filmfare*, 28 November 1952, p. 18.

56 Ajit, interviewed by Anjali Joshi, *Sunday Observer*, Delhi, 16 December 1991. For some ideas about the on-screen ramifications of Hamid Ali Khan's change of name, see my 'Dislocations', *Oxford Literary Review* 16 (1994).

57 *Filmindia*, May 1950.

58 For further reflections about Nargis's career, see Rosie Thomas, 'Sanctity and scandal in *Mother India*', *Quarterly Review of Film and Video*, 11, 3 (1989), pp. 11–30; and my "You cannot live in society – and ignore it", in Patricia Uberoi (ed.), *Sexuality, social reform and the state* (New Delhi, Sage, 1996), pp. 83–108.

59 Cases in point are *Ghulam/Enslaved* (Mukesh Bhatt, 1998) and *Zakhm/The Wound* (Mahesh Bhatt, 1999).

60   See Madhava Prasad, *Ideology of the Hindi film*, part II, for an account of how the cinematic institution was diversified in the 1970s.

61   See the arguments of Tejaswini Niranjana, 'Whose nation: tourists and terrorists in *Roja*', *Economic and Political Weekly*, 24, 3 (15 January 1994); and Madhava Prasad, 'Signs of ideological reform: from formal into real subsumption', *Journal of Arts and Ideas*, no. 29 (1996), reprinted as the epilogue to *Ideology of the Hindi film* (Delhi, Oxford University Press, 1998).

62   For a more elaborate analysis of this film, see Tejaswini Niranjana, 'Whose nation?' *Economic and Political Weekly*, 24, 3 (15 January 1994); Madhava Prasad, 'Signs of ideological reform', *Journal of Arts and Ideas*, no. 29 (1996); and Ravi Vasudevan, 'Voice, space, form: *Roja*, Indian film, and national identity', in Stuart Murray (ed.), *Not on any map: essays on post-coloniality* (Exeter, University of Exeter Press, 1997).

Acknowledgement: Parts of this chapter were originally published in Ravi S. Vasudevan, 1995: Addressing the spectator of a 'third-world' national cinema: the Bombay social film of the 1940s and 1950s. *Screen* 36(4).

9 Reception theory and audience research: the mystery of the vampire's kiss

Henry Jenkins

> Lips pressed together: two mouths tasted each other's sweetness. Louise gunned the gas pedal . . . .The Thunderbird began picking up speed as Louise headed it toward the Grand Canyon's edge.
>
> The Thunderbird arched through the cloud-wisped sky. It burst in flames, plunging to be bathed in the white flecks of the Colorado River.
>
> Two bats fluttered, their jet-black forms floating along the Grand Canyon's sheer cliffs. The winged beasts paused, a matched pair suspended in air – then took a southward direction toward Mexico.
>
> (Douglass, 1994: 63)

Susan Douglass's short story, 'Music of the night', published in the fanzine, *On the Edge*, represents one woman's response to *Thelma and Louise* (1991). Driving her green Thunderbird through the New Mexico desert, Louise glances at Thelma asleep beside her. After years of struggling for autonomy, Louise finds herself strangely drawn to Thelma, her 'streaming [red] hair', her 'dancing green eyes and rippling laughter'. Soon, the two women have sex in the moonlight, 'outlaws as lovers' as well as criminals. The two women join in other ways: Louise is a 300-year-old vampire; she 'initiates' Thelma, exchanging blood, allowing the two to 'transcend' their awaiting death.

We might contrast Douglass's story to the essay topics a writing instructor proposed to her students (Bogal, undated):

> The ending of *Thelma and Louise* is all wrong – disappointing in its message to women about their options in the United States, stupidly fanciful in its lack of realism, and unexpected and unprepared for by the movie that leads up to it [Agree or Disagree].

> Chart the ways the film shows Thelma becoming more like, or wanting to become more like, Louise through gesture, activity, speech, clothing or other props.

An event in Louise's past which is evidently of great importance to the decisions that Louise makes is never fully revealed to us. What is the effect of the omission?

The instructor's questions focus on many of the same issues as Douglass's short story. However, bright students may have already calculated how badly it would hurt their grades if they asserted that Thelma and Louise survived the crash, turning into bats and flying off to Mexico. The teacher's red pen is a powerful tool for disciplining how we interpret movies.

Teachers often claim that 'there are no right and wrong answers', but students are correct to suspect otherwise. They know, at the very least, that there are right and wrong ways to arrive at answers, right and wrong kinds of evidence, right and wrong styles of arguments, even right and wrong questions. All those rules probably do not correspond with the ways students talk about films with a friend, let alone how they think about film images in their erotic fantasies.

Such differences are the core of reception theory. Reception theory and audience research ask basic questions about how we make sense of the movies and what they mean in our lives. Within this paradigm, audiences are understood to be active rather than passive, to be engaged in a process of making, rather than simply absorbing, meanings. Meanings, interpretations, evaluations, and interpretive strategies are debated among everyday viewers as part of the 'vernacular theory' surrounding the cinema (McLaughlin, 1996). Such discussions generate shared (though usually implicit) ground-rules about what we can and cannot appropriately say about movies.

Assumptions about the audience underlie most film theories, ranging from the neoformalist conception of art as 'defamiliarizing' normal perception to the various psychic mechanisms (voyeurism, masochism, fantasy) in psychoanalytic theory. The difference between audience research and other film theory is not whether or not we discuss spectatorship, but how we access and talk about audience responses. In most other theoretical traditions, claims about spectators are derived from textual analysis, analogies, or personal introspection but not from dealing directly with the audience. Reception studies, on the other hand, seeks empirical evidence, through historical or ethnographic research, that documents the production and circulation of meaning. Other theorists speak of an 'ideal reader' or a 'subject position' created by the text, often assuming that textually ascribed meanings get reproduced fairly directly in spectator's heads. However, for audience researchers, as Tony Bennett (1983) argues, 'the process of reading is not one in which reader and text meet as abstractions, but rather one in which an intertextually organized reader meets an intertextually organized text' within a historically and culturally specific context. Text, context, and reader all play vital roles in shaping interpretation.

In television studies, most audience research has fit loosely within the framework of Anglo-American cultural studies (Fiske, 1992; Turner, 1990). In Film Studies, audience research has more eclectic roots, drawing upon reader-response criticism, cognitive science, social and cultural history, the sociology of art, and psychoanalysis (Allen, 1990; Allen and Gomery, 1985; Mayne, 1982; Staiger, 1992). Audience research bears a close relationship to issues of promotion, exhibition, and consumption. As a result, audience researchers in film studies are less likely to claim participation in a shared project than those working in television studies. However, there has been a significant body of work about film reception, appropriation, and interpretation.

In tracing various approaches to reception studies, I will return again and again to the mystery of the vampire's kiss – to 'Music of the night' and other responses to *Thelma and Louise*. Audience research has sometimes been accused of focusing on aberrant readings rather than trying to understand 'normal' acts of interpretation. The challenge, however, is to grasp the 'normality' and 'logic' of readings which 'fall outside the critical mainstream'. Less predictable readings reveal more clearly the interpretive process at work, suggesting that there is nothing inevitable about our own interpretations. However, audience research is more interested in shared patterns of meanings or in shared strategies of interpretation than idiosyncratic memories and associations. Consequently, my focus will be less on what 'Music of the night' means to Douglass than on how it relates to a succession of larger social and cultural contexts.

First, a caveat: 'Music of the night' is not, strictly speaking, an interpretation. Douglass does not understand herself to be recovering or reproducing the film's meanings. She labels her story 'a very alternate-universe version', recognizing the power of *Thelma and Louise* to limit its 'legitimate' interpretation. 'Music of the night' is an appropriation, a creative reworking of textual materials which consciously expands their potential meanings. In some senses, all interpretations are already appropriations. All readers must speculate to construct a coherent narrative from the bits and pieces of information the film provides.

Reading 'Music of the night' does not grant us unmediated access to this fan's interpretive process. We are confronting another text – an artifact not only of interpretation and appropriation but also of the discursive contexts in which it circulates. Despite its appeals to empirical research, audience study still depends upon theory and interpretation, not only upon observation and description. Whether we are looking at personal diaries and letters, trade press reports, newspaper reviews, net discussion-group debates, or focus-group interviews, we are reading the 'tea leaves' left behind by a more immediate process of reception, which we may never directly observe nor fully reconstruct (Crafton, 1996).

Texts

In an essay about *Casablanca* (1942), Umberto Eco identifies what he sees as the defining characteristics of cult movies. Rather than being 'whole' and cohesive, a cult movie must be 'already ramshackle, rickety, unhinged in itself', the coming together of various archetypes and quotations, an unstable mixture of contradictions, gaps, and irresolutions. Cult films such as *Casablanca* or *The Rocky Horror Picture Show* (1975) fall apart in our hands, 'a disconnected series of images' readily accessible as raw materials for our fantasies (Eco, 1983: 197–8). Timothy Corrigan (1986) adopts the opposite perspective, arguing that films become cult objects not so much because of their intrinsic properties as through the process of interpretation and appropriation. Cult films offer 'touristic' pleasures for people alienated from everyday life, an alternative world to visit where everything is up for grabs.

Within this debate, Eco stresses properties of texts (their fragmentation, their excesses), whereas Corrigan emphasizes the properties of audiences (their alienation, their appropriation). However, both describe an exchange of meanings which is partially determined by the film text and partially by the film-goer. Eco and Corrigan are struggling with what literary critic M.M. Bakhtin describes as 'heteroglossia', the possibility that texts may imperfectly contain or regulate meaning. For Bakhtin, there is no moment when the text stands outside cultural circulation and makes its meanings clear and unambiguous. The words and images writers use do not come from some neutral place such as a dictionary but rather from 'someone else's mouth' still dripping with meanings and associations from their previous use. All writers are already readers; their previous encounters with other texts shape what they are able to create. They can communicate only within the terms their culture gives them. Writers struggle to constrain the associations that accompany their borrowed terms, so they may fit comfortably within their new contexts. Yet, Bakhtin argues, this process never fully succeeds.

> Not all words for just anyone submit equally easily to this appropriation, to this seizure and transformation into private property; many words stubbornly resist, others remain alien, sound foreign . . . . It is as if they put themselves in quotation marks against the will of the speaker.
>
> (Bakhtin, 1981: 294)

Bakhtin examines the process by which artists 'appropriate' and 'rework' borrowed materials to fit new contexts. If Bakhtin is right, no film achieves the 'wholeness' Eco describes. All films are potential cult objects because all films are 'already ramshackled', containing both gaps and excesses, traces of cultural appropriation.

Accounts of the production of *Thelma and Louise* foreground this process of appropriative rewriting. Scriptwriter Callie Khouri wanted to 'write about two women on the screen that we haven't seen before ... women outlaws that were not involved in prostitution, who were not exploited' (Sawyers, 1991: 1). In doing so, she adopted a popular genre formula – the road picture – which historically had been associated with male fantasies of escaping from emotional commitments to women. Khouri reworked this formula into a female fantasy of escape from domestic confinement and masculine authority.

Readers, in turn, appropriate filmic images as analytic 'evidence', conversational reference points, fantasy icons, or storytelling resources. The retooling of genre conventions in *Thelma and Louise* encouraged many viewers to imagine alternative versions. Even Khouri imagined revising the film on other terms:

> If you rewrote *Thelma and Louise* and decided to have a guy come and save Thelma, there wouldn't have been an uproar. If a guy caught another guy raping a woman and killed the rapist, you wouldn't even comment on that.
>
> (Khouri, 1996: xvi)

Some rewrote the ending so that the two women enjoy more options; others reworked the story to fit more traditional patterns.

Reader-response criticism often starts with textual analysis, trying to determine points where readers must go beyond the information provided, exploring how the film shapes the range of possible inferences (Bordwell, 1985). D.A. Miller (1991), for example, notes that the protagonists' homosexuality in Alfred Hitchcock's *Rope* (1948) remains implicit, never explicitly stated, and thus open to viewer discovery and recognition. Richard Maltby (1996) points towards an ambiguous moment in *Casablanca* where a dissolve – and ellipses – leaves unresolved the question of whether or not Rick and Ilsa have slept together. How readers understand such moments depends upon their assumptions about human sexuality, the censorship process, Hollywood genres, and so forth. Talking through such differences is part of the fun of going to the movies!

One can identify many moments where *Thelma and Louise* demands viewers' participation, including gaps (Louise's 'secret' which prevents her from returning to Texas), irresolutions (the final freeze-frame of the Thunderbird hurling over the edge of the Grand Canyon), excesses (the kiss exchanged between Thelma and Louise which invites erotic interpretations of their relationship), contradictions (their repeated dependence on men despite claims of autonomy), unmotivated actions (Louise's decision to trust Thelma with her savings), and moral ambiguities (the complex circumstances surrounding the rape). At such points, readers are required to make judgements or speculations. Not surprisingly, such moments are central to most readings of the film. Khouri chose to leave some questions unanswered and to provoke controversy about characters' motives. Yet, nothing prevents readers from filling in the gaps in unanticipated ways. As Elizabeth Freund explains: 'The text does not talk back to correct one's misinterpretations; it cannot adapt, assert, defend itself or supplement its fragmented codes' (1987: 145). Textual features, however, do make some meanings more accessible than others. If you wish to read Thelma and Louise as lesbian lovers, you can do so, but some things must be explained and others added. Their one kiss can only take you so far!

Critical discourse

One important strand of reception studies has examined advertisements, film trailers, newspaper reviews, and other 'textual activators' which shape audience expectations. Tony Bennett and Janet Woollacott, for example, studied various 'moments' in the historical reception of James Bond. Bond's meanings and associations 'shifted', as Bond moved, for example, from a figure primarily understood in relation to the Cold War towards one read in relation to the sexual revolution. Their analysis centers not simply on texts but on the meanings that get 'encrusted' around the Bond phenomenon 'like shells on a rock by the seashore' as the character moves through various contexts (Bennett and Woollacott, 1988).

Drawing inspiration from Robert Hans Jauss's work on literary reputation, film historians have examined the construction of authorial 'legends' around highly visible film-makers, such as Alfred Hitchcock, Charlie Chaplin or Rainer Werner Fassbinder (Kapsis, 1992; Maland, 1989; Shattuc, 1995). For example, Barbara Klinger's *Melodrama and meaning* (1994) shows how the reputation of Douglas Sirk's films (*All That Heaven Allows* [1953], *Written on the Wind* [1956], *Imitation of Life* [1959]) have shifted dramatically as they move through different 'habitats of meaning'. In the 1950s, Universal-International Pictures sold them as 'slick, sexually explicit "adult" films', and journalistic critics denounced them for their crass commercialism. In the 1970s, academic critics rediscovered them, claiming they posed Brechtian criticisms of American middle-class culture. In the 1980s, Rock Hudson's AIDS-related death, and the revelation of his homosexuality, opened them retrospectively to camp interpretations. Such reception analysis has become a routine approach to doing film history, as writers seek more and more sophisticated accounts of what films meant in particular historical contexts (Budd, 1990; DeCordova, 1990a). Obviously, publicity-kit descriptions, journalistic reviews, movie magazine fan letters, or trade press reports are accessible to film historians whereas anonymous film-goers left little or no written traces. However, we need to be careful about ascribing to these 'textual activators' the same semiotic power once ascribed to films – that is, the power to predetermine audience response.

We also need to avoid reading critical response as if it were the same as audience response. To some degree, film critics do reflect the tastes and interests of their intended audience, as we see when the writer for an industry publication complained about negative stereotyping of truckers in *Thelma and Louise* (Siefkes, 1995), a writer for *Playboy* saw it as a feminist 'backlash' against men (Babar, 1991), and a critic for a feminist radio program compared it to Simone de Beauvoir (McAlister, undated). However, journalistic criticism operates within its own institutional contexts and interpretive rules, ensuring that critics often respond differently from casual viewers. Film critics often react to each other's reviews in the case of a high-profile and controversial film such as *Thelma and Louise*, which sparked a debate around what one male critic called its 'toxic feminism' (Schickel, 1991). Many argued whether gun-toting female outlaws constituted appropriate feminist role models and whether the film was anti-male. Film-goers were asked to choose sides between critics who had staked out radically divergent positions, often along gender lines, within ongoing debates about women and violence or 'political correctness'.

Such reviews can be seen as 'bids' for the film's potential meanings, reframing *Thelma and Louise* in various ways. Many critics read it in relation to other contemporary movies, including *Silence of the Lambs* (1991), *The Terminator 2* (1991), or *La Femme Nikita* (1990), which showed women bearing arms (Corliss, 1991: 6). Emphasizing its progressive politics, feminist critics drew parallels with the treatment of sexual violence in *A Question of Silence* (1983) or contrasted the middle-class protagonists' relative freedom to a recent Supreme Court decision restricting poor women's access to medical information (Klawans, 1991; McAlister, undated). Male critics often adopted familiar auteurist models, placing it within the career of director Ridley Scott (*Alien* [1979], *Bladerunner* [1982]), while feminist critics stressed the creative contributions of its female scriptwriter (Klawans, 1991).

Such framings of the film matter. Our initial genre classifications determine our subsequent responses to new and unfamiliar works; they shape the priority we place on particular plot details, the meanings we ascribe to various textual features, the expectations we form about likely story developments, our predictions about its resolution, and our extrapolations about information not explicitly presented (Rabinowitz, 1985). Genre classification often occurs in response to publicity mechanisms or critical discussions before we enter the theatre. Some critics complained that the advertising for *Thelma and Louise* emphasized comic aspects (in the tradition of *Smokey and the Bandit* [1977]), while their reviews reframed the film in alternative terms – as a feminist melodrama.

However idiosyncratic it may initially seem, Douglass's 'Music of the night' follows many terms set by critical discourse, adopting the female outlaws as embodiments of feminist empowerment, struggling to resolve ambiguities about Louise's past life, reading it as a female-centered road picture. In other cases, Douglass's analysis depends upon less common interpretive moves – though none without precedence in the critical discourse. Even conservative John Simon recognized some homoerotic implications: 'Are these women, consciously or unconsciously, in love with each other? Is this perhaps not just a feminist but also a lesbian feminist movie?' (1991: 48). Douglass's turn towards vampirism depends upon reading intertextually across Susan Sarandon's previous screen appearances, another familiar critical move. Stanley Kaufman (1991), for example, drew strong parallels between waitress characters which the actress played in other films, while Douglass maps Sarandon's performance as a bisexual vampire in *The Hunger* (1983) onto *Thelma and Louise*.

Exhibition

Audience research has also centered around what it means to go to the movies, a question which moves beyond the meanings which get ascribed to individual films. People go to movies for many reasons; watching specific films is only one of them. As Douglas Gomery (1992) notes, the 'movie palaces' of the 1920s often included restaurants, dance clubs, bowling allies, and day-care facilities. Movie theatres were often the first air-conditioned buildings, offering refuge on hot summer days. Going to the movies was an important social ritual, frequently linked to dating, courtship, and youth culture.

Historians document the diverse venues where people watched movies, describing film attendance in Manhattan's immigrant neighborhoods (Allen, 1979; Merritt, 1976; Singer, 1996), in vaudeville houses (Allen, 1980), in small towns (Fuller, 1996; Waller, 1995), in rural areas reached only by traveling tent-show exhibitors (Musser, 1991a, b), or in the 'combat zone', a special part of Boston devoted to adult entertainment (Johnson and Schaeffer, forthcoming). Initially, much of this research focused on economic and demographic questions, recognizing exhibition's centrality to vertically-integrated film industries. From the beginning, however, accounting for exhibition required a social and cultural history of film audiences (Allen, 1990; Haralovich, 1986; Streible, 1990). Movies do not mean the same thing when they are positioned alongside other amusement-park attractions (Rabinovitz, 1990) or within 'an evening's entertainment' which might include live stage acts, shorts, cartoons, newsreels, and coming attractions (Koszarski, 1990; Smoodin, 1993). Exhibition practices may subvert textual meanings, which occurred when black jazz bands performing for silent movies used their scores to spoof white movie stars (Carbine, 1990). Early immigrant film-goers experienced the cinema as a schoolhouse for learning American culture and values (Ewen, 1992; Hansen, 1995; Mayne, 1982).

Promotional stunts and window displays instructed patrons in gender-appropriate responses. Rhona Berenstein, for example, documents how 1930s' horror-film exhibitors would plant women in the audience to faint or scream or would position nurses in the lobby and ambulances out front to stress the dangers of watching such frightening films. She explains, 'women were classic horror's central stunt participants because they were thought to personify the genre's favored affect: fear' (Berenstein, 1996: 72). Eric Schaeffer (1994) describes how exploitation film promoters would segregate audiences into male-only or female-only showings in order to combine an aura of sensationalism with a rhetoric of public education and moral uplift.

Film theory's abstract generalizations about spectatorship often depend upon essentialized assumptions about 'archetypal' exhibition practices; theorists compare the experience of watching a movie in a darkened theatre to a dream state, or contrast the focused gaze of the film-goer with the distracted gaze of the television viewer. Such abstractions break down when we confront the eclectic history of film exhibition (Kepley, 1996). Some contexts encourage collective and vocalized responses, others foster quiet contemplation, and the conflict between these different modes of reception often marks significant class, racial, and ethnic boundaries.

The introduction of the video cassette recorder (VCR) has further expanded the contexts where films might be shown. By granting viewers access to a vast archive, the VCR breaks down traditional distinctions between different media, genres, time periods, and taste categories. For example, one university 'Womyn's Group' showed *Thelma and Louise* alongside other 'pro-women movies', including Hollywood films (*Fried Green Tomatoes* [1991], *Gorillas in the Mist* [1988]) and independent documentaries (*Not a Love Story* [1981], *Dreamworlds* [1990]). The VCR enables viewers to 'time-shift' movies so they more perfectly fit into the social dynamics of their lives. For example, Ann Gray (1992) describes a group of housewives who formed a 'movie club', getting together once a week during the day to watch videos (especially romantic comedies, historical melodramas, or musicals) which their husbands refused to see with them. The VCR enables viewers to take greater control over the flow of filmic images, using the fast-forward function to skip past dull bits or to edit together 'good-parts' tapes of special effects sequences or scenes featuring favorite actors.

The VCR enables films to move across national borders. Hamid Naficy (1993) describes how a group of recently displaced Iranian exiles cherished evenings spent eating home-cooked Persian meals with their friends and watching often faded and low-quality tapes of pre-revolutionary Iranian films. The most readily-available films were B movie comedies, melodramas, and action films, which many of these friends would not have watched in other circumstances, but which brought back the sights and sounds of their mother country. At the same time, the underground circulation of bootleg tapes of

Hong Kong action films, Hindi musicals, or Japanese anime (animated films) allow US college students to appropriate Asian popular culture for their own use. Watching anime, Annilee Newitz (1994) tells us, allows some Asian-Americans to reclaim cultural roots broken down by their parents' generation, while many white anime fans challenge American nationalism, stressing the superiority of Japanese products. The anime's foreign origins also provide some male fans with an alibi for enjoying their often 'politically incorrect' representations of female sexuality.

However, the underground circulation of videotape confronts serious technical limitations. Grass-roots distributors of bootleg Japanese and Hong Kong movies, for example, must translate films across incompatible video formats, often working from laserdisc originals. Newitz describes, for example, how some anime clubs make their own subtitled editions of videos otherwise inaccessible to most American viewers. In doing so, however, these groups shape the films' reception, selecting which videos will circulate and framing how those films will be understood through their catalog descriptions or program notes, much as Janet Staiger (1992) describes the ways that the art cinema movement shaped our current understanding of film authorship. For example, anime fandom initially concentrated around male-targeted science fiction and horror genres rather than around the female-marketed romances and historicals or cute animal stories equally prominent in Japan.

The growing centrality of the VCR to the ways audiences encounter film texts challenges film studies' attempts to 'discipline' its own borders along media-specific lines. Newitz's anime fans make little or no meaningful distinction between films made for theatrical release and series produced for airing on Japanese television; they sometimes project the tapes for large audiences at campus screenings or they watch them at home on television. Douglass's Thelma and Louise story appears in a fanzine alongside stories about characters from US (*Star Trek* [1966–1969], *Man From UNCLE* [1964–1968]) and British television (*Blake's 7* [1978–1981], *The Professionals* [1977–1983]). Her linkage between *Thelma and Louise* and *The Hunger* suggests the ready availability on video of films produced decades apart, while the story's title, 'Music of the night' comes from the Broadway musical, *Phantom of the Opera* (1925), available to Douglass through a compact disc soundtrack. An institutional division between film and television studies preserves distinctions which no longer hold descriptive validity in terms of the production, distribution, exhibition, or consumption of media texts in the 1990s. To start from this recognition may allow scholars to ask new questions about the complicated interplay of diverse media technologies (Ang, 1996; Morley, 1992).

Fandoms and other interpretive communities

Although such work has been more common in television studies, film scholars have examined the 'uses' audiences make of filmic images and meanings in their everyday lives, adopting ethnographic techniques to describe the process of media consumption. Such research explores how social factors, such as ethnicity, class, gender, age, or subcultural affiliations, influence film spectatorship and what happens when cultural materials circulate beyond the site of theatrical exhibition.

Such work has a long history. Focus-group interviews, fan writings, and personal autobiographical essays were employed by the Payne Fund researchers in the 1930s to study America's 'movie-made children' and their consumption habits (DeCordova, 1990b). The Payne studies built the case for self-regulation of film content (Jacobs, 1990; Jowett *et al.*, 1996). More recent media 'ethnographers' have had a different agenda, focusing on subcultural challenges to the media's ideological power. Earlier accounts stressed evidence that audience behavior (such as dressing like or imitating film stars) was influenced (often negatively) by film content, while more recent studies regard such behaviors as evidence of 'appropriation' or 'resistance'. This shifting perspective reflects larger changes in the nature of qualitative social science, from a period when researchers preserved a rigid distance from their research subjects towards a period when scholars have recognized the value of more proximate and engaged vantage points. Audience researchers increasingly acknowledge their own stakes in popular culture and their own membership within the fan communities they analyze (Jenkins *et al.*, forthcoming). As a result, they are less likely to portray negatively cultural processes that are part of their own lives.

Despite such shifts, audience research lags far behind dominant trends in the social sciences and still needs to become more self-conscious about the theoretical implications of its methodologies (Nightingale, 1997). At present, the term media 'ethnography' is applied loosely to all qualitative methodologies for studying the contemporary real-world contexts of media consumption. In some cases, the term gets applied inaccurately to focus-group interviews, even where the respondents did not know each other before the researcher brought them together. The term would be better applied to prolonged research into the ongoing interactions of pre-existing fan (or other subcultural) communities, especially work that extends from media consumption towards a broader range of social experiences (schooling, work, family relations).

Although film fans have existed since the beginning of cinema, their identities and activities have shifted dramatically. Many of the earliest film fans, Kathryn Fuller (1996) tells us, were men interested in cinematic technologies and the film-making process. Early film-fan magazines encouraged readers to write their own scenarios; their offices were often flooded with thousands of submissions. Only gradually did the thrust of film-fan interest shift from amateur film-making towards celebrity. In *Star gazing*, Jackie Stacey (1994) focuses on older British women's memories of their relationship to Hollywood films during World War 2 and the immediate post-war period. These women sometimes speak of the American stars as occupying a utopian space of glamour and beauty far removed from wartime shortages. The women also sought to frame the stars as like themselves, either through comparisons based on complexion, hair color, eye color, or personality traits, or through imitating the star's mannerisms and dress. The fact that these women can still remember the stars' specific costumes or gestures decades later suggests how much their relationship with these screen personalities were embedded in personal memories.

Stacey's research suggests the need for more sophisticated distinctions between different kinds of audience investments and identifications. We inhabit a world populated with other people's stories. Few of us have access to the means of production to tell our own stories through the mass media. The stories that enter our lives thus need to be reworked so that they more fully satisfy our needs and fantasies. We 'appropriate' them, or, to use another term, we 'poach' them (deCerteau, 1984). Consider, for example, one webpage which tells the story of two stray dogs their adoptive owners named Thelma and Louise. Reluctant to see these dogs as having been abandoned, the owners chose to construct a fantasy of their voluntary escape from unpleasant domestic lives, seeking freedom together on the open road. Providing these 'outlaw' pooches a home allowed the owners to claim access to the film characters' freedom and mobility.

Fans appropriate materials from film, television, and other forms of popular culture as the basis for their own cultural productions (Jenkins, 1992a). Fanzines such as *On The Edge* contain original fiction about favorite fictional characters, circulating in an underground economy. These stories emerge from – and help to perpetuate – their social interactions with other fans. In many ways, fandom extends traditional folk practices into a modern era of mass production. The difference is not that fans adopt narratives from other sources and retell them in their own terms. Shakespeare did that. So did Homer. The difference is that fans operate in an age where corporations claim exclusive ownership over core cultural narratives. Robin Hood and King Arthur belong to the British people. Kirk and Spock belong to Viacom. In that sense, fans are, indeed, 'poachers', who assert their own roles in the creation of contemporary culture, refusing to bow before pressures exerted upon them by copyright holders.

Some writers cite such fan appropriations as popular 'resistance' to dominant ideology. The situation, however, is far more complex than such formulations allow: fans relate to favorite texts with a mixture of fascination and frustration, attracted to them because they offer the best resources for exploring certain issues, frustrated because these fictions never fully conform to audience desires. Some appropriations may reflect growing disenchantment with conventional constructions of gender and sexuality; others may be highly reactionary, preserving the *status quo* in the face of potential change (Sholle, 1991). If the concept of 'resistance' carries use-value in audience research, we need continually to refine what it means to 'resist' dominant ideology; we should be more precise in examining the goals and the consequences of appropriation.

We impoverish our accounts of fan cultural production if we understand it purely in terms of ideological struggle. Fandoms do not typically understand themselves in political terms. Fans appropriate, rethink, and rework media materials as the basis for their own social interactions and cultural exchanges. As these materials enter into the transforming space of fandom, they are reshaped according to genres, which originate in part from fandoms' own cultural practices. For example, 'Music of the night' is a slash story. This fan genre posits homoerotic relations between fictional characters, most often the male partners commonly found in science fiction or action-adventure stories. Slash allows its mostly female producers to rewrite conventional representations of masculinity, to produce a more nurturing, emotionally sensitive version of the characters, and to imagine romance stories based on equality (Penley, 1992). Western culture has a long tradition of 'romantic friendships' between men, intensifying homosocial relations to the point that they blur into the homoerotic (Sedgewick, 1985). For that reason, slash fans find it relatively easy to locate suitable images in mass culture. Slash fans assert that their fantasies build on 'relationships' that are 'visible' on screen in the performers' non-verbal gestures and physical intimacy (Bacon-Smith, 1992). In most commercial texts, however, the line between the homosocial and the homoerotic is carefully policed. Slash posits a greater fluidity of emotional and erotic expression.

Slash fandom allows women a communal space for talking about their sexual fantasies, offering models for imagining alternative character relationships. Once fans have produced stories about Kirk and Spock and many other male partners, it becomes easier for Douglass to imagine Thelma and Louise as lovers and to construct a story which, she would argue, fits comfortably within the genre. Other fans, however, disagree, insisting that slash emerges specifically from the characteristics of masculine culture; female–female erotica, by its very nature, does not fit within the genre's mainstream (Green *et al.*, forthcoming). Most academic writing on slash fans asks why heterosexual women would construct homoerotic fantasies. However, a growing number of lesbian and bisexual fans appropriate the slash genre for queer pleasures. Douglass created her own zine when she found it difficult to publish female–female stories elsewhere.

Describing interpretations as 'community property', literary critic Stanley Fish (1980) sees readers as members of interpretive communities, who share common strategies for making meaning. Fish is interested in what makes an interpretation acceptable or unacceptable, plausible or implausible, novel or predictable for particular groups. Jacqueline Bobo (1995), for example, has applied Fish's notion of an 'interpretive community' to look at black women's responses to *The Color Purple* (1995). Her respondents defend such films aggressively against outside criticism, stressing the value in having even 'flawed' representations of their lives on the screen. All participants in an interpretive community do not necessarily agree about what a film means; interpretive communities do not impose rigid conformity, only set ground rules for discussion. The black women Bobo interviewed might disagree among themselves about particular characters or plot developments, yet they agreed on the film's relevance to understanding their daily lives.

One way to understand what we mean by an interpretive community would be to think about a net discussion group as a place where people exchange their views on a common topic (Clerc, 1996; Jenkins, 1995; Jones, 1995; Wexelblatt, forthcoming). Initially, as a new discussion group appears, interpretive claims might diverge wildly, yet certain consensuses emerge through discussion; members coalesce around points of mutual interest and avoid areas of dispute. Over time, the group agrees upon what kinds of posts are appropriate. In practice, larger on-line groups may bring together multiple interpretive communities with fundamentally different interests. Sometimes, the group can survive these conflicting agendas by creating alternative lines of discussion. Often, so-called 'flame wars' erupt over places where opposing interpretive communities rub against each other. The various groups cannot explain or justify their different viewpoints because they are not reading by the same rules; the only way to resolve such conflicts is to shift to another plane – a meta-level – where the interpretive communities explain the standards by which they form and evaluate interpretations. As the tension between competing interpretations mounts, the group will splinter, creating competing lists or some members may 'go underground' to protect themselves from harsh responses.

Douglass's 'Music of the night' is controversial because it is not simply a slash story but draws inspiration from alternative traditions of lesbian erotic writing. Slash fans and lesbian viewers may expand upon filmic subtexts, making visible what they see as repressed narratives of same-sex desire. Some lesbians viewers draw upon gossip about stars' personal lives, or subcultural signs (such as costuming or body language) to interpret on-screen characters as queer. Even some films, such as *Fried Green Tomatoes*, which depict lesbian relationships leave those erotic feelings implicit. Other films, such as *Alien* or *Silence of the Lambs*, develop strong cult followings because they leave the sexuality of their female protagonists unmarked, available for queer appropriation. Many lesbians 'read between the lines' as they watched *Thelma and Louise*, tracing Thelma's transformation from ultra-femme to ultra-butch as a subcultural marker of queer identity. Douglass's representation of Thelma and Louise as vampires also drew upon lesbian subcultural knowledge. Vampire films, such as *The Velvet Vampire* (1971), *Daughters of the Darkness* (1971), *The Hunger*, or *Blood and Roses* (1960) have become cult objects among some lesbians, because they explicitly represent erotic contact between women. A growing number of queer writers, including Pat Califia and Jewelle Gomez, have turned towards vampire stories as a genre of erotica (Keesey, 1993). So, in rewriting *Thelma and Louise* as a lesbian vampire story, Douglass links together two different traditions of women's amateur writing, finding a model for female–female relations otherwise unavailable to her as a slash fan.

Academic critics

Academic film studies is still struggling with the implications of this 'discovery of the reader'. In some initial accounts of reception, there was a euphoric tendency to declare the death of the text much as earlier critics had prematurely announced the death of the author. However, as we have seen, texts play central roles in shaping the terms of their reception, even if they do not totally control their meanings. Audience members may appropriate textual materials as the basis for their own cultural creations, including those which represent 'very alternate universes', but there is still a tremendous authority vested in the original that withstands most grass-roots challenges. While even the most straightforward film requires the audience to confront both gaps and excesses, allowing speculations around its margins, we are seldom confused about base-level plot details.

Audience research has increasingly rejected large-scale generalizations about spectatorship, demanding a more contingent 'case-study' approach. Slowly, academics are developing 'mixed genres' of writing which merge textual analysis with historical or ethnographic research. Some classic examples of this approach include Angela McRobbie's discussion (1991) of how *Fame* (1980) fit British youth culture or Valerie

Walkerdine's (1985) account of a working-class family watching *Rocky* (1976). Both writers took seriously what the films meant to their audiences, while offering alternative interpretations of the relationship between the films' content and their consumption contexts. Such works pose significant questions about the relative weight given popular and academic interpretations where they diverge.

If, like Lewis Carroll's Humpty Dumpty, we could make things mean whatever we wanted, then there would be no reason to struggle over access to cultural production or to bemoan sexist, homophobic, nationalistic, or racist media representations. Instead, audience research may provide new motivations for our struggles over film content, as we acknowledge the consequences of excluding certain stories from broader circulation. John Hartley (1992), for example, has called for a mode of 'intervention analysis', which takes seriously the political agendas of popular readerships while using the power and the prestige of the academy to 'intervene in the media' and in the circulation of 'popular knowledge' about media content. Gay, lesbian and bisexual critics, for example, draw upon subcultural strategies to reveal the 'queer' potential of commercially distributed texts. Cathy Griggers (1993), for example, offers an interpretation of *Thelma and Louise* which self-consciously violates conventions of academic analysis and actively 'rewrites' the film. Refusing to accept the film's closure, the protagonist's 'death sentence', Griggers takes their kiss (and their freeze-frame fall) as 'the authorizing signs to read the film's narrative as a lesbian love story, a coming out story'.

In *Making things perfectly queer*, Alexander Doty (1993: 134) challenges the notion that queer interpretations of dominant media texts should be regarded as 'alternative' or 'subtextual' rather than enjoying the same status as interpretations based on heterosexual assumptions. Doty invites us to rethink the politics of reading: If all interpretations are appropriations, why do we still read some as 'outside the mainstream' (Doty, 1993)? What allows us to read heterosexuality into films such as *The Wizard of Oz* (1939) which have no explicit romantic subtexts (Doty, forthcoming), yet reject the idea that Thelma and Louise could be lovers, despite their kiss?

Audience research has forced the academy to re-examine the institutional factors that shape canon-formation or interpretation within academic circles (Bordwell, 1989; Staiger, 1985). Some writers have challenged commonsensical assumptions about the differences between fans and academics (Jenson, 1992; Sconce, 1995). Joli Jenson contrasts the stereotypical emotionalism of fans to the rationality of academics. However, as she notes, academic writing is shaped in significant ways by the affective attachments that draw scholars to particular film-makers or theorists. Writing in a purely 'rational' voice isolates us from our own experiences as media consumers and distorts our accounts of spectatorship.

This realization has facilitated more openly autobiographical criticism. Annette Kuhn (1995), for example, has written an introspective essay about *Mandy* (1952), a favorite film from her childhood; Kuhn explores how her academic training transformed her relationship to such melodramatic works, struggling to reclaim something of what *Mandy* once meant to her. While Kuhn's refusal of academic distance remains controversial, film studies actually lags behind literary criticism, where autobiographical modes of writing have gained much broader attention and acceptance (Freedman *et al.*, 1993). Film studies may still be too uncertain about its status as a discipline to erase fully the line between academic and fan. Erecting such a boundary was the price of its admission into the academy. Yet, new modes of critical writing are more and more drawing upon traditions of fan discourse, making the way for more openly appropriative, playful, autobiographical, and inventive genres of critical analysis. Such changes will not come easily, since they go against many of the rules of conventional critical discourse. Yet, these new genres of criticism may bring us closer to understanding the affective power of popular cinema. Soon, it may be possible for us, as students and academic critics to imagine alternative endings of *Thelma and Louise* in our papers, even those that turn them into bats flying off to Mexico.

References

Allen, R.C.1979: Motion picture exhibition in Manhattan, 1906–1912: beyond the Nickelodeon. *Cinema Journal* **18**(2): 2–15.

Allen, R.C.1980: *Vaudeville and film, 1895–1915: a study in media interaction.* New York: Arno Press.

Allen, R. C., and Gomery, D. 1985: *Film history: theory and practice.* New York: Alfred A. Knopf.

Allen, R. 1990: From exhibition to reception: reflections on the audience in film history. *Screen* **31**(4): 347–356.

Ang, I. 1996: *Living room wars: rethinking media audiences for a postmodern world.* London: Routledge.

Bacon-Smith, C. 1992: *Enterprising women: television, fandom and the creation of popular myth.* Philadelphia, PA: University of Pennsylvania Press.

Bakhtin, M. 1981: *The dialogic imagination.* Austin, TX: University of Texas Press.

Barer, A. 1991: October: a male perspective on the movie, *Thelma and Louise. Playboy,* 45.

Bennett, T. 1983: The Bond phenomenon: theorizing a popular hero. *Southern Review* **16**(2): 195–225.

Bennett, T. and Woollacott, J. 1988: *Bond and beyond: the political career of a popular hero.* London: Macmillan.

Berenstein, R.J. 1996: *Attack of the leading ladies: gender, sexuality and spectatorship in classic horror cinema.* New York: Columbia University Press.

Bobo, J. 1995: *Black women as cultural readers.* New York: Columbia University Press.

Bogal, L. undated: essay questions on *Thelma and Louise.* Unpublished materials for writing instructors, Cornell University, Ithaca, NY.

Bordwell, D. 1985: *Narration in the fiction film.* Madison, WI: University of Wisconsin Press.

Bordwell, D. 1989: *Making meanings: inference and rhetoric in the interpretation of cinema.* Cambridge, MA: Harvard University Press.

Budd, M. (ed.) 1990: *The cabinet of Dr. Caligari: texts, contexts, histories.* New Brunswick, NJ: Rutgers University Press.

Carbine, M. 1990: 'The finest outside the loop': motion picture exhibition in Chicago's black metropolis. *Camera Obscura* **23**: 8–41.

Clerc, S.J. 1996: DDEB, GATB, MPPB and Ratboy: the *X-Files'* media fandom, online and off. In Lavery, D. , Hague, A. and Cartwright, M. (eds), *'Deny All Knowledge': reading the X-Files.* Syracuse, NY: Syracuse University Press, pp. 36–51; C.

Corliss, R. 1991: Why can't a woman be a man? *Time,* 5 August: 66.

Corrigan, T. 1986: Film and the culture of cult. *Wide Angle* **8**(3/4): 91–100.

Crafton, D. 1996: The *Jazz Singer's* reception in the media and at the box office. In Bordwell, D. and Carroll, N. (eds), *Post-theory: reconstructing film studies.* Madison, WI: University of Wisconsin Press, pp. 460–80.

deCerteau, M. 1984: *The practice of everyday life*. Berkeley, CA: University of California Press.

DeCordova, R. 1990a: *Picture personalities: the emergence of the star system in America*. Urbana, IL: University of Illinois Press.

DeCordova, R. 1990b: Ethnography and exhibition: the child audience, the Hays Office and Saturday matinees. *Camera Obscura* **23**: 90–107.

Doty, A. 1993: *Making things perfectly queer: interpreting mass culture*. Minneapolis, MN: University of Minnesota Press.

Doty, A. forthcoming: My beautiful wickedness: *The Wizard of Oz* as lesbian fantasy. In Jenkins, H., McPherson, T., and Shattuc, J. (eds), *Hop on pop: the politics and pleasures of popular culture*. Durham, NC: Duke University Press.

Douglass, S. 1994: Music of the night. *On the Edge*. Baltimore, MD: OTP Press, pp. 63–70.

Eco, U. 1983: *Casablanca*: cult movies and intertextual collage. In *Travels in hyperreality*. San Diego, CA: Harcourt Brace Jovanovich, pp. 197–212.

Ewen, E. 1992: City lights: immigrant women and the rise of the movies. In Ewen, E., and Ewen, S. (eds), *Channels of desire: mass images and the shaping of American consciousness*. Minneapolis, MN: University of Minnesota Press, pp. 53–74.

Fish, S. 1980: *Is there a text in this class?: The authority of interpretive communities*. Cambridge, MA: Harvard University Press.

Fiske, J. 1992: British cultural studies and television. In Allen, R. (ed.), *Channels of discourse, reassembled*. Chapel Hill, NC: University of North Carolina Press, pp. 284–397.

Freedman, D.P., Frey, O., and Zauhar, F.M. (eds) 1993: *The intimate critique: autobiographical literary criticism*. Durham, NC: Duke University Press.

Freund, E. 1987: *The return of the reader: reader response criticism*. London and New York: Methuen.

Fuller, K. 1996: *At the picture show: small-town audiences and the creation of movie fan culture*. Washington, DC, and London: Smithsonian Institution Press.

Gomery, D. 1992: *Shared pleasures: a history of movie presentation in the United States*. Madison, WI: University of Wisconsin Press.

Gray, A. 1992: *Video playtime: the gendering of a leisure technology*. London: Routledge.

Green, S., Jenkins, C., and Jenkins, H. forthcoming: 'The normal female interest in men bonking': selections from *Terra Nostre Underground* and *Strange Bedfellows*. In Harris, C. (ed.), *Understanding fandom*. New York: Hampton Press.

Griggers, C. 1993: *Thelma and Louise* and the cultural generation of the new butch-femme. In Collins, J., Radner, H., and Collins, A.P. (eds), *Film theory goes to the movies*. New York: Routledge/AFI.

Hansen, M. 1995: Early cinema, late cinema: transformations of the public sphere. In Williams, L. (ed.), *Viewing positions: ways of seeing film*. New Brunswick, NJ: Rutgers University Press, pp. 134–54.

Haralovich, M.B. 1986: Film history and social history. *Wide Angle* **8**(2): 4–14.

Hartley, J. 1992: *Tele-ology: studies in television*. London: Routledge.

Jacobs, L. 1990: Reformers and spectators: the film education movement in the thirties. *Camera Obscura* **22**: 29–50.

Jenkins, H. 1992a: *Textual poachers: television fans and participatory culture*. New York: Routledge, Chapman & Hall.

Jenkins, H. 1992b: *What made pistachio nuts?: Early sound comedy and the Vaudeville aesthetic*. New York: Columbia University Press.

Jenkins, H. 1995: 'Do you enjoy making the rest of us feel stupid?': alt.tv.twinpeaks, the trickster author, and viewer mastery. In Lavery, D. (ed.), *Full of secrets: critical approaches to* Twin Peaks. Detroit, MI: Wayne State University, pp. 51–69.

Jenkins, H., McPherson, T. and Shattuc, J. 2000: Introduction: the culture that sticks to your skin. In Jenkins, H., McPherson, T., Shattuc, J. (eds), *Hop on pop: the politics and pleasures of popular culture.* Durham, NC: Duke University Press.

Jenson, J. 1992: Fandom as pathology: the consequences of characterization. In Lewis, Lisa A. (ed.), *The adoring audience: fan culture and popular media.* New York: Routledge.

Johnson, E. and Schaeffer, E. 2000: Quarantined! A case study of Boston's combat zone. In Jenkins, H,. McPherson, T. and Shattuc, J. (eds), *Hop on pop: the politics and pleasures of popular culture.* Durham, NC: Duke University Press.

Jones, S.G. (ed.) 1995: *Cybersociety: computer-mediated communication and community.* London: Sage.

Jowett, G.S., Jarvie, I. C. and Fuller, K.H., 1996: *Children and the movies: media influence and the Payne Fund controversy.* New York: Cambridge University Press.

Kapsis, R.E. 1992: *Hitchcock: the making of a reputation.* Chicago, IL: University of Chicago Press.

Kaufman, S. 1991: *Thelma and Louise. The New Republic* 1 July: 28.

Keesey, P. 1993: *Daughters of Darkness: lesbian vampire stories.* Pittsburgh, PA: Cleis Press.

Kepley, V. 1996: Whose apparatus?: Problems of film exhibition and history. In Bordwell, S. and Caroll, N. (eds), *Post-theory: reconstructing film studies.* Madison, WI: University of Wisconsin Press, pp. 533–52.

Khouri, C. 1996: *Thelma and Louise* and *Something to Talk About:* screenplays. New York: Grove.

Klawans, S. 1991: *Thelma and Louise. The Nation,* 24 June: 86.

Klinger, B. 1994: *Melodrama and meaning: history, culture, and the films of Douglas Sirk.* Bloomington, IN: Indiana University Press.

Koszarski, R. 1990: *An evening's entertainment: the age of the silent feature picture, 1915–1928.* Berkeley, CA: University of California Press.

Kuhn, A. 1995: *Family secrets: acts of memory and imagination.* London and New York: Verso.

McAlister, L.L. undated: *Thelma and Louise,* the women's show. WMNF-FM, Tampa, FL. http://www.inform.umd.edu/EdRes/Topic/WomensStudies/FilmReviews/thelma+louise-mcalister

McLaughlin, T. 1996: *Street smarts and critical theory: listening to the vernacular.* Madison, MI: University of Wisconsin Press.

McRobbie, A. 1991: *Feminism and youth culture: from Jackie to Just Seventeen.* London: Macmillan.

Maland, C.J. 1989: *Chaplin and American culture: the evolution of a star image.* Princeton, NJ: Princeton University Press.

Maltby, R. 1996: A brief romantic interlude: Dick and Jane go to 3½ seconds of the classical Hollywood cinema. In Bordwell, D. and Carroll, N. (eds), *Post-theory: reconstructing film studies.* Madison, WI: University of Wisconsin Press, pp. 434–59.

Maslin, J. 1991: Lay off *Thelma and Louise. The New York Times* 16 June, section 2: 11.

Masonn, M.S. 1991: The movie, *Thelma and Louise* isn't just about trashing men. *The Christian Science Monitor* 1 July: 11.

Mayne, J. 1982: Immigrants and spectators. *Wide Angle* **5**(2): 32–41.

Merritt, R. 1976: Nickelodeon theatres, 1905–1914: building an audience for the movies. In Balio, T. (ed.), *The American film industry.* Madison, WI: University of Wisconsin Press.

Miller, D.A. 1991: Anal rope. In Fuss, D. (ed.), *inside/out: lesbian theories, gay theories.* London: Routedge.

Morley, D. 1992: *Television audiences and cultural studies.* London: Routledge.

Musser, C. 1991a: *High class motion picture shows: Lyman H. Howe and the forgotten era of travelling exhibition 1880–1920.* Princeton, NJ: Princeton University Press.

Musser, C. 1991b: *Before the nickelodeon: Edwin S. Porter and the Edison Manufacturing Company.* Berkeley, CA: University of California Press.

Naficy, H. 1993: *The making of exile cultures: Iranian television in Los Angeles.* Minneapolis, MN: University of Minnesota Press.

Newitz, A. 1994: Anime Otaku: Japanese animation fans outside Japan. *Bad Subjects* **13** (April); available on-line at http://magma.mines.edu/students/j/jchac/anime/otaku.txt

Nightingale, V. 1997: *Studying audiences: shock of the real.* London: Routledge.

Penley, C. 1992: Feminism, psychoanalysis and the study of popular culture. In Grossberg, L., Nelson, C., and Treichler, P. (eds), *Cultural studies.* New York: Routledge, pp. 479–93.

Rabinovitz, L. 1990: Temptations of pleasure: nickelodeons, amusement parks and the sights of female sexuality. *Camera Obscura* **23**: 70–89.

Rabinovitz, P.J. 1985: The turn of the glass key: popular fiction as reading strategy. *Critical Inquiry* **12**(2): 418–31.

Sawyers, J. 1991: Callie Khouri answers critics of *Thelma and Louise. Chicago Tribune* 7 July: 1.

Schaeffer, E. 1994: 'Bold! daring! shocking! true!': a history of exploitation films, 1919–1959. Ph.D dissertation, University of Texas at Austin, Austin, TX.

Schickel, R. 1991: Gender bender: a white-hot debate rages over whether *Thelma and Louise* celebrates liberated females, male bashers – or outlaws. *Time,* 24 June: 25.

Sconce, J. 1995: 'Trashing' the Academy: taste, excess and an emerging politics of cinematic style. *Screen* **36**(4): 371–93.

Sedgwick, E.K. 1985: *Between men: English literature and male homosocial desire.* New York: Columbia University Press.

Shattuc, J. 1995: *Television, tabloids and tears: Fassbinder and popular culture.* Minneapolis, MN: University of Minnesotta Press.

Sholle, D. 1991: Reading the audience, reading resistance: prospects and problems. *Journal of Film and Video* **43**(1–2): 80–9.

Siefkes, D. 1995: Improving the image of an industry through PR. *Marketing* (November); *http://www.siefkesgroup.com/column1.html*

Simon, J. 1991: *Thelma and Louise. National Review* 8 June: 48.

Singer, B. 1996: Manhattan nickelodeons: new data on audiences and exhibitors. *Cinema Journal* **34**(3): 5–35.

Smoodin, E. 1993: *Animating culture: Hollywood cartoons from the sound era.* New Brunswick, NJ: Rutgers University Press.

Stacey, J. 1994: *Star gazing: Hollywood cinema and female spectatorship.* London: Routledge.

Staiger, J. 1985: The politics of film canons. *Cinema Journal* **24**: 3.

Staiger, J. 1992: *Interpreting films: studies in the historical reception of American cinema.* Princeton, NJ: Princeton University Press.

Streible, D. 1990: The literature of film exhibition: a bibliography on motion picture exhibition and related topics. *The Velvet Light Trap* **25**: 80–119.

Telotte, J.P., 1991: *The cult film experience: beyond all reason.* Austin, TX: University of Texas Press.

Turner, G. (ed.) 1990: *British cultural studies: an introduction.* Boston, MA: Unwin Hyman.

Walkerdine, V. 1985: Video replay. In Burgin, V., Donald, J., and Kaplan, C. (eds.), *Formations of fantasy.* London: Routledge.

Waller, G.A. 1995: *Main street amusements: movies and commercial entertainment in a southern city, 1895–1930.* Washington, DC: Smithsonian Institute Press.

Weiss, A. 1992: *Vampires and violets: lesbians in the cinema.* London: Jonathan Cape.

Wexelblatt, A. 2000: An auteur in the age of the Internet: JMS, Babylon 5, and the Net. In Jenkins, H., McPherson, T., and Shattuc, J. (eds), *Hop on pop: the politics and pleasure of popular culture.* Durham, NC: Duke University Press.

10 Re-examining stardom: questions of texts, bodies and performance

Christine Geraghty

Stardom has been a key concept in the development of film theory, and cinema has been the key site to test and prove stardom. As Christine Gledhill wrote, 'while other entertainment industries may manufacture stars, cinema still provides the ultimate confirmation of stardom' (1991a: xiii). Others though have been less sure. Allen and Gomery, in their historical account, comment rather wearily that the term 'star' as applied to 'rock stars, athletes and soap opera actors . . . has become so overused as to become almost meaningless' (1985: 172). This chapter looks at what has happened to the concept of stars and explores what is at stake in film studies when we use a term which arguably, as Allen and Gomery suggest, now takes its meaning and energy from elsewhere. We need to look at stars in a context in which film stars may struggle for prominence. Girls' magazines which in the 1940s and 1950s featured film stars are now more likely to have pin-ups of singers, footballers, models and teenage soap actors; women's magazines reflect the same diversity and a whole magazine genre has developed around the homes and lifestyles of celebrities who are as likely to be minor royals and popular singers as film stars. In addition, for many fans there has been a shift from the cinema-based viewing of the studio years to video and television as the main means of viewing. The weekly visit to the cinema with its huge screen, darkened auditoria and (sometimes) glamorous decor has been replaced by popping in to the video store to check out the selection, followed by a viewing on a small screen in domestic circumstances.

The concept of stardom has been important in film studies because it related to the dominant ways of theorising film which developed in the 1970 and 1980s. Like genre, work on stars offered the possibility (not always taken up) of looking at the whole cinematic process through work on production, text and audiences. More specifically, the significance of stars could be explained through theories which were developed to consider how meaning was generated in the film text more generally. We can trace three overlapping theoretical developments here. First, there was the relationship between film and the real which led to a debate about film as a signifying system. Here, the influence of semiotics laid emphasis on the star as a sign; such a model emphasised the construction of the star image though, as Dyer and Ellis recognised, particular discourses of acting and presence promise access to the authentic individual behind the star's construction. This work on semiotics led to what can be defined as the second strand – an emphasis on intertextuality which linked work on stars with debates about ideology and resistance. Such work is associated with Richard Dyer's ground-breaking study (1979) and, in the emphasis on stars as sites of contradiction and resistance, provides a link between film studies and debates in cultural studies. Here work on fan cultures could be connected with that on subcultures, and questions could be asked about what audiences actually did with star images. Jackie Stacey's *Star gazing* (1994) represented an important turn to audience studies here. Stacey also drew on elements of the third strand which rooted film study in psychoanalytic work on gender. Mulvey's 1975 article, though it was not directly concerned with stardom, was premised on the different roles of male and female stars, the contrast between the female star as the fetish, the spectacle which held up the story, and the male star as the ego ideal whose mastery of the narrative made him a powerful mechanism of identification. Such an analysis was also linked to a particular view of cinema in which the darkness and the huge screen image created a particular kind of viewing relationship. Work since the 1970s has loosened up the strict gender categories so that, for instance, male 'to-be-looked-at-ness' is now a much discussed phenomenon, but the importance of the concept of the star in this area of study remains.

In this chapter, I want to look at the ways in which these understandings of film stardom can be related to the broader context indicated by Allen and Gomery. Rather than rejecting the term star because it now takes in soap actors and football players, I want to look at how the film star fits into the broader context of star within mass popular culture. By using examples mainly taken from US cinema, I want to suggest that the concepts of celebrity, cultural value and performance need to be reformulated in order to analyse how film stars make meaning in contemporary cinema and contemporary culture.

Defining stars

Definitions of stars in film studies have emphasised that the concept of stardom is sustained by a contrast between the performing presence and what happens 'off-stage'. Dyer writes of stars having 'an existence in the world independent of their screen/"fiction" appearances' (1979: 22) and describes stardom as 'an image of the ways stars live' (1979: 39). Allen and Gomery talk of 'a duality between actor and character' and, citing Edgar Morin, refer to stars as 'actors "with biographies"' (1985: 172), whereas Tasker in her work on New Hollywood describes stars as 'complex personas made up of far more than the texts in which they appear' (1993: 74). It is this duality of image which is deemed to mark a star, a duality which emphasises a balance between the site of fictional performance and life outside. Classically, the duality was based, as Dyer demonstrated, on a contrast between the glamorous film world and the surprisingly ordinary domestic life of the star. So, *Photoplay* featured Gregory Peck with a pile of chopped wood and commented that this task had to be done, regardless of status; 'life is pretty much the same – whether you are the son of a La Jolla druggist or a famous film star' (Gelman, 1972: 343). Other versions of the dual image were less wholesome and the contrast between performance and life outside could be based on more scandalous stories of affairs, drink and drugs. The contrast between the public and private, the ordinary and the extraordinary is made available through a wide range of texts which goes well beyond the films into the newspapers, fan magazines, television shows and exchanges of information and rumour between fans. Dyer's influential notion of 'the structured polysemy' of the star image (1979: 3) drew attention to this wide range of source material and emphasised the contradictory ideals which stars embody. Dyer identified 'multiple *but finite* meanings' (1979: 72, my emphasis) but later commentators have concentrated on the instability of star images. Judith Mayne is typical in arguing that 'inconsistency, change and fluctuation are characteristic of star images' (1993: 128) and suggests that the very appeal of stardom is based on 'constant reinvention, the dissolution of contraries, the embrace of widely opposing terms' (1993: 138). The emphasis on instability has been particularly strong because stars in film studies have been strongly associated with questions of identity – 'being interested in stars is being interested in how we are human now' (Dyer, 1987: 17). Psychoanalytic theory, influential in film studies, has emphasised the instability of the subject and the contradictory nature of identity. Links with cultural studies have also contributed to this sense of instability and resistance, emphasising the role of fans in making different and contested meanings. John Fiske makes this link between stars, fans and identity when he writes of the way in which audiences make meanings for their own purposes by choosing 'texts or stars that offer . . . opportunities to make meanings of their own social identities and social experiences' (1992: 35). Such possibilities are particularly associated with questions of gender. Tasker (1993) argues against criticisms of Hollywood action movies by emphasising the possibilities for resistance and contradiction offered by male action stars to their fans, and Pam Cook points to the way in which certain female stars 'resist the role assigned to them' and speculates, 'Perhaps this is where true star quality resides' (1993: xv).

Generally, then, the model for work on stars and their audiences has been that of an unstable and contradictory figure, constructed both intertextually (across different films) and extratextually (across different types of material). The relationship between the audience and star is deemed to be best figured by the fan whose knowledge comes from a wide variety of sources and who reworks the material in the interests of working through contradictory questions of identity. This emphasis on the duality of the film star and the relationship with the fan has also become established for work in popular culture more generally. In music, television, sport and beyond, the model is one of a relationship between the public sphere of performance and work and the private sphere of personal lives, of the home and personal relationships as 'revealed' through the media. Sometimes this relationship is heavily managed as can be seen in the pages of *Hello!*, the British photomagazine which invites us into the tranquil and polished homes of a range of celebrities and is always careful to emphasise the value of their work (Figure 10.1). Elsewhere, the less respectful press publicises claims of drug use, marital difficulties and personal disasters, often with an implied contrast between the control and skill of the public performance and the lack of control 'off-stage'. Princess Diana entered into the realm of stardom when knowledge of her unhappy private life could act as a counter to the glamorous public 'work'.

Figure 10.1 Cover of *Hello!* magazine.
Reproduced courtesy of Hello! Limited.

Rethinking the categories

In thinking about how film stardom now operates in popular US cinema in particular, we need to unpack this model of stardom and look at the different ways in which meaning is made through a star. In this section, I want to look at other categories – celebrity/professional/performer – which also contribute to a paradigm of the different ways in which well-known individuals 'appear' in the media and to suggest that these distinctions better help us to understand what film stars have in common with and how they differ from other mass media public figures.

The term celebrity indicates someone whose fame rests overwhelmingly on what happens outside the sphere of their work and who is famous for having a lifestyle. The celebrity is thus constructed through gossip, press and television reports, magazine articles and public relations. The 'biography' though is not matched by corresponding excellence elsewhere. Gary Whannell writes of sports stars who get to the point where 'the prominence is self-sustaining' (1992: 122), and in a British context upper-class access to parties, premieres and posh sporting events can generate celebrity status without a contrasting site of performance. Women are particularly likely to be seen as celebrities whose working life is of less interest and worth than their personal life. Liz Hurley's work as a model and actress, for instance, contributed less to her celebrity status than Versace dresses and an errant boyfriend, and even Princess Diana's celebrity was based more on personal appearance and a dramatic private life than on her public good works.

Celebrities may be contrasted to 'professionals'. These are people whose fame rests on their work in such a way that there is very little sense of a private life and the emphasis is on the seamlessness of the public persona. In television, this kind of consistency has been associated by Langer with television's personalities which 'exist as more or less stable "identities" within the flow of events, situations and narratives' (1981: 357). This consistency is evident with newsreaders, journalists, chat-show hosts and sports commentators who are particularly associated with modes of direct address to the audience. It can also be seen in fictional shows which depend on the regular appearance of recognisable fictional characters so that the actor is hidden behind the character and recognised only through that association. Regular soap and situation comedy actors would fall into this category since their fame depends on particular professional roles. The professional lacks the double image of the star though, as the case of Roseanne illustrates, the move can be made to star status when a 'biography' is brought to the audience's attention.

The third category, that of performer, is also associated with work and the public element of the star duality rather than the private life of the celebrity. In this category though, unlike that of the professional, skills and performance elements are not hidden but drawn attention to and the emphasis is on the showcasing or demonstration of skills. Tasker, in her work on action films, contrasts performers such as Chuck Norris and Claude Van Damme to stars, suggesting that the performer is characterised by the focus on particular skills such as martial arts which are showcased by the text (1993: 74). In this context, certain kinds of actors can be seen as performers whose acting skills are showcased in theatre, film and television. The actor as a performer is defined by work and is often associated with the high cultural values of theatrical performance, even when that performance takes place in film or television. The more actors are known only for their performance, the more cultural value they are likely to be given though paradoxically this may only be appreciated by a limited group. But the further an 'actor' strays from performance into the duality of the star, the more cultural value is lost, as Kenneth Brannagh and Emma Thompson discovered when their marriage break-up hit the tabloids.

Film stardom then has to be seen in the context of the drive in the media to create and exploit the status of being famous across the whole range of entertainment formats. Film, a medium in its own right, becomes also a site to be mined by other media. But cinema is a relatively inefficient way of delivering fame compared with some other formats. Cinema is slow to produce new products and while this can generate a sense of anticipation ('Batman is back') and huge audiences for the first weekend's screening the gaps between films for individual stars can be very long. Committed fans may be happy to re-view during the absence but the more regular appearances of those from spheres such as television, music or sport makes them more available to function as stars whether as pin-ups in teen magazines or as recognisable figures in press stories. I want to suggest that, in this situation, the emphasis on the polysemic film star as a site of resistance can no longer, if it ever could, account for the variety of ways in which film stars function. In a situation of intense competition for the extratextual attention of the media, there are choices, for audiences and stars, about whether to exploit the full range of mass media exposure or to establish pleasures around stardom which are specifically related to the film text and to cinema. It is these questions I wish to explore through an examination of the way in which film stars can be analysed through the categories I have outlined here.

Star-as-celebrity

The dual nature of film stardom continues to be important but in certain contexts the emphasis is almost entirely on 'biography' or the celebrity element of stardom. Films stars share this terrain with others from sport, television, fashion and music, and the material found in the press, in particular, emphasises not the work but the leisure and private life of the star. This is the area where the intertextuality may be most important since knowledge of the star's 'real' life is pieced together from gossip columns and celebrity interviews, establishing a range of discourses in which the star features. In the discourse of celebrity, film stars literally interact with those from other areas. Thus, our knowledge that Johnny Depp goes out with the model Kate Moss is in the same register as the news of footballer David Beckham marrying a Spice Girl. For young fans, in particular, the celebrity mode may be the most accessible way into film stardom precisely because it links together different entertainment formats – magazines, videos, photography, film – and reworks distant film stars into the boyfriend of the girl next door; the teenage magazine *Sugar* (Issue 32, June 1997) remarked that Gwyneth Paltrow was 'as nervous as the rest of us' at having her long hair cut. 'Only difference is, she had Brad to sit in the salon, reassuringly holding her mitt throughout her hideous ordeal!'

This emphasis on the private sphere and the interaction with other forms of fame means that in the celebrity mode the films are relatively unimportant and a star can continue to command attention as a celebrity despite failures at the box office. For Julia Roberts and Richard Gere, for instance, the balance of their star constructions shifted away in the 1990s from their relatively unsuccessful films to the complications of their personal lives. In such circumstances, the dual nature of the star construction has diminished and the balance has shifted towards that of the celebrity where there is no work to back up the emphasis on the private life. In this construction of the celebrity, it no longer makes sense to see this circulation of information and images as subsidiary or secondary to the films or indeed to see cinema as different from other entertainment arenas. It is the audience's access to and celebration of intimate information from a variety of texts and sources which are important here.

Star-as-professional

By contrast, the other categories of stardom construct a rather different relationship between star and audience, one which is based much more substantially on the film text. In these categories – the star-as-professional and the star-as-performer – it is quite possible to understand and enjoy the meaning of the star without the interdiscursive knowledge which the star-as-celebrity relies on.

The star-as-professional makes sense through the combination of a particular star image with a particular film context. It arises when we check 'whether an actor's presence in a film seems to correspond with his or her professional role' (Naremore, 1990: 262) and often involves the star's identification with a particular genre. This has become particularly important in the changed distribution situation brought about by the video market. The video shop offers the audience more films than even the multiplex, and linking the star to a genre gives a reliable indicator that a particular video will deliver what it seems to offer. In order not to limit the customer too early in the process of choosing what to rent, video stores tend not to use the more specific genre categorisations of westerns, gangster films and horror genres and employ the rather vaguer descriptions (previously confined to the trade press) such as 'action movie,' 'comedy' and 'drama'. Within those categories, however, particular stars offer a precise indication of what is on offer. Thus, certain stars such as Steve Martin, Eddie Murphy and Jim Carrey are linked to certain forms of comedy whereas the stars whom Tasker discusses – Stallone, Schwarznegger and Van Damme – are associated with quite precise variations of the action film and displays of masculine prowess.

I would suggest that for the star-as-professional a stable star image is of crucial importance. Too much difference from established star image may lead to disappointment for the intended audience. Stallone offers an interesting example of the difficulties facing a professional star who wants to change. In her study of action heroes such as Stallone, Tasker emphasises the instability of stardom, arguing that the 'truth' of a star is tied to identity which is never secured (1993: 76) and that stars work by creating space for contradictory and ambivalent identifications in the audience. She suggests that a star such as Schwarznegger managed to work on this instability by introducing an element of comedy, thus effecting a change in image away from bodybuilding and a shift into more mainstream work. But Tasker also cites the example of Stallone whose star image embodies the immigrant who achieves success in the face of the establishment. Films such as *Rocky* (1976) and *First Blood* (1982) crucially conflated fictional narratives and the story of the actor, so that certain themes – 'rags to riches', 'achievement through struggle', 'determination to succeed against all odds' – became 'central aspects of Stallone's star image' (1993: 84). Tasker's account suggests, however, that far from being unstable this image is critical to the success of his films and that repetition of the 'underdog' (1993: 84) figure is essential to the success of his work. When he tries to move away from that image by seeking to extend his range as a performer, the films fail to find an audience, as Stallone himself is reported to have recognised: 'the audience didn't want to see me in comedies. It's straight action from now on' (*Screen International*, 10 December 1993, p.21).

Stallone is also an example of the way in which two modes of stardom can run in parallel with each other without being productively contradictory in the manner described by Dyer and Mayne in their accounts of stardom. Stallone does also have an existence as a celebrity in which marriages, children, celebrity restaurants and *Hello!* spreads provide the characteristically intertextual material which accompanies a star-as-celebrity. But this success as a celebrity and the way he makes meaning as a professional star do not sit well together and it seems likely his stardom within cinema is dependent on quite a limited role in particular genres. Stallone wearing glasses and clutching babies is not merely a contradictory image; it is a dysfunctional one for the fans of his action movies.

If Stallone has had difficulties settling for being a professional star linked to particular genres, Harrison Ford is probably the most successful current exponent of this approach, a man described by *Screen International* as having 'a near perfect track record and probably the most consistent box office draw in the world' (15 December, 1995, p. 18). Ford operates in a wider generic field than many professional stars, moving smoothly between action films, thrillers and detective films with the occasional aside into comedy. Given this variation, it is noteworthy that Ford is absolutely consistent in performance, and enjoyment of a Ford film very much depends on watching the contrast between easy expressiveness of his body movements and the impassive face with its limited range of expressions. In this respect, Ford represents a continuation of the Hollywood studio style which Dyer analyses in his study of stars. He distinguished between acting styles in which the actor appears to be playing himself or herself (the radio or Hollywood studio style) and those in which there is a clear distinction between actor and character (the repertory or Broadway style) (1979: 156–60). Barry King also differentiates between 'impersonation' in which the actor's '"real" personality . . . should disappear into the part', and 'personification' in which the actor's personality is consonant with the part (1991: 168). The Hollywood star system was very much associated with personification, with the notion that the stars did not act but were themselves and that the pleasurably recognisable repertoire of gestures, expressions and movements were the property of the star not of any individual character.

So seamless is this style in Ford's case that it is easier to describe it by talking about the rare points where it is put at risk or seems to be not going to happen. Part of the power of the dance scene in *Witness* (Weir, 1985) lies in the way in which Ford is transformed, the shift from thriller to romance being marked through performance. As he approaches Rachel (Kelly McGinnis), his face is stiff and his eyes intense. Then his eyes widen, a smile breaks up the planes of his face and as he holds her and begins to move, rather stiffly and carefully, he puts the dance in quotation marks with the movement of his hands and a shrug of his shoulders. The intense, impassive expression returns as the pair nearly kiss; then, he moves his body fractionally before he turns his gaze away from her, softens his face muscles, widens his eyes and resumes the dance until it is interrupted by the arrival of Rachel's father. The tenderness of the scene depends upon the revelation, through gesture, of feeling which is normally hidden behind the Ford mask. A rather different approach occurs in *The Devil's Own* (Pakula, 1997). Here, Ford plays an ageing New York cop Tom whose happy home life is disrupted by arrival of Brad Pitt's IRA activist. In the first part of the film Ford is asked for a more expansive performance than usual, smiling at his wife, teasing his daughters, hugging this newfound 'son'. Ford seems to use his unfamiliarity in the role to underline Tom's unease with the domestic sphere. In the end, however, Ford returns to the role of the isolated pursuer of truth; his words are barked out, close-ups show the hard planes of his face, gesture is reduced to the minimum. Ford's star image has reasserted itself and *The Devil's Own* helped to take him to the number one position in *Screen International*'s analysis of the 1997 top-10 actors (12 December, 1997).

Ford and others in this category represent a continuation of the performance methods of, for instance, John Wayne (Dyer, 1979: 165–7) and Clint Eastwood.[1] The difference may only be one of degree in that for stars such as Ford the range seems to be getting narrower given the market demands for an association of the professional star with particular characters or 'franchises'; *Screen International* (9 December 1994, p. 24) commented approvingly that Ford 'has established himself as Jack Ryan in another successful franchise'. This narrowing of range is a way of giving to film the stability normally associated with long-running television series. It is usual to *contrast* the television personality and the cinema star as Langer does in suggesting that in cinema 'the star absorbs the identity of the film character' whereas on television it is the characters who are the 'memorable identities' (1981: 359). I am suggesting instead that film stars such as Ford, who work within the star-as-professional category, operate for cinema/video in the same way as a character in a television series, providing the pleasures of stability and repetition and the guarantee of consistency in the apparent plethora of choice offered by the expanding media.

Star-as-performer

This emphasis on a consistent persona underlines the claim to the uniqueness of the star-as-professional but, because of the emphasis on 'being' rather than acting, little attention is paid to the work done unless it be to the difficulties of filming hazardous action sequences. In this final category, though, attention is deliberately drawn to the work of acting so that, in a reversal of the celebrity category, it is performance and work which are emphasised, not leisure and the private sphere. This has always been a factor for certain, often theatrically based, stars, but I would suggest that it now takes on particular importance as a way for film stars to claim legitimate space in the overcrowded world of celebrity status. The expansion of the celebrity side means that film stars no longer dominate that arena and indeed the fact that soap stars and pop musicians can gain such celebrity may precisely, as Allen and Gomery note, have devalued the process. As a response to this there has been quite a pronounced shift towards performance as a mark of stardom and the concept of star-as-performer has become a way of re-establishing film-star status through a route which makes its claim through the film text rather than appearances in the newspapers. Method acting, in particular, claims cultural status by making the celebrity trappings part of the detritus which has to be discarded if the performance is to be understood; Naremore comments that De Niro, 'since becoming a famous actor, has avoided tacky celebrity interviews' (1990: 280).

Stars as performers are marked by an emphasis on 'impersonation', on a distinction between star and role which is effaced in the star-as-professional. I would speculate that what has happened is a continuation of the process which King outlined in his discussion of film acting. King suggests that film was believed by actors (and perhaps by audiences) to be 'a medium (which) regularly if not necessarily entails a deskilling process' (1991: 170). Not only did type-casting render acting apparently unnecessary but the process of 'character portrayal in film ... takes on a quasi-autonomous form' and can be carried at least in part by camera movement and *mise en scène* (1991: 177). This anxiety about the possibilities of acting in cinema has been reinforced in the 1980s and 1990s by the emphasis on blockbusters, special effects and computer graphics. Outside the cinema, stars compete for celebrity status with the glitterati from other fields; inside, they have to contend with dinosaurs, twisters and animated rabbits.

In this situation, acting has become a way of claiming back the cinema for human stars and it is not accidental that method acting has become so strongly associated with certain modes of film stardom. Colin Counsell describes the method as 'a pre-eminently *realistic* style of acting' (1996: 53) and outlines the key signs of the method as 'a new ease or "naturalness" on-stage' (1996: 54); an increased emphasis on the significance of a character's inner life and the signs by which it could be deduced; a 'heightened emotionalism' (1996: 56) which is expressed in intense outbursts of expression; and 'an underlying vision of the individual as divided between an "authentic" inner and a potentially repressed/repressive outer self' (1996: 63). Such an approach chimed with a number of cinema's claims as a medium. The emphasis on realism and naturalness fitted the Bazinian notion that cinema's key task is to reveal reality; the emphasis on emotion expressed through gesture and sound (rather than words) fitted the dethroning of the script and the word by cinema's visual possibilities; the emphasis on the expressiveness of the body could be accommodated in cinema's use of the body as spectacle; the emphasis on inner character was consonant with cinema's promotion of stars as unique and authentic individuals.

The significance of method acting for concepts of film stardom has been recognised. Both Dyer and King discuss method acting as a particularly important feature of Hollywood cinema. Gledhill, in her discussion of melodrama and stars, draws attention to the way in which the method actor '*embodies* conflicts' and suggests that this emphasis on the bodily manifestation of moral dilemmas makes 'the Method … the contemporary performance mode most able to deliver "presence"' (1991b: 224). The emphasis on the body, the promise that every gesture and grimace carries meaning in terms of character if not of narrative, the inarticulate speech which the audience has to strain for, the moments of stillness and silence where action might be anticipated – these are signs of performance which audiences now expect and understand. As Frederic Jamieson put it, in his discussion of Pacino's performance in *Dog Day Afternoon* (1975), 'the inarticulate becomes the highest form of expressiveness, the wordless stammer proves voluble, and the agony over uncommunicability suddenly turns out to be everywhere fluently comprehensible' (1990: 43). In the process, the method has been conventionalised so that audiences can recognise the signs of performance cognitively as well as responding to its emotional resonances. James Naremore comments on the irony that 'the Method was articulated in terms of "essences" but audiences looked at surfaces' (1990: 212). I am not suggesting that cinema audiences now recognise 'the Method' by name but that they do recognise modes of performing in ways which have implications for understanding how some stars (not all of whom can be directly associated with the Method) make meaning. As Lesley Stern suggests in her extremely interesting account, De Niro is not 'narrowly Method' (1995: 209) and he appears 'to relish the very game of performance' (1995: 210); it is this method-related emphasis on performance which is apparent in the work of a number of male stars.

Method acting emphasises work, craft and talent through this emphasis on performance. It restores a sense of human agency to the cinema of action. Although the aim of the method may be 'the merging of self and character' (Gledhill, 1991b: 223), the audience who follows the 1990s' performer is aware of the gap between star and character in which the performance is taking place. Some extratextual publicity may draw attention to this but the knowledge required is available in the performances. Cinematic method performances work to draw the audience into the inner depths of the character while at the same time the 'stream of behavioural minutiae' (Counsell, 1996: 56) alerts the spectator to the value of the performance itself as something worthwhile. The claim to stardom as a performer depends on the work of acting being put on display and contrasts to stars-as-celebrities who can become famous for 'being themselves' and stars-as-professionals who act as themselves. Thus, whereas in 1950s' cinema the Method was associated with the youthful naturalness and impulsive rebellion of James Dean or Marlon Brando, cinematic method acting is now a way of marking performance as work and thus claiming cultural value.

This emphasis on performance works well, in fact, for the ageing star since it has the added merit of valuing experience and allowing a career to continue well beyond the pin-up stage. Method acting directs attention to the body of the star but shifts it away from the body as spectacle (the way in which Ford and Stallone move, for instance) to the body as site of performance, worked over by the actor. In a quite conscious way, the audience is invited to recognise and admire what the actor is doing with his face and body. The revival of Al Pacino's career and the continuance of De Niro's owes much to the sense of older performers displaying well-honed skills and passing on their knowledge to the younger actors around them. Even for young male stars who are teenage pin-ups (and thus operate as celebrities) the adoption of the method approach can work as a sign of more serious intentions. Depp's shift (the thickening body, the incoherent explanations) in *Donnie Brasco* (Newell, 1997) may be an early move in that process while the languid sexuality of Brad Pitt in *Thelma and Louise* (1991) has been replaced by a more self-aware attention to the details of accent and gesture in *Se7en* (Fincher, 1995) and *The Devil's Own* (1997).

The more widespread recourse to method acting has also affected the relationship between the star and others in the film. The hierarchy of performance was always clear in classic Hollywood films in which stars were surrounded and supported by character actors and second-rank sidekicks. In acting terms, there was a difference between the personification mode of the stars and the character acting which surrounded them. That difference is now much less pronounced and this change explains what would otherwise seem to be quite a contradictory shift, on the one hand to ensemble playing and on the other to acting as confrontation and contrast. In the emphasis on ensemble, the gangster film has played a key role. Unlike the western, the gangster film has remained a consistently strong genre and its stories of male groups, explosive violence and narcissism have meshed with cinematic method acting's characteristic emphasis on internal conflict expressed through the body. An early and influential example of this can be found in *The Godfather* (Coppola, 1972) where the stars Marlon Brando and Al Pacino are surrounded by actors whose performances are similarly expressive in their apparently inarticulate reliance on gesture and facial expression. An interesting variant on this occurs in *Goodfellas* (Scorsese, 1990) where the major star, De Niro, is one of the group who supports the relatively unknown Ray Liotta, and also in *Reservoir Dogs* (Tarantino, 1991) where each of the group is given moments of playing centre stage.

The ensemble playing, which tends to position the star as 'one of the boys', is paralleled by a strong sense of performance as competition which is generated when actors, operating in the same performance mode (which itself emphasises internal conflict), are given equal weight in narratives which hinge on external conflict and opposition between them. This rivalry is internally generated by the text and its power comes from the appeal to aesthetic judgements (which is the better actor?) rather than from stories of off-screen rivalry or different fan allegiances. This aesthetic dimension is underpinned by strong associations with similar contests in sport and particularly boxing, an unsurprising analogy given method acting's strong association with issues of masculinity. The encounter between Pacino and De Niro in *Heat* (Mann, 1995) is a vivid example of this kind of contest. Both are well known as cinematic method actors. The narrative sets them in opposition as policeman and criminal and they watch, follow and photograph each other until, well over halfway through the film, they meet face to face in a coffee bar. The shot/reverse-shot system concentrates on faces, framing tighter as the scene goes on. Though both give highly restrained performances, Pacino is the more edgy, his head stretched from his shoulders like a watchful bird, his eyes more open and alert. He leans towards De Niro and the camera whereas De Niro leans back, more hunched down, his eyes narrowed. Their bodies thus mirror each other as in the dialogue they discuss how they are locked together through their work. Difference is thus displayed but a strong sense of complementary performances is also established. The cultural value of such acting was neatly summed up by the *Sight and Sound* reviewer who searched for a comparison and suggested that 'if *Heat* were a play you could imagine De Niro and Pacino swapping roles every night like Olivier and Richardson in *Othello*' (Wrathall, 1996: 44).

While De Niro and Pacino can be described as cinematic method actors, this emphasis on performance as a mark of worth can be seen in performers who owe less to that tradition. Tom Cruise, for instance, fresh from the huge court-room successes of *A Few Good Men* (Reiner, 1992) and *The Firm* (Pollack, 1993), was a controversial choice for *Interview with the Vampire* (Jordan, 1994) because his image did not conform to character as it had done in the earlier films. Instead, Cruise attempted to switch from star-as-professional to star-as-performer. The film sets Cruise up with Brad Pitt in another male pairing and makes much of the contrast between the two, as characters and performers, in terms of both physique and acting style. Where Pitt is brooding, reflective and enigmatic (much more in the method mode), Cruise is sharp in his gesture and peevish and direct in tone ('Shut up, Louis', he orders as he pulls him from the burning mansion); the famous eyes widen in annoyance; the 'multi-million dollar smile' (*Screen International*, 11 December 1992) turns to a leer to mark the desire for blood. Although this is not a method performance, it is important to note the way attention is being drawn to the distance between actor and performance as a measure of the change in Cruise's clean-cut star image.

The development of the star-as-performer as a means of reclaiming the cultural value means that we need perhaps to look again at how we understand the audience's activity in relation to stars. Dyer's emphasis on stars as a means of exploring social identity ['We're fascinated by stars because they enact ways of making sense of the experience of being a person' (1987: 17)] has been combined with an emphasis in cultural studies on the extratextual work of fans, which I discussed earlier. Polysemy and resistance thus became key terms in thinking about film stars, and the fan position, which is strongly associated with the star-as-celebrity, was assumed to be the ideal position from which to understand a star. For some kinds of stars and for some performances, however, this emphasis on the extratextual is not necessary and it is the audience's understanding of the specifically cinematic pleasures of genre and performance which needs to be foregrounded. The different modes of stardom I have described require different kinds of knowledge from audiences and although some film stars do operate as celebrities, knowledge of this is not essential to understanding their film appearances. The construction of Johnny Depp as a celebrity relies on extratextual knowledge of his bad behaviour and his stormy on/off affair with Kate Moss. For the category of performer, this extratextual information is largely irrelevant. Understanding Depp's significance in *Donnie Brasco* comes instead from textual knowledge of the performance itself, from its contrast to the rather fragile and whimsical acting styles Depp adopted in *Edward Scissorhands* (Burton, 1990) and *What's Eating Gilbert Grape?* (Hallstrom, 1993) and from the comparisons to be made with the performances of other male stars, such as De Niro and Pacino, who have used this method-influenced approach.

Analysing the female star

My discussion so far, particularly on the professional and the performer, has concentrated on male stars. I want to look now at how these categories might be applied to women film stars. In doing so, I think it is important to recognise that women stars do operate in a different context from their male counterparts. This is expressed both by the stars themselves in, for instance, complaints about the lack of good parts, and in the 'common sense' of the industry. A striking example of the common assumptions about female stars can be found in *Screen International*'s yearly assessment (since 1992) of the 'top actors' or key 'power players'. Women are both in a marked minority in the lists and the subject of generalised comments about the sheer unlikliness of women as stars. Thus, the failure of *The Scarlet Letter* (Joffe, 1995) becomes the failure of Demi More as a star, and then a question about women more generally; it raised 'the same ugly question: can she carry a film? Can *any* actress carry a film?' (*Screen International*, 15 December 1995, p. 19). Such attitudes are not new to Hollywood (stars as different as Davis, Dietrich and Hepburn had problems with how the industry dealt with them) but, given the importance of big-name stars in the ultra-high-budget films of New Hollywood (Ballio, 1998), they take on a new significance.

   The category of celebrity is one which works well for female stars. Women function effectively as spectacle in the press and on television as well as in the cinema. In addition, the common association in popular culture between women and the private sphere of personal relationships and domesticity fits with the emphasis, in the discourse of celebrity, on the private life and the leisure activity of the star. The 'biography' of the woman star then can be appropriately used to make a star-as-celebrity out of her. Drew Barrymore offers an extreme but by no means unique example of an actress whose film appearances are set in the context of a turbulent private life. Stories of love affairs, weddings and divorces bring women stars into the arena of tabloid journalism while in more staid (and stage-managed) interviews stars such as Demi Moore stress the importance of creating domestic space in which their children can grow up. Julia Roberts offers a particularly interesting example of the way in which stardom can be built on and around celebrity. Charlotte Brunsdon's analysis of Robert's most famous role, as Vivian in *Pretty Woman* (Marshall, 1990), draws attention to the way in which her nervy awkwardness is transformed by her naturalness and the unconscious 'power of her beauty' (1997: 99). Since then, her film performances have been patchy but her celebrity status is based precisely on this contrast between the successful life her beauty seems to deserve and the disasters to which her natural impulses lead her. As Brunsdon suggests, there are strong possibilities for identification in the way in which Roberts lives out of the difficulties of femininity and I would suggest that the intermittent success of her films (*Screen International*, 12 December 1998, speaks of 'yet another comeback') is less important for her role as a star than her consistent extratextual interest as a celebrity.[2]

The celebrity category also offers women the possibility of some kind of power within the system because it allows them to draw on status which has been attained outside appearances in films. For Demi Moore and Nicole Kidman, marriage to a big male star is believed to provide them with a financial clout which their films alone might not justify. In addition, celebrity status from another field can also offer a basis for female film stardom; Whitney Houston, Madonna and Cher provide good examples of the way in which the singer-as-celebrity can make a successful transition into films. Interest in them as a celebrity can then combine film, music and personal life and can thus be sustained when film appearances drop into the background.

While the celebrity category may flourish on inconsistent behaviour in the personal sphere and contradictions between public and private selves, the professional star depends on a consistent sense of self and the willingness of the industry to franchise a role. Female candidates for this category might be Sigourney Weaver in her Ripley role and Linda Hamilton as Sarah Connor in the Terminator films. Both films offered a strong female character who was identified with the actress playing it and had the emphasis on action associated with the professional category. Despite the strong sense of identification many fans felt with these actresses/characters, neither did well enough, in the industry's terms, to feature in *Screen International*'s lists or establish a secure franchise. Hamilton did not make enough films to demonstrate a consistent personna and Weaver seems to have actively tried to avoid the typing associated with the professional category. She has starred in other genres – comedy, for instance, in *Working Girl* (Nicholls, 1988), a biopic in *Gorillas in the Mist* (Apted, 1988) and artistic drama in *Death and a Maiden* (Polanski, 1994). The difference between her and Harrison Ford in *Working Girl* is instructive; while Ford maintains his professional mode by playing the hero with silent bemusement, Weaver gives a broad and excessively villainous sweep to her portrayal of Katherine, turning herself into the monster against whom the heroine struggles. Although she maintains a consistent star image as a strong woman, Weaver as an actress appears to refuse the restrictions of the professional category and hence the kind of stardom which the male action heroes have established.

The female star who comes closest to success as a professional is perhaps Whoopi Goldberg. *Screen International* commented on her success in *Sister Act* (Ardolino, 1992) by describing her as 'an unlikely star', which would seem to be a reference to her race and gender since the consistency of her roles and her identification with comedy are comparable to a male comedy star. *Screen International* indeed half recognises this by emphasising her financial worth: 'by making sure she gets her worth – namely 7 million dollars for *Sister Act II* – she also became a landmark of a different kind: an actress with the clout of a male star' (10 December 1993, p. 21). The association of money and power with masculinity even when discussing a black, female star is entirely typical. The cost for Goldberg, though, has been the restriction of her image to that of an outsider whose asexual appearance and comic mannerisms diminish any threat to white audiences (Mayne, 1993; Stuart, 1993).

It may seem easier for women to develop into stars through the category of performers, a mode in which cultural value is more important than financial pulling power. However, the codification of cinematic method acting that has worked so well for male stars has not been so helpful for their female counterparts. Counsell suggests that the method's emphasis on the divided self worked against women in that while 'the iconography of neurosis quickly became an acceptable way of representing men', the neurotic woman was 'demonised ... as victim or villainess'. 'The Method actress' he concludes 'could not be "normal" enough' for Hollywood's restricted vision of appropriate female behaviour (1996: 76).[3] Two other factors may also be at play. The method approach, emphasising as it did the repression and release of emotion, gave male actors the task of expressing feelings as well as providing action. In some senses, male stars took over the traditional role of women and provided the tears as well as the punches. In addition, the emphasis on ensemble playing has perhaps worked rather differently for women stars. While ensemble playing by women is a feature of certain kinds of women's film, such as *How to make an American Quilt* (Moorhouse, 1995), the emphasis on male groups in the more prestigious gangster and thriller genres has tended to take attention away from the actresses' performance. Thus, even in *Goodfellas* (Scorsese, 1990), a gangster film which is highly unusual in its emphasis on the home life of the gangster, Lorraine Bracco's performance as the wife cannot match the weight of the ensemble playing of De Niro, Pesci, Liotta and the rest of the gang.

It is possible, however, to see cinematic method acting in some performances by contemporary women stars. Jodie Foster's performances, for instance, in *The Accused* (Kaplan, 1988) and *The Silence of Lambs* (Demme, 1991) are marked by the way in which internal division and doubt are expressed in gestures, silences, explosions of emotion comparable to that of male stars. It is not accidental that these critically successful performances were given in thrillers/court-room dramas since in these films Foster was given access, which generally women stars do not have, to the gangster/thriller genres where the method has worked most successfully for male stars. Foster's performances in other genres – *Sommersby* (Amiel, 1993), *Nell* (Apted, 1994) – were less well received and her strong track record rests on her position as a producer and director as well as an actor though, as with Whoopi Goldberg, her success is expressed in the industry through male comparisons: 'if this is a boy's game, then Jodie plays it like the boys: with a balance of caution and boldness' (*Screen International*, 10 December 1993, p. 21). A more unusual example of a method-influenced performance, in that it occurred in a literary adaptation, was that of Nicole Kidman in *Portrait of a Lady* (Campion, 1996). Here Campion's visceral direction with its dramatic use of close-ups focused attention on Kidman's physical expression of Isabel Archer's voluntary entrapment in the way she walked, stammered and even struggled for breath.

I suggested earlier that the emphasis on performance worked to enhance certain male stars' cultural value as they aged. An interesting example of the way in which an emphasis on performance has worked differently for a female star is Meryl Streep. Streep's star status was largely based on performance – she resisted the use of her private life to turn her into a real celebrity – but the critical understanding of what was at stake in her performances was not always sympathetic. Streep's acting was understood less as the external expression of internal conflict and more as a matter of role play. Barry King (1991) suggests that method acting in cinema is underpinned by the uniqueness of the actor and that although it appears to operate as 'impersonation' (taking on a role) it actually operates as a form of personification with the 'person of the actor' as 'the consistent entity' which thus allows, in my terms, the star-as-performer to emerge. Streep's problem seems to have been that she was seen as an impersonator; the ease with which she adopted accents and changed appearance meant that she did not draw attention to the difficulty of expression which marks cinematic method acting. This lack of cultural value combined with the lack of parts for older women has seen Streep slip away, while De Niro, her co-star in *The Deerhunter* (Cimino, 1978), continues to figure in lists of top stars.

Conclusions

A final example illustrates the different way in which stars make meaning through the categories I have outlined and how gender and race inflect these categories. *The Bodyguard* (Jackson,1992) was critically derided but was a huge commercial success. bell hooks (1994) has pointed out that the film's doomed romance between the black singer Rachel Marron (Whitney Houston) and her white bodyguard Frank Farmer (Kevin Costner) is predicated on its unspoken assumptions about the impossibility of success-ful interracial relationships in Hollywood films. But *The Bodyguard* is also worth considering in terms of stars as well as narrative for what we get is a contest between the two stars which throws interesting light on film stardom in 1990s' Hollywood. The film's huge grosses put Houston into 11th position on *Screen International*'s 1996 list of top-20 screen stars, making her the first of only three female stars included. She brings to the film her star status as a singer/celebrity which is treated respectfully. The camera circles her, giving the audience both her beautiful face and long shots of her dancing, exercising and singing. The narrative makes her vulnerable and potentially a victim but we are continually reminded of her (invulnerable) star status by the songs and her composed demeanour. Costner, on the other hand, still carries with him the success of *Dances with Wolves* (Costner, 1990). Although he had a reputation as a pin-up, the film seems more concerned to emphasise his performance. He thus seeks to express his character's ambivalent obsession with his job and his fear that exposing his vulnerability in love will make him less good at it. This narrative motivation may not, as hooks indicates, be very strong but it gets its resonances from our familiarity with such internal conflicts as performed by a succession of male stars. The film thus neatly demonstrates how two big stars can be so different and need different analysis to account for their meaning. Houston is treated as a pin-up who sings; Costner is giving an acting performance. Houston is given very little space to express any feeling; Costner uses cinematic method techniques to indicate that he is trying to express the inexpressible. Houston's star status is secure in the popular enjoyment of her voice and songs; Costner is trying to claim cultural status of a different order as a serious actor. And, of course, Houston as a black woman would find it almost impossible to claim the ground on which Costner is staking his claim to stardom. In the end, it is not just the narrative but the different concepts attached to stardom which reinforce their separate worlds and send Houston back to her singing and Costner back to his work.

Endnotes

1   As is indicated here, Dyer did recognise consistency in a star image. I am suggesting that the interest in difference in film and cultural studies has overemphasised the notion of star instability in his work.
2   Brunsdon (1997: 100) draws on Jennifer Wicke's concept of 'celebrity feminism' in her analysis. The category interestingly links film stars with women academics and writers in a way which illustrates the fluidity of the star category.
3   Counsell (1996) suggests that, in an earlier period, Jane Fonda was the only method actress to be offered high-profile parts in films and compares this to the success of method actors from the 1950s onwards.

Acknowledgements: With thanks to Jim Cook for making very helpful comments on early drafts of this chapter and to Christine Gledhill for her perceptive and thoughtful work as an editor.

References

Allen, R.C. and Gomery, D. 1985: *Film history: theory and practice*. New York: Random House.
Ballio, T. 1988: 'A major presence in all of the world's most important markets': the globalization of Hollywood in the 1990s. In Neale, S. and Smith, M. (eds), *Contemporary Hollywood cinema*. London: Routledge, pp. 58–73.
Brunsdon, C. 1997: Post-feminism and shopping films. In *Screen tastes: soap opera to satellite dishes*. London: Routledge, pp. 81–102.
Cook, P. 1993: Border crossings: women and film in context. In Dodd, P. and Cook, P. (eds), *Women and film: a sight and sound reader*. London: Scarlet Press, pp. ix–xxiii.
Counsell, C. 1996: *Signs of performance*. London: Routledge.
Dyer, R. 1979: *Stars*. London: British Film Institute.
Dyer, R. 1987: *Heavenly bodies; film stars and society*. London: British Film Institute.
Fiske, J. 1992: The cultural economy of fandom. In Lewis, L. (ed.), *The adoring audience: fan culture and popular media*. London: Routledge.
Gelman, B. 1972: *Photoplay treasury*. New York: Crown Publishers.
Gledhill, C. 1991a: Introduction. In Gledhill, C. (ed.), *Stardom: industry of desire*. London: Routledge, pp. xiii–xx.
Gledhill, C. 1991b: Signs of melodrama. In Gledhill, C. (ed.), *Stardom: industry of desire*. London: Routledge, pp. 207–29.
Hooks, B. 1994: Seduction and betrayal: *The Crying Game* meets *The Bodyguard*. In *Outlaw culture: resisting representations*. New York: Routledge, pp. 53–62.
Jamieson, F. 1990: Class and allegory in contemporary mass culture: *Dog Day Afternoon* as a political film. In *Signatures of the Visible*. London: Routledge, pp. 35–54.
King, B. 1991: Articulating stardom. In Gledhill, C. (ed.), *Stardom: industry of desire*. London: Routledge, pp. 167–82.
Langer, J. 1981: Television's personality system. *Media Culture and Society* **3**(4), 351–65.
Mayne, J. 1993: *Cinema and spectatorship*. London: Routledge.
Mulvey, L. 1975: Visual pleasure and narrative cinema. *Screen* **16**(2), 6–18.
Naremore, J. 1990: *Acting in the cinema*. Berkeley, CA: University of California Press.
Stacey, J. 1994: *Star gazing: Hollywood cinema and female spectatorship*. London: Routledge.
Stern, L. 1995: *The Scorsese connection*. London: British Film Institute.

Stuart, A. 1993: The outsider: Whoopi Goldberg and shopping mall America. In Dodd, P. and Cook, P. (eds), *Women and film: a sight and sound reader*. London: Scarlet Press, pp. 62–7.

Tasker, Y. 1993: *Spectacular bodies*. London: Routledge.

Whannell, G. 1992: *Fields in vision*. London: Routledge.

Wrathall, J. 1996: Review of *Heat*. *Sight and Sound* **6**(2), 42–4.

PART 3

Questions of aesthetics

Editors' introduction

Following the dismantling in the first section of the totalising theories of the 1970s and the recontextualisation in the second section of film in the context of mass media, this section examines the consequences of such moves for the textual models and concepts that until recently governed the analysis of films. In different ways these writers look for new ways of evaluating their aesthetic and cultural significance.

Arguing our need for films 'to be about life in one way or another' (page 211), Christopher Williams addresses two monolithic and mutually supportive models of narrative which lock realism either into dominant ideology or into support for a timeless narrative continuity system. In taking apart the classic realist text developed in Colin MacCabe's influential essay of 1974, Williams undoes the identification of realism with narrative, of narrative with the image, and of both with 'dominant ideology'. Similarly, Williams relativises the role of a continuity system based on narrative logic and psychological motivation in Bordwell and Thompson's model of the classic Hollywood or narrative text. Instead Williams argues the heterogeneity of Hollywood and other cinemas which may deploy realist (or decorous) strategies alongside both anti-realist and non-realist ones. Along with the uncoupling of image, narrative and realism, Williams questions the usefulness of the concept of ideology which has been inextricably linked to realism in one strand of 1970s' theorising. Relocating film within the context of mass production and reception, he highlights the variety of narrational mechanisms and types of realism. These devices may be deployed by any film in the industry's need to engage the recognition of diverse audiences. Far from enforcing an invisible reading protocol, the resulting tensions and contradictions invite audience negotiation of intersecting aesthetic conventions, social references, and moral propositions.

Christopher Williams ends with a call to rehabilitate 'the social and aesthetic spheres' and to recuperate 'the values of ethics and humanism' (page 216). He thus moves to relocate film in the experience of the audience and refind the experience of the film. Christine Gledhill makes a similar move, in seeking a more flexible conception of genre as a switching point between industry and social history, aesthetic and critical practice. Placing the genre system within a historical understanding of melodrama as a heterogeneous and adaptive mode rather than within a timeless and formally conceived narrative classicism, Gledhill explores debates about melodrama and gender in order to highlight the insistently dialogic existence of genre as a boundary phenomenon. Insisting that the productivity of genre must be understood as operating across both the industrial production and marketing of mass culture and the range of critical practices that circulate around films, she concludes by suggesting that genre provides material to the work of cinema as alternative public sphere.

As a case study of genre in action, Carol Clover examines a genre which is so paradigmatic of how American cinema speaks to its culture that it has gone unrecognised. Her study of the trial movie details the fundamental place of the jury system in American popular consciousness, stretching across a range of legal, social, and mass media practices, including the courtroom drama or trial movie. Turning on the trope of 'empty jury box' (page 258), the trial movie invokes a spectator 'with a job to do' (page 246). Clover identifies the convention the double trial structure, in which the legal process as well as the defendant are subject to interrogation. Noting the capacity of the American imaginary to tolerate challenge to any part of the system except the jury, Carol Clover suggests how the trial movie fields the juror as American Everyman who will secure justice for all. If Miriam Hansen's concept of cinema as 'an alternative public sphere' (Chapter 18) rationalises the trope of genre as society talking to itself about itself, Carol Clover's account of the trial movie analyses a testing conversation in which films, politics, and the legal system intersect, acting out each other's dilemmas and challenges.

From movies about making judgements, Noël Carroll's chapter shifts to the problem of judging movies, returning to our attention a critical concern virtually excluded from film studies as it developed under pressure of the ideological focus of 1970s' theory. Arguing that the question of whether a movie is good or bad is a matter not only for the professional film critic or journalist, Carroll insists that it is a central activity of ordinary, movie-going practice. Essential to understanding evaluation is the assignment of a film to its category and consequent purpose. Reminding us of the problems encountered by early attempts at evolving evaluative criteria based on ahistorical conceptions of a universal cinematic essence, Carroll argues that a unitary theory of evaluation is not possible. Instead he advocates a flexible and fragmentary approach, submitting any one film to the range of generic and narrational categories which it may deploy. By such means evaluation can avoid both formalism and conservatism, taking into account the 'morality, politics and cognitive value' (page 276) bound up in generic identities, while also adjusting to the emergence of new categories as they are signalled in the wider film culture.

This section concludes with Sharon Willis's study of Tarantino's work, drawing a variety of interpretative and evaluative systems together in a complex matrix to focus the aesthetic, fantasmatic, and, in the last instance, ideological work of this most postmodern of directors. In so doing Willis brings many of the concerns of the preceeding sections to bear productively on the process of textual reading. Placing Tarantino's work squarely within mass culture, Willis constructs his work as that of a superfan feeding a taste-culture, which, combining 'funniness and scariness' (page 281) is based on 'reverse value' – turning the 'previous generation's trash'/'shit into gold' (page 284). In this context Tarantino turns to icons of African–American masculinity for a set of 'style' practices which his films deploy in insistently oedipal terms. Tarantino thus attempts to lift racialised imagery and language out of their social and historical context into a privatised sphere of interlocking public and personal oedipal fantasies. Willis concludes that these films represent symptomatic engagements in 'ongoing historical conversations with African–American cultural production' (page 294) that reveal the work of a 'public unconscious' in the privatised sphere of cinematic fantasising.

11 After the classic, the classical and ideology: the differences of realism

Christopher Williams

In a short but interesting 1992 article the British media studies academic John Corner expressed concern about the imprecise wielding of the concept of realism in much contemporary media theory. He attributed the widespread concern with realism of form to the influence of one kind of film theory:

> This influence was exerted at a time (the mid 1970s) when the ideological consequences of classical Hollywood cinematic form constituted the key focus of a newly emerging radical wing of film studies.
>
> (1992: 100)

However, this left-wing formalism did allow one kind of realism, so long as it could be presented as having explicit, politically progressive content, as in the case of the BBC Television series *Days of Hope* (1975):

> The thematic (and publicly controversial) link between television representation and social and political realities needed to be addressed within a different analytical frame from that provided by the study of form, even if finally the two had to be related. Otherwise, the issue of 'reference' would be completely displaced by that of 'signification', as often happened. An overblown notion of realism (partly parasitical on an overblown and increasingly mystical concept of ideology) acted as a block to any more incisive conceptualisation.
>
> (1992: 100–1)

The question begged by the first of these formulations is absolutely crucial: is there or was there ever a meaningful entity, effective on either the practical or the theoretical level, which could honestly or adequately be called classical Hollywood cinematic form? If there is not, it follows that media theory which assumes otherwise must be built around a shaky core. If there is or was such a form, a rider to the first question might be:

does the form have ideological consequences? If so, how can they be described or accounted for? In the second formulation the interesting problem is that of the concept of ideology itself. Is there a bad concept of ideology (overblown, mystical, misused by left-wing formalists), but perhaps somewhere behind it a good one (accurate, incisive, used by sociologists and media studies theorists)? Is it not rather the case that ideology has become an unusable term? Specifically, when we try to deal with the relations between works of art and communication, and the issues of social life and history, can the concept of ideology help in any meaningful way?

In this chapter I will argue that the intellectual mess which concerned John Corner is caused as much by the amalgam of formalist anti-realism and a hypertrophied version of ideology as by problems about the definitions of realism. In the first part I will try to unpick the notion of classical Hollywood cinematic form. Of necessity, this leads on to some discussion of language, convention, narrative and realism. In the second part I will discuss (but selectively) the archetypal 1970s' concept of ideology. Finally, I will say why the concepts of realism and its linked partner anti-realism remain important in film theory and why they merit further development.

The notion of classical Hollywood cinematic form is an amalgam of two distinct concepts: the Classic Realist Text of Colin MacCabe (1974) and the Classical Hollywood Cinema of David Bordwell, Janet Staiger and Kristin Thompson (1985).[1] These two ideas have been conflated in many an undergraduate essay and no doubt in many an academic paper since the mid-1980s, and it is this conflation that Corner reproduces without question. MacCabe's idea set a political tone, while that of Bordwell and his colleagues set an aesthetic one. I shall discuss MacCabe first.

MacCabe's initial argument was that the notions of realism and the real were both 'tied to a particular type of literary production – the nineteenth-century realist novel' (1974:8). This idea was wrong, and put the cart before the horse. There are at least four other kinds of real and realism: emotional, pragmatic, philosophical and scientific, as well as the artistic kind, of which the nineteenth-century realist novel may well be a subset. Film is not dominated by the forms of the nineteenth-century novel. It draws on a wider range of sources and inputs.

MacCabe went on to assert that the narrative prose of the novel functioned as what he called a metalanguage – a form of direct address which expressed truth claims. It aspired to states of transparency and dematerialization, and attempted to abolish the articulations of language, to deny the fact of separation between what is said and the act of saying it, to hide the fact that interpretation is deferred until after diction, or, in a word, 'to *anneal*, to make whole, through denying its own status as writing' (1974:9) and as articulation. Annealment, in ceramics, is the fusion of different materials in intense heat. Via a process akin to this fusion, it is asserted, the narrative prose of the novel becomes a metalanguage and simultaneously claims 'direct access to a final reality' (1974: 10).

The concepts of articulation, separation, and the deferment of interpretation, which MacCabe brings to this discussion from the Saussurean tradition and from Derrida, are all interesting in themselves, but I think that in this context they were never strong enough to impose the concept of a metalanguage against two more serious (and also more obvious) considerations. First, none of the narrative prose forms of the nineteenth-century realist novel – Dickens, Balzac, Eliot, Zola, Gissing, whoever – attempted to deny their own status as writing or as articulation. In fact they were, and are, only legible and interpretable through understandings of the articulations which they embody at almost every turn. Second, no mode of writing is powerful enough to operate the annealment MacCabe imagines for his metalinguistic text.[2] The signs and practices of writing have been often clear, and always noticeable, in every kind of writing, even the ones which most strenuously attempt to present or represent aspects of lived experience. The difficulty, at least for the kind of theory which wants to produce a monolithic account of these practices, is that the signs and practices vary, overlap with each other, differ, hence the importance of concepts such as convention, articulation, combination, discourse, multiplicity of viewpoint, structure and genre. These concepts have connections with (in some cases, roots in) the sciences of language, without being restricted by or contained in them. Their deployment would be an important part of the basis of a healthy theory and criticism of literature. Even a minimal deployment would make it clear how irrelevant the concepts of metalanguage and annealment are. In short, the hypothetical use of one artistic convention does not have the power to wipe out the operations of all the other conventions and practices. I say 'hypothetical' because I think that the number of literary works dependent on a single convention must be very small indeed. MacCabe approaches this area from the direction of language, but instead of using its resources he wilfully restricts them to a simplified problematic about articulation.

In turning to try to apply the fantasy of the Classic Realist Text (CRT) to film, MacCabe suddenly and uncritically adopted a term whose contemporary origins lay in the sociological and Marxist traditions. This term was 'dominance':

> does this definition carry over into films where it is certainly less evident where to locate the dominant discourse? It seems to me that it does and in the following fashion. The narrative prose achieves its position of dominance because it is in the position of knowledge and this function of knowledge is taken up in the cinema by the narration of events.
>
> (1974: 10)

Probably feeling the need to be concrete at this point, MacCabe searched for and found a cinematic equivalent for his metalinguistic narrative prose of fiction. This was nothing more nor less than the film imagetrack – the pictures. 'The camera shows us what happens' (1974: 10). MacCabe asserted for the film camera the same claims to positions of knowledge and truth he thought could be found in the nineteenth-century novel's metalanguage. It seems highly arguable whether or not the narration of events in film occupies the position or the function of knowledge. It often occupies a central, structurally important position. But can this position be equated with one of knowledge? If there were a position of knowledge, could it be located in the imagetrack alone? It certainly could not. If there were a position of knowledge (about the workings of a film narrative) it would have to be located in a combination or synthesis of several different tracks, strands or places. It would have to give some account of the emotion or idea that the narrative is devised to embody, represent or talk about. It would have to take on board the institution of characterization. It would acknowledge the crucial principle of conflict, both within and between characters, and between characters and other forces active or implied. Once it was established that idea and emotion, character and conflict, were the basic instruments of narrative articulation, it would be interested in the ways in which complication, development and outcome or resolution function as further articulations of narrative systems, and especially of the initial data. It would deal with the specific characteristics of the imagetrack (the systems often known as *mise en scène*) and with the various layers of the soundtrack.

It might also draw on the distinctions and relations made by the Russian formalists between *fabula* – the raw material of a story, the statement of the things that happen in it – and *syuzhet* – the ways in which these materials are shaped and transformed by artistic procedures.[3] It might make use of the idea of narrative function sketched out by Propp (1990) and developed by others such as Fell (1977) or Wollen (1982), in which the actions of characters are presented only in the light of their significance for the storytelling structure, but a clear idea of the parameters of one kind of structure also emerges. It might well turn to the substantial work done in the first period of film semiotics, in which Metz developed the idea of the relations between syntagmatic (sequential) and paradigmatic (lateral, alternative, vertical or static) elements in film language (1974: 31–182). It would certainly be interested in Nick Browne's (1975/76) demonstration of how the spectator engages independently and perhaps uncertainly with the experience of the film text, responding variably to the complicated interplay of the different layers of textual elements (in Browne's example these are primarily points of view and editing, but in principle extensible) and extratextual authority (here the moral outlook of the producers of the narrative, but potentially also other factors in the contexts of production or reception). It might even want to draw on Barthes's adumbration of a constantly changing network of codifications at play in the unfolding of a written narrative.[4]

In this complex, multiple network of different strands, the imagetrack will be only one feature. It may well be potent and significant, but it will not be able to 'show us what happens' or 'tell the truth against which we can measure the discourses'. It is only one of those discourses and is too imbricated with the others to attain or sustain the metalinguistics, dominating, 'final' senses MacCabe wanted to claim on its behalf.

If one does not simplify narrative into a stable, fixed formal identity, and if one sees it as significant rather than dominant, the problems about it arise in more interesting and analysable forms. MacCabe, however, remained fixated on one narrative and, behind it, one ideology, and he set the first of these fixations out clearly in the climax to the first section of the article:

> To return, however, to the narrative discourse. It is necessary to attempt to understand the type of relations that this dominant discourse produces. The narrative discourse cannot be mistaken in its identifications because the narrative discourse is not present as discourse – as articulation. The unquestioned nature of the narrative discourse entails that the only problem that reality poses is to go and look and see what *Things* there *are*. The relationship between the reading subject and the real is placed as one of pure specularity. The real is not articulated – it is. These features imply two essential features of the classic realist text:

1   The classic realist text cannot deal with the real as contradictory.
2   In a reciprocal movement the classic realist text ensures the position of the subject in a relation of dominant specularity.

(1974 : 12)

MacCabe was simply wrong when he asserted that narrative discourse is not present as discourse or as articulation. Consider the following: characterization and character function, conflict, development, structure (including exposition and outcome), *mise en scène* and the deployment of soundtracks, *fabula/syuzhet* relations, syntagm and paradigm relations, and the palimpsests of codification systems at work in most films, especially narrative ones. What on earth are all these practices if not articulations? They are the articulations which make up narrative and they have to be present in one form or another, otherwise there is no narrative. Far from being unquestioned, narrative forms and narrative discourse are frequently questioning and very frequently in conflict within and between themselves. Once one accepts that narrative is a multiple, problematic from rather than a homogenized monolith, this idea is quite easy to understand.

Now we reach the nub of the problem about realism and MacCabe's biggest mistake of all. Since narrative is in the first place a conscious arrangement of a multiplicity of artistic practices it cannot plausibly make the simple truth-claims, nor impose the hierarchy of discourses he tried to tar it with, nor can it possibly just be inviting the spectator to 'go and look and see'. The most naturalistic or documentary-style film or television programme does far more complicated things than that. Narrative and realism are not coterminous. The mistake was to have collapsed them one into the other.

Why did this come about? To understand why, it might be useful to reflect on two concepts MacCabe does not make use of. The first of these is convention. Art and communication function through varying ranges of developing devices and conventions about using them. In our culture there is still a difficulty about using the term 'convention'. Its connotations are felt to be pejorative because of the implication that there might be a given or 'correct' way of doing things, and because the repeated use of conventions is thought to deaden artistic and/or social experience. While one version of postmodernism revalidates the concept, another implies the disappearance of all conventions. Hence the pursuit of non-conventional or anti-conventional means of art and communication (which, if successful, contribute to the creation of new conventions) and also the more gradual evolution of new forms of conventions within the existing bodies and frameworks of expression.

In fact convention need not be such a scary term. What it means is a degree of agreement between a given audience or audiences and the producers. This agreement is enacted through the work, operating certain restrictions on and affording certain liberties to it. Narratives in different media use a varying range of conventions, some of which we have discussed above. Had MacCabe been able to see the multiplicity of these conventions (for serious analysis of which criticism still has a lot of space) he might have been able to avoid the homogenized fetish of his singular 'narrative discourse'. Likewise, artistic realism is also a network of differing conventions. It – or rather they – do not commit the reader or spectator to the endless pursuit of the nineteenth-century novel or similar forms, although they can make pleasant, stimulating, satisfying or disturbing reference to already existing or recycled elements. Perhaps even more importantly, they can be – and often are – linked in with non-realist or anti-realist elements. The work can combine attempts to copy life, to produce an adequate representation of it, with attempts to shape something else out of it, to stand back from it, to turn it into a spectacle and/or to pass judgement on it. The point here is flexibility: the uses of the medium remain movable within the conventions of realism; the conventions allow degrees of freedom for producers and for audiences.

The use of realist conventions does not, in itself, provide or imply provision of 'knowledge or how things really are'. On the other hand, it may, and quite often does, work within the framework of, or in relation to, social conventions involving truth or knowledge. It would be difficult to tell a love story without appealing, on one level or another, to some people's knowledge of what love is like. It is quite likely, in the construction of a mystery or detective story, that the producers will allude to the problematics of knowledge in their own right. It would be difficult to describe a situation in which one of the main points is the revelation of new elements (whether shocking or just not yet known) without some form of reliance on the concept of truth. It is also possible that the specific forms of these dependencies, allusions and references may have things in common with the social outlooks of various groups of people, with some aspect of their ideas about 'how things really are'. In the case of the cinema these relations are unlikely to be exclusive, because of the general wish to appeal to the responses of more than one audience or social grouping. Because of all these factors, the ways in which reference can be made to the notion of 'how things are' are intensely variable; the references themselves are shot through with convention. Realisms do, necessarily, tangle with conventional ways of seeing the truths and emotions of social and cultural life. But this involvement does not mean the adoption of fixed positions for the subject, the audience or the medium.

To put it another way, we as spectators make as strong demands for reference from movies as from other art and communication forms. The directions, the modes and the force of these references vary, exercizing themselves in different ways and in relation to different aspects of film and television works, and of emotional, cultural and social life. We need films to be about life in one way or another, but we allow them latitude about how they meet this need. In response to this, films offer the spectating subject and audiences a range and interplay of conventions in action: technical, formal, narrative, non-realist, generic, cultural, social, realist, specialist or some combination of these. Since this is so, the relationship between the reading subject and the film is one of negotiation and interpretation. The pure specularity to which MacCabe tries to limit it would be hopelessly inadequate to deal with so vigorous a compound. The film is articulated, and would not make sense if it were not. There was never any such thing as the CRT, but films, including realist ones (those using realist conventions among others) can deal with the real as contradictory, and in fact often do. Kazan's *On the Waterfront* (1953), in some respects a realist film, is full of contradictions, most of which it controls and explores. It also has a conception of the real, and it deals with it as contradictory. It does not ensure a position of specularity for anyone.[5]

The other concept MacCabe cannot allow into the discussion is experience. In the climate of the mid-1970s the idea was equated with illusion, ideology and anti-intellectualism, and constantly derided. If by itself it can explain little, in conjunction with other concepts such as convention, language, structure and discourse it may still help in allowing film theory to develop out of the sterility into which the false concept of the dominant metalanguage plunged it. Once the dead arm of the CRT has been disposed of, it may be helpful to remember that films draw on experience; they make it into something else which is also an experience, or create a new experience of their own and/or their genres, and the act of consuming them is yet another experience. The conventions in and through which they are made are the language in which these processes happen.

In comparison with MacCabe, David Bordwell's work on narrative has displayed several positive characteristics. The first two parts of *Narration in the fiction film* (1985) contain a useful discussion of several different theories of film narrative. In focusing positively on spectator involvement ('The viewer's activity' is the title of one chapter), Bordwell rejects the idea that film positions anybody. He also criticizes the simplified concepts of illusionism and spectator passivity which were the immediate outcome of the CRT idea and several other aspects of 1970s' theory. In three pages of another chapter, Bordwell also rejects MacCabe's metalanguage of dominant narrative in novel and film, drawing instead on a concept of heterogeneity which is derived from Bakhtin: 'Bakhtin shows that even in the most "realistic" novels, the narrator's language will interact dynamically with several discourses, not all of them attributable to direct character speech' (1985: 20). Likewise, a major contribution of Bordwell and Kristin Thompson's textbook *Film art: an introduction* (1979) has been its repeated statements of the multiplicity of the film medium, of its nature as a variable compound of different technical, stylistic, thematic and organizational layers.

How is it that despite the non-reductionist aspects of some of these positions, Bordwell and his colleagues have figured as *de facto* supporters of the CRT concept? Perhaps their doubts about MacCabe were only partial, or posed them problems which they had difficulty in dealing with at any length.

This is not really important, though, because whatever the attitude of Bordwell and his colleagues to the CRT, they have a parallel monolith of their own. This is 'The Classical Hollywood Cinema' (CHC), an entity which makes its first appearance as a subheading in the 'Narrative form' section of chapter three ('Narrative and nonnarrative formal systems') of the book *Film art*. It then grows rapidly via the section 'Narrative unity' in chapter nine ('Film criticism: sample analyses'), which consists of discussions of *His Girl Friday* (Howard Hawks, 1940), *The Man Who Knew Too Much* (Alfred Hitchcock, 1934) and *Stagecoach* (John Ford, 1939), stressing their supposed similarities. Then it bursts forth in its own big book (*The Classical Hollywood Cinema*, 1985), and lives on, simultaneously, as 'Classical narration: the Hollywood example', chapter nine of *Narration in the fiction film* (Bordwell, 1985). By the time of the 1993 edition of *Film art*, chapter three has been rejigged. After an interesting new section called 'Narration: the flow of story information' (pp. 75–81), there follows a further new section, 'Narrative conventions' (p. 81), the second subheading of which, on the very next page, turns out to be – 'The Classic Hollywood Cinema', much the same as it was in 1979, apart from one new paragraph about objectivity. In the film criticism section, towards the end of the book, there has been a real, though not properly acknowledged or addressed, broadening of the concept. It has now become 'The Classical Narrative Cinema'. *The Man Who Knew Too Much* is gone, but *North by Northwest* (Alfred Hitchcock, 1959), *Hannah and her Sisters* (Woody Allen, 1986) and *Desperately Seeking Susan* (Susan Seidelman, 1985) join *His Girl Friday* and *Stagecoach* in the classical narrative corral. In thus quietly dropping the label 'Hollywood' and replacing it with narrative (while leaving the CHC more or less the same elsewhere), Bordwell and company seem effectively to be moving closer to the CRT and 'dominant narrative' – and thus contributing the Hollywood cinematic form element to the mess which displeases John Corner.

If MacCabe's great undefined term is 'classic', Bordwell and his colleagues go for the classical, and make several unconvincing attempts to justify it.[6] It involves storytelling, unity, realism, naturalism, emotional appeal, decorum, proportion, harmony, rule-governed but self-effacing craftsmanship and 'mainstream'-ness. The cement of these qualities is continuity. For Bordwell and Thompson the 180 degree rule, the shot/reverse-shot pattern, the eyeline match and the match on action add up to what Thompson calls 'the continuity system'. The combined effect of these devices is supposed to be 'basically' forwarding the spectator's involvement in the story to the exclusion of all else. At the same time he or she is supposed not to be aware of these processes. After describing, in the first scene of *The Maltese Falcon* (John Huston, 1941), a complicated set of operations involving all the above devices, Bordwell and Thompson conclude that 'The viewer is not supposed to notice all this' (1997: 292).[7] In principle, it may be possible to imagine a completely naive spectator (an elderly person, living far from the modern media, in the 1940s, who stumbled on *The Maltese Falcon* as his or her first cinematic experience) and could see nothing in it but the way the editing presented the story. In fact, however, spectators do notice at least some, perhaps all, of the complex of devices discussed by Bordwell and Thompson, and they use what they notice of these, together with other cues and promptings, to make sense of the film and interpret it. Awareness of the operations of the devices may also be part of the pleasure the spectators take in the films.

In the end, Bordwell and Thompson exaggerate the importance of what, by a subtle but typical slippage, they come to call 'the classical continuity system' (1997: 298). It becomes the main instrument through which narrative development takes place, and through which time is made 'subordinate to causality' (Bordwell, 1985: 49) and space, or rather 'a remarkably coherent spatial system' is turned into 'the vehicle of narrative causality' (Bordwell, 1985: 59). The monolith of the 'classical' style is erected on this one-sided reading of technical practices. Nothing is allowed seriously to qualify it. Differences between genres and studios, variations in the uses of lighting and colour, and differing uses of the long take and depth of field are all briefly glanced at before being crushed into uniformity. Bordwell is concerned that the spectator should be seen as active, but this is only 'within specific limits' (Bordwell, Staiger and Thompson, 1985: 21). The spectator takes part in making the meaning of the film, but only within the framework of what the film itself (and the system it belongs to) tells him or her to do: 'The spectator must cooperate in fulfilling the film's form. It is clear that the protocols which control this activity derive from the system of norms operating in the classical style' (Bordwell, Staiger and Thompson, 1985: 8).

In fact, Hollywood has always liked the lack of decorum as well as the presence of decorum: it is concerned with form and formal relations (but these may be harmonious or non-harmonious); it both respects and strives to destroy and/or change tradition; it is interested in fantasy, construction and articulation as well as in mimesis. Its craftsmanship is real but by no means always self-effacing. It is certainly interested in the spectator's responses, and in trying to understand and perhaps control them, but without confidence about how to do so, and there is nothing particularly cool about its attitude to these concerns. Hollywood films have distinct aesthetic qualities, but these do not necessarily include elegance or unity. As for the notion of 'mainstream film style': Hollywood is the single most significant centre of filmmaking in the world, and its films by and large the most distinctive body of work. But this work is by no means so unified in its language as to function as one style. And even if it were, there are other styles culturally, socially and even economically different and vigorous enough to make the labelling of Hollywood as mainstream a crude and misleading reduction.

The concept of ideology is not one which it has been possible to use with any rigour or probity since the period in which its negative and positive connotations became inextricably entangled with each other. Coined in the early modern era (1796) to mean the philosophy of mind, it soon acquired the negative senses of abstract, unrooted thinking (Napoleon), idealist inversion and false consciousness (Marx and Engels) and illusion, sometimes biased in the interests of a given social group (common sense and some aspects of the sociological and Marxist traditions). By the early twentieth century it had also developed a new, relatively positive usage as a body of ideas of any substantial kind, usually related to a social context. Both sociology and the Althusserean Marxism of the 1960s which influenced media theory depended on conceptual distinctions between ideology (meaning either experience or speculative thought) and science (demonstrated facts or theoretical knowledge). Terry Eagleton, in his attempt to salvage something from the wreckage, proposes that both the more positive and the negative senses 'have their uses, and that their mutual incompatibility, descending as they do from divergent political and conceptual histories, must be simply acknowledged' (1991: 7). Ideology cannot be a practicable notion if it is firmly located in any one place, with the world view or interests of any one social class or group or in any specific literary, cultural or artistic style or figures of language:

> Dominant ideologies, and occasionally oppositional ones, often employ such devices as unification, spurious identification, naturalization, deception, self-deception, universalization and rationalization. But they do not do so universally; indeed it is doubtful that one can ascribe to ideology any *invariable* characteristics at all. We are

dealing less with some essence of ideology than with an overlapping network of 'family resemblances' between different styles of signification.

(1991: 222)

No critical writing has yet managed to chart such a network and make the result convincing in terms of ideologies.

What specific roles did the concept of ideology play in the 'classic Hollywood cinematic form' compound? MacCabe, having cheerfully admitted that by and large no convincing Marxist theory of ideology existed, plunged uncritically into the Lacanian/Althusserian substitute and made it his centre of operations; the purpose of ideological representations is to place the subject in position in society. The strong following wind through the second half of the 1970s meant that Bordwell and company, not really interested in the concept for its own sake, perhaps saw the utility of adopting it to support the 'mainstream' side of their otherwise apolitical, indeed largely asocial account of Hollywood. The other linking factor is a static conception of form, in which periods, origins and schools control the meanings and interpretations of works even before the works are articulated *and* when they are rearticulated and reinterpreted in later periods. MacCabe returns to this frozen formalism (still dressed up in 'political' clothes) as recently as his 1992 preface to Jameson's *Geopolitical aesthetic*:

> this postmodern medium [cinema] recapitulates the basic realism/modernism/post-modernism aesthetic development, with the classic Hollywood cinema representing realism (and a moment of innocence about the means of representation), the European cinema of the 50s and 60s reliving all the paradoxes of modernism (and Godard is here the exemplary figure) and a fully postmodern cinema having to wait until the early 70s.[8]

The decade-periodization is pretty wonky: the European cinema did more than the 'reliving' suggested here (though it should be said that the dead hand of the CRT has contributed to slowness in finding out what it did do), and postmodernism (full or half-full) is more complicated. But, above all, Hollywood has never been innocent about the means of representation. Its conventions could never be neatly aligned with realist ones.

The concept of ideology perished with Marxism, and needs to be replaced if the fields of theory and criticism associated with film and television are to come back to life and credibility after the decay and routine into which they fell, partly as a result of their association with this kind of Marxism. This replacement need not, I think, be too difficult. In many cases the Marxists and the non-Marxists who were influenced by them used the terms 'ideological' and 'ideology' to mean roughly the same as social and the social. In fact the use of the concept of ideology has become a way of avoiding discussing the social. Many of the classic Marxist writers were so disgusted by the realities of social life that they welcomed the concept of ideology as a means of escaping them via a blanket disapproval, which was what ideology, in its negative connotation, offered. Marx enjoyed designating the concern of middle-class intellectuals with social matters as hypocrisy, but the sneering tone of this condemnation[9] is all too compatible with the absolutism of Marx's fantasies of redemption via the proletariat and of revolution via the self-action of the forces of production. (Later, more academic Marxists were not so much disgusted by social realities as simply ignorant of them.) Issues to do with the problems of and in social life lose definition and focus if we choose to address them as part of ideology. They become the hunting ground of a group of people (most famously, a 'class') or the representation of (self-)interest, delusion or bad faith. The label 'ideology' does nothing to clarify them and tends to inhibit active investigation or serious discussion.

The concept of ideology should thus be replaced by whichever more concrete term is appropriate to the field under discussion. In philosophical contexts we should speak of ideas or beliefs; in linguistic ones of convention, style and diction; and in historical and political ones of social conventions and ideas and of the social itself. In the contexts of art and communication, we should start from the same bases as in thinking about language, but remembering that the conventions of art are not identical to those of communication. We will be able to make more progress with the problems of the relations between art and society through concepts of diction, expression, convention and the social than was possible with the confusions of the term ideology, by means of which distinct areas and practices were often run together into shapeless, indiscriminate amalgamations: amalgamations such as the Classic Realist Text, the Classical Hollywood Cinema and classical Hollywood cinematic form.

The recovery of both film and social life can only be accomplished by means of casting off both generalized determinism and the narrowly biased interpretations which derive from it. The latter will need to be replaced by a more responsive, honest and analytical critical language which, as well as rehabilitating the social and aesthetic spheres, is likely to be accompanied, culturally, by the recuperation of the values of ethics and humanism, both so derided in the latter-day Marxist period. This project is not necessarily incompatible with understanding or developing postmodernist ideas which, read critically, can contribute to it.

We need the concept of realism for several important reasons. Film and television continue to have flexible cognitive and cognition-related dimensions. These operate on three broad levels. First there is the project of truth-telling: the aim to say something directly or obliquely valid about an inter-individual, social or cultural situation or set of relations. This project sometimes has a strong emotional or moral base; if this is lacking, it still often refers to emotional and/or moral issues. Second, there is a positive interest in appearances: the idea that we can learn, on several levels, from how things, situations, states of affairs and aspects look, how they are presented and perceived. Finally, there is the aspiration towards a structure of cognition, whether revealed (laid bare on the surface, in the development or texture), constructed (in militant, evident form or formal relations), or deep (founded on the attempt to apply an underlying code or analysis, such as religion or history), or trying to combine aspects of these.[10] These dimensions are crucial; it is not possible to imagine film or television functioning adequately without at least selective versions of them.

At the same time, film and television are also rooted in convention and language. They display, and indeed often function through, self-consciousness about convention and language. Part of this self-consciousness is the media's sense of their own difference, of their non-reducibility to the signs or the referential contexts of the situations they deal in. These attributes of conventionality and self-consciousness have often been invoked in attempts to qualify, or substantively to dismiss, the cognitive dimensions set out above. What is needed in critical discussion of this area is a degree of discrimination. The conventional, self-conscious and different aspects of film and television do indeed qualify and set variable limits on the cognitive dimensions of each medium, shaping them so that they function both as real experiences and as mediating filters between the experiencing spectators and the materials (emotions, ideas, situations, contexts, stories) which the producers have fed into the language and structuring processes. They do not, however, dismiss the cognitive aspirations of spectators or media, or render them irrelevant. (Even less can they be said to turn them into ideology.) They use them, play with them to some extent, and reformulate them as artistic or communicative experiences from which the dimension of cognition is not absent. What role does the concept of realism have to perform in these twinned fields of cognition and convention? The answer is 'several', on condition that we confront the great mistakes of the 1970s and replace them with more serious attempts to understand. Realism is not a singular or univocal style. It is not a homogeneous or finished effect, nor is it a side-effect of genre. Different generic configurations may well make their own versions of realism, but realism in itself does not emerge out of a work conforming with generic norms to 'produce the illusion of realism' (Todorov, quoted in Corner, 1992; 99).[11] Nor can it meaningfully be divided into two distinct, antagonistic entities – illusionist realism on one side and formal and intellectual consciousness-raising anti-realism on the other, as the Toutvabienist anti-illusionism implicit in MacCabe and Bordwell tried to present them.[12] In the introduction to the Reader, *Realism and the cinema* (1980), I made the point that most useful discussion linked the two concepts of realism and anti-realism, exploring the relations between them.[13] I would like now to develop the linkage more concretely, and introduce two variations to it.

In films or television, where there is realism it is normally multiple and heterogeneous. It, or they – if, as seems preferable, we choose to formulate this multiplicity of elements as a plurality – are also accompanied either by their opposite, anti-realism, or by their non-identical different, which it might be more useful to think of as non-realism. An important part of the excitement and interest of both media is the active interplay between the elements which can be defined as realist, and the others which function simultaneously and have either a non-realist character (primarily formal, linguistic or conventional) or one which can be called anti-realist because the character of its formal, linguistic or conventional procedures specifically or explicitly tries to counteract the cognitive dimensions we have linked with realism.

To give examples of these different combinations: *Meet Me in St. Louis* (Vincente Minnelli, 1944) combines realism and anti-realism. At the same time it is multiply realist – on all three levels of emotional truth, interest in appearances and deep analytical structure – *and* anti-realist, in that it makes these levels coexist with elements of music, song and dance which simultaneously translate the work to a different level, the main concerns of which are show and performance. A strong link between the two sides is emotion, with which each side deals heavily and in depth, but it is not always precisely the same emotion, and its strength does not have the effect of collapsing the articulations between the film's aspects. In fact it can be argued that the film is dynamic precisely because it is doing both different things at once, and that criticism has some difficulty in deciding whether one side is more important than the other. Are character, discovery, fulfilment (the realist sides of the equation) more weighty than orchestrated performance (the anti-realist)? In any case the social meaning of the work (and of the experience of watching it) should be approached through this central combination rather than through contextual remarks about the significance of the family [see Bordwell and Thompson's discussion of the film (1997: 420–5)].

Many social issue and social drama films combine realist material (situations, characters and conflicts to varying extents) with non-realist devices and conventions. Thus *Gervaise* (1956), René Clément's version of Zola's novel *L'Assommoir*, chooses the heightened intensity of melodrama, not as an ironic comment on the novel's material but as authorizing a substitute set of conventions into which it and its language can be adapted. Zola's language and procedures, often traduced, in the wake of Lukács and his distinction between narration and description, as 'merely naturalistic', are in fact full of intensity and reflection. One can imagine several different ways of translating them into film terms, some of which might be anti-realistic, attempting to create a space of images to substitute a different visual experience for the literary and intellectual intensity of the novel's text. To some extent this is what happens in Franju's version of *La Faute de l'Abbé Mouret* (1970).

De Sica's *Bicycle Thieves* (1948) is an astute blending of realistic elements – the work-and-theft situation, the central characters, the social relations and some aspects of the ways they are shown – with anti-realist ones – the tragic structure, the frequent parallels, the architectural qualities of the treatment, the music. Joseph H. Lewis's *Gun Crazy* (1949) is essentially a non-realist film – the emblematic quality of its screenplay and dramatization, a degree of detachment from the issues presented, the acting, certain features which follow from the cheapness of the production values – but with striking forays into realism – moments of directness and intensity, especially in relation to the central characters – *and* into anti-realism – the simplicity of the narrative structure, the stylized effects produced by the combination of a noirish visual style with the budgetary restrictions already mentioned, the staging of the final sequence set in a mist-shrouded swamp.

Karel Reisz's *Saturday Night and Sunday Morning* (1960) deals mainly in different realist strands set alongside each other: interior (individual) psychic situation; intercharacter relation; sexuality; social situation; cultural situation and relations; landscape; the specifically British concern with focusing on the group or social dimensions of problems; but it does also include some non-realist elements. Its presentation of the Arthur Seaton character goes some way towards encouraging the sort of intensity of involvement more commonly associated with other national cinemas (including that of the USA), and this is further accentuated by the performance of the actor Albert Finney, who gives the persona the same sort of luminous quality as is achieved by the musical performers in *Meet Me in St. Louis*. A clever balance is maintained between this brightness and the search for a kind of objectivity, which in *Saturday Night and Sunday Morning* means that the relations between the film's different parts are well organized so as simultaneously to entertain, to tell a story, to discuss a state of affairs and to raise questions about it. This specific set of objectives is typical of the aspirations of much British realist film-making; but my more basic point is that it is important to recognize that the varied patterns of realism, non-realism and anti-realism evident in the five films briefly discussed here tell us quite a lot about the survival and necessity of realism. Films thrive on the articulation of their internal and external differences; realism and its alternatives are key parts of those processes of articulation.

Endnotes

1 The Classical Hollywood Cinema concept also figures in Bordwell and Thompson (1979) and in Bordwell (1985).
2 The use of the concept of 'text' became generalized following semiotics and 1970s' formalism. Appropriate for dealing with works of literature, criticism and (perhaps) information display systems, it has never been adequate for films or television. Its use tends to obscure the facts that film and television are both works and experience – constructed, made, interpreted and consumed by people.
3 See Victor Erlich, *Russian Formalism: History, Doctrine* (third edition, New Haven, Yale U.P. 1981), esp. pp. 171–286.
4 This despite Barthes's essentially negative attitude towards narrative, his constant repulsion of it into the field of the readerly (Barthes, 1970).
5 This is the point of intersection between 1970s' anti-realism and psychoanalysis. Lack of space (as well as the sense that the psychoanalytic issues are less important than the ones about realism) prevent me from going further into it here.
6 Examples are in Bordwell and Thompson (1997: 108) and in Bordwell, Staiger and Thompson (1985: 3–4).
7 The phrasing is revised since the 1979 edition, but still sloppy. Do they mean the viewer is not supposed to notice any of this or all of this?
8 Colin MacCabe, 'Preface' to Fredric Jameson, *The Geopolitical Aesthetic* (Bloomington, Ind: Indiana University Press, 1992), p. xiii.
9 As in Karl Marx and Friedrich Engels, *The German Ideology* (London: Lawrence and Wishart, 1974), part 1, sections 1a, 1b, and *The Communist Manifesto* (London: Verso, 1998), section 3.
10 In postmodernism, for instance, there is a great devotion to appearances and a real engagement with structure. Although in principle truth-telling is downgraded, in practice there is plenty of room for certain forms of it.
11 His remarks on Todorov and genre are very concise and deserve expansion.
12 They converge on the J.-L. Godard, J.-P. Gorin 1972 film in MacCabe (1974: 26) and Bordwell and Thompson (1993: 437).
13 'The two concepts have lived off each other . . . if they are opposites they tend to be inter-penetrating opposites' (Williams, 1980: 4).

References

Barthes, Roland. 1970: *S/Z*. New York: Hill and Wang.

Bordwell, David. 1985: *Narration in the fiction film*. London: Methuen.

Bordwell, David and Kristin Thompson. 1979: *Film art: an introduction*, 1st edn. Reading, MA: Addison-Wesley; 2nd edn 1986, 3rd edn 1990, 4th edn 1993 and 5th edn 1997. New York: McGraw-Hill.

Bordwell, David, Janet Staiger and Kristin Thompson. 1985: *The classical Hollywood cinema – film style and mode of production to 1960*. London: Routledge.

Browne, Nick. 1975/76: The spectator-in-the-text: the rhetoric of *Stagecoach*. *Film Quarterly* **34**(2): 26–37.

Corner, John. 1992: Presumption as theory: 'realism' in television studies. *Screen* **33**(1): 97–102.

Eagleton, Terry. 1991: *Ideology: an introduction*. London: Verso.

Fell, John. 1977: Vladimir Propp in Hollywood. *Film Quarterly* **30**(3): 19–28.

MacCabe, Colin. 1974: Realism and the cinema: notes on some Brechtian theses. *Screen* **15**(2): 7–27.

Metz, Christian. 1974: *Film language: a semiotics of the cinema*. Oxford: Oxford University Press.

Propp, Vladimir. 1990: *Morphology of the folktale*. Austin, Texas: Texas University Press, 2nd edition.

Williams, Christopher. 1980: *Realism and the cinema: a reader*. London: Routledge.

Wollen, Peter. 1982: *North by Northwest*: a morphological analysis. *Readings and writings*. London: Verso, 18–33.

12 Rethinking genre

Christine Gledhill

Genre, like the forms it produces, is a cyclical concept, once more spiralling to the forefront of debate for contemporary film studies (Neale, 1990; Collins, 1993; Maltby, 1995; Altman, 1998). It is particularly useful now for its potential to fill a gap left by the fragmenting of grand theory, which once promised to grasp films as part of a totalising 'social formation' or 'historical conjuncture'. Despite complex theories of ideology and subjectivity developed in the 1970s, the notion that mainstream films can be correlated with their social contexts still draws on more or less sophisticated models of textual 'reflection' – for example the repeated claim that the *noir* turn of Hollywood in the 1940s–mid-1950s is connected to post-war malaise following the return of men from the war and consequent drive to return women to the home. How, exactly does this happen? Steve Neale comments that the mental condition of a nation cannot be read from consumer choice at the box office (1990: 64). Equally improbable is the picture conjured of a huddle of producers, scriptwriters, and assorted film-makers planning how to make the next *film noir* direct its female audience back to their kitchen sinks. If, post grand theory, film studies is not to diminish into a conservative formalism or a conceptually unrooted empirical historicism, the question of how to understand the life of films in the social is paramount.

Genre provides the conceptual space where such questions can be pursued. In this space issues of texts and aesthetics – the traditional concerns of film theory – intersect with those of industry and institution, history and society, culture and audiences – the central concerns of political economy, sociology, and cultural studies. To understand exactly how the social and films interact we need a concept of genre capable of exploring the wider contextual culture in relationship to, rather than as an originating source of, aesthetic mutations and textual complications. If early versions of genre theory focused on the problem of what made a western a western, Richard Maltby's question – why does the western disappear in the 1970s–1980s? – demands more than ideological readings which translate forms back into social factors (1995: 122–4).

Genre is first and foremost a boundary phenomenon. Like cartographers, early genre critics sought to define fictional territories and the borders which divided, for example, western from gangster film, thriller from horror film, romantic comedy from the musical (Maltby, 1995: 107; Altman, 1998: 23–4). Not surprisingly, the process of establishing territories leads to border disputes. As a boundary concept genre is utilised by a range of different interest groups – from film studios to academic monograph writers, from review journalists to women's groups, from publishing houses to film schools – to stake out kinds of film production, and the fictional worlds and generic identities they found (Maltby, 1995: 107). The first generic boundaries, performing a class cultural function, served to demarcate literary forms as aesthetic discourse from the rest. A work belonging to a category such as tragedy, poetry, epic, or lyric could claim the identity of 'art' separate from forms of daily social usage and of low culture. Such aesthetic categories are key to the increasingly specialised and professionalised sphere inhabited by 'literature' and 'art' in the nineteenth and twentieth centuries. But as a critical concept, genre is pulled to either side of the boundary it was initially required to stake out. In painting, for example, 'genre' is associated with a turn to subject matter of everyday life in Dutch seventeenth-century painting, while in the nineteenth century, British genre painting becomes a highly narrativised form of middle-brow picture-making. With the rise of cinema, this reversal is complete. Genre, defined by familiar materials of popular cultural life and now the key to commercial fictional production, is separated from a supposedly non-generic art practice (Neale, 1990: 63–4). Latterly, as all areas of cultural production meet in a mass-mediated market place, accessible to every type of audience, postmodern culture dissolves the boundaries between high and low, the literary and the vernacular, the artistic and the commercial, threatening for more conservative critics cultural confusion and the loss of art as social critique (Collins, 1993: 249–50).

Genre was introduced into film studies as an alternative to auteurism more appropriate to a mass entertainment industry. For film critics it offered a tool capable of putting art back into popular fiction in order to reclaim the commercial products of Hollywood for serious critical appraisal. However, the process of repetition involved in the production of genres provided material for cultural historians concerned with what mass fictions reveal about society, resulting in analyses of genre films in terms of myth and ritual, or as 'reflections' of mass consciousness (Warshow, 1970; Wright, 1975; Schatz, 1981). More recently, a new historicism has investigated genre from the perspective of the film industry itself, opening a division between trade and critics' categories (Neale, 1990; Klinger, 1994; Maltby, 1995; Altman, 1998). In the contemporary moment of reinvention – of film both as medium and as discipline – genre boundaries, once seemingly securely in place if sometimes disputed, are repeatedly crossed by film-maker, critic, historian, and socio-cultural analyst. Herein, I want to suggest, lies the productivity of genre as boundaries are defined, eroded, defended, and redrawn. Genre analysis tells us not just about kinds of films, but about the cultural work of producing and knowing them.

Crucial to the development of the modern genre system and to understanding the shifting borders between high and mass culture is the rise in the nineteenth century of melodrama. Most contemporary accounts of melodrama begin with its 'notoriously' amorphous lack of distinctive boundaries. This is exemplified in recent gender disputes, whereby melodrama, reclaimed in the 1970s–1980s by feminist critics as a women's form, is now subject to historicist revision as belonging to male action genres. To understand such shifts and reversals I shall draw on the concept of modality as the sustaining medium in which the genre system operates. This chapter, then, attempts to rethink genre in its triple existence as industrial mechanism, aesthetic practice, and arena of cultural–critical discursivity.

As aesthetic practice, genre was initially conceptualised as a mode of artistic 'supervision' (Ryall, 1978). Each genre represented a body of rules and expectations, shared by film-maker and audience, which governed its particular generic 'world' and by which any new entrant was constructed and operated. The task of the genre critic was to survey the terrain of this world, identify its dramatis personae, iconography, locations, and plot possibilities, and establish the rules of narrative engagement and permutation. This taxomonic approach, seeking to define genres as exclusive categories, the identity of which rested in specific fixed features, established the first boundary skirmishes as to whether particular films fell into a particular genre and whether deviant films were valid variations or decadent corruptions. As auteurism ran out of steam, genre criticism continued the process of reclaiming by remapping Hollywood as an expanding frontier for the critical imagination of film studies, for film season and television programming, and for a burgeoning book market of pictorial and academic film histories. The western and gangster film/thriller were soon relatively well documented, but gradually less reputable or more recondite genres were recovered: the musical, science fiction, the horror film, pornography. At the same time discussion began of categories with ambiguous credentials in that they appeared to have no, or little, industrial basis: *film noir*, family melodrama, the small-town movie, and, subject of current controversy, the woman's film. Today the whole process seems to spiral out of control as genres confidently declared 'done with' return, as postmodern practices treat the past as a superstore for picking and mixing, and as film-makers take inspiration from critical as well as studio categories. A tension has always been present in this process of mapping and definition between empirically given, historical genres, and abstract theoretical structures which are thought as supervising their construction. The genre critic faced the conundrum succinctly put by Andrew Tudor: to identify a film belonging to a particular genre, the critic had to know what the features of that genre were, but equally the critic only knew that by reference to films identified as constituting the genre (Tudor, 1974: 135). Tzvetzan Todorov offered a means of addressing this tension in his proposition that whereas the historical genre is amorphous and continually growing, splitting or shrinking, the theoretical genre is provisional and subject to adjustment with every new addition to the generic corpus (Todorov, 1976: 13–14).

After 30 or so more years of post-classical Hollywood, which have foregrounded the hybridity and cyclical nature of genre production, accompanied by a period of cine-psychoanalytic theory in which all identity is perceived as dependent on a play of similarity and difference, and the obsessions of taxomonic analysis with boundary maintenance appear all but discredited. Steve Neale's 1980 study, *Genre*, argued that genres are not discrete phenomena, contained within mutually exclusive boundaries, but deal rather in a shared and changing pool of plot mechanisms, icons, and discourses. Their identity as genres depend on the particular relations they establish between a range of common elements rather than on exclusive possession of particular motifs: for example, the discourse of gunlaw in the context of the city/social alienation/mob/police precinct works differently in the gangster film from the way it works in the western, in the context of the frontier/community/outlaw/sherrif's posse. Similarly, marriage may work to integrate the warring parties in romantic comedy or produce the heterosexual conflicts of family melodrama. Thus genres hang together as an integrated system of intersecting fictional worlds. In this perspective, boundary crossings and disputes become productive sites of cultural activity: for example, the crossing of the search motif from western (*The Searchers*, 1956), into science fiction (*Star Wars*, 1978–99) and war films (*The Deer Hunter*, 1978; *Saving Private Ryan*, 1998); or the intense debate around *Stella Dallas* (1937) as a woman's film or maternal melodrama (see, *inter alia*, *Cinema Journal* 25:1, Fall 1985 and 25:4 Summer 1986).

Although many of these theorisations of genre, up to and including Steve Neale's 1980 monograph, were concerned to acknowledge the industrial foundations of mainstream cinema, they still focused on textuality, albeit industrially produced, rather than on genre as industrial mechanism. The analytical concepts developed – convention, stereotype, iconography (Alloway, 1971; McArthur, 1972), inner and outer form (Buscombe, 1970), structuring antimonies (Kitzes, 1969), syntax and semantics (Altman, 1984) – were largely formal, designed to explore how generic films produced their aesthetic and ideological effects. But a new twist in the debate follows film studies' return to history, which against critical genres poses the categories used by the industry in production schedules and marketing. Thus a decade after his monograph Steve Neale argues that 'industrial and journalistic labels ... offer virtually the only available evidence for a historical study of the array of genres in circulation or of the way in which individual films have been generically perceived at any point in time' (1990: 52). Barbara Klinger takes up this contention in her challenge to the authorial place given to Douglas Sirk as producer of what Thomas Elsaesser (1972) identified as 'sophisticated family melodramas' which, ironised by baroque *mise en scène*, were feted by cineastes and film critics as undermining the conformist ideologies of Eisenhower's 1950s' America (Klinger, 1994). By examining the 'intertextual relay' of publicity, posters, pressbooks, and review journalism, Klinger establishes that films grouped together in the 1970s as family melodramas were, in the 1950s, marketed to their audiences as 'adult movies'.

According to this perspective, reduction of melodrama to the bourgeois family within the Sirkian corpus created a retrospective genre to parallel that of *film noir*. Crucially, it brought critical attention to bear on a body of films that focused on the personal arena of domestic and heterosexual relations, culturally defined as feminine, thus inviting attention from a growing body of feminist film theory interested in what the culture dubs 'women's forms'. The intervention of feminism brought systematic ideological critique to bear on genre production in contradistinction to the auteurism that, in recuperating Douglas Sirk as a Brechtian master of ironic *mise en scène*, inadvertently drew attention to melodrama as a mode and Hollywood's production for the female audience. Given the domination of the majority of mainstream genres by the male hero and masculine action, feminist attention was drawn to any production aimed at the female audience which placed the heroine at the centre of the narrative, thus articulating the woman's film as a cross-generic corpus of films linked by their address to a female audience to be examined alongside women's fiction, women's magazines, the 'woman's page', the BBC 'woman's hour' and so on. Inevitably, given the weak twentieth-century commonsense boundary between anything labelled 'woman's' and melodrama, the woman's film and melodrama are frequently (but not invariably) treated by critics – both journalistic and academic – as one.

There have been a number of differently articulated attempts to disentangle these categories. Women's culture is distinct from, though it may use, melodrama and is as likely to relate to a tradition of domestic realism (see Gledhill, 1987; 1992; 1993). However, the most recent interventions stem from the new historicity. Thus Steve Neale in 'Melo talk' (1993) records results from an intensive perusal of the US trade press which show its limitation of the term 'melodrama' to action–sensation-dominated subgenres, assumed to be addressing male audiences – except when, as Ben Singer shows, they support a 'serial queen' such as Pearl White in the teens (Singer, 1990; 1995). Films aiming at female audiences, on the other hand, are more likely to be categorised under the more prestigious 'A' feature label, 'drama'. Richard Maltby (1995) and Rick Altman (1998) take up Ben Singer's and Steve Neale's findings to emphasise the distance between the domestic construction of the retrospectively named family melodrama of the 1950s and the presumed 'original action-oriented meaning of the term melodrama' (Altman, 1998: 35).

In thus focusing on locatable origins and singular meanings – according to Neale, Maltby, and Altman more authentically found at the site of production – the renewed historicism threatens to undo much of the valuable work achieved in theorising generic textuality. First, the presupposition of an 'original' undercuts the much discussed hybridity of genre as not only an industrial but also a cultural process. For melodrama, a form founded on plagiarism, the notion of an original or singular meaning is particularly inappropriate. Second, history is conceived as a series of successive shifts, leaving the past as done with, thus blocking perception of generic continuities. This, in turn, assumes film history has a definitive beginning this side of the emergence of the industry. But to unravel the relation of film genres and melodrama requires a history pre-dating cinema. For example, Singer's study of early film serials finds not only victimised but empowered heroines, recalling as a by-product of nineteenth-century gender ideology both cross-dressed and transvalued gender roles, whereby woman as sign of virtue may be more resiliant and competent in outwitting villany than the frequently incapacitated hero. In its focus on locatable origins and singular meanings, the empirical bent of the new historicism fails to grasp the productivity of such boundary encounters and category mixing which, amongst other things, permits the exploration of one social gender in the body of another and widens audience appeal.

Ultimately, reliance on industrial and marketing categories threatens to return us to the taxomonic trap. The process of naming is a generative process, as is demonstrated by Rick Altman's ingenious model of generic proliferation which shows how a more widely applicable adjectival attribute shifts to a singular genre-nominating noun – from musical romance and musical comedy to generic independence as *the* musical (Altman, 1998: 16–23). But names are attributed by particular organisations or groups under specific circumstances for specific purposes. Studio assignment of films for women to 'A' feature production tells us only about their placement in a production and marketing strategy, not about their cultural value, as Harry Warner made clear to Bette Davis when he told her he hated her films which nevertheless the box office dictated he make (Davis, 1962: 158). As suggested by Rick Altman's geological metaphor of the fold that exposes older rock formations, two different systems of generic naming and evaluation are at work at the same time (Altman, 1998: 22). So while there is no doubt that melodrama is a category deeply caught up in the gendering of western popular culture – in its classing and racialising as well – there is no simple identification to be made between gender, whether male or female, and melodrama at any point in its history.

What, then, do marketing labels represent? Tino Balio (1993), Klinger, Altman, and Maltby all suggest in different ways that the film industry does not work directly with genres at all. Rather, to guide production the studios look for series based on a clearly successful film or exploiting a particular asset in which they have exclusive ownership such as a star, reusable set, or particularly distinctive formula, often derived from a new mix of elements from different genres. Thus, to capture the process of industrial inception, Alloway, Maltby, and Altman favour the concept 'cycle' over genre, Tino Balio speaks of 'production trends', and Barbara Klinger of the 'local genre'. As a marketing tool genres are not only shared with rival studios, but threaten to divide audiences. Hybrid advertising identities are favoured to ensure interest for a maximal audience range (Altman, 1998: 9), while trade reviewers and video outlets work with broader categories more akin to the traditional literary types recast in popular terms – drama, adventure, comedy, thriller – under which a wide variety of films can be shelved.

Genres, nevertheless, are what journalists, critics, film scholars, and publishing houses are interested in. Altman, indeed, suggests a tension between industrially nominated cycles, which contract categories, and generic elaborations, which expand them (1998: 18). Thus there is an *inevitable* mismatch between industrial and critical histories. Richard Maltby points out, for example, that as an industrial category, the gangster film cycle lasted all of three years, while its cultural life extends to the present day (1995: 111). Genres, it would appear, represent categories whose identities are elaborated *post hoc* at a different level and elsewhere. Questions of cultural and aesthetic *value* require even more circumspection as between film-makers, trade and fan press, scholarship, and counter-cultural movements. If Rick Altman's meticulous evolutionary diagrams have all the appearance of a scientific law, the feminists mess things up by sneaking 'women's miseries' into the generic process in 'cobbling' together the woman's film, while simultaneously appropriating melodrama as a form for women (1998: 32). In a concluding coda Altman somewhat ruefully concedes that a feminist must do what a feminist must do (1998: 36), but this is precisely the wrong point to give in if we want to grasp the full productivity of genre, for boundary disputes involve contested identities.

If the return to historicist empiricism tends to conflate origins with explanations, the problem is not only, as Rick Altman argues, that the synchronic generic map does not fix things for all time. Neither do the artefacts themselves remain locked in the past. In this respect television and video stores confront the film analyst with what are givens of literary critical life – the evolving existence not only of film genres but of past exemplars of any form. 'Old' films circulate amongst us still, enabling film and critical production to hook back into the past and dust off apparently worn-out formulae for present uses and possible renaming. So the western did not die in the 1970s and, in an age dominated by postmodern *tech-noir* and action movies, romantic comedy is suddenly back. A strand of 1950s' adult movies is regrouped as family melodrama, *film noir* emerges as both critical concept and new production category, and films not initially promoted as woman's films are reconceived under this banner. The life of a genre is cyclical, coming round again in corkskrew fashion, never quite in the same place. Thus the cultural historian lacks any fixed point from which to survey the generic panorama. This is not, however, to reject the precise and close attention to specific practices and operations demanded by Neale, Klinger, Altman, and Maltby. Revealing patterns or usages lost to view – such as *Variety*'s continued use of the term 'melodrama' in only one of its varied nineteenth-century generic manifestations well into the twentieth – enables us to sharpen the questions we ask of mass popular cultural production, and alerts us to new questions not asked before. It enables us to trace the movements of cultural history, carried forward or intruding into the present, revealing hidden continuities and transformations working under new or disguising names. If male-orientated action movies are persistently termed 'melodrama' in the trade, long after the term is more widely disgraced, this should alert us to something from the past that is alive in the present and circulating around the masculine.

Melodrama is not nor ever was a singular genre. However, we may retrospectively conceive its historical effectivity in two interdependent ways: first, as an early cultural machine for the mass production of popular genres capable of summoning up and putting into place different kinds of audience; second, as a modality, understood as a culturally conditioned mode of perception and aesthetic articulation. As a genre-producing machine, melodrama is forged from the convergence of two broad-based cultural traditions: one, excluded from official culture, which contained a mix of folk and new urban entertainment forms, and another, more formally coherent, deriving from an increasingly influential middle-class fiction and theatre of sentimental drama and comedy (Figure 12.1). This forging comes about in England and France from the commercial potential of new entertainment needs and the requirement of an industrialising, democratising society for a redefined and enlarged public sphere. For the melodramatic machine, news events, popular paintings or songs, romantic poetry, successful high dramas, or circus acts generate material for theatrical enactments in which titles and posters frequently precede the manufacture of acting scripts by contracted writers; visual effects and sensations are generated before and supersede the word; and actors serve the mechanical wonders and pictorial effects of *mise en scène* and moving scenery (Booth, 1981). The subgenres which melodrama produces cohere around any one, or combination, of these mechanical features and aesthetic effects: in England, water-tanks at Sadler's Wells give rise to acquatic and nautical melodrama, the circus ring at Astley's to equestrian and military melodrama (Figure 12.2), Drury Lane's status as a legitimate theatre favours domestic, romantic, and society melodrama, while

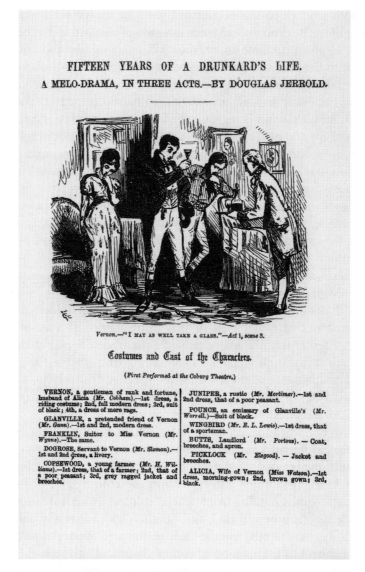

Figure 12.1 Frontispiece to J. Dicks's Standard Plays edition of *Fifteen years of a drunkard's life* (1828).

on the Surreyside the 'Bloody Vic' specialises in murders. Other subgenres abound, including gothic, society, cloak-and-dagger, cape-and-sword, sensation melodrama and, in the USA, frontier, backwoods, civil war, temperance melodrama, and so on. These melodramatic subgenres, specialising in particular materials, effects, and spectator address, compete for the loyalty of differentiated audiences, while each production site, through mixed programming, and, in the absence of copyright laws, through adpatation, plagiarism, and piracy, seeks to maximise them.

Out of this institutional context, aesthetic, cultural, and ideological features coalesce into a modality which organises the disparate sensory phenomena, experiences, and

Figure 12.2 Equestrian and military melodrama at Astley's.
Reproduced courtesy of Victoria and Albert Museum, London.

contradictions of a newly emerging secular and atomising society in visceral, affective and morally explanatory terms (see below, p. 234). The notion of modality, like register in socio-linguistics, defines a specific mode of aesthetic articulation adaptable across a range of genres, across decades, and across national cultures. It provides the genre system with a mechanism of 'double articulation', capable of generating specific and distinctively different generic formulae in particular historical conjunctures, while also providing a medium of interchange and overlap between genres. If comedy, tragedy, and romance are among the oldest and most widespread of modalities, tragedy has, in Peter Brooks's (1976) argument, largely been displaced by melodrama, while romance has radically shifted its purview from chivalric adventure to women's mass fiction (Radford, 1986). Because of its wider socio-cultural embrace, the melodramatic mode not only generates a wide diversity of genres but also draws other modes into its processes of articulation. Thus melodrama thrives on comic counterpoint, can site its fateful encounters in romance, and keeps pace with the most recent of modes, realism, which first worked in cooperation with melodrama and then disowned it. In such permeability lies the flexibility of the system necessary to the forming of a mass-produced 'popular culture' for a broadening society, drawing into public view a diversity of audiences, sometimes dividing but working more generally to unite them, while at the same time facilitating international exchange. An exemplary figure here is the actor–manager–playwright, Dion Boucicault, of French–Irish descent, who refined the energies of Surreyside blood and thunder melodrama in tune with middle-class sensibilities, recasting the 'helpless and unfriended' (Vicinus, 1981) as the respectable poor and sometimes fallen middle classes who nevertheless encounter their share of sensation and spectacle enacted in attic suicides and tenement fires, rewritten in local colour many times over to appeal to the audiences of particular cities and nations. While Charles Reade was suing rivals who had pirated his adaptation of *Les Pauvres de Paris* (1856), Boucicault staged his own multiple versions as *The Poor of New York* and *The Streets of Philadelphia* (1857), *The Poor of Liverpool, The Poor of Leeds, The Poor of Manchester, The Streets of Dublin, The Streets of Islington* (when played at Sadler's Wells), *The Streets of London* (when played at the Princess's), all produced in 1864, revived regularly thereafter (Figure 12.3), and made into films in 1913 and 1922 (see Fawkes, 1979: 147–8; Gerould, 1983: 10–11). Thus melodrama constructs a version of the 'popular' capable of producing recognition for a range of audiences from different classes, localities, and national groupings.

As a genre machine, however, melodrama brought into play a major cultural boundary of modern society, between a mass culture of content and affect-defined genres and the formally defined artistic kinds of high cultural classification – drama, poetry, prose – which provided unity, coherence, and verisimilitude to an aristocratic society of the eighteenth century and later to the cultural leadership of the intelligentsia at the turn of the nineteenth century. Where melodrama had been used to unite audiences, its name began to divide them. From its very inception the term held considerable ambivalence. Wedding two cultural traditions, and drawing together different audiences into a new public mass, melodrama is a double source of fascination and threat. Via one tradition, emerging out of and drawing on proscribed and marginalised folk and early urban entertainments, melodrama provokes, much as today, anxiety of the establishment as to the cultural degeneration and insubordination of the lower orders. Equally, however, providing an excitement and moral fervour lacking in sentimental drama and comedy, melodrama is drawn across the socially divided urban spaces to infiltrate the repertoire of established theatres in order to stem the flow of more adventurous middle-class audiences in the opposite direction. As a result the tactics of class-differentiated forms of entertainment combine. Thus action and sentiment, pathos and spectacle, presumed today to appeal to differently gendered audiences, are drawn into a composite aesthetic and dramatic modality, capable of different emphases and generic offshoots.

For twentieth-century film theorists the cultural processes of history pose the questions when and where did cinema begin and when and where did the nineteenth century end? There is now underway a vigorous debate between theatre and film scholars around the 'baton' model of stage-screen relations whereby it is supposed the practices of the popular nineteenth-century theatre are passed over to cinema, cleansed of their melodramatic trappings and made fit for the twentieth century, thus installing

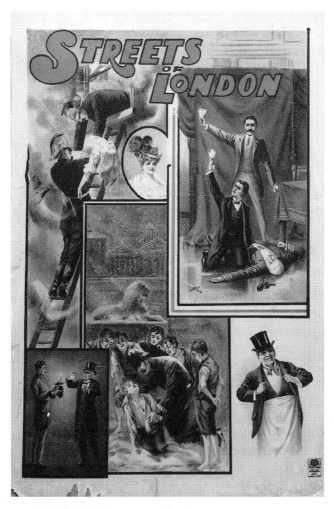

Figure 12.3 Poster for revival of *The Streets of London*.
Reproduced courtesy of Victoria and Albert Museum, London.

another boundary between 'old-fashioned' structures of moral feeling and contemporary demands for realist perception (see Mayer, 1997; Sokalski, 1997). Not only does this model misconceive the relation of melodrama and realism (to which I return below), but also it produces a paradoxical conception of film narrative. In recent years film studies, seeking to establish the historical development and formal structures of mainstream cinema, has turned predominantly to the principles of the novel or short story, as enshrined in the scenario or screenplay, for the 'classic' values of narrative causality and psychologically motivated character which are thought to displace the melodramatic. According to Steve Neale's 1980 monograph it is classic narrative which supervises the functioning of genres. And yet Richard Maltby, analysing submissions to the Production Code Administration in the mid-1940s, finds that a quarter to one-third of categories are counted as some form of melodrama (1995: 111), while Linda Williams draws on categories deployed by the American Film Institute Catalogues for 1921–30 and 1961–70 to show a 'remarkable proliferation of categories of melodrama' that 'have persisted ... in the eyes of archivists and catalogists' (1998: 51). How, then, are we to understand this persistence of melodrama, despite its widespread rejection as 'old-fashioned' and the shifting evolution of its genres into the modern age?

The presumption that cinema constitutes a modernist break with past traditions has led to neglect of melodrama's earlier history. This is reinforced by suspicion of terms denoting continuity such as Zeitgeist, world-view, social malaise, imagination, which reify generic forms in a resistance to change (see Altman, 1998: 24–5). Nevertheless, the refusal to acknowledge continuities leads, as Gill Branston points out (Chapter 2), to a fetishisation of breaks as romantically perverse as that of universals beyond culture and history. Naming contributes to a process of redrawing boundaries and redefining relationships. But such processes are neither originary nor innocent. While names are chosen to serve certain functions, they also, as Bakhtin tells us, bring with them their past histories and enter into dialogue and contest with other names (Bakhtin, 1981: 276). Behind every name are all the other uses to which it has been put. Embedded within it are all the potential new relationships it might enter into. From around 1870 through to the 1930s the terms 'melodrama' and 'realism' circulated in a fluid interchange with gender and class values as, with the rise of mass-media entertainment, the map of cultural relations reshaped itself. The 1923 advertisement for Rex Beach's *Fair Lady* in the British trade journal, *The Bioscope* (Figure 12.4), shows just such terminological vacillation, as a pitch to female audiences recalls melodrama from a different arena of cultural circulation from that associated with adventure serials.

If melodrama does indeed cross the centuries this is partly, as Thomas Elsaesser (1972), Peter Brooks (1976), and, more recently, Ben Singer (1995) suggest, because of its capacity to respond to the questions of modernity. Rather than an essentialising 'personal continuity' (Altman, 1998: 25), the term ' imagination', linked by Peter Brooks to melodrama, can be reconceived in terms of an 'imaginary', as used by several contributors to this volume. If divested of its Lacanian connotations of illusoriness, the imaginary, as James Donald and Stephanie Donald explain (Chapter 7), can be conceptualised as a public space of social imaginings within a culturally conditioned aesthetic framework. Thus a 'mode of imagination' is both culturally and historically definable. The modality of melodrama has certain priorities: the endowment of a secular world, driven by the energies of capitalist accumulation, with a significance arising out of the clash of moral imperatives. Thomas Elsaesser suggests that the rhetorical devices of melodrama – the hidden identities, misrecognitions, delayed or chance meetings, sudden reversals and climactic *coups de théâtre* – resonate in relation to and provide a means of aesthetically organising the experiences of the city and life under capitalism, which in its geographic and temporal contiguities provides stark juxtapositions between wealth and poverty, upper and working classes, social rise and fall. Ben Singer demonstrates the correlation between the growing dangers of urban and technological existence and the increasing emphasis in proletarian melodrama and yellow journalism on sensational events, which are taken into the film serials of the early teens. Such phenomenal experiences provide the dynamic rhythms, and visual textures of aesthetic

FEBRUARY 8, 1923.   BIOSCOPE   5

REX BEACH'S "Fair Lady"

SELLING MELODRAMA TO WOMEN

Wherever women go, the men go. That is certain. The preponderance of women at all performances of the popular stage hits in London and other big cities disproves the old belief that screen or stage melodrama furnishes genuine entertainment only for men audiences.

"Fair Lady" is a romantic photoplay melodrama of and for women; a melodrama of love, romance, gorgeous costumes and mystery; with thrills and action; tearful pathos and relieving comedy, and appealing directly to women of all types, classes and years.

Play up the title, "Fair Lady." It gives a direct exhibitor tie-up with every merchant, for the reason that every merchant in your city deals with women. He buys his stock, displays his goods—in fact, runs his entire business to please and cater to Fair Lady. You help him, and he'll help you!

Tie up with every first-class business man in your city. Give him neatly printed placards announcing the things he has to sell to Fair Lady. There are gowns for "Fair Lady"; hats for "Fair Lady"; shoes, hosiery, lingerie, gloves, perfumes, cosmetics, hair-goods, hair-dressing, coats, wraps, negligee, sports costumes, motoring costumes, vanity bags, travelling bags, toilet articles, confectionery,—in short, almost anything and everything that any merchant sells.

Sell "Fair Lady" to the women of your city! They'll bring the men!

No business man ever tries to sell a stock of goods without telling his patrons what he's got, and why they should buy. Selling amusement more and more is getting to be an out-and-out straight business proposition.

Allied Artists Corporation, Ltd.

Mary Pickford Charlie Chaplin Douglas Fairbanks, D. W. Griffith Hiram Abrams
Chairman

HEAD OFFICE :
86-88, Wardour Street, London, W.1

Telegrams :
" Allartisco, Wescent, London."

Telephone
REGENT 551 1778 1779

Figure 12.4 'Selling melodrama to women': advertisement for Rex Beach's *Fair Lady*, from *The Bioscope*, 8 February 1923.

Reproduced courtesy of British Film Institute.

form rendered in theatrical or pictorial terms, while at the same time bringing to the arbitrariness of an accident and coincidence-prone daily experience some kind of sense. Thus Peter Brooks suggests that sensation and aesthetic control work together to make significant the apparent randomness and atomisation of life in a capitalist world: 'making large but insubstantiable claims on meaning', the sensational effects of melodrama assert significance both in the sense of making things matter and making them mean (Brooks, 1976: 199). Melodrama's use of heightened contrasts and polar oppositions aim to make the world morally legible (1976: 42). At the threshhold of the new millennium none of these conditions, material, existential, or aesthetic, have changed. The questions how to live, who is justified, who are the innocent, where is villainy at work now, and what drives it are, as Linda Williams (1998) has forcefully argued, those which the modality of melodrama organises in the material at its disposal. The many genres of melodrama provide a range of fictional worlds in which these questions can be embodied, personified, and enacted in different social and gendered arenas and historical periods.

Melodramatic modality can do this because of its founding heterogenity and the particular aesthetic mechanisms it deploys. Despite melodrama's cultural divisiveness, the practices it separates are constantly engaged in border raids. So, for example, nineteenth-century melodramas circulate Schiller and Shakespeare, while Peter Brooks has recourse to melodrama to explain the workings of Balzac and Henry James. In writing about the genres of literature, Mikhail Bakhtin (1981) suggests that the novel's distinction lies in its capacity to reproduce all other modes of speech and writing. It is a genre of active heteroglossia, capable of drawing into itself all languages and cultural forms, high and low, literary and vernacular, past and present, setting them into dialogic exchange with each other and returning them in the process to the public sphere as literature. Melodrama might be thought as doing the same in reverse direction, drawing social, popular, and high-art cultures and discourses into its orbit, packaging them in different combinations through its cluster of genres for consumption by a newly emerging mass audience, whose social and cultural differentiations can be appealed to and exploited within a broad generic system.

Cinematic technology also delivers a medium that can reproduce all others. And like melodrama it evolves from the merging of two sets of class- and gender-differentiated traditions: fairground with parlour entertainment, the cinema of 'attractions' with a cinema of narrative fiction. If its technology and the conditions of mass production and reception usher in a qualitatively new phase of modernity, cinema's reproductive capacity makes it a site of coalescence between these and the modernising forces gathering in the previous century in melodrama's system for generic production. When studios begin to look for means of lengthening film fictions and fleshing out their generic affiliations, cinema draws on surrounding popular forms not simply from the past but still active in the music halls, vaudeville theatres, and much of the wider theatrical culture itself, as well, of course, in other sites of mass popular production: illustrated fiction, magazines, the press, public galleries, and cheap prints. Melodrama delivers a generic system as a method of production and marketing, together with a set of visual, gestural, and musical strategies which combine bodily eloquence and spectacle, already organised to address different audiences. The ascription, 'classic', to film narrative paradoxically ties cinema to a novelistic past in defiance, as Miriam Hansen suggests (Chapter 18), of its modernity. But if the novel is a form that presents all others, it too cannot partake in the purity of the 'classic'. The attempt to define mainstream film as classic neglects not only cinema's melodramatic legacy via the genre system it finds at hand but also flies in the face of the beginnings of modernity both in the melodrama machine and in the Bakhtinian novel.

Paradoxically, then, film *studies* (as opposed to the film *industry*) looks for the 'classic' while relegating melodrama as outmoded. Both moves have been facilitated by the complex history of melodrama's transition into the twentieth century and the critical vicissitudes of its name under pressures of modernisation in which class and gender played their part. A key feature in this history is the presumed superiority of cinema in delivering realism, metioned above (Vardac, 1949; Pearson, 1992). However, as David Mayer (1997) and Thomas Postlewait (1996) insist, the opposition implied between melodrama and realism simplifies the complexity of their relationship. If, as Ben Singer and Steve Neale suggest, the film industry narrows its name generically to sensational action and emotional thrills, nevertheless melodramatic modality continues to dominate mainstream cinema under the new names of Hollywood genres to the present day (Williams, 1998). To unravel this paradox requires a dialectical concept of melodrama–realism relations and of their role in modern culture's changing values, which leads practitioner-critics to disavow melodrama's name while continuing to write within its modality (Postlewait, 1996: 45).

In 'Questions of genre' (1990) Steve Neale substitutes for 'realism' the concept of cultural verisimilitude, constituted by those conventions which represent what society takes as reality, what it finds acceptable. Generic verisimilitude, on the other hand, defines what is expected of a particular kind of *fictional* world. As Neale points out, genres call on cultural verisimilitude according to their relationship to a social world – for example, the historical West in the case of the western or the contemporary urban metropolis in the case of the gangster film. However, while serving the model of bourgeois ideology which dominated 1970s' high theory, the abandonment of realism as an operative concept impoverishes the resulting model of genre culture. The conventions of verisimilitude are not static but shift under the polemic of realism, which can now be more precisely understood as that modality which makes a claim on the real, in a bid to redefine what counts as reality under pressure from struggles between established and emerging or resisting groups (Donald and Mercer, 1981). In the nineteenth century a hegemonic gender ideology of separate spheres provided ideal embodiment for the moral confrontations of a melodramatic modality. For a society governed by white, patriarchal, capitalist inequalities, yet officially committed to Christian morality, 'woman' constituted a signifier of virtue, enduring, combatative, and triumphant, or, if forswearing this role, corrupted and fatal. Functioning symbolically inside genres, such embodied representations circulate back to form social expectations and practices. However, as the socio-political formations and psychic identities of class and gender – on which Victorian melodrama depended – break free from the ideologies and representations that sustained them, the codes of verisimilitude are challenged.

With successive working-class, feminist, and civil rights movements, a reflexive self-consciousness invades an increasingly media-mediated culture: struggles to redefine cultural verisimilitude under the banner of realism follow. So if melodramatic modality aims to render everyday life morally legible and its democratic morality is locked into an aesthetic of justice, it must, in order to command recognition, acknowledge the contested and changing signs of cultural verisimilitude, bringing radical as well as conservative voices into play.

In this context, gender and class constitute key values in a contest for hegomonic control of the diversity and fluidity of a new mass culture and the mass public it brings into being. The drive to preserve cultural space and leadership for a middle-class intellectual elite polarises melodrama and realism as critical values. This had profoundly ambivalent effects for those endeavouring to claim respectability for the industry they depended on, whether studio heads or a critical intelligentsia seeking to promote cinema as an art form. In this context the 'feminine' is recruited to both sides of the struggle. On the one hand, realism, in its association with restraint, underplaying, and the reasoning mind, is valued as masculine, relegating emotion and pathos as feminising. On the other hand, analysis of feeling and dialogue are nurtured in women's fiction, which becomes a staple source for scenario writers of genres labelled 'drama' or given the prefix 'psychological' and aimed at female audiences, who were crucial to raising the cultural respectability of cinema (Neale, 1993).

Thus the name of melodrama is preserved by the film industry for genres which emphasise action and spectacle while minimising (though rarely abandoning) sentiment and pathos in a more direct appeal to urban, proletarian audiences, imagined in the masculine. But how the industry tries to position its product and how film-makers or critics, each with their own stakes in mass culture, respond are very different things. Bette Davis had to fight to retain the dialogue of Olive Higgins Prouty's *Now, Voyager* (1942), while camerawork, lighting, and Max Steiner's score melodramatise the more attenuated domestic realism of women's fiction (Allen, 1984). Critical literature and review press are scattered with giveaway phrases which attempt to distanciate the effects of the presumed feminising aspects of emotion while finding protective classic names to remasculinise and dignify genres to be rescued for serious critical attention. Thus the first generic mapping of Hollywood reclaims the western as epic, the gangster as tragic hero, and melodrama, inescapable in Douglas Sirk's Hollywood œuvre, is at last acknowledged only through the ancient Greek terms, *aporia* and *peripeteia*, as ironising devices deployed to undercut what are described as the hollow sentimentalities derived from a feminised consumerist culture (Gledhill, 1987: 10–11). But all the ancient Greek terminology in the world cannot disguise the melodrama that exploits a realism associated not only with the rich repertoire of sexualised images derived from popular Freudism, but with the intensifying expressive violence of the western, thriller, action movie, and horror film. The taciturnity of masculine realism is the seedbed of melodramatic emotion (Figure 12.5), while the talk that characterises women's cultural forms threatens to dissipate melodrama in analytic discourse.

Application of 'classic' labels, however, is not simply a bid to claim elite cultural values. When André Bazin talked of the 'classical' maturity of Hollywood in the 1930s

Figure 12.5 The taciturnity of masculine realism as seedbed of melodramatic emotion: Clint Eastwood in *The Outlaw Josey Wales* (1976).

and 1940s, he was looking to identify 'the genius of the system' (Bazin, 1968: 154) – a phrase taken up since by David Bordwell *et al.* (1985) and Thomas Schatz (1988) to connote the smooth working of a well-oiled aesthetic machine. In popular usage 'classic' suggests the realisation of a distinctive fictional world, working within familiar rules (Maltby, 1995: 112–14; Ryall, 1998: 336). This world is both like and not like ours, its boundaries permitting safe encounter with what lies the other side. But submitted to the model of classic narrative, genre's fictional worlds are conceived as formal and ideological systems which programme audience reading or secure compliant subjects. From this perspective, cine-psychoanalysis, with its uncompromising relegation of narrative to 'secondary elaboration' of a primary, underlying psychic substrate, deconstructes the boundary as some kind of regressive security blanket. However, boundaries serve not only to separate and contain but also constitute meeting points, instituting contact between spheres the dominant culture seeks to divide. Definition through differentiation brings new terrain into view. Desire is generated at the boundaries, stimulating border crossings as well as provoking cultural anxieties. This is particularly the case where social identities – gender, class, ethnicity, sexuality – are shifting.

Melodramatic modality is peculiarly attuned to the frisson of the boundary in its search for polarising juxtapositions founded in referential recognition. Symptomatic of such border activity is the cry of outrage heard from British critics when the Italians used the Eastwood persona to inject into the western a newly sexualised, proletarianised male violence, making a new claim on realism and cutting across the genre's 'classic' codes of honour. In this respect melodrama's protagonists hover between symbolic functions for the genre and the renewal of performance gestures that will command cultural recognition. Importantly, Steve Neale's (1990) account of generic and cultural verisimilitude allows a crossover effect as media fictions circulate in society, supplying generic signs as cultural signposts, and, conversely, reabsorbing cultural codes into generic worlds as markers of authenticity or contemporaneity. An exchange takes place between generic symbol and signifier of the real. Protagonists classed, gendered, or ethnically marked for our cultural recognition take up symbolic positions in a moral and affective drama. Melodramatic modality articulates social, as aesthetic questions, and vice versa. It asks of the protagonists and actors available: who can personify – body forth in their physical presence, in the particularities of personality in their social representativeness – the cause of innocence, justice, hope? Who embodies the oppression and allure of demand run rampant which dares break taboos, releasing desires we disown as threatening destruction? Bodies, gestures, looks, the grain of the voice perform affective scenarios in which aesthetic involves moral and social drama.

Melodrama, as an organising modality of the genre system, works at western culture's most sensitive cultural and aesthetic boundaries, embodying class, gender, and ethnicity in a process of imaginary identification, differentiation, contact, and opposition. But, as we have seen, bodies belong not only to generic worlds. They circulate as representations of ourselves within cultural verisimilitude and are subject to challenge. In a media-saturated society, now aware of sexism, racism, and homophobia, contest over ownership of the image is intensified. In the early stages of genre analysis a common metaphor used of genre was that of a society *talking to itself* (McArthur, 1972) – a metaphor that prefigures Miriam Hansen's development of the concept of cinema as an 'alternative public sphere'. It is now possible to conceptualise the intuitive reach of this metaphor in the tripartite meeting between Bakhtinian dialogism, melodramatic modality, and the boundary encounters of the generic system. In this activity operate the processes by which society enters genre production. Genres construct fictional worlds out of textual encounters between cultural languages, discourses, representations, images, and documents according to the conventions of a given genre's fictional world, while social and cultural conflicts supply material for renewed generic enactments. Heteroglossia and dialogism are built into the genre product's need both to repeat, bringing from the past acculturated generic motifs, and to maintain credibility with changing audiences by connecting with the signifiers of contemporary verisimilitude, including signs of struggles to shift its terms in the name of the real, of justice, of utopian hope. In each addition to a genre, 'thousands of living dialogic threads ... [are] woven by socio-ideological consciousness around the given object of an utterance ... it cannot fail to become a participant in social dialogue' (Bakhtin, 1981: 276). Melodrama capitalises on this Babel-like condition, courting the excitement and novelty of sometimes violent, sometimes startling, encounters at the boundaries – giving us, for example, the serial queen, or the 'true woman', as today's action heroine – and orchestrating proceedings in an eruption of moral and emotional consequences staged in terminal conflicts and clarifying resolutions.

But it is not just inside the fictional worlds constructed by genres that society talks to itself. If taxomonic definition cannot be justified at a meta-discursive level, the zeal with which genre identities such as the western or woman's film are contested demonstrates that naming remains culturally and politically significant. Moreover, just as critics participate in audiences, audiences may also become critics. Thus the women's movement rejected the place Hollywood carved out for women, and reinterprets particular historical cycles and trends from the perspective of a specific social group in a later decade. The new historicity, however, looks for empirical authenticity in the film industry and questions such interventionist critical constructions as bids for cultural prestige or academic advancement – as if historians were not also on the academic payroll. An examination of publicity tells us about a certain 'horizon of expectations' within which films circulate and are positioned for audiences. But the film industry is neither an originating source of categories, nor are such categories the measure of audience response. Putting, as Tom Ryall (1978) recommends, industry, genre product, audiences, and critical institutions back into their shared cultural and social formation makes productive the tension between industry and genre histories. Where, for example, do the names called on by the film industry come from? Barbara Klinger (1994) shows how the term 'adult movie' wins at the box office because it cues into culturally resonant material and attitudes. In claiming maturity with the promise of censored material for adults only, it combines the prestige of the sexually more adventurous European movie with the sensationalism of the 'true confessions' magazine. But while the identification of the category 'adult movie' pinpoints a marketing niche, this does not of itself tell us about the aesthetic or ideological productivity of the films. Indeed, Klinger suggests that these conditions of production and circulation, rather than displacing the family melodrama as an analytical frame, explain why the form retrospectively so named served the adult movie well. The massness of films is so often treated as a direct conduit to social concerns, the historical and cultural analyst may forget what textual understanding of narrative and generic processes can reveal of cinematic experience as yet unarticulated. Audiences may be summoned and aesthetically moved by, and film-makers drawn to, fictional and filmic processes without the critical apparatus that accounts for why. Marketing names, aesthetic practices, and critical values are not coterminous and may conflict.

In producing trends, cycles, and local genres the film industry provides material for the wider process of genre-making, conceived as a process of cultural identity or social imaginary formation in which a range of different agents participate. Genres are central to this process, because they provide public imagery as the building material for the construction of alternative, fictional worlds, while their overlapping boundaries and pool of shared images and conventions mean that they are ripe for reconstruction and retrospective imagination. The job that critics do, then, whether journalistic, academic, or counter-cultural, is to make connections across generic boundaries, to bring into view previously unperceived configurations and patterns – for example: *film noir*, the small-town movie, the woman's film – that were present if unarticulated in a previously figured terrain of an earlier period, and which hold a different significance for us now.

Such configurations become available for new uses by film-makers, audiences, critics, and, if widespread enough, production publicists. In this sense the small-town movie, despite *The Last Picture Show* (1971) and *Blue Velvet* (1984), has not yet made it, whereas *film noir* has not only returned but is generating its own subgenres, 'neo-*noir*' and 'tech-*noir*'. Thus the genre system's inevitable historicity, intensified by postmodernity, reinforces the revisiting and reworking of past practices and discourses (Collins, 1993: 246–8).

Recovering the concept of melodramatic modality – as distinct from melodrama's subgenres – forestalls reduction of the symbolic productivity of genre to a form of social or cultural reflection. Because melodramatic modality supervises many but is not identified with any one genre, it offers maximum flexibility, while the permeable boundaries between generic and cultural verisimilitude support two-way exchanges between melodramatic personifications and new signifiers of the 'real'. However, while melodrama as genre machine fosters heteroglossic encounters and dialogic exchanges that play on what Bakhtin (1981: 275) terms 'the elastic environment' of signs, as a polarising modality it drives generic signifiers towards binary oppositions, making signs declare themselves in identification with singular social, affective moral forces (Brooks, 1976). This aesthetic necessity creates conditions in which what cannot be said officially may appear dramatically. Thus melodramatic modality, personifying social forces as psychic energies and producing moral identities in the clash of opposites, is committed to binaries which bring the 'others' of official ideologies into visibility. The body images of liberation and struggle created by the women's movement, black power, and gay liberation – along with a repertoire of gestures, looks, dress codes, character traits, and so on – provide material to melodrama for enactments of heroic resistance against tyranny and of world-transforming hope to counter the terrible fascinations of power at work (Figure 12.6). *If* the ideological conditions and signs of cultural verisimilitude allow, any 'body' can occupy these positions. Significant are those increasingly numerous occasions when the mantle of victim–survivor–saviour is passing from the white to the black woman or man: 'I'm poor, black, I may even be ugly, but dear God, I'm here!' (*The Color Purple*, 1985). *The Siege* (1998), predictably perhaps, casts terrorism from the Middle East as source of fascinating villainy. But unlike *The Deer Hunter* (1978), which went to Vietnam to find the corruption at the heart of Middle America, *The Siege* (1998), shown in London when the USA and Britain were bombing Iraq and the Clinton impeachment was at its height, uses terrorism as a dramatic catalyst to trigger the aesthetic derangement of white militaristic masculinity in Bruce Willis's American general as the ultimate dystopic threat, against whom Denzel Washington's black crusading policeman fights to protect a vision of original multicultural innocence. Such films can neither be reduced to an ideological substrate nor simply be referred to the conventions which establish a genre as a discrete fictional world. Melodramatic modality is double. Ideologies provide material for symbolic actions and the aesthetic process hands back to the social affective experience and moral perceptions.

Thus genres provide fictional worlds as sites for symbolic actions, but the combination of generic and cultural verisimilitude ensures a fluidity not only between the boundaries that divide one genre from another but also between fictional and social imaginaries. In

Figure 12.6 The body images of liberation: *The Color Purple* (1985).

the process genre itself becomes a dialogised category and, as we have seen, occasion of contest. The historicity of the genre system complicates the uses of film history, for through genre production history is never done with; historical research does not provide a true identity we can find once for all in some past origin but is itself, as Steve Neale, Richard Maltby, and Rick Altman demonstrate, an object of appropriation, struggle, and, moreover, still in the making. Genres are fictional worlds, but they do not stay within fictional boundaries: their conventions cross into cultural and critical discourse, where we – as audiences, scholars, students, and critics – make and remake them. The metaphor of society talking to itself – the notion that film can provide an alternative public sphere – is seen in action as a growing secondary genre industry in film criticism, television shows, film seasons, and pictorial encyclopedias produce a widely diffused film culture increasingly conscious of its own history, calling a range of new stakeholders into implicit or explicit struggle for ownership. Dialogic discourses gather round each genre and we need to be sensitively attuned to what is being said in what arenas and for what purposes by the contradictory voices that mingle there.

References

Allen, J.T. 1984: Introduction. In Allen, J.T., ed., *Now, Voyager*. Madison, WI: University of Wisconsin Press.

Alloway, L. 1971: *Violent America: the movies 1946–64*. New York: Museum of Modern Art.

Altman, R. 1984: A semantic/syntactic approach to film genre. *Cinema Journal* **23**(3): 6–18; reprinted in expanded form in Grant, B. (ed.), 1995; *Film genre reader*, 2nd edn. Austin, TX: University of Texas Press, 26–40.

Altman, R. 1998: Reusable packaging: generic products and the recycling process. In Browne, N. (ed.), *Refiguring American film genres: theory and history*. Berkeley, CA: University of California Press, 1–41; revised as, Are genres stable? In Altman, R. 1999: *Film/genre*. London: BFI Publishing, 49–82, [as this second volume appeared after this chapter was completed, all references are to the earlier, 1998, version].

Bakhtin, M.M. 1981: Discourse and the novel. In *The dialogic imagination: four essays*, edited by Michael Hollquist, translated by Caryl Emerson and Michael Holquist. Austin, TX: University of Texas Press, 259–422.

Balio, T. 1993: *Grand design: Hollywood as a modern business*. New York: Scribner's.

Bazin, A. 1968: La politique des auteurs. In Graham, P. (ed.), *The new wave*. London: Secker and Warburg, 137–57.

Booth, M.R. 1981: *Victorian spectacular theatre 1850–1910*. London: Routledge.

Bordwell, D., Staiger, J. and Thompson, K. 1985: *The classical Hollywood cinema: film style and mode of production to 1960*. New York: Columbia University Press.

Brooks, P. 1976: *The melodramatic imagination: Balzac, Henry James, melodrama, and the mode of excess*. New Haven, CT, and London: Yale University Press.

Buscombe, E. 1970: The idea of genre in the American cinema. *Screen* **11**(2): 33–45.

Collins, J. 1993: Genericity in the nineties: eclectic irony and the new sincerity. In Collins, J., Radner, H. and Preacher Collins, A. (eds), *Film theory goes to the movies*. New York: Routledge.

Davis, B. 1962: *The lonely life*. New York: Putnam.

Donald, J. and Mercer, C. 1981: Reading and realism, unit 15, block 4, *Popular culture*. Milton Keynes: Open University Press, 69–98.

Elsaesser, T. 1972: Tales of sound and fury: observations on the family melodrama. *Monogram* **4**: 2–15; reprinted in Gledhill, C. (ed.) 1987: *Home is where the heart is: studies in melodrama and the woman's film*. London: British Film Institute, 43–69.

Fawkes, R. 1979: *Dion Boucicault: a biography*. London: Quartet Books.

Gerould, D. 1983: *American melodrama*. New York: Performing Arts Journal Publications.

Gledhill, C. 1987: Mapping the field. In Gledhill, C. (ed.), *Home is where the heart is: studies in melodrama and the woman's film*. London: British Film Institute, 5–39.

Gledhill, C. 1992: Speculations on the relationship between melodrama and soap opera. *Quarterly Review of Film and Video* (Fall): 103–24; reprinted in Browne, N. (ed.), 1993: *American television: economies, sexualities, forms*. New York: Harwood, 123–44.

Gledhill, C. 1993: Between melodrama and realism: Anthony Asquith's *Underground* (1927) and King Vidor's *The Crowd* (1927). In Gaines, J. (ed.), *Classical Hollywood cinema: paradigm wars*. Durham, NC: Duke University Press, 129–67.

Kitzes, J. 1969: *Horizons West*. London: Secker and Warburg/British Film Institute.

Klinger, B. 1994: 'Local' genres: the Hollywood adult film in the 1950s. In Bratton, J., Cook, J., and Gledhill, C. (eds), *Melodrama: stage, picture, screen*. London: British Film Institute, 134–46. Revised in Klinger, B. 1994: *Melodrama and meaning: history, culture, and the films of Douglas Sirk*. Bloomington, IN: Indiana University Press.

McArthur, C. 1972: *Underworld USA*. London: Secker and Warburg/British Film Institute.

Maltby, R. 1995: Genre. In Maltby, R., *Hollywood cinema: an introduction*. Oxford: Basil Blackwell, 107–43.

Mayer, D. 1997: Learning to see in the dark. *Nineteenth Century Theatre* **25**(2), (Winter): 92–114.

Neale, S. 1980: *Genre*. London: British Film Institute.

Neale, S. 1990: Questions of genre. *Screen* **31**(1): 45–66.

Neale, S. 1993: Melo talk: on the meaning and use of the term 'melodrama' in the American trade press. *The velvet light trap* **32**(Fall): 66–89.

Pearson, R. 1992: *Eloquent gestures: the transformation of performance style in the Griffith's Biograph films*. Berkeley, CA: University of California Press.

Postlewait, T. 1996: From melodrama to realism: the suspect history of American drama. In Hays, M. and Nikolopoulou, A. (eds), *Melodrama: the cultural emergence of a genre*. New York: St Martin's Press, 39–60.

Radford, J. 1986: Introduction. In Radford, J. (ed.), *The progress of romance: the politics of popular fiction*. London: Routledge and Kegan Paul.

Ryall, T. 1978: *Teachers' study guide No. 2: the gangster film*. London: BFI Education.

Ryall, T. 1998: Genre and Hollywood. In Hill, J. and Church Gibson, P. (eds), *The Oxford guide to film studies*. Oxford: Oxford University Press, 327–38.

Schatz, T. 1981: *Hollywood genres: formulas, filmmaking and the studio system*. New York: Random House.

Schatz, T. 1988: *The genius of the system: Hollywood filmmaking in the studio era*. New York: Pantheon.

Singer, B. 1990: Female power in the serial-queen melodrama: the etiology of an anomaly. *Camera Obscura* **22** (Winter) 89–129.

Singer, B. 1995: Modernity, hyper-stimulus, and the rise of popular sensationalism. In Charney, L. and Schwartz, V.R. (eds), *Cinema and the invention of modern life*. Berkeley, CA: University of California Press, 72–99.

Sokalski, J. 1997: From screen to stage: a case study of the Paper Print Collection. *Nineteenth century theatre* **25**(2) (Winter): 115–38.

Todorov, T. 1976: The origin of genres. *New Literary History*, **8**(1), (Autumn).

Tudor, A. 1974: *Theories of film*. London: Secker and Warburg/British Film Institute.

Vardac, N. 1949: *Stage to screen: theatrical origins of early film from Garrick to Griffith*. Cambridge, MA: Harvard University Press.

Vicinus, M. 1981: Helpless and unfriended: nineteenth-century domestic melodrama. *New Literary History* **13**(1), (Autumn).

Warshow, R. 1970: The gangster as tragic hero and Movie chronicle: the westerner. In Warshow, R., *The immediate experience*. New York: Atheneum Books.

Williams, L. 1998: Melodrama revised. In Browne, N. (ed.), *Refiguring American film genres: theory and history*. Berkeley, CA: University of California Press, 42–88.

Wright, W. 1975. *Sixguns and society: a structural study of the western*. Berkeley, CA: University of California Press.

13 Judging audiences: the case of the trial movie

Carol J. Clover

The American trial has always been an entertainment – a cross between soap opera, spectator sport and morality play.

(Alan Dershowitz, *Reversal of Fortune*)[1]

Spreckels, 62, is a veteran court-watcher – she has been attending Los Angeles-area trials off and on for 46 years. Procedure, not personalities, is what keeps her coming back, she says. . . . 'I like the courtroom atmosphere, the discipline, the points of law, the brilliance of people coming up with a better lie and telling it often enough to be believed.'

(*Los Angeles Times*)[2]

In their country [the United States], the jury is introduced into the games of schoolboys.

(Alexis de Tocqueville, *Democracy in America*)[3]

It was one of Tocqueville's great insights that because there were in America 'no nobles or literary men, and the people are apt to mistrust the wealthy', it was men of law – lawyers and judges – who consequently formed 'the highest political class and the most cultivated portion of society' and whose ways were emulated by the larger public much as the ways of the European aristocracy were emulated by common folk.[4] And how did Americans come by their knowledge, such as it was, of lawyers and the legal system? In two ways, Tocqueville declared. One was through public life: because judges and lawyers frequently went into politics, they inevitably 'introduce[d] the customs and technicalities of their profession into the management of public affairs'. But a far more important mechanism for the generalization of legal thinking, Tocqueville observed, was the jury system, and on this point his reasoning seems astonishingly modern. He declared:

> The jury extends this habit to all classes. The language of the law thus becomes, in some measure, a vulgar tongue; the spirit of the law, which is produced in the schools and courts of justice, gradually penetrates beyond their walls into the bosom of society,

where it descends to the lowest class, so that at last the whole people contract the habits
and tastes of the judicial magistrate.

By bringing common people to the law, the jury brings the law to common people, and
hence the thought of the legal aristocracy 'extends over the whole community and
penetrates into all the classes which compose it; it acts upon the country imperceptibly,
but finally fashions it to suit its own purposes'.[5]

What interests me here are not so much the mechanism of discipline and the process
of political interpellation that Tocqueville so approvingly outlines as the shaping force
he ascribes to the judicial system in the hands of a citizenry of once and future jurors.[6]
That system constitutes a common language, a rhetorical and logical template that gives
shape to all manner of social forms above and beyond the court of law. So it is that
'scarcely any political question arises in the United States that is not resolved, sooner or
later, into a judicial question', that 'all parties are obliged to borrow, in their daily
controversies, the ideas, and even the language, peculiar to judicial proceedings', and
that 'the jury is introduced into the games of schoolboys'.[7]

Just what 'games of schoolboys' Tocqueville had in mind we don't know, but the spirit
of the remark is clear enough: so fundamental is the jury in the American imaginary that
it turns up in and structures even the sheerest forms of play. No one even vaguely
acquainted with American culture can help being struck by the truth of his observation.
We watch television programs like *You Be the Judge* (which summarizes the arguments
of real trials and has viewers call in their verdicts on a 1-900 number) and *Jones and the
Jury* (in which audience members are 'impaneled' to decide which of the disputants
should get custody, or pay damages, or whatever).[8] We marvel at gameshow gimmicks
like the 'OJ-ometer', an electronic register of the reactions – 'good for OJ' as it rose and
'bad for OJ' as it fell – of button-pushing audience members as they viewed the
preliminary hearings of the OJ Simpson trial. We read books like *You be the jury* or
You're the jury: solve twelve real-life court cases along with the juries who decided them and
Trial of the century: you be the juror, a guide to all the Simpson witnesses and the points
of law that will be engaged in the examination of them ('See the OJ trial through the eyes
of a juror'). We play board and computer games based on trials, and we used the the
interactive 'jury simulation software', *You Be the Jury*, that 'allows you to review actual
presentations made to the [OJ Simpson] jury during the trial … the closest thing to
being there!'[9] Some of us attend real trials as so-called courtwatchers, producing and
reading the *Courtwatchers Newsletter*. Others of us content ourselves with live-coverage
television ('If I were on the jury', the callers on Court TV's 'Open Line' begin their
comments, or, on the television commentator's side, 'We got a call from one of our
jurors – sorry, I mean viewers – asking whether demeanor evidence is fair'.)[10] The first
filmed series made especially for television, *Public Prosecutor* (1947–48), was subsequently turned into a panel show in which a group of three mystery writers or buffs
watched an episode and then, right before the climax, tried to guess who the guilty party
was. We have juror therapy and advice columns, and we have, or once had, a school for
jurors, offering courses on such topics as 'duties of jurors considering evidence; jury
service law; qualifications of jurors; exception from jury service; and court procedure'.[11]

And of course we watch and read what seems an endless stream of documentary and quasi-documentary forms (*The Trial of Lee Harvey Oswald*, *The Thin Blue Line*); courtroom dramas proper (*Witness for the Prosecution*), and, finally, narratives that duplicate the structure and operations of the trial though they may never actually set foot in the courtroom (lots of detective mysteries and thrillers). My interest in this chapter is in the cinematic version of the next-to-last category, the courtroom drama or trial movie – a category widely acknowledged though never treated as a genre – and in the ways that it positions us not as passive spectators but as active ones, viewers with a job to do.

It is perhaps no accident that the courtroom drama or trial movie that most clearly declares the relation between juries and audiences is probably the very first: the 1907 biograph picture *Falsely Accused!* This short feature begins with the murder of an inventor in his studio. His daughter is found beside the body clutching the murder weapon (a letter opener), and she is arrested and charged with the crime. Her boyfriend believes her falsely accused and begins poking around the studio looking for clues. He notices a motion picture camera and realizes that it was running at the time of the murder.[12] He removes the film, takes it into a darkroom, and puts it in the chemical bath. We cut to a close-up of the chemical tray to see the film as it develops.[13] Armed with the film, the boyfriend rushes into court just as the daughter is about to be convicted, and he demands to project his footage. The judge agrees, and two men mount chairs behind the witness stand and stretch a sheet between them. On this screen, in the film's climactic scene, is projected the footage that reveals the murderer to have been someone else.[14]

The courtroom scene of *Falsely Accused!* has been noted as the first in which D.W. Griffith appeared in film (as one of the men holding the sheet),[15] but surely its greater significance lies in the way it prefigures, with startling clarity, the terms of a form that will be a staple of US cinema for a century to come. *Falsely Accused!* is not just a movie about a trial. It is a trial movie that spells out the natural fit between trials and movies. By having a motion picture give testimony (note the placement of the film screen at the witness stand), *Falsely Accused!* turns the courtroom into a movie theater and the jury into a film audience. And to the extent that we, the audience of *Falsely Accused!*, are aligned with the diegetic jury at that moment, both of us looking to the film for evidence, we too are in the geometry. At just the moment that the cinema of 'attractions' began to give way to the cinema of 'narrative integration', in other words, we get a courtroom drama – and not just any courtroom drama, but one that is as clear a program statement for the genre as we could ever hope to find.[16]

There is a difference between the diegetic and extradiegetic juries of *Falsely Accused!*: having witnessed the crime as it happened, we know more than they do. With the courtroom screening, they see for the first time what we see for the second. This split-knowledge arrangement, in which we know more than the jury does until the end, will persist and remains a standard format to this day, typically in films that turn on the question of why or how (*Compulsion*, for example, or, more recently, *Mortal Thoughts*) rather than who or whether. But its alternative, in which the diegetic jury and the extradiegetic one are in the same position with respect to the evidence, also puts in an early appearance in cinema history. Consider the 1913 film *By Whose Hand?* (also known as *Who Killed Simon Baird?*). As the American Film Institute catalogue sums it up:

> Edith and John Maitland will allow David Sterling to marry their daughter Helen as soon as he earns five thousand dollars, so David tries to sell one of his inventions to Simon Baird for that amount. Simon, unable to make up his mind, is found murdered the next day, and David is arrested with five thousand dollars of Simon's money in his possession. At the trial, Edith confesses to the murder, saying that Simon had wronged her years before, and that she took his money and gave it to David so that he could marry Helen. David refutes this testimony, though, and claims to be the murderer himself. In the end, the audience must decide for itself the identity of the killer.[17]

If *Falsely Accused!* announced the equations

film audience = jury

and

film diegesis = evidence

By Whose Hand? simply enacts them in a form in which the film diegesis is the sole iteration of the evidence, and the film audience and the jury are in the same shoes doing the same job – in this case, trying to figure out which of the four suspects is the culprit. The word 'diegesis' is peculiarly appropriate in this connection, given its original Greek referent: the recital of facts in a court of law. The term was imported into film studies by Étienne Sauriau, from Aristotle, who in the *Rhetoric* speaks of the 'survey of actions', the account of 'the actions themselves', and in a lawsuit, a form of 'narration'.[18]

By Whose Hand? is an extreme case, but in degree, not kind. As contemporary reviews make clear, the you-are-the-jury, you-decide format was not unprecedented, though it was more familiar in serials than in feature films. *The Trial of Vivienne Ware* (1932) appeared first as a six-part serial run simultaneously in a newspaper and on radio, accompanied by an offer of 'money prizes for the best verdicts that listeners sent in'.[19] In our own day, the question mark ending is more characteristic of documentary or based-on-real-trial features – *The Trial of Lee Harvey Oswald* (1977), for example, which closes with a crawl that reads, 'In creating the trial of Lee Harvey Oswald we have relied on documented fact. We have assumed the roles of prosecutor and defense attorney. We do not assume the role of the jury. The judgment is yours.'[20] Or consider *Free, White, and 21* (1963), about a trial of a black businessman charged with raping a young Swedish woman (a Freedom Rider) in which, after the two attorneys have delivered their closing arguments and the judge his instructions directly to the camera, the scene cuts to a close-up of a clock and a voiceover that says:

> Ladies and gentlemen, you are the jury. When you entered this theater, you were given a subpoena, a summons that put you in the jury box in the case of the People v. Ernie Jones. The judge has charged you to render a judgment of guilty or not guilty on the question of consent. Greta Mae Hanson was free, white, and twenty-one – the age of consent. If she did not consent, then it was rape, and Ernie Jones was guilty. If she

consented, then Ernie Jones is not guilty and should leave the courtroom a free man. Now weigh your conscience. Follow the instructions on your summons. See if your decision coincides with the actual verdict brought in by the jury in and for the State of Texas. You have approximately three minutes, while the managmnent polls you, the jury!

The voiceover ceases, and for two and a half soundless minutes we stare at this clock. When the three minutes are up, we cut back to the courtroom and hear a verdict of 'not guilty'.[21] Rising and facing the camera, Ernie Jones thanks us from the bottom of his heart.

Although overt 'jury challenges' of this sort crop up periodically in the following decades, most courtroom dramas after the early period eschew obvious forms of apostrophe in favor of devices more in keeping with the invisible apparatus of classical Hollywood narration. There is an interestingly intermediate form of jury address in MGM's first all-talking picture, *The Trial of Mary Dugan* (1931). A showgirl friend of Mary's who takes the stand keeps addressing her answers to the examining attorney, who is standing before her to her right – an arrangement that shows them both in semi-profile. He, in turn, keeps reminding her to 'please address the jury' and with a bodily flourish directs her gaze away from himself to a focal point some 45º to her left. Following his prompt, she turns directly to the camera and completes her testimony looking flatly into our eyes. This happens no fewer than four times in her short stint on the stand, each a more brazen breach of classical cinematic protocol than the one before. (Her striking eyes make the moments all the more remarkable.) The point is driven home by the judge when, toward the end of the trial and film, he instructs the jury:

> *You* [he pauses for emphasis] are the sole judges of the facts in this case, of the guilt or innocence of this woman. You are not here to say who killed Edgar Rice. Your sole function is to determine the guilt or innocence of Mary Dugan. The jury will now retire and reach a verdict.

Before this speech, he was looking in another direction, but with the word '*You*', he turns emphatically to the camera and looks us straight in the eye, a position he holds until he is done. The moment is doubly transgressive: it addresses the camera, and it names the addressee: '*you*', 'the jury'.[22]

The jury challenge in mainstream cinema has for the past couple of decades been largely relegated to the promotional materials (videocassettes, posters, sometimes trailers), which by tradition speak the language of second-person address: 'Was the "Scarsdale Diet" doctor murdered, or was it a tragic accident?'; 'Was Randall Adams murdered – or was he an innocent scapegoat?'; 'What are the limits of justice? Of social responsibility?'; 'Was she simply malicious, or was she sick?'; and so on.[23] This is not to say that modern films jury-box their audiences any less. It is to suggest that with the fixing of the narrative and cinematic codes, we have come to need less overt discipline. We know our place and just what our job will be even before we take our seats.

Still, even the most discreet of trial movies may tip its hand now and then. At the end of *Compulsion*, the 1959 film based on the Leopold-Loeb case, defense attorney Wilk (based on Clarence Darrow and played by Orson Welles) delivers himself of what is said, at some 15 minutes, to be the longest speech ever delivered on-screen. In it, he begs in impassioned terms for a sentence of life imprisonment rather than the death penalty. 'Life!' he exhorts: 'Any more goes back to the hyena!'

Wilk came late to the case, only after the parents of the accused men had grasped the seriousness of the situation and also, as it turned out, after their sons' guilt had been irrevocably established, thus forcing Wilk to forgo a jury for a judge, to plead guilty by virtue of a species of insanity, and to beg for a merciful sentence. We saw the earlier jury: a bunch of flinty older men. But that jury is dismissed, and now, as Wilk takes over, the camera takes pains to show the jury box empty, almost lingering on the void. When Wilk/Darrow/Welles begins to speak, we see him in a frontal shot, as though he were addressing us or a space proximate to us. Because we know that the judge is the object of the performance, we feel ourselves positioned in his vicinity. But then, still facing us – looking us virtually in the eye – and without missing a beat in his peroration, Wilk changes his orientation somewhat, turning some 30° to the right, and leans one forearm on the telltale rail. The space so insistently established as empty some minutes ago has now been filled, as it were, by us.[24]

Again, the equations are clear. Although the diegesis, echoing the historical facts of the case, draws a strong distinction between judge and jury (dismissing the latter in favor of the former), the cinematography puts them together again. By positioning us first at the judge's bench and then, through a rotation, in the jury box, the camera links the two, reminding us that they are versions of one another and that a speech meant for the one will do for both. But even more striking is the equation the camera draws between the diegetic jury and the film's spectators. The fact that there *is* no diegetic jury in this sequence only makes more pointed the camera's invitation. It is as though the diegetic jury box, explicitly drained of diegetic jurors, has been extended out into the movie theater to embrace us. What we are asked to judge is not the facts of the matter, which are no longer in dispute, but the sentence. More generally, we are asked to pass judgment on the death penalty, that act that 'takes us back to the hyena', in principle. Lest we doubt who the real addressee is of that 15-minute speech, we might recall that it was issued separately for sale as a phonograph record.

The homiletic tone of *Compulsion*, once a regular feature of trial movies, has fallen out of favor. But the trope of the empty jury box lives on. Consider *Presumed Innocent* (1990). The film opens with the shot of a vacant courtroom. Our vision pans ever so slowly to the right until it arrives at the jury box. We pause. Then, at an almost imperceptible rate, we start moving forward. The empty, ornate chairs of the jury loom larger and larger in our vision, and as the credits crawl over them, we hear a man's voice intone:

> I am a prosecutor. I am a part of the business of accusing, judging, and punishing. I explore the evidence of a crime and determine who is charged, who is brought to this room and tried before his peers. I present my evidence to the jury, and they deliberate upon it. They must determine what really happened. If they cannot, we will not know whether the accused deserves to be freed or punished. If they cannot find the truth, what is our hope for justice?

What is most striking about the voiceover here is not so much its words as its almost incantatory tone. It is as though we are being ushered into that empty courtroom, directed to those empty chairs, and sworn in. Two hours later, we will revisit this scene – same shot of the empty courtroom and jury seats, voiceover in the same monotone. The time in between we spend not in the courtroom, but following the fortunes of the speaker, District Attorney Rusty Sabich, as he investigates the murder of his colleague Carolyn Polhemus, with whom, it emerges, he had been having an affair. In fact, the finger of suspicion begins to point to him: the blood type matches his, and a glass found in her apartment has his fingerprints on it. The visualized story roams into Sabich's obsessive relationship with Carolyn, into his home life with his wife Barbara, a woman angry at the affair with Carolyn and dissatisfied with her role as bedmaker (she is at work on a dissertation but it is slow going), into his relation with his lawyer Sandy Stern, and (typically enough) into District Attorney Horgan's political ambitions and shady connections. Even when we finally arrive in the courtroom, some 80 minutes into the film, our narrative and cinematic focus remains stubbornly on Sabich and his lawyer Stern as we approach the bench with them, go to chambers with them, and so on.

Despite all this mobility in time and space, however, and despite our engagement with the figure of Sabich, we are functionally never very far from the jury box of the opening scene. We study exhibits and demeanor, speculate on motive, consider other candidates, wrestle with the presumption of innocence of the title.[25] In fact, when it comes right down to it, Sabich's own 'work' is pretty much the work of the jury – at least until some point in the last third of the film, when something seems to dawn on him that does not dawn on us. At that moment, he splits off from us, leaving us behind with the diegetic jury, with whom we 'vote', in the end, for a verdict of not guilty, not because we positively know otherwise, but simply because the prosecution did not meet the standard of reasonable doubt. The fact that we subsequently learn who really did it (Sabich's wife) does not mean that we have finally transcended our role as jurors in the rhetorical economy of the film; it only means that we are jurors who learned more after the fact, as jurors sometimes do. (*Presumed Innocent* lets us off easier than films such as *Anatomy of a Murder*, in which we realize that we are jurors who may have screwed up, and *Witness for the Prosecution*, in which we learn that we are jurors who surely *did* screw up.) Our position and our predicament are slammed home in the film's closing scene, which returns us to the scene – same courtroom, same empty jury seats – and the sound – same flat voiceover – of the opening, the only difference being that this time the voice tells us, in effect, that the search for justice sometimes fails. At no time during the film's two hours do we catch so much as a glimpse of the jury actually trying the case – an omission all the more striking in light of the attention lavished on the empty seats in the beginning and again at the end. The point could hardly be clearer: we are it.

We are similarly ushered into and out of *Reversal of Fortune* (1991), but there is a difference: the voiceover and images are those of the victim. Alan Dershowitz's account of Claus von Bülow's second trial for attempting the 'insulin murder' of his heiress wife Sunny, *Reversal of Fortune* opens with a blue-tinted static image of Sunny, lying in a hospital bed in a coma. After a pause, a voiceover begins – hers, recounting the history of the first trial. This rather lengthy synopsis ends with the following words: 'On March

16, 1982, he was found guilty on both counts. Even Alexandra Ives testified against him. You are about to see how Claus von Bülow sought to reverse, or escape from, that verdict.' And then, in grave tones, '*You* tell *me*.' Now, with history in place and the jury charged, the movie proper starts.

Reversal of Fortune plays a sly game. Its 'you tell me' suggests a balanced two-story set-up: the prosecution case, brought by the children, who believe Claus murdered Sunny, versus the defense case, spearheaded by Dershowitz and his team of Harvard law students, who argue that Sunny overdosed: so the opening shots suggest, and so suggests the Rashomon-like visualization of different scenarios for how Sunny came to be lying in a faint on the bathroom floor with her gown hiked up to her waist. Both enact voiceovers. In the first, we see Sunny in the bedroom popping pills, then walking to the bathroom, turning on the sink faucet, lifting her skirt to use the toilet, and fainting. In the second, we see her overdose and Claus let it happen, after which he drags her to the bathroom (hence the hiked-up skirt) and deposits her on the floor. The sequences are of the same length and mode and both are plausible.

Nor does the film ever give us an answer. The crime is presented as a mystery and left as such. Claus is played (by Jeremy Irons) as inscrutable. 'Is it the truth?' Dershowitz asks him. 'Of *course* it's the truth', he answers, 'But not the *whole* truth. I don't *know* the whole truth. I don't *know* what happened to her.' The film's final dialogue line is spoken by Dershowitz to von Bülow as they part ways at an elevator: 'One thing, Claus. Legally, this was an important victory. Morally, you're on your own.' If that were not enough, we cut at the end to Sunny in her coma, her voiceover saying, 'Claus von Bülow was given a second trial and acquitted on both counts. This is all you know, all you can be told. When you get where I am, you will know the rest.' This is not quite the '*you* are the jury, *you* decide' ending of *By Whose Hand?*, but it comes awfully close – the jury challenge in modern drag. It is in fact strikingly like *Presumed Innocent*, ending as it began with the same static image and the same flat voiceover. The precise similarity of that triadic structure, in which the ending is a version of the beginning and both of them are discursively different from the long middle, to the triadic structure of the Anglo-American jury trial is a subject I consider in some detail elsewhere. Suffice it to note here that it is a standard structure of both trials and trial movies.

But *Reversal of Fortune* is not only about Claus von Bülow. It is also – even more so – about the business of defense lawyering. Long stretches of the film have a law-school how-to quality: how to value even the smallest detail, how to extract multiple meanings from a fact, how to question whether 'facts' really are facts, and how to give oneself over to one's imagination in the creation of an alternative story. Piece by piece, we watch Dershowitz and his team of students construct another explanation for the set of givens: black bag, insulin levels, room temperature, and so on. We also get a dose of moralizing about the goodness of a system that guarantees everyone, even Claus von Bülow, the right to a defense. To judge from its proportions, *Reversal of Fortune* is less interested in the case at hand – the guilt or innocence of von Bülow – than it is in criminal defense as a process and a moral project in Anglo-American law. It is in any event more than a best-possible-case-for-the-defense movie. It is also a best-possible-case-for-the-criminal-defense-lawyer movie. More particularly, it is a best-possible-case-for-Dershowitz movie, mounted by Dershowitz himself,[26] thus the double-trial structure: the explicit diegetic trial of von Bülow and the implicit trial of defense lawyer Dershowitz. On the matter of von Bülow's guilt or innocence, the film claims if not neutrality then eternal mystery, which from the defense standpoint amounts to the same thing.[27] The 'trial' of Dershowitz by contrast urges us to a verdict of not guilty (of all the bad things people think about criminal defense attorneys).

The double-trial structure is fundamental to trial narratives. Films about rape or wife-beating typically mount a second, unofficial trial on the legal system's ability to serve (female) victims of intimate crimes. *The Accused* (1988), for example, is about the New Bedford gang rape trial, but its dramatic tension lies as much in whether one female lawyer can buck a male system set in its ways and a male law structurally biased against victims of rape. Consider films such has *Burning Bed* (1984), in which the first trial turns on a wife's murder of her husband and the second on the failure of criminal law to appreciate what is now called battered-wife syndrome; *The Murder of Mary Phagan* (1988), in which the first trial is based on the Leo Frank case and the second makes the case for a miscarriage of justice; and *Sergeant Rutledge* (1960), a western in which the first trial has Rutledge charged with murder and the second asks whether a black man can get a fair trial. *Breaker Morant* (1979), like most court-martial and war-crimes movies, asks not only whether the accused committed the deed, but what is the nature of an order and what is the range of interpretation allowed the individual, and indeed, in this case, whether the convictions and executions were done in the name of law or of propaganda. The official trial of *Class Action* (1991) is a civil suit resembling the Ford Motors Pinto case, but its unofficial trial turns on lawyers who sell out to corporate big bucks. In the overwhelming majority of trial movies, from the beginning of cinema, the unofficial trial turns on an aspect of the legal system. Is the system fair across various social differences – class, race, gender? Can it be corrupted? Does money buy people off? Are lawyers human? Should the death penalty exist? Can the system really get at the truth? Can it distinguish between technical justice and real justice? Does it convict innocent people? Does it too often acquit the guilty?

What it almost never questions, however, is the institution of the jury. Even when the system has gone manifestly wrong, blame is laid at the door of a sleepy judge, an ambitious district attorney, a greedy lawyer, a dishonest witness, a misleadingly charming or offensive defendant, the general clubbiness of the legal profession, politics at large – but not the jurors or the jury system. The institution of the jury has been much debated in the press in recent years, but it remains for the most part oddly secure in the movies.

It is also oddly invisible. We seldom see movie juries. When we do, it is usually momentarily and at a distance, commonly by way of a pan across the courtroom or in the occasional cutaway – a shot in either case too briefly held for us to register such vitals as sex, race, or ethnicity, much less individual characteristics. The faces that loom so large in courtroom sequences include those of just about everybody in the courtroom, even gallery spectators (wives, journalists, etc.), but not those of jurors. (The camera goes into the jury room in *Call It Murder*, but once there shows us only the close-up hands of the jurors – folded attentively, tapping nervously, thumb-twiddling, and so on.) If we look carefully as the camera pans across the courtroom, we are likely to see a group of people (not focusing on any one) as nondescript as they are impassive: not too fat or thin, not too young or old, not too strangely dressed, and expressionless but for a certain look of attention. In either case, such shots usually add up to no more than a couple of minutes of the film's two hours. The avoidance of the jury box is all the more striking in light of the fact that courtroom camerawork is often rather inventive, as if to counter the claustrophobia that inheres in the situation.

The shunning of the jury as both visual object and political subject is too consistent and too patterned to be accidental. The reason that juries are largely unseen in trial movies and the jury system largely uncontested within the regime of cinema is surely that we understand the jury to constitute a kind of necessary blank space in the text, one reserved for occupancy by us. To critique the system in a courtroom drama would involve us with jurors in a way that is incompatible with our own position in the text. To know about Juror Number Four in any detail would detract from the puzzle we came to solve, to add another dimension to what is to be interpreted. We can imagine an art film focused on the jury and individual jurors, but would we then perceive that film as courtroom drama? I suspect we would feel it as something else – that what we expect in a courtroom drama is a form that presents itself as a trial and us as its jury, and that draws us into its text by addressing us visually (as in *The Trial of Mary Dugan* and *Compulsion*), by directing us to a vacant jury box (as in *Presumed Innocent* and *Incident at Oglala*), by gesturing to a jury so generic that we can take it as not as a competing body but as a vague surrogate, or by simply skipping it altogether. The rule, in the televising of real trials, that the jury cannot be shown is a rule we have lived with in fiction for decades (and is arguably a rule we would not know how to live *without*).

Of course there are odd cases – thrillers in which a juror forms a relationship with someone he shouldn't (*Suspect*) as well as generically offbeat films such as *Knock on Any Door, Rampage, Tomorrow,* and a few others.[28] But within the category courtroom drama, there is just one significant exception to the rule of jury avoidance: *Twelve Angry Men.* And a mighty exception it is. Showing nothing *but* the jury and taking place entirely *within* the jury room, *Twelve Angry Men* not only breaks the rules, it reverses them utterly – and yet it is in the eyes of many the defining example of the courtroom drama as a category. How are we to explain the emergence and canonical status of such a deviant case?

Twelve Angry Men was written as a teleplay by Reginald Rose in 1953. It aired in 1954, and in 1956 Henry Fonda proposed to Rose that he expand it to feature length. He did so, and Sidney Lumet was assigned the project as his directorial debut. The film, which appeared in 1957, retains the teleplay's theatricality and sense of enchamberment. It opens with some outdoor shots of the courthouse and courthouse steps, and the pre-credit sequence show us some courtroom interiors, including a scene in which a bored judge instructs the jury and we get a haunting head-shot of the accused, a dark-skinned, large-eyed young man of 18 years. The credits roll over a shot of the jury room, empty in the beginning, into which the jurors file one by one. The credits end when the room is full, and the drama begins. It opens with a preliminary vote: eleven guilty and only one, Juror Eight (Henry Fonda) not guilty. Other jurors try to bring Eight into line, but he will not be moved. Maybe the boy did do it, he says, but does the evidence really prove it beyond a reasonable doubt? So the debate goes for 90 minutes, with all the jurors' personalities and personal stakes slowly emerging. As Juror Eight questions the prosecution's evidence, piece by piece, others join him, one by one, in his doubt. Finally, even the most recalcitrant of the group crumbles, and the jury delivers a verdict of not guilty. In yet another turn on the triadic structure, the film closes as it began, outdoors on the courthouse steps, as Juror Eight and the old-man juror exchange names on parting.

The first thing to be noted about *Twelve Angry Men* is that it appears to have been inspired by a French original: the 1950 film *Justice est faite*, written and directed by André Cayatte and distributed in the United States as *Justice Is Done* and *Let Justice Be Done*. ('Strangely enough', writes Thomas J. Harris, 'as of 1957 the subject of the jury had only received one serious treatment in all of world cinema – by French writer-director André Cayette in his 1950 film *Justice est faite*.'[29]) The film recounts a seven-member jury's deliberation in the trial of a woman doctor who had euthanized her terminally ill lover at his request.[30] *Justice est faite* is perhaps as anomalous among French trial movies as *Twelve Angry Men* is among American ones in light of the fact that the jury is seldom used in France and has little place in the public imaginary, much less cinema. In any event, for whatever reason, Cayatte (himself a lawyer) made *Justice*, and perhaps just because the trial movie is not the chestnut of French cinema that it is of Anglo-American, he was not so bound by a tradition that he could not experiment with the dramatics of an underappreciated element of the system. And the result moved Rose to a similar experiment.

But if Cayatte's was an experiment in something like a vacuum, Rose's was one in what would seem a downright inimical context. To understand why *Twelve Angry Men*'s breach of the jury-avoidance rule did not disqualify the film with American audiences, we need to look more closely at its narrative operations. To begin with, there is the question it asks. The issue in *Justice est faite* is not who did it, which is clear, nor even whether it is right or wrong ('the partisan script asserts flatly, at the outset, that [the woman] should not be guillotined, nor even imprisoned'),[31] but why (out of mercy as his lover, or out of greed as his heir?). *Twelve Angry Men* asks the typical Anglo-American trial-movie question: did the accused man do it or not? More to the point, it goes about answering that question in the same way that Anglo-American trial movies have always gone about it: by casting it in strongly adversarial terms and by putting the audience through the steps and processes of the trial itself.

The discussion around and about the preliminary vote sets the terms: 11 of the jurors agree more or less summarily that the evidence against the defendant, a young man accused of stabbing his father to death, is overwhelming: a woman saw him (from the other side of the elevated train tracks); an old man downstairs heard him; he had bought a switchblade that day; he was known to fight with his father and to shout that he wanted to kill him; and he had been in trouble with the law before. Juror Eight balks: he doesn't know whether to believe the defendant's story or not, but given his miserable life (dead mother, felonious father, orphanage) and the fact that a guilty vote would send him to death, the least they owe him is a serious deliberation. He introduces in clear terms the cornerstone of every criminal defense when, in response to one juror's argument that the boy must be guilty because nobody proved otherwise, he declares, 'Nobody has to prove otherwise. The burden of proof's on the prosecution. The defendant doesn't even have to open his mouth. That's in the Constitution.' In other words, the first five minutes of the jury drama sound for all the world like opening statements in a trial: prosecution first (the evidence will show guilt beyond a reasonable doubt), and then the defense (the evidence does *not* meet the burden of proof beyond a reasonable doubt).

With the two sides in place, the jury drama moves into a different phase. It is introduced by a second poll, in which each of the 11 pro-guilt jurors is to state his reasoning. Thus the text shifts from generalities to details, each of which is subject to dispute as the jurors interrupt one another with objections, questions, and, increasingly, insults. There is no order to the discussion of evidence: it comes in bits and pieces as they occur to jurors. But one by one, the items of evidence are submitted to the process of examination: first direct, then cross, and often redirect and recross as well. An exemplary exchange turns on the switchblade knife with which the man was killed and that the defendant claimed to have bought and lost on the same day. One juror cites it, during the second poll, as the piece of evidence that seemed to him incontrovertible. They ask to see it and it is brought in. The juror enumerates all the incriminating facts about the knife. He ends by stabbing it into the table so it stands upright and declaring, 'Take a look at this knife. It's a very unusual knife. I've never seen one like it, and neither had the storekeeper who sold it to the boy. Aren't you [turning to Juror Eight] asking us to accept a pretty incredible coincidence?' 'I'm just saying a coincidence is *possible,*' Juror Eight replies, reaching into his pocket to produce an identical knife, which he stabs into the table next to the other one.

Point, counterpoint; direct examination, cross-examination. So the film goes, with every piece of prosecution evidence effectively answered by one or another of the jurors: the eyewitness had indentations on the bridge of her nose, meaning she wore glasses and could not have seen what she claimed; the old man downstairs had a bum leg and could not have covered the space he said he did in the time available; the grip on a switchblade precludes a downward stabbing motion, and so on. At one point, the most vehemently pro-guilt juror becomes so angry at Juror Eight that he shouts 'I'm gonna kill him!' – thus undoing the force of the testimony about the defendant's having similarly shouted at his father. Piece by piece, what seemed a watertight assemblage of facts comes apart, and, juror by juror, they change their votes, until at the end, we have moved from the prosecution view of the case to the defense side, which is to say the side of reasonable doubt.[32]

A full account of the ways that trial movies enact the structure and narrative procedure of real trials is beyond the scope of this chapter. But even this short account should suffice to suggest that *Twelve Angry Men* is in all respects but one playing by the rules. It may transpire in a jury room (as other courtroom dramas may transpire in judge's chambers, police stations, lawyer's conference rooms, jail cells, morgues) instead of a courtroom, and the players may be citizen-jurors instead of lawyers, but in its triadic shape, adversarial mode, X–not-X opposition (and the insistence on the reasonable-doubt basis of not-X), the cross-examining quality of the discussions of evidence, the programmed shift from prosecution to defense, and the sense of truth-crisis that attends that shift, *Twelve Angry Men* is a consummate courtroom drama. Most crucially, despite its jury-room setting, it still plays to an offscreen jury. Perhaps it is because we sense our position as the film's object of address to be so secure that we can ignore or get beyond our diegetic competition. In any case, *Twelve Angry Men* is on closer inspection not quite the exception it at first seemed.

Perhaps *Justice est faite* is not quite the exception *it* seemed, either. American commentators, in any case, found it too much interested in the characters of the jurors (whose lives are explored in detail) and too little in the trial and the crime. The *Variety* reviewer thought that the film put 'too much emphasis on its jurists [*sic*], detracting not only from the trial but from the killing itself'.[33] Another commentator noted that 'The scenario covers the various phases of a big criminal trial, but contrary to the usual formula in this type of film, the main role is not assigned to the accused, or to the victim, or even to the judges . . .'.[34] Another writes:

> Among this French picture's many unusual features . . . is the fact that its central
> character is not the woman who is on trial for murder, not her victim whom we never
> see at all – but the jury members who have to decide [her] fate.[35]

The decidedly hostile *Cine* reviewer noted that insofar as the film 'focuses its camera on the seven jurors rather than the accused', it lives up to its subtitle: *The Secret Lives and Loves of a French Jury*.[36] The same reviewer also found alien the way the film instructed its audience, right at the outset, as to the proper moral position. Bosley Crowther was also bothered by the apparent absence of procedure (the 'casualness' and the 'conspicuous eccentricity of practices') in the trial scenes.[37] These are telling remarks, for they suggest that by American lights what is wrong with *Justice Is Done* is that it is not a *trial* movie, as though any film focused on a jury ought to be considerably, if not mainly, about the trial, and to adopt the posture and conventions of an American trial movie. Rather, it is a philosophizing set of character studies and as such not so different from other French and European films of its time. In naturalizing the jury story to Anglo-American expectations, *Twelve Angry Men* reversed the priorities, not only putting the trial front and center, but following the narrative procedures of the standard courtroom drama.

To say that we accepted *Twelve Angry Men* is not to say we loved it, however. The film was a great success among critics, but it was a box-office mediocrity, not even close to the 10 top-grossing films of that year.[38] It apparently played best to the art-film crowd in its heyday. That those critics and that crowd won the day eventually is clear from the subsequent installation of *Twelve Angry Men* at the top of the courtroom drama list. It may deserve that place. But it is important to remember that the public at large demurred. Perhaps that was because of the film's staginess, its philosophizing, its refusal of romance and action – features that suited the tastes of the late-1950s' art-movie crowd but not those of public at large. But perhaps it was also because, for all its virtues, *Twelve Angry Men* got something wrong. In any event, it did not start a trend.[39] The big courtroom dramas of the following few years – *I Want to Live!* (1958), *Anatomy of a Murder* (1959), *Compulsion* (1959), *Inherit the Wind* (1960), *To Kill a Mockingbird*

(1962) – revert to the cipher-jury formula. Again, there are exceptions, but they are occasional and brief. *Twelve Angry Men* remains a blip on the American scene – not so odd as to be discursively unrecognizable (on the contrary, it is discursively old hat), but too odd to catch on.

Twelve Angry Men was widely reviewed as a 'penetrating indictment' of the jury system.[40] Insofar as it reminds us how overdetermined jurors' reactions can be, it is indeed sobering. Were it not for one man in the right place at the right time, the defendant would have gone to the chair. Still, that one man was there, and all of the other men are rational enough to be brought around when the evidence is put before them. And we are also repeatedly reminded that 12 heads are better than one, an observation that has particular force in a film in which the one head, that of the judge, is so manifestly bored that it must be propped up with an arm – apparently because it regarded the conclusion as foregone. Not even this odd-duck film in the American cinematic tradition, in other words, not even an art film with social–critical ambitions and a French prototype, seems to be able to take on the jury system in any real or sustained way. To take on the jury system seriously would be to repudiate the judgment of citizens in favor of the judgment of professionals, and that is not a step that *Twelve Angry Men* comes even close to taking. The judge's role is small, but it blows open the film's politics. Frightening though a jury may be, given the number of 'angry men' in the world, it is better than the alternative.

The jury may be up for grabs in the world of law and politics, but, in the world of popular culture, it remains by and large serenely untouchable. In movies, citizen juries make mistakes only when the system misleads them (*Presumed Innocent*), not because they do not understand the issues or are irrational bigots. Surely this has to do with the fact, as Tocqueville might point out, that movie audiences are made up of citizen jurors – both actual ones (people who have served or almost served on juries) and 'generalized' ones (movie viewers who identify with and do the work of jurors). It is no surprise, given the effort of movies to suture audiences into the jury position and given the desire of audiences to be engaged as triers of fact, that films should be friendly to the idea of the citizen jury: to be otherwise would be to bite the hand that feeds them. What the editors of *Cahiers du Cinema* wrote of *Young Mr. Lincoln* (1939), that it is 'America itself which constitutes the Jury, and who cannot be wrong, so that the truth cannot fail to manifest itself by the end of the proceedings',[41] and Norman Miller said of *Twelve Angry Men*, that the 'jurors function precisely as representatives of the American people in the pursuit of Justice … a multi-bodied American Everyman',[42] pretty much go for trial movies in general, which indeed often show us, in a final shot, a monumental courthouse or an American flag or both. An American courtroom drama could no more critique the jury than a game of Cowboys and Indians could critique racism.[43]

Such is our relation to the form and the tradition that when juries are discussed, we know to take it personally. When the lawyer Michael in *Class Action* coaches a witness, 'Keep your words short; don't talk above the jury – though that wouldn't be hard', we register the insult, sensing that at some level he means us, and mark Michael as the villain. By the same token, we know how to take it when, in *Anatomy of a Murder*, as the lawyers are waiting for the verdict to come in, one philosophizes:

> Twelve people, with twelve different minds, with twelve different sets of experiences . . .
> and in their judgment they must become of one mind – unanimous. That's one of the
> miracles of man's disorganized soul, that they can do it, and in most instances do it quite
> well. God bless juries!

The fact that this is one of those instances in which we are not at all sure the jury *did*
do it quite well should not bother us unduly, given that the lead defense attorney
(played by Jimmy Stewart in one of his most winning roles) is not quite sure either.
We do the best we can with what we get, and much of the art of trial movies, like
much of the art of trials, lies in playing the ambiguity for all it is worth.

Tocqueville was right: we are a nation of jurors, and we have created an entertainment
system that has us see just about everything that matters – from corporate greed to child
custody – from precisely that vantage and in those structural terms. Just as the legal system
has always drawn on the entertainment system, playing to the spectator in us all, so, from
Falsely Accused! to *Philadelphia* and trial after trial on Court TV, the entertainment system
draws on the legal system, playing to the juror in us all. In the coverage of real trials, and
in the advertising for the coverage of real trials, not only on Court TV but on the networks,
the stock visual image is an empty jury box (and it was over just that image, in the absence
of real courtroom footage, that news of the Simpson civil and McVeigh trials was voiced
night after night). If Tocqueville were to return tomorrow, he would no doubt relate the
trial-mania of our current popular culture to the fact that, of the world's jury trials, 90
per cent are now American, and that in the year 1989 about 80 million Americans, 45 per
cent of all adults, had been called for jury duty.[44] Nor would he be surprised at the way
that the American legal imagination, as it plays itself out among the 'common people',
inhabits first and foremost not the judge's bench, not the attorney's chair, not the witness
stand, not even the jail cell or the electric chair, but the jury box. The visible player, the
protagonist, may be any of these other people (commonly one of the lawyers, in line with
Tocqueville's observation that jurors are would-be jurists), and the fiction may take us
into the judge's chambers, or back in history to the scene of the crime, or with the
investigator on his quest for clues, but at bottom our stance with respect to the evidence
is always that of the citizen asked to decide: the trier of fact. It is hard to imagine a more
generative exercise in American popular culture than this one. *Diegesis*, in its first form,
may be our most favorite kind of narrative.

Endnotes

1   Alan Dershowitz, *Reversal of Fortune* (New York: Simon and Schuster/Pocket, 1986), p. xv.
2   Amy Wallace, 'Courthouse is clubhouse for the Menendez watchers', *Los Angeles Times*, 15
    January (1994), p. A33.
3   Alexis de Tocqueville, *Democracy in America*, vol. 1 (New York, Random House/Vintage,
    1990), p. 318.
4   Tocqueville, *Democracy in America*, vol 1, p. 278.
5   Tocqueville, *Democracy in America*, vol. 1, p. 280.
6   Where modern readers will see the machinery of discipline and the means of political
    interpellation, Tocqueville saw a splendid form of education:

> The jury contributes powerfully to form the judgment and to increase the natural intelligence of a people; and this, in my opinion, is its greatest advantage. It may be regarded as a gratuitous public school, ever open. … I think that the practical intelligence and political good sense of the Americans are mainly attributable to the long use that they have made of the jury in civil cases. … Thus the jury, which is the most energetic means of making the people rule, is also the most efficacious means of teaching it how to rule well.
>
> (*Democracy in America*, vol. 1, pp. 285–7)

Although Tocqueville is speaking here of the civil trial, his remarks apply in the main to the criminal one as well.

7   Tocqueville, *Democracy in America*, vol. 1, pp. 280, 318.

8   On Fox and CBS respectively in 1994–95.

9   Another software game, *In the 1st Degree* (Brøderbund, 1995), puts the player in the role of prosecutor:

> Some artists die for their art. James Tobin killed … or did he? As San Francisco's D.A., you must prove he did, in what has become the most sensational murder case to hit the Bay Area in years. Every reluctant witness and shred of evidence is required to paint a homicidal portrait as chilling and surreal as one of Tobin's own paintings. Call your first witness, Counsellor. Can you prove murder? *In the 1st Degree?*

Insofar as the prosecutor here seems to know no more than a juror, the game illustrates perfectly Tocqueville's point about identification upwards.

10   Court TV commentator Cynthia McFadden (on *Prime Time Justice*, Sunday, 28 April 1993).

11   So reported *Law Notes* in May 1937 (as quoted in Osborn, *The Mind of the Juror*, pp. 232–33). The school was established that year in Newark, NJ, at the instigation of 'the desire of federal jurywomen to know more about jury service'. Classes were open to any of the talesmen who wish to avail themselves of the excellent opportunity of becoming familiar with court procedure'.

12   The topos of the accidently photographed or filmed crime scene also has a long history. Dion Boucicault's *The Octoroon* is often cited as the literary ancestor. For early film examples, see especially Tom Gunning, 'Tracing the individual body, aka photography, detectives, early cinema and the body of modernity', in Vanessa R. Schwartz and Leo Charney, eds, *Cinema and the Invention of Modern Life*, (Berkeley, CA: University of California Press, 1995), and 'What I saw from the rear window of the Hotel des Folies-Dramatiques, or the story point of view films told', in André Gaudreault, ed., *Ce que je vois de mon ciné …* , (Paris, Klincksieck, 1988); I am also grateful to Jim Lastra for sharing his unpublished manuscript on the subject. That the idea is going strong after 90 years is clear from the 1995–96 ABC television serial *Murder One*. In the last two episodes (22–23 April 1996), the defense lawyer realizes that the murder in question must have been captured on videotape, finds and views the tape, and, in the series finale, plays it to the court, thus revealing the identity of the real murderer and establishing the innocence of his own client – the plot of *Falsely Accused!* updated for video.

13   This 'skilful cut-in of film being developed in a darkroom tray' [John L. Fell, 'Motive, mischief, and melodrama: the state of film narrative in 1907', in John L. Fell, ed., *Film before Griffith* (Berkeley, CA: University of California Press, 1983), p. 279] may be the first instance of what will become a standard gesture in evidence-based movies.

14 The surviving print is incomplete at this point (the screen in the courtroom has not yet been matted with the images of the murder sequence, which come next on the reel). Writes Fell: 'The last sequence is visible in the Museum nitrate print, first with spectators staring at a blank sheet mounted behind the bench, then with the yet-to-be-matted-in murder footage positioned to accommodate the preceding image' ('Motive, mischief, and melodrama', p. 279). See also Eileen Bowser, 'Griffith's film career before *The Adventures of Dollie*', in *Film before Griffith*, pp. 367–8).

15 Bowser, 'Griffith's film career before *The Adventures of Dollie*', p. 367.

16 Gunning's categories in his 'The cinema of attraction: early film, its spectator, and the avant-garde', *Wide Angle*, 8 (1986).

17 *The American Film Institute Catalogue*, vol. F1 (Berkeley, CA: University of California Press, 1988), q.v. *By Whose Hand*. It was a five-reel picture (Equitable).

18 Étienne Sauriau, 'La structure d'univers filmique et le vocabulaire de la filmologie', *Revue Internationale de Filmologie*, **7/8** (undated), p. 233. See also Edward Lowry, *The Filmology Movement and Film Study in France* (Ann Arbor, MI: University of Michigan Press, 1985), pp. 84–5. Aristotle writes:

> There must, of course, be some survey of the actions that form the subject-matter of the speech. ... [One of the two parts of this speech] is not provided by the orator's art, viz. the actions themselves.... Nowadays it is said, absurdly enough, that the narration [*diegesis*] should be rapid. Remember what the man said to the baker who asked whether he was to make the cake hard or soft: 'What, can't you make it *right*?' Just so here. We are not to make long narrations, just as we are not to make long introductions or long arguments. Here, again, rightness does not consist either in rapidity or in conciseness, but in the happy mean; that is, in saying just so much as will make the facts plain, or will lead the hearer to believe that a thing has happened to some one, or that the man has caused injury or wrong to some one, or that the facts are really as important as you wish them to be thought: or the opposite facts to establish the opposite arguments.
>
> (*The Rhetoric and Poetics of Aristotle* (New York, Modern Library, 1984 [originally published in 1954], *Rhetoric*, pp. 1416b: 18–1417a:3)

19 *American Film Institute Catalogue*, vol. F3, q.v. *The Trial of Vivienne Ware*. The serial ran first in New York and subsequently by the Hearst papers elsewhere in the USA. The parts of judge and lawyers in the radio broadcast were played by well-known figures in the political and legal arena. The film, however, fixed the ending. The 1941 film based on Ayn Rand's play of the same name is a similar case: the stage play of 1935 used a jury recruited from the audience at each performance, and, depending on their vote, one of Rand's multiple finales was played out; but the film chose one ending and played the case straight. Wrote the *Variety* reviewer:

> The film version of 'Night of Jan. 16' will hardly emulate the success of the Ayn Rand play in 35–36 because the show hinged on a trick of audience participation which the picture obviously cannot employ. Result is a moderate feature destined to play in support.
>
> [*Variety Film Reviews*, (New York, Garland, 1983), 10 September 1941]

20 For example *Scene of the Crime* (1984–85) is described as 'a trio of intricate and spine-tingling cases each presenting a rogues' gallery of celebrity suspects and asking you to discover whodunit' and *Free, White, and 21* (1963) is described as:

The defense argues consent in the trial of a black hotel owner accused of raping a white civil rights worker. The trial culminates with both attorneys making their final arguments and the judge giving jury instructions directly to the camera. The screen fades to black, a clock appears, and the movie audience, having previously been handed a 'summons', is asked to decide the verdict.

(Marlyn Robinson, comp., 'Law in popular culture: feature films; an annotated list of films in the law and popular culture collection, Tarlton Law Library, University of Texas School of Law', *http://www.law.utexas.edu*)

21 A very short coda shows us the two lawyers alone in the courtroom, musing on the case. 'Of course you know she took a polygraph test . . .', says the prosecutor. 'Oh, yeah, I know – told she was telling the truth, didn't it?', replies the defender. Prosecutor: 'How do you square that with a verdict of not guilty?' Defender: 'It's a matter of definition. In her heart, she thought she'd been raped. By Texas law, she consented. Law is the best thing we've to go by on this earth. If you're black, or if you're white.' The prosecutor then utters the last words of the film: 'Is it that we love negroes more, or that we love intruders even less?' (Much is made in the film of the Swedish woman's outsider status.)

22 This is so in the majority of narrative cinema, in any case. For recent work (in which earlier positions are discussed) considering exceptions and their significance, see especially Wheeler Winston Dixon, 'It looks at you: notes on the "look back" in cinema', *Post Script*, 13, 1 (1993): 77–87; Marc Vernet, 'The look at the camera', *Cinema Journal* 28, 2 (Winter 1989): 48–63.

23 From the video box covers for *The Trial of Jean Harris*, *The Thin Blue Line*, *The Accused*, and from Court TV's Prime Time Justice tag for the Susan Smith trial (July 1995), respectively.

24 The classic *noir* film *Knock on Any Door* similarly has the lawyer (Humphrey Bogart), as he pleads for mercy for his client, look the camera, and us, straight in the eye. Early in the film, as he was about to give his opening statement, the lawyer sized up the jurors in an internal monologue (accompanied by very brief shots of each): 'Manicurist. Conscious of a person's looks ... Social worker: good. Grandmother: firm believer in the gentle Christ. Good. Jewish refugee, ex-professor, naturalized; *he'll* know about persecution and slums. Truck driver [holding a portable chess board]. Plays chess. Good. Mix them well and shake before using.'

25 On the irony of the title, see Christine Alice Corcos, 'Presuming innocence: Alan J. Pakula and Scott Turow take on the great American legal fiction', forthcoming in the *Oklahoma City University Law Review*.

26 Dershowitz's novel, on which the film is based, is clear about the autobiographical stakes and is written in Dershowitz's first person (especially 'Setting the Stage', pp. xv–xxvi). The Magill's entry explains the film's defense bias as a function of libel law, a problem that often dogs films about still-living characters. Thus the stepchildren are sketchily drawn as 'passive and almost nonexistent' because the film-makers feared a lawsuit, whereas the Dershowitz father and son are depicted as fiery, passionate, emotional, and vibrant.

Because the film is based, for the most part, on Dershowitz's book of the same name and was co-produced by his son Elon, the film-makers had little to worry about lawsuits from Dershowitz and his family and had more freedom to add substance to these characters and more fully dramatize their points of view.

[*Magill's Survey of Cinema*, English Language Films, second series (Englewood Cliffs, NJ, Salem Press, 1981), q.v. *Reversal of Fortune*]

27   Said writer Nicholas Kazan of his open ending,

> I certainly could never convince myself that this man was totally innocent in the more primitive sense of having nothing on his conscience. So I didn't want to make a film which wildly professed his innocence if, you know, when I met my maker I'd be tapped on my shoulder: 'By the way, this is a dreadful thing, but Claus was guilty'. . . . Hence the end of the film . . . I did want to leave it open, because I feel the essence of the human condition is that we never know for sure.

Quoted in Suzanne Gibson Shale, 'The conflicts of law and the character of men: writing *Reversal of Fortune* and *Judgment at Nuremberg*', *University of San Francisco Law Review*, 30: 4 (1996): 991–1102.

28   *Tomorrow* is a particularly interesting example. It begins and ends in a jury room, and its long middle is a flashback recounting the life of the one juror (Robert Duvall) who refused to join the others in a not-guilty verdict. The flashback is introduced with a voiceover, that of a lawyer saying that had he known then what he knows now (that the juror is the adoptive father of the murder victim) he would never have allowed this man to serve on the jury. The entire film, in other words, is about the making of a juror.

29   Harris, *Courtroom's Finest Hour*, p. 2. The evidence for influence is circumstantial, but powerful and generally assumed. See Thomas J. Harris, *Courtroom's Finest Hour in American Cinema* (Metuchen, NJ, and London: Scarecrow Press, 1987), p.2. Cayatte's film was released in France in 1950 and won the International Grand Prix at the Venice Film Festival that year. It was also released and reviewed in the USA in 1950 and seems to have had a second run in 1952–53, at which time it was quite widely reviewed. Rose's teleplay was first broadcast as a CBS Studio One production in 1954. Rose continued with trials, writing *The Sacco-Vanzetti Story* (1959) and *The Defenders* (1961–65).

30   Bosley Crowther wrote in his review of 3 March 1953,

> Actually, this terse investigation of seven assorted jurors' private lives as they sit in solemn judgment on a woman accused of the mercy killing of her paramour is simply a study of the natures and the reactions of human characters when called upon to render a decision involving the straight intepretation of law and morals. It is a crisp and absorbing demonstration of how people generally respond to the moral aspects of a situation according to the sort of people they are. And, as such, it becomes an exposition of consummate social irony, for the question it leaves with the viewer is whether justice or unfairness has been done.
>
> [*New York Times Film Reviews* (New York: *New York Times*)]

The *Variety* review (1 November 1950) also finds something amiss in the trial treatment: 'The film puts too much emphasis on the jurists, detracting not only from the trial but the killing itself.'

31   *Films In Review*, 4 (1953): 199. Like many American reviewers, this one roundly disliked the film: 'In this French film euthanasia is condoned and the jury system of determining guilt and innocence is derided', he begins, sarcastically.

32   Writes US Circuit Judge Alex Kozinski of his first viewing of *Twelve Angry Men*:

> As I sat there watching, struggling a bit with the language, trying to figure out the jury's function in American law . . . my whole adolescent conception of certainty, of knowledge itself was shaken. The case against the defendant sounded so airtight; the

reasons offered by the eleven sounded so irrefutable. I couldn't imagine how (or why) anyone could reach a different conclusion. Then, as one reason after another started to come apart, as inconsistencies crept into the picture, as jurors began changing their votes, I came to understand that truth does not spring into the courtroom full-blown, like Athena from the head of Zeus.

> [in Paul Bergman and Michael Asimow, *Reel Justice: The Courtroom Goes to the Movies* (Kansas City, KS: Andrews and McMeel, 1996), p. xiv]

On the different status of truth in the adversarial and the inquisitorial systems as well as in the narrative entertainments derived from those systems, see Chapter 4 of my *Trials, Movies, and the Adversarial Imagination*.

33 *Variety Film Reviews*, 1 November 1950.

34 'A French winner at Venice', *Films In Review*, 1, 7 (October 1950): 8.

35 *The Commonweal*, 57 (27 February 1953): 522.

36 *Cine*, 61 (1963): 112.

37 *New York Times Film Reviews* (3 March 1953). American reviewers were also taken aback by the French trial system. 'Sitting with them [the jurors], in court and out, is the president, who seems to combine the functions of foreman, judge, prosecuting attorney, and God', worried the *Saturday Review* , 36 (28 February 1953): 39.

38   Released as a conventional booking in large theaters (rather than being distributed only to small art houses, where it might have gained a major following and run for months on the strength of the uniformly favorable reviews it received), the film failed to make a profit, and Fonda never received his deferred salary.

> (*The Motion Picture Guide*, eds. Jay Robert Nash and Stanley Ralph Ross
> (Chicago, IL: Cinebooks, 1987), q.v. *Twelve Angry Men*

After noting its commercial failure, Pauline Kael remarked that 'the social psychology of the film is attuned to the educated audience' [*5001 Nights at the Movies* (New York, Henry Holt, 1991; originally published in 1982)], q.v. *Twelve Angry Men*.

39 Actually, there have been occasional television programs (for example *Picket Fences* and *Happy Days*) that re-enacted the *Twelve Angry Men* scenario. *Murder Most Foul* (1964), begins by presenting Miss Marple as the sole holdout juror in a murder case – though we learn this by report after the fact, not through direct observation of jury deliberations. There is a Tony Hancock spoof and various international versions or remakes, including the Hindi *One Man Stopped the Action* (1986) and a recent Japanese satire *The Gentle Twelve*. Even a spoof of the jury system (inspired by Menendez and Simpson) such as *Jury Duty* refers to *Twelve Angry Men* (same room, rounded windows, venetian blinds). On Sunday, 17 August 1997, HBO premiered a remake, starring Jack Lemmon as Juror Eight. Reviews tended to echo Caryn James's assessment that it is (and has always been) less a lesson in justice than 'a theatrical stunt, an excuse to bring together a dozen top actors, lock their characters in a sweltering room and let them go at it' [*New York Times*, The Arts (Saturday, 16 August, 1997), p. 12]. But remakes, spoofs, and homages exactly point up *Twelve Angry Men*'s failure to generate a real cycle of textual offspring (the way *Psycho* generated the terror film).

40 Harris, *Courtroom's Finest Hour*, p. 20.

41 'John Ford's *Young Mr. Lincoln*', in Bill Nichols, ed., *Movies and Methods*, vol. I (Berkeley, CA: University of California Press, 1976), p. 519. Originally published in *Cahiers du Cinema*, 223 (1970).

42   The sports fanatic, the former slum-kid, the Swiss-German immigrant, the educated doctor, the advertising man, the self-made businessman, the bigot. As symbolic representatives, even names are unnecessary . . . The trial of an accused is simply a broader trial of the functioning of America as democracy.
                    (Norman Miller, *International Dictionary of Films and Filmmakers*, vol. 2)
                                                                    q.v. *Twelve Angry Men*

Compare lawyer Bogart's internal monologue as he looks at the jury in *Knock on Any Door* (see endnote 24).

43   This is not to say that the jury is entirely beyond jokes and pot-shots. *The Juror* is an extended joke about jurors (clearly prompted by Simpson and Menendez).

44   *The Defense Research Institute's Report on Jury Service in the United States* (Chicago, IL, 1990), especially 3–8.

Acknowledgement: This chapter is adapted from a chapter of my (provisionally titled) *Trials, movies, and the adversarial imagination* (Princeton, NJ: Princeton University Press, forthcoming).

14 Introducing film evaluation

Noël Carroll

When we first think of evaluating films, we think initially of film critics. These are people who are in the business of pronouncing on the value of films. There are so many films to see and so little time. Thus, almost all of us have to fall back on the recommendations of film critics in order to inform our choice of viewing fare.

There are several different ways in which the role of a film critic may be pursued. Some critics attempt to function as consumer reporters – trying to predict which films most of their readership will enjoy. For such readers, these critics serve as consumer guides. Other critics aim at being taste-makers – identifying which films are special, and in the best of cases, suggesting how the rest of us might go on to appreciate them. Readers who prefer their tastes confirmed will gravitate toward the consumer guides. Those who want their taste expanded are likely to admire the critics who are able to pick out singular cinematic achievements and to contextualize and explain them.

However, though the role of the film critic commands an important position in cultures awash with movies (both in movie theaters, and on television and video cassettes), it would be a mistake to think of film evaluation as exclusively a professional matter. For evaluating films is something that we all do all of the time.

Nor do I mean by this merely that we automatically form preferences for some of the films we see over others and rank some of them as better than the rest. As humans, we tend to do this with respect to most of our experiences. But with regard to film viewing, this is not something that simply happens to us automatically. It is something that we avidly pursue. Evaluating films is part of our everyday film culture. When we talk about films with others, most of our time is spent trading evaluations, comparing them, sometimes sharing them, and often arguing about them. Indeed, we frequently read critics after we have seen a film in order to enter imaginary conversations of this sort with them.

Film viewing is often portrayed as a solitary affair in which each spectator communes with a brightened screen in a dark room. But film viewing is more sociable than that. Film viewing is part of our social life. After we have seen a film, we want to talk about it with others. We want to tell them what we have seen, to exchange ideas with others who have seen the same films, and to discuss our reactions and theirs. Film viewing is a natural pretext for sociability. And film evaluating is at the crux of this very elemental form of social exchange and consolidation. It is through such encounters that we express and develop ourselves as cultural beings.

That is to put the matter very abstractly. But what I have in mind can be clarified by recalling a very common experience. You attend a film with some friends. Afterwards you go out for coffee, or sweets, or a drink. You talk about the film you have just seen, remarking on the parts you liked or disliked. But, of course, quite frequently the conversation does not just end with a summary of personal preferences. The discussion may often turn to whether or not the film is good or whether it worked. That is, there is an almost ineluctable tendency for the conversation to move from reports of subjective enjoyment or boredom to questions of objective evaluation.

Experiences like these are part of the typical life of film-going – which is to claim that evaluation is at the heart of this practice for most of us. It adds zest to the activity. It is something that ordinary film-goers care about deeply. It is something that they want to do. And yet it is this aspect of film-going to which recent film scholarship pays little attention. Where ordinary film viewers probably care more about evaluation, contemporary film scholars are more obsessed with interpretation. So, by way of balance, attention, in this chapter, will shift to certain selected issues concerning evaluation. Let us talk to the film-goer where she or he lives. Specifically, in what follows, I will discuss certain kinds of selected problems that arise inevitably in the course of film evaluation, the traditional way in which classical film theorists attempted to resolve those problems, and I will conclude with some programmatic remarks about alternatives to the classical solution.

Some problems of film evaluation

I have suggested that film evaluation is something that we come to almost naturally. So in what sense could it be problematic? Well, recall the scenario I alluded to above. Suppose a group of us has just seen a film together – for example, *Speed* (1994). You like it; I do not. As often as not, the conversation will not stop there. You are apt to defend your liking of the film by saying that it is good. I may reply that I do not deny that you liked the film, but I add that that does not prove that it was good. It is perfectly consistent, I say, for you to like that film and for the film to be bad at the same time. Moreover, I add that *Speed* is a bad film.

At this point, notice that we have left off talking about our likes and our dislikes and we have entered the realm of objective evaluation. You are claiming that any reasonable and informed viewer should regard *Speed* as a good film, whereas I am denying that. In other words, we both accept each other's likes and dislikes. There is no more arguing about that than there is about our preferences in ice cream. But we are *arguing* – our discussion revolves around coming up with *reasons* that we believe should sway or even compel others to accept our viewpoint.[1]

A subjective report of a like or a dislike is a fact about us. It does not command the agreement of others. If you dislike spinach that is not a reason for me to dislike spinach, since reasons – as opposed to mere likings – are objective. Reasons are offered to others with an implicit claim on their assent. Thus, if you provide a reason for saying that *Speed* is a good film and if that reason is relevant and acceptable, you expect others to concur with your assessment. In our discussion of *Speed*, our behavior – our exchange of reasons – gives every appearance of being committed to objectivity. We do not pound the table and shout 'But I like it!' We try to find objective reasons that will convince others that our assessment is correct.

Here, in a nutshell, is the central problem of film evaluation (and, indeed, of all aesthetic evaluation). It emerges from a stubborn fact with which we are all familiar. That is the fact of disagreement. We disagree about our evaluations of film. Moreover, as I have already indicated, we do not act as though these disagreements are merely a matter of personal whims or preferences, since we argue about them, we advance reasons on their behalf, and we attempt to defend them.

When you say that *Speed* is good, you are advancing an objective claim, and your conversational behavior implies that you believe that your evaluation can be rationally adjudicated. But how is that possible? How can such disagreements be resolved rationally?[2] How can you hope to defend your assessment objectively?[3] Those are some of the central questions of film evaluation.

In order to get some sense of how such disagreements might be negotiated rationally, let us follow our imaginary dispute about *Speed* a little further. You say it is good; I say it is bad. What happens next? Very often we start mentioning other films. You might refer to other suspense films, such as *Die Hard* (1988) or *The Man Who Knew Too Much* (1934, 1956). Your purpose here might be to get me to agree that they are good films. For if I agree that they are good films, you will argue that consistency (a test for rational objectivity) demands that I agree *Speed* is also good, on the grounds that *Speed* shares essential features with the other suspense films that I have already conceded are good.

Here the conversation could go in several directions. I might deny that *Speed* is really analogous to the paradigms you have adduced, or I might deny that the other films you have mentioned are good. Let us explore the second option. Suppose that I deny that any of the three films are any good. At this point, you will begin to wonder what I think makes for a good film, and you may challenge me to produce an example of one. Say my example is *Riddles of the Sphinx* (1977), an avant-garde film that mixes disjunctive editing with dense, philosophical voiceover narration.

You agree that *Riddles of the Sphinx* is a good film, yet you cannot but feel that somehow I have missed the point. You say that that is not the kind of film that *Speed* is. *Speed* and *Riddles of the Sphinx* belong to different categories – they serve different purposes, and, in consequence, they have different standards of evaluation.

Perhaps one thing that this debate reveals so far is that when we evaluate films, part of that process involves placing the film in question in a certain category. This is a psychological fact about us. To evaluate, one categorizes.[4] The reason for this is that categories are generally connected to purposes and standards. When we categorize a piece of cutlery as a steak knife, we recognize that its purpose is to slice through thick pieces of beef and that, in consequence, a good-making feature of it is its sharpness. Sharpness, in other words, is a standard of goodness in steak knives because it is in virtue of its sharpness that a steak knife can discharge its purpose. In this way, categories, purposes, and standards form a matrix.

When we view a film, we also – as a matter of psychological fact – place it in a category, one that shapes our expectations and standards. Our dispute about *Speed* in the preceding example turns on the fact that we have situated *Speed* in different categories or comparison classes.

But, as I have said, this is only a psychological fact, not a logical one. We do not resolve the question of whether *Speed* is good by citing the different categories in which we regard *Speed*. That may clarify our differences, but it does not settle them. Our disagreement will not be adjudicated rationally until we are able to determine which of our competing categories is the *correct* one (or, at least, the more correct one).

Our dispute about the goodness or badness of *Speed*, then, has escalated, so to speak, into a disagreement about categories. Which category (or categories) is (are) appropriate or correct in this case? Our debate looks like it can be brought to a reasonable resolution only if we can determine which category is the correct one to bring to bear on the case of *Speed*. A great many problems about film evaluation could be resolved, if only we had a way to fix the correct category or categories for evaluating the film in question.[5] But how does one determine a correct category? That is the million dollar question. For without an answer to that question, it looks like our disagreement is just as rationally intractable as the question of whether or not *Speed* is good.

The classical solution

As we have just seen, one of the central problems of film evaluation is what we can call 'the problem of the correct category'. This is not a problem that has concerned recent film scholarship. However, there is a way of looking at classical film theory – film theory prior to the advent of semiotics and post-structuralism – such that the problem of the correct category turns out to be one of the central issues, if not sometimes *the* central issue, with which film theorists, such as Rudolf Arnheim (1957) and Siegfried Kracauer (1960) were wrestling.[6]

Classical film theory is generally preoccupied with isolating the essence of film – what some people call the *cinematic*. The cinematic is what differentiates film from other artforms, such as theater and painting. Moreover, classical film theorists were not simply concerned with what in fact differentiated film from other artforms. The differentiae they sought were also often normative. That is, they were concerned with the way in which film *should* be different from other arts. Stated obscurely, they thought that films should be cinematic. Various classical theorists defined what constituted being cinematic in different ways. But for most of the classical theorists, they had a conception of what counted as cinematic. And for them, the failure of a film to be cinematic was a defect.

What does this notion of the cinematic have to do with the problem of the correct category? Well, effectively, for the classical film theorist, *all films* – or at least all the films that we would want to talk about from an aesthetic point of view – fell into one category which we might call *film as film*. Thus, debates about the goodness or badness of a given film could be referred back to the question of whether or not the film under discussion was cinematic, that is, whether it was a proper instance of the category of film as film. Consequently, if we want to determine whether *Speed* is a good film, then what we have to do is to show that it is cinematic.

One obvious advantage of a classical approach to the problem of the correct category is that it makes film evaluation a very unified practice. The notion of the cinematic, in the hands of a given classical theorist, provides a single scale on which all films can be weighed and compared. Whether or not a film is good (relative to the category of film as film) can be established by showing that it is cinematic, while how good it is can be gauged in light of how cinematic it is. Similarly, one can say that a film is bad if it fails to be cinematic, or that it is flawed to the degree that uncinematic elements intrude into its style. Moreover, films can be compared and even ranked as good, bad, better, and worse in accordance with a single measure – their degree of cinematicity.

This is a very tidy program. It would provide a way of rationally negotiating disagreements about evaluating films just in case one were able to characterize satisfactorily what counts as cinematic. But there is the fly in the ointment. For, as is well known, different classical film theorists tended to argue for different and often conflicting (or non-converging) conceptions of the cinematic.

Early film theorists, for instance, tended to locate the cinematic in terms of two contrasts – that which differentiated film from theater, on the one hand, and that which differentiated film from the slavish recording of reality, on the other hand. They emphasized the difference between film, properly so called, and mere recording, in order to establish the credentials of film as an artform – something that did not simply duplicate reality but that could reconstitute it expressively and creatively.

But they also differentiated film from theater. The point here was to demonstrate that film was a *unique* artform, an artistic category unto itself – film as film. Thus, these early film theorists, of whom Rudolf Arnheim (1957) is a leading example, argued that film, properly so-called, was neither an imitation of nature, nor an imitation of any other artform, notably theater.

Whereas theater narration typically relies on words, cinematic narration, it was asserted, could and should emphasize movement, image, and action. If theater was primarily verbal, cinema, ideally, was primarily visual. Likewise, cinema had resources, particularly editing, that enabled film-makers to manipulate spatial and temporal transitions with more fluidity than was customary in theater. Thus, editing, or montage, was generally celebrated as the most important, essential characteristic of cinema. On this view, film was essentially visual, its natural subject of representation was animated action, and its primary means of expression was editing or montage.

Other techniques were also regarded as cinematic – including close-ups, camera angulation, trick photography, visual devices such as fades, wipes, and superimposition, camera movement, and the like. As with editing, these techniques were prized because they both declared the difference between film and theater (inasmuch as the effects available through these devices were not easily achieved in theater) and departed from the 'straight' recording of reality. In other words, the use of these devices standardly indicated that film differed from theater and from what was thought of as 'normal perception'. They displayed film as a unique artistic category – film as film.

A feature of a film was cinematic, then, as long as it deployed techniques that underscored the putatively unique capacities of cinema. Stylistic features that failed to do this – such as the use of extended dialogue or stolid tableaux shots – were uncinematic. Excessive reliance on words at the expense of animated action, or the use of a single camera position to record the declamation of dialogue (rather than exploiting the powers of editing) was not only uncinematic, but downright theatrical. And to be theatrical or uncinematic flew in the face of the canonical standards of film as film. Theatrical or uncinematic films were bad films, inappropriate or defective examples of the category.

A film such as *Speed* does very nicely on this conception of film. Dialogue here is in the service of action, of which there is quite a lot, which, in turn, is magnificently articulated through the editing. On the other hand, a film such as *Riddles of the Sphinx* would probably fare badly on this approach because of its extensive use of language. This approach to film evaluation could settle our earlier dispute in short order, if only its account of the essence of cinema were compelling.

But this conception of cinema is hardly incontestable. In fact, it was challenged by later film theorists in the classical tradition. These later classical theorists, of whom Siegfried Kracauer (1960) is a noteworthy example, are often called realists because they thought that the essential feature of cinema is photography and that this feature committed cinema to meeting certain standards that emphasized the recording and disclosure of reality.

So whereas earlier classical theorists, such as Arnheim, thought that the capacity of film to diverge from the recording of reality implied that cinema should employ assertive devices such as editing to reconstitute reality, realist theorists, such as Kracauer, looked more favorably on cinema's provenance in photography and inferred that this argued for the realistic usage of film. Both Arnheim and Kracauer were classical film theorists – both believed in the cinematic. But they disagreed not only about what constituted the category but also about what standards, as a result, were suitable to bring to bear in evaluating films.

Indeed, their theories led them in opposite directions. Highly stylized films of the sort favored by Arnheim's theory were apt to be castigated by Kracauer's lights because of their disregard for the canons of realism. From Kracauer's view, for instance, a film such as *Speed* would be uncinematic because of the various ways in which it violates Kracauer's conception of the (normative) essence of cinema. Specifically, Kracauer thinks that cinematic realism requires a disposition toward the use of open-ended plot structures, whereas the narrative world of *Speed* is closed, and, by Kracauer's lights, unrealistically contrived.

In the debate over the cinematic, proponents of the earlier view – that film should reconstitute reality – and proponents of the later view – the realists – could both score points against each other. Each side could argue that the other side failed as a comprehensive theory of the nature of film, because each side was blind to certain kinds of cinematic achievement. The defender of realism could claim that theorists such as

Arnheim ignored the accomplishments of films whose style gravitated more toward recording, such as the work of the Italian neo-realists (whose aspirations, of course, could be effectively explained from a realist point of view).

On the other hand, those who favored stylization and editing could explain many avant-garde experiments which were anything but realistic. Each side pretended to be a comprehensive theory of the nature of film, but opponents of either side could point out that the other side ignored or attempted to sublate or to substract, in an *ad hoc* manner, massive amounts of the data of film history.

Furthermore, it did not appear possible to patch up this problem by simply combining these two schools of classical film theory because, in important respects, they contradicted one another. Adding the two lines of theory together would not lead to a more comprehensive theory, but only to an inconsistent one.

One explanation of how these two strands of classical film theory failed to deliver the goods is that, though each side presented itself as a comprehensive theory of all film, this was not, in actuality, what either of these theoretical approaches was about. Both were really characterizations of different stylistic tendencies that crystallized at different points in film history. Theorists such as Arnheim and Russian montagists, like V. I. Pudovkin (1960), were particularly sensitive to stylistic developments in the period of silent film-making, whereas realist theorists such as Kracauer and the French writer André Bazin (1967, 1971) were especially attuned to stylistic developments of the sound film of the 1940s and early 1950s.

Both sides mistook certain period-specific developments in film history to reveal the essence of cinema. This is why their theories were suited to certain bodies of work, while being insensitive to achievements from other stylistic traditions. Whereas a theory of the nature of film should apply to films of all styles, these theorists inadvertently privileged certain styles over others to the extent that certain avenues of accomplishment were deprecated by them as uncinematic. Thus, their theories failed to be comprehensive because they were biased.

Undoubtedly, another – logically less flattering – way to put it was that these theorists proposed to demonstrate that certain options of film stylization were uncinematic by deducing the essence of cinema; but, in fact, what they did was to allow their stylistic preferences to shape their conception of the essence of cinema. Kracauer asserts that photography is the essential feature of cinema. But how does he know that photography rather than editing is the essential feature? The answer is because he already presumes that realist film-making demarcates the recognized body of achievement in the medium. But this, of course, begs a question.[7] And this fallacy is rampant throughout the corpus of classical film theorizing.[8]

One very ingenious attempt to reconcile the differences between the different schools of classical film theory can be found in Victor Perkins's excellent book *Film as film* (1972). This is an especially interesting text from our perspective because it is an explicit effort to provide a rational foundation for film evaluation. Though Perkins would probably bridle at this characterization, his book is an example of classical film theory, as his title – *Film as film* – indicates. Like other classical theorists, Perkins tries to develop a unified canon of evaluation for all films, irrespective of genre and period.

This canon is rooted in combining some of the insights of theorists such as Arnheim and realists such as Kracauer in a single, non-contradictory formula. From Perkins's view, in order to be good, a film must abide by certain realist standards of verisimilitude. This pays homage to the theoretical tradition of people such as Kracauer and Bazin.

But Perkins also pays his respects to the tradition of assertive stylization in classical film theory. For he maintains that the extra degrees of goodness that a film accrues (over and above the minimal accreditation as good that it receives for being realistic) are to be calibrated in terms of the extent to which the film is stylized – via editing, set design, camera angulation, camera movement, costume, and so on – just as long as that stylization is articulated within the bounds of realism. A film such as *Elmer Gantry* (1960), for example, can employ hyperactive montage metaphors just insofar as those metaphors are motivated realistically in the world of the film.

Here, realism and stylization do not contradict each other. Rather, realism constrains the legitimate compass of stylization. That is, realism and stylization are coordinated by a rule that says a good film contains both, but only to the extent that stylization stays within the bounds of realism. In *Elmer Gantry*, expressive cutting between a swelling fire and a religious frenzy is acceptable cinematically because the fire that comments on the frenzy is of a piece with the naturalist settings and narration of the fictional world. This use of editing contrasts to Eisensteinian montage, which sometimes resorted to similes that intruded upon the decoupage from outside the setting of the fiction.

By requiring that stylization be constrained by realism, Perkins proposes a principled way for films to exploit both of the tendencies advocated by the conflicting strands of classical film theory. It is a brilliant compromise solution between two opposing schools of thought. It seems to realize the dream of classical film theory – to solve the problem of the correct category by ascertaining a standard of evaluation applicable to all films.

However, if Perkins's approach represents one of the highest points in classical film theory, it is also unfortunately vulnerable to some of the same criticisms we brought against earlier forms of this sort of theory. We have already noted that a recurrent failing of classical film theorists involved their hypostatization of certain period-specific film styles – their tendency to mistake these styles for the very essence of cinema itself.

A similar problem is evident in Perkins's book. Perkins takes the exploration of stylization within the bounds of realism to be the quiddity of film as film. But why take this to be more representative of the essence of film than experiments in avant-garde irrealism? Why is Preminger more cinematic than Godard?

When one looks at the data base of Perkins's theory, the answer seems very apparent. Those examples come predominantly from Hollywood films of the 1950s and early 1960s. During that period, constraining stylization within the bounds of realism was, so to say, a rule of the practice. But in this respect, what Perkins has done, like Arnheim, Kracauer, and Bazin before him, has been to mistake an essential (or fundamental) feature of a specific practice for the essence of cinema as a whole. That is, Perkins's preference for a certain kind of film-making has biased his account of the nature of, as he himself calls it, film as film.

One of the greatest promises of classical film theory was that it would solve the problem of the correct category. For, if we could make a classical film theory work, we would have the one and only category for evaluating all films. By identifying an essence of film – one with normative implications – we would have a standard that could be brought to bear to resolve rationally most disagreements about the quality of given films. But the search for this kind of essence has proven chimerical.

In most cases, classical theorists have proceeded by begging the question. They have built in their stylistic preferences as premises in their deductions of stylistic imperatives and cinematic canons. This is rather like the magician who puts the rabbit in the hat and then draws it out. What is not really magic is not logic either.

Unfortunately, this sort of error recurs throughout the body of classical film theory, even in its most sophisticated representatives, such as Perkins. Thus, until this failing is repaired, the prospects for solving the problem of the correct category by means of the strategies of classical film theory appear foreclosed, and this suggests that another alternative needs to be explored.

An alternative approach

What we had hoped to inherit from classical film theory was a solution to the problem of the correct category. This problem is a pressing one for film evaluation, because if we are able to find a way to establish the correct category for evaluating a given film, then we are on our way to resolving many (though not all) of the disagreements that arise when we attempt to assess films. Unfortunately, we have seen that so far classical film theory has failed in this regard.

Undeniably, the failure of film theory is instructive. It shows something, but we need to be careful about what it reveals. It does not show that there cannot be correct categories for evaluating films. Rather, it only shows that it is unlikely that we can evolve a unitary theory of evaluation based on a *single* category such as film as film. That is, it only suggests that there is not a universal litmus test – such as the cinematic – for goodness in film. But the failure of classical theory does not show that categories as such are irrelevant to film evaluation.

The problems of classical film theory may incline us toward skepticism about whether there is a single evaluative category that subsumes all films. But this should not make us skeptical about whether films fall into various different categories, many of which come with perfectly respectable standards of evaluation. That film practices are too diverse to be all assimilated usefully under the sort of essential category that classical theorists hoped to discover hardly implies that films cannot be categorized.

Indeed, it is obvious that films can be categorized. We have lots of film categories, such as suspense films, horror films, structural films, trance films, neo-realist films, art films, and so on. Nor is there any reason to think that regarding films under these categories rather than others is not often correct. Additionally, many of these categories come with subtending purposes and standards of accomplishment attached to them.

For example, some films are correctly categorized as melodramas. Part of the point of a melodrama is to move the audience to feel – at least for some segment of the duration of the film – sadness or pity for one of the protagonists. A correctly categorized melodrama that failed in this respect would be *prima facie* defective. A melodrama that succeeds in this regard would be *prima facie* a good melodrama. Likewise, a correctly classified classical detective film that fails to prompt speculation about whodunit (perhaps because the answer is too obvious) and a comedy whose gags are so disastrously timed that every laugh line falls flat are both presumptively failures. That is, if nothing can be said to justify the ways in which such films deviate from the standards of the categories by which they are fittingly described, then we can rationally ground negative assessments of these works.

Returning to the question of *Speed*: you said that it was good; I said that it was bad. However, in the course of our discussion, it became apparent that the likely basis for my negative assessment was that I evaluated *Speed* relative to an incorrect category. I compared it with *Riddles of the Sphinx* – a film in the category that is sometimes called the New Talkie – and clearly the aims and standards relevant to that category differ wildly from those appropriate to suspense films. New Talkies are designed to raise philosophical questions, and, though some suspense fictions may also do this, explicitly raising philosophical questions is not a standard expectation that we require every (or any) suspense film to fulfill. The failure to raise philosophical questions is not a basis for charging that a film correctly categorized as suspense is bad. Thus, if you can advance objectively creditable reasons for classifying *Speed* as a suspense film while also challenging my grounds for comparing it with a New Talkie, then you have a rational basis for dismissing my allegations. And if I cannot undermine your categorization with reasons, nor defend my own categorization, I should (rationally speaking) concede your point.

In this example, I have placed a great deal of emphasis on the role of reasons in supporting or dismissing categorizations. But this may strike the reader as obscure. What are these reasons and in what sense are they objective? In this regard, three kinds of reasons come into play most frequently (see Walton, 1970).[9] The first kind of reason pertains to the structure of the work: if it possesses a large number of features that are typical of films existing in a certain category, then that is a strong reason to classify it as, for example, a suspense film. Conversely, the fewer features a film contains of the sort that are typical for a certain category, such as that of the New Talkie, the less likely it is that the film belongs to that category. The number of relevant features a film possesses or lacks may not always provide conclusive reasons in favor of one categorization over another, but statistics such as these generally provide evidence in the direction of one classification over another. Moreover, these reasons are objective inasmuch as it can be a matter of intersubjectively ascertainable fact that a film possesses or lacks a certain number of clearly defined features and that said features are typical of a certain category of film.

Another kind of reason that is relevant to the question of the categorization of a film concerns authorial intention. How a film-maker or group of film-makers intended a work to be categorized is quite often an intersubjectively ascertainable matter of fact, and, in a great many of the remaining cases, a highly plausible hypothesis about the intended categorization of a given film is available. Again, authorial intentions may not always provide conclusive reasons for categorization, though they may support a presumption in favor of one categorization over another. And when evidence of authorial intention can be wedded to structural evidence of the sort alluded to in the previous paragraph, the grounds for rationally preferring one categorization over another mounts appreciably.

Further reasons on behalf of the categorization of a film can be adduced from the historical and/or cultural context from which the film emerged. That is, if a certain category of film-making is alive and abroad in the historical and/or cultural context from which the film emerged (especially when competing categories are not), then that supplies rational grounds for film categorization. This too is a question of fact. That suspense films are common currency in the cultural enclave of Hollywood-type movie-making and that New Talkies and, for that matter, art films are not provides us with contextual reasons for arguing that *Speed* belongs to the comparison class of suspense films as opposed to many of the alternative categories against whose standards *Speed* might be discounted as defective.

Structural, intentional, and contextual considerations supply us with strong reasons for categorizing films one way rather than another. Where we have reasons of all three kinds, their combined force may sometimes be conclusive. Often these kinds of reasons dovetail, since contextual considerations frequently count as evidence of authorial intention – inasmuch as film-makers generally have an interest in addressing audiences in terms of the categories with which they are familiar and since authors typically signal the category they have in mind by exhibiting well-entrenched structural features of the intended genre. Of course, in some cases, our categorization may not depend on all three kinds of reasons. Sometimes structural (or authorial or contextual) reasons alone will be sufficient, particularly where there are no persuasive, countervailing reasons available for competing categorizations.

Where does this leave us? First, it lends support to our conviction that there are objective grounds for categorizing films one way rather than another. Thus, if the objective evaluation of films depends upon our ability to categorize films correctly, then we have shown that this requirement can be met sometimes, if not often. Moreover, if we possess the wherewithal to categorize films correctly – and to defend certain categorizations over others – then we have the means to settle rationally some – indeed, I suspect many – disagreements concerning film evaluation. In order to defend our own evaluations of films against competing ones, we will often proceed by demonstrating that our evaluation rests upon a correct categorization of the film in question, while also arguing that rival evaluations depend on incorrect, unlikely, or, at least, less plausible ones. This will not resolve every disagreement about film evaluation, but it may dissolve a great many of them, thereby implying that, in large measure, film evaluation is a reasonable activity.

This approach to film evaluation is not as unified as the one proposed by classical film theory. Since classical film theory acknowledged only one category, it supplied a unitary metric according to which every film might be ranked. Every film could be compared for its cinematicity. The approach that I have been discussing is far more fragmentary, since I maintain that there are many different categories which we may call upon to evaluate different types of films.

This may dishearten some. They might complain that my approach makes the qualitative comparison of films of different categories impossible especially when contrasted to the capacity of the classical tradition to rank all films on a single grid. However, I find these objections exaggerated, on the one hand, and utopian, on the other. The worry that my approach makes all comparison between films of different categories impossible is hyperbolic because there is no reason to suppose that there are never shared, cross-categorical dimensions of evaluation, such as, for instance, narrative coherence.

At the same time, the wish to be able to compare all films with all other films has always seemed to me unrealistic. Why suppose that the best narrative film is strictly commensurable with *Last Year at Marienbad* (1961)? Sometimes it is a case of apples and oranges.

Another objection to my method is that it is formalist, since it primarily involves assessing films in virtue of things such as generic canons. But here the charge of formalism is misplaced if that means bracketing considerations of morality, politics and cognitive value, since many film categories themselves countenance such considerations. A social problem film that failed to portray injustice effectively would be a defective specimen of the category.

Perhaps a deeper concern is that my view makes a fundamental ontological mistake. It seems to suppose that there is one and only one category into which each film falls. And that is just false. But, of course, I readily agree that films may inhabit more than one category. However, that does not show that my approach is flawed. It only entails that evaluation may be more complicated than my examples have suggested so far. Films may be evaluated in light of several categories. Moreover, this may lead to mixed results. A film may turn out to be good in respect to one category to which it belongs, but bad in respect to another. But this should come as no surprise. Mixed results often figure in our assessments of films even when considering a film in light of only one category. That is, mixed results are just something – like gravity – that we have to learn to live with.

A related anxiety might be that my approach is too conservative. It appears to presume that categories are fixed. But film categories are also mutating. Some are disappearing, others are changing, and new ones are coming into existence. How can I handle films from categories that are in the process of evolution as well as films that herald the onset of new genres? Surely, I cannot deny the existence of such phenomena.

Nor would I want to. But film categories, like the films themselves, do not come from nowhere. New categories arise from earlier ones by well precedented processes of development – such as hybridization, amplification, repudiation, and other processes. Consequently, it is possible to track emerging categories along with their purposes and standards *in media res*. With respect to avant-garde cinema, this is even facilitated by the existence of manifestos and a lively film culture as well as frequently through the existence of related aspirations in adjacent art forms which suggest the rationale behind new developments. The category of the New Talkie, for instance, was comprehended virtually with the arrival of the first examples. Thus there is no reason to fear that talk of categories precludes receptivity to novel forms of film-making.

Finally, it may be said that, at best, this chapter only gets us as far as evaluating films in terms of whether they are good, bad, better, or worse specimens of a kind or category. But we do not evaluate films only as good of a kind or genre. We may also wish to evaluate genres, arguing, for example, that some genres are better than others. This charge is fair but not decisive. Throughout I have said that my method resolves only *some* problems of film evaluation. One reason for that qualification is that I acknowledge that problems such as this one remain to be tackled.

At the same time, the question of ranking film genres and categories ultimately involves not only issues of film criticism and practice narrowly construed, but also general questions of axiology – such as whether the philosophizing of the New Talkie is more valuable than the emotional engagement of the suspense film. That is no reason to neglect this topic. But it may be a justification for breaking off an introductory chapter narrowly concerned with *film* evaluation at just this point and for holding off these larger issues for another time and place.

Nevertheless, though there is much work still to be done, one should not take that as a reason to dismiss the work done so far. We have traveled quite a distance since the beginning of this chapter. We started with the problem of disagreement, which from many viewpoints appears insuperable. However, we have argued that for a great many cases, disagreements can be resolved objectively and we have shown how this might be done. Indeed, I suspect that the considerations advanced in this chapter afford the tools to dismantle most of the disputes that arise in informal discussions about film. Of course, whether my arguments have been successful must be weighed carefully. But that too is something that can be done rationally.

Endnotes

1   It is just this – our appeal to third parties and their standards of argument and evidence – that marks our discussion as objective (that is, as playing by intersubjective rules of rationality).

2   In this chapter, I will try to show how at least *some* of these debates can be resolved rationally. I will not attempt to show that *all* evaluative disagreements can be so resolved. This chapter should not be understood as claiming that, on the basis of its argumentation, all evaluative disputes are rationally decidable. But some may be, and that is all I want to establish in an introductory chapter like this. An interesting question for students to pursue with respect to this chapter is to identify the kinds of disputes that the approach in this chapter leaves unsolved. An even more interesting problem is for students to think about how some of those disputes might be rendered rationally tractable.

3   Some readers may feel that there is a short answer to questions such as these – namely, that these disagreements cannot be rationally resolved, nor can film evaluations ever be defended objectively. All these invocations of rationality and objectivity are really nothing but masks for something else – personal taste, the will to power, the play of class interests, gender biases, racial prejudices, and so on. Those are all positions represented in the literature. They are what are called 'debunking arguments'. However, for a debunking argument to get off the ground, it needs to be shown that there really is no prospect for rationality in this arena. Thus, students who want to dismiss the possibility of rational film evaluation need to show first that the procedures recommended in this chapter are fallacious or fantastical before they go on to reveal them as exercises of an elitist will to domination.

4   There may be certain exceptions to this generalization. If Kant is correct, judgments of what

he calls free beauty would defy it. But this is not the place to discuss Kant's theory of aesthetic judgment (Kant, 1987). For heuristic purposes, I will pass over this complication except to say that the evaluations discussed in this chapter are what Kant might have considered to be judgments of dependent beauty.

5   As this sentence indicates, though I think that figuring out the correct way to categorize a film solves a *great many* problems of film evaluation, I do not think that it settles them all. Even when one agrees on the correct category of a specific film, there will be many remaining questions, such as which standards are the ones appropriate to the category in question, whether or not the film under discussion truly meets those standards, and what is the worth of the relevant category relative to other categories of film. Thus, I do not suppose that all disagreement will disappear automatically with the determination of the correct category (or categories). My point in this short chapter is only to suggest that many problems may be rationally resolved in this way. Showing that much is as ambitious as I am prepared to be in such an introductory discussion.

6   For a discussion of classical film theory, see Carroll (1988).

7   In order to see this argument worked out in detail, see Carroll (1997).

8   This argument is developed in Carroll (1996).

9   Walton (1970) speaks of four categories, but I am only convinced of three of them.

References

Arnheim, Rudolf. 1957: *Film as art.* Berkeley, CA: University of California Press.

Bazin, André. 1967, 1971: *What is cinema?*, trans. by Hugh Gray. Berkeley: University of California Press.

Carroll, Noël. 1988: *Philosophical problems of classical film theory.* Princeton, NJ: Princeton University Press.

Carroll, Noël. 1996: Forget the medium! In Tjarks, M. and Tillman, F. (eds) *A cinema of ideas.* Honolulu, HI: Hawai Pacific University, 44–9.

Carroll, Noël. 1997: Kracauer's theory of film. In Lehman, P. (ed.), *Defining cinema.* New Brunswick, NJ: Rutgers University Press, 111–31.

Kant, Immanuel. 1987: *Critique of judgement,* trans. Werner Pluhar. Indianapolis: Hackett.

Kracauer, Siegfried. 1960: *Theory of film.* Oxford: Oxford University Press.

Perkins, V.F. 1972. *Film as film.* Baltimore, MD: Penguin Books

Pudovkin, V.I. 1960: *Film technique and film acting.* New York: Grove Press.

Walton, Kendall, 1970: Categories of art. *The Philosophical Review* **79**: 334–67.

15 'Style', posture, and idiom: Tarantino's figures of masculinity

Sharon Willis

If Quentin Tarantino has been celebrated as the embodiment of 'cool', it may be because his tightly crafted films offer a distinctive blend of affective forces – combining astonishing violence with explosive hilarity – while carefully calibrated irony allows them to push relentlessly at aesthetic and discursive boundaries. Such a structure offers the thrill of transgression with the promise that the ironic frame will manage and contain it. If irony is an unmistakably social and intersubjective form, however, the world of affective intensities seems inevitably linked to privacy and subjective interiority. That world is also, of course, the world of fantasy. And when we speak of fantasy, our most flexible interpretive tool may be psychoanalysis.

Long-standing and often implicit debates within film studies and cultural studies concern suspicions that psychoanalytic readings invariably understand social conflict through models of individual subjectivity, thus reducing the social to the psychic. However, I want to argue that, in fact, popular representations themselves elaborate social anxieties through fantasmatic structures that are apparently 'private'. Collective or public fantasies about social difference, then, take shape through representations that seem to draw on private or subjective intensities. To the extent that social difference continues to provide some of the most striking material for the collective fantasies elaborated in cultural representations, we cannot really afford to dispense with psychoanalytic tools. From this perspective, Quentin Tarantino's work offers a case in point since the steadfastly oedipal framing of his dramas works to 'privatize' his violent images and to evaporate any historical specificity or social referentiality from them. Articulating the fantasies it deploys through signature stylistic effects, *Pulp Fiction* (1994) codes them as 'subjective', as emanating from and ultimately referring to only the director himself.

A close reading of *Pulp Fiction* that remembers *Reservoir Dogs* (1991) and Tony Scott's (1993) *True Romance*, for which Tarantino wrote the screenplay, may allow us to chart

Tarantino's consistent construction of blackness, and especially of black males, as a specific cultural icon. However, we must also examine the production of Tarantino's vivid authorial style in the consumer context of promotion and reception. By exploring our current working conceptions of an 'auteur' and their social meanings, we may disclose the discursive interactions that shape audiences in relation to a specific authorial persona. Closely linked to the consolidation of audiences as taste cultures, the contemporary auteur figures as an embodiment of 'style'. But this emphasis on style often obscures the social and cultural situation that underwrites it. This reading of *Pulp Fiction* seeks to discern the social side of style by exploring the ways that 'race' works for Tarantino and for his imagined audience, particularly in relation to gender identity, erotics, and fantasy. In discussing fantasy here, I mean to explore the unstable and obscure intersection where collective or public fantasies remain tightly bound in reciprocally shaping relations with the private ones that we consider to be the product of a particular subjectivity.

Quentin Tarantino's characters spend a lot of time in the bathroom, and because they do, the bathroom acquires a dramatic centrality in his work. The bathroom is an ambivalent site, since the activities that take place there become in these films structurally both world-making and earth-shattering. In *Pulp Fiction* the bathroom anchors a dense nexus that connects blood and violence to anal eroticism and smearing. It thus permits delicate intersections that connect aggressive soiling impulses with tense efforts to consolidate, to clean, and to retain, at the literal level, and, at the figurative level, with social hygienic dreams of sanitizing a word such as 'nigger'. In the process, the bathroom also realigns cultural authority in relation to refuse, or trash, on the one hand, and to 'race', on the other.

To read the relationship between private and public fantasy in Tarantino's work, however, we must look at the privy and the threat of exposure. Often, like *Pulp Fiction*'s Vincent Vega (John Travolta), Tarantino's characters get caught with their pants down. We might even understand that as the film's central metaphor. Not only does Vince Vega get killed as a consequence of an untimely visit to the john, but the anal rape of Marcellus Wallace is the most deeply embedded episode in its interlocked plot structure. Wallace (Ving Rhames), Vega's boss, is the central figure who organizes all the characters diegetically, and who orchestrates the narratives' intertwining. So, in some sense, the film is about catching the big boss with his pants down literally, even as the other characters strive to keep from being caught that way.

Getting caught with one's pants down seems to be the prevailing effect these films aim to produce in the spectator as well. Tarantino addresses this effect – provocatively – in connection with his film's most discussed scene. Tarantino tells Dennis Hopper in an interview:

> The thing that I am really proud of in the torture scene in *Dogs* with Mr. Blonde, Michael
> Madsen, is the fact that it's truly funny up until the point that he cuts the cop's ear off.
> While he's up there doing that little dance to 'Stuck in the Middle with You', I pretty
> much defy anybody to watch and not enjoy it . . . And then when he starts cutting the ear
> off, that's not played for laughs . . . . So now you've got his coolness and his dance, the

joke of talking into the ear and the cop's pain, they're all tied up together, and that's why I think that scene caused such a sensation, because you don't know how you're supposed to feel when you see it.

(1994a: 17)

To be caught laughing when something horrific happens, gasping at the mismatch between our affective state and the next image, reproduces or recalls the embarrassment, or even shame, of being caught in a breach of social discipline. Tweaking our internal social censorship mechanisms through such uncomfortable intersections of the funny and the horrifying, these films leave us to manage that affective excess, which we may do by turning shock into embarrassment, or by taking satisfaction in the alibi they provide for us to get away with laughing when we should not.

Curiously, the film-maker addresses this kind of excess through references to taste, food, and consumption, a category definitively mismatched with the bathroom and its functions. '"Funniness and scariness", in the words of the film geek-turned-auteur are "two great tastes that taste great together"' (Kennedy, 1994; 32). By appropriating a jingle this way, Tarantino mimes the discourse of *Pulp Fiction*, a film that, like *Reservoir Dogs*, self-consciously speaks fragments of popular culture. As these films consume the soundtrack of daily life and recycle it, bits of discourse, figures, and fragmented texts from television, radio, and print become found objects that circulate as residue or trash. That circulation may be linked to the films' metaphorics of shit.

Part of the reason that bloodletting can be humorous in Tarantino's work is that blood really operates like feces, so that the spilling of blood is very much like smearing. In all its evocation of infantile activity, smearing not only provokes laughter, but also implies violence. Though this connection between blood and shit might seem at first far-fetched, a look at Tarantino's signature effects suggests that it is not. While the celebratory clamor about his emergence as the American auteur for the 1990s turns on his wizardry with violence and its eroticized possibilities, the film-maker's own appearance as a figure in his films is as closely associated with shit as with violence. Tarantino's character in *Reservoir Dogs* loudly proclaims this in so many words. Complaining to his boss about his alias, Mr Brown, he asserts: 'Brown, that's a little too close to shit.'

Soiling and cleaning are, of course, the central subject of episode titled 'The Bonnie Situation'. This sequence's sustained comic gag means to rewrite and contain the film's violence as entirely 'over the top', and thereby to ironize retroactively much of what has gone before. Vince Vega precipitates 'the Bonnie situation' when he accidently shoots Marvin, the only survivor of the opening confrontation, in the face, blowing blood, skull, and brain matter all over the back seat and into his and Jules's (Samuel L. Jackson's) hair. This moment echoes one of *Reservoir Dogs*'s central images, as Mr Orange (Tim Roth) spends most of the film's duration writhing and slipping in an ever-growing pool of blood. Here, the image of blood veers away from the violence that produces it, and begins to refer more definitively to the shocking aesthetic effects the smears of red on white background produce.

Tarantino's character, Jimmy, who appears only in this episode, is frantic to clean up all the bloody evidence of Jules's and Vince's visit to his home. In a central and particularly hilarious moment, Jules, clearly the film's best cleaner, as well as its most articulate speaker, is infuriated by Vince's poor bathroom habits, since he leaves the washcloth stained with blood, and looking like a 'maxipad'. As this sequence foregrounds hygiene in an uproarious way, its structural link between blood and the bathroom reinforces our sense that bloodletting is Tarantino's way of 'smearing'. Soiling and cleaning, then, become central organizing processes for these films – at the literal and the figurative levels.

What can happen inside the bathroom? Somebody can, for instance, consolidate his position or his image, as Vince Vega does when he spends several minutes in Mia's (Uma Thurman's) bathroom posing before her mirror and earnestly talking himself out of sleeping with her. Of course, when Vince returns from his trip to the bathroom he finds a full-blown crisis: Mia is comatose, drooling and bleeding from the nose. Similarly, in the closing segment of the film's framing sequence, Vince emerges from the bathroom to find the Hawthorne Diner in the middle of a full crisis. In *Pulp Fiction*, emerging from the bathroom sometimes has the status of an emergency. With striking frequency, people return from the john to find that the world has changed in their absence, as the situation has exploded or imploded.

But the bathroom's relationship to anality and aggression is, of course, what underlies its connection to emergencies, to world-making and earth-shattering change. The infantile lining to the fantasies Tarantino's films mobilize around this site discloses itself across the story, 'The Gold Watch', the second of *Pulp Fiction*'s three embedded narratives. From its opening this story establishes both its pleasures and its shocks as rooted in infantile regression to anal sadism and the satisfactions of producing a 'gift'. The gift is, of course, the father's watch, the gold watch of the title.

This sequence opens with a cartoon image that fills the screen, later to be matched on the television in the child Butch Coolidge's living room. As spectators, then, we are watching Coolidge's childhood television of the 1960s. Butch becomes the character the film links most closely to the television; for instance, the sound of automatic weapons fire from the television is ambient when Butch wakes up in his motel room. This soundtrack recalls the opening of the story, where the child Butch receives his dead father's watch from a Viet Nam war buddy, Captain Koons, played by Christopher Walken.

Walken himself operates as an icon of 1970s' readings of the Viet Nam war, through his performance in *The Deer Hunter* (1978). As he tells Butch the story of the watch's itinerary through family history, and through men's bodies – explaining to Butch that the watch is a paternal legacy that goes back to his great-grandfather, and that passes from father to son as an amulet to protect them in war – he reproduces the deranged voice and look of his character in the earlier film. He recounts that the watch's most recent passage from man to man has transpired in the prisoner-of-war camp where Koons and the senior Coolidge have been incarcerated. There, Koons tells Butch, with blunt force, his father hid the watch 'up his ass'. When the father dies of dysentery (the inability to retain anything at all), Koons installs the watch in his own rectum – for two years. So the adored fetish for which Butch risks his life later in this episode is a gift that issues from the father's ass. Metaphorically, then, this is a gift from the very site of the father's death, and one that passes from man to man in an exchange forcefully coded as anal. Here the relentless focus on the anal indicates the persistence of pre-oedipal impulses underlying the oedipal structures. Indeed, as *Pulp Fiction* unfolds, we might see it as producing an increasingly tense friction between oedipal organization and ferocious pre-oedipal impulses.

At the level of dialogue, this scene is quite funny, especially as Walken's character moves from solemn reverence about his war buddy and his own surrogacy in fulfilling the paternal legacy to a vulgar diatribe about the discomforts of carrying a watch in one's rectum. Equally ironic, the father surrogate's appearance is heralded by a television image, and the television continues to play throughout this sequence. Television and televised visions of the Viet Nam war have come to coincide with the figure of the father. It is as if the television, and war movies of the 1970s, were Butch's father, at least to the extent that the television inscribes the father's images as endless reruns. That is, Butch has Viet Nam war movies and video footage in place of the absent father. And when Captain Koons enters the living room, we see Christopher Walken in his function as an image retrieved from a repertoire of 1970s' television and movie versions of ruined masculinity in search of rehabilitation.

In this sequence the gray light of the television presiding over the scene seems to inscribe a ghostly paternal gaze. Where the previous sequences have unfolded under Marsellus's absent but ambient gaze, this story substitutes a paternal gaze emerging from the concreteness of the television set, the site of a different kind of unlocalizable gaze. But even more important, figurally, this effect coheres with a reading of the film's overarching project as a drive to turn shit into gold. That might also be a way of describing the project of redeeming and recycling popular culture, especially the popular culture of one's childhood, as is Tarantino's inclination. To follow out this logic, then, Walken himself is part of the detritus that is being recycled here, as are John Travolta, Dennis Hopper in *True Romance*, and Harvey Keitel, both as Winston Wolf in this film, and as Mr White in *Reservoir Dogs*.

Harvey Keitel figures an interesting link between the well-known actors of this generation who function to anchor both the ensembles of these films and the popular culture of Tarantino's own past that circulates through and animates their narrative and image repertoires. Keitel, however, also figures as a father. Not only is he the co-producer of Tarantino's first film, *Reservoir Dogs*, but his character incarnates a certain paternal authority of experience. Likewise, his character in *Pulp Fiction*, Winston Wolf, who orchestrates the clean-up in Jimmy's house, brings a certain paternal force to bear on the situation, instructing and ordering Jules and Vince to perform their tasks, reassuring Jimmy about his ability to restore order to the suburban home. He is also, of course, in this sequence, a director figure, orchestrating the action, and referring to the people involved as 'the principals'. It is surely no accident that this kind of director figure appears to discipline and reassure the character played by Tarantino himself here, a man desperate with anxiety that he will not be able to fulfill domestic responsibilities presumably set out by his wife, Bonnie. Tarantino's person, then, figures as irresponsible in ways that have interesting resonances for the rest of the film, particularly concerning his repeated use of the word 'nigger', a term that the film keeps in volatile circulation. But this sequence also evokes the director-as-auteur, his persona for the press.

What is interesting about Tarantino in this connection is that he provides both a phantom presence within the film and an extratextual commercial performance – which is probably why he has emerged so spectacularly as the auteur of the 1990s. This ability to combine two types of authorial function is no doubt part of Tarantino's debt to the French New Wave, and part of his appeal to 'art' audiences. In this regard, he fulfills what James Naremore describes as the 'two faces' of auteurism. 'Marginalized social groups,' he writes, 'can declare solidarity and create a collective identity by adopting authors as culture heroes – names that signify complex, coded meanings.' 'Once these same culture heroes have been established and widely recognized, however,' Naremore continues, 'they can become icons of mass memory or touchstones in a "great tradition"' (1990: 21). Tarantino's function as an icon of mass memory like those he recycles is certainly worth serious attention. But this should be understood in the context of his appeal to cult and fan formations, and perhaps most particularly because he presents himself as a superfan.

In this respect, the rapidity with which Tarantino has developed a huge fandom may have to do with what Timothy Corrigan describes as the increasing importance of cult viewing in relation to auteurship, where the auteur operates 'as a commercial strategy for organizing audience reception, as a critical concept bound to distribution and marketing aims that identify and address the potential cult status of an auteur' (Corrigan, 1991: 103). And perhaps this is why Tarantino is so intent on inscribing himself, multiply, in his films.

Butch Coolidge is only one of a series of characters who all represent some defiance of paternal authority, such as Clarence Worley, Mr Orange, Vince Vega, Vic Vega (Mr Blonde), and, of course, the characters Jimmy and Mr Brown, whose presence inscribes the author as the kind of 'fanboy' – a film buff drawn to a collective male youth culture that he both identifies with and seeks to attract. Tarantino's auteur status is closely coincident with his cult status because both his persona and his films embody a nostalgia for a 1970s that is continually circulating in television, video, and radio.

This is the popular culture that formed the previous generation – the parent generation – now the shapers of dominant critical discourse about popular culture. And if that generation experienced as children the formative effects of a popular culture whose nostalgia and recollection were seeking to make some sense, through cultural artifacts and repetitions, of the 1960s, later appropriations of the products of the 1970s recycle them as a kind of nostalgia to the second degree: nostalgia for nostalgia. Tarantino's work stresses the absolute contemporaneity – the contemporaneity of the always already 'missed' – that television and radio recycling posit for these cultural artifacts. And this artificial contemporaneity operates as a kind of utopian eternal present. In relying on these artifacts as central organizing devices, his films offer the perfect salvage operation, redeeming a past for the generation that inhabited it, but that also 'missed' it. To redeem a previous generation's trash may be, metaphorically, to turn its shit into gold, and to posit a certain reversibility of cultural authority in the process. At the same time, we need to explore how this obsessive return to oedipal narratives and images for processing a cultural history produces a powerful – even structuring – equation in Tarantino's work between African-American masculinity and popular culture.

Butch circulates through episodic structures that are governed by another figure who also emerges under the sign of the father and of the law. This is Marsellus Wallace, the 'big man', the boss that Jules and Vince keep referring to in the preceding sequence. While Marsellus is absent from all but the opening scene of this segment, he is clearly constructed as the ultimate authority in Jules and Vince's work-world, as well as the central narrative organizing principle, to the extent that he holds all the plot lines together. Operating as the intersection of plots, Marsellus himself is the link that connects the divergent episodes and initially unrelated characters. Having established him as the unseen law of this world, the film introduces his physical presence at the beginning of 'Vince Vega and Marsellus Wallace's Wife', in a sequence that we will later understand to be a snippet of the 'Gold Watch' segment.

At first Marsellus is only a voice instructing Butch Coolidge. When he does appear, we see only the back of his head, dilated to fill most of the frame. In place of a face, we see the blank screen of his shaved head, a surface interrupted only by the risible mark of a bandaid, of that pinkish beige color that white people often once called 'flesh'. This puny and familiar little object, placed as it is in the middle of the back of Marsellus's skull, operates as a blemish, a mark that highlights this character's skin tone in a world that is white-bound at the level of the most banal everyday object. This scene, which turns on Marsellus's transaction with Butch, paying him to lose a boxing match, also establishes his relationship to Vince and Jules. Upon noticing Vince at the bar, Marsellus greets him jauntily as 'my nigger'. Where Jules, the avenging angel, is the character who first employs this term, and thus associates its use with his own moral/spiritual authority, Marsellus is the character with the lexical authority to displace its reference, making it apply to Vince, a white guy.

However, to understand the many functions of Marsellus as authority or law, we must first read him as a disembodied figure who is most powerful in his absence – as, for instance, a voice on the phone. Though he is initially invisible, since Marsellus is soon transformed into a spectacular body, we must explore the resources and effects of this embodiment. It does not seem accidental that the two white 'hillbillies' in the gun shop-surplus store choose Marsellus as their rape victim. It seems all the less accidental as the film establishes these characters as racist through their recitation of 'eeny-meeny miney moe, catch a nigger by the toe'. Intentionally or not, this moment establishes the non-accidental character of the very chance that is invoked here. And, as we will see, part of the reason this is not an accident is that *Pulp Fiction* depends ambiguously and ambivalently on the very racism it wishes to establish as its own outside, or its 'elsewhere'. Consequently, it is worth considering how the film's apparently critical edge of suggested anti-racism, which is built as much out of interviews with its author as out of its diegetic handling of racial material, is implicated with the racist discourse it seeks to dislodge or hold up for our examination.

The smugly superior distance the film provides on these 'hillbilly' characters – for itself and for us – may be more than slightly akin to the concept of 'white guilt' and its social functioning that Judith Butler describes in *Bodies that matter*.

> For the question ... is whether white guilt is itself the satisfaction of racist passion, whether the reliving of racism that white guilt constantly performs is not itself the very satisfaction of racism that white guilt ostensibly abhors ... for white guilt ... *requires* racism to sustain its sanctimonious posturing. ... Rooted in the desire to be exempted from white racism, to produce oneself as the exemption, this strategy virtually requires that the white community remain mired in racism; hatred is merely transferred outward, and thereby preserved, but it is not overcome.
>
> (1993: 227, note 14)

The emphasis in *Pulp Fiction* clearly lies more on the side of the will to exemption than on the posture of guilt, but the two seem deeply interrelated. The substitution of an acrimonious, ironic, and aggressive posture for a sanctimonious one hardly slips the social knot that ties together guilt and a desire to exempt oneself from racism.

In their effort to humiliate Marsellus before they rape him, these characters reduce the 'big man' by calling him 'boy'. And this may be the point at which the embedded symbolics of the film's most anxious and horrifying moment of suspense emerge, because the reduction of man to boy in the context of this anal aggression returns us to the problem of fathers and sons, and to the oedipal–pre-oedipal tonality with which the whole film, like Tarantino's work in general, is tinged. As spectators, we are implicated in this scene's construction as a primal scene; we are required to wait anxiously, staring at the closed green door while we hear groans of bodily strain that could easily be confused with sexual sounds. We might find in this position a certain analogy with a curious child outside his or her parents' bedroom, or waiting outside the bathroom door. Straining to see beyond the wall, but fearing the moment of disclosure, we find ourselves in a position which might put us in mind of the film's opening sequence, where, at a certain point, the screen goes black, and we anxiously await the return of the image. When it does, we are looking up at Vince and Jules, and we retroactively locate the camera in the trunk of the car. This is the position that Marvin's body will soon occupy, once Vince has accidentally blown his head off. So *Pulp Fiction*'s spectator position might resemble that of the victim abducted and thrown in the gangster's trunk.

At the same time, the rape scene emphatically replays the familiar Tarantino effect: it catches us laughing inappropriately. While Marsellus is concealed in the closed room, Butch manages to get free. In a visible, but unaccountable, 'change of heart' that is a familiar move for Tarantino's characters, he goes to seek a weapon with which to rescue Marsellus. Our enjoyment of Butch's slow, deliberate choice of weapon, ending up with the least appropriate, the samurai sword, is abruptly interrupted by the revelation of the rape in progress behind the door. So we get caught laughing at an anal rape; we are caught, figuratively, at the very moment when Marsellus is caught with his pants down literally.

The violence and aggression that attend this literalization produce an affective force that is somewhat hard to localize, and this may be because of the reversibility suggested by our own position as spectators – caught off guard and rendered vulnerable. In the sadomasochistic economy that drives the film's most gleefully violent sequences, the spectator seems subject to a constant oscillation between the position of subject and object of violence, an oscillation in which we are at constant risk of being caught out. It is as if the film were addressing an audience whose visual and aural appetite for knowledge – curiosity – were the unmistakable counterpart of that anal aggressivity.

Another indication that *Pulp Fiction*'s fantasies are steadfastly infantile is that in its universe everything is reversible. As soon as he is freed, Marsellus retaliates by shooting his rapist, Zed, in the crotch, and by threatening him with distinctly racialized violence: 'I'll get a couple of hard pipe fitting niggers to go to work on Mr. Rapist here with a blowtorch and pliers'. If the film had any ambition to sanitize the anal rape of its racial overcodings, this moment certainly reinstates the racialized edge to this homo-erotophobic attack.

On the other hand, I think the image of this anal rape becomes only fully legible if we set it in the context of the obsessional patterns that emerge around the bathroom, and around violence not only in relation to race, but to sexuality, paternity, and culture in Tarantino's films. In *Pulp Fiction*'s elaborate performances, race is coded as culture, through its figuration as pure linguistic expression. 'Race' becomes a kind of switch point here, lying at the center of a knot that condenses oedipal rivalry with homo-erotophobic attraction–repulsion, an attraction and repulsion that is also aligned with anxieties and desires about feminization. In this vortex of reversible infantile fantasies of anal aggression, raping the father reverts to being raped by him. At the same time, however, 'race' becomes a transformative term, placed at the border where identification rubs against murderous hostility.

This is because the obsessive rehearsal of oedipal structures – and of the pre-oedipal ones that underlie and break through them – intersects with ambivalent racial meanings with suspicious frequency, as it does in the figure of Marsellus Wallace. Such intersections produce negotiations that often flip-flop between idealization and abjection, two processes that may operate in a dialectical interplay around the father and extend to other figures as well. But is Daddy black or white? We might be moved to ask about the fantasmatic father's race and its impact on the oedipal dramas the film is playing out its their collisions of cultural artifacts. *Pulp Fiction* seems to channel an ambivalent mix of desire and hostility through recourse to adolescent, 'boyish', bathroom humor. And both desire and hostility seem to be directed at fathers, in attacks staged to win the approval of women and black men. Notably, in many instances, the father figures are represented as popular culture icons in films that depend centrally on a structure that repeatedly effects a displacement and substitution of authority between an idealized absent black male peer – represented by a figure such as Marsellus Wallace – and the white father, frequently associated with the popular culture industry, as either its star, or its abject or residue, such as Travolta and Walken.

The over-the-top hilarity and adolescent glee at merging racial slur with sexual insult between the two smirking characters here combine the pleasure of transgressive hate speech in the safe container of highly staged artifice – performance – with the pleasure of having Daddy for an audience. Part of the power of the scene's effect is its ambiguity about what its primary point is. That ambiguity is bound to the possible satisfactions and pleasures in hearing spoken elsewhere what remains censored and unavailable to speech. It depends, that is, on imagining that some of us – individually or collectively – must be working to censor such speech. It imagines, in other words, something like a cultural id that functions on an analogy with individual unconscious processes.

Tarantino's films seem to map social differences as competing cultures, where icons of African-American culture are constructed as an intervention, a critical challenge to Daddy's culture of the 1970s. Racial difference, figured as cultural capital or expressivity, operates fantasmatically to interrupt white paternal authority, as young white men watch their white father under the intervening gaze of an imaginary black male, either alternate father or rival brother.[1]

In *Pulp Fiction*, the father's watch – his gift, his excrement – is a source of obsessive fascination that reminds us of the gaze and surveillance as well; it is as if the watch, like the television, and popular culture in general, were an instrument of the reversible gaze. In this web of reversible infantile fantasies, authority and its gaze are linked to shit. But which father is watching? If the repetition of oedipalized couplings of men perhaps provides us some clue about the address of the masculine posturings that emerge as the central subjects of Tarantino's films, this may suggest that the point of address is as important as the performance itself.

To understand Marsellus Wallace's function as a paternal figure, saturated with racial meanings, we need to see this figure in relation to *Pulp Fiction*'s other black male authority: Jules. Jules the avenger, quoting redemptive verses from Ezekiel to his victims, is the only character who judges the universe these characters inhabit. Finding it insufficient, he retreats from it. Effectively, by exiting when he does, he puts an end to the potentially endless series of episodes that might unfold here. If Jules is the ultimate judge, and the would-be redeemer of Honey Bunny and Pumpkin, he is also the film's most consistent viewpoint and mouthpiece; he sees and analyzes everything. By contrast, we never see things from Marsellus's point of view directly. This effect helps to establish his perspective as omniscient and unsituated, as the patriarchal god who commands and judges, where Jules mediates and redeems. There is one exception to the Law of Marsellus's indirect point of view, however, one shot that seems anchored to and governed by his gaze. This is the moment when Jimmy's absent wife, Bonnie, is given to our sight, as Marsellus, talking on the phone with Jules about the 'situation', imagines her coming home to find the disarray. This shot, assigned to Marsellus's knowledge or fantasy, establishes Bonnie as a black woman.

If Marsellus Wallace may figure the law of the film, his authority is superseded by that of the black woman, Jimmy's wife, whose image, after all, he supplies for us. Whereas the other women in *Pulp Fiction* appear as narrative agents only to the extent that they produce accidents for the men to handle – Fabian's forgetting Butch's watch, for instance, or Mia's heroin overdose – the woman is the whole point of the Bonnie situation. The segment is conditioned by and addressed to her absence. When Jules and Vince retreat to Jimmy's suburban house to clean their car and to dispose of Marvin's body, the situation goes into comic overdrive as Marsellus calls in a specialist, Mr Wolf, to mobilize the bumbling group in a desperate cleaning binge. As this segment devotes itself entirely to the men's anxiety about a woman's anger, it is shaped by a parodic address to Mommy.

This very address shows the father to be deficient. The figure of the black woman interrupts his authority, since even Marsellus fears Bonnie. Of course, this is part of the segment's comic effect: all these violent, aggressive males, including the most hypermasculinized, Marsellus, are intimidated by the absent, unseen nurse – the phallic Mommy. And we know this because the fantasy of Bonnie's return to catch the boys in the act is visualized from Marsellus's point of view. Hence, the black father is completed and complemented by an address to an absent black woman. And the phallic overtones assigned to racial inflection are the most significant symptoms of the specific racial fetishism that conditions Tarantino's filmic universe.

We've seen this before: the men's behavior in the Bonnie situation echoes the fumbling band of boy fans who fetishize blaxploitation heroine Pam Grier in *Reservoir Dogs*. These guys may remind us that *Pulp Fiction*'s male group at Jimmy's house is like a bunch of fans. And perhaps the fans in the films, and the fans imagined to be in the audience, are a group of guys that it's fun to hang out with, but that you would not want Mom to see? Perhaps this is why the Bonnie situation is so compellingly essential to the narrative intricacies of *Pulp Fiction*, because it discloses a central motivation for the film's excesses, playing with what you wouldn't want Mom to see or hear: shit, genitals, and obscene language. Such a reading is consistent with the status of feminine authority in the Bonnie situation. This status, in turn, is consistent with the film's gendered universe, where all challenges to authority are marked as oedipally addressed: to Mommy or Daddy.

But there is another aspect to this authority as well. Tarantino's character expresses his rage and anxiety in a characteristic riff where dialogue comes close to pure performance. He rants on and on: 'What do you think this is? Dead nigger storage?' This explosive eruption, coming from the white actor, and repeated four times, is clearly meant to shock. In the context of this episode and the absent authority who presides over it, the film aims to place racist epithet at the same level as obscenities. Everything proceeds as if, by figuring Jimmy's wife as African-American, the film could insulate the director's own image from the racist edge of his discourse. Bonnie functions, then, as his alibi; she is supposed to exempt him from cultural rules, from ordinary whiteness. This alibi function is consistent with many popular cultural representations of interracial relationships, where each partner's racial identity is imagined to be interrupted, realigned, and exempted from its own category by virtue of the other partner's difference.

Given the way the film sets her up as the ultimate judge of the men's housekeeping operation, Bonnie both authorizes this moment of verbal smearing and spewing, and symbolically cleans it up, or sanitizes it. Thus, this moment emerges as contained by the female authority to whom it is addressed. Equally important, the condensation of aggression, abjection, and authority here constitutes the implosion of the oedipal narrative into the pre-oedipal figure it both addresses and wards off, the phallic mother. A central address to absent feminine authority might explain some of the pleasures of Tarantino's films for the young males who largely constitute his fan audience. But it may also account for an appeal to certain female spectators as well. Tarantino's films are nothing if not symptomatic. If the absence of women in *Reservoir Dogs*, for example, or in 'The Bonnie Situation' does not put off female spectators, it may be because

Tarantino's films display a masculinity whose worst enemy is itself. Or, it may be because the film interpellates women spectators into the reassuring posture of judge, adjudicator, or evaluator. In this case, self-deconstructing adolescent white masculinity is on parade before the discerning, and perhaps satisfied, feminine gaze, a gaze that can take its distance from a transgressive eruption designed precisely to provoke her.

In this particular structural sense, it is worth considering that the viewing pleasures that Tarantino's films mobilize resemble pornographic ones. That is, they may draw on some of the same energies that are at play for the presumed masculine addressees of certain versions of heterosexual pornography, and, specifically, on the structure of the fourth look. Paul Willemen describes this fourth look and its effects as follows. The possibility of the 'overlooking-look' that haunts our exercise of the scopic drive, he argues:

> gains in force when the viewer is looking at something she or he is not supposed to look at, either according to an internalized censorship (superego) or an external, legal one (as in clandestine viewings) or, as in most cases, according to both censorships combined.
>
> (1992: 174)

The fourth look, then, articulates internal psychic processes with a social dimension. Interestingly, for Willemen, there is reason to speculate that the fourth look is most often imagined as a feminine spectator overlooking the male viewer. It may be specifically in relation to the possibility of a feminine fourth look catching the viewer unawares that his pleasure emerges.

In the viewing structures Tarantino's films offer us, the pleasures of transgressive viewing are secured in the framework that mobilizes a judging gaze, which both threatens the spectator with exposure and also guarantees a certain containment. The figure of the woman overlooking the scene, like Bonnie, for instance, represents the social and its censoring demands, while she also serves as a reproachful addressee. Consequently, within the pleasurable structures of reversibility that allow the viewer to be both subject and object of the look, she might be imagined to be the origin as well as the addressee of the fantasies, and specifically the fantasy of the phallic woman who can manage all the men.

At the same time, the film inscribes an address to two audiences, the one performing for the other. If the fourth look is assigned to women and African-Americans, mostly males, the specular aggressive posturing and display that animates the gang in *Reservoir Dogs*, much as it does the group in the Bonnie situation, seems designed to capture the fascinated and transgressive identifications of white male fans. Tarantino's films imagine a fandom for 'boys' that would recognize itself through an identification with a bad boy fan auteur. The films and the fandom, however, depend upon a reinscription of sexual and racial difference to mark the border that sets this band apart. [We remember that Tarantino's films appear under the logo 'band apart' films, in a reference to Godard's *Bande à part* (*Band of Outsiders*) (1964).]

Outsiders become insiders in view of a virtual gaze overlooking their specular posturing for each other, and overhearing the stream of insults and obscenities with which they amuse themselves. We might ask how this circuit of specularities and identifications is linked to *Pulp Fiction*'s drive to lift the word 'nigger' out of its web of social meanings, and how its ruse that this is a simple lifting of repression, like any other, can only fail. One reason for this failure is, of course, that the pleasurable charges the film means to mobilize as the word erupts from its characters are structurally associated with obscenity and anal aggression.

Within the rather resolute oedipality of these structures, Bonnie figures as the ultimate condensation of gendered and racialized authority, an authority that seems to preside over the circulation of racial epithets as a form of transgressiveness that is exactly equivalent to obscenity. But this is a false analogy, and we need to inquire why obscenity and aggression continually accumulate at the borders of racial difference. This overcharged friction around racial difference seems to blend abjecting and idealizing impulses, just as it mingles fetishism – in the fantasy that blackness is phallic – with projective identifications. Part of what Bonnie authorizes, I want to suggest, is white male posturing in imitation of *images* of black men. Of course, Jimmy's 'dead nigger storage' riff is a paradigmatic example of this posturing.

Tarantino's universe seems to depend intimately on just such an iconic construction of African-American masculinity. This is the universe in which *Pulp Fiction* posits that the term 'nigger' can be neutralized through a generalized circulation in which it designates anyone at all, of whatever race. Race plays similarly in *Reservoir Dogs*. One of the more hilarious moments in that film involves a problem of color and naming. As Joe Cabot prepares his men for 'the job', he assigns them aliases: Brown, Blonde, Blue, Orange, Pink, and White. Pink's name is the subject of much joking and of dissatisfaction to its bearer: 'pink, faggot, pussy'. One character demands to know why they cannot pick their own names. 'It doesn't work out', Cabot replies. 'Put four guys in a room and let them pick their own colors, everybody wants to be Mr Black.' 'Black' is the coolest name, and, for these characters, the only other 'cool-sounding' name is 'white'. It is this boyish association of 'blackness' with 'cool' that forms the context in which we may examine the circulation of the word 'nigger' among the interlocutors who inhabit *Pulp Fiction*.

Through white men's identifications with them, black men become icons, gestural repertoires, and cultural artifacts, as the threads of cross-racial identification wind around a white body that remains stable. Perhaps more important, these fantasmatic identifications maintain an aggressive edge: the white subject wants to be in the other's place, without leaving its own. These are identifications that still operate through a gaze that is imagined to remain stable before the volatile image it wants to imitate. What results is a re-inscription of black masculinity as an image, a cultural icon, seen through white eyes. And this why neither Bonnie nor Marsellus Wallace really has a point of view.

In a commentary for the *Chicago Tribune*, Todd Boyd examines and contests the use of the word 'nigger' in *Pulp Fiction*. For Boyd, in our current cultural context, 'the recurrent use of the N-word has the ability to signify the ultimate level of hipness for white males who have historically used their perception of black masculinity as the embodiment of cool' (1994: 2C). This use of the word, Boyd contends, allows for persistent reference to 'one's own whiteness without fear of compromise'. In effect, Tarantino's films seem to re-territorialize and re-stabilize whiteness. In the process, however, they offer up explicit anxieties about race for critical scrutiny. Such anxieties clearly emerge in the fascination invested in a masculinity that expresses itself as racialized *and* as constituted by the exclusions it continually memorializes.[2] But, in the context of ongoing cultural work that remakes 'race' both for and against racism, we need to entertain the possibility that *Pulp Fiction* might re-secure racialized representations for a racist imaginary, even as it tries to work them loose from it.

Pulp Fiction parades an identificatory delirium, where white men posture as 'talking black', and thus confuse speaking as and speaking with their objects of identification. Like its author, the film seems to believe there is a certain inoculating effect to code mixing and repetition.[3] What the film forgets to remember is that social force of words cannot be privatized, that it cannot cite the word 'nigger' outside a context formed by its enunciative conditions, which include the author's social location, as well as the word's history. Indeed, the word functions to highlight the ways the very racism the film discourse wants to abject instead forms the border against which it takes shape. Equally important, this dream of sanitation ignores the force of the unconscious speaking through us. But what if, in a spectacular misfire, that word becomes the signifier that organizes all the others, much the way Marsellus Wallace's body seems to organize all the other bodies? What if the word itself remembers history? It then remembers *for* the film, and it acts like the film's unconscious.

Given the public enthusiasm with which the author persona connects his 'will to cool' with his desire to imitate his own cultural fantasy of black males, Todd Boyd's analysis of the uses of 'the N-word' seems all the more compelling. As he indicates, this word also circulates frequently through a wide variety of African-American authored popular culture. This circulation may be precisely what allows Tarantino to appropriate the term as an artifact from the culture with which his films seem to entertain a playful and admiring rivalry. Tarantino's use of the word has as much to do with the wish to mark himself as a cultural 'outsider' with the privilege of an 'insider' within the 'outsider' culture he fetishizes. And the word stands as the mark of precisely that fetishization.

The steadfastly oedipal nature of the author's relations to popular culture – so that he can pick the term up as found object and combine it with an address to the fantasmatic black male rival through display and impersonation – may be what allows him to go on insisting on the politically progressive possibilities in his 'sanitizing' project. Similarly, his recourse to blaxploitation images, for instance, operates as a false social anchor, a mere referencing in a universe where all artifacts have equal weight. For the world of Tarantino's films is a world without history – a world where all culture is simultaneous, where movies only really watch other movies. *Pulp Fiction* is relentless in its refusal to inhabit any specific historical moment; its very collision of styles and signs undermines any effort to stabilize it historically. A variety of details recall recent decades in a dense jumble – from the twist scene and the club in which it takes place as iconic of the 1960s, to Bruce Willis's '1950s' face', to Samuel L. Jackson's incoherent hair – combining 1970s' sideburns with 1980s' jheri curls.[4]

Tarantino's characters, like his films, live in no community, none but the public space that is built into television, radio, and videotapes – a community of popular culture users and cult viewers. As Timothy Corrigan has described cult films:

these movies by definition offer themselves for endless reappropriation: their worn out tropes become the vehicles not for original connotations but for the viewer's potentially constant re-generation of connotations, through which the audience reads and re-reads itself rather than the film.

(1991: 90)

In a world of equal 'users', like Tarantino's, we are allowed to imagine that the meanings of a word in popular circulation can be interrupted and reshaped by a set of individual speech events. Similarly, the films which seek to disalign body from speech, names, and race forget their own dependence on the bodies of actors – familiar and often iconic faces and gestures – recycled and reprocessed. The same cinematic moves that figure history as cultural nostalgia, as generational trash to be collected and recombined, produce a fantasy that 'race' could be susceptible to private manipulations, as videos are to private screenings.

Pulp Fiction knows that no one 'owns' race, or culture, either individually or collectively. But it does not quite own up to the differences in the ways that we, as specific social subjects, remain dispossessed of the very processes of racialization that nevertheless circumscribe our cultural locations. And that is why all its efforts to render 'race' as performance, much as they symptomatically highlight the instability of 'race' as a category, and much as they challenge any imaginary coherence between appearance and identity, cannot escape capture in a circuit of cultural meanings that strive to restabilize race. More important, *Pulp Fiction* depends on the fantasy that the category of white men is meaning-free in order to cast it as the blank screen upon which racial meanings may be written – and voluntarily at that. Even in a filmic world which seeks to disarticulate meaning from appearance, white men figure as not meaning anything by themselves or to themselves or to anyone else. And what a privilege this is.

In Tarantino's privatized public sphere, memory and history become entirely contemporary in the user's use. It is as if these films offered history as the screen for one's own fantasies. What kind of identification does one make with this screen? In the end, the obsession to organize history oedipally upholds the powerful and curious equation that structures Tarantino's filmic universe: the equation of African-American masculinity and popular culture. So we need to ask why his films map the sphere of popular culture as thoroughly oedipalized. Their insistently oedipal account of cultural production and exchange displaces or erases social conflicts in favor of the drama of fathers and sons.

Pulp Fiction dreams of offering a screen beyond history, since history is figured in the textures of recycled and replayed popular music, television and movies, sound and image tracks we all share, and whose continual contemporariness functions as the mark of a nostalgia untethered from a historical moment. How should we take its aggressive figuration of a cultural legacy and history as refuse, a refuse whose emblem is surely the father's gold watch stashed in his rectum? It is precisely an oedipal imaginary that seems to govern this work's relation to the popular culture debris it gathers and redistributes. If popular culture artifacts are stepchildren to be adopted, Tarantino as auteur presents himself as a stepson, claiming fathers such as Oliver Stone, or Jean-Luc Godard, and seeking to be affectionately adopted by his male fans.

So, Tarantino's films seem to posit that we might read history by sifting through the father's waste. But then they do not go on to read what they find there. If they posit, likewise, that history is what catches you with your pants down, they do not examine the social context in which such an event takes on meanings. Still, their symptomatic edge extends in several directions. For better, and for worse, these are white-authored films that understand masculinity as racialized, and that understand their own context as multicultural. These may be the first films of their genre to play so explicitly and self-consciously on a multicultural field.

We may not like *Pulp Fiction*, or we may not *want* to like it. But, then, films are rarely about what we say we want, or what we consciously want. Instead, they tend to produce what works on us by appealing to our pleasure, our anger, fear, or anxiety, or by appealing to what we do not want to own. And this is why it is worth exploring the stunning asymmetry of the equation that seems to underlie Tarantino's aggressive identifications with the icons of African-American masculinity that he presents as exact equivalents of Elvis, for example, or 1970s music. Such an equation emerges at a moment when the dominant white culture might begin to take seriously the ongoing historical conversations with African-American cultural production that have always been centrally structuring to its very fabric.[5] Tarantino's ahistorical reading of these conversations is deeply fetishistic. But other readings, respecting history, might ask what US culture would look like without this conversation, saturated with struggle though it has been. Critically analyzing and contesting the work that acknowledges this conversation may be our best means of owning up to the ways in which we do not own culture.

Endnotes

1   For a study that may help to set Tarantino's borrowings of 'style' in a long history of white appropriations of African-American cultural forms, see Carole Clover's brilliant essay, 'Dancin' in the rain' (*Critical Inquiry* 1995, 21: 4). Clover contends that *Singin' in the Rain*'s symptomatic moments of unacknowleged borrowing from African-American dance styles may be characterized as: '"memories" in the framework of "forgetting"' (1995: 737).

2   Amy Taubin has analyzed the fascination with rap culture that emerges in *Reservoir Dogs* and has theorized what underlies it, specifically in connection to Tarantino's violence.

> If the unconscious of the film is locked in competition with rap culture, it's also desperate to preserve screen violence as a white male privilege. It's the privilege of white male culture to destroy itself, rather than to be destroyed by the other.
>
> (1992: 5)

3   On the relationship of self-consciousness to African-American vernacular styles and their consequent susceptibility to a variety of appropriations, see Kobena Mercer (1994).

4   See 'Pulp Instincts', for Tarantino's take on this: 'Bruce has the look of a 50s actor. I can't think of any other star that has that look. he reminds me of Aldo Ray in Jacques Tourneur's *Nightfall*' (1994b: 10). Meanwhile, Jackson shed his jheri curl wig for the film's publicity still, increasing its effects of incoherence.

5   Paul Gilroy makes a sustained and detailed argument about the centrality of the African or black diaspora to Western culture, most particularly in the USA and England, in *The black Atlantic: modernity and double consciousness* (1993).

References

Boyd, Todd 1994: Tarantino's mantra, *Chicago Tribune*, 6 November, p. 2C.

Butler, Judith 1993: *Bodies that matter: on the discursive limits of 'sex'*. New York and London: Routledge, 277.

Corrigan, Timothy 1991: *A cinema without walls*. New Brunswick, NJ: Rutgers University Press.

Gilroy, Paul 1993: *The black Atlantic: modernity and double consciousness*. Cambridge, MA: Harvard University Press.

Kennedy, Lisa 1994: Natural born filmmaker. *Village Voice* (25 October) 32.

Mercer, Kobena 1994: *Welcome to the jungle*. New York and London: Routledge.

Naremore, James 1990: Authorship and the cultural politics of film criticism. *Film Quarterly*, 20.

Tarantino, Quentin 1994a: Blood lust snicker snicker in wide screen. Dennis Hopper interviews Quentin Tarantino. *Grand Street* **49** (Summer).

Tarantino, Quentin 1994b: Pulp instincts. Interview. *Sight and Sound* (May) 10.

Taubin, Amy 1992: The men's room. *Sight and Sound* **2** (December): 8.

Willemen, Paul 1992: Letter to John. *The sexual subject*. London and New York: Routledge.

PART 4

The return to history

Editors' introduction

The history of the art, technology and business of film has always been necessary to any understanding of the medium. However, in the 1970s and early 1980s – the period of the academic legitimization of film studies in the USA and Britain – film history became what Tom Gunning has called the 'poor relation' of film studies. At this time the major 'advances' in the field were seen to be in theory, especially the semiotic study of film language, the psycho-analytic study of the cinematic imaginary, the Althusserian study of film ideology. Amid such heady theorizing the historical 'poor relation' seemed hopelessly naïve and passé, devoted to a quixotic recovery of objective historical facts. In the past decade, however, history has seemed to have its revenge on theory. The energy of the field has shifted to what might be called theoretically informed historical inquiries. Theory itself has been historicized. If film theories are, as Bill Nichols claims in his contribution to this volume, simply historically situated conceptual frameworks for thinking about the meaning of the medium, and if these frameworks are themselves inextricable from the historical forces of twentieth-century modernity and post-modernity, then it becomes self-evident that all history is written from within some conceptual framework. Similarly, all conceptual frameworks work within the parameters of some history. Today the most relevant theorists and historians are those who recognize the degree to which history and theory work closely with one another. Indeed, as we shall see in many of the chapters in this section, it is often difficult to tell where the theorist leaves off and the historian begins.

Vivian Sobchack's chapter, 'What is film history?, or, the riddle of the sphinxes', sets the stage for the new film history's theoretically informed historicizing of its objectives. No longer a simple matter of 'excavating' original documents and material traces and causes of an objectively existing past, film history has taken on a self-reflexive awareness of its own discursive processes of writing and mediation. Taking the excavation of the buried 'City of the Pharoah' set from Cecil B. DeMille's *The Ten Commandments* as a telling allegory of the shifting ground of the traditional historical enterprise, Sobchack herself excavates the new complexities of writing a history of our media past that now includes the 'fabricated and second-order "fantasy histories" of dreamers such as DeMille and Disney' (page 309). Her allegory deftly encapsulates the extent to which film history has always been about the excavation of 'fantasy lands' and the extent to which film historians' new awareness of the transformative nature of mediation and representation has given this excavation its own second-order dimension of fantasy production. As we shall see, all of the chapters in this section are in something like the position of the film-maker–archeologist Sobchack describes attempting to excavate DeMille's buried set: while excavating a past whose objective reality is forever shifting, they are at the same time utterly serious about the need to continue to dig.

Cinema is one of the few art forms whose development is recent enough to be apprehended within relatively recent memory. James Agee, who writes movingly of growing up with silent film has grandiosely compared witnessing the invention of narrative cinema in the films of D.W. Griffith to being present at the invention of the wheel. Cinema historians have understandably been drawn to the drama of such moments of 'origin'. Even if these dramas soon give way to more sophisticated genealogies, the excitement of capturing something like the beginning of a new art, an art that is also a quintessentially modern technology, is unmistakable among historians of early cinema. We can see this excitement in the second chapter in this section, Tom Gunning's account of the development of cinema in '"Animated pictures": tales of cinema's forgotten future'. For even as Gunning demonstrates that precise moments of origin are impossible to chronicle, his enthusiasm for a past when cinema's future was not yet known becomes a way of understanding our own end-of-century where the future of moving images is equally unknown. While Gunning sketches a similarity between the state of crisis and flux that the incipient cinema encountered in the late nineteenth century with the crisis and flux of the end of the twentieth century, he demonstrates that it may be precisely this uncertainty about the future of any particular point of 'invention' that is the source of our enthusiasm. Certainly the 'multiple scenarios' of cinematic invention that Gunning traces through uncanny and insubstantial fantasmagoria of magic lantern shows, on the one hand, and instantaneous photography, on the other, do not point to any unitary object. They point rather to the uneasy coexistence of rival claims of scientific demonstration and visual wonder that persists in the present day.

Just as Gunning's theoretically informed historiography of cinema's beginnings places in doubt what exactly was invented with the invention of cinema, so Miriam Hansen's investigation of the mass-produced industrial nature of this popular entertainment form rethinks what has been designated under the umbrella term of 'classical cinema'. In particular, Hansen is concerned to chart the relation of the conventional notion of the 'classical' text to modernity and modernism. Pointing out that the term 'classical cinema' has been used variously by critics and historians to designate a timeless ideal of classic perfection derived from neoclassicism and a quite different tradition of nineteenth-century realism, Hansen observes that neither of the meanings that accrue to the term fully address the hegemonic mechanisms by which Hollywood became the 'first global vernacular' mediating cultural discourses on modernity and modernization. The classical appeal of Hollywood, in other words, has not been very carefully calibrated with the mass-produced appeal to the senses. Aiming to restore historical specificity to a style and mode of production that has gained worldwide hegemony, Hansen does not abandon the term 'classical' but modifies it with the notion of a modernism that most successfully globalized a particular historical experience.

While Miriam Hansen explores the vernacular modernism of the 'classical' cinema, Linda Williams uses a case study of Alfred Hitchcock's *Psycho* (1960) to probe another vernacular appeal to the senses, in this case claiming it as exemplary of a new postmodern cinema. By exploring the critical place of *Psycho* within a high modernist tradition of film studies that asserted the importance of the film in terms of its ability to castigate and punish viewers identified with its fiction, and thus within a classical tradition that asserted the film's importance in terms of its ability to absorb subversive moments, Williams argues that both the high modernist and the low classical appropriations of the film have missed the sensory appeal of a roller-coaster ride seeming to careen wildly out of control. The sensory appeal of this ride constituted the unique fun of the film's first release. This newly destabilized, out-of-control fun is characteristic of the shocks that the postmodern 'cinema of attractions' now delivers to its viewers. At the same time, however, Williams argues that the flip side of these destabilizing 'wild rides' was the historical institution of a new discipline at the heart of going to the movies: the requirement, uniquely policed in *Psycho*'s opening run, but soon institutionalized throughout the American cinema, that audiences arrive on time for performances.

Although Gunning, Hansen and Williams's chapters may on the surface appear to fall into a neat periodization of the pre-classical cinema of attractions, a classical cinema of Hollywood hegemony and a post-classical cinema of destabilized shock, the real interest of these chapters may be the way each challenges the conventional way of thinking about their respective periods. Ultimately, all three writers share a concern with the sensory appeal and visceral pleasures that underlie the entire history of cinema. By questioning the meaning of some of the fundamental conceptual frameworks with which cinematic history has been written, they advance history even as they advance theory.

16 What is film history?, or, the Riddle of the Sphinxes

Vivian Sobchack

> The world and all its beauty come to us secondhand – a twice-told tale, as it were, a double-storied mystery.
>
> (David Harlan, 1997: xx)

> Something fundamentally unsettling happens when history begins to write its own history.
>
> (Pierre Nora, 1989)

What is film history? At the end of the twentieth century and in the pervasive context of mass-mediated and high-technology culture, the responses to this question are much more complex than they once were. Some 50 years or so ago, the general response would have been that film history, as both practice and product, is the excavation, accumulation, and dissemination of knowledge about the cinema's progressive temporal evolution as an art form, an industry, a technology, and a cultural artifact. Hardly anyone would have noticed – let alone argued with – the choice and connotations of such words as 'progressive' (with its linear and teleological implications of advancement as improvement) or 'evolution' (with its unthreatening implications of change in time as a gradual, continuous, and homogeneous process). Nor was it likely that anyone would have immediately interrogated the discrete categories or hierarchical order into which the cinema and film history were usually divided: that is, aesthetic history kept relatively distinct from (and untainted by) economic or technological history, or cinema as an art form privileged above movies as a cultural artifact.

Today, however, the question of film history is much more vexed than it was mid-century when the infant discipline of film studies was first attempting to legitimate both itself as an academic enterprise and the cinema as an aesthetic (and secondarily historical) form worthy of serious scholarly attention. Indeed, until the late 1970s and early 1980s, film history seemed sure of what its 'proper' object was, where its focus should be, what events and people were important enough to be deemed fit as historical subjects. Up until this time, as Thomas Elsaesser suggests, most film scholars (whether writing surveys or more focused investigations) wrote 'accounts which told the history of the cinema as the story of fearless pioneers, of "firsts", of adventure and discovery, of great masters and masterpieces' (1990: 3). Although it was certainly acknowledged that there could be, indeed must be, multiple histories of the cinema because no one historian could do it all, this multiplicity was regarded as cumulative: despite the individual historian's necessarily selective focus and particular 'objective' interpretation of historical facts, collectively film historians would come up with the 'whole story', would complement each other's work to fill in vexing 'gaps' in historical knowledge, and together would create a relatively continuous, coherent, and unified explanatory narrative that was both comprehensive and comprehensible. The primary task of the film historian was to uncover previously unknown historical facts and to interpret and represent them as objectively as possible so as to add to the cumulative storehouse of film historical knowledge.

Today, however, our interests in the field (let alone our circumscription of it) have complicated our notions of both 'film' and 'history'. In the first instance, influenced by the transformations of cinema brought about by television, video cassette recorders (VCRs), and computers, the definition of 'film' as an object of study has not only broadened considerably but has also been increasingly destabilized as an object and form. In the second instance, influenced by feminism, cultural studies, and a variety of 'post' theories (particularly postmodernism and post-colonialism), the definition of 'history' has also undergone a significant broadening and destabilization of its objects and forms. Indeed, both the idea of history as an 'objective science' and the totalizing coherence of 'grand narratives' have been criticized and deconstructed – as has the discipline's primary focus on political and military events and the individual power and achievements of 'great' – and 'white' – men.

Today, both as practitioners and as writers, historians in all fields (including film and media studies) question not only whether historical objectivity is possible but also whether it is desirable. Grand, coherent, and evolutionary narratives have given way to local and micro histories – and the gaps and ruptures in our knowledge of the past are foregrounded rather than smoothed over. The privileging of political and military history also has given way to heightened interest in social and cultural history and in the past practices of 'everyday' life. Thus, focus has shifted from the much-noted deeds of elite and prominent white men to the less-documented actions and accomplishments of those previously marginalized in historical inquiry. Even more significantly, as historians have become increasingly self-conscious of history's always-constructed and representational nature and its always-motivated and selective focus, history has lost its stability as the grounded site upon which knowledge of the past is accumulated, coherently ordered, and legitimated; rather, it has become an unstable site in which fragments of past representations do not necessarily 'add up' or cohere but, instead, are subject to 'undisciplined' (and often 'undisciplining') contestation and use.

Ungrounding terra firma

All this is to say that in the past 50 years or so, both as participating members of an increasingly mass-mediated culture and as film scholars, we have become increasingly aware of the highly invested and hardly objective nature of representation of *any* kind – and of historical representation in particular. That is, now that we are fully conscious of our pervasively 'mediated' relation not only to the past but also to our own supposedly 'immediate' present, we are hermeneutically suspicious of any representation's 'warranting' of events and experience as 'real' and/or 'true' – and especially suspicious of that particular form of warranting privileged as 'historical' representation.

Indeed, the practice and writing of film history are bound irreducibly to our current consciousness of 'history' and its representation in general – and that consciousness has been complicated by our own historically-altered sense of what 'being-in-time' in relation to 'the past' feels like and what it means in a culture of pervasive mass-mediation and 'present' second-hand experience. Thus questions of what the object of film history is or should be, what form such history takes, and for whom and to what purpose it is constructed are not merely local questions related to a specific film historical project but also entail larger philosophical and theoretical questions that riddle the discipline – and 'disciplining' – of history as a whole. These questions imply others, themselves always solved and re-solved not for all time, but historically, institutionally, locally, contingently: What is worthy of being considered an 'historical event'? What is an 'historical fact'? What constitutes 'historical evidence'? What does it mean to 'narrate' and 'emplot' past events through the arrangement and tone of their telling? Is history an objective science able to make 'truth claims' about the past or is it a mode of invested, ideological, and moral 'fabulation', a 'realist fiction' privileged for its re-presentation of a past that is constructed through particular conventions of temporal logic and verisimilitude comprehensible to those in its historical present?

Certainly, with regard to its status as both representation and narrative, history has always been explicitly, and from the very first, understood as a 'twice-told tale' (Harlan, 1997: 10): that is, as a mode of representation, a research activity, and eventually an academic discipline whose particular goals and problems emerge from the fact that it is self-consciously removed in time from the very events it seeks to reconstruct, understand, and relate to the present. However, despite this initial understanding of history as always and inherently 'twice-told', it is only relatively recently that history has become explicitly, and at the very least, a 'thrice-told tale' – that is, removed yet further from a sense of the 'actual' past as its 'original' and 'grounding' object of study by a novel awareness of the mediating and transformative nature of representation itself. Up until fairly recently, as philosopher of history Pierre Nora writes:

> The historian's ... role and place in society were once simple and clearly defined: to be the spokesman of the past and the herald of the future. In this capacity his person counted less than his services; his role was that of an erudite transparency, a vehicle of transmission, a bridge stretched as lightly as possible between the raw materiality of the document and its inscription in memory – ultimately, an absence obsessed with objectivity.
>
> (1989: 18)

Now, however, historians are aware that they are hardly 'an erudite transparency' or an 'absence'. Not only do they understand their own presence and responsibility as mediators between the 'raw materiality' of past documents and their temporal reclamation by the present, but also they have come to a novel 'hyper-realization' that the very 'raw', 'primary', and 'grounding' materials upon which they based their 'objective' historical accounts are nothing more (or less) than themselves mediating and suspect representations. That is, 'original' documents and 'authentic' material traces of past events are now widely recognized as never given to us by the past or taken up by us in the present as 'raw' – and, consequently, their previous overvaluation as the 'authentic' evidence and 'primary sources' that provided historians privileged access to the 'truth' or 'real' meaning of past events is diminished by our contemporary awareness that no matter how historically 'old', no re-presentation of the past is ever original.

At the present moment, then, the once merely 'twice-told tales' called history are now understood as 'thrice-told' – that is, further and exponentially elaborated through the mass-mediated proliferation of any number of representational forms and foci, through a multitude of contestatory narratives, and through a variety of present desires and ideological investments. Thus, the historian's once relatively transparent object – 'real' past events – and the historian's once relatively secure and clear goal – an objective 'reconstruction' of the chronology, motivations and causes, consequences, and meanings of these events – now seem murky and opaque, obscured (and, yes, quite literally 'crazed') by complex networks and palimpsestic overlays of historically subjective narrations that command our attention and (for some traditionalists) 'get in the way' of coherent and 'objective' historical reconstruction. In this sense, the initial object of history – 'real' past events – and the historian's initial goal – the 'reconstruction' of their 'original' causes and meanings – are themselves so mediated that both are fundamentally 'unsettled' and, at best, are seen through a glass darkly.

This contemporary hyper-realization of the extent to which history is estranged from its 'original' object has partially displaced history's initial focus on 'real' past events and their remains in 'raw' evidence to a focus on the relationship between past and present re-presentations. Historical consciousness thus becomes also *historiographical* consciousness (consciousness of the process of writing and representing history). And with this shift in focus to representation, 'history begins writing its own history' (Nora, 1989: 10). That is, history focuses as much attention on understanding its own desires, criteria, and representational structures for achieving historical coherence and meaning as it does on reconstructing a coherent and meaningful past. Furthermore, history sees its 'truth value' relative to an 'actual' past as less compelling, persuasive, and achievable than its 'use value' as an explicit exploration of its own subjective purposes and practices and its narrative as a 'double-storied mystery'. This recognition of additional 'layers' of mediation and estrangement from history's 'original' – and always lost – object and this heightened sense of reflexivity about history's own historical desires and practices have led to the recent emergence of what Nora describes as a 'new type of historian'. This is a historian 'who, unlike his precursors, is ready to confess the intimate relation he maintains to his subject. Better still, he is ready to proclaim it, deepen it, make of it not the obstacle but the means to his understanding' (1989: 18).

Thus, historical coherence and grand narratives are now riddled not only by holes, gaps, and omissions in our historical *knowledge* that once we might have tried to cover over or fill in, but they are also riddled by the questions and investments of past and present *desire*. And the 'new type of historian' described above now regards both the original object of history and the objectivity of history as always already in *ruins*. That is, the field, or site, of history is now seen as unstable and shifting, and its material and temporal excavations are understood as yielding only fragments, traces, and potsherds – and these not of 'the past' but of its earlier representations. And like the ruin, history has become open and unfixed and available for different kinds of dreams than that of objectivity. Thus it is no accident that, constructed as it is from scattered and scarce fragments of past representations and the explicit force of present feminist desire, the title of one of the major works of this new type of film history, written by Guiliana Bruno, is *Streetwalking on a ruined map* (1993).

The significance and consequences of this contemporary and novel 'ruination' of history have been most eloquently summed up by Iain Chambers:

> Now that the old house of criticism, historiography and intellectual certitude is in ruins, we all find ourselves on the road. Faced with a loss of roots, and the subsequent weakening of the grammar of 'authenticity', we move into a vaster landscape. Our sense of belonging, our language and the myths we carry in us remain, but no longer as 'origins' or signs of 'authenticity' capable of guaranteeing the sense of our lives. They now linger on as traces, voices, memories, and murmurs that are mixed with other histories, episodes, encounters.
>
> (1994: 18–19)

Its house now in ruins, history is opened up as a 'site of discourse where multifarious identities, memories, nostalgias, stories, and experiences, reside' (Gabriel, 1993: 218). And opened up in this way, although in ruins, history is hardly 'over' – nor are we, in fact, over it. History's ruination has reinvigorated both its practice and its writing: indeed, it has never been so much a popular (as well as academic) object of desire as it is now. As one critic aptly remarks: 'History has seen, at one and the same time, its truth-value crumble and its approval ratings soar' (Shatz, 1998: 25).

An archaeology: history in ruins

Which brings us (at last!) to the 'double-storied mystery' and 'thrice-told tale' that is contemporary film history – and quite literally to the riddle of the sphinxes in my title, cryptically posed not to Oedipus but to us by a 'real' film historical ruin of an ersatz Egyptian city buried since the early 1920s beneath the sand dunes on a stretch of California coastline. At this site, the material and temporal excavation of film history stands not only as an *actual* archeological enterprise but also as an *allegorical* one. That is, the dig is simultaneously both a literal example and a symbol of the destabilized grounds of contemporary historical theory and practice – for here in the sand it is impossible to stand on solid historical ground, to uncover historical artifacts that are 'authentic', to hit the bedrock of historical 'origins'. Indeed, from the initial creation of this archeological site in 1923 to its partial excavation in the present day, we are quite literally confronted with 'twice-told tales', with 'history writing history', with a 'site of discourse where multifarious identities, memories, nostalgias, stories, and experiences reside'. Here, in the Guadalupe Dunes, is a *mise en abîme* of historical and historiographic representation whose 'double-storied mystery' cannot be solved by traditional historical logic. Under literally shifting ground, the 'concrete' historical 'facts' to be found in this historical ruin challenge and mock the enterprise of the traditional historian: not only are they fragmentary, highly fragile, and susceptible to crumbling into dust, but also – and from the beginning – these 'concrete' historical 'facts' were, in fact, themselves 'reconstructions'. That is, most were not concrete but plaster-of-paris.

Consider, then, the following newspaper item:

> Guadalupe, Calif. – an ancient Egyptian eye, unblinking in the sandy wind, stared up at Peter Brosnan. And Peter Brosnan, a bearded Angelino with $10,000, a borrowed ground-penetrating radar system and a crazy dream, stared back. 'Take a look at this guy', said Brosnan. 'That's the Pharaoh.'
>
> And that's why Brosnan, 38, a screenwriter, teacher and documentary filmmaker, started digging in the dunes near this Santa Barbara County city of 5,500 in 1983. This is where Cecil B. DeMille filmed the silent movie version of 'The Ten Commandments' in 1923, and where DeMille buried and abandoned one of the largest sets in feature film history – the City of the Pharaoh, with walls that rose 110 feet and sprawled 750 feet in width, its entrance flanked by 21 sphinxes and four 35-foot Pharaoh statues.
>
> (Reynolds, 1990: F1)

Embedded in this story – and the site – is, of course, a much more elaborated narrative history. Indeed, if we consider 'just the facts, ma'am' (however plaster-of-paris most of them may be) as if we could really objectively, empirically, and through a linear chronology 'get to the bottom' of this site, then there is much more that we 'know' about the history of Brosnan's film historical enterprise and its object: their respective 'origins' and sources, their progress and frustrations.

To begin, DeMille's 'lost' City of the Pharaoh (also referred to as the City of Rameses) was only 'generally' and 'materially' lost since not only has one been able to see it both in the film which is still available for viewing and in production stills, but also DeMille had written about the site in his autobiography; Brosnan, however, was the one who found and eventually mapped its exact location. [For photos and maps, see the web pages 'DeMille's "Lost City"' (1999) and 'Hollywood fantasy/archaeology reality' (1999) detailed at the end of this chapter.] Designed by Paul Iribe and constructed for the biblical prologue of what was in 1923 the most expensive film ever made in Hollywood (it cost US$1.4 million), the lavish set evoked not only Egypto-fantasies of the biblical past (particularly the Exodus), but it also captured the more contemporary Egypto-imagination of a mass public entranced by the discovery and excavation of the tomb of King Tutankhamun only a year before in November 1922. The entrance to the walled Egyptian city was the set's primary and most massive structure and it was guarded on both sides by 21 supine plaster sphinxes. Against its walls were four 35-foot seated plaster statues of Rameses, each weighing 27 tons, and two rampant lions flanked each statue's throne. Along the expanse of wall was also a bas-relief pair of monumental horse-drawn chariots. And 'in the distance, to the left of the massive gate, a pyramid pierced the sky of a limitless, arid landscape' (Higashi, 1994: 184). Although accounts of the amount of materials used for the set's construction vary, film historian Sumiko Higashi describes both the preproduction publicity and the fact sheet in *The Ten Commandments*'s souvenir program as indicating that the massive entrance to the City of Rameses 'required 300 tons of plaster, 55,000 board feet of lumber, 25,000 pounds of nails, and 75 miles of cable and wiring' (1994: 182).

Building the city and filming in and around it for the film's biblical prologue required the expenditure of enormous resources. DeMille describes some of these in his autobiography (1959: 252–3), and Higashi, using *Motion Picture News* as a more elaborated source, tells us that motion picture exhibitors 'read about the installation of a twenty-four-square-mile tent city to house 2,500 inhabitants and 3,000 animals, including horses, camels, burros, poultry, and dogs, assembled for scenes of the exodus'. Furthermore, 'a complete utilities system providing water, electricity, and telephones had been built in addition to transportation facilities' (1994: 182). There was also initial trouble with transporting the sphinxes from Los Angeles to the Guadalupe Dunes by truck. DeMille writes:

> No one had thought to measure the clearances of the bridges along the route. There were some anxious moments when our majestic and mysterious sphinxes were ignominiously halted by a bridge too low for them to pass under. No one lost his head though, except the sphinxes, who were decapitated long enough to pass under the bridge and then had their heads restored for the remainder of their progress.
>
> (1959: 253)

Nonetheless, and despite this restoration, after filming was complete, the entire set was partially dismantled and then buried in the Guadalupe Dunes – supposedly because DeMille did not want anyone to use or copy it before his film was released.

If we now turn to Brosnan's more contemporary history with the site, we know that he first heard about DeMille's 'lost city' from a film school friend. Traveling to the Guadalupe Dunes in 1983, his first 'find' was a plaster horse's head – and it was then he resolved not only to map and excavate the buried set but also to make a documentary of the process. This, of course, would require extensive fundraising. Furthermore, there were permission problems: the dunes were 'private property' and also constituted a delicate ecosystem whose disruption might harm local shore birds. Indeed, in 1988, the site passed into the management of The Nature Conservancy which endorsed efforts to save the set; and Hollywood Heritage, a Los Angeles preservation group, became its non-profit sponsor, acting as the umbrella organization handling donations and inquiries about the proposed excavation. (The hope – as yet unfulfilled – was that the wealthy Hollywood community would provide major funding.)

By 1990 (the date of the news item above), Brosnan was able to get a US$10 000 grant – donated by the Bank of America through Hollywood Heritage – to make an archaeological survey of the site. [Bank of America became involved because DeMille, 'a former bank employee and personal friend of bank founder A.P. Giannini', had been able to finish the troubled and over-budget production 'by persuading Giannini to make him a loan' (Reynolds, 1990: F2; see also DeMille, 1959: 258).] Brosnan and archaeologist Dr John Parker, with the aid of geophysics specialist Dr Lambert Dolphin, spent two weeks mapping and videotaping the site which 'covers the area of two football fields and contains historical cultural material to a depth of six feet' ['Out of the Sands' (1999) web page]. Ground-penetrating radar indicated 'several large objects beneath the sand just where the old sphinxes should be', and archaeologist Parker said 'several other findings match[ed] with old charts and suggest[ed] that while many objects have been dismantled or damaged, most features remain largely where they were in 1923' (Reynolds, 1990: F1). Indeed, initial mapping confirmed that two-thirds of the set material was still buried in the dunes. Among a few other artifacts, Pharaoh's head (at least his eye and head-dress) was also exposed – only to be reburied until funding was secured. Registered as site CA-SBA-2392H with the State of California, DeMille's 'lost city' became an official archaeological site (thus tampering with or removing artifacts from it without permission is a felony). Brosnan, however, still had no permits or funding to begin excavation and, as the newspaper article reports, although the Smithsonian was interested, 'no museum made any commitments to display anything' (Reynolds, 1990: F2).

Throughout the 1990s, Brosnan has struggled to raise money to excavate the site properly. There has been an almost completed detail surface mapping and, of course, additional filming. [A computer-generated contour map of the site can be seen at the 'Out of the Sands' (1999) web page.] Discovery of the location of buried lumber has also allowed theoretical reconstruction of the original alignment of the set walls. Although surface indications suggest the location of much buried material, there is no way for Brosnan to recover the fragile plaster items intact without funding to support specialized excavation techniques as well as purchase particular chemicals to harden the soft plaster and allow its removal. In 1993, for example, a lion's head and torso was discovered but had to be reburied until it could be safely removed and restored. That same year, the National Endowment for the Humanities turned down a grant request for the project, indicating that they felt funding should come from Hollywood.

The year 1998 marked the 75th anniversary of DeMille's 1923 *The Ten Commandments* and the film was shown with orchestral accompaniment at the second (or 'twice-told') 'grand opening' of Graumann's Egyptian Theatre in Los Angeles – newly restored to its 1922 inaugural Orientalist glory from years of decay and degradation (before it was closed for remodeling, its most recent use had been as a porn theater). Speaking at the grand opening, Charlton Heston (the star of DeMille's 1956 remake of *The Ten Commandments*) championed the archaeological project while some financial help from the American Cinémathèque enabled the display of a few of the site's surface artifacts. Brosnan apparently still needs US$175 000 to excavate the site although he has now secured the necessary permits and permissions from appropriate state agencies. He has also raised sufficient money over the years to film over 40 hours of interviews with DeMille's associates, including those who worked on the film (all now deceased) – with the stipulation that this material is eventually to be donated to the Arts and Communications Archives at Brigham Young University which houses DeMille's collected papers. In addition to excavating the site and completing his own film, Brosnan's goal is eventually to 'pack the choicest artifacts off to an American museum or use them as centerpieces for an educational center at the dunes site' (Reynolds, 1990: F2). However, given the crumbling truth-value of history and yet its soaring approval ratings, it is more likely that, once excavated, DeMille's City of Rameses may end up not as an 'educational center', but the center of a 'theme park' or 'heritage museum'.

A genealogy: the runes of history

What you have read thus far – related in a traditionally historical, chronologically linear, causally motivated, and relatively detailed fashion – is a 'twice-told tale' of the background and discovery of the 'lost' movie set of the City of Rameses. But this twice-toldness does not fully satisfy our curiosity or address the giddiness and fascination this particular historical site provokes. DeMille's lost movie set is both an example of a real archaeological and film historical 'artifact' and an example of archaeological and film historical 'artifice'. That is, it historically represents a fabricated version of yet another lost Egyptian city whose 'authenticity' and 'origins' are irrecoverable, unknowable, and hence historiographically 'fabulous'. Thus, the history to be found and written here is literally more than merely twice-told. Now in ruins, made of plaster-of-paris, and buried in the shifting California sands, this lost city provokes in us the desire not for fixed chronologies and causes, but rather for forms of historiographic reflexivity that match its own. It also calls us to wander, to follow its residue of 'multifarious identities, memories, nostalgias, stories and experience' across different times and spaces in what might be called a kind of *historical nomadism*. As Teshome Gabriel notes further of the ruin: 'Moving through time and space along a varying path, this form of discourse rejects fixed positions' (1993: 217). Indeed, even DeMille foresaw the historical and historiographic problem of time and space travel that his lost city might present to the future – albeit as a gentle joke. He writes of the site in his autobiography: 'If, a thousand years from now, archaeologists happen to dig beneath the sands of Guadalupe, I hope they will not rush into print with the amazing news that Egyptian civilization, far from being confined to the valley of the Nile, extended all the way to the Pacific coast of North America' (1959: 253).

In sum, all the previous historical 'facts' – plaster-of-paris or concrete – do not help us to understand the deep (dare I say 'buried'?) historical meanings of the 'double-storied mystery' of the ruins resting silently beneath the Guadalupe Dunes. At this moment in historical time and practice, there is something unsatisfying and flat about the previous chronological and linear narrative about 'origins' and teleological 'progress'. Indeed, this narrative seems much more historically interesting and meaningful as an allegory for the present than as an 'objective' retelling of the past. As Nora writes most eloquently: 'It is no longer genesis that we seek but instead the decipherment of what we are in the light what we are no longer' (1989: 18). Decipherment and loss are the operative words here. Faced with fragments not of some 'authentic' past but of what we now accept as an always already represented and irrecoverable past, we need new hermeneutic strategies with which to fabricate – and confabulate – the stories and meanings of historical ruins and the ruination of history. (In this context, and amidst the ruins of history, it is worth noting the psychological definition of 'confabulation' as precisely the invention of imaginary experiences to fill gaps in our memory – here, our collective memory.)

In this sense, the historical fragments of DeMille's representation of an unknowable lost city stand also as what might be called (and I do not pun lightly) historical 'runes' – that is, as cryptic signs of secret or hidden lore carved in wood or stone (in this case, plaster-of-paris) and believed to have magical power or significance. And, deciphered, their hidden and powerful message is a revelatory allegory and confabulation not about the past but about the historical reality of our mass-mediated present: namely, our increased estrangement from and desire to recuperate a history we know we never knew. Thus, as Nora suggests, 'the practice of history' (here, the excavation of a fabulous representation of a lost Egypto-biblical city made to be represented in an ersatz historical movie) becomes 'a repository for the secrets of the present' (1989: 18).

And what might those secrets of the present be? We can find them revealed in the *Los Angeles Times* article cited above (Reynolds, 1990). Meta-historian Hayden White has written: 'Every historical discourse contains within it a full-blown, if only implicit, philosophy of history' (1978: 127). In 1990 (when he was interviewed for the article), Jarell Jackman, then executive director of the Santa Barbara Trust for Historical Preservation, contemplated the significance of the DeMille movie site and enthusiastically commented: 'This is utterly unique, and it gives you a sense of time having passed – that movies are now a part of history. Some archeologist may be uncovering Disneyland 500 years from now' (Reynolds, 1990: F1). Given previous discussion, Jackman's remark seems uncanny: that is, it is at once familiar and strange. On the one hand, this professional historian is fully aware of the mischievously troublesome nature of this archeological historical site under which is buried both a 'fake' ancient Egyptian city and a 'real' old movie set and he clearly recognizes that the 'stuff' or 'evidence' of history now includes the explicitly fabricated and second-order 'fantasy histories' of dreamers such as DeMille and Disney. On the other hand, however, he also unreflectively embraces and seems transparently unaware of the novel complication of traditional concepts of 'history' and historiography generated by these 'extra layers' of historical 'stuff' that were themselves constructed as historical representations. Indeed, both historically aware and transparent, Jackman's remarks speak directly of the familiarity of our increased estrangement from and desire for the past. And, in this regard, the DeMille historical site is 'utterly unique' only insofar as it is a literal and blatant example of what is now the commonplace relationship that members of contemporary culture have to history as always already a thrice-told tale ready to be told yet again.

Thus, the secret of the present found in the buried ruins of DeMille's ersatz Egyptian city is a new philosophy of history. Indeed, for Jarell Jackman, for members of mass-mediated culture in general, and for the 'new type of historian' in particular, both the historical 'ground' and the 'grounding' of traditional film history now seem as shifting and unstable as the Guadalupe Dunes. Both the stuff of history and the stuff of moving images seem unstuck in time and space, intermingle, and effluvially layer themselves in our representations and our cultural and collective memory and historical consciousness. Yet *what* precisely it is that is being unstuck and re-presented is not at all clear. The blank stare (but perhaps raised eyebrow) of that early twentieth-century 'ancient Egyptian eye, unblinking in the sandy wind' challenges not only the 'crazy dream' of would-be documentarian/archeologist Peter Brosnan to complete his film, but also challenges the 'crazy dream' of a traditional empiricist film history whose temporal trajectory, causations, and meanings can be excavated, represented, and understood in terms of some linear, unidirectional, and progressive notion of 'original' events and chronological 'order' based upon the 'coherence', 'consistency', and 'reliability' of an accumulation of 'authentic' trace 'evidence' left by the past.

Today, the 'crazy dream' of such a redeemable (and redemptive) order of history – and history of order – raises not only Pharaoh's eyebrow, but also our own. Indeed, in the face not only of DeMille's Pharaoh but also of what Nora sees as the 'disintegration of history-memory' in the culture at large, the increasingly reflexive doublings and exponential layering of historical representation (that is, history writing its own history, or filming it *ad infinitum*) have transformed our historical consciousness (for better and worse) into an 'artificial hyper-realization of the past' (1989: 18). The 'secrets of the present' to be deciphered from the historical runes found in the Guadalupe Dunes are those that make us confront this transformation and its paradoxical nature. This paradox is that, during the past quarter century in particular, the past and present have drawn ever closer together in our historical consciousness through the accelerations of mass-mediated representation and this makes the past seem temporally closer and more familiar to us; at the same time, however, the proliferation of mass-mediated representation has also led us to feel distanced and estranged from the past which we now know we cannot 'know' and whose image we both fetishize and mistrust as a substitution for the 'real' and irrecoverable thing.

That is, we live in a temporally accelerated and re-presentational culture in which the temporal distance between past and present that has hitherto constituted 'history' is now extraordinarily foreshortened. Partly a function of the accelerated pace of the temporal 'connectivity' enabled by mass media and high technology and partly a function of an ever-increasing accumulation of past and present images into a temporal palimpsest (and pastiche), there seems to be a great deal less 'time' between the present and past than there used to be. Indeed, we are now a culture that does not have the time or desire to contemplate the past from a distance; we want to immerse ourselves sensually in it, to enliven and live it (hence the extraordinary rise in heritage museums and historically re-creational and participatory activities such as weekend re-stagings of Civil War battles). Furthermore, in the culture of mass-media, we no longer can separate our present experience and the historical past by virtue of the former's 'natural immediacy' and the latter's 'mediated nature'; that is, our present is so rapidly re-presented and revalued as a spectacle for us to look at and comment upon that 'immediate' experience is less transparently experienced as 'immediate' and no longer distinctly different from mediated images and narratives of the past.

We can see this historically novel 'foreshortening' of present and past both in our heightened historical consciousness and in the temporal palimpsests of representation explicitly articulated all around us and very much a function of historically novel technologies – in the fact that people walk around now 'immediately recording' their 'direct experience' of present events with camcorders and an eye to getting 'historical' footage on the evening television news or, alternatively, they rush to the scene of an event they know is being filmed so that they can 'be in history'. We can also see this collapse of past and present in such a recently popular phenomenon as the History Channel ('the new channel for all ages') whose trade-marked catch phrase is 'All of history. All in one place'. (Other promotional material tells us: 'Don't miss your chance to be there when it happens again'.) And while the cover of a recent *TV Guide* announces ever so boldly, 'The past is now', it features a thoughtful reflection on televisual histories written for a mass audience by Neil Gabler which discusses the medium as redefining '*what* history is' and also '*how* history is presented' (1998: 21). History has even become a major subject for an unprecedented number of Broadway musicals including hits such as *Ragtime* (1997) and *Titanic* (1998), all of which hired historians as consultants and one of which – *The Civil War* (1999) – even featured a song whose lyrics, though thoroughly banal, were also historiographically conscious: 'When this war is over and we all have passed away/There'll be some damn fool in some damn school who'll write about today' (Vinciguerra, 1999: 36).

Indeed, not just historians but also a media-savvy public are highly reflexive about historical representation. A movie such as *Forrest Gump* (1994) – centered on our increasing technological and psychological capacity to collapse temporality and confabulate history through representation – could never have been so popular if we had not already learned its lessons: representation is now history and history is now representation. Thus many of us, although we live in 'the present', always already self-consciously tend to see our lives 'as history'. (Here the vernacular phrase 'You're history' resonates.) Which is to say that we live in a culture whose members (individually and collectively) not only reflexively regard themselves and present events as the proto-televisual (or cinematic) material of historical re-presentation, but also recognize that the historical past only presently exists through multiple layers of unrelenting mediation.

Consider, for example, the reflexive and historically conscious commentary on his own 'present' experience offered by Tim Foneris, unknown to 'history' until he caught the ball from Mark McGwire's 'historic' 62nd home run – and then gave it back to him (certainly, in our commodified culture in which the ball was possibly worth a cool million, a historic event in itself). Suddenly and explicitly a part of 'history', Foneris was invited to appear on a large number of television shows, went to Disneyland as a VIP, and met President Clinton at the White House (all filmed by the media). Featured (for the briefest of image and sound bites) on television's *Access Hollywood* (1998) and asked about this whirlwind experience, Foneris replied: 'I felt just like Forrest Gump superimposed over all these places. When I see the pictures, I'll believe it.' So much for our belief in the 'primary' evidence of 'direct' experience; now we need 'secondary' evidence – although, as indicated by Foneris's reference specifically to *Forrest Gump*, such 'evidence' is itself understood as a 'superimposition', a fabricated 'writing over' of an 'original' event that was, from the first, lost to direct experience and belief.

These are the 'secrets of the present' that reside in and are allegorized by an archaeology and genealogy of the 'real' ruined movie set buried in the Guadalupe Dunes. Itself fancifully 'reproduced' for and in an Egypto-biblical historical epic and providing the 'sand-bound legacy' that will be the historical stuff of yet another – this time 'documentary' – film, DeMille's historical representation of the City of the Pharaoh materializes quite literally the fact that 'something fundamentally unsettling happens when history begins to write its own history'. Indeed, the *Los Angeles Times*'s response to the DeMille site and Brosnan's entire project could stand also as a response to the riddle posed to us about film history by the 21 buried sphinxes: 'The imponderables remain nearly as imposing as the walled city once was' (Reynolds, 1990: F2).

A tropology: turning in time

Given these 'imponderables' and a historiography that has self-reflexively 'entered its epistemological age' (Nora, 1989: 18), what then characterizes the 'new type of historian' whom Nora contrasts to the traditional type of historian, that 'erudite transparency' who once set the modern standard for what constituted the objects and objectivity of 'legitimate' history? Certainly, as Nora suggests, this new historian is in readiness to confess and proclaim a subjective and 'intimate relation' to a given historical project. Certainly, and as a consequence of our heightened understanding of representation and mass mediation, this new historian knows that historical investigation does not just 'find' a historical object; it 'produces' it as historical. Thus, any material trace of the past (whether judged to be really 'old' or fairly recent, elite or popular, significant or trivial) can become a 'proper' historical object and, partially produced in the present, a much broader range of things can be said about – and through – it.

Certainly, the new type of historian understands history as something much more – and other – than merely chronological, causally linear, and teleologically progressive. Indeed, this mode of understanding finds no mutual exclusivity of present, future, and past and it engages in temporal investigations (and representations) that may productively 'go back and forth' in time 'like a shuttle' or branch out in all directions 'from one central core of meaning' like the spokes on a 'wheel'; that may double back on themselves in recursive and palimpsestic iterations or spread themselves out as a field; that may take turn upon turn, detours with no end in sight, or may move associatively in time 'along paradigmatic threads' or themes (Portelli, 1991: 65).

Certainly, also, the new type of historian recognizes history as inherently discursive, rhetorical, figural, tropological – 'turning' both on itself and its being in time and language, veering off in strange directions from the straight and narrow, constituting itself in narratives and allegories. It is thus no accident that the title of one of Hayden White's books which historicizes historiography is called *Tropics of discourse* (1978). And it is also worth noting that 'trope' has a philosophical definition as well as a rhetorical one: a 'trope' is a figural use of language but it is also an argument advanced by a skeptic. And, indeed, the new historian is a tropologist in both senses of the word: fully aware and productively suspicious that history is always being imaginatively 'figured' as it is seemingly 'figured out'.

Thus, contemporary history is practiced and written not in the certitude of concrete 'historical facts' but rather in the productive unreliability and partiality of lived and invested memories, murmurs, nostalgias, stories, myths, and dreams. Indeed, the new historian realizes that 'errors, inventions, and myths lead us through and beyond facts to their meanings', that the 'dubious reliability' of such 'wrong' tales enhances their historical value in that they 'allow us to recognize the interests of the tellers, and the dreams and desires beneath them' (Portelli, 1991: 2, 11). Acknowledging, then, both his or her own fascinations and interests in the present as well as the fascinations and interests of those in the past, acknowledging that history is always writing itself over and writing over itself, this new type of historian, as Nora puts it, 'is one who prevents history from becoming *merely* history' (1989: 18).

My previous – and relatively traditional – history of DeMille's buried movie set and Brosnan's desire to excavate and film it is at once both fascinating and '*merely* history'. If I similarly had the time and obsession of a DeMille or Brosnan, I might wander forever in the sand, turning literally and troping figurally among the site's historical fragments and heterogeneities, its murmurs, nostalgias, stories, myths, its other episodes and histories. For example, as new historian Antonia Lant has done in 'The curse of the pharaoh, or How cinema contracted Egyptomania' (1992), I might turn in the direction of Egypt and the discovery of King Tut's tomb in 1922 which 'influenced the exploitation strategy of *The Ten Commandments*' (Higashi, 1994: 180), the building of the Egyptian Theatre in Hollywood where the film premiered, and held sway over the US imagination and press for eight years. I also might veer off to write a tangential history of the site which points outward to other Egypto-orientalist fantasies of the period, not only in cinema, but also in painting, architecture, popular music, and museology (in this regard, DeMille was wrong: 'Egyptian civilization, far from being confined to the Valley of the Nile', did indeed extend 'all the way to the Pacific Coast of North America').

Were there world enough and time, I might also twist and turn along the historical path of re-creation to trace not only the re-making of *The Ten Commandments* in 1956, but also the 1998 re-creation of the Egyptian Theatre: the desires and investments that led to both, the myths that grew from them, the current obsession with historical 'preservation' and 'restoration'. I might also follow the scent of money and excess and quantification that hangs about the site – and epic films – as a commodity form (Sobchack, 1990). Or I might pause in singular contemplation of Pharaoh's head and the role of plaster-of-paris in Hollywood. In a more contemporary mode, I might spend hours on the Internet, moving out from the historical site to the web sites that commemorate it for they, too, are part of the site's history – and its historiography. Or I might focus in on the history of Brosnan's enterprise: its entailments with environmental agencies, public funding agencies, historical trusts, preservation societies, and its implications for a philosophy of history .

Once, the ruin of a 1922 movie set buried in the Guadalupe Dunes would not have been considered a 'proper' film historical object nor would it have spoken to us of the power of plaster-of-paris to cause cracks in the bedrock of history. Instead, it would have been considered too 'material', too 'recent', too 'trivial', or too 'kitschy' to warrant an excavation or a history. And, more significantly, historians would not have known what to do with it, what to make of it, how indeed to 'figure' it out. The site's 'uncanny' admixtures of temporality, its *mise en abîme* of representation, would have been as terrifying as the 21 'mongrel' sphinxes blurring the boundaries not only between 'human' and 'animal' but also between 'history' and 'fiction'.

Today, however, this Egypto-biblical 'lost' city exists beneath the sands and in our historical imagination as what Walter Benjamin called a 'dialectical image' – a 'montage' fragment of the past blasted out of its historical continuum, a heterogeneous historical object that contains within it temporal and cultural contradictions that cannot be resolved or synthesized. Indeed, this particular historical object in the Guadalupe Dunes concretizes quite literally the contradictory temporal elements that Benjamin saw as constituting an uncanny historicity able to shock us into historical awareness: it is simultaneously a 'fossil', a 'fetish', a 'wish image', and a 'ruin'. A fossil, this buried movie set is a 'trace' of a seeming 'natural history': the 'visible remains of the ur-phenomena' that is the Hollywood past. A fetish, this Egypto-biblical city is a piece of 'phantasmagoria': DeMille's orientalist fantasy (the period's fantasy) marks a 'mythic history', an 'arrested form of history' that presents 'the new as always the same'. A wish image, the grandeur and excess of the city stand as 'symbol' of a 'mythic nature': a dream form of Hollywood's vast potential and its longing for revolutionary effects and collective awakenings. And, as ruin, this 'lost' and dismantled city is an 'allegory' of an 'historical nature': appearing, that is, not only as the rubble of the past, but also as 'loosened building blocks (both semantic and material) out of which a new order can be constructed' (Buck-Morss, 1991: 211–12).

In sum, DeMille's 'lost' and Brosnan's 'found' City of Rameses buried in the sand along the California coastline is an historical site ripe for tropological excavation and for what Samuel Weber (1996) calls a 'deconstructive history'. Such a history – like the dialectical image itself – would resist 'the mutual exclusivity of what we call past, present and future', would refuse inserting its heterogeneous materials 'in a chain of causal explanation', and would instead rethink them in relation to representation, finitude, and 'the role of *repetition* in regard to a history no longer construed in terms of totalization or progress'. The representations and repetitions found in the Guadalupe Dunes are historically dizzying – and uncanny. Thus, as Weber recognizes:

> A deconstructive history would have to leave far more space for the uncanny than has hitherto been done . . . . It is entirely possible that what emerges from this kind of rethinking will no longer be 'historical' in the way that many have traditionally used that term. But if 'facts' and the 'empirical' are understood as being inseparably bound up with the heterogeneous, then a deconstructive history would involve the effort to *respond* to their appeal rather than trying – or pretending – not to listen.
>
> (1996: 217–18)

The empirical facts to be found in the Guadalupe Dunes are indeed heterogeneous: both plaster-of-paris and concrete. Responding to their uncanny appeal, we should look directly into Pharaoh's unblinking eye and listen to the sphinxes: what they murmur, remember, and narrate is not the question 'What is film history?' but its answer.

References

Access Hollywood. 1998: National Broadcasting Corporation. 10 September.

Bruno, Giuliana. 1993: Streetwalking on a ruined map: cultural theory and the city films of Elvira Notari. Princeton, NJ: Princeton University Press.

Buck-Morss, Susan. 1991: The dialectics of seeing: Walter Benjamin and the Arcades Project. Cambridge, MA: MIT Press.

Chambers, Iain. 1994: Migrancy, culture, identity. London: Routlege.

DeMille, Cecil B. 1959: The autobiography of Cecil B. DeMille, ed. Donald Hayne. Englewood Cliffs, NJ: Prentice-Hall.

Elsaesser, Thomas. 1990: Introduction. In Thomas Elsaesser with Adam Barker eds, Early cinema: space, frame, narrative, London: British Film Institute 1–8.

Gabler, Neil. 1998: History is prime time. TV Guide. 23–29 August: 18–21.

Gabriel, Teshome. 1993: Ruin and the other: towards a language of memory. In Hamid Naficy and Teshome H. Gabriel, eds, Otherness and the media: the ethnography of the imagined and imaged. New York: Harwood Academic Publishers, 211–19.

Harlan, David. 1997: The degradation of American history. Chicago, IL: University of Chicago Press.

Higashi, Sumiko. 1994: Cecil B. DeMille and American culture: the silent era. Berkeley, CA: University of California Press.

Lant, Antonia. 1992: The curse of the pharaoh, or How cinema contracted Egyptomania. October **59**: 86–112.

Nora, Pierre. 1989: Between memory and history: Les lieux de mémoire. Translated by Marc Roudebush. Representations **26**: 7–25.

Portelli, Alessandro. 1991: The death of Luigi Trastulli, and other stories: form and meaning in oral history. Albany, NY: State University of New York Press.

Reynolds, Christopher. 1990: An Archeology spectacular: unearthing the set of DeMille's 1923 'Ten Commandments'. The Los Angeles Times 20 November: F1–2.

Shatz, Adam. 1998: Being there. Lingua Franca (April): 25–6.

Sobchack, Vivian. 1990: 'Surge and splendor': a phenomenology of the cinematic historical epic. Representations **29**: 24–49.

Vinciguerra, Thomas. 1999: Getting it right dept. The New Yorker 10 May: 36–7.

Weber, Samuel. 1996: Mass mediauras: form, technics, media, ed. Alan Cholodenko. Stanford, CA: Stanford University Press.

White, Hayden. 1978: Tropics of discourse: essays in cultural criticism. Baltimore, MA: Johns Hopkins University Press.

Web pages

DeMille's 'Lost City'. 1999: On-line posting 31 May: http://www.lostcitydemille.com/

Hollywood fantasy/archaeology reality. 1999: On-line posting 31 May: http://www.tcsn.net/sloarchaeology/10com3.html

Out of the sands. 1999: On-line posting 31 May: http://www.tcsn.net/sloarchaeology/10com2.html

17 'Animated pictures': tales of cinema's forgotten future, after 100 years of films

Tom Gunning

A visit to the kingdom of shadows

> If you only knew how strange it is to be there.
> (Maxim Gorky, 1896)

In 1896 Maxim Gorky attended a showing of the latest novelty from France at the All Russia Nizhni-Novgorod Fair – motion pictures produced and exhibited by the Lumière brothers, Auguste and Louis. The films were shown at Charles Aumont's Theatre-concert Parisian, a recreation of a *café chantant* touring Russia, offering the delights of Parisian life.[1] A patron could enjoy the films in the company of any lady he chose from the 120 French chorus girls Aumont featured (and who reportedly offered less novel forms of entertainment to customers on the upper floors). Gorky remarked a strong discrepancy between the films shown and their 'debauched' surroundings, displaying family scenes and images of the 'clean toiling life' of workers in a place where 'vice alone is being encouraged and popularized'.[2] However, he predicted that the cinema would soon adapt to such surroundings and offer 'piquant scenes of the life of the Parisian demi-monde'.[3]

But it was not the place of exhibition alone that made Gorky uneasy about his first experience of motion pictures. The spectre-like monochrome and silent films themselves disturbed him, appearing like harbingers of an uncertain future: 'It is terrifying to see this gray movement of gray shadows, noiseless and silent. Mayn't this already be an intimation of life in the future? Say what you will – but this is a strain on the nerves.'[4]

The cinema made a strong impression on Gorky, but he did not display the reaction often assumed to be common for the first viewers of cinema – gaping astonishment at this new mastery of realism and technology. Instead Gorky experienced the first films as powerful in their uncanny and disturbing effect:

This mute gray life finally begins to disturb and depress you. It seems as though it carries a warning, fraught with a vague but sinister meaning that makes your heart grow faint. You are forgetting where you are. Strange imaginings invade your mind and your consciousness begins to wane and grow dim.[5]

A century later, this record of cinema's origins recalls a time when cinema possessed a future rather than a past. Cinema as a commercial industry has always been founded on novelty (one early film magnate even compared the industry to the ice business, selling goods whose value lessened every minute).[6] Consequently, its past has not only been neglected but systematically discarded and destroyed. We now possess only a fragment of our film culture, with less than 20 per cent of silent cinema existing. No art form has ever been placed so directly in harm's way, the result of a combination of material fragility (the celluloid film base itself, as well as emulsion and color dyes) and institutional indifference. But excavating the first years of cinema history uncovers not only a neglected past, but a forgotten future,[7] an often troubling vision of its potentials and perils. If there is a rationale for celebrating cinema's centennial, remembering the complexities of an earlier imagined future may supply one.

Celebrating 100 years of cinema, like any centennial, courts the danger of asserting continuities where they do not exist and charting linear narratives of progress that suppress detours and paths not taken. Centennials tend to construct homogenies and to legitimate dominant forces, providing reassurances which run counter to the dynamic potential of historical research to upset assumed genealogies and de-familiarize habitual practices and assumptions. But if centennials primarily express institutional delight over the tidiness of round numbers, they also carry within them a destabilizing force, a return to origins that are foreign because they have been – if not repressed – at least subject to amnesia.

Cinema at this present moment, the culmination of its first complete century, hardly stands in a position of institutional power or economic stability. Flux and uncertainty seem to threaten not only film's continued existence but its very definition. While the technological prophets of cinema's demise by the turn of the twentieth century seem to have been premature, there is no question that cinema now means something very different than it did even a generation ago. Is video a form entirely different from cinema, or simply a new means of distribution of what now might be best referred to generically as 'motion pictures'? Are the technological differences between film and video strong enough to determine an aesthetic disparity or do they simply represent alternate modes of exhibition? Certainly, a technological essentialist position seems harder to support today when so much of the film industry's profits come from the video market. However, an enormous transformation of movie watching has taken place – from a public theatrical event to an increasingly private act of domestic consumption. In the first half of the twentieth century film theory labored to endow cinema with a unique identity, to differentiate it from the older arts and provide it with a new aesthetics. At the beginning of cinema's second century we find this identity fraying, dispersed into a number of new image technologies. The last modern art form seems to be dissolving into a postmodern haze.

I will not exercise dubious gifts of prophecy by attempting to foresee cinema's second century. Instead I claim the historian's privilege of retrospection and point out that cinema's apparently chaotic present recalls in many respects its origins about a century ago. This *déjà vu* goes beyond recognizing the recurrence of historical cycles (whether tragical or farcical). Recalling cinema's origins at this point in time should open up a non-linear conception of film history within which a chaotic and protean identity holds utopian possibilities and uncanny premonitions. In place of a well-rounded century of film history, this approach to cinema's centennial aspires to Walter Benjamin's description of true historical thinking: 'to seize hold of a memory as it flashes up in a moment of danger'. To do this one must, as Benjamin demands, 'blast open the continuum of history'[8] and discover in the past the shards of a future discarded or disavowed.

This centennial marks not only the first century of film history, but also the first century of history captured by motion pictures. In a sense motion pictures literally embody Benjamin's description of the historical imperative, seizing hold of the flash of memory in a century of danger. But the danger inherent in modern life derives from cinema as well. The proliferation of moving images threatens, as in the myth of the invention of writing offered in Plato's *Phaedrus*, to destroy rather than preserve memory, substituting widely circulated institutional images for the most personal resources of imagistic recall. Images in their mass-produced form recall less those 'honeycombs of memory'[9] that Proust sought, than recycled discards of the all-too-familiar. It may well be that the warnings offered by the ghost-like flickering images Gorky watched in 1896, downstairs from a bordello, included this eclipse of authentic memory by a barrage of stock footage. The forgotten future of cinema that we seek must take seriously the unease Gorky experienced when first viewing film's spectral world, an unease partly due to the uncanny presence of realistic detail within an insubstantial fleeting imagery composed of shadow and light. Cinema has always pirouetted about the poles of providing a new standard of realist representation and (simultaneously) projecting a sense of unreality, a realm of impalpable phantoms.

Lanterna magica: images edged in light

> I pretend to be neither priest nor magician; I have no wish to deceive you; but I know how to astonish you.
>
> (Paul Philidor, inventor of the Fantasmagoria, 1793)

At its appearance, cinema was often referred to as 'animated pictures'. Cinema seemed to add the surplus of life-like movement to images previously experienced as static. While this animation supplied the innovation offered by the inventions of Edison, Lumière, Skladanowsky and others at the end of the nineteenth century, it also related cinema to a host of technologies of vision that had already gained popularity during the nineteenth century, all of which manipulated images to make them more intense and more exciting, whether by the addition of motion, color, three-dimensionality or intense illumination. The century-long pursuit of 'animated pictures' reveals cinema's imbrication within new experiences of technology, time and visual representation.

In other words, the identity of cinema which theorists took pains to define from the 1910s to the 1960s has its origin in a morass of modern modes of perception and new technologies which coalesced in the nineteenth century. To trace back cinema's origins leads not to a warranted pedigree but to the chaotic curiosity shop of early modern life. The genealogy of cinema (from the magic lanterns of the seventeenth century through the 'philosophical toys', experiments with vision and still photography of the nineteenth century) takes on a tidy appearance when these diverse threads are spun together teleologically to culminate in the invention of cinema. However, if we follow the thread backward into the labyrinth of the nineteenth century, it unravels into a disparate series of obsessions and fascinations. What has commonly been called the 'archaeology of the cinema' fragments into multiple scenarios.

Images projected by light are one trajectory in this ancestry of motion pictures. While projected images can be traced back to the shadow and light plays of antiquity, an actual historical filiation only appears with sixteenth-century experiments with optics and light. Ahistorical theories may find the source of cinema in the shadow play exhibited in Plato's cave, but the historical genesis of the light play of cinema derives from an intersection between a Renaissance preoccupation with the magical power of images (typified by Guilio Camillo's and Giordano Bruno's theaters of memory[10]) and a secular discovery of the processes of light and vision.

This extraordinary confluence of an ancient magical imagistic tradition and a nascent scientific enlightenment seesaws between a desire to produce thaumaturgic wonder and an equally novel interest in dissolving the superstitious mystification of charlatans via the demonstrations of science. Although the Enlightenment contributed a scientific purpose and method to these optical experiments, it is often difficult to separate a naïve sense of wonder from learned awe at the demonstration of the laws of nature. The magic lantern (as well as earlier optical devices which preoccupied scholars in the seventeenth century, such as the catoptric mirror and camera obscura) derives from the tradition of natural magic, an intersection between earlier occult traditions and the new spirit of the late Renaissance and dawning Enlightenment. For Giambatista della Porta, whose *Magiae naturalis sive de miraculis rerum naturalium* was published in Naples in 1589, the realm of natural magic included not only the magical powers of images, stones and plants and descriptions of the celestial influences which bathe our planet but also chemical and optical experiments. Among these, della Porta offered a plan for an optical theater using the camera obscura to create a shifting and varied visual entertainment whose magical effects were attributable entirely to the laws of optics.[11]

Optics became increasingly popular as a form of scientific entertainment during the seventeenth century. The Jesuit polymath Athaneus Kircher devoted a whole volume to the *Ars magna lucis et umbrae*, a work completed in 1644. Describing a variety of optical phenomena, natural and artificial, Kircher followed della Porta in envisioning spectacles created by a camera obscura or reflections from focused and inscribed catoptric mirrors. As Charles Musser has pointed out in his sketch of the history of 'screen entertainment' in his book *The emergence of cinema*, Kircher demanded that impresarios of such entertainment explain their scientific basis and demystify any appearance of sorcery or magic that might cling to them.[12] In the era of the Inquisition (which had burned Bruno at the stake for his devotion to imagistic magic), such advice indicates not only a growing scientific spirit but also a strong sense of self-preservation. By 1833 David Brewster (himself the inventor of two important visual devices – the kaleidoscope and the stereoscope) in his *Letters on natural magic* had abandoned any reference to celestial influence or magical images and explained optical illusions and the wonders of natural magic from a purely scientific viewpoint.[13]

But optical entertainments retained a powerful uncanny effect despite their rationally explainable processes of light and vision. This may explain why Christian Huygens, who invented the magic lantern (the first projection device using both an artificial light source and a lens, and therefore cinema's first direct ancestor) in 1659, chose not to display it publicly and even avoided association with it, preferring to be known for his astronomical discoveries via the telescope or his perfection of accurate clocks.[14] As Laurent Mannoni has shown in the most recent (and best) description of cinema's archaeology, *Le grand art de la lumière et de l'ombre*, the magic lantern spread across the globe as a device of entertainment and instruction. With a modest beginning at the end of the seventeenth century, it became a highly commercialized form of public and home entertainment by the nineteenth century. However, the great familiarity that followed the commercial expansion of this optical toy did not entirely overcome its uncanny associations. Pierre Petit, one of the lantern's first public exhibitors, called it, in fact, the '*lanterne du peur*'.[15]

The most elaborate visual entertainment using the magic lantern, the fantasmagoria of Philidor and Robertson, invoked the supernatural by projecting images of spirits of the dead in highly stage-managed eerie surroundings while simultaneously obeying Kircher's dictum on demystification.[16] Robertson (who offered his spectral entertainment in Paris at the end of the eighteenth century, nearly in the shadow of the guillotine) repeatedly stressed that his phantoms were merely applications of the laws of optics and perspective. He portrayed himself as one of the '*physicien-philosophes*' of the Enlightenment, dedicated to destroying the old enchanted world of superstition. Fantasmagoria productions of mysterious projected images appeared throughout the Western world during the first half of the nineteenth century. A show of projected spirits in Cincinnati, Ohio, in 1811, for instance, maintained the seemingly contradictory attractions of Robertson's spectacle, advertising itself as 'scientific, rational and astounding'.[17]

The ghost-raising spectacles of the fantasmagoria could only have appeared in the wake of the Enlightenment and subsequent secularization. Formerly sacred concepts, stripped of official sanction, could now serve as entertainment. But the residue of faith produced the uncanny shudder which these projected apparitions drew from spectators. The magic lantern of the fantasmagoria, with its powerfully illuminated images which seemed to move and float in mid-air, discovered the fissure between skepticism and belief as a new realm of fascination. These optical entertainments exemplify the state of suspended disbelief Octave Mannoni describes as 'I know very well, but nonetheless . . .'.[18] In a new realm of visual entertainment this psychic state might best be described as 'I know very well, and yet I see . . .'. The purveyors of magical illusions learned that attributing their tricks to explainable scientific processes did not make them any less astounding, because the visual illusion still loomed before the viewer, however demystified by rational knowledge that illusion might be.

Although any connection of the magic lantern with the supernatural had been officially repressed by the nineteenth century, it returned in the memory of adults recounting their childhood experiences of projections on bedroom walls or sheets hung in the family parlor. Marcel Proust found that his delight in the magic lantern slide shows projected in his bedroom and narrated by his great-aunt was undercut by the sudden uncanny unfamiliarity it introduced into the center of his domestic environment:

> it substituted for the opaqueness of my walls, an impalpable iridescence, supernatural
> phenomenon of many colors, in which legends were depicted as on a shifting transitory
> window. But my sorrows were only increased thereby, because this mere change of
> lighting was enough to destroy the familiar impression I had of my room, thanks to
> which, save for the torture of going to bed, it had become quite endurable. Now I no
> longer recognized it and felt uneasy in it.[19]

Harriet Martineau in her autobiography records a similar childhood reaction in which rational daytime knowledge was overthrown by the irrational power of the projected image:

> I used to see it [the magic lantern] cleaned by daylight, and to handle all its parts –
> understanding its whole structure; yet such was my terror of the white circle on the wall,
> and of the moving slides, that, to speak the plain truth, the first apparition always
> brought on bowel-complaint.[20]

Although polite, Martineau's Victorian terminology clearly expresses the plain truth that even a domesticated '*lanterne de peur*' scared the shit out of well-bred children. Such memories were not restricted to decadent aesthetes or Victorian neurasthenics. In 1897 the pioneering San Francisco woman journalist who wrote under the pseudonym Alice Rix (a tough cookie who had undertaken exposés of white slavery in Chinatown and reported on Sausalito pool rooms) concluded her review of the Veriscope, an early motion picture projector which exhibited films of prizefights, with her childhood memory of magic lantern shows:

> I am reminded suddenly of a long-forgotten childish terror of the Magic Lantern show.
> The drawing-room in darkness, the ghastly white plain [*sic*] stretching away into the
> unknown world of shadows. It was all very well to call it a linen sheet, to say it was
> stretched between innocent familiar folding doors, it nevertheless divided the known
> and safe from the mysterious beyond where awful shadows lived and moved with a
> fearful rapidity and made no sounds at all.
>   And they were always awful, no matter how grotesquely amusing the shape they took,
> and they followed me to the nursery in after hours and sat on my heart and soul the
> black night through. And sometimes even morning light could not drive them quite
> away. And now, forsooth, it seems they have withstood the years.[21]

Even a tough and modern 'new woman' at the dawn of the twentieth century retained this memory of the ontological instability of projected images and the terror they could inspire, a memory that surfaced on her first exposure to the modern motion pictures.

If the tradition of optics and projected images provides one branch of cinema's ancestors, another aspect displays even less coherence and includes a wide variety of devices which attempted to endow images with a surplus of lifelikeness, ranging from three-dimensionality to effects of transformation and movement. Many of these, such as Daguerre's diorama, wedded traditional perspectival arts to the control of light mastered in the magic lantern tradition. Daguerre's huge paintings on transparent materials were presented in darkened theaters and illuminated from behind, giving them an intensely virtual nature, as if the viewer were gazing into an actual landscape. Manipulation of the light behind the picture could give the effect of changing light and shade or even of complete transformation from daylight to night.

The famous story that a spellbound child observing one of Daguerre's dioramas declared that it 'was more beautiful than nature itself'[22] accents the contradictory aspect of these enhanced realist illusions, their 'more than real' effect. If the recreation were powerful enough it could surpass reality in intensity and animation. These images with their carefully devised effects were successively (or perhaps even simultaneously) experienced as mere images, as accurate simulacra of reality and as images more perfect or more pleasing than reality itself. While avoiding supernatural content, such enhanced images partook of the magical effect of the fantasmagoria, creating images so real they seemed to blur the distinction between model and copy, or even render the original source inferior to its imagistic realization. We encounter here again the spectral nature of cinema's sources, not only creating detailed realist images but also fashioning a world of images that threaten to replace the actual experiences they represent.

The image of an instant

> Horses in the air
> Feet on the ground
> Never seen
> This picture before.
> (Philip Glass, 'The photographer')[23]

The invention of photography (partly through Daguerre's next innovation, the daguerreotype) derives directly from other nineteenth-century optical devices which shared this obsession with enhanced images endowed with a surplus of realism. Nowhere is this better demonstrated than in the stereoscope, one of the most popular forms of nineteenth-century photography. The stereoscope was an optical device which gave specially made photographs (known as stereographs) an illusion of three-dimensionality. Creating an image with the appearance of relief and recession, the stereoscope caused its enthusiasts to claim it provided the perfect image of reality.[24] However, as Jonathan Crary has pointed out, the fascination of the stereoscope seems to outrun its realist claims, or to redefine them. The strangely layered three-dimensional image it offers strikes the viewer precisely as an illusion – something which exceeds common sense and perception. Again, the reality effect functions as a surplus, a magical addition to an image, rather than an integrated mode of representation. We see an image endowed with three-dimensionality through an optical illusion rooted in the physiology of human vision, an illusion which in fact frequently takes a moment or two to swim into focus before the viewer's eyes.[25]

However, the form of photography that led directly to the cinema differed greatly from the daguerreotypes or other forms of still photography possible for most of the nineteenth century. The long exposure time required for early photographs (an hour or longer for the first photographic images and several seconds through the 1860s) meant that photography for most of the nineteenth century lagged behind the accelerating pace of modern life. Charles Baudelaire praised the quickly sketching crayon of illustrators such as Constantin Guys for capturing the smack of the instant, but the ephemeral moment of modernity initially eluded the camera.[26] Film theorists (including André Bazin and Siegfried Kracauer) have often derived essential aspects of cinema's identity from its dependence on photography. But the major debt cinema owes to photography must be credited to a very specific practice that appeared only in the 1870s: instantaneous photography.

It is not clear that when Fox Talbot, Niepce and Daguerre conceived of photography in the first half of the nineteenth century they were concerned about capturing a brief instant of time.[27] Early photography seemed more suited to what Baudelaire (rather slightingly) called its 'secretary' function, capturing with unprecedented accuracy the forms of works of art (engravings and sculpture), recording the multitude of hieroglyphics on an ancient monument or even providing an inventory of a shelf of books.[28] Still photography was initially confined to still subjects. Rather than seizing an instant on the wing, photography was vaunted as a hedge against time, a souvenir preserving an accurate memory of those things – relatives, landscapes or works of art – which time would decay. While the goal of freezing a moment of time, of capturing a subject in full flight, became increasingly seductive after mid-century, it remained technically elusive. The motion studies Eadweard Muybridge began in 1873 did not anticipate the cinema simply because they consisted of a series of images recording the stages of a motion, like the succession of frames in a motion picture film. Even as single images Muybridge's photographs announced the unique ability of cinema, capturing the impression of an instant of time beyond the capacity of the human eye to retain it.[29]

If cinema derives from this diverse genealogy of optical fascinations which twine about the separate poles of optical entertainment and scientific demonstration, the actual invention of moving picture devices in the late nineteenth century by Marey, Demeny, Edison and Lumière rehearsed this *pas de deux* with compressed elegance. Once again the rival claims of scientific demonstration and visual wonder came together. This time, however, the contest no longer pitted a waning occultism against a dawning secular science. Instead, an empirical science, increasingly suspicious of visual evidence, confronted a popular culture reaching constantly expanding audiences through a mechanical reproduction of visual attractions.

The career of Étienne-Jules Marey, the man who can best claim the title of inventor of the cinema, re-enacted this conflict with instructive clarity (including dramas of personal betrayal). As Marta Braun demonstrates in her authoritative study of this French physiologist, the center of Marey's research lay in a search for precision machines sensitive enough to record the processes of the body which are too subtle for direct perceptual observation.[30] Marey's 'obsession with the trace' initially led to a series of mechanisms which could provide an objective record of bodily processes through time, whether the pulse of circulating blood or the rhythm of the muscles. These apparatuses replaced direct visual observation with precise graph-like diagrams of those processes the human body has always performed but which no one had previously recorded accurately.[31] Marey's curiosity extended to patterns of movement beyond the human, including the flight of birds and insects, the gait of horses and other animals and the currents of liquid and air.

At first Marey must have regarded photography with some suspicion. He made no use of the medium until new thresholds of film sensitivity transformed this clumsy visual simulacrum into a new form of observation – instantaneous photography. Photography's new receptivity and speed transformed its relation to human knowledge. Photography no longer was restricted to the role of secretary and *aide-mémoire* but could provide a glimpse of a new realm of temporality beyond direct human perception. Before the 1870s photography was basically limited to reproducing the already seen, the *déjà vu* of sights already available to the human eye. With the mastery of the instant, photography left human vision behind and opened up a world from which the naked eye had been excluded. The enormous controversy that greeted Muybridge's first publication of his instantaneous photographs of galloping horses heralded a new era in representation, a visual image simultaneously concretely recognizable and intellectually confounding. No one had seen what Muybridge showed and therefore no one could believe it. Visual wonder once again confounded common perceptual sense, but in this case no illusion was involved. Instead an unfamiliar accuracy loomed before the viewer.

A much more thoroughly trained and serious scientist than Muybridge, Marey already had obtained evidence of the patterns of a horse's strides from his pressure-sensitive motion recorders. Marey had preferred these non-imagistic devices because they avoided the fallibility of sensual representation with evidence presented in an abstract quasi-mathematical manner. But Muybridge's photographs presented an image that seemed to contradict human habits of seeing by means of a new scientific vision that Marey could countenance. Marey's own chronophotographic images strove to overcome the chaotically overspecific imagery of ordinary photography. Cloaking his photographic subjects in black tights and hoods, decorated with white strips outlining the basic limbs, Marey converted human beings into abstract stick figures. Even animals submitted to this passion for the essential over the anecdotal. Heroic chargers were spangled with dots marking key joints, converting galloping horse flesh into a series of points describing an arc of motion. To obtain these graph-like streaks of motion. Marey effaced photography's visual icons, privileging its new ability to retain the trace of the smallest increments of time.

The analysis of motion which Marey's chronophotography allowed could also be regathered into a synthesis, a recreation of motion providing proof of the accuracy of his process of recording. But for Marey the reproduction of motion was decidedly secondary. After all, such reproduction merely presented what the eye already saw – a walking man, the galloping horse – rather than the transformation of vision which the non-human sensitivity of instantaneous photography allowed. Edison and the Lumière brothers observed demonstrations of Muybridge's and Marey's breakdown of the visual continuum and decided to reverse the process. This photographic analysis could be adapted to a series of visual toys which had reproduced motion since the 1830s, including the phenakistiscope, the zootrope and Reynauld's praxinoscope. All these visual devices had taken advantage of discoveries in the physiology of vision (and especially in the possibility of tricking the eye into seeing something that did not exist, as in the stereoscope's illusion of depth) to produce illusions of motion. However, these devices had previously depended on drawings for their images, since photography had not been able to capture the stages of motion (unless artificially posed). If Marey saw instantaneous photography as a penetration into what Benjamin has called 'unconscious optics',[32] Edison and Lumière saw a new means for fooling the eye, astounding viewers with illusions produced by scientific means.

Marey recognized this difference between his work and that of purveyors of scientific entertainment. The popularity of the new inventions founded on his work which reproduced movement photographically did not surprise him, but their effects did not interest him greatly, because of their lack of scientific observation, 'however satisfying and astonishing that resurrection of movement may be'.[33] Motion pictures may fascinate audiences, but:

> What they show the eye can see directly. They add nothing to the power of our vision, they banish none of sight's illusions. Whereas the true character of a scientific method is to supplement the weakness of our senses and to correct our errors.[34]

The bitter split between Marey and his chief assistant Georges Demeny emerged partly from his protégé's desire to exploit chronophotography as a means of entertainment, a project which filled Marey with grave suspicion and even distaste. When Edison's kinetoscope appeared in Paris a few years later as the first widespread commercial utilization of motion picture photography, one journalist described the innovation it represented in terms of its deviation from Marey:

> M. Marey had only a scientific end in view, he applied himself to research in physiology or physics .... Examining his films in a zootrope is extremely instructive and interesting, but it isn't amusing. Mr. Edison, on the other hand, desires nothing but to give pleasure, science being not the end, but the means.[35]

Myths of total illusion

> It is precisely when it appears most truthful, most faithful and most in conformity to reality that the image is most diabolical.
>
> (Jean Baudrillard, 'The evil demon of images', 1987)[36]

Ultimately, however, the testimony of Gorky and others makes us wonder how familiar and ordinary the sight of projected motion pictures really was. If nineteenth-century viewers of the cinema were rarely the unsophisticated gawkers before a totally new invention some accounts of early cinema would like us to imagine, nonetheless the première of moving photographic images represented a new move in a long-existing game of fooling the senses and the uncanny pleasures it evoked. André Bazin, in his famous essay (in fact a review of the first volumes of Georges Sadoul's *Histoire générale du cinéma*), declared that the invention of cinema was simply a partial realization of a 'myth of total cinema' which appeared in various forms throughout the nineteenth century, 'a total and complete representation of reality … a perfect illusion of the outside world in sound, color and relief'.[37] In one sense, I have been surveying in this chapter precisely that tradition. However, for Bazin, writing in 1950s (a decade which saw a resurgence of realist illusions in the cinema, including three-dimensional films, Cinerama and Cinemascope), it seemed this myth was on the verge of completion, hence his reassuring and idealist understanding of cinema's relation to reality and illusion.[38]

Myths, as Bazin well knew, always express ambivalence. There is no question that cinema at the end of the nineteenth century appeared amidst a welter of hyper-realistic forms of representation, which included not only the devices of projection and photography I have discussed, but other forms of mass entertainment, such as the wax museum and the world expositions. What are we to make of this obsession with realism?

I believe it would be simplistic to treat such an obsession as naïve belief in the efficacy of representation. I have tried to demonstrate in this sketch of cinema's origins that the appearance of animated images, while frequently invoking accuracy and the methods of science, also provoked effects of astonishment and uncanny wonder. Innovations in realist representation did not necessarily anchor viewers in a stable and reassuring situation. Rather, this obsession with animation, with super-lifelike imagery, carries a profound ambivalence and even a sense of disorientation.

The discourse surrounding all these realist modes of visual attraction balanced claims of realism with proclamations of wonder, dazzling effects, reactions verging on disbelief. Audiences could not believe their eyes and were dazzled by these displays of alternative realities. Gorky's unease before motion pictures may be of a peculiarly sophisticated sort, but it expresses an ambivalent experience of animated pictures that was shared by many early viewers.[39] The more real such illusions were, the more their deficiencies were evident (the lack of sound or color, the disappearance of moving figures at the border of the screen). The more perfect the illusion, the more unreal and phantom-like such illusion seemed, reflecting back on the viewer's sense of her or his deluded perception as much as on the referent portrayed.

Could it be that the nineteenth century became obsessed with this task of an ever-progressive and always elusive total and complete illusion precisely from an anxiety about the loss of concrete experience? Edgar Allan Poe offered in his story 'The oval portrait' (written in 1842, three years after the first public discussions of the daguerreotype – and two years after Poe himself wrote several brief articles on this new invention)[40] a fable of the pursuit of realist representation that serves as a cautionary tale. In this brief story Poe first describes a painting whose 'life-likeliness of expression' first startled and 'finally confounded, subdued and appalled' a viewer, and then tells the tale of its creation. A young artist obsessed with his craft paints a portrait of his wife, shutting her up in a turret as he paints her, unaware of the debilitating effect this has on her. The portrait at length completed, the artist stands before it and proclaims, 'This is indeed Life itself.' He turns 'to regard his beloved – She was dead'.

From the perspective of the end of the first century of cinema, one might wonder whether ever-increasing powers of realist illusion are not counterbalanced by, and indeed a response to, a constantly increasing sense of a loss of a shared reality. I believe that it is only during periods of a temporary stability that the ambivalence of such representations can be forgotten. Perhaps fortuitously, the full cycle of the century brings us back to this sense of crisis in representation and medium. Cinema was devised as the medium that could not only deliver the most intense impression of animated pictures but also serve as a record of the most aleatory and instantaneous events. It should not surprise us that in both its form and history cinema reflects this mercurial and ambiguous mission.

A century ago cinema emerged from various strands of visual entertainments and new forms of intensified visual representation. Curiously, when film began to define its own aesthetic identity in the teens and twenties, the extreme variety of its origins most often was reduced to a differentiation from theater. Now, a century later, cinema seems to define itself in relation to another evil twin, the specter of television. But if cinema is now inconceivable on many levels without television (as a component in financing production and as a dominant mode of distribution and exhibition), this should not produce the illusion that this new medium has a stable identity. It is a grave mistake to analyse television primarily in terms of the material produced for it (the game shows, news reports, soap operas, etc.) rather than as a domestic form of access to a range of various programs offered simultaneously.

As Wim Wenders has said, anywhere a television set is turned on automatically becomes the center of the world.[41] Television seems less involved with intensifying vision than with providing immediate access to anything whatsoever. Clearly, this drive for access and coverage emerges as one of the extreme points in the spectralization of reality. But television itself possesses no solid identity beyond this dream (or nightmare) of immediate access to all of time and space. Movies remain one of the things carried by television, and watching movies on television is not just watching television. In spite of widespread predictions of cannibalization and total absorption, the two forms remain distinct; they seem to articulate in different ways the crisis of image and representation that an age of information brings to light.

Benjamin demonstrated half a century ago that cinema, as a mode of mechanical reproduction, could never be treated as a traditional form of high art. The elusive nature of the film commodity deprives it of a traditional aura of uniqueness. Unlike the traditional high arts, as an industrial product film depends less on individual ownership and unique artifacts than on circuits of distribution. Film culture is based less on objects than on the intangible effects of memory and shared experiences. It is important that the accumulated thickness of film history does not make us assume that cinema is simply an art like all the others, and that its contemporary crisis threatens an established sacral identity. In fact, there is no single identity to guard, and cinema in its origins was founded on the transformation of sacred rituals into irreverent entertainments.

I do not want to indicate that we should react either passively or optimistically to the current adulteration of the film image by video technology, to the loss of public experiences and discourse that the eclipse of the film theater implies or to the irreparable loss of film prints through corporate greed or bureaucratic inaction. However, in defending our film culture we need to recognize that cinema itself was conceived as a protean form and its permutations are far from played out. The crisis of cinema does not consist in the passing away of a century-long fashion in popular entertainment but embodies a crisis in our way of life in the age of information. It was as a harbinger of this crisis that film emerged about a century ago; now it once again focuses our understanding of this situation with greater clarity. Cinema has long been a skeleton at a feast, but at the same time, as in a fantasmagoria program, a Méliès trick film or a Disney cartoon, cinema is also a feast of skeletons, a carnival which simultaneously acknowledges our progressive loss of shared realities and provides a festive ground on which this loss can be anticipated, celebrated, mourned and perhaps even transcended. There is still a future, even if only an apocalyptic one, for this century-old illusion.

Endnotes

1   Gorky wrote two reviews of these films. One, signed with the pseudonym I. M. Pacatus, appeared in *Nizhegorodski listok* on 4 July 1896. This review is translated in Jay Leyda, *Kino: a history of the Russian and Soviet film* (London, George Allen & Unwin, 1960), pp. 407–9, translated by 'Leda Swan'. The other review apparently appeared in an Odessa newspaper and is translated as 'Gorky on the Films, 1896', ed. Herbert Kline *New theater and film: 1934 to 1937, an anthology* translated by Leonard Mins (San Diego, Harcourt Brace Jovanovich, 1985), pp. 227–31. I have quoted from both reviews. Gorky also wrote a short story about this screening, entitled 'Revenge'. Background on these reviews and the story, as well as an insightful discussion of them, can be found in Yuri Tsivian. *Early cinema in Russia and its cultural reception*, translated by Alan Bodger, (London, Routledge, 1994), pp. 36–7.
2   Gorky, *Kino*, p. 409.
3   Gorky, *New theater and film*, p. 229. Gorky was actually slightly behind the times here. Henri Joly, working for Charles Pathé, had already shot *Le Bain d'une mondaine* in October 1895. See Laurent Mannoni, *Le grand art de la lumière et de l'ombre* (Paris, Éditions Nathan, 1994), p. 402.
4   Gorky, *New theater and film*, p. 229.
5   Gorky, *Kino*, p. 408.
6   This was Frank Dyer, head of the Edison film interests, testifying in the government anti-trust suit against the MPPC in 1914. *United States v. Motion Picture Patents Company*. 225 F. 800 (E.D. Pa., 1915) Record, 1627.
7   By this phrase I pay tribute to the series of super-8 films made by Lewis Klahr known as 'Tales of the forgotten future'. But Miriam Hansen points out to me that the phrase was also used by Walter Benjamin.
8   Walter Benjamin. 'Theses on the philosophy of history', ed. Hannah Arendt, *Illuminations* (New York, Schocken Books, 1969), p. 255.
9   The phrase is Benjamin's, in 'The image of Proust', *Illuminations*, p. 203.

10 This tradition is discussed by Frances Yates in her controversial works, such as *The art of memory* (Chicago, IL, University of Chicago Press, 1966) and in Ioan P. Couliano, *Eros and magic in the Renaissance* (Chicago, IL, University of Chicago Press, 1987).

11 For a discussion of natural magic and of della Porta (whose name is also often given as Giovanni Battista della Porta) see Lynn Thorndike, *History of magic and experimental science* (New York, Columbia University Press, 1941), vol. vi, especially pp. 418–23. Della Porta published an earlier edition of this book in 1558, but this theater is described in the later edition. My summary comes from the section quoted in Mannoni, *Le grand art de la lumière et de l'ombre*, p. 20.

12 The best discussions of Kirchner's optical works in relation to the cinema appear in Mannoni, *Le grand art de la lumière et de l'ombre*, pp. 29–35, 61–63, and in Charles Musser, *The emergence of cinema; the American screen to 1907* (New York, Charles Scribner's Sons, 1990), pp. 17–22.

13 David Brewster, *Letters on natural magic* (London, John Murray, 1933).

14 Mannoni supplies a detailed and focused treatment of Huygens's invention of the magic lantern as well as his near disowning of it, in *Le grand art de la lumière et de l'ombre*, pp. 44–52. See, as well, his article 'Christian Huygenes et la "lanterne de peur" ', in *1895* no. 11 (December, 1992), pp. 49–78. Perhaps the first scholar to indicate Huygens' priority in the invention of the magic lantern was H. Mark Gosser, in 'Kircher and the magic lantern – a re-examination', *Journal of the Society of Motion Picture and Television Engineers*, 90 (October 1981), pp. 972–8.

15 See Mannoni, *Le grand art de la lumière et de l'ombre*, p. 55, and 'Christian Huygens', p. 69.

16 There are many descriptions of the fantasmagoria (sometimes spelled 'phantasmagoria'). The best are Mannoni, *Le grand art de la lumière et de l'ombre*, pp. 135–68; X. Theodore Barber, 'Phantasmagorical wonders: the magic lantern ghost show in nineteenth century America', *Film History*, 3, no. 2 (1989), pp. 73–86; Richard Altick, *The shows of London* (Cambridge, MA, Harvard University Press, 1978), pp. 217–19 (focused on the version presented in London); Olive Cook, *Movement in two dimensions* (London, Hutchinson, 1963), pp. 19–21.

17 Barber, 'Phantasmagorical wonders', p. 82.

18 Octave Mannoni, 'Je sais bien, mais quand même . . .', in *Clefs pour l'imaginaire ou l'autre scène* (Paris, Éditions du Seuil, 1969). This idea is founded upon Freud's concept of 'disavowal'. See 'Fetishism', *The standard edition of the complete psychological works of Sigmund Freud*. edited and translated by James Strachey, vol. XXII, pp. 152–7.

19 Marcel Proust, *Remembrance of things past; vol. I: Swann's Way*, translated by C.K. Scott Moncrieff and Terence Kilmartin (New York, Vintage Books, 1982), pp. 9–10.

20 Quoted in Altick, *The shows of London*, p. 233.

21 Alice Rix is quoted in the dissertation by Daniel Gene Streible, 'A history of the prizefight film, 1894–1915' (Austin, TX, University of Texas at Austin, 1994). Mr Streible is the first, I believe, to have unearthed this fascinating account. My information on Ms Rix comes from this excellent dissertation.

22 Helmut Gernstein and Alison Gernsheim, *L.J.M Daguerre: the history of the diorama and the daguerreotype*, p. 18. On the diorama see also Mannoni, *Le grand art de la lumière et de l'ombre*, pp. 177–82; Altick *The shows of London*, pp. 163–74; and Cook, *Movement in two dimensions*, pp. 36–43.

23 Philip Glass, 'The photographer', 'A Gentleman's Honor' (New York: CBS Records, 1983).

24 See, for instance, Oliver Wendell Holmes's famous essay, 'The stereoscope and the

stereograph', ed. Alan Trachtenberg, *Classic essays on photography* (New Haven, CT, Leete's Island Books, 1980), pp. 71–82.

25   Jonathan Crary, *Techniques of the observer: on vision and modernity in the nineteenth century* (Cambridge, MA, MIT Press, 1990), especially pp. 116–35. This important book has had a strong influence on this chapter.

26   Charles Baudelaire, 'The painter of modern life', edited and translated by Jonathan Mayne, *The painter of modern life and other essays* (London, Phaidon, 1965), p. 13.

27   Geoffrey Batchen, *Burning with desire: the conception of photography* (Cambridge, MA, MIT Press, 1997), pp. 90–1, indicates that the early photographers were greatly interested in the temporal nature of photography, but this seems to me primarily to indicate an interest in preserving, by fixing them in a photograph, phenomenon that are ephemeral, that fade quickly, such as Talbot's shadows, rather than the brief instant which exceeds human perception.

28   Baudelaire, 'The salon of 1859', edited and translated by Jonathan Mayne, *Art in Paris 1845–1862* (London: Phaidon, 1965), p. 154. The use of photography in recording hieroglyphics is suggested in Arago's 1839 'Report to the French Commissioner of Deputies on the daguerreotype', reprinted in Trachtenberg, p. 17.

29   The bibliography on Muybridge is extensive. Besides Muybridge's own books of plates, *The human figure in motion and animals in motion*, both reprinted by Dover Press, the most thorough works are Robert Haas, *Muybridge: man in motion* (Berkeley, CA, University of California Press, 1976); and Gordon Hendricks, *Muybridge: the father of the motion picture* (New York, Grossman, 1975). Brian Coe's *Muybridge and the chronophotographers* (London, Museum of the Moving Image, 1992) provides a more recent and an excellent condensed contextual account. Muybridge's relation to the development of motion pictures is sketched well in both Mannoni, *Le grand art de la lumière et de l'ombre*, and Musser, *The emergence of cinema*.

30   Marta Braun, *Picturing time: the work of Étienne-Jules Marey (1830–1904)* (Chicago, IL, University of Chicago Press, 1992). This is not only the definitive work on Marey but an extremely careful placement of his work within cultural history. Braun provides a thorough discussion of Marey's relation to motion pictures. In addition, Marey's work is discussed in relation to motion pictures in Coe, *Muybridge and the chronophotographers*, Jacques Deslandes, *Histoire comparée du cinéma* (Paris, Casterman, 1966), vol. I, pp. 107–77; and Mannoni, *Le grand art de la lumière et de l'ombre*, pp. 299–337. See as well Francois Dagognet's excellent book-length essay on Marey, *Étienne-Jules Marey: a passion for the trace* (New York, Zone Books, 1992).

31   Both Braun, *Picturing time*, and Dagognet, *Étienne-Jules Marey*, provide descriptions of these devices. They include the sphygmograph for recording the pulse, the cardiograph for measuring the heart beat, and the myograph for recording muscular contractions. These are illustrated in Braun on pages 17, 20 and 25.

32   Walter Benjamin; 'The work of art in the age of mechanical reproduction', *Illuminations*, p. 237.

33   Quoted in Braun, *Picturing time*, p. 196.

34   Quoted in Deslandes, *Histoire comparée du cinéma*, p. 144, my translation.

35   Quoted in Mannoni, *Le grand art de la lumière et de l'ombre*, p. 372, my translation.

36   Jean Baudrillard, 'The evil demon of images', *Powers Institute Publication* no. 3, (Sydney: Powers Institute, 1987), p. 13.

37   André Bazin, 'The myth of total cinema', *What is cinema?*, vol I (Berkeley, CA, and Los Angeles, CA, University of California Press, 1967), p. 20.

38 However, Bazin is always more subtle than his detractors make out. Notice his comment in a footnote in 'The myth of total myth of total cinema':

> Besides, just as the word indicates, the aesthetic of trompe-l'oeil in the eighteenth century resided more in illusion than in realism, that is to say, in a lie rather than the truth ... To some extent, this is what the early cinema was aiming at, but this operation of cheating quickly gave way to an ontogenetic realism.
>
> (1967: 19)

39 In a previous essay, ' "Primitive cinema", a frame-up? or The trick's on us' (anthologized in Thomas Elsaesser, *Early cinema: space, frame, narrative* (London, British Film Institute, 1990), I have discussed the following scene from Frank Norris's novel *McTeague* in which Mack and Trina accompany Trina's mother, Mrs Sieppe, to an early projection of motion pictures. After the younger couple express amazement, the older immigrant woman intervenes:

> 'It's all a drick', exclaimed Mrs. Sieppe with sudden conviction. 'I ain't no fool; dot's nothun but a drick'.

> 'Well, of course, Mamma', exclaimed Trina; 'it's–'.
> But Mrs. Sieppe put her head in the air. 'I'm too old to be fooled', she persisted. 'It's a drick'. Nothing more could be got out of her than this.
> [*McTeague* (New York, New American Library, 1964), p. 79]

This admittedly fictional exchange (written only a couple of years after Gorky's piece – *McTeague* was published in 1899) portrays an unsophisticated reaction that is as aware as Gorky is of the ambiguous nature of the image.

40 Edgar Allan Poe, 'The oval portrait', *Poe: poetry and tales*, ed. Patrick F. Quinn (New York: Library of America, 1984), p. 484.
41 Wim Wenders, Soundtrack of film *Tokyo Ga* (1984).

Acknowledgements: A version of this chapter has previously been published in *Michigan Quarterly*, vol. 34, no. 4 (1995).

18 The mass production of the senses: classical cinema as vernacular modernism

Miriam Bratu Hansen

In this chapter, I wish to reassess the juncture of cinema and modernism, and I will do so by moving from the example of early Soviet cinema to a seemingly less likely case, that of the classical Hollywood film. My inquiry is inspired by two complementary sets of questions: one pertaining to what cinema studies can contribute to our understanding of modernism and modernity; the other aimed at whether and how the perspective of modernist aesthetics may help us elucidate and reframe the history and theory of cinema. The juncture of cinema and modernism has been explored in a number of ways, ranging from research on early cinema's interrelations with the industrial–technological modernity of the late nineteenth century, through an emphasis on the international art cinemas of the interwar and new wave periods, to speculations on the cinema's implication in the distinction between the modern and the post-modern.[1] My focus here will be more squarely on mid-twentieth-century modernity, roughly from the 1920s through the 1950s – the modernity of mass production, mass consumption, and mass annihilation – and the contemporaneity of a particular kind of cinema, mainstream Hollywood, with what has variously been labelled 'high' or 'hegemonic modernism'.

Whether or not one agrees with the postmodernist challenge to modernism and modernity at large, it did open up a space for understanding modernism as a much wider, more diverse phenomenon, eluding any single-logic genealogy that runs, say, from Cubism to Abstract Expressionism, from Eliot, Pound, Joyce, and Kafka to Beckett and Robbe-Grillet, from Schönberg to Stockhausen. For more than a decade now scholars have been dislodging that genealogy and delineating alternative forms of modernism both in the West and in other parts of the world – modernisms that vary according to their social and geopolitical locations, often configured along the axis of post/coloniality, and according to the specific subcultural and indigenous traditions to which they responded.[2] In addition to opening up the modernist canon, these studies assume a notion of modernism that is 'more than a repertory of artistic styles', more than sets of ideas pursued by groups of artists and intellectuals.[3] Rather, modernism encompasses a whole range of cultural and artistic practices that register, respond to, and reflect upon processes of modernization and the experience of modernity, including a paradigmatic transformation of the conditions under which art is produced, transmitted, and consumed. In other words, just as modernist aesthetics are not reducible to the category of style, they tend to blur the boundaries of the institution of art in its traditional, eighteenth-century and nineteenth-century incarnations that turn on the ideal of aesthetic autonomy and the distinction of 'high' versus 'low', of autonomous art versus popular and mass culture.[4]

Focusing on the nexus between modernism and modernity, then, also implies a wider notion of the aesthetic, one that situates artistic practices within a larger history and economy of sensory perception which Walter Benjamin for one saw as the decisive battle-ground for the meaning and fate of modernity.[5] While the spread of urban–industrial technology, the large-scale disembedding of social (and gender) relations, and the shift to mass consumption entailed processes of real destruction and loss, there also emerged new modes of organizing vision and sensory perception, a new relationship with 'things', different forms of mimetic experience and expression, of affectivity, temporality, and reflexivity, a changing fabric of everyday life, sociability, and leisure. From this perspective, I take the study of modernist aesthetics to encompass cultural practices that both articulated and mediated the experience of modernity, such as the mass-produced and mass-consumed phenomena of fashion, design, advertising, architecture, and urban environment, of photography, radio, and cinema. I am referring to this kind of modernism as 'vernacular' (and avoiding the ideologically overdetermined term 'popular') because the term vernacular combines the dimension of the quotidian, of everyday usage, with connotations of discourse, idiom, and dialect, with circulation, promiscuity, and translatability. It is in the sense of the latter, finally, that this chapter will also address the vexed issue of Americanism, the question as to why and how an aesthetic idiom developed in one country could achieve transnational and global currency, and how this account might add to and modify our understanding of classical cinema.

I begin with an example that takes us back to one standard paradigm of twentieth-century modernism: Soviet cinema and the context of Soviet avant-garde aesthetics. At the 1996 festival of silent film in Pordenone, the featured program was a selection of early Soviet films, made in the period 1918–24, that is, before the great era of montage cinema, before the canonical works of Eisenstein, Pudovkin, Vertov, Dovzhenko. The question that guided the viewing of these films was, of course, how Russian cinema got from the Old to the New within a rather short span of time; how the sophisticated *mise en scène* cinema of the Czarist era, epitomized by the work of Yevgenij Bauer, was displaced by Soviet montage aesthetics. Many of the films shown confirmed what film historians, following Kuleshov, had vaguely assumed before: that this transformation was mediated, to a significant degree, by the impact of Hollywood. American films began to dominate Russian screens as early as 1915 and by 1916 had become the main foreign import. Films made during the years following 1917, even as they staged revolutionary plots for 'agit' purposes, may display interesting thematic continuities with Czarist cinema (in particular, a strong critique of patriarchy) and still contain amazing compositions in depth.[6] Increasingly, however, the *mise en scène* is broken down according to classical American principles of continuity editing, spatio-temporal coherence, and narrative causality. A famous case in point is Kuleshov's 1918 directorial debut, *Engineer Prait's Project*, a film that employed Hollywood-style continuity guidelines in a polemical break with the slow pace of Russian 'quality pictures'.[7] But the 'American accent' in Soviet film – faster cutting rate, closer framing, and breakdown of diegetic space – was more pervasive and can be found as well, in varying degrees of consistency, in the work of other directors (Vladimir Gardin, Ceslav Sabinskij, Ivan Perestiani). Hyperbolically speaking, one might say that Russian cinema became Soviet cinema by going through a process of Americanization.

To be sure, Soviet montage aesthetics did not emerge full-blown from the encounter with Hollywood-style continuity editing; it is unthinkable without the new avant-garde movements in art and theater, without Constructivism, Suprematism, Productivism, Futurism – unthinkable without a politics of radical transformation. Nor was continuity editing perceived as neutral, as simply the most 'efficient' way of telling a story. It was part and parcel of the complex of 'Americanism' (or, as Kuleshov referred to it, 'Americanitis') which catalysed debates on modernity and modernist movements in Russia as it did in other countries.[8] As elsewhere, the enthusiasm for things American, tempered by a critique of capitalism, took on a variety of meanings, forms, and functions. Discussing the impact of American on Soviet cinema, Yuri Tsivian distinguishes between two kinds of Americanism: stylistic borrowings of the classical kind described above ('American montage', 'American foreground'); and a fascination with the 'lower genres', with adventure serials, detective thrillers, and slapstick comedies which, Tsivian argues, were actually more influential during the transitional years. If the former kind of Americanism aspired to formal standards of narrative efficiency, coherence, and motivation, the latter was concerned with external appearance, the sensual, material surface of American films: their use of exterior locations, focus on action and thrills, physical stunts and attractions; their tempo, directness, and flatness; their eccentricity and excess of situations over plot.[9]

Tsivian analyses the Americanism of the 'lower' genres as an intellectual fashion or taste. Discerning 'something of a slumming mentality' in Eisenstein's or FEKS' fascination with 'serial queen' melodramas, he situates the preference of Soviet film-makers for 'cinematic pulp fiction' (Victor Shklovsky) in the context of the leftist avant-garde's attack on high art, cultural pretensions, and Western ideals of naturalism.[10] What interests me in this account is less the intellectual and artistic intertext than the connection it suggests *across* the distinction, between the two faces of American cinema: the classical norm, as an emergent form that was to dominate domestic as well as foreign markets for decades to come, and the seemingly non-classical, or less classical, undercurrent of genres that thrive on something other than or, at the very least, oblique to the classical norm. What also interests me in the dynamics of Americanism and Soviet film is the way it urges us to reconsider the relationship between classical cinema and modernism, a relationship that within cinema studies has habitually been thought of as an opposition, as one of fundamentally incompatible registers.

The opposition between classicism and modernism has a venerable history in literature, art, and philosophy, with classicism linked to the model of tradition, and modernism to the rhetoric of a break with precisely that tradition.[11] In that general sense, there would be no problem with importing this opposition into the field of cinema and film history, with classical cinema falling on the side of tradition, and alternative film practices on the side of modernism. If, however, we consider the cinema as part of the historical formation of modernity, as a larger set of cultural and aesthetic, technological, economic, social, and political transformations, the opposition of classical cinema and modernism, the latter understood as a discourse articulating and responding to modernity, becomes a more complicated issue.

I am using 'classical cinema' here as a technical term that has played a crucial part in the formation of cinema studies as an academic discipline. The term came to serve as a foundational concept in the analysis of the dominant form of narrative cinema, epitomized by Hollywood during the studio era; in that endeavor, 'classical cinema' referred to roughly the same thing whether you were doing semiotics, psychoanalytic film theory, neo-formalist poetics, or revisionist film history. This is not to say that it *meant* the same thing, and just a brief glimpse at its key moments will illustrate the transvaluations and disjunctures of the term.

Not coincidentally, the reference to Hollywood products as 'classical' has a French pedigree. As early as 1926, Jean Renoir uses the phrase 'cinematic classicism' (in this case referring to Chaplin and Lubitsch).[12] A more specific usage of the term occurs in Robert Brasillach and Maurice Bardèche's *Histoire du cinéma*, in particular the second edition of 1943, revised with a collaborationist bent, in which the authors refer to the style evolved in American sound film of 1933–9 as the 'classicism of the "talkie"'.[13] After the Occupation, critics, notably André Bazin, began to speak of Hollywood film-making as 'a classical art'. By the 1950s, Bazin would celebrate John Ford's *Stagecoach* (1939) as 'the ideal example of the maturity of a style brought to classic perfection', comparing the film to 'a wheel, so perfectly made that it remains in equilibrium on its axis in any position'.[14] This classical quality of American film, to quote Bazin's well-known statement, is a result not of individual talent but of 'the genius of the system, the richness of its ever-vigorous tradition, and its fertility when it comes into contact with new elements'.[15]

The first major transvaluation of the concept of classical cinema came with post-1968 film theory, in the all-round critique of ideology directed against the very system celebrated by Bazin. In this critique, formulated along Althusserian and Lacanian lines and from Marxist and later feminist positions, classical Hollywood cinema was analysed as a mode of representation that masks the process and fact of production, turns discourse into diegesis, history into story and myth; as an apparatus that sutures the subject in an illusory coherence and identity; and as a system of stylistic strategies that weld pleasure and meaning to reproduce dominant social and sexual hierarchies.[16] The notion of 'classical cinema' elaborated in the pages of *Cahiers du Cinéma*, *Cinéthique*, *Screen*, *Camera Obscura*, and elsewhere was less indebted to a neoclassicist ideal (as it still was for Bazin and Rohmer) than to the writings of Roland Barthes, in particular *S/Z* (1970), which attached the label of a 'classic', 'readerly', ostensibly transparent text to the nineteenth-century realist novel.[17]

Another turn in the conception of 'classical cinema' entails the rejection of any evaluative usage of the term, whether celebratory or critical, in favor of a more descriptive, presumably value-free and scientifically valid, account. This project has found its most comprehensive realization to date in David Bordwell, Janet Staiger, and Kristin Thompson's monumental and impressive study, *The classical Hollywood cinema: film style and mode of production to 1960* (1985). The authors conceive of classical cinema as an integral, coherent system, a system that interrelates a specific mode of production (based on Fordist principles of industrial organization) and a set of interdependent stylistic norms that were elaborated by 1917 and remained more or less in place until about 1960. The underlying notion of classical film style, rooted in neo-formalist poetics and cognitive psychology, overlaps in part with the account of the classical paradigm in 1970s' film theory, particularly with regard to principles of narrative dominance, linear and unobtrusive narration centering on the psychology and agency of individual characters, and continuity editing. But where psychoanalytic–semiotic theorists pinpoint unconscious mechanisms of identification and the ideological effects of 'realism', Bordwell and Thompson stress thorough motivation and coherence of causality, space, and time; clarity and redundancy in guiding the viewer's mental operations; formal patterns of repetition and variation, rhyming, balance, and symmetry; and overall compositional unity and closure.[18] In Bordwell's formulation, 'the principles which Hollywood claims as its own rely on notions of decorum, proportion, formal harmony, respect for tradition, mimesis, self-effacing craftsmanship, and cool control of the perceiver's response – canons which critics in any medium usually call "classical"'.[19]

Such a definition is not just generally 'classical' but more specifically recalls neoclassicist standards, from seventeenth-century neo-Aristotelian theories of drama to eighteenth-century ideals in music, architecture, and aesthetic theory.[20] (I do not wish to equate eighteenth-century aesthetics at large with the neoclassicist tradition, nor with an ahistorical reduction to neo-formalist principles: the eighteenth century was at least as much concerned with affect and effect, with theatricality and sensation, passion and sentiment, as with the balance of form and function.) As in literary and aesthetic antecedents that invoke classical antiquity as a model – recall Stendhal's definition of classicism as a style that 'gives the greatest possible pleasure to an audience's ancestors'[21] – the temporal dynamics of the term classical as applied to the cinema is retrospective; the emphasis is on tradition and continuity rather than newness as difference, disruption, and change.

I can see a certain revisionist pleasure in asserting the power and persistence of classical standards in the face of a popular image of Hollywood as anything but decorous, harmonious, traditional, and cool. But how does this help us account for the appeal of films as diverse as *Lonesome, Liberty, Freaks, Gold Diggers of 1933, Stella Dallas, Fallen Angel, Kiss Me Deadly, Bigger Than Life, Rock-a-Bye Baby* (add your own examples)? And even if we succeeded in showing these films to be constructed on classical principles – which I am sure can be done – what have we demonstrated? To repeat Rick Altman's question in an essay that challenges Bordwell, Thompson, and Staiger's model: 'How classical was classical narrative?'[22] Attempts to answer that rhetorical question have focused on what is left out, marginalized, or repressed in the totalizing account of classical cinema – in particular, the strong substratum of theatrical melodrama, with its uses of spectacle and coincidence, but also genres such as comedy, horror, and pornography which involve the viewer's body and sensory-affective responses in ways that may not exactly conform to classical ideals.[23] What is also minimized is the role of genre in general, specifically the affective–aesthetic division of labor among genres in structuring the consumption of Hollywood films. An even lesser role is granted to stars and stardom, which cannot be reduced to the narrative function of character and, like genre but even more so, involve the spheres of distribution, exhibition practices, and reception. *The classical Hollywood cinema* explicitly and, it should be said, with self-imposed consistency brackets the history of reception and film culture, along with the cinema's interrelations with American culture at large.

It is not my intention to contest the achievement of Bordwell, Staiger, and Thompson's work: the book does illuminate crucial aspects of how Hollywood cinema works and goes a long way toward accounting for the stability and persistence of this particular cultural form. My interest is rather in two questions that the book does *not* address, or addresses only to close off. One question pertains to the historicity of classical cinema, in particular its contemporaneity with twentieth-century modernisms and modern culture; the other question is to what extent and how the concept can be used to account for Hollywood's worldwide hegemony. To begin with, I am interested in the anachronism involved in asserting the priority of stylistic principles modelled on seventeenth-century and eighteenth-century neo-classicism when we are dealing with a cultural formation that was, after all, perceived as the incarnation of *the modern*, an aesthetic medium up-to-date with Fordist–Taylorist methods of industrial production and mass consumption, with drastic changes in social, sexual, and gender relations, in the material fabric of everyday life, in the organization of sensory perception and experience. For contemporaries, Hollywood at its presumably most classical figured as the very symbol of contemporaneity, the present, modern times: 'this our period', as Gertrude Stein famously put it, 'was undoubtedly the period of the cinema and series production'.[24] And it held that appeal not only for avant-garde artists and intellectuals in the USA and the modernizing capitals of the world (Berlin, Paris, Moscow, Shanghai, Tokyo, São Paulo, Sydney, Bombay), but also for emerging mass publics both at home and abroad. Whatever the economic and ideological conditions of its hegemony – and I wish by no means to discount them – classical Hollywood cinema could be imagined as a cultural practice on a par with the experience of modernity, as an industrially produced, mass-based, vernacular modernism.

In cinema studies, the juncture of the classical and the modern has, for the most part, been written as a bifurcated history. The critique of classical cinema in 1970s' film theory took over a structuralist legacy of binarisms, such as Barthes's opposition between the 'readerly' and 'writerly', which translated into the binary conception of film practice as either 'classical/idealist', that is, ideological, or 'modernist/materialist', that is, self-reflexive and progressive. This is particularly the case for the theory and practice of 'counter cinema' that David Rodowick has dubbed 'political modernism' – from Jean-Luc Godard and Peter Gidal through Noel Burch, Peter Wollen, Stephen Heath, Laura

Mulvey, and others – which owes much to the revival or belated reception of the 1920s' and 1930s' leftist avant-garde, notably Brecht.[25] Moreover, the polarization of classical cinema and modernism seemed sufficiently warranted by skepticism *vis-à-vis* Hollywood's self-promotion as 'international modern', considering how much the celebration of American cinema's contemporaneity, youth, vitality, and directness was part of the industry's own mythology, deployed to legitimate cut-throat business practices and the relentless expansion of economic power worldwide.

While Bordwell and Thompson's neo-formalist approach is to some extent indebted to the political–modernist tradition,[26] *The classical Hollywood cinema* recasts the binarism of classicism and modernism in two ways. At the level of industrial organization, the modernity of Hollywood's mode of production (Fordism) is subsumed under the goal of maintaining the stability of the system as a whole; thus major technological and economic changes (such as the transition to sound) are discussed in terms of a search for 'functional equivalents' by which the institution ensures the overall continuity of the paradigm.[27] In a similar vein, any stylistic deviations of the modernist kind *within* classical cinema – whether imports from European avant-garde and art films, native *films noir*, or work of idiosyncratic auteurs such as Welles, Hitchcock, and Preminger – are cited as proof of the system's amazing appropriative flexibility: 'So powerful is the classical paradigm that it regulates what may violate it.'[28]

To be sure, there is ample precedent, outside film history, for the assimilation of the modern to classical or neo-classicist standards; after all, art historians speak of 'classical modernism' (Picasso, de Chirico, Léger, Picabia) and there were related tendencies in music (Reger, Stravinsky, Poulenc, de Faya, to name just a few).[29] In modern architecture (Le Corbusier, Gropius, the Bauhaus), we can see the wedding of machine aesthetics to a notion of presumably natural functions, and in literary modernism we have self-proclaimed neo-classicists such as T.E. Hulme, Wyndham Lewis, Ernst Jünger, and Jean Cocteau. In the genealogy of film theory, one of the founding manifestos of classical cinema is Hugo Münsterberg's *The psychology of the photoplay* (1916), a treatise in neo-Kantian aesthetics applied to the cinema. Its author was actually better known for books on psychology and industrial efficiency that became standard works for modern advertising and management. Yet, these examples should be all the more reason for the historian to step back and consider the implications of these junctures – junctures that reveal themselves as increasingly less disjunctive with the passing of modernity, the disintegration of hegemonic or high modernism, and the emergence of alternative modernisms from the perspective of postmodernity.

A key problem seems to lie in the very concept of the 'classical' – as a historical category that implies the transcendence of mere historicity, as a hegemonic form that claims transcultural appeal and universality. Already, in its seventeenth-century and eighteenth-century usages, the neo-classicist recourse to tradition, in whatever way it may misread or invent a prior original, does not take us through history but instead to a transhistorical ideal, a timeless sense of beauty, proportion, harmony, and balance derived from *nature*. It is no coincidence that the neo-formalist account of classical cinema is linked and elaborated in Bordwell's work to the project of grounding film studies in the framework of cognitive psychology.[30] *The classical Hollywood cinema* offers an impressive account of a particular historical formation of the institution of American cinema, tracking its emergence in terms of the evolution of film style (Thompson) and mode of production (Staiger). But once 'the system' is in place (from about 1917 on), its ingenuity and stability are attributed to the optimal engagement of *mental* structures and perceptual capacities that are, in Bordwell's words, 'biologically hard-wired' and have been so for tens of thousands of years.[31] Classical narration ultimately amounts to a method of how optimally to guide the viewer's attention and how to maximize his or her response by way of more intricate plots and emotional tensions. The attempt to account for the efficacy of classical stylistic principles with recourse to cognitive psychology coincides with the effort to expand the reign of classical objectives to types of film practice outside Hollywood that had hitherto been perceived as alternative (most recently in Bordwell's work on Feuillade and other European traditions of staging-in-depth) as well as beyond the historical period demarcated in the book (that is, up to 1960).[32]

How can we restore historical specificity to the concept of 'classical Hollywood cinema'? How can we make the anachronistic tension in the combination of neo-classicist style and Fordist mass culture productive for an understanding of both classical Hollywood cinema and mass-mediated modernity? How do we distinguish, within the category of the classical, between natural norm, canonical cultural form, and a rhetorical strategy that perhaps enabled the articulation of something radically new and different under the guise of a continuity with tradition? Can there be an account of classicality that does not unwittingly reproduce, at the level of academic discourse, the universalist norms mobilized, not least, for purposes of profit, expansion, and ideological containment? Or would we not do better to abandon the concept of 'classical cinema' altogether, and instead, as Philip Rosen and others have opted to do, use the more neutral term 'mainstream cinema'?[33]

For one thing, I do not think that the term 'mainstream' is necessarily clearer, let alone neutral or innocent: in addition to the connotation of a quasi-natural flow, it suggests a homogeneity that locates side-streams and counter-currents on the outside or margins, rather than addressing the ways in which they at once become part of the institution and blur its boundaries. For another, I would argue that, for the time being, 'classical cinema' is still a more precise term because it names a regime of productivity and intelligibility that is both historically and culturally specific, much as it gets passed off as timeless and natural (and the efforts to do so are part of its history). In that sense, however, I take the term to refer less to a system of functionally interrelated norms and a corresponding set of empirical objects than to a scaffold, matrix, or web that allows for a wide range of aesthetic effects and experiences – that is, for cultural configurations that are more complex and dynamic than the most accurate account of their function within any single system may convey, and that require more open-ended, promiscuous, and imaginative types of inquiry.[34]

From this perspective, one might argue that it would be more appropriate to consider classical Hollywood cinema within the framework of 'American national cinema'. Such a reframing would allow us, among other things, to include independent film practices outside and against the pull of Hollywood (such as 'race films', regional, subcultural, and avant-garde film practices). While this strategy is important especially for teaching American cinema, the issue of Hollywood's role in defining and negotiating American nationality strikes me as more complicated. If we wish to 'provincialize Hollywood', to vary on Dipesh Chakrabarty's injunction to 'provincialize' European accounts of modernity,[35] it is not enough to consider American cinema on a par with any other national cinema – inasmuch as that very category in many cases describes defensive formations shaped in competition with and resistance to Hollywood products. In other words, the issue of classicality is bound up with the question of what constituted the hegemony of American movies worldwide, what assured them the historic impact they had, for better or for worse, within a wide range of different local contexts and diverse national cinemas.

The question of what constitutes Hollywood's power on a global scale returns us to the phenomenon of Americanism discussed earlier in connection with Soviet film. I am concerned with Americanism here less as a question of exceptionalism, consensus ideology, or crude economic power – though none of these aspects can be ignored – than as a question of cultural circulation and hegemony. Victoria de Grazia has argued that Americanism still awaits analysis, beyond the polarized labels of, respectively, cultural imperialism and a worldwide spreading of the American Dream, as 'the historical process by which the American experience was transformed into a universal model of business society based on advanced technology and promising formal equality and unlimited mass consumption'.[36] However ideological these promises may, or may not, turn out to be, de Grazia observes that, unlike earlier imperial practices of colonial dumping, American cultural exports 'were designed to go as far as the market would take them, starting at home'. In other words, 'cultural exports shared the basic features of American mass culture, intending by that term not only the cultural artifacts and associated forms, but also the civic values and social relations of the first capitalist mass society'.[37]

Regarding classical cinema, one could take this argument to suggest that the hegemonic mechanisms by which Hollywood succeeded in amalgamating a diversity of competing traditions, discourses, and interests on the *domestic* level may have accounted for at least some of the generalized appeal and robustness of Hollywood products *abroad* (a success in which the diasporic, relatively cosmopolitan profile of the Hollywood community no doubt played a part as well). In other words, by forging a mass market out of an ethnically and culturally heterogeneous society (if often at the expense of racial others), American classical cinema had developed an idiom, or idioms, that travelled more easily than its national–popular rivals. I do not wish to resuscitate the myth of film as a new 'universal language', whose early promoters included D.W. Griffith and Carl Laemmle (founder of the Universal Film Company), nor do I mean to gloss over the business practices by which the American film industry secured the dominance of its products on foreign markets, in particular through control of distribution and exhibition venues.[38] But I do think that, whether we like it or not, American movies of the classical period offered something like the first global vernacular. If this vernacular had a transnational and translatable resonance it was not just because of its optimal mobilization of biologically hardwired structures and universal narrative templates but, more important, because it played a key role in mediating competing cultural discourses on modernity and modernization, because it articulated, multiplied, and globalized a particular historical experience.

If classical Hollywood cinema succeeded as an international modernist idiom on a mass basis, it did so not because of its presumably universal narrative form but because it meant different things to different people and publics, both at home and abroad. We must not forget that these films, along with other mass cultural exports, were consumed in locally quite specific, and unequally developed, contexts and conditions of *reception*; that they not only had a levelling impact on indigenous cultures but also challenged prevailing social and sexual arrangements and advanced new possibilities of social identity and cultural styles; and that the films were also changed in that process. Many films were literally changed, both for particular export markets (for example, the conversion of American happy endings into tragic endings for Russian release) and by censorship, marketing, and programming practices in the countries in which they were distributed, not to mention practices of dubbing and subtitling.[39] As systematic as the effort to conquer foreign markets undoubtedly was, the actual reception of Hollywood films was likely a much more haphazard and eclectic process, depending on a variety of factors.[40] How were the films programmed in the context of local film cultures, in particular conventions of exhibition and reception? Which genres were preferred in which places (for instance, slapstick in European and African countries, musical and historical costume dramas in India), and how were American genres dissolved and assimilated into different generic traditions, different concepts of genre? And how did American imports figure within the public horizon of reception which might have included both indigenous products and films from other foreign countries? To write the international history of classical American cinema, therefore, is a matter of tracing not just its mechanisms of standardization and hegemony but the diversity of ways in which this cinema was translated and reconfigured in local and translocal contexts of reception.

This means that Americanism, notwithstanding Antonio Gramsci (as well as recent critiques of Gramsci and left Fordism), cannot simply be reduced to a regime of mechanized production, an ideological veneer for discipline, abstraction, reification, new hierarchies, and routes of power. Nor can it be reduced to the machine aesthetics of intellectual and high modernism.[41] We cannot understand the appeal of Americanism unless we take seriously the promises of mass consumption, and the dreams of a mass culture often in excess of and conflict with the regime of production that spawned that mass culture ('Americanization from below').[42] In other words, we have to understand the material, sensory conditions under which American mass culture, including Hollywood, was received and could have functioned as a powerful matrix for modernity's liberatory impulses – its moments of abundance, play, and radical possibility, its glimpses of collectivity and gender equality (the latter signalled by its opponents' excoriation of Americanism as a 'new matriarchy').[43]

The juncture of classical cinema and modernity reminds us, finally, that the cinema was not only part and symptom of the crisis and upheaval as which modernity was experienced and perceived; it was also, most importantly, the single most inclusive, cultural horizon in which the traumatic effects of modernity were reflected, rejected or disavowed, transmuted or negotiated. That the cinema was capable of a reflexive relation with modernity and modernization was registered by contemporaries early on, and I read Benjamin's and Siegfried Kracauer's writings of the 1920s and 1930s as, among other things, an effort to theorize this relation as a new mode of reflexivity.[44] Neither simply a medium for realistic representation (in the sense of Marxist notions of reflection or *Widerspiegelung*), nor particularly concerned with formalist self-reflexivity, commercial cinema appeared to realize Johann Gottlieb Fichte's troping of reflection as 'seeing with an added eye' in an almost literal sense, and it did so not just on the level of individual, philosophical cognition but on a mass scale.[45] I am also drawing on more recent sociological debates on 'reflexive modernization' (Ulrich Beck, Anthony Giddens, Scott Lash), a concept deployed to distinguish the risk-conscious phase of current post- or second modernity from a presumably more single-minded, orthodox, and simple, first modernity. However, I would argue (though I cannot do so in detail here) that modernization inevitably provokes the need for reflexivity and that if sociologists considered the cinema in aesthetic and sensorial terms rather than as just another media of information and communication they would find ample evidence, in American and other cinemas of the interwar period, of an at once modernist and vernacular reflexivity.[46]

This dimension of reflexivity is key to the claim that the cinema not only represented a specifically modern type of public sphere, the public here understood as a 'social horizon of experience', but that this new mass public could have functioned as a discursive form in which individual experience could be articulated and find recognition by subjects and others, including strangers.[47] Kracauer, in his more utopian moments, understood the cinema as an alternative public sphere – alternative both to bourgeois institutions of art, education, and culture and to the traditional arenas of politics – an imaginative horizon in which, however compromised by its capitalist foundations, something like an actual democratization of culture seemed to be taking shape; in his words, the possibility of a 'self-representation of the masses subject to the process of mechanization'.[48] The cinema suggested this possibility not only because it attracted, and made visible to itself and society, an emerging, heterogeneous mass public ignored and despised by dominant culture; the new medium also offered an alternative because it engaged the contradictions of modernity at the level of the senses, the level at which the impact of modern technology on human experience was most palpable and irreversible. In other words, the cinema not only traded in the mass production of the senses but also provided an aesthetic horizon for the experience of industrial mass society.

While Kracauer's observations were based on movie-going in Weimar Germany, he attributed this sensory reflexivity more often than not to American film, in particular slapstick comedy, with its well-choreographed orgies of demolition and clashes between people and things. The logic he discerned in slapstick films pointed up a disjuncture within Fordist mass culture, the possibility of an anarchic supplement generated on the same principles:

> One has to hand this to the Americans: with slapstick films they have created a form that offers a counterweight to their reality. If in that reality they subject the world to an often

unbearable discipline, the film in turn dismantles this self-imposed order quite forcefully.[49]

The reflexive potential of slapstick comedy can be (and has been) argued on a number of counts, at the levels of plot, performance, and *mise en scène*, and as depending on the particular inflection of the genre: in addition to articulating, and playing games with, the violence of technological regimes, mechanization, and clock time, slapstick films also specialized in deflating the terror of consumption, of a new culture of status and distinction.[50] Likewise, the genre was a vital site for engaging the conflicts and pressures of a multi-ethnic society (think of the many Jewish performers who thematized the discrepancies between diasporic identity and upward mobility, from Larry Semon and Max Davidson to George Sydney). And, not least, slapstick comedy allowed for a playful and physical expression of anxieties over changed gender roles and new forms of sexuality and intimacy.

But what about other genres? And what about popular narrative films that conform more closely to classical norms? Once we begin looking at Hollywood films as both a provincial response to modernization and a vernacular for different, diverse, yet also comparable experiences, we may find that genres such as the musical, horror, or melodrama may offer just as much reflexive potential as slapstick comedy, with appeals specific to those genres and specific resonances in different contexts of reception. This is to suggest that reflexivity can take different forms and different affective directions – both in individual films and directorial œuvres and in the aesthetic division of labor among Hollywood genres – and that reflexivity does not always have to be critical or unequivocal; on the contrary, the reflexive dimension of these films may consist precisely in the ways in which they allow their viewers to confront the constitutive ambivalence of modernity.

The reflexive dimension of Hollywood films in relation to modernity may take cognitive, discursive, and narrativized forms, but it is crucially anchored in sensory experience and sensational affect – in processes of mimetic identification that are more often than not partial and excessive in relation to narrative comprehension. Benjamin, writing about the elimination of distance in the new perceptual regimes of advertising and cinema, sees in the giant billboards that present things in new proportions and colors a backdrop for a 'sentimentality . . . restored to health and liberated in American style', just as in the cinema 'people whom nothing moves or touches any longer learn to cry again'.[51] The reason slapstick comedy hit home and flourished worldwide was not critical reason but that the films propelled their viewers' bodies into laughter. And adventure serials succeeded because they conveyed a new immediacy, energy, and sexual economy, not only in Soviet Russia and not only among avant-garde intellectuals. Again and again, writings on the American cinema of the interwar period stress the new physicality, the exterior surface or 'outer skin' of things (Antonin Artaud), the material presence of the quotidian; as Louis Aragon put it, 'really common objects, everything that celebrates life, not some artificial convention that excludes corned beef and tins of polish'.[52] I take such statements to suggest that the reflexive, modernist dimension of American cinema does not necessarily require that we demonstrate a cognitive, compensatory, or therapeutic function in relation to the experience of modernity but that, in a very basic sense, even the most ordinary commercial films were involved in producing a new sensory culture.

Hollywood did not just circulate images and sounds; it produced and globalized a new sensorium; it constituted, or tried to constitute, new subjectivities and subjects. The mass appeal of these films resided as much in their ability to engage viewers at the narrative–cognitive level, or in their providing models of identification for being modern, as it did in the register of what Benjamin troped as the 'optical unconscious'.[53] It was not just *what* these films showed, what they brought into optical consciousness, as it were, but the way they opened up hitherto unperceived modes of sensory perception and experience, their ability to suggest a different organization of the daily world. Whether this took the shape of dreams or of nightmares, it marked an aesthetic mode that was decidedly not 'classical' – at least not if we literalize that term and reduce it to neo-classicist formal and stylistic principles. Yet, if we understand the 'classical' in American cinema as a metaphor of a global sensory vernacular, rather than a universal narrative idiom, then it might be possible to imagine the two Americanisms operating in the development of Soviet cinema, the modernist fascination with the 'low', sensational, attractionist genres, and the classicist ideal of formal and narrative efficiency, as vectors of the same phenomenon, each contributing to the hegemony of Hollywood film. This may well be a fantasy: the fantasy of a cinema that could help its viewers negotiate the tension between reification and the aesthetic strongly understood, the possibilities, anxieties, and costs of an expanded sensory and experiential horizon – the fantasy, in other words, of a mass-mediated public sphere capable of responding to modernity and its failed promises. Now that postmodern media culture is busy recycling the ruins of both classical cinema and modernity, we may be in a better position to see the residues of a dreamworld of mass culture that is no longer ours – and yet to some extent still is.

Endnotes

1   See, for instance, Leo Charney and Vanessa R. Schwartz (eds), *Cinema and the invention of modern life* (Berkeley, CA, University of California Press, 1995); John Orr, *Cinema and modernity* (Cambridge, Polity Press, 1993); Anne Friedberg, *Window shopping: cinema and the postmodern* (Berkeley, CA, University of California Press, 1993). In addition, of course, there have been numerous studies on the impact of cinema on experimentation in other media, especially fiction, painting, and theater.

2   See, for instance, Marshall Berman, *All that is solid melts into air: the experience of modernity* (New York, Simon and Schuster, 1982); Andreas Huyssen, *After the great divide: modernism, mass culture, postmodernism* (Bloomington, IN, Indiana University Press, 1986); Peter Wollen, 'Out of the past: fashion/orientalism/the body' (1987), in *Raiding the icebox: reflections on twentieth-century culture* (Bloomington, IN, Indiana University Press, 1993); Richard Taruskin, 'A myth of the twentieth century: *The Rite of Spring*, the tradition of the new, and "music itself"', *Modernism/Modernity* 2, 1 (January 1995), pp. 1–26; Rosalind Krauss, *The originality of the avant-garde and other modernist myths* (Cambridge, MA, MIT Press, 1985); Griselda Pollock, 'Modernity and the spaces of femininity', in G. Pollock, *Vision and difference* (London, Routledge, 1988), pp. 50–90; Molly Nesbit, 'The rat's ass', *October*,

56 (Spring 1991), pp. 6–20; Matthew Teitelbaum (ed.), *Montage and modern life 1919–1942* (Cambridge, MA, MIT Press, 1992); Houston A. Baker, Jr, *Modernism and the Harlem Renaissance* (Chicago, IL, University of Chicago Press, 1987); Michael North, *The dialect of modernism* (New York, Oxford University Press, 1994); Paul Gilroy, *The black Atlantic: modernity and double consciousness* (Cambridge, MA, Harvard University Press, 1993); Homi Bhabha, *The location of culture* (London and New York, Routledge, 1994), ch. 12; Tejaswini Niranjana, P. Sudhir, and Vivek Dhareshwar (eds), *Interrogating modernity: culture and colonialism in India* (Calcutta, Seagull Books, 1993); Arjun Appadurai, *Modernity at large: cultural dimensions of globalization* (Minneapolis, MN, University of Minnesota Press, 1996); Néstor García Canclini, 'Latin American contradictions: modernism without Modernization?', in *Hybrid cultures: strategies for entering and leaving modernity*, translated by C.L. Chiappari and S.L. Lopez (Minneapolis, MN, University of Minnesota Press, 1995), pp. 41–65; and Sharan A. Minichiello (ed.), *Japan's competing modernities: issues in culture and democracy 1900–1930* (Honolulu, HI, University of Hawaii Press, 1998).

3   Lawrence Rainey and Robert von Hallberg, 'Editorial/Introduction', *Modernism/Modernity* 1, 1 (1994): 1.

4   Peter Bürger, following Adorno, asserts that the very category of 'style' is rendered problematic by the advanced commodification of art in the twentieth century and he considers the refusal to develop a coherent style (as in Dada and Surrealism) as a salient feature of avant-gardist, as distinct from modernist, aesthetics; see Bürger, *Theory of the avant-garde*, translated by Michael Shaw (Minneapolis, MN, University of Minnesota Press, 1984), especially ch. 2.1, 'The historicity of aesthetic categories'. The opening up of modernist and avant-garde canons, however, shows a greater overlap between the two, just as the effort, on the part of particular modernist artists and movements, to *restore* the institutional status of art may well go along with avant-gardist modes of behavior and publicity; see Miriam Hansen, *Ezra Pounds frühe Poetik zwischen Aufklärung und Avantgarde* (Stuttgart, Metzler, 1979). Also see Huyssen, *After the great divide*, in particular ch. 2, 'Adorno in Reverse: from Hollywood to Richard Wagner'. On style as historical category, see also Frederick J. Schwarte, 'Cathedrals and shoes: concepts of style in Wölfflin and Adorno', *New German Critique*, 76 (Winter 1999), pp. 3–48.

5   In his famous essay, 'The work of art in the age of mechanical reproduction' (second version, 1935), Benjamin wrote of 'the theory [*die Lehre*] of perception that the Greeks called aesthetics' [*Gesammelte Schriften*, vol. VII, eds R. Tiedemann and H. Schweppenhäuser (Frankfurt am Main, Suhrkamp, 1989), p. 381], and he conceived of the politics of this essay very much as an effort to confront the aesthetic tradition narrowly understood, in particular the persistence of aestheticism in contemporary literature and art, with the changes wrought upon the human sensorium by industrial and military technology. See Susan Buck-Morss, 'Aesthetics and anaesthetics: Walter Benjamin's artwork essay reconsidered', *October* 62 (Fall 1992), pp. 3–41; also, see Hansen, 'Benjamin and cinema: not a one-way street', *Critical Inquiry* 25, 2 (Winter 1999), pp. 306–43.

6   On the cinema of the Czarist period, see Yuri Tsivian, 'Some preparatory remarks on Russian cinema', in *Testimoni silenziosi: Filmi russi 1908–1919/Silent witnesses: Russian films 1908–1919*, eds Paolo Cherchi Usai *et al.* (Pordenone, London, British Film Institute, 1989); Tsivian, *Early cinema in Russia and its cultural reception* (1991), translated by Alan Bodger (1994; Chicago, IL, University of Chicago Press, 1998); also see the contributions of Paolo Cherchi Usai, Mary Ann Doane, Heide Schlüpmann, and myself to two special issues of the journal *Cinefocus* (Bloomington, IN) 2, 1 (Fall 1991) and 2, 2 (Spring 1992).

7   Yuri Tsivian, 'Between the Old and the New: Soviet film culture in 1918–1924', *Griffithiana* 55/56 (1996), 15–63; 39; Tsivian, 'Cutting and framing in Bauer's and Kuleshov's films', *Kintop: Jahrbuch zur Erforschung des frühen Films*, 1 (1992), pp. 103–13; Kristin Thompson and David Bordwell, *Film history: an introduction* (New York, McGraw-Hill, 1994), p. 130.

8   See, for instance, *The Weimar Republic source book* (Berkeley, CA, University of California Press, 1994), section 15; and Antonio Gramsci's famous essay, 'Americanism and Fordism', in *Selections from the Prison notebooks* [1929–1935], edited and translated by Quintin Hoare and Geoffrey Nowell Smith (New York, International Publishers, 1971), pp. 277–318. Also, see Mary Nolan, *Visions of modernity: American business and the modernization of Germany* (New York, Oxford University Press, 1994); Thomas J. Saunders, *Hollywood in Berlin: American cinema and Weimar Germany* (Berkeley, CA, University of California Press, 1994), especially chs 4 and 5; Alf Lüdtke, Inge Marßolek, Adelheid von Saldern (eds), *Amerikanisierung: Traum und Alptraum im Deutschland des 20. Jahrhunderts* (Stuttgart, Franz Steiner, 1996); Jean-Louis Cohen and Humbert Damisch (eds), *Américanisme et modernité: L'idéal américain dans l'architecture* (Paris, EHESS, Flammarion, 1993).

9   Tsivian, 'Between the Old and the New', pp. 39–45.

10 Tsivian, 'Between the Old and the New', p. 43. A related recruiting of 'low' popular culture for the programmatic attack on the institution of art can be found in Western European avant-garde movements, in particular Dadaism and Surrealism.

11 Robert B. Pippin, *Modernism as a philosophical problem* (London, Basil Blackwell, 1991), p. 4.

12 See Thomas Elsaesser, 'What makes Hollywood run?', *American Film*, 10, 7 (May 1985), pp. 52–5, 68.

13 Robert Brasillach and Maurice Bardèche, *Histoire du cinéma*, 2nd edn (Paris, Denoël, 1943), p. 369, quoted in David Bordwell, *On the history of film style* (Cambridge, MA, Harvard University press, 1997), p. 47. With regard to the earlier edition (1935), which bestows the term 'classic' on international silent film of the period 1924–29, Bordwell remarks that the invocation of the term recalls 'the common art–historical conception of classicism as a dynamic stablity in which innovations submit to an overall balance of form and function' (p. 40). On the political stance of the authors, in particular Brasillach, see Alice Kaplan, *Reproductions of banality: fascism, literature, and French intellectual life* (Minneapolis, MN, University of Minnesota Press, 1986), chs 6 and 7, and Bordwell, *On the history of film style*, pp. 38–41.

14 André Bazin, 'The evolution of the western', *What is cinema?*, selected and edited by Hugh Gray (Berkeley, CA, University of California Press, 1971), vol. II, p. 149. In 'The western: or the American film par excellence', Bazin invokes Corneille to describe the 'simplicity' of western scripts as a quality that both lends them 'naive greatness' and makes them a subject for parody (p. 147). Also, see Bazin, 'The evolution of the language of cinema', in *What is cinema?*, vol. I, p. 29. Dudley Andrew has drawn my attention to Eric Rohmer who during the same period developed a notion of cinematic classicism that more broadly linked 'modern' cinema to the eighteenth-century tradition. See Rohmer, *Le Goût de la beauté*, ed. Jean Narboni (Paris, Éditions de l'Étoile, 1984), esp. part I, 'L'Age classique de cinéma', pp. 25–99; also see Bordwell, *History of film style*, p. 77.

15 André Bazin, 'La Politique des auteurs', in ed. Peter Graham, *The New Wave* (New York, Doubleday, 1968), pp. 143, 154.

16 See, for example, Jean-Louis Comolli and Jean Narboni, 'Cinema/ideology/criticism', in *Screen Reader 1* (London, SEFT, 1977); Janet Bergstrom, 'Enunciation and sexual difference (part I)', *Camera Obscura*, 3–4 (1979); as well as writings by Comolli, Jean-Louis Baudry,

Christian Metz, Raymond Bellour, Stephen Heath, Laura Mulvey, and Colin MacCabe in Philip Rosen (ed.), *Narrative, apparatus, ideology: a film theory reader* (New York, Columbia University Press, 1986).

17 See Judith Mayne, 'S/Z and film theory', *Jump Cut* 12/13 (December 1976), pp. 41–5. A notable exception to this tendency is Raymond Bellour who stresses the formal and stylistic principles at work in classical cinema (patterns of repetition–resolution, rhyming, symmetry, redundancy, interlacing of micro and macro structures) by which classical films produce their conscious and unconscious meanings and effects. See Bellour, *L'analyse du film* (Paris, Éditions Albatros, 1979), which includes the texts translated as 'Segmenting/analyzing' and 'The obvious and the code', in Rosen, *Narrative, apparatus, ideology*, pp. 66–92, 93–101.

18 In *The classical Hollywood cinema* (New York, Columbia University Press, 1985), p. 19, 'realism' is equated with verisimilitude and as such figures as one of four types of narrative motivation (compositional, realistic, intertextual, artistic). While this qualification seems appropriate *vis-à-vis* the diversity of Hollywood genres (think of the musical, for instance), it does not make the issue of cinematic 'realism' go away, whether as rhetorical claim, ideological fiction, or aesthetic possibility. In this context, see Christine Gledhill's interesting attempt to understand 'realism' as American cinema's way of facilitating the 'modernization of melodrama'; Gledhill, 'Between melodrama and realism: Anthony Asquith's *Underground* and King Vidor's *The Crowd*', in Jane Gaines, ed., *Classical Hollywood narrative: the paradigm wars* (Durham, NC, Duke University Press, 1992), p. 131.

19 David Bordwell, Janet Staiger, and Kristin Thompson, *The classical Hollywood cinema*, pp. 3–4.

20 Rick Altman discusses the problematic relationship of Bordwell's concept of cinematic classicism with its French literary antecedents in his essay, 'Dickens, Griffith, and film theory today', in Gaines, ed., *Classical Hollywood narrative*, pp. 15–17.

21 Bordwell *et al.*, *Classical Hollywood cinema*, pp. 367–8.

22 Altman, 'Dickens, Griffith, and film theory today', p. 14.

23 The debate on melodrama in cinema studies is extensive; for an exemplary collection see Christine Gledhill (ed.), *Home is where the heart is: studies in melodrama and the woman's film* (London, British Film Institute, 1987), especially Gledhill's introduction, 'The melodramatic field: an investigation', pp. 5–39; Gledhill, 'Between melodrama and realism', in Gaines, ed., *Classical Hollywood narrative*; Linda Williams, 'Melodrama revised', in Nick Browne, ed., *Refiguring American film genres: theory and history* (Berkeley, CA, University of California Press, 1998). On genres that involve the body in non-classical ways, see Linda Williams, 'Film bodies: gender, genre, and excess', *Film Quarterly* 44,4 (Summer 1991), pp. 2–13. On the intrinsically competing aesthetics of slapstick comedy, see Donald Crafton, 'Pie and chase: gag, spectacle and narrative in slapstick comedy', in Kristine Brunovska Karnick and Henry Jenkins, eds, *Classical Hollywood comedy* (New York and London, Routledge, 1994), pp. 106–19; also see William Paul, *Laughing screaming: modern Hollywood horror and comedy* (New York, Columbia University Press, 1994).

24 Gertrude Stein, 'Portraits and Repetition', in *Lectures in America* (New York, Random House, 1935), p. 177. For a critical account of the industrial, political, and cultural dimensions of Fordism, see Terry Smith, *Making the modern: industry, art, and design in America* (Chicago, IL, University of Chicago Press, 1993).

25 D. N. Rodowick, *The crisis of political modernism: criticism and ideology in contemporary film theory* (Urbana and Chicago, IL, University of Illinois Press, 1988); also see Sylvia Harvey,

May '68 and film culture (London, British Film Institute, 1978), ch. 2; Martin Walsh, *The Brechtian aspects of radical cinema*, ed. Keith M. Griffiths (London, British Film Institute, 1981). For a graphic example of the binary construction of this approach, see Peter Wollen, 'Godard and counter-cinema: *Vent d'est*' (1972), reprinted in Rosen (ed.), *Narrative, apparatus, ideology*, pp. 120–9.

26 See, for instance, Kristin Thompson and David Bordwell, 'Space and narrative in the films of Ozu', *Screen*, 17, 2 (Summer 1976), pp. 41–73; Thompson, *Breaking the glass armor: neoformalist film analysis* (Princeton, NJ, Princeton University Press, 1988), part 6; Bordwell, *Narration in the fiction film* (Madison, WI, University of Wisconsin Press, 1985), ch. 12.

27 Bordwell *et al.*, *The classical Hollywood cinema*, p. 304.

28 Bordwell *et al.*, *The classical Hollywood cinema*, p. 81. Such statements bear an uncanny similarity to Max Horkheimer and Theodor W. Adorno's analysis, in *Dialectic of Enlightenment* (1944/47), of the 'Culture industry' as an all-absorbing totality though obviously without the despair and pessimism that prompted that analysis.

29 The Basel Kunstmuseum mounted an impressive exhibition of classicist modernism in music and the arts; see the catalogue, *Canto d'Amore: Klassizistische Moderne in Musik und bildender Kunst 1914–1935*, eds Gottfried Boehm, Ulrich Mosch, Katharina Schmidt (Basel, Kunstmuseum, 1996), and the collection of essays and sources accompanying the concurrent concert series, *Klassizistische Moderne*, ed. Felix Meyer (Winterthur, Amadeus Verlag, 1996).

30 Bordwell *et al.*, *The classical Hollywood cinema*, pp. 7–9, 58–9; Bordwell, *Narration in the fiction film,* chs 3 and *passim*; Bordwell, 'A case for cognitivism', *Iris* 5, 2 (1989), pp. 11–40. Also see Dudley Andrew's introduction to the issue, devoted to 'Cinema and cognitive psychology', 1–10, and the continuation of the debate between Bordwell and Andrew in *Iris* 6, 2 (Summer 1990), pp. 107–16. In the effort to make cognitivism a central paradigm in film studies, Bordwell is joined, among others, by Noël Carroll; see Bordwell and Carroll (eds), *Post-theory: reconstructing film studies* (Madison, WI, University of Wisconsin Press, 1996), pp. 37–70; also see Carroll, *Theorizing the moving image* (Cambridge and New York, Cambridge University Press, 1996).

31 Bordwell, '*La Nouvelle Mission de Feuillade*; or, What was mise-en-scène?', *The Velvet Light Trap*, 37 (1996), p. 23; also see Bordwell, *On the history of film style*, p. 142, and Bordwell, 'Convention, construction, and cinematic vision', in *Post-theory*, pp. 87–107.

32 Bordwell, '*La Nouvelle Mission de Feuillade*', *On the history of film style*, ch. 6, and *The classical Hollywood cinema*, ch. 30. Kristin Thompson's new study is concerned with the persistence of classical principles past 1960, see 'Storytelling in the new Hollywood: the case of *Groundhog Day*', paper presented at the Chicago Film Seminar, 3 October 1996.

33 Rosen, *Narrative, apparatus, ideology*, p. 8.

34 Patrice Petro, drawing on the work of Karsten Witte and Eric Rentschler, contrasts this centrifugal quality of Hollywood cinema to the literalization of classical norms in Nazi cinema: 'The Nazi cinema [in its strategies of visual enticement and simultaneous narrative containment] represents the theory (of classical Hollywood narrative) put into practice rather than the practice (of Hollywood filmmaking) put into theory'. ['Nazi cinema at the intersection of the classical and the popular', *New German Critique*, 74 (Spring/Summer 1998), p. 54.]

35 Dipesh Chakrabarty, 'Postcoloniality and the artifice of history: who speaks for "Indian" pasts?' *Representations*, 37 (Winter 1992), pp. 1–26; 20.

36 Victoria de Grazia, 'Americanism for export', *Wedge*, 7–8 (Winter–Spring 1985), pp. 74–81;

73. Also, see de Grazia, 'Mass culture and sovereignty: the American challenge to European cinemas, 1920–1960', *Journal of Modern History*, 61, 1 (March 1989), pp. 53–87.

37 De Grazia, 'Americanism for export', p. 77. Mica Nava argues for a similar distinction (i.e. between a commercial culture of cosmopolitan modernism shaped in the USA and the cultural imperialism of colonial regimes) in her essay 'The cosmopolitanism of commerce and the allure of difference: Selfridges, the Russian Ballet and the tango 1911–1914', *International Journal of Cultural Studies*, 1, 2 (August 1998), pp. 163–96.

38 On the role of foreign markets for the American film industry, see Kristin Thompson, *Exporting entertainment* (London, British Film Institute, 1985); Ian Jarvie, *Hollywood's overseas campaign: the North Atlantic movie trade, 1920–1950* (Cambridge and New York, Cambridge University Press, 1992); David W. Ellwood and Rob Kroes (eds), *Hollywood in Europe: experiences of a cultural hegemony* (Amsterdam, VU University Press, 1994); Ruth Vasey, *The world according to Hollywood, 1918–1939* (Madison, WI, University of Wisconsin Press, 1997). On the celebration of film as a new 'universal language' during the period 1910–19, see M. Hansen, *Babel and Babylon: spectatorship in American silent film* (Cambridge, MA, Harvard University Press, 1991), pp. 76–81, 183–7.

39 On the practice of converting happy endings of American films into 'Russian endings', see Yuri Tsivian, 'Some preparatory remarks on Russian cinema', *Silent witnesses: Russian films 1908–1919*, eds Paolo Cherchi Usai *et al.* (Pordenone, London, British Film Institute, 1989), p. 24; also see Mary Ann Doane, 'Melodrama, temporality, recognition: American and Russian silent cinema', *Cinefocus* (Bloomington, IN), 2, 1 (Fall 1991), pp. 13–26.

40 See, for instance, Rosie Thomas, 'Indian cinema: pleasures and popularity', *Screen*, 26, 1 (1985), pp.116–31; Sara Dickey, *Cinema and the urban poor in South India* (New York, Cambridge University Press, 1993); Stephen Putnam Hughes, 'Is there anyone out there?': exhibition and the formation of silent film audiences in South India, PhD thesis, University of Chicago, IL, 1996; Onookome Okome and Jonathan Haynes, *Cinema and social change in West Africa* (Jos, Nigeria, Nigerian Film Corporation, 1995), ch. 6; also, see Hamid Naficy, 'Theorizing "Third World" film spectatorship', *Wide Angle*, 18, 4 (October 1996), pp. 3–26.

41 For an example of such a critique, see Peter Wollen, 'Modern times: cinema/Americanism/ the robot' (1988), in *Raiding the icebox*, pp. 35–71.

42 The phrase 'Americanization from below' is used by Kaspar Maase in his study of West German youth culture of the 1950s, *BRAVO Amerika: Erkundungen zur Jugendkultur der Bundesrepublik in den fünfziger Jahren* (Hamburg, Junius, 1992), p. 19.

43 On the different economy of gender relations connoted by American culture in Weimar Germany, see Nolan, *Visions of modernity*, pp. 120–27; and Eve Rosenhaft, 'Lesewut, Kinosucht, Radiotismus: Zur (geschlechter-)politischen Relevanz neuer Massenmedien in den 1920er Jahren', in Lüdtke, Marßolek, von Saldern, eds., *Amerikanisierung*, pp. 119–43.

44 Hansen, 'Benjamin and cinema', and 'America, Paris, the Alps: Kracauer (and Benjamin) on cinema and modernity', in Charney and Schwartz, eds, *Cinema and the invention of modern life*, pp. 362–402.

45 Quoted in Ulrich Beck, Anthony Giddens, and Scott Lash, *Reflexive modernization: politics, tradition and aesthetics in the modern social order* (Stanford, CA, Stanford University Press, 1994), p. 175.

46 See Beck, Giddens, and Lash, *Reflexive modernization*; also see Giddens, *Modernity and self-identity* (Stanford, CA, Stanford University Press, 1991). Lash criticizes his coauthors both for the notion of a 'high' or 'simple' modernity and for their neglect of the 'aesthetic dimension', but he does not develop the latter in terms of changes in the institution of art

and the new regimes of sensory perception emerging with mass-mediated modernity; Lash, 'Reflexive modernization: the aesthetic dimension', *Theory, Culture and Society*, 10, 1 (1993), pp. 1–23.

47 This is not to say that the cinema was unique or original in forging a modern type of publicness. It was part of, and borrowed from, a whole array of institutions – department stores, world fairs, tourism, amusement parks, vaudeville, etc. – that involved new regimes of sensory perception and new forms of sociability; at the same time, the cinema represented, multiplied, and deterritorialized these new experiential regimes. My understanding of the public sphere as a general, social 'horizon of experience' is indebted to Oskar Negt and Alexander Kluge, *The public sphere and experience* (1972), translated by Peter Labanyi, Jamie Daniel, and Assenka Oksiloff, introduced by M. Hansen (Minneapolis, MN, University of Minnesota Press, 1993).

48 S. Kracauer, 'Berliner Nebeneinander: Kara-Iki – Scala-Ball im Savoy – Menschen im Hotel', *Frankfurter Zeitung*, 17 February 1933; also, see 'Cult of Distraction' (1926) and other essays in Kracauer, *The mass ornament: Weimar essays*, translated, edited, and introduction by Thomas Y. Levin (Cambridge, MA, Harvard University Press, 1995).

49 Kracauer, *Frankfurter Zeitung*, 29 January 1926.

50 See, for instance, Eileen Bowser, 'Subverting the conventions: slapstick as genre', in Bowser, ed., *The slapstick symposium,* May 1985, The Museum of Modern Art, New York (Brussels, Fédération Internationale des Archives du Film, 1988), pp. 13–17; Crafton, 'Pie and Chase'; Charles Musser, 'Work, ideology and Chaplin's tramp', *Radical History*, 41 (April 1988), pp. 37–66.

51 Benjamin, 'One-way street' (1928), translated by Edmund Jephcott, in *Selected writings*, eds Marcus Bullock and Michael W. Jennings (Cambridge, MA, Harvard University Press, 1996), p. 476 (translation modified).

52 Antonin Artaud, 'The shell and the clergyman: film scenario', *Transition*, 29–30 (June 1930), p. 65, quoted in Siegfried Kracauer, *Theory of film* (1960; Princeton, NJ, Princeton University Press, 1997), p. 189; Louis Aragon, 'On decor' (1918) in Richard Abel, ed., *French film theory and criticism: a history/anthology, 1907–1939*, 2 vols (Princeton, NJ, Princeton University Press, 1988), vol 1, p. 165. Also see in Abel, *French film theory and criticism*, Colette, 'Cinema: the cheat', Louis Delluc, 'Beauty in the cinema' (1917) and 'From Orestes to Rio Jim' (1921), Blaise Cendrars, 'The modern: a new art, the cinema' (1919), Jean Epstein, 'Magnification' (1921); 'Bonjour cinéma and other writings by Jean Epstein', translated by Tom Milne, *Afterimage*, no. 10 (undated), especially pp. 9–16; and Philippe Soupault, 'Cinema U.S.A.' (1924), in Paul Hammond, ed. and intr., *The shadow and its shadow: surrealist writings on the cinema* (London, British Film Institute, 1978), pp. 32–3.

53 Benjamin develops the notion of an 'optical unconscious' in 'A short history of photography' (1931), translated by Stanley Mitchell, *Screen*, 13 (Spring 1972), pp. 7–8, and in his famous essay, 'The work of art in the age of mechanical reproduction' (1936), *Illuminations*, ed. Hannah Arendt, translated by Harry Zohn (New York, Schocken, 1969), pp. 235–7. Also see his defense of *Battleship Potemkin*, 'A discussion of Russian filmic art and collectivist art in general' (1927), in Kaes, Jay, and Dimendberg, eds, *The Weimar Republic source book*, p. 627.

Acknowledgements: For critical readings, research, and suggestions I wish to thank Paula Amad, Dudley Andrew, Bill Brown, Susan Buck-Morss, Jean Comaroff, Michael Geyer, Tom Gunning, Lesley Stern, Yuri Tsivian, and Martha Ward, as well as inspiring audiences and commentators in various places where I presented versions of this chapter.

19 Discipline and fun: *Psycho* and postmodern cinema

Linda Williams

> If you've designed a picture correctly, in terms of its emotional impact, the Japanese audience would scream at the same time as the Indian audience.
> (Alfred Hitchcock, quoted in Houston, 1980: 448)

Talk to psychoanalytic critics about *Psycho* and they will tell you how perfectly the film illustrates the perverse mechanisms of the medium. Talk to horror aficionados and they will tell you how the film represents the moment horror moved inside the family and home. Talk to anyone old enough to have seen *Psycho* on first release in a movie theater, however, and they will tell you what it felt like to be scared out of their wits. Fear of showers in the aftermath of the film's famous shower-murder ran rampant throughout the 1960s. Yet if it is popularly remembered how *Psycho* altered the bathing habits of the nation, it is oddly less well remembered how it fundamentally altered viewing habits.

The following study of the place of Alfred Hitchcock's *Psycho* (1960) in film studies is interested in the critical and popular reception of a film that I believe has been crucial to the constitution of new ways of seeing, and new ways of feeling, films. As we shall see, these ways of seeing and feeling are simultaneously more distracted and more disciplined than previous cinema. Released in the summer of 1960 – a date which has been seen by some to mark the end of the 'classical' Hollywood style and mode of production and the beginning of a much more amorphously defined 'post-classical', postmodern cinema – *Psycho* has nevertheless not previously been viewed as a quintessentially postmodern film.[1]

The term postmodern is enormously complicated in its application to cinema by the way the medium of cinema has, since its inception, automatically, but unreflectingly, been equated with modernity. Fredric Jameson (1984) sees postmodernism in cinema as a relatively recent occurrence determined by the 'cultural logic of late capitalism' manifested in a schizophrenic, decentered subjectivity that can be seen in popular cinema in the pervasive mode of nostalgia and pastiche that flattens all time, or, more recently, in the prevalence of paranoid conspiracy thrillers in which communication technologies are often central metaphors. Anne Friedberg (1993) and Miriam Hansen (this volume, Chapter 18), on the other hand, have both argued for the need first to sort out cinema's problematic relation to the modern, before leaping to embrace the 'p' word. For Friedberg the very apparatus of the cinema makes the stylistic categories of modernism and postmodernism inappropriate since it constructs a 'virtual, mobilized gaze' through a photographically represented 'elsewhere and elsewhen' that is already postmodern. Thus for Friedberg there is no precise moment of temporal rupture between the modern and the postmodern, but only a subtle transformation produced by the increasing centrality of the image-producing and reproducing apparatuses (1993: 170). For Hansen, the difficulty is the relation of the modernity of cinema and its so-called 'classical' Hollywood tendencies. Since cinema history has so often been presented as the juncture between the classical popular and the modernist avant-garde, it has been difficult to perceive the extent to which the quintessentially modern phenomenon of movies have also been popular.

I agree with Friedberg that the basic elements of the so-called postmodern condition consist in the 'instrumentalized acceleration of spatial and temporal fluidities' that have always operated in cinema (1993: 179). In this sense all cinema *is,* as Friedberg puts it, 'proto-postmodern'. A mere thematics of nostalgia – or in this case of schizophrenia – does not adequately define a postmodern film. I also agree with Hansen that from the contemporary perspective of postmodernity, it becomes possible to see the limitations of both a purely 'high modernist' understanding of cinematic modernism and a seemingly ahistorical popular 'classicism'. However, the temptation to identify specific films or genres which emphatically perform the kind of acceleration of fluidities Friedberg mentions and the kind of challenge to the 'classical' Hansen mentions remains. My own particular temptation is to locate within the history of cinematic reception a moment in which audience response to postmodern gender and sexual fluidity, schizophrenia, and irony began to become not only central *attractions* of 'going to the movies' but the very basis of new spectatorial *disciplines* capable of enhancing these attractions.

The place of *Psycho* in film studies

In order to argue for the postmodern nature of *Psycho*'s discipline and distraction, let me briefly survey the film's changing status within the field of film studies. David Bordwell's (1989) survey of the rhetoric of *Psycho* criticism is a good place to begin to identify what might be called the modernist appropriation of the film – approaches that Bordwell wishes to disparage. Bordwell's account of the interpretations of *Psycho* traces a remarkable process of legitimization whereby a film initially seen as a minor, low-budget, black-and-white Hitchcock 'thriller', not up to the 'master's' usual standards, was 5 years later the subject of an extremely influential chapter of a major auteur study, 10 years later a classic worthy of close analysis, and 15 years later an example of a subversive work of modernism. All subsequent interpretations, including those by Rothman (1982), Jameson (1990), and Zizek (1992), assume the centrality of the film to cinema studies as constituted and legitimized by reigning psychoanalytic paradigms of film theory in the 1970s. Yet, as Bordwell shows, what is missing from such interpretations is a quality mentioned by Hitchcock himself and cited in an epigraph to Robin Wood's influential auteur study: this quality is 'fun'.

> You have to remember that *Psycho* is a film made with quite a sense of amusement on my part. To me its a *fun* picture. The processes through which we take the audience, you see, its rather like taking them through the haunted house at the fairground.
>
> (Bordwell, 1989: 229; Wood, 1965: 106)

With *Psycho*'s entrance into the canon of the 20 or so most frequently taught and critically revered films, discussion of this fairground appeal to sensational fun fell by the wayside. The more exalted Hitchcock's critical reputation became, the less he, or anyone else, learned about the secrets of this fun. As he once noted, 'My films went from being failures to masterpieces without ever being successes' (Spoto, 1983: 456–7). So interested was Hitchcock in understanding the powerful effect *Psycho* had on audiences that he proposed that the Stanford Research Institute devote a study to understand its popularity. But when he found out they wanted US$75 000 to do the research, he told them he was not that curious (Spoto, 1983: 457).

One reason so much academic film criticism has passed over the question of the film's fun has to do with psychoanalytic and feminist paradigms aligned with what David Rodowick has called the discourse of political modernism in which the notion of an endlessly deferred, unsatisfiable *desire* was central and the notion of visual pleasure (let alone 'fun') was anathema.[2] Within these paradigms *Psycho*'s modernism could only be understood as a rupture with 'readerly', and 'classical' forms of visual pleasure. This 'classical' pleasure might be understood judgmentally as transparent realism's support of bourgeois ideology (as in most 1970s' film theory) or, somewhat more neutrally, as a dominant style and mode of production (as in Bordwell, Thompson, and Staiger's monumental work, *The classical Hollywood cinema: film style and mode of production, 1917–1960* (1985)). Of course it makes a difference which form of classicism a work like *Psycho* is seen to rupture.

For Kaja Silverman, it ruptures the classical 'system of suture' whereby coherent forms of meaning and unified subject positions are upheld. Silverman asserts the exceptional and deviant status of a film that obliges its viewing subjects 'to make abrupt shifts in identification', at one juncture inscribed as victim, 'at the next juncture as victimizer' (Silverman, 1983: 206). However, Silverman's psychoanalytic character-ization of the viewer as 'castrated' comes close to presenting the experience of viewing the film as a form of punishment. For her – and for most critics who wrote about the film in this mode – the film is about painful castration and perversely thwarted desires. Spectators who are first identified with the neurotic desires of Marion are abruptly cut off from her and subsequently unwittingly caught up in the perverse and psychotic desires of Norman and are then, presumably, punished for such errant identification by a narrative that does not follow the 'classical' realist narrative trajectory of resolution and reassurance.[3] For Silverman, and many others, the transparency and unity of the suture system are 'synonymous with the operations of classic narrative' and its ideological effects (1983: 214).

In contrast, in the Bordwell–Thompson paradigm of the 'classical' cinema, classicism stands not so much for realism and suture as for Aristotelian (and neo-Aristotelian) values of unity, harmony, and tradition that have endured in American cinema since the late 'teens'. This classicism is seen as consisting in a strong narrative logic, coherence of cause and effect, space and time, psychological motivation, and character-driven events. To Bordwell and Thompson it is so stable and permanent a style that it is capable of absorbing whatever differences are introduced into the system. This is precisely what Bordwell argues with respect to *Psycho*. Noting that it is 'certainly one of the most deviant films ever made in Hollywood' because of its attack on such fundamental classical assumptions as the psychological identity of characters and the role accorded to narration, he nevertheless argues that '*Psycho* remains closer to *His Girl Friday* than *Diary of a Country Priest*' (Bordwell *et al.*, 1985: 81).

For Bordwell, *Psycho*'s deviation from 'classical' unity is transitory and fleeting: 'in Hollywood cinema, there are no subversive films, only subversive moments' – moments ultimately absorbed by the relatively static hegemony of the group style (Bordwell *et al.*, 1985: 81). For Silverman, *Psycho*'s deviation from classical style *is* subversive, but it is a subversion that partakes of the unpleasure – even the quasi-punishment – of high modernism. Thus, although the answer to the questions of what *Psycho* ruptures, and how it does so, differs slightly depending on whether it is the 1970s' version of 'classical realist narrative' – often equated with the novel – or the 'classical Hollywood style' – often traced back to the well-made play, and to neo-classical values – the common wisdom of both approaches is that the classical can be opposed to the innovation and rupture of the modern. Classicism thus seems to acquire something akin to a universal static appeal in tension with, but ultimately overpowering any deviation posed by, the modern.[4]

What is missing from both Bordwell's and Silverman's account of *Psycho*'s deviance from 'classical' norms is any sense of the popular, sensory pleasures of either the mainstream cinema from which it supposedly deviates or the specific nature of the different and 'deviant' pleasures of *Psycho* itself. The deeper problem may be, as Miriam Hansen has suggested, that the very category of the classical verges on anachronism when we are using the term to refer to 'a cultural formation that was, after all, perceived as the incarnation of *the modern*' in its methods of industrial production and mass consumption (page 337, emphasis in original). In other words, the category of the classical to which Bordwell wants to assimilate *Psycho*, and from which Silverman and others want to differentiate it, might better be reconceived as a form of what Hansen calls 'popular modernism'. From this perspective, the Bordwell–Thompson–Staiger model of the tendency of the classical cinema to devour and assimilate the modern, and the 1970s' film theory model of classical realism's neutralization of the modern, are both inadequate to the task of understanding what was new, and fun, in popular, mainstream cinema.

My project with *Psycho* is therefore to account for some of its more sensational and 'fun' appeals. However, this fun does not represent a completely radical rupture with a popularly conceived, mainstream, Hollywood cinema in the business of providing sensually based thrills and pleasures. It represents, rather, a new intensification and destabilization of the gendered components of that pleasure. Following both Anne Friedberg and Miriam Hansen, then, I would like to argue that *Psycho* offers an intensification of certain forms of visuality, and certain appeals to the senses through the image-producing and reproducing apparatuses that were already evident in what is more properly called the popular modernism of mainstream Hollywood cinema, but which changed under the incipient pressures of postmodernity.[5]

Psycho's story of an eye

Alfred Hitchcock's *Psycho* opens on a famous 'bird's eye' view of the Phoenix skyline; after surveying the city laterally the camera moves forward towards a half-open window blind, then through the window to allow us to become voyeurs of the aftermath of illicit sex in a sleazy hotel. Marion Crane and her lover Sam are half naked after a lunch-hour tryst. Never before in the history of mainstream American film had an erotic scene been played horizontally on a bed (Rebello, 1990: 86). Never before had a film so blatantly enlisted voyeuristic pleasures. Marion begins the scene supine, in bra and slip; Sam, with his shirt off, stands over her. Soon he joins her on the bed; they kiss and express frustration at having to meet like this.

Marion later steals $40 000 in order not to have to meet in cheap hotels. When she gets lost *en route* to Sam, she meets Norman Bates who seems, like herself, caught in a 'private trap'. After a cathartic conversation with Norman in the parlor of the motel, Marion decides to return the money. Norman peers through a peephole as she prepares for her shower. In extreme close-up we see a gigantic (male) eye gazing at a partly disrobed (female) body. Yet the twist of *Psycho* will turn out to be that this 'male gaze' unleashes not a conventional, masculine heterosexual desire (or assault) but a new being: the schizo-psychotic Norman–Mother who will act to foil Norman's heterosexual desire.

The sudden, unexplained violence of the attack in the shower came as a great shock to audiences who had been set up by the first third of the film to expect the slightly tawdry love story of Marion and Sam. The shower-murder's destabilizing effect on audiences was perfectly enacted by the shots that followed this attack. The same roving, voyeuristic camera eye that began the film appears to want to pick up the pieces of a narrative trajectory. But where should it go? What should it now see? The inquisitive, forward-propelled movement that inaugurated the story is now impossible; the camera can only look at the bloody water washing down the drain. Tracking 'down the drain' graphically enacts what has just happened to all narrative expectation with the murder of the film's main character and star. From the darkness of the drain, and echoing the counter-clockwise spiral of the swirling water, vision re-emerges in a reverse pull-back out of the dead, staring, eye of Marion.

This baroque camera movement 'down the drain' and back out of a dead, unseeing eye enacts a spectatorial disorientation that was one of the most striking features of watching *Psycho*. In a moment this abyss will be filled by a new focus on Norman who will enter to clean up the mess and protect 'Mother'. But from this point on, the audience cannot comfortably settle into a conventional narrative trajectory. What it will do instead is begin to anticipate 'Mother's' next attack and to register the rhythms of its anticipation, shock, and release.

The above are familiar observations about *Psycho*'s abrupt rupture with supposedly 'classical' narrative expectation. Yet anyone who has gone to the movies in the past 20 years – a period in which the influence of Hitchcock in general and *Psycho* in particular has become increasingly apparent – cannot help but notice how elements of this 'roller-coaster' sensibility – a sensibility that is grounded in the pleasurable anticipation of the next gut-spilling, gut-wrenching moment – has gained ascendance in popular moving-image culture.[6] Although *Psycho* is certainly not the direct antecedent of all these films, it does mark the important beginning of an era in which viewers began going to the movies to be thrilled and moved in quite visceral ways, and without much concern for coherent characters or motives.

The new 'cinema of attractions'

Scholars of early cinema have recently shown the importance of visual sensation in this period (see Gunning, this volume, Chapter 17). As these scholars have learned to appreciate the sensational pleasures of this pre-narrative, pre-'classical' cinema, they have often noted affinities between this cinema and the contemporary return to sensation in special effects, extreme violence, and sexual display. While narrative is not abandoned in ever more sensationalized cinema, it often takes second seat to a succession of visual and auditory 'attractions'. Tom Gunning's work on the early 'cinema of attractions' is based on this cinema's dual ability visually to 'show' something new or sensational and to 'attract' viewers to this show. Gunning shows how most early cinema before Griffith placed a premium on calling attention to the ability of the apparatus to offer attractions over its ability to absorb spectators into a diegetic world (Gunning, 1986). The term attraction is borrowed from Sergei Eisenstein whose theory of the 'montage of attractions' laid stress on the 'sensual or psychological impact' of images on spectators in their ability to disrupt spectatorial absorption into 'illusory depictions' (Eisenstein, 1988: 35). It was, in fact, the destabilizing, shock effect of the fairground roller coaster that Eisenstein had most in mind when he coined the term.[7] And it is very much a quality like a roller-coaster ride that is the primary attraction of the new cinema described above.

The point of invoking the term 'attractions' (and the further association of the actual roller-coaster ride) is not to argue that contemporary postmodern American cinema has reverted to the *same* attractions of early cinema. While there is certainly an affinity between the two, this new regime entails entirely different spectatorial disciplines and engages viewers in entirely different social experiences.[8] We might distinguish between these experiences by considering the attractions of the fair which beckon to viewers, surrounding them with sights and shows from which they might choose, to the experience of being caught up in the literal sensations of falling, flying, careening in the roller coaster. Film historian Thomas Schatz has attempted to specify the institutional, economic, technological, and generic changes that have constituted the new attractions of what he prefers to call 'the New Hollywood' (Schatz, 1993). Schatz isolates a common feature of 'high-cost, high-tech, high-speed thrillers' which, in his predominantly negative account, were most dramatically ushered in by the 1973 blockbuster *Jaws* and followed by the *Star Wars*, *Close Encounters*, *Raiders of the Lost Ark*, *E.T.*, *Exorcist*, and *Godfather* mega hits.[9] He characterizes these 'calculated blockbusters' as genre pastiches which are 'visceral, kinetic, and fast-paced, increasingly reliant on special effects, increasingly "fantastic" … and increasingly targeted at younger audiences' (Schatz, 1993: 23).

What is especially interesting in Schatz's description is the attention to the new packaging of thrills and the connection of these thrills not simply to the fairground of Eisenstein's attractions but to the postmodern theme park of Baudrillardian simulacra. For the crucial point about all the films Schatz mentions is not simply that some of them actually *are* theme-park rides (for example, Universal's 'E.T.' and Disneyland's 'Star Tours'), but that many films now set out, as a first order of business, to simulate the bodily thrills and visceral pleasures of attractions that not only beckon to us but take us on a continuous ride punctuated by shocks and moments of speed-up and slow-down. Since Schatz wrote his essay, one of the highest grossing movies ever is a film about a dinosaur theme-park ride run amok (*Jurassic Park*, 1993). The fact that this film has now itself become a theme-park ride only confirms the observation that the destabilized ride, the ride that seems to career most wildly out of control, is the one we increasingly want to take.

We might consider as well a telling moment in *Titanic* (James Cameron, 1997), the film that has now passed *Jurassic Park* to become the biggest box-office hit of all time. Just before the stern end of the Titanic – the only part of the ship still afloat – sinks, it rides high up into the air and poises perpendicular to the water. With desperate passengers clinging to the railings, the towering upended stern pauses a breathless moment before plunging straight down into the deep. During this moment, behaving for all the world like a kid on a roller coaster preparing to ride the downhill plunge after the dramatic pause at the top, the film's hero Jack Dawson (Leonardo DiCaprio) cries out with more excitement than fear: 'This is it!' Dawson's exclamation, pinpointing the exact moment of the ride's greatest anticipation and fear speaks for the roller-coaster thrill of yet another film ride that has careened wildly out of control. Can the theme-park simulation be far behind?

Perhaps the best way to understand this specific appeal to the roller-coaster sensibilities of contemporary life is to compare a traditional roller-coaster ride – say the rickety wood and steel affair on Santa Cruz CA's boardwalk, part of the fun of which is riding high above the boardwalk, beach, and ocean – with the roller-coaster-style rides at Disneyland. These latter rides borrow from cinema in one of two ways. Either they simulate a diegetic world through cinematic *mise en scène* – but still literally move the body through actual space – such as the 'Matterhorn', or they are elaborate updates of early cinema's Hales Tours, 'moving' the audience through virtual, electronically generated, space, such as Tomorrow land's motion-simulation 'Star Tours'. This ride, which literally goes nowhere, feels just as harrowing as an actual roller coaster, even more so when the added narrative informs us that the robot pilot has malfunctioned causing us nearly to collide with a number of objects. The narrative information that we are out of control enhances the virtual sensation of wild careening.

In both forms of ride, traditional roller coasters have become more like the movies; and movies, in turn, have become more like roller coasters. In this convergence of pleasures the contemporary, postmodern cinema has reconnected in important ways with the 'attractions' of amusement parks. But these attractions have themselves been thematized and narrativized through their connection with the entire history of movies. (Even the Matterhorn is based on a now forgotten 1959 movie, *Third Man on the Mountain*.) It would be a mistake, therefore, to think of these new forms of attractions as simply reverting (or regressing) to the spectatorial sensations of early cinema. Rather, we need to see them as scopic regimes demanding specific kinds of spectatorial discipline.

One aspect of that discipline was already being cultivated in the long lines beginning to form in the late 1950s at the newly built Disneyland. Just as the newly thematized roller coasters such as the Matterhorn and the later motion-simulation roller coasters such as Star Tours base their thrills on destabilizing movement through real, or simulated, narrativized space, so a film such as *Psycho* introduced, long before the blockbusters Schatz describes as defining the New Hollywood, what might be called a roller-coaster concept to the phenomenon of film viewing. For *Psycho* the ride began, like the rides at Disneyland, with the line and its anticipation of terror. It continued in the film proper with an unprecedented experience of disorientation, destabilization, and terror. When the forward-moving, purposeful voyeuristic camera eye 'washes' down the drain after the murder of Marion and emerges in reverse twisting out of her dead eye, audiences could, for the first time in mainstream motion picture history, take pleasure in losing the kind of control, mastery, and forward momentum familiar to what I will now resist calling the 'classical' narrative and will instead call popular modern cinema.

Billy Crystal's joke at the 1993 Academy Awards ceremony that *The Crying Game* proved that 'white men *can* jump' offers a good example of the kind of pleasurable destabilization that I am trying to identify. The shocking attraction of this film is the appearance of a masculine mark of gender where none was expected. This gender shock would not have been possible without the remarkable ability of audiences and critics to keep the secret of a key protagonist's gender. Gender shock is, of course, what *Psycho* also gave to its audience. The 'shock' of the surprise depends on the discipline of the kept secret. *Psycho* is the film that first linked an erotic display of sexual attractions to a shocking display of sexualized violence. But its attractions were no longer deployed within a stable heterosexual framework or within the hegemony of an exclusive masculine subjectivity. This new twist on some very 'basic instincts' is at the heart of postmodern gender and sexuality in popular cinema.

Psycho and genre study

If today it is becoming possible to recognize *Psycho* as fun, it is partly because the popular contemporary slasher film has taught us this lesson through generic repetitions of what was once so strikingly original in *Psycho*. But it is also because genre study has sometimes been the one place in film studies where repeatable audience pleasures, as opposed to thwarted or punitive desires, have been scrutinized. Genre study is also the place where some of the major truisms of contemporary film theory have been most thoroughly re-examined in the face of the social experiences of spectators. It is thus not surprising that it is in the study of the horror genre that we have received, however indirectly, an implicit appreciation of *Psycho*'s pivotal place in the transition to a postmodern visual culture.

Approached as a horror film, *Psycho* is often regarded as a turning point in the history of the genre: the moment when horror moved, in Andrew Tudor's words, 'from collective fears about threatening forces somewhere "out there"' to a 'sexuality, repression and psychosis' that is frighteningly close to home and potential in us all (1989: 46–7). Carol J. Clover's study of contemporary horror film, *Men, women, and chain saws*, has also commented on the enormous influence of a tale 'of sex and parents' (1992: 49) inaugurated by *Psycho*. In her chapter on the contemporary 'slasher film' that forms the nucleus of her book, Clover notices how powerfully a masculine viewer casts his emotional lot with a 'female-victim-hero'.[10] This 'final girl', survivor of gruesome slice and dice mayhem, is, in her knife-wielding or chain-saw-wielding triumph at the end, anything but passive and not very feminine. Where traditional views of the horror genre have too simply polarized gender to active male monster and passive female victim, Clover's analysis of the low exploitative subgenre of the slasher film discovers that a vicarious 'abject terror, gendered feminine' is crucial to the genre, and that this terror is merely the starting point of a roller-coaster ride that careens wildly, between the gendered poles of feminine abjection and masculine mastery.

Clover develops Kaja Silverman's insight that identification in *Psycho* shifts between victim and victimizer, though she develops this mostly in relation to the contemporary horror tradition spawned by this film and she develops it as masochistic *pleasure*, not punishment. In order to understand sadomasochistic pleasures that are perhaps more basic to contemporary film viewing than any modernist rupture, Clover argues that all forms of contemporary horror involve the thrill of being assaulted – of 'opening up' to penetrating images. Using horror's own meta-commentary on itself to fill in what she calls the 'blind spots' of theories of spectatorship by Metz and Mulvey, Clover asserts the importance of 'gazes' that do not master their objects of vision but are reactive and introjective (Clover, 1992: 225–6).

Today, *Psycho*'s relation to the slasher genre and its peculiar gendered pleasure seems obvious. Yet, it is only in retrospect that we can place it 'in' the slasher subgenre, or perhaps only if we wish to include its sequels of the 1980s – *Psycho* II, III, and IV – as part of its text.[11] What, then, is *Psycho*? Or, more precisely, what was *Psycho* on first viewing and what has it become since? Through subsequent viewings it has become the familiar antecedent for familial 'slice and dice' horror. But audiences who first went to see it did not go to see a slasher horror film; they went to see a *Hitchcock* thriller with a twist – about which there was a great deal of excitement and quite a bit of mystery. The crucial significance of *Psycho*, measurable today in terms of its influence on the slasher film, but measurable then in its new 'attractions' challenging certain production code taboos against depictions of both sex and violence, is not that it actually showed more sex or more violence than other films – which it, literally speaking, did not – but rather, as Clover notes, that it sexualized the motive, and the action, of violence (Clover, 1992: 24).

Just how we understand this sexualization of violence seems to be the key issue in assessing the impact, the influence, and the postmodernity of *Psycho*'s particular roller-coaster ride of attractions. The shower sequence is one of the most analysed sequences in all American film. Certainly, part of its fame derives from the technical brilliance of the way it is cut. Many a film teacher, myself included, has taught the importance of editing by punning on its powerful effects of cutting – of both flesh and film.

It was almost a reflex of post-structuralist psychoanalytic criticism to 'read' the shower sequence as an act of symbolic castration carried out on the presumably already 'castrated' body of a woman with whom spectators have identified. Marion's body – insisted on by some form of undress in two scenes prior to the shower murder – unleashes Norman's desire for her which in turn unleashes 'Mrs Bates', the mother who kills to protect her son from the sexual aggressions of 'loose' women. As I once put it: 'the woman is both victim and monster . . . . Norman, the matricide and killer of several other women, is judged the victim of the very mother he has killed' (Williams, 1984: 93–4). The female monster unleashed by the female victim seemed to permit the simultaneous vilification and victimization of women. Yet as Carol Clover has correctly pointed out, such a feminist critique does not do justice to the obvious bisexuality of the slasher killers spawned by Norman, nor to the new-found strength and resourcefulness of the female victims spawned by Marion and her sister (Clover, 1992: 21–64).

Barbara Creed has tried to argue that what has been missing from psychoanalytically based studies of horror film has been an appreciation of the disturbing power of the 'monstrous feminine'.[12] Creed has a point about the Kristevan powers of (abject, female) horror. However, because she points to the monstrous feminine as an archetype, she fails to account for the remarkable emergence of this monstrosity in the wake of the influence of *Psycho*, or for the historical importance of *Psycho* itself. For the really striking fact about this film is not its illustration of a previously unacknowledged archetype, but its archetype's influential emergence in 1960. This is not to say that there had not been female monsters before *Psycho* or that conventional male monsters of classic horror were not often sexually indeterminate.[13] It is to say, however, that *Psycho*'s array of dislocations – between normal and psychotic; between masculine and feminine; between Eros and fear; even between the familiar Hitchcockian suspense and a new, frankly gender-based horror – are what make it an important precursor of the thrill-producing visual attractions Schatz discusses as crucial to the New Hollywood and which I would like to identify as postmodern. Thus Hitchcock's decision to make the traditional monster of horror cinema a son who dresses up as his own mummified mother was a decision not so much to give violent power to 'the monstrous feminine', but, much more dramatically, to destabilize masculine and feminine altogether.

'He's a transvestite!' says the district attorney in a famously inadequate attempt to explain the root cause of Norman's disturbance. The line has been criticized, along with the psychiatrist's lengthy speech about how Norman became his mother, as Hitchcock's jab at the inadequacies of clinical explanation. Certainly Norman is not a mere transvestite – that is, a person whose sexual pleasure involves dressing up as the opposite sex – but rather a much more deeply disturbed individual whose whole personality had at times, as the psychiatrist puts it, 'become the mother'. Yet in the scene that supposedly shows us that Norman has finally 'become the mother', what we really see is Norman, now without wig and dress, sitting alone in a holding area reflecting, in the most feminine of the many voices given Mrs Bates, on the evil of 'her' son.

In other words, while ostensibly illustrating that Norman now 'is' the mother, the film provides a visual and auditory variation on Norman's earlier sexual indeterminacy. The shock of this scene is the combination of young male body and older female voice: visual evidence of male, aural evidence of female. It is thus not the recognition of one identity overcome by another that fascinates so much as the slippage between masculine and feminine poles of an identity. The film's penultimate image drives this home. Briefly emerging as if from under Norman's face is the grinning mouth of Mrs Bates's corpse. Again, the shock is that of indeterminacy: both Norman *and* mother. Thus the psychiatrist's point that Norman is entirely mother is not visually or aurally proven. Instead, these variations of drag become overtly thematized as ironic, and almost camp, forms of play with audience expectations regarding the fixity of gender.[14] Norman is not a transvestite but transvestitism is a major 'attraction' of these scenes for audiences.

A similar point can be made for the earlier climax of *Psycho* during Norman–Mrs Bates's thwarted attack on Lilah in the fruit cellar. Here again the 'attraction' is neither the appearance of Mrs Bates as woman, nor the revelation, when 'her' wig falls off in the struggle, that 'she' is her son. At the precise moment that Norman's wig begins to slip off in his struggle with Sam – when we see a masculine head emerging from under the old-lady wig – we witnessed what was at the time a truly shocking absence of gender stability. Gender of the monster is revealed in this film in very much the terms Judith Butler offers: as an imitation without an origin, a corporeal style of performance, a construction (1990: 138–9).

There can be no doubt, however, that one primary 'attraction' of the film's horror is its spectacular mutilation of a woman's naked body. Abject terror, as Clover puts it, is 'gendered feminine' (1992: 51). There is also no doubt that the introduction of certain psychoanalytic conventions on screen conspire to vilify the mother and her sexuality as cause of Norman's derangement. These are certain misogynist features of a film that, for a variety of reasons, struck a responsive chord with American audiences in a way that Michael Powell's similar, but more truly modernist, 'laying bare' of the device of voyeurism in *Peeping Tom* (also 1960) did not.[15] Over the next 20 years the horror genre would begin to establish a formula for reproducing, and refining, the various sexual and gendered elements of this experience in ways that would not lessen the attraction of the violence against women but which would empower the 'final girl' to fight back and invite spectators to identify alternately with her powerless victimization and the subsequently empowered struggle against it.

Psycho thus needs to be seen not as an exceptional and transgressive experience working against the classical norms of visual pleasure but rather as an important turning point in the pleasurable destabilizing of sexual identity within what would become the genre of slasher horror: it is the moment when the experience of going to the movies began to be constituted as providing a certain generally transgressive sexualized thrill of promiscuous abandonment to indeterminate, 'other' identities. To undergo this abandonment, however, audiences had to be *disciplined*, not in Silverman's sense of being punished, but in Foucault's sense of voluntarily submitting to a regime.

Disciplining fear: 'the care and handling of *Psycho*'

From the very first screenings of the film, audience reaction, in the form of gasps, screams, yells, and even running up and down the aisles, was unprecedented. Although Hitchcock later claimed to have calculated all this, saying he could hear the screams when planning the shower montage, screenwriter Joseph Stephano claims, 'He was lying .... We had no idea. We thought people would gasp or be silent, but screaming? Never' (Rebello, 1990: 117).

No contemporary review of the film ignored the fact that audiences were screaming as never before. Here are some typical reviews:

> Scream! Its a good way to let off steam in this Alfred Hitchcock shockeroo, . . . so scream, shiver and shake and have yourself a ball.
>
> (*LA Examiner*, 8 November 1960)

> So well is the picture made ... that it can lead audiences to do something they hardly ever do any more – cry out to the characters, in hopes of dissuading them from going to the doom that has been cleverly established as awaiting them.
>
> (Callenbach, 1960: 48)

And on the negative side:

> Director Hitchcock bears down too heavily in this one, and the delicate illusion of reality necessary for a creak-and-shriek movie becomes, instead, a spectacle of stomach-churning horror.
>
> (*Time*, 27 June 1960: 51)

> *Psycho* is being advertised as more a shocker than a thriller, and that is right – I am shocked, in the sense that I am offended and disgusted .... The clinical details of psychopathology are not material for trivial entertainment; when they are used so they are an offense against taste and an assault upon the sensibilities of the audience ... it makes you feel unclean.
>
> (Robert Hatch, *The Nation*, 2 July 1960)

Having unleashed such powerful reactions, the problem now was how to handle them. According to Anthony Perkins the entire scene in the hardware store following the shower-murder, the mopping up and disposal of Marion's body in the swamp were inaudible due to leftover howls from the previous scene. Hitchcock even asked Paramount Studio head Lew Wasserman to allow him to remix the sound to allow for the audience's vocal reaction. Permission was denied (Rebello, 1990: 163).

Hitchcock's unprecedented 'special policy' of admitting no one to the theater after the film had begun was certainly a successful publicity stunt, but it had lasting repercussions in its transformation of the previously casual act of going to the movies into a much more *disciplined* activity of arriving on time and waiting in an orderly line. As Peter Bogdanovich (1963) has noted, it is because of *Psycho* that audiences now go to movies at the beginning. One popular critic wrote in a Sunday arts-and-leisure section about the new policy:

> At any other entertainment from ice show to baseball games, the bulk of the patrons arrive before the performance begins. Not so at the movies which have followed the policy of grabbing customers in any time they arrive, no matter how it may impair the story for those who come in midway.
>
> (*View*: 1)

This reviewer then takes it upon himself to advocate the exhibition policy so important to *Psycho*'s success and impact on audiences: that no one be admitted late to the film. Hitchcock defended this policy in an article published in the *Motion Picture Herald* saying that the idea came to him one afternoon in the cutting room.

> I suddenly startled my fellow-workers with a noisy vow that my frontwards-backwards-sidewards-and-inside-out labors on 'Psycho' would not be in vain – that everyone else in the world would have to enjoy the fruits of my labor to the full by seeing the picture from beginning to end. This was the way the picture was conceived – and this was how it had to be seen.
>
> (6 August, 1960: 17–18)

This 'policy', unheard of in the USA at the time, necessitated important changes in the public's movie-going habits: audiences had to be trained to learn the times of each show; if they were late they had to wait for the next screening; and, once they bought their tickets, they had to be induced to stand patiently in ticketholder lines. The theater managers new buzzwords were to 'fill and spill' theaters efficiently at precise intervals, thus affording more screenings. The unprecedented discipline required to 'fill and spill' the theater was in paradoxical contrast to the equally unprecedented thrills of the show itself.[16]

Here is how another columnist described the discipline and thrill of seeing the film over a month after its release:

> There was a long line of people at the show – they will only seat you at the beginning and I don't think they let you out while it's going on . . . . A loudspeaker was carrying a sound track made by Mr. Hitchcock. He said it was absolutely necessary – he gave it the British pronunciation like 'nessary'. He said you absolutely could not go in at the beginning. The loudspeaker then let out a couple of female shrieks that would turn your blood to ice. And the ticket taker began letting us all in. A few months ago, I was reading the London review of this picture. The British critics rapped it. 'Contrived', they said. 'Not up to the Hitchcock standards'. I do not know what standards they were talking about. But I must say that Hitchcock . . . did not seem to be that kind of person at all. Hitchcock turned us all on. Of all the shrieking and screaming! We were all limp. And, after drying my palms on the mink coat next to me, we went out to have hamburgers. And let the next line of

people go in and die. Well, if you are reading the trade papers, you must know that 'Psycho' is making a mint of money. This means we are in for a whole series of such pictures.

(Delaplane, 1960)

How shall we construe this new disciplining of audiences to wait in line? Michel Foucault writes that 'discipline produces subjected and practiced bodies, "docile" bodies' (1978: 138). He means that what we experience as autonomy is actually a subtle form of power. Obviously the bodies of the *Psycho* audience were docile. Indeed, the fun of the film was dependent upon the ability of these bodies to wait patiently in line in order to catch the thrills described above. No one coerced them to arrive on time and wait in line. This discipline is for fun. And the fun derives partly from the exhilaration of a group submitting itself, as a group, to a thrilling sensation of fear and release from fear. In this highly ritualized masochistic submission to a familiar 'master', blood turns to ice, shrieking and screaming are understood frankly as a 'turn on', followed by climax, detumescence, and the final the recovery and renewal of (literal and metaphorical) appetite.

The passage also offers a rich mix of allusions to gender, class, and nationality: the mink coat next to the columnist is clear indication that these pleasures were not for men only, as well as evidence that a wide variety of the public participated. Hamburger counters mink; snooty English 'standards' are foils to America's favorite fantasy of the leveling democratic entertainment of 'the movies'. What we see here is a conception of the audience as a group with a common solidarity – that of submitting to an experience of mixed arousal and fear and of recognizing those reactions in one another and perhaps even performing them for one another.[17]

This audience, surveilled and policed with unprecedented rigor outside the theater, responding with unprecedented vocalized terror inside the theater, is certainly disciplined in the sense of Foucault's term. But it is also an audience with a new-found sense of itself as bonded around the revelation of certain terrifying visual secrets. The shock of learning these secrets produces a camaraderie, a pleasure of the group, that was, I think, quite new to motion pictures. A certain community was created around *Psycho*'s secret that gender is often not what it seems. The shock of learning this secret helped produce an ironic sadomasochistic discipline of master and slave with Hitchcock hamming up his role as sadistic master and with audiences enjoying their role as submissive victims.

An important tool in disciplining the *Psycho* audience were three promotional trailers, two quite short and one six-minute affair that has become a classic. All hinted at but, unlike most 'coming attractions', refrained from showing too much of the film's secret. In the most famous of these Hitchcock acts as a kind of house-of-horrors tour guide at the Universal International Studio set of the Bates Motel and adjacent house (now the Universal Studios Theme Park featuring the *Psycho* house and motel). Each trailer stressed the importance of special discipline: either 'please don't tell the ending, it's the only one we have' – or the importance of arriving on time. But there was also another trailer, not seen by the general public but even more crucial in inculcating audience discipline. Called 'The care and handling of *Psycho*' this was not a preview of the film but a filmed 'press book' teaching theater exhibitors how properly to exhibit the film and police the audience.[18]

The black-and-white trailer begins with a scene outside the DeMille Theater in New York where *Psycho* began a limited engagement before being released nationwide. To the accompaniment of Bernard Herrmann's driving violin score we see crowds in line for the film. A man in a tuxedo is a theater manager, the narrator urgently informs us, in charge of implementing the new policy, which the trailer then explains. The sly voice of Alfred Hitchcock is heard over a loudspeaker explaining to the waiting audience that 'This queuing up is good for you, it will make you appreciate the seats inside. It will also make you appreciate *Psycho*.' The mixture of polite inducement backed up by the presence of Pinkerton guards, and a life-size lobby card cut-out of Hitchcock pointing to his watch, add up to a rather theatrical, sadomasochistic display of coercion. We hear Hitchcock induce the audience to keep the 'tiny, little horrifying secrets' of the story while insisting on the democracy of a policy that will not even make exceptions for the Queen of England or the manager's brother.

Perhaps the most striking thing about this trailer is that it worked; not only did audiences learn to arrive on time but they eagerly joined the visible crowds on the sidewalks waiting to see the film. When shaken spectators left the theater they were grilled by those waiting in line but never gave away the secret (Rebello, 1990: 161). By exploiting his popular television persona as the man who loves to scare you, and the man audiences love to be scared by, Hitchcock achieved the kind of rapt audience attention, prompt arrival, and departure, that would have been the envy of a symphony orchestra. Yet, he achieved this attention with the casual, general audience more used to the distractions of amusement parks than the discipline of high culture.

On 17 July 1955 Disneyland had already opened its doors to large numbers of visitors taking in the total visual attraction of a variety of film-orientated 'fantasy lands'. In August 1964 Universal Studios began offering tramride tours of its movie sets and would eventually expand to a more movie-related and thrill-inducing competitor to Disneyland, including the *Psycho* set and a presentation of how certain scenes from the film were shot.[19] Clearly, the sort of discipline that Hitchcock was teaching was more like that of the crowds at these theme parks than any kind of simple audience taming. Lawrence Levine has written compellingly about the taming of American audiences during the latter part of the nineteenth century. He argues that while American theater audiences had in the first half of the nineteenth century been a highly participatory and unruly lot, spitting tobacco, talking back to actors, arriving late, leaving early, stamping feet, applauding promiscuously, they were gradually tamed by the arbiters of culture to 'submit to creators and become mere instruments of their will, mere auditors of the productions of the artist' (1988: 183).

Levine tells, for example, of an orchestra conductor in Cincinnati in 1873 who ordered the doors to be closed when he began to play, admitting no one until the first part was finished. When he was resisted his argument was 'When you play Offenbach or Yankee Doodle, you can keep your doors open. When I play Handel ... they must be shut. Those who appreciate music will be here on time' (1988: 188). Levine argues that this late-nineteenth-century American audience lost a sense of itself as an active force, a 'public', and became instead a passive 'mute receptor' of the will of the artist through this discipline. New divisions between high and low meant that it was more and more difficult to find audiences who could serve as microcosms of society, who felt like participants in a general culture, and who could articulate their opinions and feelings vocally (Levine, 1988: 195).

With Hitchcock's policy trailer we certainly see some elements of Levine's tamed audience: Pinkerton guards, loudspeakers, 'docile bodies' waiting patiently in line, not to mention Hitchcock's disembodied voice insisting that seeing the film from the beginning is 'required'. Certainly, Hitchcock asserts 'the will of the artist' over the audience. However, this will is in the service of producing visceral thrills and ear-splitting screams that are a far cry from the politely suppressed coughs of the concert hall. It seems that the efficiency and discipline demonstrated outside the theater need to be viewed in tandem with the unprecedented patterns of fear and release unleashed inside.

Hitchcock's discipline, like that of the emerging theme parks, was not based on the stratification of audiences into high and low, nor, as would later occur in the ratings system, was it based on the stratification of different age-groups. Nor was it based on the acquisition of the same kind of passivity and silence that Levine traces in late-nineteenth-century America. In Hitchcock's assumption of the persona of the sadist who expects his submissive audience to trust him to provide a devious form of pleasure, we see a new bargain struck between film-maker and audience: if you want me to make you scream in a new way and about these new sexually destabilized secrets, the impresario seems to say, then you must line up patiently to receive this thrill.

Hitchcock is, of course, only doing what he often did in his trailers: teasing the audience with their paradoxical love of fear, shock, surprise, and suspense – all emotions which he can rely upon audiences to know that he will manipulate for maximum pleasure. His famous cameos in the early parts of most of his films are another way of teasing the audience, though also of disciplining them to pay close attention. Like the patient crowds standing in line at Disneyland, or the crowds that would eventually stand in line to see the *Psycho* house and motel at Universal Studios,[20] these disciplined audiences were a far cry either from 1970s' film theory's notion of distanced, voyeuristic mastery or Levine's passive, mute receptors.

Psycho is popularly remembered as the film that violated spectatorial identification with a main character by an unprecedented killing off of that character in the first third of the film. But in order for audiences to experience the full force of that violation, Hitchcock required the kind of rapt entrance into the spell of a unified space and time that the so-called 'classical' theories of spectatorship assume but which the popular Hollywood cinema, with its distracted viewers wandering into theaters at any old time, had perhaps only rarely delivered. *Psycho* thus needs to be viewed as a film in which disciplined audiences arrived on time in order to be attentively absorbed into the filmic world and narrative, and in which distracted 'attractions' of the amusement-park variety are equally important. The more rapt viewers' initial attention, the more acute the shock when the rug was pulled out from under them.

Lawrence Levine's analysis of the nineteenth-century taming of the audience argues a singular process of repressing unruly body functions. Theaters, opera houses, large movie houses were, for him, agents in teaching audiences to adjust to new social imperatives, training them to keep strict control of emotional and physical processes. Levine may be right that bodily repression was necessary to concert and theater goers. But the (mostly unwritten) history of cinema reception[21] will require more than a concept of bodily repression to understand the various disciplines of film-going that have taken place in this century. It will certainly require a more Foucauldian concept of discipline as productive of certain precise bodily regimes of pleasure rather than the mere repression of the physical. For, as we have seen, *Psycho* simultaneously elicits more bodily reaction along with greater bodily discipline.[22]

The lesson of the 'care and handling' of *Psycho* is thus how first Hitchcock, and then Hollywood, learned how greater spectatorial discipline could pay off in the distracted attractions of a postmodern cinema. *Psycho* needs to be seen as an historical marker of a moment when popular American movies, facing the threat of television, in competition and cooperation with new kinds of amusement parks, began to invent new scopic regimes of visual and visceral 'attraction'. In this moment visual culture can be seen getting a tighter grip on the visual pleasures of film spectators through the reinstitution of a postmodern cinema of attractions.

One way of picturing the variety of these regimes and this perhaps unique moment of discipline and distraction that was *Psycho* is to consider an entire series of publicity photos of audiences watching *Psycho* published in the same trade publication. These photos were taken at the Plaza Theatre, London, during the film's first run in Britain. Figure 19.1 shows fragments of a very intense-looking audience, jaws set, looking hard except for a few people with averted eyes. We can note here the somewhat defensive postures indicating moments of anticipation – arms crossed; one person holding ears, suggesting the importance sound has in cueing the anticipation of terror.

Figure 19.2 shows closer detail of what may be the same audience. Here we begin to note significant gender differences. Whereas the men look intently, most women cringe, refusing to look at the screen as I had once suggested women do at horror films (Williams, 1984), or they cover their ears [Figure 19.2(a)]. On the other hand, Figure 19.2(b) shows just how dramatically male viewers seem to assert their masculinity by looking (note the 'cool' man with clenched jaw who both looks and clutches his tie).

Let us suppose, for the sake of argument, that these scared women in the audience are looking at one of the following: the 'scary woman' (Mrs Bates) or a terrified woman being attacked (Marion, Figure 19.3). What is the best way to describe the specifically gendered reactions of these women spectators? Consider the experience of watching the first attack on Marion in the shower. At this point in the film all viewers can be assumed to be somewhat identified with Marion and to be relatively, though not completely, unprepared for the attack – after all the film is called *Psycho*. They are taken by surprise by this first irrational irruption of violence, mystified by the lack of a distinct view of the attacker, shocked by the eerie sound and rhythms of screaming violins blending with screaming victim, and energized by the rapid cutting of the scene. This much is true for all spectators. Why then do women appear so much more moved, often to the point of grabbing ears, averting and covering eyes? The question, it seems, is whether female viewers can be said to be more closely identified with Marion, especially at the height of her fear and pain, than the males? Do we identify more, and thus find ourselves more

Figure 19.1 Fragment of the audience at the Plaza Theatre, London: bracing itself to view *Psycho*.
Reproduced courtesy of The Academy of Motion Picture Arts and Sciences.

Figure 19.2 Fragment of the audience at the Plaza Theatre, London: gendered responses to *Psycho*. Reproduced courtesy of The Academy of Motion Picture Arts and Sciences.

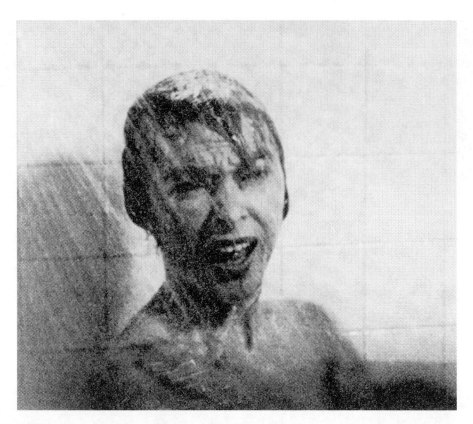

Figure 19.3 Marion in the shower, Psycho (1960).
Reproduced courtesy of The Academy of Motion Picture Arts and Sciences.

terrorized, because we are insufficiently distanced from the image in general and from this tortured image of our like in particular?

Men, in contrast, may identify with Marion but they forcefully limit their correspondence to her. Since terror is itself, as Carol Clover aptly notes, 'gendered feminine', the more controlled masculine reaction immediately distances itself from the scared woman on the screen. It more quickly gets a grip on itself (as does the man with his tie) and checks its expression. Yet at the same time that it exercises this control, this masculine reaction fully *opens up* to the image to, as Clover puts it, 'take it in the eye' (1992: 202). If, as Clover argues, all forms of contemporary horror involve the masochistic and feminine thrill of 'opening up' to, of being 'assaulted' by, penetrating images, we might say that the men can be seen to open up more because they feel they 'correspond' less to the gender of the primary victims (and to the femininity of fear itself).

For the woman viewer, however, this 'taking it in the eye' pleasures her less, initially, than it does the man. Because women already perceive themselves as more vulnerable to penetration, as corresponding more to the assaulted, wide-eyed, and opened-up female victim all too readily penetrated by knife or penis, women's response is more likely to *close down*, at least initially, to such images. This is to say that the mix of pleasure and pain common to all horror viewing, and aligned with a feminine subject position, is negotiated differently by men than by women. Thus all viewers experience a second degree of vicarious pain that is felt as feminizing. But in their greater vulnerability, some women viewers react by acting to filter out some of the painful images. I once took the woman's refusal to look at the screen as a sensible resistance to pain (Williams, 1984). Now I am more inclined to think that, like the general audiences who were disciplined to arrive on time, a much more complex and disciplined negotiation of pleasure and pain is taking place, and that this negotiation takes place over time, as we watch first this film and then its host of imitators – something these instantaneous photos cannot register.

In involuntarily averting their eyes, for example, women viewers partially rupture their connection with the female victim. In the process, we may also establish a new connection with the other women in the audience whose screams we hear. This new connection then itself becomes a source of highly ritualized feminine pleasure. We enjoy being scared *with one another* – a camaraderie that also allows us to measure our difference from Marion. Notice, for example, the smile on the half-hidden mouth of the woman in Figure 19.4.

Thus, while our first reactive, introjective experience of fear may elicit almost involuntary screams and the 'closing down' response of not looking, we do not stop feeling

Figure 19.4 Fragment of the audience at the Plaza Theatre, London: the gendered pleasure of fear. Reproduced courtesy of The Academy of Motion Picture Arts and Sciences.

the film because we stop looking. In fact, our reliance on musical cues may even induce us to feel more at this juncture. What are the violins saying about the danger of looking again? What is my girlfriend's posture as she leans into me telling me about how I might respond? Eventually, however, through the familiarity afforded by the film's repeated attacks, we begin to discipline ourselves to the experience of this reactive, introjective gaze. At this point some women may discipline themselves to keep their eyes more open.

Of course, these pictures do not really tell what audiences felt, and like all still images these are frozen moments, a few hundredths of seconds out of a 109-minute film. They could also have been faked. Nevertheless they dramatize, in acute body language, some general points about the changing distractions and disciplines of film spectatorship inaugurated by *Psycho*.

The first point is that however much we speak about the disembodied and virtual nature of cinematic, and all postmodern, forms of spectatorship, these are still real bodies in the theater, bodies which acutely feel what they see and which, even when visually 'assaulted', experience various mixes of vulnerability and pleasure. These people are on a kind of roller coaster which they have been disciplined to ride, and discipline is an enormously important part of the social experience of going to the movies.

A second point is that this discipline may involve the audience in a new level of performativity. While learning to enjoy the roller-coaster ride of a new kind of thrill, the audience may begin to perceive its own performances of fear as part of the show. As we also saw in the extended description of seeing *Psycho* by the columnist, these performances – screaming, hiding eyes, clutching the self as well as neighbors – may be important to the pleasures audiences take, as a group, in the film. Such spectatorial performances are certainly not new with *Psycho*. However, the self-consciously ironic manipulations of 'the master' eliciting these performances from audiences in a film that is itself about the performance of masculinity and femininity represents a new level of gender play and destabilization that I take to be a founding moment of the greater awareness of the performativity of gender roles increasingly ushered in by a postmodern, 'post-classical' reception of cinema.

A final point is that the discipline involved here – both inside and outside the theater – takes place over time. Spectators who clutched themselves, covered eyes, ears, and recoiled in fear at the shower-murder may have been responding involuntarily, the first time, to an unexpected assault. But by the film's second assault this audience was already beginning to play the game of anticipation and to repeat its response in increasingly performed and gender-based gestures and cries. By the time the game of slasher-assault became an actual genre in the mid-1970s, this disciplined and distracted, this attentive, performing audience will give way to the equivalent of the kids who raise their hands in roller-coaster rides and call out 'look 'ma, no hands!'

To find the experience of the popular, fun *Psycho* beneath the layers of high modernist critique or an all-embracing classicism is neither to denigrate the film's intelligence, nor the intelligence of the audiences who have enjoyed it. It is to recognize, rather, how important the visual and visceral experience of narrativized roller coasters have become and how assiduously audiences have applied themselves to the discipline of this fun.

Endnotes

1   Slavoj Žižek, for example, claims that it is 'still a "modernist" film because it has maintained a dialectical tension between history and the present' which he sees embodied in the contrast between the old family house and the modern hotel (Zizek, 1992: 232). Psychoanalytic critics seem to agree with this assessment. David Bordwell, as we shall see below, goes to some trouble to argue for the film's 'classical' status despite the fact that the release date of the film corresponds with the endpoint of his and his colleagues study of the classical Hollywood era of cinema. This date would be quite convenient for the argument I propose about the postmodernity of *Psycho* if Bordwell, Thompson and Staiger actually argued that 1960 represented a real change in the Hollywood style of film-making. In fact, however, they argue that while the mode of production has changed, moving from studio system to a package-unit system relying on the enormous profits of occasional blockbusters to drive economic expansion into related acquisitions in the leisure field, the Hollywood style has not changed that much (1985: 360–77). I think it has and that *Psycho* is a good example of the nature of this change.

2   One measure of the high seriousness of this tradition could be seen in Robin Wood's straight-faced interpretation of Mrs Bates's famous line about the fruit cellar – 'Do you think I'm fruity?' – as offering the 'hidden sexual springs of his behavior' yet then simply explicating the line as 'the source of fruition and fertility become rotten' – with not a word about the gay implications of Norman's fruitiness.

3   In this passage, Silverman introduces the seeds of a sadomasochistic dynamic that she and others have fruitfully developed in later work. But she cannot develop it here, in relation to *Psycho*'s viewing pleasure because her analysis is still wedded to a Mulveyan formula that sees all viewers seeking to escape an unpleasurable threat of castration. Since such escape is presumably thwarted by *Psycho*, the film seems to Silverman to disrupt classical narrative. However, this disruption was, in effect, saved from popular and suspect pleasures by its supposed enactment of castration: 'When the stabbing begins, there is a cinematic cut with almost every thrust of the knife. The implied equation is too striking to ignore: the cinematic machine is lethal; it too murders and dissects' (1983: 211).

4   For an excellent critique of limitations of this way of formulating cinema history see Miriam Hansen, this volume (Chapter 18). For a critique of the glaring omission of the mode or genre of melodrama from this history, see Altman (1992), Gledhill (1987), and Williams (1998).

5   This unfortunately leaves open the vexed problem of what to call this cinema, given the general acceptance of the term classical by so many scholars. I have become convinced that very often the old-fashioned, industry term melodrama – along with additional descriptive terms (western melodrama, gangster melodrama, racial melodrama) – offers a more precise description of both the narrative form and the spectatorial pleasures of a certain mainstream Hollywood product than does the term classical. But that is a matter for another essay (see Williams, 1998).

6   Consider, for example, the collections of films that have often (rather loosely) been called thrillers: erotic thrillers as different as *Blue Velvet* (1986), *Fatal Attraction* (1987), and *Basic Instinct* (1992); older-style paranoid political thrillers such as *The Parallax View* (1974) or *All the President's Men* (1976); or the more recent political thrillers *JFK* (1991) and *The Pelican Brief* (1993); action thrillers, whether of the slightly more realistic Harrison Ford variety or the more stylized Hong Kong-influenced variety; older-style gross-out horror such as *The Texas Chain Saw Massacre* (1974) or *Halloween* (1978) and the hundreds of sequels of these

and many other titles, or the newer-style mainstream horror thrillers (with similar 'psycho-killer' monsters) such as *The Silence of the Lambs* (1991); or, finally, the paranoid political thriller turned gender-destabilized romance of *The Crying Game* (1992).

7   Gunning writes, for example, 'the relations between films and the emergence of the great amusement parks, such as Coney Island, at the turn of the century provides rich ground for rethinking the roots of early cinema' (1990 reprint: 58). A similarly rich ground for rethinking postmodern cinema might be to consider the relation between cinema and the theme parks of the second half of the twentieth century.

8   Miriam Hansen, for example, has (sibilantly) argued that American films have in some ways returned to attractions which 'assault the viewer with sensational, supernatural, scientific, sentimental or otherwise stimulating sights' (Hansen, 1995). Yet, as Hansen certainly is aware, it is also important to see how these sensational and stimulating sights have changed.

9   Though Schatz himself would have no truck with such theoretical grand narratives as the rupture of the modern by the postmodern, his description of the appeal of these films nevertheless exemplifies both Jameson's 'cultural logic of late capitalism' as well as Friedberg's more modest description of the gradually increasing centrality of the image-producing and reproducing apparatuses.

10 Clover does not consider the female viewer as a significant component of the audience of slasher films.

11 Although the basic conventions of gender-confused psycho 'killer', 'terrible place', 'phallic weapon', and 'multiple victims' are already in place with *Psycho*, the convention of the powerful and triumphant 'final girl' is only incipient with the survival (though not yet the self-rescue) of Marion's sister Lilah. Since this 'girl's' reversal from abject victim to triumphant victor is crucial to the energy of the genre it is possible to say that *Psycho* does not fully 'fit' the psycho-killer genre.

12 This power challenges the prevalent view – especially in discussions of horror cinema – that femininity constitutes passivity. Creed goes on to argue in a chapter on *Psycho* that the really important story of this film is precisely the story of the castrating mother. While it has become conventional to interpret the phallic mother as endowed with a fantasy phallus whose function is to disavow the male fear of castration – and thus the 'actual' 'lack' in the mother's body – Creed insists that *Psycho* does not offer an image of a phallic mother disavowing lack, but of a castrating mother whose power is located, presumably, in her difference from the male. Creed does not make this point about difference specifically in relation to *Psycho*, but she does make it generally with respect to the monstrous feminine.

13 Rhona Berenstein's study of classic horror film (1995), for example, extends Clover's insights into an earlier realm of horror often considered the province of the sadistic 'male gaze' to argue that viewing pleasures were a more complicated form of role play than even Clover's masochistic pleasure of being assaulted can account for. In a genre in which monsters are masked and unmasked, heroes are feminized and doubled with monsters, heroines are both victimized and aligned with the monster's potency, viewer pleasure cannot be accounted for by simple binaries of masculine/feminine, Oedipal/preOedipal, homo/hetero. Berenstein thus argues not for a subversion of a monolithic male gaze through a challenge to pleasure but for an account of viewing pleasures that entails a play of shifting gender and sexual identifications. Audiences themselves, Berenstein argues, become performers of gender roles in the game of attraction–repulsion played out in the genre.

14 See, for example, Butler (1990), Garber (1992) and Berenstein (1995).

15 Both films are about knife-wielding psycho killers. Both begin with illicit sex – sex in a hotel room in *Psycho*; the initial filmed assignation-murder of a prostitute in *Peeping Tom* – both then travel down a circuitous garden path to sexually motivated murder. Both films were more 'graphic' in their displays of sex and violence than previous narratives. In both we are led to identify with the impulses of murdering peeping Toms who are presented as sympathetic and with young men beleaguered by oppressive parents – Norman by his dead mother, Mark by his dead film-maker father. The films differ, however, in one very important respect: Hitchcock initially fools us, in effect, about the perversions in which we are enlisted. Powell 'plays fair' and lets us know immediately that the nice boy who is so damaged by his private family romance is in fact a psycho killer who murders women while filming them and then projects what amounts to a snuff film for his private pleasure. Hitchcock, on the other hand, plays devious and does not let on that the nice young man who seems to be protecting his mother is really a sexually confused psychotic condemned to murder anyone who interferes with his totally psychotic relation to his mother–himself. Thus Powell's construction of the audience's relation to Mark, who is actually a moral being who destroys himself rather than destroy the 'good' woman who breaks into his psychotic repetition compulsions, is ironically more threatening to moral and psychological certainty than Hitchcock's construction of the audience's relation to Norman. For Norman has no moral awareness of his deeds at all since they are done 'by' Norman-as-mother. Thus *Peeping Tom* is the film that took the critical heat for being truly perverse while *Psycho* acquired the reputation of the self-reflexive critique of perversion. Powell claims that the strong negative reaction to this film, coupled with its poor box office, virtually ended his career. In contrast, the initially negative critical reaction to *Psycho* did Hitchcock no harm at all.

16 This is not to say that absolute mayhem inside the theater contrasted to absolute discipline in the lines formed outside. Hitchcock's project was, after all, to control the audience reaction inside the theater as well: 'If you've designed a picture correctly, in terms of its emotional impact, the Japanese audience would scream at the same time as the Indian audience' (Penelope Houston, 1980: 448). To the extent that he could not remix his film, Hitchcock did not, finally, obtain optimum control over audience reaction.

17 In 1971 film critic William Pechter pinpoints this camaraderie of the audience in his own description of how it felt to watch *Psycho*:

> The atmosphere ... was deeply charged with apprehension. Something awful is always about to happen. One could sense that the audience was constantly aware of this; indeed, it had the solidarity of a convention assembled on the common understanding of some unspoken *entente terrible*; it was, in the fullest sense, an audience; not merely the random gathering of discrete individuals attendant at most plays and movies.
>
> (1971: 181)

18 The recent Universal Studios 'rides' – with the possible exception of the fanciful flight on E.T.'s bicycle, or the more jolting experiences of catastrophic earthquake (*Earthquake*) and fire (*Backdraft*) seem to operate in the more sensationalizing, blockbuster, Hitchcock tradition of catastrophe and terror, to move audiences quite seriously. In April 1992 the guide on the tram ride portion of the tour showed how thoroughly the Hitchcockian model of assault on the body had been absorbed: 'At Universal Studios we not only like to show you the movies, we like you to feel them too'. For an excellent discussion of the 'hypercinematic' nature of the Disney experience see Scott Bukatman (1991).

19   It is worth noting that Hitchcock's next project was to have been a film set against the background of Disneyland with Jimmy Stewart as a blind pianist whose sight is restored in an operation and who goes to Disneyland in celebration. While there he discovers that the eyes he has been given are those of a murdered man. He thus begins to hunt down 'his' killer. After the manifest perversions of *Psycho*, the then child-centered and family-centered Disney claimed that not only would he not permit Hitchcock to shoot in his park, he would not permit his own children to see *Psycho* (Spoto, 1983: 471).

20   Hitchcock was greatly disappointed. Yet he may have had at least partial revenge. In a filmed address made sometime later to a British film society, we can see Hitchcock inventing the rudiments of what would one day become the Universal Studio's Tour. Called the Westcliffe Address – basically a filmed speech overlaid with documentary shots of the Universal Studio backlots featuring, of course, as the movie-centered amusement park now does, the *Psycho* house as one of its main attractions – the speech is fascinating for its anticipation of the Hollywood rival to Disneyland which would include a more catastrophic, Hitchcockian, assaultive, approach to its attractions. As we have already seen, what Hitchcock anticipated, not only in this address but in *Psycho* itself, was the process whereby amusement parks would become more like movies and movies would become more like the new amusement parks. The Westcliffe Address is in the archives of the Margaret Herrick Library.

21   One important exploration in the theory and practice of cinematic reception study is Janet Staiger's *Interpreting films* (1992).

22   Berenstein (1997) argues that such performances were a common feature of 'classic' horror cinema. She cites the publicity stunt of a woman planted in the audience of each screening of *Mark of the Vampire* as an extreme example. Her task was to scream and faint at predetermined moments so that ushers would whisk her away in a waiting ambulance.

Acknowledgements: This is a revised and altered version of an essay from *Culture and the problem of the disciplines* edited by John Rowe. Copyright © 1998 by Columbia University Press. Reprinted with permission of the publisher.

Thanks to Agnieszka Soltysik for much of the research concerning the reception of *Psycho*, to Nita Rollins and Christine Gledhill for the significance of roller coasters, to Michael Friend of the Margaret Herrick Library for all sorts of advice and information, including access to 'The care and handling of *Psycho*'. Thanks also to members of the University of California Irvine Critical Theory Institute, and to many other University of California Irvine colleagues, and to the Bay Area Film Consortium, for helpful suggestions.

References

Altman, Rick. 1992: Dickens, Griffith and film theory today. In Jane Gaines, ed., *Classical Hollywood narrative*, Durham, NC: Duke University Press, pp. 9–47.

Berenstein, Rhona. 1995: Spectatorship as drag: the act of viewing and classic horror cinema. In Linda Williams, ed., *Viewing positions: ways of seeing film*. New Brunswick, NJ: Rutgers University Press, pp. 231–69.

Berenstein, Rhona. 1996: *Attack of the leading ladies: gender and performance in classic horror cinema*. New York: Columbia University Press.

Bogdanovich. 1963: *The cinema of Alfred Hitchcock*. New York: Doubleday.

Bordwell, David. 1989: *Making meaning: inference and rhetoric in the interpretation of cinema*. Cambridge, MA: Harvard University Press.

Bordwell, David, Janet Staiger and Kristin Thompson. 1985: *The classical Hollywood cinema: film style and mode of production, 1917–1960*. New York: Columbia University Press.

Bukatman, Scott. 1991: There's always Tomorrow land: Disney and the hypercinematic experience. *October* **57**: 55–78.

Butler, Judith. 1990: *Gender trouble: feminism and the subversion of identity*. New York: Routledge.

Callenbach, Ernest. 1960: *Film Quarterly* **XIV** (1): 47–9.

Clover, Carol. 1992: *Men, women and chain saws: gender in the modern horror film*. Princeton, NJ: Princeton University Press.

Creed, Barbara. 1993: *The monstruous feminine: film, feminism, psychoanalysis*. London: Routledge.

Delaplane, Stan. 1960: *Los Angeles Examiner*, 12 August.

Eisenstein, Sergei. 1988: The montage of attractions. In *Eisenstein, Writings, vol. 1, 1922–1934*, edited and translated by Richard Taylor. Bloomington, IN: University of Indiana Press.

Foucault, Michel. 1978: *Discipline and punish: the birth of the prison*. Translated by Alan Sheridan. New York: Vintage Books.

Friedberg, Anne. 1993: *Window shopping: cinema and the postmodern*. Berkeley, CA: University of California Press.

Garber, Marjorie. 1992: *Vested interests: cross-dressing and cultural anxiety*. New York: Routledge.

Gledhill, Christine. 1987: The melodramatic field: an investigation. In Christine Gledhill, ed., *Home is where the heart is: studies in melodrama and the woman's film*. London: British Film Institute, pp. 5–39.

Gunning, Tom. 1986: 'The cinema of attractions: early film, its spectator and the avant-garde'. *Wide Angle* **8**(3–4): 63–70; reprinted in Thomas Elsaesser and Adam Barker, eds, *Early cinema: space, frame, narrative*. London: British Film Institute, 1990, 56–62.

Hansen, Miriam. 1995: Early cinema, late cinema: transformations of the public sphere. In Linda Williams, ed., *Viewing positions: ways of seeing film*. New Brunswick, NJ: Rutgers University Press.

Hatch, Robert. 1960: *The Nation*, 2 July.

Hitchcock, Alfred. 1960: *Motion Picture Herald*, 8 August, pp. 17–18.

Houston, Penelope. 1980: Alfred Hitchcock: I. In Richard Roud ed., *Cinema: a critical dictionary. vol. I*. Norwich: Martin Secker and Warburg, pp. 487–502.

Jameson, Fredric. 1984: The Cultural logic of late capitalism. *Postmodernism or, the cultural logic of late capitalism*. Durham: Duke University Press.

Jameson, Fredric. 1990: *Signatures of the visible*. New York: Routledge.

Jameson, Fredric. 1992: *The geopolitical aesthetic: cinema and space in the world system*. London and Bloomington, IN: Indiana University Press.

Levine, Lawrence. 1988: *Highbrow/lowbrow: the emergence of cultural hierarchy in America*. Cambridge, MA: Harvard University Press.

Pechter, William S. 1971: *Twenty-four times a second*. New York: Harper and Row.

Rebello, Stephen. 1990: *Alfred Hitchcock and the making of* Psycho. New York: HarperCollins.

Rothman, William. 1982: *The murderous gaze*. Cambridge, MA: Harvard University Press.

Schatz, Tom. 1993: The new Hollywood. In Jim Collins, Hilary Radner and Ava Preacher Collins, eds, *Film theory goes to the movies*. New York: Routledge, pp. 8–36.

Silverman, Kaja. 1983: *The subject of semiotics*. New York: Oxford University Press.

Silverman, Kaja. 1992: *Male subjectivity at the margins*. New York: Routledge.

Spoto, Donald. 1983: *The dark side of genius: the life of Alfred Hitchcock*. New York: Ballantine.

Staiger, Janet. 1992: *Interpreting films: studies in the historical reception of American cinema*. Princeton, NJ: Princeton University Press.

Tudor, Andrew. 1989: *Monsters and mad scientists: a cultural history of the horror movie*. Oxford: Basil Blackwell.

Williams, Linda. 1984: When the woman looks. In Mary Ann Doane, Patricia Mellencamp, and Linda Williams, eds, *Re-Vision: essays in feminist film criticism*. The American Film Institute Monograph Series, vol. 3. Frederick, MD: University Publications of America, pp. 83–99.

Williams, Linda. 1998: Melodrama revised. In Nick Browne, ed., *Refiguring American film genres*. Berkeley, CA: University of California Press, pp. 42–58.

Wood, Robin. 1965: *Hitchcock's films*. New York: Paperback Library.

Zizek, Slavoj (ed.) 1992: *Everything you always wanted to know about Lacan but were afraid to ask Hitchcock*. London and New York: Verso.

PART 5

Cinema in the age of

global multimedia

Editors' introduction

Contributors to this section take up the question of what cinema has become
in an era of postmodern, post-colonial, and global multimedia in which
Hollywood still rules although no longer in the same ways. Robert Stam and
Ella Shohat frame the concerns of this section with an understanding of the
inherently globalized, multicultural, and transnational nature of film arguing,
like Tom Gunning in the previous section, that moving-image media today are
very much situated as they were a hundred years ago. In their essay 'Film
theory and spectatorship in the age of the "posts"' they show that then, as
now, everything is possible; visual media of all sorts proliferate, and theatrical,
feature exhibition is only one possibility. Although Stam and Shohat
acknowledge the often one-way cultural imperialism of Hollywood, they also
point to the many ways in which the global media are now more interactive,
and to the way post-colonial theory and post-colonial cinema present new
kinds of cultural contradictions and syncretisms in a mass-mediated world.
They also suggest the ways in which the long-heralded celluloid specificity of
film has been 'dissolving into the larger bitstream of the audio-visual media'
(page 394) as media blur and become transnational and as the notion of
passive spectators gives way to more active participants.

Rey Chow, addressing the international post-colonial, transnational appeal
of contemporary Chinese cinema, asks the hard question of how to read these
films beyond the simple fact of their difference from Hollywood films. In
'Digging an old well: the labor of social fantasy in a contemporary Chinese

film', she focuses on the sensuous beauty of a number of contemporary Chinese films, pointing out that Western eyes perceive the gorgeous colors of the dye mill in *Joudou* as the films' exotic, 'third world difference' and that this social fantasy is indeed the cultural labor of the 'third world' for the 'first world': to provide the first world with a sense of its own freedom and democracy. However, Chow suggests that this 'third world difference' is also a way in which China explores its own relation to an inner, primitive alterity, which she examines through the 1987 film *Old Well*. Reading the film as an allegory of the nation's fascination with a primitive otherness that can stand in for an infinite regress of lacks, Chow shows how nostalgic social fantasy works to create a Chinese identity of collective work in the face of the failure of the Cultural Revolution.

In 'Facing up to Hollywood' Ana López traces an economic and cultural history of the different ways Latin American cinemas have 'faced up' to the hegemony of Hollywood cinema. Although her chapter traces a history that leads up to the contemporary era of global multimedia, her emphasis on the many ways in which Hollywood cinema and those that have 'faced up to it' have always been international and global is significant for the concerns of this section. Citing the example of Mexican cinema in the 1930s, López shows how a national cinema arose in the very shadow of Hollywood, to capture Latin American markets with a popular genre vision of Mexico. López compares this popular success with the Vera Cruz studios in Brazil in the 1950s which attempted to imitate Hollywood universalism, and the New Latin American cinema of the 1960s which opposed Hollywood politically, aesthetically, and economically. Both these later film movements failed to capture the popular imagination of national viewers. Today, López describes a more intensely globalized situation in which the relation to Hollywood is neither that of imitation nor that of antagonism but a fairly regular series of transnational border crossings.

This section ends, fittingly, with 'The end of cinema: multimedia and technological change'. In this chapter Anne Friedberg explores some of the global media changes discussed by Stam and Shohat. Demonstrating precisely how the media specificity of film has been 'dissolving into the larger bitstream of the audio-visual media', Friedberg opens up a new world of interactive exchange even as she describes the end of cinema as we know it. At the same time, Friedberg also shows us the endurance of our relationships to screens, whether these screens offer the dialogic interactivity of telephones or a relation akin to the old-fashioned absorption of cinema. While cinema 'itself' may not endure as film becomes more and more embedded in new technologies, our continuing relations with a screen intensify and invite our future scrutiny.

20 Film theory and spectatorship in the age of the 'posts'

Robert Stam and Ella Habiba Shohat

Our purpose in this chapter is to address the inherently globalized, multicultural, and transnational nature of film (and film theory), from the beginnings to the present, in the light of the diverse 'posts': post-structuralism, postmodernism, post-colonialism, and, we would add, 'post-film'. Obviously, we cannot survey all of film theory from this perspective; rather, we will focus on the globalized nature of some key 'moments'; the beginnings of cinema, the moment of structuralism and post-structuralism, and the contemporary moment of the 'posts'. Although some speak apocalyptically of the 'end of cinema', the current situation uncannily recalls the situation at the beginnings of cinema as a medium. 'Pre-cinema' and 'post-cinema' have come to resemble each other. Then, as now, everything seems possible. Then, as now, film 'neighbors' a wide spectrum of other simulation devices. Just as early cinema neighbored scientific experiments, burlesque, and sideshow, new forms of 'post-cinema' neighbor home shopping, video games, CD-ROMs, and IMAX. And then as now we find not only egalitarian possibilities but also entrenched assymetries of international power.

Since all social struggle in the postmodern era necessarily passes through the simulacral realm of mass culture, the media are absolutely central to any discussion of multiculturalism, transnationalism, and globalization. The contemporary media shape identity; indeed, many argue that they exist close to the very core of identity production. In a transnational world typified by the global circulation of images and sounds, goods and populations, media spectatorship impacts complexly on national identity, political affiliation, and communal belonging. By facilitating a mediated engagement with 'distant' peoples, the media circulate across national boundaries and thus 'deterritorialize' the process of imagining communities. And while the media can destroy community and fashion solitude by turning spectators into atomized consumers or self-entertaining monads, they can also fashion community and alternative affiliations.

Beyond the nation-state

The centrifugal forces of the globalizing process, and the global reach of the media, virtually oblige the contemporary media theorist to move beyond the restrictive framework of the nation-state. The cinema, for example, is now, and arguably always has been, a thoroughly globalized medium. In terms of personnel, we have only to think of the role of German émigrés in Hollywood, of Italians in Brazil's Vera Cruz, or of the Chinese in Indonesian film. Globalization has also been aesthetic. India's 'Bollywood' borrows and spices up Hollywood plots, while Brazilian comedies parody American blockbusters; thus *Jaws* (1975) becomes *Bacalhau* (1976) ('Codfish'). Moreover, Hollywood has by now been internalized as an international *lingua franca* which inhabits, as it were, virtually all cinemas, if only as a constant temptation or as the demonized other of national cinema. But it is not only Hollywood that has international influence. In the 1940s neo-realism became an influence in India (Ray) and Egypt (Chahine) and all around Latin America (dos Santos, Birri). The French New Wave and *cinéma verité* cast their spell over the African francophone countries. Nor is the influence unidirectional. Herzog, Coppola, and Scorcese express admiration for Brazil's Cinema Novo; Quentin Tarantino registers the impact of Hong Kong action films. Formerly 'Third World' film-makers are not limited to Third World locations. Mexican film-makers such as Alfonso Arau and Guilhero del Toro, for example, work in the United States, while the Chilean Raul Ruiz is based in France but also works elsewhere.

Although many regard the only 'real' cinema as the Hollywood-style fiction feature, much as American tourists abroad ask for prices in 'real money', in fact 'real' cinema takes many forms. Hollywood, furthermore, despite its hegemonic position, contributes only a fraction of the annual worldwide production of feature films. From its very inception, film production has been international. Although cinema began in Europe, it spread quickly throughout the world, with capitalist-based film production appearing roughly simultaneously in many countries, including in what are now called 'Third World' countries. Brazil's cinematic *bela epoca* (golden age), for example, occurred not in the 1960s but rather between 1908 and 1911, before the country was infiltrated by American distribution companies in the wake of World War 1. By the 1920s, India was producing more films than Great Britain. Today, the cinemas of Africa, Asia, and Latin America constitute the majority cinema of the world, just as people of color form the majority population. 'Third World cinema', taken in a broad sense, actually produces most of the world's feature films. If one excludes made-for-television films, India is the leading producer of fiction films in the world, producing between 700 and 1000 feature films a year. Asian countries, taken together, produce over half of the yearly world production.

Although arguably the majority cinema, 'Third World' cinema is rarely featured in cinemas, video stores, or in academic film courses. The yearly Oscar ceremonies inscribe Hollywood's arrogant provincialism; the audience is global, yet the product promoted is almost always American, the 'rest of the world' being corraled into the ghetto of the 'foreign film'. In this sense, the cinema inherits the structures laid down by the communication infrastructure of empire, the networks of telegraph and telephone lines and information apparatuses which literally wired colonial territories to the metropole, enabling the imperial countries to monitor global communications and shape the image of world events. In the cinema, this hegemonizing process intensified shortly after World War 1, when US film distribution companies (and secondarily European companies) began to dominate Third World markets, and was further accelerated after World War 2, with the growth of transnational media corporations.

In the postmodern age the old imperial hegemonies are more 'dispersed' and 'scattered'.[1] At the same time, even within the current situation of dispersed hegemonies, the historical thread or inertia of Western domination remains a powerful presence. Despite the close imbrication of 'First' and 'Third' worlds (now redubbed 'North' and 'South'), the global distribution of power still tends to make the First World countries cultural 'transmitters' and to reduce most Third World countries to the status of 'receivers'. The problem lies not in the exchange but in the unequal terms on which the exchange take place. One paradoxical by-product of this situation is that First World minorities have the power to project their cultural productions around the globe, which are then appropriated and 'indigenized'. (The *beur* films made by North Africans in France, for example, display the pervasive influence of African American hiphop culture, a case of one African diasporic community identifying with the cultural products of another African diasporic community.) Yet while the Third World is inundated with North American films, television series, popular music, and news programs, the First World receives precious little of the vast cultural production of the Third World, and what it does receive is usually mediated by transnational corporations. One telling index of this global Americanization is that even Third World airlines program Hollywood suburban comedies as their idea of 'universal' fare.

At the same time, the media imperialism thesis needs drastic retooling in the contemporary area. First, it is simplistic to imagine an active First World simply forcing its products on a passive Third World. Second, global mass culture does not so much replace local culture as coexist with it, providing a cultural *lingua franca*. Third, the imported mass culture can also be indigenized, put to local use, given a local accent as in the example of *beur* cinema above. Fourth, there are powerful reverse currents as a number of Third World countries (Mexico, Brazil, India, Egypt) dominate their own markets and become cultural exporters. The Indian television version of the *Mahabharata* won a 90 per cent domestic viewer share during a three-year run, and Brazil's Rede Globo now exports its *telenovelas* to more than 80 countries around the world. One of the biggest television hits in the new Russia is a venerable Mexican soap opera called *Los Ricos Tambien Lloran* ('The rich also cry'). We must distinguish, furthermore, between the ownership and control of the media – an issue of political economy – and the specifically cultural issue of the implications of this domination for the people on the receiving end. The 'hypodermic needle' theory is as inadequate for the Third World as it is for the First: everywhere spectators actively engage with texts, and specific communities both incorporate and transform foreign influences.

The global cultural situation is now more interactive; the USA is no longer the puppeteer of a world system of images, but only one mode of a complex transnational construction of 'imaginary landscapes'. In this new conjuncture, some argue, the invention of tradition, ethnicity, and other identity–markers becomes 'slippery, as it is swept up in the fluidities of transnational communication'.[2] Now the central problem becomes one of tension between cultural homogenization and cultural hetero-genization, in which hegemonic tendencies, well documented by Marxist analysts such as Mattelart and Schiller, are simultaneously 'indigenized' within a complex, disjunctive global cultural economy. At the same time, we would add, discernible patterns of domination channel the 'fluidities' even of a 'multipolar' world; the same hegemony that unifies the world through global networks of circulating goods and information also distributes them according to hierarchical structures of power, even if those hegemonies are now more subtle and dispersed.

The aporias of globalization

The term 'globalization' usually evokes a recent phenomenon involving complex realignments of social forces engendering an overpowering wave of international political, cultural, and economic interdependency. The term evokes the volatility and mobility of capital, the internationalization of trade and tariffs, a salutary 'competitiveness' on the part of labor, and the transformation of the world into a seamlessly wired global village. In its more euphoric versions, it evokes a cybernetic dance of cultures, 'one planet under a groove', the transcendence of rigid ideological and political divisions, and the worldwide availability of cultural products and information, whether it be CNN, world music, American serials, or Latin American *telenovelas*. The more dystopian view of globalization, in contrast, evokes the homogenization of culture, the annihilation of local political and cultural autonomy, and ultimately ecological catastrophe, as an untenable consumerist model is spread around a globe that can ill afford it. Recent financial crises in Asia, Africa, and Latin America, furthermore, suggest that globalization is not the panacea it has often been proclaimed to be.

What is often forgotten is that 'globalization' is not a new phenomenon; it forms part of the much longer history of colonialism going at least as far back as 1492. Columbus, in this sense, performed the founding gesture of globalization. Although colonization *per se* pre-dated European colonialism, what was new in European colonialism was its planetary reach, its affiliation with global institutional power, and its imperative mode, its attempted submission of the world to a single 'universal' regime of truth and power. This movement reached its apogee at the turn of the century. Globalization theory, in this sense, is what J.M. Blaut calls 'diffusionist';[3] it imagines Europe benevolently spreading its people, ideas, goods, and political systems around the world. Colonialist diffusionism, we would argue, began with colonialism's 'civilizing mission'. It transmuted into 'modernization' theory in the late 1940s and 1950s (the idea that Third World nations would achieve economic 'take-off' by emulating the historical progress of the West), and finally metamorphosed into neoliberalism and globalization in the 1980s and 1990s.

The cinema, as a product and symptom of modernity, forms part of this global history. Although the cinema as a technology is often seen as inherently 'Western', this is a misnomer. Until recent decades, Europe was largely a borrower of science and

movement, here too we encounter reciprocal influence within global relations. Post-structuralism had its long-term historical origins not only in European philosophy but also in a series of events that undermined the confidence of European modernity: the Holocaust (and in France the Vichy collaboration with the Nazis), and the post-war disintegration of the last European empires. Third World thinking had an undeniable impact on First World theory. The early structuralists codified, on some levels, what anti-colonial thinkers had been saying for some time. The subversive work of 'denaturalization' performed by what one might call the left wing of semiotics – for example Roland Barthes's famous analysis of the colonialist implications of the *Paris Match* cover showing a black soldier saluting the French flag – had everything to do with the external critique of European master narratives performed by Third World Francophone decolonizers such as Aimé Césaire and Frantz Fanon.[9] In the wake of decolonization, Europe started to lose its privileged position as model for the world. Lévi-Strauss's crucial turn from biological to linguistic models for a new anthropology, for example, was motivated by his visceral aversion to a biological anthropology deeply tainted by anti-semitic and colonialist racism. Indeed, it was in the context of decolonization in the early 1950s that UNESCO asked Lévi-Strauss to do research on *Race and history*, where the anthropologist rejected any essentialist hierarchy of civilizations.

In the late 1960s, structuralism came under attack from Derridean deconstruction – thus leading to post-structuralism. On one level, post-structuralism forms part of the anti-foundationalist wave going back to Nietzsche, Freud, and Heidegger, and notably to the 'hermeneutics of suspicion' (Paul Ricoeur) that interrogates the inevitable slips that corrode attempts to fix and stabilize meaning. But, on another level, post-structuralism coincided with a veritable legitimation crisis in Europe itself. Derrida's decentering of Europe as 'normative culture of reference' was clearly indebted to Fanon's earlier decentring of Europe in *The wretched of the earth*. Many of the source thinkers of structuralism and post-structuralism, as Robert Young points out in *White mythologies*,[9] were biographically linked to what came to be called the Third World: Lévi-Strauss did anthropology in Brazil; Foucault taught in Tunisia; and Althusser, Cixous, and Derrida were born in Algeria, the same country where Bourdieu did his field work.

While supportive of post-structuralism's decentering of Europe, some Third World and later post-colonial thinkers quarrelled with the dissolution of the subject proposed by post-structuralism. With post-structuralism, the notion of a coherent subject identity, let alone a community-identity, came to seem epistemologically suspect. Debra P. Amory expressed Third World feminist frustration with this (dis)articulation of the subject:

> Doesn't it seem funny that at the very point when women and people of color are ready to sit down at the bargaining table with the white boys, that the table disappears? That is, suddenly there are no grounds for claims to truth and knowledge anymore and here we are, standing in the conference room making all sorts of claims to knowledge and truth but suddenly without a table upon which to put our papers and coffee cups, let alone to bang our fists.[10]

Metrocentric theory announces the demise of what others still want to achieve – nation, narrative, subjecthood. In this sense, much of postmodern theory constitutes a sophisticated example of what Anwar Abdel Malek calls the 'hegemonism of possessing minorities'.[11] The center proclaims the end of its privileges, ironically, just when the periphery begins to lay claim to them. Elizabeth Fox-Genovese writes:

> Surely it is no coincidence that the Western white male elite proclaimed the death of the subject at precisely the moment at which it might have had to share that status with the women and peoples of other races and classes who were beginning to challenge its supremacy.[12]

Thus thinkers from the center, blithely confident in national power and international projection, denounce non-metropolitan nationalisms as atavistic and *passé*. Metropolitan writers announce the 'death of the author' just as 'peripheral' writers begin to win their Nobel Prizes. All these 'divestitures' reflect a privilege available only to the already empowered, for the proclamation of the end of margins does not short-circuit the mechanisms that effectively disappropriate peoples of their culture or nations of their power.

How, then, should the struggle to become subjects of history be articulated in an era of the 'death of the subject'? Should Third Worldist notions of becoming 'subjects' of history be dismissed as a pathetic lure and mystification? And does the decentering of identities mean that it is no longer possible to draw boundaries between privilege and disenfrachisement? At least provisionally, identities can be formulated as situated in geographical space and 'riding' historical momentum. That identity and experience are mediated, narrated, constructed, caught up in the spiral of representation and intertextuality does not mean that all struggle has come to an end. Diana Fuss distinguishes between 'deploying' or 'activating' essentialism on the one hand, and 'falling into' or 'lapsing into' essentialism on the other.[13] What Spivak calls 'strategic essentialism' and what Hall refers to as 'the fictional necessity of arbitrary closure', are crucial for any multicultural struggle that hopes to allow for communities of identification, even if those communities are multiple, discontinuous, and partially imaginary.

The politics of postmodernism

Contemporary media theory has of necessity to confront the phenomena summed up in the mercurial term 'postmodernism', a term which implies the global ubiquity of market culture, a new stage of capitalism in which culture and information become key terrains for struggle. 'Postmodernism' is on one level not an event but a discourse, a conceptual grid which has by now been 'stretched' to breaking point. As Dick Hebdige points out in *Hiding in the light* (1988),[14] postmodernism has shown a protean capacity to change meaning in different national and disciplinary contexts, coming to designate a host of heterogeneous phenomena, ranging from details of architectural decor to broad shifts in societal or historical sensibility. Hebdige discerns three 'founding negations' within postmodernism: the negation of totalization, that is an antagonism to discourses which address a transcendental subject, define an essential human nature, or proscribe collective human goals; the negation of teleology (whether in the form of authorial purpose or historical destiny); and the negation of utopia, that is a scepticism about what Lyotard calls the '*grands récits*' of the West, the faith in progress, science, or class struggle.[15] A *boutade* summed up this position as: 'God is dead, so is Marx, and I'm not feeling too well myself'.) The empty sequentiality of the 'post' corresponds to a preference for prefixes which begin in de or dis – decentering, displacement – which suggest the demystification of pre-existing paradigms.

But with postmodernism too, as with post-structuralism, we have to acknowledge the force of the anti-colonial and anti-racist critique which helped provoke this legitimation crisis in the West. Postmodernism too can be seen as on some levels as a symptom of Europrovincialism, the assumption that when the First World sneezes, the whole world catches a cold. Eurocentrism makes the local global, the provincial 'universal'. Indeed, Third World critics have argued that 'postmodernism' was merely another way of the West naming itself, passing off its provincial concerns as universal conditions. 'For the African,' writes Denis Epko, 'the celebrated postmodern condition [is] nothing but the hypocritical self-flattering cry of overfed and spoiled children.'[16] Latin American intellectuals, meanwhile, pointed out that neologistic Latin American culture (for example Brazilian modernism and Mexican *mestizaje* in the 1920s), in its precocious embrace of hybridity and syncretism, had been aesthetically postmodernist *avant la lettre*. This global synchronicity was missed even by such a generally acute cultural theorist as Fredric Jameson, who in his unguarded moments seems to conflate the terms of political economy (where he projects the Third World into a less developed, less modern frame), and those of aesthetic and cultural periodization (where he projects it into a 'pre-modernist' or 'pre-postmodernist' past). A residual economism or 'stagism' here leads to the equation of late capitalist = postmodernist and precapitalist = pre-modernist, as when Jameson speaks of the 'belated emergence of a kind of modernism in the modernizing Third World, at a moment when the so-called advanced countries are themselves sinking into full postmodernity'.[17] Thus the Third World always seems to lag behind, not only economically but also culturally, condemned to a perpetual game of catch-up in which it can only repeat on another register the history of the 'advanced' world.

Postmodernism as a discursive/stylistic grid has enriched film theory and analysis by calling attention to a stylistic shift toward a media-conscious cinema of multiple styles and ironic recyclage – for example the relation between Madonna's song 'Material girl' and *Gentlemen prefer blondes* (1953), Much of the work on postmodernism in film has involved the positing of a postmodern aesthetic, exemplified in such influential films as *Blue Velvet* (1982), *Blade Runner* (1987), and *Pulp Fiction* (1994) Jameson discerns in such 'neo-*noir*' films as *Body Heat* (1981) a 'nostalgia for the present'. Films such as *American Graffiti* (1973) for Americans, *Indochine* (1992) for the French, and the 'raj nostalgia' films (*Heat and Dust* (1983), *Passage to India* (1984)) for the English, convey a wistful sense of loss of what is imagined as a simpler and grander time. For this stylistically hybrid postmodern cinema, both the modernist avant-garde modes of analysis – with the cinema as the instigator of epistemological breakthroughs – and the modes of analysis developed for 'classical' cinema, no longer quite 'work'. Instead, libidinal intensities compensate for the weakening of narrative time, as the older plots are replaced by an 'endless string of narrative pretexts in which only the experiences available in the sheer viewing present can be entertained'.[18]

The important point that postmodernism makes is that virtually all political struggles now take place on the symbolic battleground of the mass media. Instead of the 1960s' slogan 'the revolution will not be televised' it seems in the 1990s that the only revolution will be televisual. The struggle over representation in the realm of the simulacra homologizes that of the political sphere, where questions of representation slide into issues of delegation and voice. At its worst, postmodernism reduces politics to a passive spectator sport where the most we can do is react to pseudo-events (but with real-world effects) such as the 'Bill and Monica show'[19] through polls or call-in tabloid news programs. At its best, postmodernism alerts us that new times demand new strategies.

Film and the post-colonial

What was once called 'Third World' theory has now largely been absorbed into the field of the 'post-colonial'. Post-colonial discourse theory refers to an interdisciplinary field (which includes history, economics, literature, the cinema) which explores issues of the colonial archive and of post-colonial identity often in highly theoretical work inflected by Lacan and Derrida. Post-colonial theory is a complex amalgam fed by diverse and contradictory currents; studies of nationalism (for example Benedict Anderson's *Imagined communities*), the literature of 'Third World allegory' (Ismail Xavier, Fredric Jameson, Aijaz Ahmad), the work of the 'Subaltern Studies Group' (Ranj Guha, Partha Chatterjee), and the work of the 'post-colonial critics' *per se* (Edward Said, Homi Bhabha, and Gayatri Spivak).[20]

Post-colonial theory built on and assumed earlier anti-colonial theory (Aimé Césaire, Frantz Fanon, Albert Memmi, Amikar Cabral). Although Fanon never spoke of 'Orientalist discourse', his critiques of colonialist imagery provide proleptic examples of anti-Orientalist critique. Within colonial binarism, according to *Wretched of the earth*, 'the settler makes history; his life is an epoch, an Odyssey, while against him torpid creatures, wasted by fevers, obsessed by ancestral customs, form an almost inorganic background for the innovating dynamism of colonial mercantilism'.[21] The foundational text for post-colonial theory in academe, however, was Edward Said's *Orientalism* (1978), where Said used Foucauldian notions of 'discourse' and the power/knowledge nexus to examine the ways that Western imperial power and discourse constructed a stereotypical 'Orient'.[22] Post-colonial theory builds on the insights of post-structuralism – Said draws on Foucault, Spivak on Derrida, and Bhabha on both Lacan and Derrida – but in some ways it has an adversary relation to postmodernism, for which it forms, as it were, a kind of reverse field. If postmodernism is Eurocentric, narcissistic, flaunting the West's eternal newness, post-colonial criticism argues that the West's models cannot be generalized, that the East is in the West and vice versa, that we are here because you were there.

The wide adoption of the term 'post-colonial' to designate work thematizing issues emerging from colonial relations and their aftermath, in the late 1980s, clearly coincided with the eclipse of the older 'Third World' paradigm. The 'post' in 'post-colonial' suggests a stage 'after' the demise of colonialism, and it is therefore imbued with an ambiguous spatio-temporality. 'Post-colonial' tends to be associated with 'Third World' countries that gained independence after World War 2, yet it also refers to the 'Third World' diasporic presence within 'First World' metropolises. The term 'post-colonial' blurs the assignment of perspectives. Since most of the world is now living 'after' colonialism, the 'post' neutralizes significant differences between France and Algeria, Britain and Iraq, the USA and Brazil. By implying that colonialism is over, furthermore, 'post-colonial' risks obscuring the deformative traces of colonialism in the present. While most of the 'posts' suggest the supersession of outmoded philosophical aesthetic paradigms – post-structuralism, postmodernism – post-colonialism suggests both a movement beyond a specific point in history (European colonialism) and the supersession of an intellectual paradigm (anti-colonialist discourse), resulting in a tension between philosophical and historical temporalities.

If the nationalist discourse of the 1960s drew sharp lines between First World and Third World, oppressor and oppressed, post-colonial discourse replaces such binaristic dualisms with a more nuanced spectrum of subtle differentiations, in a new global regime where First World and Third World are mutually imbricated. Notions of ontologically referential identity metamorphose into a conjunctural play of identifications. Purity gives way to 'contamination'. Rigid paradigms collapses into sliding metonymies. Erect, militant postures give way to an orgy of 'positionalities'. Once secure boundaries become more porous; an iconography of barbed-wire frontiers mutates into images of fluidity and crossing. A rhetoric of unsullied integrity gives way to miscegenated grammars and scrambled metaphors. Colonial tropes of irreconcilable dualism give way to complex, multilayered identities and subjectivities, resulting in a proliferation of terms having to do with various forms of cultural mixing: religious (syncretism); biological (hybridity); linguistic (creolization); and human-genetic (*mestizaje*).

Black skin, white masks, Isaac Julien's post-Third-Worldist documentary about Frantz Fanon, gives voice to these discursive shifts.[8] While accepting the basic anti-colonialist thrust of Third Worldist discourse, the film also interrogates the limits and tensions within that discourse, especially in terms of infra-national having to do with race, gender, sexuality, and even religion. On another level, *Black skin white masks* stages the diasporic chronotope (space/time) lived by the biographical Fanon, the film's scene ultimately constituting a dispersed, fractured chronotope. The film's 'home' location is the psychiatric ward in Blida-Joinville, where Fanon went in 1953, yet the film's 'story' evokes Martinique, France, Algeria, Tunisia, while still other spaces 'enter' the film through radio broadcasts alluding to the black struggle in the USA.

The emphasis on various forms of 'mixedness' in post-colonial writing calls attention to the multiple identities, already present under colonialism, but now further complicated by the geographical displacements characteristic of the post-independence era, and presupposes a theoretical framework, influenced by anti-essentialism post-structuralism, that refuses to police identity along purist 'either/or' lines. But while reacting against the colonialist phobias and the fetish of racial purity, contemporary hybridity theory also counterposes itself to the overly rigid lines of identity drawn by Third Worldist discourse. The celebration of hybridity (through a switch in valence for what were formerly negatively connoted terms) gives expression, in the era of globalization, to the new historical moment of the post-independence displacements which generated dually or even multiply hyphenated identities (Franco-Algerian, Indo-Canadian, Palestinian-Lebanese-British, Indo-Ugandan-American, Egyptian-Lebanese-Brazilian).

A number of 'post-colonial' films – Stephen Frear's *Sammy and Rosie Get Laid* (1989), Gurinder Chada's *Bhaji on the Beach*, (1994), and Isaac Julien's *Young Soul Rebels* (1991) – bear witness to the tense hybridities of the former colonized growing up in what was once the 'motherland'. In the multicultural neighborhood of *Sammy and Rosie Get Laid*, the inhabitants have 'lines out', as it were, to Asia and the Caribbean and other formerly colonized parts of the globe. Many 'post-colonial hybrid' films focus on diasporas in the First World: the Indian diaspora in Canada (*Massala*, 1991) and the USA. (*Mississippi Massala*, 1991); the Iranian diaspora in New York (*The Mission*, 1985; *The Suitors*, 1988); Ghanians in England (*Testament*, 1988); Turks in Germany (*Farewell to False Paradise*, 1988); North Africans in France [*Le Thé du Harem d'Archimède* ('Tea in the Harem', 1985)]; Chinese in the USA. (*Full Moon over New York*, 1990).[23] Such films also reflect a real-world situation of multiple national allegiances, where Mexican and Pakistani 'immigrants' to the USA, for example, keep in close touch with their home communities thanks to cheap flights, and new technologies such as e-mail, satellite television, and faxes, not to mention local cable stations featuring programs in Spanish or Urdu. Old-style assimilation gives way to the active maintenance of multiple loyalties, identities, and affiliations.

Post-colonial theory deals very effectively with the cultural contradictions and syncretisms generated by the global circulation of peoples and cultural goods in a mass-mediated and interconnected world, resulting in a kind of commodified or mass-mediated syncretism. The culinary metaphors typical of post-colonial discourse often imply a fondness for this kind of *mélange*. Significantly, Indian film-makers speak of blending the massalas – literally, Hindi for 'spices', but metaphorically evoking the creation of 'something new out of old ingredients' – as a key to their recipe for making films. Indeed, the word massala forms part of the titles of two Indian diasporic films, one Indian-Canadian (*Massala*) and the other Indo-American (*Mississippi Massala*). In the former film, the god Krishna, portrayed as a gross hedonist, appears to a nostalgic Indian grandmother thanks to an interactive video cassette recorder (VCR). While mocking the official multiculturalism of Canada, the filmic style itself serves up a kind of massala, where the language of the Hindu 'mythological' mingles with the language of MTV and the mass media.

Post-colonial theory has been critiqued for: its elision of class (not surprising given the elite origins and status of many of the theorists themselves); its psychologism (the tendency to reduce large-scale political struggles to intra-psychic tensions; its elision of questions of political economy in an age where economics is the driving force behind the very cultural changes registered by post-colonial theory; its ahistoricity (its tendency to speak in the abstract without specifying historical period or geographical location); its denial of the pre-colonial past of non-European societies; its ambiguous relation to indigenous peoples; its ambiguous relation, in academe, to 'ethnic studies', where post-colonial theory is projected as sophisticated (and unthreatening) while 'ethnic studies' is seen as militant and crude.[24]

Indigenous media

While post-colonial thought stresses deterritorialization, the artificial, constructed nature of nationalism and national borders, and the obsolescence of anti-colonialist discourse, indigenous or 'Fourth World' peoples emphasize a discourse of territorial claims, symbiotic links to nature, and active resistance to colonial incursions. In this sense, post-colonial theory, like Third World theory before it, elides the presence of the 'Fourth World' existing within all of the other worlds, to wit, those peoples variously called 'indigenous', 'tribal', or 'first nations', in sum the still-residing descendants of the original inhabitants of territories subsequently taken over or circumscribed by alien conquest or settlement.

Fourth World peoples often appear in 'ethnographic films,' which of late have attempted to divest themselves of vestigial colonialist attitudes. While in the old ethnographic films self-confident 'scientific' voiceovers delivered the 'truth' about subject peoples unable to answer back (while sometimes prodding the 'natives' to perform practices long abandoned), the new ethnographic films, in the wake of post-structuralist anthropology, strive for 'shared film-making', 'participatory film-making', 'dialogical anthropology', 'reflexive distance', and 'interactive film-making', as artists experience a salutary self-doubt about their own capacity to speak 'for' the other.[25] Film-makers/theorists discard the covert elitism of the pedagogical or ethnographic model in favor of an acquiescence in the relative, the plural, and the contingent. (Anthropology, as the *boutade* has it, has become 'Anthro-Apology'.) The question, ideally, is no longer how one represents the 'other', but rather how one collaborates with the 'other', or better how to critique the practices which generate otherness. (In the end, there are no 'others', only 'otherization'.) The goal, rarely realized, becomes to guarantee the effective participation of the 'other' in all phases of production, including theoretical production.

Indigenous people themselves, meanwhile, have undertaken to represent themselves, more or less without mediation. We now have the first independent narrative fiction feature film written, produced, directed, and acted by native Americans: *Smoke Signals* (1998), adapted from a book by Sherman Alexie (Spokane), *The Lone Ranger and Tonto fistfight in heaven*, and directed by Chris Eyre (Cheyenne), it tells a coming-of-age story about two young Coeur d'Alene men bound together by the loss of their fathers. In New Zealand, Lee Tamahori's *Once Were Warriors* (1994) was the first Maori feature to become an international hit. But the most remarkable recent development has been the emergence of 'indigenous media', that is, the use of audio-visual technology (camcorders, VCRs) for the cultural and political purposes of indigenous peoples. Within this new form of cultural production, which emerged in the late 1970s in North America, and in the 1980s in Australia and Brazil, the producers are themselves the receivers, along with neighboring communities and, occasionally, distant cultural institutions or festivals such as the Native American film festivals held in New York and San Francisco. Indigenous media is an empowering vehicle for communities struggling against geographical displacement, ecological and economic deteriotion, and cultural annihilation.[26] Indigenous film and video-makers confront what Faye Ginsburg calls a 'Faustian dilemma':[27] on the one hand, they use new technologies for cultural self-assertion, on the other they spread a technology that might ultimately only foster their own disintegration.

Indigenous people have used camcorders to document their traditional knowledge of the forest environment and record the transmission of myths and oral history. For people such as the Kayapo of Brazil, as Turner puts it, video media have become 'not merely a means of representing culture', but are themselves the ends of social action and objectification in consciousness.[28] Widely disseminated images of the Kayapo wielding video cameras, appearing in *Time* and *The New York Times Magazine*, derive their power to shock from the premise that 'natives' must be quaint and allochronic; 'real' Indians don't carry camcorders.

The leading anthropologists studying indigenous media, such as Ginsburg and Terence Turner, see such work not as locked into a bound traditional world but rather as concerned with 'mediating across boundaries, mediating ruptures of time and history', and advancing the process of identity construction by negotiating 'powerful relationships to land, myth and ritual'.[27] Rather than a mere adaptation of Western visual culture, Faye Ginsburg argues, we are dealing with a 'new form of collective self-production'.[28] At the same time, 'indigenous media' should not be seen as a magical panacea either for the concrete problems faced by indigenous peoples or for the aporias of anthropology. Such work can provoke factional divisions within indigenous communities, and can be appropriated by the media as facile symbols of the ironies of the postmodern age.[29]

Post-celluloid: digital theory and the new media

While Fourth World peoples make territorial claims, the media more and more 'deterritorialize' subjectivity. Contemporary spectatorship must therefore also be considered in the light of changing audio-visual technologies. The cinema in its long-heralded specificity now seems to be dissolving into the larger bitstream of the audio visual media, be they photographic, electronic, or cybernetic, changing not only the 'identity' of the cinema but also that of those who consume it. Indeed, changing audio-visual technologies dramatically impact on virtually all of the perennial issues engaged by film theory: specificity, auteurism, apparatus theory, spectatorship, realism, aesthetics. As Henry Jenkins puts it:

> E-mail poses questions about virtual community; digital photography about the
> authenticity and reliability of visual documentation; virtual reality about embodiment
> and its epistemological functions; hypertext about readership and authorial authority;
> computer games about spatial narrative; MUDs about identity formation; webcams
> about voyeurism and exhibitionism.[30]

The new media 'blur' media specificity; since digital media potentially incorporate all previous media, it no longer makes sense to think in media-specific terms. In terms of auteurism, purely individual creation becomes even less likely in a situation where multimedia creative artists depend on an extremely diversified network of media producers and technical experts. Digital imaging also leads to the de-ontologization of the Bazinian image. With the dominance of digital image production, where virtually any image becomes possible, 'the connection of images to solid substance has become tenuous . . . images are no longer guaranteed as visual truth'.[31] The artist need no longer search for a pro-filmic model in the world; one can give visible form to abstract ideas and improbable dreams. The image is no longer a copy but rather acquires its own life and dynamism within an interactive circuit, freed of the contingencies of location shooting, weather conditions, and so forth.

Computer graphics, interactive technologies and virtual reality carry the bracketing of social positions to unprecedented lengths. Within cybernetic paraspace, the flesh-and-blood body lingers in the real world while computer technology projects the cybersubject into a terminal world of simulations. Such technologies expand the reality effect exponentially by switching the viewer from a supposed passive to a more interactive position, so that the raced, gendered censorial body could be offered, theoretically, a constructed virtual gaze, becoming a launching site for identity travel. Yet it would be naïve to place exaggerated faith in these new technologies, for their expense makes them exploitable mainly by corporations and the military. As ever, the power resides with those who build, disseminate, and commercialize the systems.[32] All the technological sophistication in the world, furthermore, does not guarantee empathy or trigger political commitment. The point is not merely to communicate sensations but rather to advance structural understanding and promote change.

While it has been argued that the classical film was a well-oiled machine for producing emotions, one which urged the spectator to follow a linear structure which provoked a sequenced set of emotions, the new interactive media allow the participant – the word spectator seems too passive – to forge a more personal temporality and mould a more personal emotion. The screen becomes an 'activity center', a cyberchronotope where both space and time are transformed. While it makes sense to ask the 'length' of a film, it is meaningless to ask the same question of an interactive narrative or game or CD-ROM. The participant decides the duration, the sequence, the trajectory. CD-ROMs such as *Myst* and *Riven* use high-definition image and stereo sound to bring the participant into a film-like dietetic world with multiple byways and exits and endings. Now the key word becomes 'interactivity', rather than enforced passivity, whence the obsolescence of the Baudry–Metz style analyses of spectatorship and the apparatus.

At the same time, digital cameras and digital editing (AVID) facilitate low-budget film-making and new montage possibilities. And in terms of distribution, the Internet makes it possible for a community of strangers to exchange texts, images, video sequences, thus enabling a new kind of translational communication, hopefully more reciprocal and multicentered than the old Hollywood-dominated international system. Thanks to fiber-optics, we can look forward to 'dial-up cinema', the capacity to see, or download, a vast archive of films and audio-visual materials. The shift to the digital makes for infinite reproducibility, without loss of quality since the images are stored as pixels, with no 'original'.[33] We are also now being promised computer–generated actors, desktop computers that can produce feature films, creative collaborations across geographically dispersed sites.

Just as Umberto Eco suggested in *Foucault's pendulum* that literature would be changed by the existence of word-processors, so film (and film theory) will be irrevocably changed by the new media.[34] These changes have led some to a euphoric discourse, reminiscent in some ways of that which greeted the cinema a century earlier. But the idea that the new media can make possible the transcendence of race and class and nation and gender distinctions ignores the historical inertia of socially generated stratifications. Any serious discussion of the new media has to speak of their uses and potentialities in specific times and spaces, suggesting not only their advantages but also their limitations. Even what qualifies as 'new' or as high-tech is relative; in the USA for Europe it might be IMAX or the World Wide Web; in the Amazon it might be camcorders, VCRs, and satellite dishes. And despite all the talk of democratization and interactivity, techo-futurist discourse often resorts to gendered tropes rooted in colonial domination or conquest: trail-blazing, space conquest, 'homesteading of the electronic frontier'. The cyber-discourse of *Wired* magazine speaks in the language of the Western to evoke the Internet's 'wide-open-spaces', where one 'stakes a claim' in 'new territory' guided by a 'pioneer/settler philosophy' of 'self-reliance and direct action'. The 1993 *Newsweek* cover story on interactive technologies, similarly, invoked 'virgin territory', literally 'there for the taking'. But facile talk about democratization can hide the new media's complicity in military/entertainment/information culture. The danger is that multimedia democratization will be limited to a tiny privileged sphere, that cybernetic democracy will resemble other partial democracies, like that of the slave-holding democracies of ancient Athens and the American revolution. Given the *realpolitik* issues of political economy and differential access, the progressive uses of the new media could still be relegated to the off-ramps of the 'Infobahn'. Islands of information affluence might neighbor with what Mitchell calls 'electronic Jakartas' for the 'bandwidth disadvantaged'.[35]

While being aware of the dangers of cyber-authoritarianism, it would be short-sighted to ignore the progressive potential of digital media. Allucquere Rosanne Stone, in *The war of desire and technology at the close of the mechanical age*,[36] invokes the Native American myth of Coyote, the shapeshifter, to laud digital media as subverting fixed social identities and stable configurations of power. Digital media have been linked both to the military–industrial complex and to counterculture. Henry Jenkins speaks of the 'surprisingly comfortable fit' between the hacker subculture battling media conglomerates and cultural studies concepts of 'poaching' and 'resistance'.[37] Can multimedia, as Janet Murray implies in *Hamlet on the holodeck*, turn mute, inglorious nerds into 'cyberbards'?[38]

Despite the social ambiguities of the new technologies, they do open up intriguing possibilities for both film and film theory. Interestingly, some contemporary theorists now 'do' theory through the new electronic and cybernetic media. Semioticians such as Umberto Eco, film theorists such as Henry Jenkins, filmmakers such as Peter Greenway, Chris Marker, and Jorge Bodansky, video artists such as Bill Viola, have all turned to the new media. We are now seeing CD-ROMs of film analysis by Henry Jenkins and Marsha Kinder in the USA, by Jurandir Noronha and Zita Caravalhosa in Brazil. Marsha Kinder deconstructs race and gender in her computer game *Runaways* (1998). Brazilian film-maker Jorge Bodanksy, who made films such as *Iracema* (1975) in the Amazon in the 1970s, is now creating what amounts to a kind of cybernetic updating of Hales Tours, a CD-ROM which allows the 'voyager' to visit the Amazon, to click on a tree which reveals the animals inside it, to trigger a fire or deforestation and see its ecological consequences.

Spectatorship in the wake of the 'posts'

How, then, do all these developments impact the study of film spectatorship? If the film theory of the 1970s psychoanalyzed the apparatus and the situation of the spectator, film theory in the 1980s and 1990s has become more interested in differentiated spectatorship. *Contra* earlier apparatus theory, it was now argued that the strong 'subject effects' produced by narrative cinema cannot be separated from the desire, experience, and knowledge of historically situated spectators, constituted outside the text and traversed by sets of power relations. If the earlier theory had acknowledged, since Laura Mulvey's landmark essay in 1975 that spectatorship was gendered, theory was also beginning to recognize that the spectator was sexualized, classed, raced, nationed, and regioned.

The culturally variegated nature of spectatorship derives from the diverse locations in which films are received, from the temporal gaps of seeing films in different historical moments, and from the conflictual subject-positionings and community affiliations of the spectators themselves. In its quasi-exclusive focus on sexual as opposed to other kinds of difference, and in its privileging of the intra-psychic as opposed to the intersubjective and the discursive, psychoanalytic film theory often elided questions of culturally inflected spectatorship. In his essay on 'black spectatorship', Manthia Diawara argues that black spectators cannot 'buy into' the racism of a film such as *Birth of a Nation* (1915). They disrupt the functioning of Griffith's film, rebelling against the 'order' imposed by its narrative.[39] bell hooks, meanwhile, speaks of the 'oppositional gaze' of black female spectators, which problematizes and complexifies the issue of female identity, representation, and spectatorship.[40]

At the same time, there is no racially, culturally, or even ideologically circumscribed essential spectator – *the* white spectator, *the* black spectator, *the* latino/a spectator, *the* resistant spectator. Such categories repress the heteroglossia within spectators themselves, who do not have single monolithic identities but are rather involved in multiple identities (and identifications) having to do with gender, race, sexual preference, region, religion, ideology, class, and generation. Moreover, socially imposed epidermic identities do not strictly determine personal identifications and political allegiances. It is not only a question of what one is or where one is coming from, but also of what one desires to be, where one wants to go, and with whom one wants to go there. Within a complex *combinatoire* of spectatorial positions, members of an oppressed group might identify with the oppressing group (Native American children being induced to root for the cowboys against the 'Indians', Africans identifying with Tarzan, Arabs with Indiana Jones), just as members of privileged groups might identify with the struggles of oppressed groups. Spectatorial positioning is relational: communities can identify with one another on the basis of a shared closeness or on the basis of a common (scapegoated) antagonist. Spectatorial positions are multiform, fissured, schizophrenic, unevenly developed, culturally, discursively, and politically discontinuous, forming part of a shifting realm of ramifying differences and contradictions. That spectatorial identification is culturally, discursively, and politically discontinuous, that it is fissured, even schizophrenic, suggests a series of gaps; the same person might be crossed by contradictory discourses and codes. That the spectator is the scene of proliferating differences and contradictions does not mean that an opposite, conglomerating process of cross-racial and cross-cultural identifications and alliance imagining does not also take place. Amending Raymond Williams, we have argued elsewhere for the existence of 'analogical structures of feeling', that is, for a structuring of filmic identification across social, political, and cultural situations, through strongly perceived or dimly felt affinities of social perception or historical experience.[41] In a context where one's own community goes unrepresented, analogical identifications become a compensatory outlet. A member of a marginalized group might look for himself or herself on the screen, but, failing that, might identify with the next closest category, much as one transfers allegiance to another sports team after one's own team has been eliminated from the competition.

Far from being essentially regressive and alienating, the space of media spectatorship is politically ambivalent. Nor are Hollywood films monolithically reactionary. Even hegemonic texts have to negotiate diverse community desires – Hollywood calls it 'market research'. As Fredric Jameson, Hans Magnus Enzensberger, Richard Dyer, Jane Feuer, and Jane Gaines have all argued,[42] to explain the public's attraction to a text or medium one must look not only for the 'ideological effect' that manipulates people into complicity with existing social relations, but also for the kernel of utopian fantasy reaching beyond these relations, whereby the medium constitutes itself as a projected fulfillment of what is desired and absent within the *status quo*. Symptomatically, even imperialist heroes such as Indiana Jones and Rambo are posited not as the oppressors but as the liberators of subject peoples.

A purely cognitive approach to film reception allows little space for such differences. It does not explore how spectators can be made to identify with tales told against themselves, or how films can become a catalyst for collective desire. It does not allow for the potential misogynistic response of the spectator of *Fatal Attraction* (1987), the possible homophobic response of the spectator of *Cruising* (1981), or the anti-Arab racism of the spectator of *Siege* (1999). Privileging denotation over connotation, a cognitive model has little room for what one might call cultural schemata or ethnically-inflected cognition, that is the fact that an anti-semitic film such as *The Jew Suss* might resonate with the common sense of the anti-semite but not with that of Jews and their sympathizers. Different reactions to films are symptomatic of different historical experiences and social desires.

Transnational spectatorship can also mold a space of future-orientated desire, nourishing the imaginary of 'internal émigrés', actively crystallizing a sense of a viable 'elsewhere', giving it a local habitation and a name, evoking a possible 'happy end' in another nation. Given the inequitable distribution of power among nations and peoples, such movements are often one-directional, and the desire for an elsewhere is often frustrated by the law of green cards and border patrols. Cross-cultural spectatorship, in other words, is not simply a utopian exchange between communities, but a dialogue deeply embedded in the asymmetries of power. Brian Larkin speaks of 'parallel modernities' to account for African spectators who 'participate in the imagined realities of other cultures as part of their daily lives' in a situation where Western media offer only one of many choices where the Hausa, for example, have the choice of 'watching Hausa or Yoruba videos, Indian, Hong Kong or American films, or videos of Qur'anic *tafsir* (exegesis) by local preachers'.[43]

Within postmodern culture, the media not only set agendas and frame debates but also inflect desire, memory, phantasy. By controlling popular memory, they can contain or stimulate popular dynamism. The challenge, then, is to develop a media practice by which subjectivities may be lived and analyzed as part of a transformative, emancipatory praxis.[44] The question then becomes: given the libidinal economy of media reception, how do we crystallize individual and collective desire for emancipatory purposes? In this sense, media culture must pay attention to what Guattari calls the 'production machines' and 'collective mutations' of subjectivity. As right-wing forces attempt to promote a super-egoish 'conservative reterritorialization' of subjectivity, those seeking change in an egalitarian direction must know how to crystallize individual and collective desire.

Since cultural identity, as Stuart Hall has pointed out, is a matter of 'becoming' as well as 'being', belonging to the future as well as the past,[45] multicultural media activism might serve to protect threatened identities or even create new identities, a catalyst not only for the public sphere assertion of particular cultures but also for fostering the resistant intersectionality of an emergent transcultural community.

Endnotes

1   A similar concept, 'scattered hegemonies', is advanced by Inderpal Grewal and Caren Kaplan who use the phrase in 'Introduction: transnational feminist practices and questions of postmodernity', *Scattered hegemonies: postmodernity and transnational feminist practices* (Minneapolis, MN, University of Minnesota Press, 1994).

2   Appadurai posits five dimensions of these global cultural flows: (1) ethnoscapes (the landscape of persons who constitute the shifting world in which people live); (2)

technoscapes (the global configuration of technologies moving at high speeds across previously impermeable borders); (3) financescapes (the global grid of currency speculation and capital transfer); (4) mediascapes (the distribution of the capabilities to produce and disseminate information and the large complex repertoire of images and narratives generated by these capabilities; and (5) ideoscapes (ideologies of states and counter-ideologies of movements, around which nation-states have organized their political cultures). See Arjun Appadurai, 'Disjunction and difference in the global cultural economy', *Public Culture*, 2, (Spring 1990).

3   J.M. Blaut, *The Colonies modelled the world* (New York, Grove Press, 1993), p. 11.
4   Frantz Fanon, *The wretched of the earth* (New York, Grove Press, 1963), p. 102.
5   Quoted in Jay Leyda, *Dianying: electric shadows* (Cambridge, MA, MIT Press, 1972), p. 2.
6   Haile Gerima, interview with Paul Willemen, *Framework*, nos 7–8 (Spring 1978), p. 32.
7   Frantz Fanon, *Black skin, white masks* (New York, Grove Press, 1967), pp. 152–3.
8   Frantz Fanon, *Black skin, white masks*, pp. 112–16.
9   Roland Barthes, *Mythologies* (New York, Wang & Hill, 1972), Aimé Césare, *Discourse in colonialism* (Monthly Review Press, 1972), Fanon, *The wretched of the earth*.
10   Robert Young, *White mythologies* (New York, Routledge, 1990). Debra P. Amory, 'Watching the table disappear: identity and politics in Africa and the Academy', paper given at the African Studies Association (1990).
11   Anwar Abdel Malek, 'Orientalism in crisis', *Diogenes* 44 (Winter 1963): 107–8.
12   Elizabeth Fox-Genovese, 'The claims of a common culture: gender, race, class and the canon', *Salmagundi*, 72 (Fall 1986): p. 121.
13   See Diana Fuss, *Essentially speaking* (London, Routledge, 1989), pp. 20–1.
14   Dick Hebdige, *Hiding in the light* (London, Routledge, 1988).
15   François Lyotard, *The postmodern condition* (Minneapolis, University of Minnesota Press, 1984).
16   Denis Epko, Towards post Africanism. *Textual Practice* No. 9 (Spring 1995).
17   Fredric Jameson, *The geopolitical aesthetic: cinema and space in the world system* (Bloomington, IN, Indiana University Press, 1992), p. 1.
18   Fredric Jameson, *The cultural turn* (London, Verso, 1998), p. 129.
19   Proceedings surrounding Monica Lewinsky's accusations of sexual misconduct by US President Bill Clinton were heavily covered on television.
20   Benedict Anderson, *Imagined communities* (London, Verso, 1991).
21   Frantz Faron, *Wretched of the earth*, p. 51 For more on 'post-Third-Worldism', see Ella Shohat and Robert Stam, *Unthinking Eurocentrism: multiculturalism and the Media* (London, Routledge, 1992), and Ella Shohat, 'Post-Third Worldist culture: gender, nation, and the cinema', in Jacqui Alexander and Chandra Talpade Mohanty, eds, *Feminist genealogies, colonial legacies, democratic futures* (London, Routledge, 1996), pp. 183–209.
22   Edward Said, *Orientalism* (New York, Pantheon, 1978).
23   The Hybrid State Films, curated by Coco Fusco in 1991, was a program of 'parallel history', a year-long interdisciplinary project produced by Exit Art and directed by Jeanette Ingberman and Papo Colo.
24   See Ella Shohat, Notes on the post-colonial, *Social Text* 31–32 (Spring 1992); Grewal. 1994; Anne du Cille, *Skin trade* (Cambridge, MA, Harvard University Press, 1996).
25   See, for example, David McDougall, 'Beyond observational cinema', in Paul Hockings, ed., *Principles of visual anthropology* (The Hague, Mouton, 1975).
26   Indigenous media have remained largely invisible to the First World public except for

occasional festivals (for example, the Native American Film and Video Festivals held regularly in San Francisco and New York City, or the Latin American Film Festival of Indigenous Peoples held in Mexico City and Rio de Janeiro).

27 Faye Ginsburg, 'Indigenous media: Faustian contract or global village?', *Cultural Anthropology*, 6, 1 (1991).

28 See Terence Turner's account of his long-standing collaboration with the Kayapo, in 'visual media, cultural politics and anthropological practice', *The Independent*, 14, 1(Jan/Feb 1991).

29 For a critical view of the Kayapo project, see Rachel Moore, 'Marketing alterity', *Visual Anthropology Review*, s, 2 (Fall 1992); James C. Faris, 'Anthropological transparency: film, representation and politics', in Peter Ian Crawford and David Turton, eds, *Film as ethnography*' (Manchester, Manchester University Press, 1992). For an answer by Turner to Faris, see 'Defiant images: the Kayapo appropriation of video', Forman Lecture, RAI Festival of Film and Video in Manchester 1992, forthcoming in *Anthropology Today*.

30 Henry Jenkins, in Toby Miller and Robert Stam, eds (1999).

31 W.J.T. Mitchell, 'The pictorial turn', *Art Forum*, 30, 3 (1992), pp. 89–94.

32 Anne Friedberg, *Les flaneurs du mal (1): cinema and the postmodern condition* (Berkeley, CA, University of California Press, 1992).

33 Toby Miller, 'Discourses of technology', in Toby Miller and Robert Stam, eds (1999).

34 Umberto Eco, *Foucault's pendulum* (London, Martin Secker and Warburg, 1989).

35 William J. Mitchell, *City of bits* (Cambridge, MA, MIT, 1995), p. 171.

36 Allucquere Rosanne Stone, *The war of desire and technology at the close of the mechanical age* (Cambridge, MA, MIT Press, 1996).

37 Henry Jenkins, Textual poachers: television fans and participatory culture. New York: Routledge, Chapman & Hall, 1992.

38 Janet Murray, *Hamlet on the holodeck* (Cambridge, MA, MIT, 1997).

39 Manthia Diawara, *Film theory and criticism*, in Leo Braudy and Marshall Cohen. New York: Oxford University Press, 1999.

40 bell hooks, *Black looks: race and representation* (Boston, MA, South End Press, 1992), pp. 115–31. Jane Gaines, some years earlier, had pursued similar lines of questioning in her essay 'White privilege and looking relations: race and gender in feminist film theory', in Patricia Erens, ed., *Issues in feminist film criticism* (Bloomington, IN, Indiana University Press, 1990). For more on the issue of the raced and gendered spectator, see E. Deidre Pribram, ed., *Female spectators* (London, Verso, 1988).

41 See Shohat and Stam, *Unthinking Eurocentrism: multiculturalism and the media* (London, Routledge, 1994).

42 Fredric Jameson, *The political unconscious: narrative as a socially symbolic act* (Ithaca New York: Cornell University Press, 1981); Richard Dyer, *Only entertainment* (New York and London: Routledge, 1992); Jane Feuer, *The Hollywood musical* (Bloomington: Indiana University Press, 1982); Jane Gaines, this volume, Chapter 6.

43 Brian Larkin, 'Hausa dramas and the rise of video culture in Nigeria', in Jonathon Haymnes, ed., *Nigerian video films* (Ibadan, Nigeria, Kraft Books, 1997), p. 409.

44 See Rhonda Hammer and Peter McLaren, 'The spectacularization of subjectivity: media knowledges, global citizenry and the new world order', *Polygraph* 5 (1992).

45 Stuart Hall, 'Cultural identity and cinematic representation', *Framework*, 36 (1989).

21 Digging an old well: the labor of social fantasy in a contemporary Chinese film

Rey Chow

Allegorizing the 'Third World': opposition or narcissism?

> All third-world texts are necessarily ... to be read as what I will call national allegories.
>
> (Fredric Jameson)[1]

> Allegory ... means precisely the non-existence of what it presents.
>
> (Walter Benjamin)[2]

> Perhaps the nearest thing to thought about nationalism inspired by the Third World – outside the revolutionary left – was a general scepticism about the universal applicability of the 'national' concept.
>
> (E.J. Hobsbawm)[3]

What does the term 'Third World' conjure up these days? In the realm of cinema, a response to this question would have to be twofold. It would need to register, first of all, the legacy of Western imperialism, which gives rise to the hierarchical divisions of the world according to their stages of 'development'; it would also need to recognize the indelible imprints of Hollywood as an instance of that imperialism. A system which is as capable of restricting possibilities of reception to its ethnocentric norms as it is of circulating its own products worldwide, Hollywood has something of the global currency of English – a contemporary *lingua franca* with which film-makers and audiences, whether or not they like it or know it, must come to terms. It is in an attempt to undermine such domination of Hollywood – and with it, the ubiquitous domination of Western cultural imperialism – that various notions of alternative practices have been mobilized. The 'Third World' is one such notion.

In the academic circles of North America, therefore, the 'Third World' is often used as a signifier for opposition, resistance, anti-imperialism, anti-colonialism, struggles for national and cultural autonomy, and so on. When we examine 'Third World' cinema, our expectations also tend to follow these major notions, which operate by identifying Western imperialism of the past few hundred years as the chief enemy.

But the idealistic postulation of a 'third world difference'[4] is not without its own problematic – and equally ethnocentric – assumptions. Arguments for 'Third World' cinema are often such that the 'Third World' becomes an extension of the European Marxist avant-garde tradition, and such that its cultures are loaded, by way of interpretation, with residues of the European Enlightenment with an emphasis on cognitive lucidity, on production, on experiment, and on emancipation.[5] What dominates the understanding of the 'Third World' is thus a masculinist leftism for which 'nationalism' becomes the 'Third World' revenge on 'First World' imperialism.[6] The 'Third World' is attributed an 'outside' position from which criticism can be made about the 'First World'. This outside position is part and parcel of what Gayatri Spivak calls 'the continuing subalternization of Third World material'[7] by 'First World' critics, who condemn 'Third World' cultural production in the age of postmodernism to a kind of realism with functions of authenticity, didacticism, and deep meaning.

One question that the inscription of 'Third World' cultures in opposition does not seem to be able to deal with is what else there is in such cultures besides the struggle against the West. What if the primary interest of a 'Third World' culture is not that of resistance against Western domination? How are we to read the processes of signification that actually fall outside the currently hegemonic reading of Third World cultures, the reading that insists on their *oppositional* alterity to the West only?

The currency of Jameson's notion of 'national allegories' is evident in its application by scholars who are otherwise different in their political, national, and gender interests. Rather than simply agreeing or disagreeing with Jameson and his followers, let us first reconsider what Jameson means by 'allegory': 'the allegorical spirit is profoundly discontinuous, a matter of breaks and heterogeneities, of the multiple polysemia of the dream rather than the homogeneous representation of the symbol'.[8] Although he defines 'the allegorical spirit' with care, Jameson has not applied it to the word 'nation'. Using his own definition of allegory, we may ask: why has not the notion of 'nation' and 'the Third World nation' been allegorized and made 'discontinuous'? For whom is the nationness of 'Third World' nations unquestionable in its collectivity? For whom does 'Third World' collectivity equal the 'nation'? Even though 'national allegories' might have currently locked the West's others into a particular kind of reading, the notion as such cannot sufficiently account for the 'breaks and heterogeneities' and 'multiple polysemia' of 'Third World' texts.

Contemporary Chinese cinema is fascinating because it problematizes the facile notions of oppositional alterity, including especially the notion of a distinct, unquestionable *nationality*, that have for so long dominated our thinking about the 'Third World'. Those readers who have seen something of this cinema would know that the Chinese films that manage to make their way to audiences in the West are usually characterized, first of all, by visual beauty. From Chen Kaige's *Yellow Earth* (1984) to Tian Zhuangzhuang's *Horse Thief* (1986), to Zhang Yimou's *Red Sorghum* (1988), *Judou* (1990), and *Raise the Red Lantern* (1991), we see that contemporary Chinese directors are themselves so fascinated by the possibilities of cinematic experimentation that even when their subject matter is – and it usually is – oppression, contamination, rural backwardness, and the persistence of feudal values, such subject matter is presented with stunning sensuous qualities. One would need to ask whether some of these films are not compelling because of their aesthetic purity and beauty rather than simply because of their content of the 'lack of enlightenment'. If so, what kinds of issues do they engender for cross-cultural inquiry?

The sharp distinction between the often grave subject matter and the sensuously pleasing 'enunciation' of contemporary Chinese film – a distinction we can describe in terms of a conjoined subalternization and commodification, as a subalternized commodification and/or a commodified subalternization – points to the economics that enable the distribution and circulation of these films in the West.

Some may therefore say that contemporary Chinese directors know how to 'package' their stories of oppression with fashionable techniques and that, if not for such packaging, the films would not sell. The presumption of this kind of argument is that 'packaging' is superfluous – something that the films can or should do without. What contemporary Chinese films demonstrate, however, is that packaging is now an inherent part of cultural production. Even the most gruesome story needs to be shot exquisitely, so that it can contend for attention in metropolitan markets. If we follow this understanding of 'packaging' – that is, packaging as a kind of production, the production not of deep meanings but of exotic surfaces – we would need to redefine cultural labor and value production as these appear in contemporary 'Third World' cinema.

To illustrate this point, let us consider briefly a film that attracted quite a bit of attention some years ago: Zhang Yimou's *Judou*. Based on the story 'Fuxi Fuxi' by Liu Heng,[9] the film is about the secret, illicit relationship between Yang Tianqing and Wang Judou, a man and a woman who are, in family kinship terms, nephew and aunt (Judou is the young wife of Tianqing's uncle, Yang Jinshan). In the film, incest and adultery lead to the birth of a son, Tianbai, who officially remains Tianqing's 'younger brother' since he is thought to be the offspring of Jinshan and Judou. Tianbai eventually kills both his father-by-name and his biological father.

Rather than simply focusing on the sexual content, which caused the film to be banned in China when it was first completed and constituted its main interest for audiences overseas, I want to argue how this film transforms our notions of 'Third World' cultural production. This can be seen in the changes Zhang made in the story. Among these changes, the most interesting one is the background of a dye-mill, which is not in the original story by Liu Heng.

With the dye-mill come the possibilities of experimenting with colors as part of the visual language of the film, and it is in such visual aspects of *Judou* that the historical conditions of 'Third World' cultural production are most pronouncedly truthful – not because it represents 'China' as such, but because it signifies that which is not purely 'Chinese'. Another way of defining this impurity is to say that the 'ethnicity' of contemporary Chinese cinema – 'Chineseness' – is already the sign of a *cross-cultural* commodity fetishism.

Jean Baudrillard defines the semiological relation between commodity fetishism and ideology in these terms:

> the fetishization of the commodity is the fetishization of a product emptied of its concrete substance of labor and subjected to another type of labor, a labor of signification, that is, of coded abstraction (the production of differences and of sign values.) It is an active, collective process of production and reproduction of a code, a system, invested with all the diverted, unbound desire separated out from the process of real labor and transferred onto precisely that which denies the process of real labor.[10]

For those intent on looking for the 'Third World difference', the dye-mill would be one of those sites of 'Third World' labor that can be used to contrast with 'First World' metropolitan centers. A predictable set of dichotomizations would thus follow to oppose the 'Third' and 'First' worlds in terms of rural versus urban life, manual versus mental labor, simplicity and innocence versus complexity and experience, and so forth. And yet, in *Judou*, the setting of the dye-mill does not so much enable us to understand the labor of dyeing cloths in the Chinese countryside in the 1920s as it provides the metaphoric and cinematic staging for the romance, the physical violence, and the human tragedy that unfold in the course of the story. The dyed cloths that are hoisted to the roof of the village house, the visual effects of layeredness as pieces of brightly dyed cloths fall and fold upon each other at crucial moments (such as the lovers' first episode of love-making), the disturbed colors in the dye-basin in which the two men die – all these are part of a kind of production that is other than the 'realistic' portrayal of the labor of Chinese peasants living in the feudal countryside. Instead, an age-old labor activity is now given a second-order signification, that of cinema, in order to project a very different concept of labor altogether. This is the cultural labor of the 'Third World' in the 1990s, in which the 'Third World' can no longer simply manufacture mechanical body parts to be assembled and sold in the 'First World'. What the 'Third World' has been enlisted to do *also* is the manufacture of a *reflection*, an alterity that gives (back) to the 'First World' a sense of 'its' freedom and democracy while it generously allows the 'Third World' film to be shown against the authoritarian policies of 'Third World' governments. But an 'alterity' produced this way is a code and an abstraction whose fascination lies precisely in the fact that it is artificial and superficial; as Baudrillard says, '*it is the artifact that is the object of desire*'.[11]

Once we shift our thinking of production to that of image production, we can no longer theorize 'labor' as purely physical or manual, that is, emanating from the human body and therefore more genuine and unalienated. The production of images is the production not of things but of relations, not of one culture but of *value between cultures*: even as we see 'Chinese' stories on the screen, therefore, we are still confronted with an exchange between 'China' and the West in which these stories seek their market. In the case of films from the People's Republic, this is especially evident when excellent films receiving applause outside China are banned at home. (*Judou*, for instance, was nominated for 'best foreign film' at the Oscars in 1991 while being banned in China until the spring of 1992.) What this means is that the labor of Chinese film-makers is, to use the language of classical Marxism, literally alienated from its home use. Contemporary

Chinese film production serves in this instance to redefine 'Third World' cultural production as first and foremost alienated. Alienation is the very form of cultural production, which 'Third World' cultures, precisely because of their histories, make manifest. And the first symptom of such alienation is usually the emotional insistence on a 'national' essence such as the 'Chinese'. It is as if the more indisputable the interference and intervention of the 'foreign' have become, the stronger the insistence on cultural self-containment must be.[12]

The simultaneous fascination with traditional activities of physical labor and the abstraction of such labor in the form of beautiful images (as is the case of wine-making in *Red Sorghum* and the nomadic livelihood of Tibetan people in *Horse Thief*) mean that questions of 'Third World' cinema cannot be posed simply in terms of a uniform nationality or nationalistic opposition to the 'First World'. Instead, the production of images foregrounds the much more difficult issue of *value*, which, precisely because it is intangible, can be distributed, absorbed, and reproduced far more easily than actual objects. But in posing the question of 'Third World' cultural production in terms of images, I am not, I want to emphasize, making an argument for criticizing the 'incorrect' images and finding the 'correct' images of the West's others, since I would, in order to do that, need to presume the existence of an unalienated labor which can be matched onto a correct image. The much more disturbing issues of cultural exchange – the exchange of ideologies, values, and images – mean that what need to be fundamentally revamped are not so much positivistic representations as the critical bases on which 'Third World' cultures are currently being examined.

Here, the history of China *vis-à-vis* the West can be instructive in a number of ways. Unlike India or countries in Africa and America, most parts of China were, in the course of modern European imperialism, never territorially under the sovereignty of any foreign power, although China was invaded and had to grant many concessions throughout the nineteenth century to England, France, Germany, Russia, Japan, and the USA. Major political movements in China, whether for the restoration of older forms of government (1898) or for the overthrow of the dynastic system (1911), whether led by the religious (1850–64), the well-educated (1919), the anti-foreign (1900, 1937–45), or communists (1949), were always conducted in terms of China's relations with foreign powers, usually the West. However, my suggestion is that the ability to preserve more or less territorial integrity (while other ancient civilizations, such as the Inca, the Aztec, and those of India, Vietnam and Indochina, Algeria, and others, were territorially captured) as well as linguistic integrity (Chinese remains the official language) means that as a 'Third World' country, the Chinese relation to the imperialist West, until the communists officially propagandized 'anti-imperialism', is seldom purely 'oppositional' ideologically; on the contrary, the point has always been for China to become as strong as the West, to become the West's 'equal'. And even though the Chinese communists once served as the anti-imperialist inspiration for other 'Third World' cultures and progressive Western intellectuals, that dream of a successful and consistent opposition to the West on ideological grounds has been dealt the death blow by more recent events such as the Tiananmen Massacre of 1989, in which the Chinese government itself acted as viciously as if it were one of its capitalistic enemies. As the champion of the unprivileged classes and nations of the world, communist China has shown itself to be a failure, a failure which is now hanging on by empty official rhetoric while its people choose to live in ways that have obviously departed from the communist ideal.

The point of summarizing modern Chinese history in such a schematic fashion is to underscore how the notion of 'coloniality' (together with the culture criticisms that follow from it), when construed strictly in terms of the *foreignness* (that is, exteriority) of race, land, and language, can blind us to political exploitation as easily as it can alert us to it. In the history of modern Western imperialism, the Chinese were never completely dominated by a foreign colonial power, but the apparent absence of the 'enemy' as such does not make the Chinese case any less 'Third World' (in the sense of being colonized) in terms of the exploitation suffered by the people, whose most important colonizer remains their own government. China, perhaps because it is the exception to the rule of imperialist domination by race, land, and language involving a foreign (external) power, in fact highlights the effects of the imperialistic transformation of value and value production more sharply than in other 'Third World' cultures.

Once we see national culture as a kind of value production, the predicament faced by many 'Third World' nations becomes lucid. While the history of Western imperialism relegates all non-Western cultures to the place of the other, whose value is 'secondary' in relation to the West, the task of nationalism in the 'Third World' is that of (re)inventing the 'secondary' cultures themselves as primary, as the uncorrupted origins of 'Third World' nations' histories and 'worth'. In the case of China, for instance, the state authorities insist to this day on the separation of China from the West as summarized in the nineteenth-century dictum, *zhong xue wei ti, xi xue wei yong* – 'Chinese learning for fundamental structure, Western learning for practical use'. This dictum, often interpreted as a sign of the conservative nature of China's attitude toward the West, actually signifies in an elegant way the difficulty inherent in the value production that is otherwise known among 'Third World' intellectuals as the construction of national culture. According to this dictum, 'China' is the foundation of cultural value, a foundation that determines other cultures' relation/relevance to itself rather than the other way around. 'China' was there 'before' the West, which might be added on for practical purposes but which cannot usurp China's place as the origin of value. And yet, the predicament of China in modern times is, of course, precisely that of the paradox inscribed in all 'Third World' nations' attempts to construct their own identities: the notion that 'China' is first and original is already a *response* to the exchange with the West, a claim that is made *after* the onslaught of the West has become irreversible. If an original 'Chineseness' somehow persists and thrives as collective belief, it is only because 'China' continues to be circulated among entities that are not-Chinese. To prove the 'Chineseness' of the Chinese culture, the only way is through difference, which means inserting 'China' among others in processes of cross-cultural production – processes that render the fantasy of an original 'Chinese' value untenable.

Precisely because the processes of labor's alienation – exchange, commodification, circulation – are inevitable to the definition of value, the insistence on an original 'Chinese' culture is the insistence on a kind of value that is outside alienation, outside the process of value-making. The wish to return a culture to an original (native or national) value is thus the wish to remove that culture from the process in which it appears 'original' in the first place. In modern Chinese texts, filmic or literary, this kind of predicament and paradox of the production of national culture as original value repeatedly occur. Unlike, say, modern India, where the British left behind insurmountable poverty, a cumbersome bureaucracy, and a language in which to function as a 'nation', but where therefore the sentiment of opposition can remain legitimately alive because there is historically a clearly identifiable *foreign* (external) colonizer, the Chinese continue to have 'their own' system, 'their own' language, and 'their own' problems. Chinese intellectuals' obsession remains 'China' rather than the mere opposition to the West. The cultural production that results is therefore narcissistic and self-conscious, rather than purely oppositional, in structure. Whatever oppositional sentiment there exists is an oppositional sentiment directed internally toward the center that is itself – 'China', the 'Chinese heritage', the 'Chinese tradition', the 'Chinese government', and variants of these.

This structure of narcissistic value-making explains the current interest on the part of Chinese film-makers to search for China's 'own' others. The films about the remote areas of China such as Tibet, about emperors, empresses, and eunuchs, about the agrarian lives of the nameless and voiceless peasants in the past, as well as about the lingering forces of feudalist oppression that persist in spite of the revolutions – all such films partake of what we may call a post-structuralist fascination with the constructedness of one's 'self' – in this case, with China's 'self', with China's origins, with China's own alterity. In the wish to go back to 'China' as origin – to revive 'China' as the source of original value – the 'inward turn' of the nationalist narrative precisely reveals 'China' as other than itself. This narcissistic structure then (mis)translates into the more familiar paradigm of 'China as oppositional alterity to the West' through the international cinematic apparatus and the not-so-innocent apparatuses of cross-cultural interpretation.

In the following, I examine the problems that surface in such a narcissistic exploration of a 'native' culture. Foremost among my questions is how narcissism informs the reconstruction of origins, the truncating of libidinal economies, and the imaginary reinvestments that make up the 'labor' moving within a 'Third World' culture as well as between the 'First' and 'Third' worlds.

The futurity . . . the futility of the nation

The film I will discuss now is *Lao jing* or *Old Well*, directed by Wu Tianming and produced in 1987. Like many contemporary Chinese films, *Old Well* is based on a novel by the same name.[13] The author of the novel, Zheng Yi, also wrote the film script.

Old Well is a village located far into the Taiheng Mountains. There are endless stony mountains, but no water. Over the generations, the Old Well villagers have dug 127 wells, but they have all been dry. The deepest was over 50 meters. The greatest hope of all the villagers is that they will find water on their own land. The protagonist is an educated youth called Sun Wangquan ('Sun', his family name, also means 'grandson', and 'Wangquan' means 'auspicious for flowing stream'). When the film begins, Wangquan has returned to his village and is determined to use his knowledge to find water. His own

family is very poor. To reach his goal and to help his brothers get married, he marries
Duan Xifeng, a young widow with a daughter, and gives up his love relationship with
another woman, Zhao Qiaoying. After many failed attempts, including one in which
Wangquan and Qiaoying are trapped at the bottom of a well, where Wangcai,
Wangquan's younger brother, is killed, Wangquan finally succeeds in digging a well by
applying his newly acquired hydraulic knowledge. For the first time in many
generations, Old Well village has water.

Old Well can, of course, be read as a 'national allegory'. According to this type of
reading, everything in the film would be assigned a national – that is, Chinese –
significance. The struggle of the protagonist and the village would then be microscopic
versions of the 'nation' and its people struggling to consolidate their identity.[14] It would
be a story with a positive ending. But what if the supposedly 'national' sign 'Chinese'
itself is more than the 'Third World nation' that is conferred upon it by modernity?
Once we stop using the 'nation' to unify the elements of the film text, other questions
begin to surface. A careful allegorical reading of *Old Well* would demonstrate that the
allegory of the 'nation' is, paradoxically, the nation's otherness and non-presence.

The 'nation' reading is impossible because a national *enemy* is absent. Instead, the
space of an enemy, which is crucial for the unification of a community, is occupied by
two 'others' – the dry well and the romantic woman. Why would a 'Chinese' film of the
1980s concentrate on enemies other than 'national' enemies?

In the readings of recent world events, it is commonly recognized that the breakdown
of communism in Eastern Europe since 1989 has not led to democratic prosperity in
accordance with anti-communist beliefs, but has instead caused the resurgence of old
ethnic conflicts which were neutralized and covered up under communism. The
prominence of nationalistic sentiments in the states previously dominated by the former
USSR indicates that nationalism was actually the repressed side of communism, a
repressed side that boils over once the lid of communism is removed.

In China, where ethnic differences are relatively undisruptive (except in Tibet and
Xinjiang) and where the centrality of the Han culture remains relatively uncontested by
other ethnic groups, many of whom have been assimilated for generations, nationalism
has functioned in the past 40 years to fuel communism rather than serving as
communism's repressed side. As communism gradually loses its hold on the populace
(even though it is still the official policy), what surfaces as the 'social disorders' that are
repressed under communism? The answer is two related things: sexual difference, which
communism neutralizes, and 'the West', which is communism's adversary but also
communism's founding source. The surfacing of these disorders means not only the
relative indifference to communism but also an implicit questioning of communism's
ally in China – nationalism itself.

Female sexuality and the nation

The eruption of romantic love in contemporary Chinese cinema continues the
'modernized' interest in the controversies of love and sexuality among Chinese

intellectuals since the beginning of the twentieth century. Why is romantic love such an issue?

If the conception of 'woman' was in the past mediated by women's well-defined roles within the Chinese family, the modern promotion of the nation throws into instability all those traditional roles. How are women's sexuality, social function, economic function, contribution to cultural production, and biological reproduction to be conceived of outside the family and in terms of the nation? This is the historical juncture when, in what appeared to be a sudden 'liberation' of the traditional constraints on Chinese women's identity, romantic love became, in the early twentieth century, a leading social issue. For what is 'romantic' about romantic love is not sex but the apparent freedom in which men and women could 'choose' their sexual partners, in a way that differed from arranged marriage. And since the traditional family system was paternalistic – that is, resting on the sexual stability, chastity, and fidelity of women while men were openly promiscuous and/or polygamous – the new freedom meant first and foremost the production of a new female sexuality. In other words, because the conception of the nation sought to unify the culture regardless of sexual and class difference, it left open many questions as to how women's sexual identities, which were carefully differentiated and monitored within the traditional kinship system, should be reformulated. This is why, one could say, in the discourse of modernity, the Chinese woman suddenly became a newly discovered 'primitive' – a body adrift between the stagnant waters of the family, whose oppressiveness it seeks to escape, and the open sea of the nation, whose attention to 'woman' is only such that her sexual difference and history become primarily its support while she 'herself' is erased.

The emotional as well as economic forms of the family, on the other hand, die a slow and drawn-out death. Especially because the modern discourse of the nation has not really provided real alternatives other than an apparently emancipated 'body' with no constraints, the tenacious bonds of the family live on. And this is ironically even more so under the communist revolution. When Mao Zedong upheld women as 'equal' to men in the public spheres of work and economic production for the nation, and when Western feminists were delighted to see Chinese women being honored without discrimination with the same tasks as men, the family continued to thrive in the ideological vacuum left by the creation of the communist nation, simply because women's labor in the home, unlike their kinship roles and positions which could be taxonomically classified, remained real and material but traditionally unclassified and unpaid, and hence much more difficult to reclassify in the new system. The consequence is that the oppressiveness resulting from such labor remains intact to this day, leaving its imprint on cultural productions even when such productions are not overtly about gender, sexuality, or women.

In *Old Well*, the kinship-bound and modernized female sexualities are represented by Wangquan's different relationships with Xifeng and Qiaoying. From the beginning, the two women are portrayed stereotypically, in accordance with the literary and historiographic conventions of understanding Chinese modernity. While Qiaoying is, like Wangquan, coming back to the village after having been in the outside world, Xifeng is the woman who remains at home. Qiaoying's attractiveness is associated with her 'novelty': she brings back with her modern items such as a television set. Xifeng, although widowed, is clearly more 'stable': her stability is represented by the support she has from the multiple roles she plays within the kinship system, in which the women are as strongly functional as the men.

Xifeng has a mother, who supervises her sexual life, and is herself a mother. All she needs is a husband who would make her female social identity complete. Qiaoying, on the other hand, is an unknown entity: one of the reasons Wangquan's grandfather disapproves of her is because he thinks she would not stay put in the village. Even though, in terms of social progress, Qiaoying is much closer to man himself than the woman-at-home, in the rural village her avant-garde ontological proximity to masculinity is eyed with suspicion and distrust. The modernized, educated woman signifies romantic freedom – that is, 'choice' over her own body – and thus social instability. Qiaoying is represented as without family relations. Like a mysterious signifier unleashed from centuries of anchorage to kinship, she does not know where she is heading.

What is most remarkable, however, is the way this *convention* of understanding modernity – the convention of exorcizing the romantic woman and romantic love from traditional society – surfaces in post-Cultural-Revolution cultural production. What does this convention do here?

First, it helps consolidate the traditional female sexuality represented by Xifeng and her relation to Wangquan, whose genealogical as well as career stability is guaranteed through marriage. Wangquan 'receives' not only food, cigarettes, and money from Xifeng, but finally, though reluctantly, also her body. Toward the end of the film, Xifeng is pregnant. By contrast, the romantic woman is turned into an outcast. Qiaoying is the 'enemy' to the economic basis of the village community who must be exiled.

Second, in the aftermath of the Cultural Revolution, the affirmation of traditional family values comes as an attempt to mask the lack created by the bankruptcy of communism and nationalism, even though nationalism may persist by reinscribing itself in traditional forms. The main point is that the central roles played by the family and village community are here signs of the *dismantling* of the modernist revolution from 'family' to 'nation'. 'Woman' is now caught between the bankruptcy of nationalism/communism, in which the sexes are 'equal' and women's problems do not exist, and the resurgence of older patriarchal forms of community, in which female sexuality is strictly managed for purposes of kinship reproduction.

A film such as *Old Well* demonstrates that the 'Chinese nation' itself does not have to exist in order for the social and sexual issues to be circulated and negotiated. Like the female body emancipated from traditional kinship bonds, the 'nation' is *nowhere* except in the politics which uses it to fight the past (be that past primitive, ethnic, feudalist, or colonized). Like the female body thrown into 'romantic love', the nation is theoretically capable of all kinds of dangerous libidinal possibilities. Because it is fundamentally empty, the 'nation' has to be controlled by a more locally grounded production and reproduction. In their relative silence on the subject of the nation, contemporary Chinese films seem to say: 'It is the "nation" with all its extravagant promises that has led to the internal catastrophes in modern China. But – still, we must continue to seek such extravagant promises elsewhere!'

The barrenness of romantic love

If the decline of the 'nation' is as elusive as its rise, this elusiveness finds a convention of staging itself in the romantic woman.

In spite of Wangquan's marriage to another woman, Qiaoying loves him, and we feel, through his silence and guilty expressions, that he still loves her. After Wangquan is married, Qiaoying has been going out with Wangcai, who earlier had a quarrel with Wangquan about his own lack of everything, in particular his lack of experience with women. Qiaoying's association with Wangcai is clearly presented as futile and futureless: Wangcai is an example of the 'decadent' younger generation of contemporary China with no long-term plan and no concern for society's future. During a well-digging accident, Wangcai is killed by rubble falling into the well.

Because of the accident, however, Qiaoying is finally able to 'consummate' her love for Wangquan. In this 'love scene', we have perhaps one of the most romantic portrayals of romantic love in contemporary Chinese cinema. Its romanticism lies in an excessiveness that can only belong to film.

From under the well, the image of the two lovers kissing in passion is superimposed with the cosmic landscape – the sky, the mountains, the trees – in a series of shots that are, like the accompanying music, in motion rather than still. The lovers' entrapment inside the well thus becomes, in a dream-like fashion, the freedom one can find in 'nature' outside the confines of human wants and desires. If this moment 'captures' romantic fulfillment, it is also, I suggest, a capturing of the uncapturable through the juxtaposition of that which is temporally and geographically specific – romantic love – with that which is timeless and placeless – the cosmos. As that which is here and now, love does not and cannot reproduce itself outside the circuit of the two lovers. The sacrifice it requires, as well as the meaning of its intense 'presence', is that of an unrecuperable death. Romantic love is thus literally experienced as death, at a moment when the lovers have lost hope of getting out alive. It is in death that they can dream of being at one with each other and with the cosmos, in a way that – thanks to the imaginary possibilities of the cinema – transcends the constraint of the specific here and now. This transcendence is fantastical but anti-social. Romantic love becomes the signifier of emptiness – the emptiness and emptying of the social.

After this death, society goes on. The fantasy of romantic love is from now on remembered with nostalgia, as what happened at a different time in a different place. Importantly, it is the woman, Qiaoying, who carries death with her. She eventually leaves the community and donates her dowry to the cause of continual well-digging. Wangquan, who found himself a mistress in the depths of his failed social labor, re-emerges as a cultural hero who is aided not only by his mistress but also by his wife, who calls upon the entire village to give what they can to help his cause. While one woman gets nothing and the other retains her husband, Wangquan keeps his family, the memory of love, and leaves himself a name.

The futility of the nation is thus signified by the barrenness of romantic love, the consummation of which takes place in the depths of a dry well at the moment of a collapsed effort at drilling. Romantic love is barren not because it is impoverished but because it is surplus: its excessiveness threatens economic productiveness because it prevents that productiveness from being stabilized. Another way of putting this is to say that the sacrifice of romantic love is pure: unlike the attempt to drill a well, it cannot be rewarded nor 'completed' in the way the 'In Memoriam' plaque, as I will go on to argue, completes and rewards the sacrifices of men's lives down the centuries. If well-digging generates the 'value' that compensates for the loss of lives, the barrenness of romantic love lures modernity against itself and back toward the long-disputed family.

The labor of social fantasy

ethnicity *can* mobilize the vast majority of its community – provided its appeal remains sufficiently vague or irrelevant.

(E.J. Hobsbawm)[15]

how is one to interpret the fact that large numbers of people collectively hold beliefs that are false?

(Partha Chatterjee)[16]

If one 'foreign enemy' to the community is the romantic woman, who must be cut off, the other 'foreign enemy' is the lack that is inside Old Well village – the dry wells themselves. This lack awaits being filled, and, once filled, will give meaning to the community.

The theme of dry wells repeats the obsession that has characterized 'Chinese modernity' since the nineteenth century: the power of technology. Although we are familiar with the many technological inventions that owe their origins to the Chinese – the compass, paper, printing, fireworks, gunpowder, deep drilling, to name just a few – in the modern period, notably after Western imperialism became unavoidable, one might argue that 'technology' situates the Chinese culture *vis-à-vis* the West in the form of a lack. Political trends in the twentieth century shift back and forth between the desire to fill this lack and the pretense that China needs nothing. In the post-Cultural-Revolution period, following Deng Xiaoping's modernization campaigns, we see once again the openness to technology, from the most mundane items for household use to computers. Contemporary Chinese films necessarily reflect these developments. One of the narratives that have sustained China's relationship with Western modernity can thus be described as a quest for technology – a quest for that 'power' without which China cannot become strong.

At the same time, in this film, the quest for technology is legitimated not so much in terms of the elusive 'nation' as it is in terms of a post-Cultural-Revolution *humanism* that tries to preserve the traditional in modernization. As such, the film also repeats one of the basic fantasies that have run throughout the course of Chinese modernization since the nineteenth century, which is expressed in the aforementioned phrase 'Chinese learning for fundamental structure, Western learning for practical use'. The fantasy is that the Chinese can have part of the West – technology – without changing its own social structure. Today, this fantasy continues in the evident split between official

Chinese rhetoric, which still remains loyal to the classical themes of Marxism, Leninism, and Maoism, and Chinese social practice, which now includes all kinds of Western and capitalistic ventures and enterprises. Such fantasy is crucial to the narcissistic value-making that I suggest as the alternative way of understanding 'Third World' cultures.

This narcissistic value-making is, moreover, masculinist. The film begins with shots of part of a naked male body against a dark background hammering away in sweat. We read 'determination' into these signifiers. The ending of the film completes these opening signifiers with an 'In Memoriam' plaque indicating the lives (presumably all male) that have been lost in the centuries of failed attempts at well-digging. The completion is the completion of the sacrificial process: finally, the film seems to say, the sacrifices pay off.

From the perspective of Wangquan, technology is strictly a means to an end. Technology is instrumental in fulfilling the mandate which is loaded on him and which he cannot resist. He cannot protest against that mandate because in it lies a communal meaning of responsibility; he cannot decline it because in it lies the very personal identity he receives from society as a reward. The mandate does not only take from him his life energy; it also gives him his life and his immortality.

What is interesting is not the simple affirmation of humanistic values and a process of identity production through stamina, effort, and willingness to self-sacrifice, but how such an affirmation is at the same time part of that cultural narcissism which exoticizes its own alterity, its own otherness. The fact that the affirmation of humanistic values takes place not in metropolitan centers such as Shanghai and Beijing, but in backward villages in remote mountains, suggests that the reinvestment in humanism in contemporary Chinese cultural production is at the same time an uncanny *ethnographic* attempt to narrate a 'noble savagery' that is believed to have preserved the older and more authentic treasures of the culture, in ways as yet uncorrupted by modernity.

To this extent, *Old Well* provides an excellent example of the complex that I call 'primitive passions', a complex that may be briefly explained as follows. At a moment of *cultural crisis*, an interest in the 'primitive' arises, typically involving fantasies of an origin. These fantasies are played out through a *generic* realm of associations, often having to do with the animal, the savage, the countryside, the indigenous, the people, and so forth, which *stand in* for that 'original' something that has been lost. (Re)constructed in this manner, the fantastical origin is now imagined as a *common* point of knowledge and reference that was there prior to a group's present existence and, even though it is a man-made artifice, appears to be timeless *nature* itself.

At the center of the primitive treasures to be preserved in *Old Well* is a system of production in which the will to work will be duly rewarded – if not in the form of an immediate gratification to the individual, then definitely in the form of the reproduction and continuance of the life of a community. The fascination not only with technological production or genealogical reproduction alone but with the welding of the two in the successful perpetuation of a culture is probably the most important fascination of the post-Cultural-Revolution period, in which the diversion from the mindless destructiveness of the previous two decades needs to graft itself onto something substantial and concrete. These two kinds of production together make up the economy of the third kind – the production of value/ideology, a production which is at the same time a series of translations, decodings, and recodings between 'contemporary' and 'rural' China, between communism (with its emphasis on loyalty to the party) and humanism (with its emphasis on loyalty to the clan and the family, and on individual effort), between China's status as the-other-to-the-West and the status of the 'other' cultures of China's past and unknown places to China's 'present self'. In *Old Well*, the 'lack' of China (in terms of technology) is projected onto the 'lack' of China's rural area, which is further projected onto an actual lack, the lack of water. In this series of projections and substitutions, the 'lack', always frustrating and empowering at once, finally gives way to a filling which stabilizes signification for survival.

At this point, we need to say, But wait, it is not only the 'filling' and the production of water that enable the survival of the community! The *failure* to produce water is what has already sustained the culture of Old Well village for generations!

What indeed is the old well?

In terms of narrative structure, the old well is, of course, nothing: it is the lack that makes narrative possible. The old well is the obsession that, precisely because it remains unfulfilled, perpetuates itself in the village as a kind of collective memory, collective responsibility, and collective desire. Do the men in Old Well village know what they really want? Or do they continue digging simply because their ancestors have formed that habit – simply because it has become a *tribal ritual*? The sense of absurdity that figures in what looks like a revered tradition is clearest in the scene where villagers from a neighboring village attempt to close up a well that the Old Well villagers claim to be theirs. This competition over the rights to the well leads to the question as to the whereabouts of the plaque indicating the well's 'ownership'. Finally, it is the women who produce the 'original' plaque, which has, it turns out, long become a latrine stone.

But the absurdity of this discovery does not change the powerful impact the obsession has on the village. And such is the power of social fantasy: even when the 'original' plaque has been turned into a latrine stone and is thus shown to be, after all, *no more than a (shitty) stone*, the belief that it is *more* persists. In a discussion of Eastern Europe after the collapse of communism, Slavoj Žižek writes about the fantastical nature of what he calls the 'nation-Thing' in a way that is equally applicable to the old well:

> The Thing is not directly a collection of these features [composing a specific way of life]; there is 'something more' in it, something that is present in these features, that appears through them. Members of a community who partake in a given 'way of life' believe in their Thing, where this belief has a reflexive structure proper to the intersubjective space: 'I believe in the (national) Thing' is equal to 'I believe that others (members of my community) believe in the Thing'. The tautological character of the Thing – its semantic void, the fact that all we can say about it is that it is 'the real Thing' – is founded precisely in this paradoxical reflexive structure.[17]

This fantasy turns all accidents – events that cannot be accounted for coherently but that nonetheless are real – into *mere* accidents, mere errors, which have no place in the actual functioning or *labor* of the fantasy. Similarly, all the lives that have been sacrificed in the course of searching for water are simply meaningless until the first well is successfully dug. Until then, we can say that the lost lives do not *matter*: they remain chance components waiting to be materialized into the full-blown fantasy peopled with real bodies. Instead of describing the history of Old Well village as one in which the villagers are united by a hope for the future (when water will be found), therefore, we should describe it this way: the discovery of water validates the sacrifices *retroactively* as parts of a concerted communal effort at well-digging. This is the paradox of the ending, at which we are shown a close-up of the plaque that is 'in memoriam' of all the well-digging martyrs, with the dates of their failed efforts and their deaths. Superimposed upon the rolling image of this plaque is the author's/director's inscription documenting Sun Wangquan's accomplishment: 'January 9, 1983: Water was found, and fifty tons of water were produced every hour from the first mechanized deep well'. The current 'success' proves by its chance occurrence that 'it' is what all the previous generations have been slaving for and that, moreover, their deaths were finally *worthwhile*.

The act of discovering water, in other words, is like a signifier which enigmatically constitutes the identity of the past by its very contingent presence or randomness. If, because of its success, this act becomes endowed with the value of a 'primary' act, then 'primary' value itself must be described not as an absolute origin but instead as a supplementary relation: like all previous attempts at well-digging, the latest attempt is a random event; at the same time, this latest attempt is marked by an *additional* randomness – the discovery of water, the accident of 'success'. This additional randomness, this accident that is more accidental than all the other accidents, marks the latest attempt at well-digging apart from the others, thereby constituting in the same moment the 'necessary' structure that coheres the entire series of events in a meaningful signifying chain, a signifying chain that I have been referring to as social fantasy. The labor of social fantasy, then, comprises not only the random physical efforts at well-digging and their failures but also the process of retroactive, supplementary transformation in which the random and physical becomes the primary, the necessary, and the virtuous, and henceforth functions and reproduces itself ideologically as such.

Crucial to this social fantasy is the danger represented by the romantic woman and the recurrent dry well, both of which are 'taken care of' at the end. The fantasy is that the village can have the technology of the running well without the technology of the new (running) woman, that the village can turn into a self-sufficient community with only as much outside help as it wants – precisely at a time when Chinese countryside self-sufficiency, like that of other 'Third World' rural areas, has been irredeemably eroded by 'modernized' production, distribution, and the permeation of global capitalist economics.

A film such as this, which demonstrates the fundamental nothingness of the labor of social fantasy, inevitably lends itself to a reading that is exactly the opposite. Attesting to that is *Old Well*'s warm reception by Chinese audiences at home and overseas, and its success at the Second Tokyo International Film Festival of 1987,[18] in contrast to the regular official censorship of films by the Fifth Generation directors that are consciously critical of Chinese culture. The intense appeal of a film that celebrates the rewarding of a communal, collective effort makes little sense unless we understand the magnitude of the fantasy of collectivity on the largest scale – the Cultural Revolution – and its collapse. The emotional vacuum left behind by the latter awaits the legitimating *work* of some other thing. This other thing is increasingly being sought in China's old and remote areas, where social fantasy, whose creation of a present identity is always through a nostalgic imagining of a permanent other time and other place, can flourish most uninhibitedly. And so, beyond the futility of the nation and the barrenness of love, the labor of social fantasy, like the muscular masculine arms at the film's beginning, hammers on.

Endnotes

1   Fredric Jameson, 'Third-World literature in the era of multinational capitalism', *Social Text*, No. 15 (Fall 1986), p. 69. For the most widely cited piece of criticism of Jameson's position, see Aijaz Ahmad, 'Jameson's rhetoric of otherness and the "national allegory"', and Jameson, 'A brief response', *Social Text*, 17 (Fall 1987), pp. 3–25; 26–7. [See also the relevant pages in Ahmad, *In theory: classes, nations, literatures* (London, Verso, 1992).] For a criticism of Jameson's 'A brief response', see Kwai-cheung Lo, 'Crossing boundaries: a study of modern Hong Kong fiction from the fifties to the eighties', M.Phil dissertation, University of Hong Kong, 1990, pp. 165–73. For Jameson's reinstatement of the concept of national allegory, see his 'Foreword: in the mirror of alternate modernities', Karatani Kōjin, *Origins of modern Japanese literature*, a collective translation edited by Brett de Bary (Durham, NC, Duke University Press, 1993), pp. vii–xx; see in particular pp. xix–xx, in which he issues the call for a moral rectification of 'our' (that is, US) 'national' character.

2   Walter Benjamin, *The origin of German tragic drama*, translated by John Osborne (London, New Left Books, 1977), p. 233.

3   E.J. Hobsbawm, *Nations and nationalism since 1780: programme, myth, reality* (New York, Cambridge University Press, 1990), p. 152.

4   This phrase is Chandra Talpade Mohanty's. See 'Under Western eyes: feminist scholarship and colonial discourses', in Chandra Talpade Mohanty, Ann Russo, and Lourdes Torres, eds, *Third World Women and the Politics of Feminism* (Bloomington, IN, Indiana University Press, 1991), p. 53. An earlier version of this essay was published in *boundary 2*, 12, no. 3/13, no. 1 (Spring–Fall 1984) and reprinted in *Feminist Review*, 30 (Autumn 1988).

5   For instance, see Paul Willemen, 'The Third Cinema question: notes and reflections', in Jim Pines and Paul Willemen eds, *Questions of Third Cinema* (London, British Film Institute Publishing, 1989), pp. 1–29.

6   '[The] dominant *radical* reader in the Anglo–U.S. reactively homogenizes the Third World and sees it only in the context of nationalism and ethnicity', Gayatri Chakravorty Spivak, *In other worlds: essays in cultural politics* (New York, Methuen, 1987), p. 246: emphasis in the original.

7   Spivak, *In other worlds*, p. 254. By 'subalternization', Spivak is referring to the tendency to place in a lower, inferior, or less important position in the hierarchy of society or the hierarchy across cultures.

8   Jameson, 'Third-World literature', p. 66.

9   Liu Heng, 'Fuxi Fuxi', in Wang Ziping and Li Tuo, eds, *Zhongguo xiaoshuo yi jiu ba ba* (Chinese fiction 1988) (Hong Kong, Sanlian shudian, 1989), pp. 80–171. For an informative analysis of the story, see Marie-Claire Huot, 'Liu Heng's *Fuxi Fuxi*: what about Nuwa?', in Tonglin Lu, ed., *Gender and sexuality in twentieth-century Chinese literature and society* (Albany, NY, State University of New York Press, 1993), pp. 85–105.

10 Jean Baudrillard, *For a critique of the political economy of the sign*, translated with an introduction by Charles Levin (St Louis, MO, Telos Press, 1981), p. 93.

11 Baudrillard, *For a critique*, p. 94; emphasis in the original.

12 The recent films by Chen Kaige and Zhang Yimou obtained financial support from Hong Kong, Taiwan, Japan, England, Germany, and Holland.

13 Zheng Yi, *Lao jing* (Taipei, Haifeng chubanshe, 1988). The novella was first published in a literary magazine in China in February 1985. It is also available in English. See Zheng Yi, *Old Well*, translated by David Kwan, with an introduction by Anthony P. Kane (San Francisco, CA, China Books and Periodicals, 1989).

14 Such a reading informs, for instance, the discussions collected in Jiao Xiongping, ed., *Lao jing* (*Dianying/Zhongguo mingzuo xuan*, no. 1) (Taipei, Wanxiang tushu gufen youxian gongsi, 1990).

15 E.J. Hobsbawm, *Nations and nationalism since 1780*, p. 169, emphasis in the original.

16 Partha Chatterjee, *Nationalist thought and the colonial world – a derivative discourse?* (The United Nations University, Tokyo, Zed Books, 1986), p. 11.

17 Slavoj Žižek, 'Eastern Europe's Republics of Gilead', *New Left Review*, 183 (September/October 1990), p. 53. As he argues in another context, social fantasy is 'precisely the way the antagonistic fissure is masked . . . . Fantasy is a means for an ideology to take its own failure into account in advance.' See Žižek, *The sublime object of ideology* (London, Verso, 1989), p. 126.

18 *Old Well* won 4 of the 13 awards given by the festival, including the 'special affirmation award by international film critics'.

Acknowledgement: This chapter is an excerpt, with significant abridgements and modifications, from *Primitive passions: visuality, sexuality, ethnography, and contemporary Chinese cinema* by Rey Chow. Copyright © 1995 Columbia University Press. Reprinted with permission of the publisher.

22 Facing up to Hollywood

Ana M. López

Although resolutely national, the US film industry – Hollywood – has always also been profoundly international. Hollywood's international presence has had acute effects not only on Hollywood itself – upon its production and textual practices – but on all other film-making nations. One way or another, all other nations aspiring to produce a 'national' cinema have always had to deal with Hollywood's presence or, sometimes, its absence. For almost a century, Hollywood films have been a constant source of entertainment pleasure for international audiences and the Hollywood style of production the goal that national cinemas have striven to achieve. Perceived as the industrial 'vanguard', Hollywood always seems to lead the way in technology, capital investments, and pleasure-producing innovations. Yet paradoxically, 'Hollywood' and everything it stands for have also been the nemesis of national cinemas throughout the world: the seductive polish, production values, and constant presence of Hollywood films invariably precluded or prejudiced the industrial development of indigenous production.

Understanding the impact of Hollywood's international ubiquity and developing strategies to 'face up' to it is a considerable challenge for producers in other cultural/national contexts. This chapter begins by providing a summary of the context in which Hollywood acquired its hegemony over international markets and then traces the historical development of the strategies and theoretical rationales that have been deployed to deal with it. In the period between the coming of sound and the 1950s, national cinemas generally 'faced up' to Hollywood by addressing specific market segments (art/high culture or language-based, for example) and/or by imitation. I will illustrate these strategies via two 'case studies', the development of a film industry in Mexico in the 1930s and the attempt to create a 'Brazilian Hollywood' by the Vera Cruz Studios in the late 1940s/early 1950s. In the 1960s, the theories of dependency that emerged from Latin America, coupled with post-World-War-2 alternative models of film production and expression such as Italian neorealism and the French New Wave, altered this paradigm. Rather than an admired ideal, Hollywood's ubiquity became a predominant symbol of the strength of US cultural imperialism, and its practices and appeals were to be shunned in the interests of national cultural specificity. The most illustrative cinematic response to this conceptual and political shift was the New Latin American Cinema movement of the 1960s and 1970s. By the 1970s and 1980s, however, a recognition of new patterns of economic and cultural exchanges led to an important reconceptualization of the cultural imperialism approach. The concepts of globalization and postmodernity, acknowledging the growing speed and international interdependence of contemporary economics and culture, have opened a space for rethinking the strategies through which Hollywood needs to be 'faced' and the histories of national cinemas.

How Hollywood became an international force: economics, politics, and ideology

Even before the full establishment of the classical Hollywood studio system of production in the late 1910s, the cinema was already global, in the sense that it was recognized as an international business. The first attempt to monopolize the industry, Thomas Alva Edison's Motion Picture Patents Company ('the Trust'), strategically included significant non-American film concerns: its 'continental wing' comprised alliances with two French companies, Pathé Frères – at the time the most powerful international company, already vertically integrated – and Georges Méliès's Star Films.

Nevertheless, despite the Trust's early efforts, the US film industry did not really acquire hegemony over world markets until World War 1 (Thompson, 1985). Previously, the huge size of its domestic audience and its vertiginous growth had kept the industry more than profitable, since the domestic market fully amortized production expenses. In fact, several European companies (Pathé from France, Nordisk from Denmark) who depended upon export revenues to amortize production because of their small domestic markets had already a well-established competitive presence within the USA. But by the immediate pre-war years, the industry had organized and consolidated its activities sufficiently to saturate the domestic market and expand into foreign markets by tailoring its pricing structures and establishing new distribution procedures. Since production costs could be recouped in the domestic market, international film sales could be priced differentially, according to what specific national/regional markets could bear and undercutting the local competition. This made Hollywood films very attractive to local exhibitors and distributors, who quickly saw that they could gain higher profits by showing Hollywood films rather than local productions. Furthermore, rather than relegate all international trade to agents in London, Hollywood producers began to open their own local offices in the major foreign markets. In Brazil, for example, the sudden appearance of well-funded branches of Hollywood studios who bought out local distributors essentially wiped out all domestic production (Johnson and Stam, 1995).

In general industrial terms, World War 1 was a godsend for Hollywood because it allowed for the solidification of its international operations. First, while the war raged in Europe, film-making there was disrupted and production plummeted, while the US cinema prospered: Cook, citing Lewis Jacobs, estimates that while in 1914 the USA produced slightly over half the world's films, by 1918 it was making nearly all of them (1996: 47). Simultaneously, the US industry took advantage of its competitors' distractions by aggressively going after the export markets they had previously dominated, especially Australia, New Zealand, and Latin America. By eroding the European industry's international base of support, Hollywood permanently weakened the formerly strong European producing countries. Since 1919, overseas receipts have regularly been factored into Hollywood's budgets and, since the 1930s, foreign markets have provided between a third and a half of all industry revenues. World War 1 – and later World War 2 – placed the US industry in a position of indisputable economic and productive leadership that, with variations, it would never again relinquish.

Economic strategies and political alliances

To never again loosen its hold of the international film marketplace, the Hollywood industry developed complex strategies to sustain and augment its power. In economic terms, this has been described as the industry's flexible managerial structure and open and innovative financial systems (Acheson and Maule, 1994). However, most important in the immediate post-World-War-1 years was establishing the terms of Hollywood's relationship to Europe. A first step was to co-opt foreign producers. For example, Germany, which had emerged from the war with a relatively strong industry, was resisting the US takeover of its market and had innovated with protective legislation (quotas on imports since 1921). Therefore, when for complex reasons the powerful and very successful German producer UFA found itself in dire financial trouble in 1925, Paramount and Metro Goldwyn Mayer stepped in with a large loan in exchange for the right to release 10 UFA films annually in the USA and the creation of a joint distribution company, Parufamet, to distribute Paramount/MGM films in Germany. Offering much-needed capital to financially strapped foreign producers who could conceivably have an edge in some important foreign market to establish binational production and distribution agreements would continue to be a favorite Hollywood strategy.

A second, ancillary strategy involved attempts to diversify the Hollywood talent pool. Consciousness of the international market led producers to seek out foreign actors, positioning Hollywood as the home base of a broad constellation of international stars. Thus, for example, a canny producer imported Dolores Del Rio from Mexico in the 1920s and made her a star who could fit the exotic foreigner role to perfection. European talent was always particularly attractive. In fact, immediately after the Parufamet agreement, many UFA artists and technicians migrated to Hollywood. Director Ernest Lubitsch and actress Pola Negri, in Hollywood since the early 1920s, were joined by several directors (among them, F.W. Murnau and Michael Curtiz), cinematographer Karl Freund, actors Emil Jannings, Conrad Veidt, and Greta Garbo, producer Erich Pommer, and set designer Carl Mayer. Others, from Germany and elsewhere in Europe, would join them throughout the late 1920s and through the 1940s, among them Jean Renoir from France, Alfred Hitchcock from England, and Fritz Lang, Robert Siodmak, Douglas Sirk, Billy Wilder, and Otto Preminger from Germany. The studios also eagerly sought talent from less-well established film producers who had nevertheless established a firm regional reputation: Mexican heart-throbs Pedro Armendáriz and Arturo de Cordova, for example, worked for Hollywood studios in the 1940s and 1950s.

Beyond purely financial and importation deals, however, the Hollywood studios also established a firm connection with the US State Department and other governmental agencies that allowed the industry to wield extraordinary diplomatic clout – always, of course, in the service of its own international position. In 1922, the US studios established a trade association, the Motion Pictures Producers and Distributors of America (MPPDA) and hired the well-connected ex-Postmaster General Will Hays to direct it. Although primarily designed to clean up Hollywood's somewhat tarnished national image, the MPPDA was also empowered to represent the industry's trade interests abroad. In fact, the MPPDA and its offshoot since World War 2, the Motion Picture Export Association of America (MPEAA), have acted as a legal cartel for foreign trade. Both the MPPDA and the MPEAA have successfully negotiated with foreign governments to fight quota legislations curtailing the presence of Hollywood films in particular countries. Representing the entire industry, they could not only threaten – and carry out – boycotts, but also negotiate enforceable agreements. Furthermore, the US government often fully backed their endeavors, either via the Motion Picture Division of the Department of Commerce (established in 1929) or directly via the State Department. Jack Valente, head of the MPEAA since the 1940s, endearingly dubbed the agency 'the little State Department' because of its close alliances with US policy and ideology (Guback, 1969).

These alliances were more than strengthened during and after World War 2, when the government saw Hollywood films as propaganda for democracy and 'the American way of life' (Schatz, 1988) and facilitated film exports through Commerce Department initiatives and diplomatic pressures. During the war, the Hollywood cinema was perceived as a crucial weapon, extraordinarily valuable to maintain not only national morale but also the political alliances of the USA's South American 'neighbors'. Not coincidentally, these South American neighbors were also one of the industry's few remaining foreign markets, since this war again paralysed the market in continental Europe (which had previously provided the industry with 25 per cent of its foreign revenues). Reviving the dormant 'Good Neighbor Policy', the State Department created the Office of the Coordinator of Inter-American Affairs in 1940 to combat pro-Axis sentiment in Latin America, and its Motion Picture division worked with Hollywood producers to ensure the production of films to please this suddenly significant market: Latin American themes, locations, rhythms, and talent invaded Hollywood films during the war (Woll, 1980).

Similarly, the post-World-War-2 dismantling of the film industries of the former Axis nations fully complemented Hollywood's economic plans with the USA's anti-fascist and anti-communist political agendas. The alliance between the MPEAA and the State Department continues to this day. For example, in 1970–71, the MPEAA collaborated with the USA's efforts to undermine president Salvador Allende's Popular Unity government by participating in an 'invisible blockade' against Chile. The majors stopped shipping prints and demanded advance payments on rentals, which effectively eliminated Hollywood films from Chilean screens, further discredited the regime, and increased popular dissatisfaction (Chanan, 1974). In contrast, the US government collaborated explicitly with MPEAA efforts: in 1985 Congress and the US embassy demanded that South Korea allow Hollywood to establish its own distribution companies and shortly thereafter South Korea became Hollywood's second largest market in Asia (Bordwell and Thompson, 1994).

Beyond economics

As a complement to the canny business and lobbying practices that transformed the USA into the world leader of cinema, Hollywood also had a stake in making its own nationality invisible. Since its earliest days, the cinema had often been posited as a *universal* medium that could surmount linguistic differences, overcome distances, and be understood by all, and Hollywood had a particular practical interest in promoting this position as it came to dominate world markets (Sklar, 1993). That the cinema was a universal medium was a specially handy counter-argument against those wishing either to use film to represent national/local interests or to erect import barriers. And it also served to naturalize Hollywood's own nationality by equating the Hollywood cinema's undeniable American 'accent' with a universal language. Given Hollywood's worldwide prominence and the rhetoric of universality, the style and practice of film-making developed by Hollywood in the late 1910s and 1920s became international norms: studio-based production, expensive production values, rapid cutting, shot variety, continuity editing. However, to the same degree that people in all countries could see and understand the Hollywood cinema, when it represented those peoples and nations it did so, invariably, though its own very American eyes. As Sklar argues, the aspiration to global leadership was not accompanied by an effort to construct a global perspective on human lives and cultures. The Mexican government's reaction to Hollywood's hegemony on Mexican screens in the 1920s is especially telling in this respect. Whereas other nations demanded protective legislation (such as quotas) on economic terms, Mexico was the first country to protest against the USA on ideological grounds. Offended by the too-frequent stereotypical representation of Mexicans as 'greasers', evil bandidos, and sexy señoritas, in 1922 the Mexican government banned the films of any company making films portraying Mexicans offensively, even when the films themselves were not distributed in Mexico (García Riera, 1987: 109–11, 125–6). Because the Mexican market was already lucrative enough to be of interest, US producers promised to comply. In fact, one of the earliest charges of the MPPDA, included in lists of 'Don'ts and Be Carefuls' to producers, was to ensure that 'foreigners' were not depicted offensively. In practice, the greasers and señoritas did not disappear, but the narratives in which they appeared were relocated from Mexico to imaginary tropical nations or to unidentified 'Spanish' California locales.

The effects of Hollywood's international dominance: the problems of national cinemas

The range and depth of the Hollywood industry's historical control over international film markets have forced film-makers aspiring or struggling to produce national cinemas always to have to establish a dialogue with Hollywood. If not a universal medium, the very presence of Hollywood films everywhere proved that the cinema was at the very least international and, outside Hollywood, raised questions of national provenance with which Hollywood had not previously been concerned. What could be deemed 'national' in film? National ownership of the means of production, distribution, and exhibition? The nationality of the creative personnel? Narrative content/style and their cultural specificity (Crofts, 1993)?

In Europe, after World War 1, the dominance of Hollywood films was seen 'as a crisis not only of cinema, but of civilization' (Sklar, 1993: 126). It gave rise to significant comparative debates over economic, aesthetic, and social issues. Was the dominance of Hollywood films a purely economic factor, linked to the industry's ability to gain distribution and exhibition outlets and cutting film rental prices below that of local producers? Or was it that Hollywood films were indeed better than national efforts; that is, that their polish and technological sophistication offered greater entertainment value and textual pleasure? Or was their popularity perhaps a sign of the disintegration of the national culture and its values, part of the process of commercialization into a homogenous international mass culture driven by consumerism and technology in the service of capital? In this context, what responsibility does the state have to protect and/or foster a national cinema?

In one form or another, these debates have been echoed since then in all nations or regions aspiring to indigenous cinematic production since the end of World War 1. After the coming of sound, Hollywood became more entrenched in international markets, although it had become, obviously, less universal when speaking English. Because the costs of the transition to sound were enormous – wiring theaters, acquiring new equipment – local investment throughout most of the world lagged behind that of Hollywood and allowed the industry to maintain its dominance. However, the difficulties of translation did open up a potential window of opportunity for local producers in non-English-speaking markets who suddenly had, on the surface, an easy answer to the question of 'national' differences in the cinema: language and music.

Hollywood's efforts to produce foreign-language versions (for example, the 'Hispanic Cinema') and multiple language versions of its films for export had been singularly unsuccessful. They were expensive to produce and, worse of all, usually box-office failures because they failed to offer audiences any kind of cultural specificity or the lure of the appeal of established stars (Durovicova, 1992). But resorting to subtitling automatically eliminated the segment of the popular audience that was either unable or unwilling to read at the movies, while dubbing produced a singular disruption of the spectatorial experience and the requisite suspension of disbelief. Furthermore, in some areas of the world linguistic commonalities seemed to offer natural well-differentiated markets for regional exploitation, creating a favorable climate for the development of industries, for example, in the larger Spanish-speaking nations such as Mexico, Argentina, and Spain. The history of the development of the Mexican sound cinema – its 'Golden Age' – provides an especially illustrative example of the complex issues and negotiations involved in creating a national cinema in the face of Hollywood's international dominance.

The case of Mexico: a 'national' cinema in the shadow of Hollywood

By the late 1920s (and despite earlier achievements), Mexican production had come to an almost complete standstill. The crisis was so dire that then minister of Public Education José Vasconcelos even argued that the cinema was 'a typically US cultural product impossible to develop as a national form' (De la Vega, 1995: 79). But after the success of the first sound films and the failure of the 'Hispanic films', Mexico attempted to compete with Hollywood on its own terms. A group of exhibitors and journalists committed to the idea of a national cinema invested in optical sound-on-film production using a system patented by two Mexican engineers who had lived in Los Angeles, the brothers Joselito and Roberto Rodríguez. They produced an adaptation of *Santa* (Antonio Moreno, 1931), a canonical novel by Federico Gamboa (the Mexican Zola) about a prostitute with a heart of gold, that established a basis for the future development of the desired national film industry. *Santa* also included the romantic music of Agustín Lara and established an important connection between the cinema and the national radio and record industries which promoted the development of a regional mass culture industry.

The production of *Santa* coincided with a campaign led by a group of deputies to raise the consciousness of Mexicans to consume only national products (De la Vega, 1995: 81). Although this campaign was short-lived, it helped to establish protectionist trade barriers that facilitated the production of *Santa* and its subsequent success. In other words, the state was finally supporting, even if only indirectly, a Mexican film industry. *Santa* also coincided with the arrival of a famous and polemical visitor: Sergei Eisenstein, who had obtained funding from Upton Sinclair to shoot a paean to Mexican culture, *Que Viva Mexico*. Eisenstein was never able to complete his film, but left an undeniable legacy to the Mexican cinema in his translation to film of some of the visual characteristics of the muralist, engraving, and photography movements that were cultivated in Mexico in the 1920s as part of the post-Revolutionary 'national culture' project (for example, the murals and paintings of Diego Rivera, José Clemente Orozco, and David Alfaro Siquieros).

Thus, by 1932, the Mexican cinema already possessed some of the essential requirements for the development of industrial film production: a trustworthy sound system, an idea of a nationalist aesthetic, and the precedent of state support. Furthermore, Mexico was in the last stages of its post-Revolutionary national reconstruction and, for the first time in decades, enjoying the benefits of political stability and capitalist development. What was needed to infiltrate the market, however, were distinctively local themes and genres. Given that Hollywood had not yet abandoned 'Hispanic' films, even though they were in crisis, the incipient Mexican cinema bourgeoisie had sufficient time to experiment and to find a type of cinema to woo the Spanish-language foreign market; this was the only way to develop the national film industry.

The generic experimentation of the period 1933–37 was broad-based, aesthetically and commercially successful, and encompassed a variety of approaches to the medium.

Some directors approached the cinema primarily as a business and were primarily concerned with box-office receipts and offering entertainment value. Perhaps the most prototypical was the Spanish-Mexican Juan Orol, producer and director of lachrymose melodramas directly influenced by the popularity of serial radio dramas. Clearly a part of an incipient pan-Latin-American mass culture industry, these films were among the first to prove successful in non-Mexican markets, especially in Central America and the Caribbean, and began to establish a distribution base for Mexican producers. At the opposite end of the spectrum, we find the avant-garde playwright Juan Bustillo Oro whose films followed a more traditional artistic model, influenced by literary trends and German expressionist styles. Between these two extremes, a third strand of films benefitted from state support. Under the influence of the radical social policies of president Lázaro Cárdenas (1934–40), the state funded the production of films with a marked social content, including *Redes* (Nets, Fred Zinnemann, and Emilio Gómez Muriel, 1934), *¡Vámonos con Pancho Villa!* ('Let's Go With Pancho Villa!'; Fernando de Fuentes, 1935) and many documentaries and newsreels exalting the popular politics and economic progress of the Cárdenas regime. Yet a fourth tendency was exemplified by directors who managed to articulate commercial and aesthetic demands with extraordinary results, for example Arcady Boytler in *La mujer del puerto* ('The Woman of the Port', 1933), a brilliant brothel melodrama; Fernando de Fuentes in *El fantasma del convento* ('The Convent Ghost', 1934), an innovative horror film; and José Bohr, whose delirious but well-made gangster-detective trilogy is often considered among the best work of the period: *¿Quién mató a Eva?* ('Who Killed Eva?', 1934), *Luponini* (*El terror de Chicago*) ['Luponini (The Chicago Terror)'] and *Marihuana* (*El Monstruo Verde*) ['Marijuana (The Green Monster)'] shot, respectively, in 1935 and 1936.

Mexican cinematic nationalism took two distinct forms in this period. On the one hand, some films explicitly reflected the liberal nationalism of Lázaro Cárdenas's policies and were influenced by Eisenstein's visualization of Mexico and the prevalent musical nationalism of art music (composers such as Manuel Castro Pasilla, Silvestre Revueltas, Manuel M. Ponce, and Carlos Chávez). On the other hand were films that focused on the pre-Revolutionary agrarian world (ruled by the dictator Porfirio Díaz and called the *Porfiriato*), 'putting aside the social changes brought about by the Revolution and defending the established order', which were influenced by popular theater and music rather than elite culture (De los Reyes, 1987: 187). The international success of one of these, Fernando de Fuentes's *Allá en el Rancho Grande* ('Over There in the Big Ranch', 1936) determined the nature of the Mexican industry, which would develop commercially under the influence of popular cultural forms – popular music, comedy/vaudeville, melodrama – to the detriment of a state-sponsored cinema inspired by elite art forms.

To understand this shift, consider a brief analysis of the textual work of *Allá en el Rancho Grande*. *Rancho Grande* is set in the present, but in a bucolic mythical rural area where neither the Revolution nor the recent Agrarian Reform has left any traces and where conflicts emerge only from love affairs, wounded male pride, and misunderstandings. Its narrative is pure melodrama: a landowner falls for the girlfriend of his foreman, with whom he has been friends since childhood. The former friends become enemies, but ultimately, despite macho attitudes and fights, the bonds of their friendship prevail and all are reconciled with the aid of much singing and dancing. Beyond its nostalgia for an imaginary past in which such simple relationships could have been conceived, the film reworks a series of popular and folkloric elements that would define the *comedia ranchera* genre: popular music in the form of *ranchera* songs; a loose, episodic narrative structure derived from variety theater in which songs often take the place of dialogue; and familiar yet picturesque character types (*charros*, innocent *señoritas* with long braided hair, peppery old housekeepers) and situations (cock fights, fiestas, horse races, etc).

The film was eventually very popular and was even more widely distributed after cinematographer Gabriel Figueroa received the Mexican cinema's first international festival prize for its cinematography in Venice. Nationally, it spurred investment in the industry and production. The year *Rancho Grande* was released (1936), Mexico produced 25 films. By 1937 production grew to 38 films, of which 20 followed the *ranchera* model. In 1939 production again increased: out of 57 films, 20 exploited the ranchera formula and 'local color'.

Rancho Grande was also seen throughout the Spanish-speaking Latin American market and subtitled versions were even released in the USA (always the market most resistant to cinematic imports). But this first moment of nationalist expansion was already mediated by Hollywood. International distribution was coordinated by United Artists, who struck a most advantageous agreement with the film's producer (60–40 per cent split of gross revenues). Until United Artists got out of Latin American distribution in the 1950s, *Rancho Grande* was one of its highest grossing films, in 1939 surpassed only by *Modern Times* and *The Garden of Allah* (de Usabel, 1992: 140–1). As would be the case throughout most of its history, the Mexican cinema expanded with the cooperation of Hollywood, which favored it more than any other Latin American film producer. As Paulo Antonio Paranaguá has succinctly expressed it: 'Poor Mexico, so far from God and so close to Hollywood' (1995: 9).

In any case, the release of *Rancho Grande* in Latin America could not have occurred at a more propitious moment. Other Spanish-language cinemas which had competed for the Latin American market were going through difficult times. Spain was involved in a bloody civil war that would temporarily cripple production. Argentine films – of much higher technical quality than the Mexican but also becoming very Europeanized – were waning in popularity, and Argentine production, although increasing, had not matched the levels of the Mexican industry (Argentina produced 15 films in 1936, 28 in 1937, and 41 in 1938). The *Rancho Grande* formula unearthed what Latin American audiences seemed to have been looking for in the Mexican cinema: the presentation of a 'Mexican' vision of Mexico that coincided with their expectations of the nature of national 'local color'. As Emilio García Riera has argued, after *Rancho Grande*, the Mexican cinema 'enjoyed the prestige of authenticity granted by even the most adulterated folklore' (1987: 111). The *ranchera* vision of Mexico, albeit decidedly distinct from other Latin American national stereotypes, was simultaneously still recognizable. It combined an appealing exoticism with a comforting familiarity that easily won over Latin American audiences looking for points of cinematic identification. Furthermore, the nostalgia for an imaginary bucolic past where macho pride and true love always prevailed invoked by *Rancho Grande* and its successors also echoed throughout other Latin American countries where, despite different political histories, the present was burdened by the legacies of colonization and the frustrations of independence (López, 1994).

Rancho Grande opened the doors, the industry rushed to keep them open: the Mexican cinema consolidated its strength by copying, expanding, and improvising upon the formula of the *comedia ranchera*, introduced variations of other well-rehearsed generic formulas such as the maternal melodramas and the picaresque comedy, and attempted to develop a 'star system' of its own comparable to that of Hollywood. Some 57 features were produced in 1938, and the Mexican film industry was officially born. The industrial transformation of the Mexican cinema involved the defeat of the Hollywood 'Hispanic' cinema and constant supremacy over the other Spanish-language producers. But the other US-produced cinema never lost its hegemony over Latin American or Mexican screens: of the 3081 feature films premiered in the capital in the 1930s, 2338 (76 per cent) were from the USA, 544 (18 per cent) were from other foreign nations, and only 199 (6 per cent) were Mexican (Ayala Blanco and Amador, 1980). In this sense, neither the Mexican cinema nor the cinemas of other underdeveloped nations have ever been a serious threat to Hollywood.

The case of Vera Cruz: the failure of studio-based Brazilian production

The Companhia Cinematográfica Vera Cruz, in existence between 1949 and 1954, represents the most concerted effort to implement studio-based film-making in Brazil. In Rio de Janeiro, other companies such as Atlântida and Cinédia were also studio-based, but unlike them Vera Cruz was modern, well-equipped, and, since it was backed by the wealthy São Paulo bourgeoisie, well-financed. For its founders, the great industrialists Francisco Matarazzo Sobrinho and Franco Zampari, Vera Cruz – like the Museu de Arte Moderna and the Teatro Brasileiro de Comédia which they had also created – was a symbol not only of their own cultural aspirations but of the modernity and effervescence of the São Paulo bourgeoisie in general. If anyone could, they would be the ones finally to produce a Brazilian cinema of international 'quality', the opposite of the much-detested *chanchadas* or carnivalesque comedies produced by the Rio de Janeiro companies. Their 'internationalism' was inspired by Hollywood's universality (and the studio mode of production), but the technical know-how for the company was all European. Among the talent imported by Vera Cruz were British cinematographer Chick Fowle, Austrian editor Oswald Haffenrichter, Danish sound engineer Eric Rasmussen, and several Italian directors (Adolfo Celi, Luciano Salce, and Ruggero Jacobbi) associated with the Teatro Brasileiro de Comédia. Of course, the principal 'import' was not really an importation, but the return of a prodigal son: Vera Cruz hired as its executive producer the Brazilian-born director–producer Alberto Cavalcanti, who had begun his career with the French avant-garde, worked at Joinville in multilingual productions, had participated in the establishment of the British documentary movement, and greatly contributed to the success of the Ealing studios. Under his tutelage, Vera Cruz established a complex system of studio production, fully staffed and with large facilities (Galvão, 1981; Johnson and Stam, 1995; Ramos, 1987).

In its five years of intense activities, Vera Cruz produced some documentaries (including two shorts directed by Lima Barreto) and 18 feature films, ranging from historical and contemporary melodramas to biographical films, historical epics, and comedies. Its greatest success was Lima Barreto's *O Cangaceiro* (1953), which won two awards at Cannes and was distributed worldwide. Vera Cruz's output, coupled with increasing film-making activity in São Paulo itself and in Rio, led to a general euphoria over the real possibilities of Brazilian film-making: national film production rose from 10 films in 1947 to 20 in 1950. Above and beyond production numbers, it was also evident that the Vera Cruz studios had, almost overnight, improved the technical quality of Brazilian cinema, especially in relation to cinematography, sound, editing and lab work. As Johnson and Stam argue, 'through their themes, genres, and production values they achieved the "look" of First World Cinema' (1995: 28).

Nevertheless, critics complained about the lack of national specificity in this 'international style'. Vera Cruz films were accused of 'foreignness' because of their foreign technical personnel as well as the perceived inauthenticity of its formal paradigms. And the markets were much more difficult to conquer than Vera Cruz had estimated. Inexplicably, Vera Cruz did not take into account the limitations of the domestic market and the difficulties of breaking into the international market. Returns on investment were simply too slow to sustain big studio production: its big-budget films (the average Vera Cruz film cost 10 times more than a Rio *chanchada*), extraordinarily high overhead costs, and, eventually, its indebtedness to the Bank of Brazil and the Bank of the State of São Paulo, bankrupted the company. Even the 1953 success of *O Cangaceiro*, the first Vera Cruz film to break into the international market, came too late. Strapped by debts the company sold its international distribution rights to Columbia Pictures, which was the only one to profit from the film's ground-breaking success.

Although Vera Cruz's failure proved the economic unsuitability of Hollywood-modeled studio film production in Brazil, its achievements were very significant. Beyond its individual films, the company and its foreign technicians trained a cadre of professionals in the field which would later contribute greatly to Brazilian film and television production (López, forthcoming). Furthermore, the extraordinary impact of its failure led to a broad debate among critics and film-makers and a search for new aesthetic and production models more appropriate to the social and economic conditions of the nations which would eventually evolve into the Cinema Novo movement of the 1960s.

Dependency theory and cultural imperialism: facing up to Hollywood in the 1960s

The nations in the periphery of the international superpowers have always been cognizant of the uneven nature of cultural flows, especially of the cinema, and of the potentially negative effects of Hollywood's pleasure machine on national cultures. People all over the world and in every conceivable cultural and social context were exposed not only to narrative and spectacular pleasures, but also, as part of the 'American way of life', to the wonders of US modern consumer technology (cars, furniture, fashions, etc.). That Hollywood films clearly created a desire for US-made consumer goods was not lost upon Hollywood exporters or national agencies, which regularly protested against specific market disruptions caused by films. In the mid-1930s, for example, a group of Argentine merchants protested to the US Embassy about Clark Gable's lack of an undershirt in a crucial scene of It Happened One Night (1934) because it had created a surplus of undershirts in their warehouse (King, 1990: 32).

However, beginning in the post-World-War-2 period, and especially among poorer nations, this discourse took on different overtones. In an environment in which exported consumer goods and modernized markets were positioned as important contributors to modernizing developmental processes, social critics foregrounded the capitalist media as the principal vehicles for the commodification and political and economic exploitation of their societies. Development through commercialism meant dependence: slow economic growth, disenfranchised local cultures, emergent local ruling classes reliant on foreign capital and ideology (Mattelart, 1979; Tomlinson, 1991; Turnstall, 1977).

Significant international political realignments in 1959–60 added an additional facet. While in Africa the old European colonial empires crumbled and new nations were quickly emerging, in Latin America, cultural renewal and political debates acquired a new urgency and viability after the spectacular success of Fidel Castro's guerrilla forces against a dictator in Cuba (Castro took power on 1 January 1959). The non-aligned movement of the 1950s, which had sought a way out of the polarizations of the Cold War, soon became a 'third' way and those nations collectively known as the 'Third World'.

Perhaps the most sustained attempt to translate dependency theory into practice in the realm of culture and cultural critique occurred in the debates and films of the New Latin American Cinema (NLAC) movement. A central focus of this movement, which emerged as the synthesis of a series of 'new' national cinemas in Argentina (La Nueva Ola), Brazil (Cinema Novo), and Cuba, was the rejection of the mode of production, style, and ideology of the Hollywood cinema. Film-makers and critics were influenced by the aesthetic innovations and new modes of production of European film movements, especially Italian neorealism and the French New Wave, which proved the viability of non-studio-based production. They were also, simultaneously, immersed in the maelstrom of political and social debates and revolutions that traversed the continent from Cuba to Patagonia and were eager to 'liberate' the cinema; that is, to change its social function. The 'new' cinemas would serve as forms of national expression but would also be active weapons in the transformation of the under-development and political oppression that characterized Latin America (López, 1990). Manifestos such as Julio García Espinosa's 'For an Imperfect Cinema' (Cuba) and the Grupo Cine Liberación's 'Towards a Third Cinema' (Argentina) critiqued the 'perfection' and ideological complicity of Hollywood films while arguing for the need for a new, imperfect, cinema of liberation for the continent. Film-makers throughout the continent attempted to put theory into practice and produced some of the most innovative and far-reaching works of the decade, ranging from, in Cuba, Tomás Gutiérrez Alea's *Memories of Underdevelopment* (1968) and Humberto Solas's *Lucia* (1968); in Argentina Fernando Solanas and Octavio Getino's *The Hour of the Furnaces* (1968); in Chile, Miguel Littin's *The Jackal of Nahueltoro* (1971) and Patricio Guzman's *The Battle of Chile* (1975–79); in Bolivia, Jorge Sanjines's *Blood of the Condor* (1969); and, in Brazil, Glauber Rocha's *Terra em Transe* (1967) and *Antonio das Mortes* (1969), Nelson Pereira dos Santos's *Vidas Secas* (1963) and Joaquim Pedro de Andrade's *Macunaima* (1968).

The films of the NLAC were often revolutionary and explicitly political, taking on the medium as political instrument. In the fictional realm, they were films which took on the cinema as a medium for entertainment but attempted to transform and demystify its standard parameters, resorting either to 'realism' or to 'history' as privileged realms. They were not, however, industrial films. Above all, these were independent films, marginal cinemas on the fringes of existing industries or artisanal practices in nations without a national cinematic infrastructure such as Chile, Uruguay, and Bolivia. Cuba has been a case apart because of the stability (until recently) and extraordinary longevity of the Castro regime.

Unlike Cuba, almost all other Latin American nations underwent cataclysmic political changes in the 1970s and 1980s which undermined the viability of an alternative revolutionary cinematic movement such as the NLAC: repressive regimes, military *coup d'états*, failed socialist experiments, ballooning foreign debts, and deteriorating economic conditions. Furthermore, the NLAC was simultaneously challenged by another problem. Despite its challenges to dominant cinemas and its desire to subvert and demystify, the NLAC was also interested in fostering the national presence of the cinema and to encourage sustained production. These kinds of concerns cannot be addressed from the margins, but must be articulated in relation to mainstream national cinematic production, state protection of the national cinema, and the cinema's popular or commercial potential. Thus, in nations with developed or developing national industries, the NLAC, in its search for ways to become popular, gradually found itself incorporated into mainstream – albeit somewhat modified – commercial operations. When combined with political pressures, this trend towards industrial practices conclusively altered the NLAC project.

In Brazil, for example, the Cinema Novo disappeared under the hegemonic power of the state agency for the cinema Embrafilme. After democratization, Argentine film-makers focused on redeveloping the industrial film-making sector. In Cuba, although still a case apart, the longevity of the state agency for the cinema (ICAIC) has also meant that the Cuban cinema is an official (rather than a marginal) cinema with different national imperatives.

Perhaps even more conclusive from a theoretical perspective, some of the basic premises underpinning the NLAC have also been put into question. For example, the articles and manifestos that denounced Hollywood's cinematic imperialism also rejected the 'classic' cinemas produced in Latin America between the 1930s and 1950s as imitative of Hollywood, unrealistic, alienating, and ideologically complicit and servile to the interests of the dominant classes. The old cinema's principal sin was, as the Cuban critics Enrique Colina and Daniel Díaz Torres argued in 1972 in the pages of *Cine Cubano*, its melodramatic proclivities. Making the melodrama synonymous with the Hollywood cinema, they argued that these Latin American films were little else than a poor imitation 'which opened the floodgates to a manifold process of cultural colonization' in Latin America (1971: 15). However, Colina and Díaz Torres did not take into account that this was the first indigenous cinema to dent the Hollywood industry's pervasive presence in Latin America; the first consistently to circulate Latin American images, voices, songs, and history; the first to capture and sustain the interest of multinational audiences throughout the continent for several decades (López, 1991).

The melodramatic was so easily identified with cultural colonization because of its popularity. Simplistically reproducing an elitist mistrust of mass communication and popular culture, critics influenced by theories of cultural imperialism were often unable to see in the popularity of the melodrama or other forms of popular culture anything but the alienation of a mass audience controlled by the dominant classes' capitalist interests. With little differentiation or attention to the processes of reception and identification, they rejected the melodrama as 'false' communication. It is ironic, however, that the new cinema's efforts to establish so-called 'real' communication – as important as they have been – have rarely attained the levels of popular acceptance of the old cinemas. And when that popular success has been achieved, as in *La Historia Oficial* ('The Official Story', Luis Carlos Puenzo, 1986, Argentina), for example, it has been precisely by recourse to the melodramatic.

This example points to some of the fatal flaws of the cultural imperialism thesis and dependency theory, in particular their inability to address the specificity of cinematic reception and identification, what Miller calls, 'the mediation of Hollywood's output by indigenous cultures' (1998a: 375). An additional flaw proved to be the unproblematized approach to 'national' cultures, which assumed the existence of some authentic core of national issues/concerns that the cinema had to address and, furthermore, privileged all national producers irrespective of their mediations and relationships with international practices. However, the discussions mobilized by cultural imperialism and dependency theory did allow for the recognition of important cultural inequalities, and pointed the way for the reconceptualization of differences and cultural specificity which constitutes the core of the globalization approach.

To be or not to be . . . global

In the late 1990s, this can hardly be the question. Whether individuals or nations recognize it or no, we are 'global'. Since the 1970s the speed and range of economic and cultural exchanges have increased vertiginously, allowing companies to sell to customers all over the world. Technology transfers have also contributed to globalization, accelerating the flow of information across, and often without regard to, national borders. These days, financial decisions and events in one part of the world have immediate ripple effects throughout the rest (witness the collapse of the Asian financial markets and its reverberations on Mexico and the USA). Corporations are increasingly multinational and unfettered by national policies and legislation (or attempts to curb them). Whether Mercedes Benz constructs factories in the USA and Brazil or whether US fund managers invest millions in Thai stocks, the economies of individual nations are increasingly integrated by private, cross-border financial flows. In this sense, Hollywood is part of the USA perhaps only in theory, since the major production companies are owned by large international conglomerates, almost half of them not even US-based (as with Sony, Rupert Murdoch). In general terms, industrial production – a practice firmly rooted in a location, the factory – has become both increasingly mobile (the maquiladoras in the US–Mexico border) and insignificant: the real profits are to be made trading and speculating on securities and selling services rather than products. Similarly, the production of films is no longer necessarily the main source of profits for conglomerates that sell everything from books and magazines to sneakers, toys, and breakfast cereals: for blockbusters, the ancillary products are often as profitable as box-office revenues (Wasko, 1994). International credit policies have meant the end of import-substitution industrialization for 'developing' nations and the institution of export-based economies linked to an 'open' world marketplace, limited perhaps only by regional trade agreements [North Atlantic Free Trade Agreement (NAFTA), General Agreement on Tariffs and Trade (GATT) etc.]. Thus commodities are increasingly produced for specific international markets: Chile sells its extraordinary Pacific fish to the Japanese for sushi, Sean Connery remains a 'star' because of his appeal to European audiences, and Kevin Costner's *Dances with Wolves* (1990) is sold to the French as a semi-documentary on Native Americans (Danan, 1995). As Miller argues, in the era of globalization, the national has become paradigmatic: 'new forms of rationalization standardize the acknowledgment of difference as part of capital's need for local marketability' (1998a: 377). The speed and frequency of cultural transfers have given consumers throughout the world 'global' tastes, accelerating the demand for cultural imports of all kinds – from movies and music to fashion and food. And this has taken place, at a somewhat similar pace, throughout the world, irrespective of first, second, or third 'barriers'.

Some of the changes we have seen in the cinema include the growth and mutation of co-productions. Originally, the Hollywood studios used co-productions to defeat restrictions upon earnings imposed by foreign nations after World War 2 (reinvesting the frozen funds in 'local' productions which would have the benefits of two nationalities for distribution quotas elsewhere). They were seen as a strategy that undermined the potential of the national cinema, yet another one of Hollywood's unfair competitive advantages. Yet, as the studios purchased facilities throughout the world to take advantage of lower labor costs, production increasingly shifted away from the locatedness of 'Hollywood' and became ever more global. At the same time, co-productions have also become the lifesaver of struggling national cinemas. For example, since the 1970s Latin American film-makers have eagerly sought co-production arrangements – either with European and/or with Hollywood producers – as sometimes the only way to make any kind national production possible. Such has been the extreme case of Cuba in the 1990s, when the financial crisis brought about by the collapse of the Soviet Union (known as the 'special period') abruptly immersed the formerly isolated nation into the global arena and decimated the national cinema: the only films that can be made in Cuba today are ones with international financing. A less extreme example is that of Brazil, where the new cinema legislation enacted in the mid-1990s encouraging local investments in culture via tax breaks has proven useful primarily in conjunction with international co-production deals.

In a global universe, 'facing up to' Hollywood has become an increasingly amorphous project. The extreme globalization of film production has made the idea of national cinemas more problematic than ever before. Alongside the eternal desire to use the medium to address national history and cultural values, all producers of national cinemas are also aware that much greater profits and prestige are to be found in a reconfigured international film market now driven by 'global' tastes. The US market has never been more open to exotic – and profitable for the US distributors representing them – imports. Thus the spectacular success of *Like Water for Chocolate* (Alfonso Arau, 1991) – the highest grossing foreign film in US history – must be understood as a function of the film's canny recycling of Mexicanisms in a global context: its re-imagining of the iconography of 1940s' Mexican revolutionary melodramas through the metaphor of its own international consumption.

At the same time, the growing traffic in cultural products inherent to globalization has also meant that film-makers and creative personnel cross borders with increasing regularity. International success may also mean following the inevitable road to the Hollywood 'Mecca'. Like Alfonso Arau, for example, Mexican director Guillermo del Toro followed up the international success of his quirky *Cronos* (1995) produced with the support of IMCINE (the Mexican state agency for the cinema) by moving to Hollywood and making the big-budget horror *Mimic* (1997). Mexican star Selma Hayek, a new national icon, is currently attempting to fill (or create) a space for a Latina actress in Hollywood productions such as *Fools Rush In* (1996). But these kinds of exchanges are rarely unidirectional now. Brazilian director, Bruno Barreto – who was responsible for some of the greatest box-office successes of Brazilian cinema in the 1970s and 1980s such as *Dona Flor and her Two Husbands* (1976) – has lived and worked in the US for a decade. But he also directed *O que que isso companheiro?* (1997) in Brazil, which was nominated for the foreign film academy award. Meanwhile, Carlos Marcovich, who has worked primarily in music videos and advertising in Mexico City, went to Cuba to direct *¿Quién diablos es Juliette?* (1996), to date the most incisive analysis of the intersection of globality and gendered identities in contemporary Cuba. Another, among many other transnational travelers, is the Brazilian José Araujo, who works as an independent sound editor in US independent productions (such as Lourdes Portillo's *El diablo nunca duerme/The Devil Never Sleeps* (1995), but directed his well-received *opera prima*, *O Sertão das memorias* (1996), in his native state of Ceará exclusively with local funding. In yet another ironic contemporary transnational twist, the renowned Cuban director Tomás Gutiérrez Alea became a Spanish citizen to facilitate co-production deals – and enable his last film, *Guantanamera* (1995) – a few years before his death in 1996.

These multiple and diverse 'border crossings' point to the fact that film production, despite the continued financial hegemony of the Hollywood machine, has become as deterritorialized, diasporic, and transnational as the rest of our world. While Hollywood's own profitability has never been more dependent on foreign revenues, the industry has never been more open to the differences to be found elsewhere. And while we may sometimes worry about its absorption of different cultures, knowledges, and landscapes, it is also true that globalization has contributed to the spread of cinematic activity and to the recognition of film-makers and film-making traditions that had never appeared on the US motion picture map. This may not constitute an assault on Hollywood's hegemony, but it is a visible and significant constant reminder of difference, perhaps globality's greatest contribution to our understanding of culture.

Our critical awareness of global forces and practices has had a significant impact upon the theorization of international cinematic relations, that is, on the practices and consequences of 'facing up to' Hollywood. Earlier approaches such as purely economic analyses or the cultural imperialism/dependency thesis have given way under the pressure of the shifting cultural paradigms of globality to what we may call 'transnational' film studies. Under the banner of transnationality, scholars have begun to question many central paradigms of the field through relational (rather than merely comparative) prisms which reposition the center/periphery and national/foreign dichotomies. Thus, for example, Ella Shohat and Bob Stam's *Unthinking Eurocentrism* (1994) brilliantly unpacks complex international textual and productive relationships through the lens of multiculturalism and post-colonialism. Without negating the uniqueness of the contemporary situation, what Toby Miller has dubbed the 'New International Division of Cultural Labor' (1998: 171), scholars have also begun to apply the lessons of the present to their historical research. One privileged object of study has been the Mexican Golden Age cinema (1930s–1950s), traditionally considered the most stalwartly nationalistic of all Latin American cinemas. Fein, O'Neil and I have begun an important reconsideration of this period as already profoundly transnational: Fein (1998) has focused on the imbrication of Mexican and US interests in a series of productions during and after World War 2, O'Neil (1998) has analysed Hollywood's second attempt to make Spanish-language films in the late 1930s as illustrative of the Mexican cinema's own hybridity; and I (López, 1998a) have chronicled the 'reverse-flow' of Dolores Del Rio, who left Hollywood and became the foremost icon of the Mexican cinema, and have explored the impact of intercontinental traveling auteurs such as José Bohr, Juan Orol, and others in the development of the industry (López, 1998b). Similarly, Ann Marie Stock's anthology *Framing Latin American Cinema* gathers recent work which focuses on the transactions and interconnections in the history of Latin American cinema, while Chon Noriega's collection *Visible nations*, returns to the question of the national in Latin American cinema with a difference, placing the nation itself under the lens of a transnational gaze.

Rather than a face-off between Hollywood and its others, what we now seek to understand is a broader zone of cultural debate and economic relationships in which we can trace the tensions and contradictions between national sites and transnational processes. It is in this zone, after all, that the cinema is and has been 'lived' as a part of public culture (Appadurai and Breckenridge, 1995).

References

Acheson, K. and Maule, C. 1994: Understanding Hollywood's organization and continuing success. *Journal of Cultural Economics* **18**(4): 271–300.

Appadurai, A. and Breckenridge, C. 1995: Public modernity in India. In Breckenridge, C. ed., *Consuming modernity: public culture in a South Asian world*. Minneapolis, MN: University of Minnesota Press, 1–22.

Ayala Blanco, J. and Amador, M.L. 1980: *Cartelera Cinematográfica 1930–39*. Mexico City: UNAM.

Bordwell, D. and Thompson, K. 1994: *Film history: an introduction*. New York: McGraw-Hill.

Chanan, M (ed.), 1974: *Chilean cinema*. London: British Film Institute.

Colina, E. and Díaz Torres, D. 1971: Ideología del Melodrama en el Viejo Cine Latinoamericano. *Cine Cubano*, no. 73-74-75: 12–20.

Cook, D. 1996: *A history of narrative film*, 3rd edn. New York: Norton.

Crofts, S. 1993: Reconceptualizing national cinema/s. In López, A. and Butzel, M., eds, Mediating the national. *Quarterly Review of Film and Video* **14**(3): 49–67.

Danan, M. 1995: Marketing the Hollywood blockbuster in France. *Journal of Popular Film and Video* **23**(3): 131–40.

De la Vega Alfaro, E. 1995: Origins, development and crisis of the sound cinema (1929–64). In Paranaguá, P. ed., *Mexican cinema*. London: British Film Institute, 79–93.

De los Reyes, A. 1987: *Medio siglo de cine Mexicano (1886–1947)*. Mexico City: Trillas.

de Usabel, G.S. 1982: *The high noon of American films in Latin America*. Ann Arbor, MI, Michigan: UMI Research Press.

Durovicova, N. 1992: Translating America: the Hollywood multilinguals 1929–1933. In Altman, R., ed., *Sound theory, sound practice*. New York: Routledge, 138–53.

Fein, S. 1998: Transnationalization and cultural collaboration: Mexican film propaganda during World War II. In López, A. ed., *Popular cinemas/popular cultures. Studies in Latin American Popular Culture* **17**: 105–28.

Galvão, M.R.1981: *Burguesia e cinema: o caso Vera Cruz*. Rio de Janeiro: Civilização/Embrafilme.

García Espinosa, J. 1970/1983: For an imperfect cinema. In Chanan, M., ed., *Twenty-five years of the New Latin American Cinema*. London: British Film Institute.

García Riera, E. 1969: *Historia Documental del Cine Mexicano*, vol. II. Mexico City: Ediciones Era.

García Riera, E. 1987: *México visto por el cine extranjero*, vol. 1.Guadalajara, Mexico: Ediciones Era/Universidad de Guadalajara

Guback, T. 1969: *The international film industry: Western Europe and America since 1945*. Bloomington, IN: Indiana University Press.

Johnson, R. and Stam, R. (eds), 1995: *Brazilian cinema: expanded edition*. New York: Columbia University Press.

King, J. 1990: *Magical reels: a history of cinema in Latin America*. London: Verso.

López, A.M. 1990: An 'other' history: the New Latin American cinema. In Sklar, R. and Musser, C., eds, *Resisting images: essays on cinema and history*. Philadelphia, PA: Temple University Press, 308–30.

López, A.M. 1991: Celluloid tears: melodrama in the classic Mexican cinema. *Iris* no. 13 (Summer): 29–52.

López, A.M. 1994: A cinema for the continent. In Noriega, C. and Ricci, S., eds, *The Mexican cinema project*. Los Angeles, CA: UCLA Film Archives, 7–12.

López, A.M. 1998a: From Hollywood and back: Dolores Del Rio, a transnational star. In López, A., ed., *Popular cinemas/popular cultures. Studies in Latin American Popular Culture* **17**: 5–32.

López, A.M. 1998b: Historia nacional, historia transnacional. In Burton-Carvajal, J., Torres, P., and Miquel, A., eds, *Horizontes del segundo siglo: investigación y pedagogía del cine mexicano, latinoamericano y chicano*. Guadalajara: Universidad de Guadalajara/IMCINE, 75–81.

López, A.M. forthcoming, 1999: The São Paulo connection: the Companhia Cinematográfica Vera Cruz and *O Cangaceiro*. *Nuevo Texto Crítico*.

Mattelart, A. 1979: *Multinational corporations and the control of culture: the ideological apparatuses of imperialism*. Atlantic Heights, NJ: Humanities Press.

Miller, T. 1998a: Hollywood and the world. In Hill, J. and Church Gibson, P. eds, *The Oxford guide to film studies*. London: Oxford University Press, 371–81.

Miller, T. 1998b: *Technologies of truth: cultural citizenship and the media*. Minneapolis, MN: University of Minnesota Press.

O'Neil, B. 1998: Yankee Invasion of Mexico or Mexican invasion of Hollywood? Hollywood's renewed Spanish-language production of 1938–39. In López, A., ed., *Popular cinemas/popular cultures. Studies in Latin American Popular Culture* **17**: 79–104.

Paranaguá, P.A. 1995: Ten reasons to love or hate the Mexican cinema. In Paranaguá, P.A. ed., *The Mexican cinema*. London: British Film Institute, 1–13.

Ramos, F. (ed.), 1987: *Historia do cinema Brasileiro*. São Paulo: Art Editora.

Schatz, T. 1988: *The genius of the system: Hollywood filmmaking in the studio era*. New York: Pantheon.

Shohat, E. and Stam, R. 1994: *Unthinking Eurocentrism: multiculturalism and the media*. London: Routledge.

Sklar, R. 1993: *Film: an international history of the medium*. New York: Prentice-Hall.

Solanas, F. and Getino, O. 1969/1976: Towards a third cinema. In Nichols, B., ed., *Movies and methods*. Berkeley, CA: University of California Press.

Thompson, K. 1985: *Exporting entertainment: America in the world film market, 1907–1934*. London: British Film Institute.

Tomlinson, J 1991: *Cultural imperialism: a critical introduction*. London: Frances Pinter.

Turnstall, J. 1977: *The media are American: Anglo-American media in the world*. London, Constable.

Wasko, J. 1994: *Hollywood in the information age: beyond the silver screen*. Austin, TX: University of Texas Press.

Woll, A. 1980: *The Latin image in American film*. Los Angeles, CA: UCLA Latin American Series.

23 The end of cinema: multimedia and technological change

Anne Friedberg

Figure 23.1 'Now playing. Movies for your computer': a 1995 advertisement from Gametek Cinema/Digital Movies, announcing movies on CD-ROM. 'Gametek presents six cult classic movies: *Metropolis, Robotech, R.G. Veda, Reefer Madness*, Troma's *Toxic Avenger* and *Class of Nuke em High*'.

The screen featured here (Figure 23.1) faces its audience: the regimented rows of a computer keyboard, each key in the fixed position of a cinema spectator. The image – of the transformative moment in *Metropolis* when the metallic robot Maria is infused with the life-force of electricity – suggests another moment of transformation. The cinema screen has been replaced by its digital other, the computer screen.

As this millennium draws to an end, the cinema – a popular form of entertainment for almost a century – has been dramatically transformed. It has become embedded in – or perhaps lost in – the new technologies that surround it. One thing is clear: we can note it in the symptomatic discourse, inflected with the atomic terms of 'media fusion' or 'convergence' or the pluralist inclusiveness of 'multimedia' – the differences between the media of movies, television, and computers are rapidly diminishing. This is true both for technologies of production (that is, film is commonly edited on video; video is transferred to film; computer graphics and computer-generated animation are used routinely in both film and television production) and for technologies of reception and display (that is, we can watch movies in digitized formats on our computer screens or in video formats on our television screens.) The movie screen, the home television screen, and the computer screen retain their separate locations, yet the types of images you see on each of them are losing their medium-based specificity.

When Marshall McLuhan proclaimed 'the medium is the message' in 1964, this sound-bite aphorism drew attention not only to the *media*tion that the media incurred but also to the specificity of each separate medium. McLuhan inveighed against content-based studies: 'The "content" of any medium,' McLuhan wrote, 'blinds us to the characteristics of the medium.' Instead, he prescribed an account of the effects – 'the change of scale or pace or pattern' – that each particular medium might produce. McLuhan analysed the interrelatedness of media in an evolutionary scheme ('The content of any medium is always another medium'), and he insisted that each new medium would 'institute new ratios, not only among our private senses, but among themselves, when they interact among themselves' (McLuhan, 1964: 8–9, 53). In the new media environment of the 1990s, the media of radio, telephone, television, movies, computer not only interact among themselves, but their cross-purposed interactions pose new questions about their technological specificities. German media theorist Friedrich Kittler anticipated this convergence of media when he wrote: 'The general digitalization of information and channels erases the difference between individual media'(1986: 102). Yet Kittler predicted that the installation of fiber-optic cable was the technology that would turn film, music and phone-calls into a 'single medium'. Given the suggested reconfiguration of screens and their spectators in the image of *Metropolis* on the computer monitor figured here (Figure 23.1), we must now ask: how have the material differences between cinematic, televisual, and computer media been altered as *digital* technologies transform them?

Nicholas Negroponte answers this question with a counter-polemical aphorism, turning McLuhan's 'the medium is the message' on its head. 'The medium is not the message in the digital world,' declares Negroponte, 'It is an embodiment of it. A message might have several embodiments automatically derivable from the same data' (1995: 71). Digital imaging, delivery, and display effectively erase the 'messages' implicit in the source 'medium'. The digitized *Metropolis* illustrates how almost all of our assumptions about the cinema have changed: its image is digital, not photographically-based, its screen format is small and not projection-based, its implied interactivity turns the spectator into a 'user'.

The following chapter addresses two related issues. The first part examines a number of technologies introduced in the 1970s and 1980s which began to erode the historical differences between television and film. The video cassette recorder, the television remote control, and the growth of cable television significantly altered the terms of both televisual and cinematic viewing. As I will argue, these technologies led to a convergence of film and television technology that began without fiber-optic cable, occurred before the digitalization of imagery, and preceded the advent of the home computer.

Secondly, as a result of these initial reconfigurations and as our visual field has been transformed by newer technologies, the field of 'film studies' finds itself at a transitional moment. We must add computer screens (and digital technologies), television screens (and interactive video formats) to our conceptualization (both historical and theoretical) of the cinema and its screens. *Screens* are now 'display and delivery' formats – variable in versions of projection screen, television screen, computer screen, or headset device. *Film* is a 'storage' medium – variable in versions of video, computer disks, compact discs (CDs), high-density compact video-disc players (DVDs), databanks, on-line servers. *Spectators* are 'users' with an 'interface' – variable in versions of remotes, mice, keyboards, touch screens, joysticks, goggles and gloves and body suits. Just as the chemically-based 'analog' images of photography have been displaced by computer-enhanced digital images; the apparatus we came to know as 'the cinema' is being displaced by systems of circulation and transmission which abolish the projection screen and begin to link the video screens of the computer and television with the dialogic interactivity of the telephone. Multimedia home stations combining telephone, television, and computer (what will we call these: tele-puters? image-phones?) will further reduce the technical differentiation of film, television, and the computer.

It now seems that a singular history of 'the film' without its dovetailing conspirators – the telephone, the radio, the television, the computer – provides a too-narrowly constructed geneology. Once thought to be the province of 'information science' and not part of the study of 'visual culture', histories of the telephone and the computer become significant tributaries in the converging multimedia stream.[1] In this way, perhaps, Charles Babbage's 1832 'analytical engine' could be measured as significant in the contemporary remaking of visual imagery as Joseph Plateau's 1832 phenakistiscope. Babbage's 'analytical engine' – a mechanical precursor to modern digital computing – could store a number, retrieve it, modify it, and then store it in another location (Figure 23.2). Plateau's phenakistiscope – an optical toy now considered a key pre-cinematic apparatus – demonstrated how movements analyzed into their static components could be perceived as moving images when perceived through the slits of a spinning disc (Figure 23.3). The 'analytical engine' turned information into discrete, manipulable units; the phenakistiscope turned images into discrete and manipulable units. The historical coincidence between these two devices only emerges as significant in light of recent technologies of digital imaging and display.

Figure 23.2 Charles Babbage's analytical engine (1832). The 'analytical engine' – a mechanical precursor to modern digital computing – could store a number, retrieve it, modify it, and then store it in another location.

Figure 23.3 Joseph Plateau's phenakistiscope (1832) – an optical toy now considered a key pre-cinematic apparatus – demonstrated how movements analysed into their static components could be perceived as moving images when viewed through slits of a spinning disc.

The new media environment

But there were a number of pre-digital technologies that significantly changed our concept of film-going and television-viewing before the digital 'revolution'. The video cassette recorder (VCR), cable television, and the television remote control (Figure 23.4)

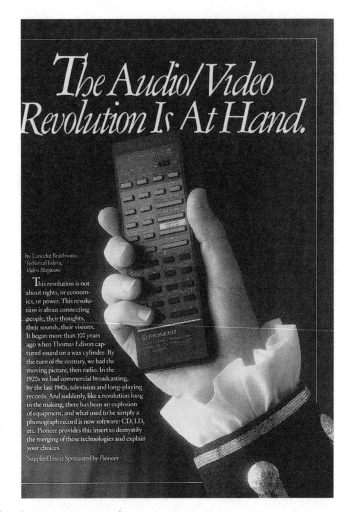

Figure 23.4 The television remote control.

have prepared us for the advent of computer screens with wired (Internet) connections – for interactive 'usage' instead of passive spectatorship – and continue to produce profound changes to our sense of temporality.[2] If television's innate 'liveness' – its ability to collapse the time of an event with the time of its transmission – was one of its key apparatical distinctions from the movies, the VCR collapsed these separations. Television's mode of absolute presence, as Jane Feuer has eloquently argued, became a key determinant of televisual aesthetics (1983: 12–22). The VCR demolished the aura of live television and the broadcast event, freeing the television screen from its servitude to the metaphysics of presence. Whereas the cinematic apparatus had the potential for re-seeing a film built into its means of mechanical reproduction, television had to await the advent of videotape recording and playback features of the VCR. The VCR introduced the potential to 'time-shift' (to view what you want, when you want), to 'zip' (to fast-forward and/or reverse the video cassette, effectively skipping portions of the taped program (with televised programming, this usually meant commercials)), and also made it easier to re-see a film or program over (and over) again. With the VCR, both the cinematic and the televisual past became more easily accessible and interminably recyclable.

Cable television not only changed the quality of and criteria for television reception, but expanded its offerings with increased channel choice, effectively breaking the monopolies of network broadcasting. In turn, the television remote control allowed the viewer instantaneously to change televised channels (to 'zap'), to fast-forward and/or reverse the video cassette (to 'zip'), to switch between live and taped programming, and to eliminate the lure or distraction of television's sound (to 'mute'). As a result of these technologies, the premises of cinema spectatorship and televisual viewing changed radically.[3]

The VCR

The time-shift machine

As the VCR became widely available in the mid-1980s, the number of VCR households grew in a parallel 'penetration' of the American home to the growth of television in the 1950s. In 1952 fewer than 250 000 sets were owned by American households; by 1960, 80 per cent of American homes had television; by 1993 there were 93.1 million television households, with a near total saturation, in the high 90 per cent. The marketing of the VCR followed this curve. While there were a variety of video cassette systems marketed in the 1970s, it was not until the early 1980s that the VCR became a common household appliance. In 1985, only 20 per cent of American households had VCRs; in 1989 the figure was 65.5 per cent. But by 1993 the total reached 80 per cent and by 1997, 88 per cent of American homes had VCRs (Lipton, 1991; Nielsen, 1996).

A videotape machine with the capacity for recording and playback on video cassettes, the VCR not only solved broadcast television's reception difficulties, but also freed the television viewer from its programming limitations and rigid timetable. In 1970, there were six competing 'cassette TV' systems in development, set for target marketing dates in mid-1971 or early 1972. [Five of these – Avco, Sony, Ampex, Magnavox, Norelco – relied on videotape. CBS' EVR – Electronic Video Recording – used a photographic film which was scanned and converted to a television signal (Kern, 1970: 46–55).] The Sony Betamax, introduced in 1975, used ½ inch videotape in a cassette format that could record for an hour; and a competing ½ inch format VHS (Video Home System) was introduced in 1976. The VHS format initially had the advantage of recording for up to two hours. Since cassette recorders were first used primarily for recording broadcast feature films, the two-hour cassette made a difference in the competitive market (Lardner, 1987).

VCRs were first used for recording off the air, but through the 1980s as more and more pre-recorded video cassettes became available, a rental market (an entirely new industry) developed for movies, exercise videos, educational, and self-help material. Hence, the VCR – originally intended by its marketers to be used as a recording and 'time-shifting' device – became essentially a playback device. Both formats – Betamax and VHS – quickly adopted 1) pause buttons so that the viewer could eliminate commercials while recording; 2) timers that allowed the viewer to record while not at home; 3) devices that allowed the viewer to view one program while taping another; and 4) still frame and variable-speed playback features. The sales of VCRs soared beyond expectations.[4] As the major film studios sold video rights to their archives, slowly, through the 1980s, most films – even foreign – were transferred to video.

There was only a small cloud over the steamrolling success of the VCR in the marketplace: the issue of copyright. In 1976, Universal and Disney sued the Sony Corporation claiming that any machine that could record, hence 'copy', copyrighted material was in violation of basic copyright laws and should not be manufactured. In 1979, a federal judge sided with Sony, declaring that recording and viewing television program material in the home were 'fair use'. An appeals court reversed this decision, and it was not until a 1984 Supreme Court decision ruled that home taping does not violate copyright laws that the machine itself was in the clear.[5]

As the VCR became a fixture in American living rooms, its penetration of the global market also proceeded apace. A 1983 study showed that VCR penetration of the Third World exceeded television growth. VCRs were used for viewing videotapes, especially of banned material: Indian films in Pakistan and Bangladesh, Western films in Eastern Europe, pornography everywhere. VCRs became an easy 'open door' for cultural contraband – material kept out of cinemas and off television but available for viewing on this playback box. Video cassettes and VCRs also penetrated countries bereft of television; offering uncensored mass entertainment by supplying the immediacy of television without its political impediments. [Statistics from 1982 demonstrated some interesting things about cross-cultural usage: 92 per cent of television homes in Kuwait had VCRs; 82 per cent in Panama, 70 per cent in Oman, 43 per cent in Bahrain, whereas in 1984, in France the figure was 10 per cent, Japan 26 per cent, Singapore 62 per cent, United Arab Emirates 75 per cent, UK 30 per cent (Ganley and Ganley, 1987).]

Despite the initial fear of theater owners and film producers that VCRs would detract from their box-office receipts, the statistical evidence from the 1980s did not support this fear: movie-goers attended in record numbers and still rented videos. While 40 per cent of feature-film viewing is done on VCRs, movie attendance is still strong; as if the use of VCRs actually stimulates movie-orientated activity. Nielsen reports that movie rentals cut into only a small percentage of total television use (Nielsen, 1996). So, if the statisticians have it right, television use has not decreased, movie attendance has not decreased while VCR usage has increased. This would lead us to conclude that in the past 15 years we have spent more time watching television and films and videotapes of both.

A new temporality: when will then be now? Soon!

Now that 'time' is so easily electronically 'deferred' or 'shifted' one can ask: has the VCR produced a new temporality, one that has dramatically affected our concept of history and our access to the past? The VCR treats films or videotapes as objects of knowledge to be explored, investigated, deconstructed as if they were events of the past to be studied.[6]

The 1987 film *Spaceballs* (Mel Brooks, 1987) parodies some of the changes in movie reception produced by the VCR and the rental marketing of video cassettes. In the film, Dark Helmet (Rick Moranis) and his commander, Colonel Sanders, chase an intergalactic 'winnebago' driven by a space-bum-for-hire Lone Star (Bill Pullman) and his canine sidekick, Barf (John Candy). Dark Helmet and Colonel Sanders stand by the spaceship's video scanner screen when Sanders introduces a 'new breakthrough in video marketing – instant cassettes'. The riff between Helmet and Sanders toys with the new temporality produced by the video cassette: 'Prepare to fast forward . . . go past this part . . . the part on ridiculous speed'. When they suddenly stop the tape at a frame that matches the moment they are in, they do a double take between the screen and each other:

> 'When does this happen? Then?'
> 'Now.'
> 'When will then be now?'
> 'Soon!'

The jumbled tenses of present and past here form a parody on the very paradoxes of televisual presence ('Now') and the VCR's deeper challenges to time and memory ('When will then be now? Soon!').

Paul Virilio has described the new temporality made possible by the VCR:

> The machine, the VCR, allows man [*sic*] to organize a time which is not his own, *a deferred time*, a time which is somewhere else – and to capture it. . . . The VCR . . . creates two days: a reserve day which can replace the ordinary day, the lived day.
>
> (1988)

For Virilio, the VCR produces a time that is shifted, borrowed, made asynchronous. The VCR is like an electronic melatonin, resetting the viewer's internal clock to a chosen moment from the past.

While these new attributes of televisual time often lead to liberatory rhetoric about the VCR – freeing its viewers from the tyranny of standard time and broadcast choices with button-pushing empowerment – there remain limits to the choices available. Richard Dienst forecloses any emancipatory potential of this new temporality, reminding us that the privilege of individual prerogative ultimately profits 'paranational . . . conglomerates':

> VCRS do nothing but extend the range of still and automatic time, offering an additional loop of flexibility in the circulation of images, bringing new speeds and greater turnover. . . . video allows people to operate another series of switches, a privilege bought with more time, money and subjective attachment. . . . who profits from this new and immense expansion in the volume of overall televisual time? . . . paranational electronic manufacturers and entertainment conglomerates.
>
> (1994: 165–6)

And now that the VCR has become a well-entrenched consumer durable, electronics companies are trying to supplant it with laser disc technology, hoping that the DVD player will become the next VCR, just as audio CD machines have supplanted record players in the past decade (Bauman and Harmon, 1994). DVD technology offers some advantages: as with the larger laser disc formats, one can access a different section of the disc in a near instant; there is no fast-forwarding or rewinding required. But owing to more sophisticated image compression algorithms, a DVD, unlike larger laser discs and CD-ROM technology, can hold an entire feature film on a single disc. As Figure 23.1 illustrates, CD-ROM technology promised to bring 'movies' to your computer, with new playback possibilities, but the DVD may be the format that succeeds in doing so.

Cable television

Cable television is almost as old as commercial broadcast television. Because broadcast television required a clear 'line of sight' between the transmitter and the receiving set for adequate 'reception', cable television developed in areas where broadcast television was not easily received, where antennae could not 'see' each other, and where alternative methods were needed for transmitting broadcast signals. But cable television also offered some additional advantages: because it delivered television signals on coaxial cable it could carry more than one channel on the coaxial cable and import distant signals which were received by one master antenna (or, later, by one master satellite dish) and retransmit them.

In 1975 – the year that began the Betamax/VHS format wars – a dramatic change in cable programming occurred: Home Box Office (HBO) began distributing special events (beginning with the Ali-Frazier 'Thriller in Manila' fight) and movies via satellite. Shortly after HBO launched its service, Viacom launched a competing pay television service (Showtime) in 1976, and Warner Communication followed with The Movie Channel (which showed movies 24 hours a day) in 1979. These 'pay' or 'premium' cable channels relied heavily on the programming of feature films.

And not long after HBO began using satellite transmission, the owner of a low-rated UHF station in Atlanta put his station's signal on satellite to be seen nationwide. This station, WTBS, owned by Ted Turner, became known as a 'superstation' because of its national availability. Turner's 'superstation' was a 'cable network' which made economic sense both to subscribers and to local cable companies. Cable subscribers were not charged for an extra station, the local cable company was only charged a dime a month per subscriber, and the extra service increased subscribers. And even though the revenues from the local cable companies did not cover the superstation's costs, the superstation could charge higher advertisement fees because it could boast a bigger audience. The core programming on WTBS consisted of Hollywood's movie past. [In 1986 Turner bought MGM and its film library; in 1987 Turner bought rights to an additional 800 RKO films (Gomery, 1992: 263–75).]

In the late 1970s and early 1980s cable television grew phenomenally. Most of what we know now as 'basic cable' – CNN, MTV, Nickelodeon, C-Span, the superstations TBS, WOR, USA Network – were born within a timespan of a few years. In 1993, 64 per cent of television owners subscribed to cable; by 1996, the figure was 68.5 per cent (Nielsen,

1996). While studies on the movie-going habits of basic and pay cable subscribers have shown mixed results, indicating both a decrease and increase in movie-going (Austin, 1986: 93–4), one thing is certain: the increase in VCR users and cable subscribers meant that the cinematic spectator became a televisual viewer.

The television remote control

A third technology that transformed televisual viewing (and exacerbated its differences from film spectatorship) is the television remote control. The television remote control penetrated the American household as rapidly as VCRs and cable: in 1976, 9.5 per cent of televisions were sold with remote controls; by 1990, 90 per cent of them were (Napoli, 1999); in 1985, only 29 per cent of households had remote controls, in 1996, 90 per cent of US household had at least one (Nielsen, 1996). Versions of the television 'remote' control device were marketed in the 1950s – first tethered to a wire and later as a wireless light-sensor remote – but these offered fewer options to the couch-bound viewer of 1950s' broadcast television than the same device did for the later VCR or cable subscriber. With a television remote control, the viewer becomes a *montagiste*, editing at will with the punch of a fingertip, 'zipping', 'zapping', and 'muting'. Television programmers have noted that to capture the armchair channel-surfer requires more and more 'visual' programming – relying less on plot and characterization and more on fast rhythmic editing. Some studies have shown that this form of viewing even changes the ability to follow linear arguments (Meyerowitz, 1985). And, as if to demonstrate its teleological relation to computer usage, the television remote control is now – retronymically – referred to as an 'air mouse'.

The film screen, the television screen, the computer screen

Certainly, much of the early competition between film and television centered around screen size and format; the television providing a 10–12 inch screen tailored to the domestic scale of the home, the movie screen differentiating its offerings with color, three-dimensional, and wider screen formats, compensating for what the black-and-white flat screens of television could not supply. Television 'viewing' altered some of the protocols of cinema 'spectatorship': unlike the cinema spectator, the television viewer watches a light-emanating cathode ray box in a partially darkened room. The optics of television do not rely on persistence of vision and projection but on scanning and transmission. [Our eyes have grown accustomed to NTSC 525 lines per image at 30 frames per second; or phase alteration line (PAL) at 624 lines at 25 frames per second; high definition television (HDTV) has 1125 lines per image.] And, as television scholars are quick to note, the placement of televisions in the home significantly alters the function of such spectatorship. Lynn Spigel, for example, likens the television's screen – a form of 'home theater' – to the 1950s' architectural use of the picture window, a 'window-wall' designed to bring the outside in (1992: 102).

Although both the content and the form of television competed with the film industry for viewers, television also became a delivery system for motion pictures – first in broadcast and syndicated format and later in basic and premium cable movie channels (Gomery, 1992: 247–75). As films were shown on television, changes in cinema screen aspect ratios meant that films were either panned and scanned or – more appropriately – 'letterboxed' to fit in the 4:3 rectangular format of the television screen. The television 'viewer' could now view films in a space that was, as Roland Barthes described it, 'familiar, organized, tamed' (Barthes, 1975). In 1974, Raymond Williams predicted: 'The major development of the late seventies may well be the large screen receiver: first the screen of four by six feet which is already in development; then the flat-wall receiver' (Williams, 1974: 136). As HDTV flat screen technology improves and screens replace real windows with a kind of 'inhabited television', a 'windows environment' may come to mean a virtual 'window-wall'.

The scale and domestic place of the television have prepared us for the screens of the 'personal' computer. Computer 'users' are not spectators, not viewers. Immobile with focused attention on a cathode ray screen, the computer 'user' interacts directly with the framed image on a small flat screen, 'using' a device – keyboard, mouse, or, in the case of touch screens, the finger – to manipulate what is contained within the parameter of the screen.[7] While computers have been designed to 'interface' with humans in ways that emulate the associative patterns of human thought (Bush, 1945), to become dyadic partners in a metaphysical relationship (Turkle, 1995), complaints about the awkwardness of this relationship are surfacing. As one critic has proclaimed: 'Using computers is like going to the movie theater and having to watch the projector instead of the film' (Kline, 1997).

Reinventing 'film studies'

As the field of 'film studies' has been redefining itself, both revising its internal historical accounts and opening up its field to the emerging multiplicities of 'cultural studies' and 'visual studies', much of this work has been coincident with the campaign for the academic legitimacy of film studies as a republic separate from its former disciplinary overlords. But as new technologies trouble the futures of cinematic production and reception, 'film' as a discrete object becomes more and more of an endangered species, itself in need of asserting its own historicity. In the past decade or so, first with the VCR and more recently with on-line and digital technologies, the methods and source material for film and television scholarship have been radically transformed.[8]

Here it seems necessary to describe the following historiographical conundrum: David Bordwell and Kristin Thompson, arbiters of film history-as-text (and as text-book) have marked the history of film as a field of academic research 'no more than thirty years old' (1994: xxvi). Yet in the past several decades, while film scholars have been reworking the histories of cinema's past – adjusting or refuting its teleologies, challenging its grand narratives – our concept of and access to not just the cinema's past but to the past itself have also radically been transformed and this due in no small part to the cinema. Hence, there is a troubling paradox in the way in which the ascendency of film historical discourse in the past several decades may have worked to mask the very *loss* of history that the film itself inflicted. What I am invoking here are a familiar set of historiographic questions about the ways in which we can know the past, the truth claims of histories, and the nature of historical knowledge. As the field of 'film history' has flourished in its vitality, the concomitant changes to our concept of the past produce a reflexive problematic. Cinema spectatorship, as one of its essential features, has always produced experiences that are not temporally fixed, has freed the spectator to engage in the fluid temporalities of cinematic construction – flashbacks, ellipses, achronologies – or to engage in other time frames (other than the spectator's moment in historical time, whether watching the diegetic fiction of a period drama or simply a film from an earlier period).

Without the discourse of film history, films would lose their historical identity, would slip into the fog of uncertain temporality. (As an exercise in my undergraduate film history classes, I ask them to turn on TNT in the middle of the night, without their television guides in hand, and to try to identify a rough production date for the films they are watching.) But even with the discourse of film history, films continue to reconstitute our sense of historical past. Recent films which have digitally 'revised' film footage from the 1960s – *Nixon*, *JFK*, *Forrest Gump* – illustrate the compelling urge to reprogram popular memory. And as the past is dissolved as a real referent and reconstituted by cinematic images which displace it, Charles Baudelaire's 1859 cynical prophesy about photography's 'loathing for history'[9] meets Fredric Jameson's (1983) dystopic syptomology of history's 'disappearance'.[10]

And just as soon as film scholars have undone the set of teleologies which read film history backward from the classical Hollywood model, a newly constructed teleology seems to be in the making. If a 1995 *New York Times* front-page story, 'If the medium is the message, the message is the Web', is any indication, a new *telos* is beginning to appear. In a feature-spread headlined, 'How the earlier media achieved critical mass', separate articles on the printing press, the motion picture, radio, and television were juxtaposed, suggesting a synergy of the mythic moments that have transformed each medium from one with technological potential into one with 'critical mass', that is, into a medium of mass reception. In this article, Molly Haskell's account of 'the defining moment for motion pictures as a mass medium' formulaically replays *Birth of a Nation*'s New York premiere as the event 'that catapulted the medium from its 19thc peep-show origins into its status as the great new popular art form of the 20th century' (1995: C5). While *The New York Times* did not directly assert the World Wide Web as *the* heir to the cultural centrality of the motion pictures and television ('there will be no certainty that this medium will achieve the critical mass that capitalism demands of its mass media'), the Web was positioned as a challenging successor which, unlike 'each previous mass medium . . . does not require its audience to be merely passive recipients of information'. Certainly, as the World Wide Web has become the *modem* (*modus*) *operandi* of everyday life, media savants have had to change their predictions about the electronic future of the 500-channel information highway and adjust for a much more computer-based key to the electronic future (Levy, 1995).

And now as the cynical futurologists prophesy the future of each new technology, it is worth recalling that in 1895, Louis Lumière boasted 'the cinema is an invention with no future'. While we have some indications of where new technologies might take us, we still have no clear sense of what will be a 'sustainable' technology in market terms. Even the current storage and display media – CD-ROMs and video cassettes – may be seen as transitional technologies as films and other visual material move on-line. And yet it is more than apparent that with the speed of such rapid and radical transformations, our technological environments cannot be conclusively theorized.

The history of 'film studies' in its own way parallels the history of film itself, with a lag of perhaps 40 years. In what has been called the 'classical' Hollywood period of film history there was a consensus not only as to what constituted narrative 'content' but also as to the size, shape, color, and scope of the screen. Similarly, during the 'classical' period of film studies there has been a general agreement as to what constitutes the size, shape, and scope of the discipline's objects. Now, a variety of screens – long and wide and square, large and small, composed of grains, composed of pixels – compete for our attention without any arguments about hegemony. Not only does our concept of 'film history' need to be reconceptualized in light of these changes in technology, but our assumptions about 'spectatorship' have lost their theoretical pinions as screens have changed, as have our relations to them.

Endnotes

1   In the United States, the 1995 Telecommunications Bill introduced pro-competitive deregulatory policies which encouraged the merging of technology industries, thus erasing many of the historical bases for their separation.

2   These three technologies fit as examples of Raymond Williams's tripartite typology of communication technologies as: *amplificatory* (distributing messages), *durative* (storing messages), and *alternative* (altering the form of messages) (Williams, 1980). In this way, the VCR is 'durative', cable television is 'amplificatory', and the television remote is 'alternative'.

3   Hence, the schoolyard epithet: 'Your folks are so old, they get up to change the channels'. More recently, as 'picture in picture' television sets allow for the simultaneous viewing of multiple channels, the sequential tide of television 'flow' no longer applies.

4   The VCR became a basic household appliance, but the puzzle of programming a VCR became a running national gag. President George Bush joked at a commencement speech at Caltech in 1991: 'The seventh goal of education should be that by the turn of the century, Americans must be able to get their VCRs to stop flashing 12:00' (Ferguson, 1993: 72).

5   Soon after Sony won the copyright battle it lost the format battle. Betamax was a format that – although it offered better picture quality – lost its market share as the majority of new VCR buyers bought VHS.

6   The Mia Farrow character, Cecilia, in *Purple Rose of Cairo* (Woody Allen, 1985) was a pre-VCR viewer who had a viewing repetition compulsion made possible by the cinematic potential to for re-seeing/re-experiencing the identical film over and over.

There seems to be little statistical evidence on how often films were re-viewed by the same viewer, or how often the same viewer re-viewed a film over time – in its original release and then again in its re-release, or its release in repertory. Television viewing was always thought of as more transient. The pleasures of re-viewing television programs, once only available on the cycle of summer re-runs, have been more fully discovered since cable networks become repertories for revisiting the televisual past and since the VCR has made it technologically possible to capture and replay them on videotape. In this regard, it is worth considering how we commonly listen to an audio recording repeatedly, while visual media is thought to be more disposable and, in fact, is often constructed as such.

7 When Microsoft trademarked its second-generation software as Windows™ they emphasized the metaphoric nature of much of our computer usage – 'mice' which scurry under our fingers at the fluid command of wrist and palm; 'desktops' which defy gravity and tranform the horizontal desk into a vertical surface with an array of possible colors and digital textures. The computer 'window' is only a portion of the computer screen, scalable in size. Windows can overlap, stack, or abut each other. The windows 'environment' makes the screen smaller and allows for simultaneous applications. As an 'interface', Windows™ extends screen space by overlapping screens of various sizes; each 'window' can run a different application; you can scroll through a text within a 'window', arrange windows on your screen in stacked or overlapping formations, decorate your windows (with wallpapers, textured patterns). A paradox begins to emerge: the more the image becomes digital, the more the interface tries to compensate for its departure from reality-based representation by adopting the metaphors of familiar objects in space.

8 For example: as part of an on-line collection deemed 'American Memory' the Library of Congress has made films in their 'Early Motion Picture Collection' available for down-loading off the World Wide Web along with hyperlinked texts detailing the historical context of 'America at the turn of the century', complete with a selected bibliography. (Although conclusions drawn from these films have to take into account that in their digitized format, 5–10 per cent of the original film frames are lost in the transfer.)

9 In 1859, Charles Baudelaire indicted photography as being a 'cheap method of disseminating a loathing for history'. Baudelaire was an early declaimer of the dangerous transformations of history and memory that the photographic image would produce. Despite photography's 'loathing for history', Baudelaire also recognized it as a technique that could preserve 'precious things whose form is dissolving and which demand a place in the archives of our memory' (1862: 153).

10 In a 1983 essay, Fredric Jameson, one of the key diagnosticians of postmodernity, catalogued some of its symptoms as:

> *the disappearance of history*, the way in which our entire contemporary social system has little by little begun to *lose its capacity to retain its own past*, has begun to live in a perpetual present and in a perpetual change that obliterates traditions.
>
> (1983: 125, emphasis added)

References

Roland Barthes 1975: En Sortant du cinéma. *Communications* **23**, translated by Bertrand Augst and Susan White, in *Apparatus*, edited by Theresa Hak Kyung Cha. New York: Tanam Press, 1980, 1–4.

Charles Baudelaire 1862: The salon of 1859. In *Art in Paris 1845–1862: salons and other exhibitions*, translated and edited by Jonathan Mayne. Oxford: Phaidon Press, 1965, 144–216.

Adam S. Bauman and Amy Harmon 1994: Rival systems of VCR 'Replacement' could spark standards war. *Los Angeles Times* 14 September 1, D1, D4.

Robert V. Bellamy, Jr and James R. Walker 1996: *Television and the remote control: grazing on a vast wasteland*. New York: Guilford Press.

David Bordwell and Kristin Thompson 1994: *Film history: an introduction*. New York: McGraw-Hill, xxvi.

Vannevar Bush 1945: As we may think. *Atlantic Monthly*, July.

Sean Cubitt 1991: *Time shift: on video culture*. New York: Routledge.

Richard Dienst 1994: *Still life in real time: theory after television*. Durham, NC: Duke University Press, 165–6.

Andrew Ferguson 1993: Charge of the couch brigade. *National Review* **45**(19) 4 October.

Jane Feuer 1983: The concept of live television: ontology as ideology. In E. Ann Kaplan, ed., *Regarding television*. Los Angeles, CA: American Film Institute Monographs, 12–22.

Gladys D. Ganley and Oswald H. Ganley 1987: *Global political fallout: the VCR's first decade*. Cambridge, MA: Program on Information and Resourses Policy, Harvard University.

Douglas Gomery 1992: *Shared pleasures: a history of movie presentation in the United States*. Madison, WI: University of Wisconsin Press.

Molly Haskell 1995: 'The Birth of a Nation', the birth of serious film. *The New York Times* 20 November: C5.

Frederic Jameson 1983: Postmodernism and consumer society. In Hal Foster, ed., *The anti-aesthetic*. Port Townsend, WA: Bay Press, 111–25.

Edward Kern 1970: Cassette TV: the good revolution. *Life* **69**(16) (16 October) 46–55.

Friedrich Kittler 1986: *Grammophon, film, typewriter*. Berlin: Brinkmann and Bose. Translated by Dorthea Von Mücke with the assistance of Philippe L. Similon, as 'Gramophone, film, typewriter', *October* **41**: 101–18.

David Kline 1997: The embedded Internet. *Wired Magazine* **5**:2, February.

James Lardner 1987: *Fast forward: Hollywood, the Japanese, and the VCR wars*. New York: New American Library.

Steven Levy 1995: *The New York Times*, 24 September.

Lauren Lipton 1991: VCR: very cool revolt. *Los Angeles Times*, TV Times cover story, 'How we tape', 4 August.

Marshall McLuhan 1964: *Understanding media*. Cambridge, MA: MIT Press, 1994.

Joshua Meyerowitz 1985: *No sense of place: the impact of electronic media on social behavior*. New York: Oxford University Press.

Lisa Napoli 1999: A gadget that taught a nation to surf: the TV remote control. *The New York Times* 11 February: D10.

Nicolas Negroponte 1995: *Being digital*. New York: Alfred Knopf.

A.C. Nielsen 1996: *The home technology report*. A.C. Nielsen Company, July.

Lynn Spigel 1992: *Make room for TV: television and the family ideal in postwar America*. Chicago, IL: University of Chicago Press.

Sherry Turkle 1995: *Life on the screen: identity in the age of the Internet*. New York: Simon and Schuster.

Paul Virilio 1988: The third window: an interview with Paul Virilio. *Cahiers du Cinema*, translated by Yvonne Shafir, in *Global Television*, edited by Cynthia Schneider and Brian Wallis. Cambridge, MA: MIT Press: 185–97.

Raymond Williams 1974: *Television: technology as cultural form*. New York: Schocken.

Raymond Williams 1980: Means of communication as means of production. In *Problems of materialism and culture*. London: New Left Books.

The New York Times, 1995: If the medium is the message, the message is the Web. 20 November, pp. A1, C5.

Index

Italic page numbers refer to figures.